Flight into Darkness

Flight into Darkness:
A Political Biography of
Shapour Bakhtiar

by Hamid Shokat

translated from the Persian
by M.R. Ghanoonparvar

Ibex Publishers,
Bethesda, Maryland

Flight into Darkness: A Political Biography of Shapour Bakhtiar
by Hamid Shokat
Translated from the Persian by M.R. Ghanoonparvar

Manufactured in the United States of America

The paper used in this book meets the minimum requirements of the American National Standard for Information Services—Permanence of Paper for Printed Library Materials, ANSI Z39.48–1984
Ibex Publishers strives to create books which are complete and free of error. Please help us with future editions by reporting any errors or suggestions for improvement to the address below or:
corrections@ibexpub.com

Ibex Publishers, Inc.
Post Office Box 30087
Bethesda, Maryland 20824
Telephone: 301–718–8188
Facsimile: 301–907–8707
www.ibexpublishers.com

Library of Congress Cataloging-in-Publication Data

Shawkat, Ḥamīd, author. | Ghanoonparvar, M.R. (Mohammad R.), translator.
Flight into darkness : a political biography of Shapour Bakhtiar / by Hamid Shokat ; translated from the Persian by M.R. Ghanoonparvar.
Parvāz dar ẓulmat. English
Bethesda, Maryland : Ibex Publishers, 2019. | Includes bibliographical references and index.
LCCN 2018047001 | ISBN 9781588141866 (hardcover : alk. paper)
Bakhtiar, Chapour. | Prime ministers—Iran—Biography. | Statesmen—Iran—Biography. |
Iran—Politics and government—1941-1979. | Iran—History—Revolution, 1979.
DS318.84.B35 S5213 2019 | DDC 955.05/3092 [B]—dc23

Contents

To my daughter, Mina,
the melody and song of my life…

Translator's Note

Although the country that Shapour Bakhtiar called his homeland was known to its own people as well as the people of the Middle East and South Asia by its endonym, Iran, since ancient times, Europeans and other people in the West officially referred to the same country as Persia until 21 March 1935, when on the request of the Persian government, the international name of Persia was changed to Iran, thereby also changing the international name of its people from Persian to Iranian. On the other hand, the name of the official state language spoken by Iranians remained the same, "Persian." In this translation, the term Persia is used to refer to the country with regard to events that took place prior to 1935 and Iran regarding occurrences after that date. Similarly, the term Iranians is used to refer to its people only after 1935. For the same reason, the original English name of the Anglo-Persian Oil Company (APOC) was changed to Anglo-Iranian Oil Company (AIOC) in the same year, although its Persian name, "Sherkat-e Naft-e Iran va Engelis," did not change until 1951, when Iran nationalized its oil industry and the oil company's name was changed to National Iranian Oil Company (NIOC). In rendering the name of the company, this translation uses one or the other name in English, depending on the date to which a reference to it is made. With few necessary exceptions, all dates from the Persian solar calendar and Islamic lunar calendar have been converted to Common Era dates.

In rendering the Persian names and terms in the English alphabet, I have used more of a transcription rather than transliteration method, although in many instances they are the same. I have basically followed Naser Sharifi's system in *Cataloguing Persian Works* (Chicago: American Library Association, 1959), with the following exceptions: (1) Other than the Persian letter *qaf* represented by "q" and the letter *gheyn* represented by "gh," no other distinction is made between consonants that are pronounced alike in Persian and represented by different letters. (2) No diacritical marks are used to distinguish between long and short vowels in this translation. Hence, the long "a" as in the pronunciation of "tall" and the short "a" as in "hat" are transcribed the same. (3) The apostrophe (') is used to represent the letter *eyn* and the sign *hamzeh* but is omitted in the initial position. (4) Although words containing a *tashdid* (emphatic consonant represented by double letters in English) are transcribed according to the aforementioned system, a single letter is used in the case of the letter "y" when preceded by an "i"; hence "Feyzi-yeh" rather than "Feyziyyeh." Unless quoted from an English-language source, the transliteration of Shapour Bakhtiar's name, as well as those of the members of his family and the Bakhtiari tribe, follows a more or less internationally used spelling rather than following the transliteration system used in this translation.

Persian names in English transcription often seem long and difficult to pronounce. This is especially true of nineteenth-century Persian titles customarily bestowed upon prominent individuals by the monarchs. Suffixes such as "dowleh" (of the state) as in Vosuqoddowleh (trustee of the state) and "saltaneh" (of the monarchy) as in Qavamossaltaneh (pillar of the monarchy) were commonly used with the names of such individuals, which might confuse readers as to how to identify the person's first and last names. In most instances, translators break up these titles into their components and transcribe them in the Arabic style of transliteration, such as Vosuq al-Dowleh or Vosuq od-Dowleh and Qavam al-Saltaneh or Qavam os-Saltaneh. To make these names more easily identifiable, I have refrained from these Arabic-style tran-scriptions.

For readers who may not be familiar with specific names and events in Iranian history and the culture-specific references made in this book, an alphabetized list of "Explanatory Notes" is provided at the end of the volume. A bibliography of books and articles (excluding online and archival materials) extracted from the footnotes and endnotes of the original Persian has also been added to this rendition.

This translation is based on a slightly modified text of the second printing of Hamid Shokat, *Parvaz dar Zolmat: Zendegani-ye Siyasi-ye Shapour Bakhtiar* (Köln, Germany: Forough Publishing, 2016).

Preface

*I naturally think about a specific audience, about those
who are searching without being certain that they have
found what they are seeking.*
—Paul Valéry

The political life of Shapour Bakhtiar, the last prime minister of the monarchical regime in Iran, is tied to our historical destiny. From his childhood in the midst of a nomadic tribe, his teenage years and young adulthood in Beirut and Paris, and his political struggles in the Iran Party (Hezb-e Iran) and the National Front of Iran (Jebheh-ye Melli-ye Iran) to his confrontation with Mohammad Reza Shah and Ayatollah Khomeyni, each is emblematic of a past that has left a lasting impact on our time. This is a time during which, in a sense, the battle between freedom and despotism formed the personality of such a politician as Bakhtiar and made him for some the distinct symbol of resistance against the autocracy of religion and state. In a different sense, however, the tragic end of Bakhtiar also is a mirror of a time that, like a vicious circle, has left an indelible mark on our historical memory of little more than murder and exile, or incarceration and migration. In this sense, Bakhtiar is the offspring of his own time, and was nurtured in his own time. Hence, a discussion of his life as a historical figure is itself a discussion about the events of the age in which Bakhtiar lived, and a chance to have a better understanding of those events. But, "how can one understand an irreversible past with the aid of indicators and impacts that human beings of that past have left behind?" Undoubtedly, in such an experiment as investigating the political life of a historical personality, we face difficulties and complexities. The French historian Lucien Febvre says: "Describing what we see is not very difficult. Seeing what must be described, this is where the actual difficulty lies hidden."[1]

Thus it is that in reconstructing historical events and portraying the life of a historical figure, by studying the etchings on the weapons of soldiers in battles that he has not witnessed, by describing the designs of the tiles of buildings that have been destroyed, and by searching the margins of half-burnt and faded documents and papers of a distant past, the historian perceives that past of a society and understands and makes comprehensible the present. This task is similar to that of an astrologer who, by searching the galaxies and discovering a new planet, better and further understands the position of the solar system, and the position of the earth in it, and helps others understand it; and all this resembles an archeological investigation that cannot be completed hastily—like finding a piece of bone or a coin, an image on a rock, or a sign on an earthenware vessel, in the same way that for many long years he rummages through and delves into an inscription from the Achaemenid era to learn how some ceremony or other was held at the beginning of a season, or a song at the conclusion of some ritual. It is a task that seems insignificant and marginal, but for the reconstructing and discovering of the cyphers and secrets of a thousand and one points that remain concealed behind the curtain of bygone eras, it is an undeniable necessity.

In this experiment, that which is thought to be indisputable truth must be constantly the subject of critical assessment and revision under a new light, an effort that will undoubtedly be met with the hostility of the dogmatic defenders of official narratives. Such are dogmatic thinkers, who in praising absolute truths regard every instance of skepticism to be the same as blasphemy and every question to be deserving of excommunication; thus, in the tedious sanctifications of past "glories," they replace knowledge with faith and history with mythology, whereas probing historical judgment requires rethinking and revision, and establishes its roots with an approach toward the past always from the perspective of the present, yet at the service of the future. Such a future becomes meaningful under the light of reexamination and audacious critiquing of past occurrences.

Another aspect of this approach is concealed in the comprehension of the argument that even though history concerns the past, it is not the same as the past. In the reconstruction of the past, what is imagined to be the truth is more or less a manifestation and an aspect of the truth, that upon which, by creating a creative picture, the historian bestows meaning and a new hue and luster. For this reason, in the book and the court of history, we face not one but various narratives of the same events, either bringing us closer to or further away from what has occurred. In this arena, posing questions that will bring us closer to historical truth is essential, and for that matter, with a ceaseless reminder that it is not sufficient to merely state what happened, but, like Ibn Khaldun, we must ask why it happened as it happened. Through an understanding of the past, we must make an effort to find new evidence by observation coupled with transparent doubt and conscientious searching, so that upon reopening and reviewing the seemingly closed cases of the past, we can erase fictive stories from history, understand the secrets and mysteries of the present, and pave the way toward the future. We must, however, be mindful that following such a path will ultimately bring us closer, not to an overall understanding of the truth, but, at best, to an understanding of some of its aspects, a truth that in historical judgments is without a doubt always, and inevitably, biased. Even though biased, this truth has not overlooked the need for criticism, revision, and reconsideration.

• • •

In a discussion of Bakhtiar's political life, his acceptance of the position of prime minister on the threshold of the revolution has a special place. Many have considered the reason for this decision, to the extent that it relates to his character and individual characteristics, to be related to his ambition. Bakhtiar, however, without any false humility, considered ambition "the engine of a political man." Hence, he saw no need to refute such a characteristic, nor to consider it incorrect. Nevertheless, he regarded the main reason for his decision to accept a position of responsibility under those critical conditions to be his increasing concern over the future that threatened Iran. Years before rising in opposition to Ayatollah Khomeyni, he considered courage and frankness to be an important factor in political life and said: "The problem is that some people in all stages of their lives pursue a comfortable and peaceful social

situation and at the same time prefer residence in Paradise to all alternatives of life... In any case, every country needs pious and patriotic
individuals; but such pious and patriotic individuals will not bring this
ship to shore. A number of strong and willful individuals are necessary."[2]

From the time he stepped into the arena of politics, because of his
individual and family strengths, Bakhtiar enjoyed the possibility of
making what he called political ambition a reality by setting aside his
own beliefs. His kinship with Sorayya Esfandiyari, the Shah's second
wife, and Teymur Bakhtiar, the head of the Organization of National
Intelligence and Security (SAVAK), was an advantage, in each case, one
that could pave his way to the peak of fame and power. Because of the
values he believed in, however, he turned away from all this. In the early
days after the fall of Mosaddeq's cabinet in August 1953, he refused the
offer of membership in Zahedi's cabinet; and on the threshold of the
revolution, when he saw that gaining power by the National Front was
within reach, despite all his disagreements with Allahyar Saleh, he
regarded him as the right nominee for the position of prime minister. At
another opportunity, Bakhtiar made every effort to ensure the premiership of Karim Sanjabi; and when the name of Gholamhoseyn Sadiqi for
that position was being mentioned, he spoke well of him with the Shah.
Finally, when he saw that the existence of his homeland was being
threatened, like a fearless leader, he stepped into the arena, and with
courage that stemmed from his self-confidence and tribal lineage, like a
"storm petrel," he hurried in the direction of an ill-fated battle, a storm
petrel flying into darkness.

Bakhtiar knew that in the fast pace of the chariot of politics, history
requires truth, and truth, courage. He stated: "True courage means calm
and patience in the face of great events."[3] And this may be another
indication of why he was on the scene and others, in the shadows. His
historic act, however, in accepting the position of prime minister, when
even his closest allies did not see much chance of his success, also had
other consequences, the extent of which went beyond comprehending
such a reality, a reality the awareness of which does not become mean-

ingful merely in terms of his characteristics, such as fearlessness and self-confidence, or reliance on aspects of lineage and character, or his political outlook.[i]

At the height of the unrest, when the masses of the people and the educated elite sought the secret to their peace and security in unequivocal, uncomplicated answers to their difficult and complex questions, Bakhtiar did not overlook any effort to speak with them about all that he regarded as knowledge and wisdom, without, in his doomed effort, having the good fortune of opening a path for them, and by breaking the unbroken spell of foolishness, showing the way to their good fortune and better days. Without being able to find a solution for confronting the increasing hardships that he faced during his premiership, he raised a question the answer to which continues still to be on the agenda of the Iranian society on the thirty-fifth anniversary of the revolution. This reality might perhaps be an indication of the importance of his historic action at a destiny-making time in the history of the country that he loved, and perhaps someday the historical conscience of the people of that country will entrust the name of Bakhtiar to their memory.

• • •

The fate of Bakhtiar in the Iranian Revolution has been compared with that of Kerensky, the head of the provincial government in the February 1917 Russian Revolution. Despite the clear differences between these two men, such a comparison is not without foundation. Following the Bolshevik Revolution in October 1917, Kerensky fled to France, wrote his memoir, tried his luck once more, and by establishing a political organization, he nurtured the hope for the "liberation of Russia" in his mind, until finally he shifted his seat from premiership to that of university professor. Like Kerensky, Bakhtiar also studied philosophy and law, turned to politics, and dreaming about establishing a constitu-

---

[i] An old friend of Bakhtiar, Aliqoli Bayani, had said about his decision to from a cabinet: "Under these circumstances, accepting the position of prime minister requires more courage than entering the cage of a hungry tiger." This writer's interview with Hamid Zonnur, Paris, 11 December 2007.

tional monarchy, he faced that which to him was the nightmare of the revolution. He fled to France, organized the "National Resistance Movement" (Nehzat-e Moqavemat-e Melli), published his memoir, and in the end, in the final years of his life, bewildered and heartbroken, he decided to wash his hands of politics and teach at the university.

The October Revolution of 1917 and the February Revolution of 1979, one in the early years and the other in the final years of the twentieth century, also left astonishing impacts, at times astonishingly similar. When we examine these two events, on the threshold of both revolutions, the consequences of which extended far beyond the borders of the two neighboring countries, we face a dual power. One is the official power of the government cabinet of ministers, the military, and the executive organizations that is disintegrating without any support, and the other is the unofficial power that has the support of the masses of the people. The leaders of both revolutions spent a period of migration and exile away from their country with steadfastness, stubbornness, and self-confidence that stemmed from an unwavering belief, without having had much hope of returning in the final years of migration and exile. Nevertheless, one of them in the "ten days that shook the world"[ii] eradicated tsarism, and the other, ten days after returning to his country, removed the monarchical system. Despite all their differences, both revolutions pursued exporting and expanding themselves; they both faced foreign aggression; and they both spoke of freedom and justice and the establishment of a promised paradise. And in a sharp and rapid turnabout, both revolutions attributed any statement other than what they considered permissible to the counterrevolution and actualized a wave of suppression and migration which was virtually unprecedented in the modern history of their countries.

[ii] *Ten Days that Shook the World* is the title of a famous book by the American journalist, John Reed, about the Russian Bolshevik Revolution. With a short introduction written by Lenin, this book is the most important work published in 1919 about that revolution. The book is especially important because its author was an eyewitness to the formation and the developments of the 1917 October Revolution.

Another surprising similarity between the two revolutions was their command centers, both of which were in girls' schools, Lenin's residence in the Smolny school and the residence of Ayatollah Khomeyni in the Refah school.

The Smolny Institute for Noble Maidens was built as a convent between 1806 and 1808 on the order of Elizabeth I, the Empress of Russia, as a place of rest for her in her old age. In the nineteenth century, it was the place for educating the daughters of the nobility, in order to familiarize them with the customs and protocols of aristocracy and foreign languages for attending high-level gatherings. The October Revolution was also planned there. With the fall of Kerensky's government, the first government of the Soviets was formed in that school. After the 1917 October Revolution, Smolny became the headquarters of the provincial government; and for four months, it was Lenin's residence. Some of the ministers in Kerensky's government and the leaders of the former regime were detained in the rooms of this school. Interrogations of the "counterrevolutionary" elements who were prisoners in detention in Smolny were conducted in the rooms of the same school.

Refah Girls' School, which was established in the 1960s by individuals who played an important role in the Islamic Revolution and was chosen as the command headquarters of the revolution, strangely resembled Smolny. Upon his return to Iran, Ayatollah Khomeyni took up residence in that school; and the first meetings of the Revolution Council also were held there. After the fall of the monarchy in February 1979, some of the heads of the former regime were imprisoned in the rooms of this school, and a number of them were put on trial there and executed on the roof of Refah School.

•   •   •

Shapour Bakhtiar had a well-mannered, reclusive, shy, and witty disposition. With the exception of a few people, he addressed everyone else with the formal second-person pronoun in Persian. He had enormous respect for his family, but he would not socialize and rarely visited anyone's home lest his political activities would cause problems for others. In the 1940s, he was occasionally invited by Sorayya, the Shah's wife, to the Royal Court, which he also declined. He liked sports and music; he was especially fond of classical music and the works of Mozart and Beethoven; and Iranian music filled him with "joy and rapture." He was a mountain hiker, and most weekends or on Fridays, he went to Pasqal'eh and Tuchal on the slopes of the Alborz Mountains with five or six of his friends.[4]

Other people needed to make an appointment to go to his house. At home, he always wore Lor tribal pants; and in the presence of others, he appeared in a suit and tie or in a dress shirt with an open collar. In Tehran, he had rented a house in a respectable neighborhood in which he lived with his French wife Madlaine and his children. Later on, he bought a plot of land in the Farmaniyeh area of Tehran on which he had a house built with installment payments, and on the wall of the basement parlor of which were inscribed poems by Hafez. That was where he occasionally held literary gatherings in which he read poetry with his friends or held political meetings. His daughter, France, remembers: "I recall that from the same house, they took my father to prison several times. He knew himself when they were going to take him. With his suitcase ready at the door, he would sit in the parlor until they came. When I would see this scene, I would realize that Dad was leaving. They would come, knock on the door, and say politely, 'Mr. Bakhtiar, please come with us. We have a few questions to ask you.' That was it, and I would not see my dad for a while. Sometimes it happened that when I came home, I saw that my father was not there. They would tell me that they had taken Dad away. When he would come back from prison, he had lost a lot of weight, but he was strong and determined; he was always like that." He lived in the same house in the Farmaniyeh area until the revolution.[5]

Bakhtiar read profusely, in particular, Persian poetry and literature. He was exceptionally fond of Hafez, and he recited a few couplets on every occasion and regarding any issue. He was said to have memorized hundreds of couplets. "In his non-political gatherings in the evening, as soon as he found someone who was interested in poetry and literature, he would change the conversation to Hafez, and he would not let any other topic be discussed." He listened to the news on the radio, and his favorite radio program was a Persian-style poetical crambo program, and he constantly criticized the contestants for having made mistakes in their recitation of poems. Among the newspapers, he read *Keyhan*, *Le Monde*, and some other French newspapers. For a while, he was a member of the French Club in Tehran, and occasionally, he took his children there. He did not meddle too much in what his sons Guy and Patrick did, but he was somewhat strict with his daughters, Viviane and France.[iii] His restrictions were mostly the sort common with Iranian fathers, such that, for example, he did not want his daughters to go to parties. When he separated from his first wife, Madlaine, he sent his elder son to France and he registered his other son and his youngest daughter in French schools in Tehran.[6]

Bakhtiar avoided gatherings and societies. On Mondays, he often went to the sauna, and if necessary, he had his hair cut there. He did not like to sit in a barbershop; and occasionally, the barber came to his house to cut his hair. He was not a gambler, and he did not go to movie theaters. Only once, he agreed to accompany his daughters to a movie theater to see *The Bridge on the River Kwai*, an event that became an indelible memory for them. He suffered from ulcers, and he often was careful about what he ate. He would say, "You shouldn't eat a heavy dinner," and he always had a bottle of vodka on ice, which he drank with lemon and soda. Once, Haj Mahmud Maniyan, one of the well-known members of the National Front, who was witty by nature, on the threshold of the revolution told him: "The bazaar merchants asked me what kind of man you are." Bakhtiar asked: "What did you tell them?" Haj Maniyan said: "I told them, I've seen him drinking many times, but I've not seen him perform his prayers, not even once."[7]

Mohammad Moshiri-Yazdi, Bakhtiar's old friend and his deputy when he was prime minister, states: "Bakhtiar did not know how to make a

---

iii For Bakhtiar's first son, they had chosen the French name Guy, but they often called him Giv, an Iranian name.

living at all. A bit was left of the inheritance from his father, which was
not much. Perhaps some property was also left to him, from the sale of
which he did not gain much. In fact, he lacked the means for a comfortable lifestyle; but he was not a person to reveal it. I should even say—
though I should not say it—that he lived off of the sale of what was left
to him from his father, carpets, dishes, and such things. Of course, his
relatives, such as his paternal cousin Teymur Bakhtiar, while they
worked in the government, did not want him to live like a pauper; but
he was not the kind of person to stoop to asking anyone for help.
Subsequently, after a while, he had to get some sort of a job. After the
1953 coup d'état, he no longer pursued government employment. So,
he was hired in a few private institutions. But it would happen that the
government would not allow him to be employed; they would cause
trouble for him."[8] Bakhtiar worked in Vatan Textile Factory and
Shahinshar Construction Company in Isfahan, and he became the CEO
of Daktiran Company, which operated with joint Iranian and French
investments. Then he worked for Hamun Contract Company, and for a
while he was in charge of the legal and judicial affairs of the French
Saser Company that was involved in the building of Latyan Dam.[9]

Following the failed experience of the period of Ali Amini's premiership, the disintegration of the Second National Front, and the suppression of the riots on 5 June 1963, when the political climate of Iran was
becoming more stifling, Bakhtiar faced serious political and financial
hardships, to the point that he decided to leave Iran. According to
SAVAK documents, in a letter to the Shah, he asked the Shah to agree
to his and his children's "emigration" from Iran. The Shah ordered an
investigation into the matter, after which SAVAK wrote in this connection: "The aforementioned has financial problems and owes a certain
amount of money." Earlier, as well, in a report on the request of Bakhtiar to leave Iran, SAVAK had written: "Outside Iran, even if personally he does not wish to engage in activities contrary to the interests of
the regime, political deviants might pressure him and force him to
become active. Hence, because the aforementioned is currently suffering
from financial hardship and his main motivation in leaving the country

stems from this issue, it seems that if arrangements are made for him to continue to reside in Iran and in some way he is placated and assisted, such would be beneficial." Hence, the agreement to permit him to leave the country was no longer an issue.[10]

Hints about Bakhtiar's financial difficulties are made in another report prepared by SAVAK regarding private conversations of some of the members of the National Front. There is even talk about his intent to commit suicide. The report states: "Ebrahim Karimabadi at the home of Hoseyn Shah-Hoseyni's sister says, 'Because of his large amount of debt, Dr. Bakhtiar wanted to commit suicide, but they had come to his rescue and prevented him.' Shah-Hoseyni said, 'Yes, he is in a dire situation. He needs 500,000 *tumans* to get him going.'"[11]

As those close to him have said, Bakhtiar would readily trust others and was excessively optimistic. Some have considered "his nomadic tribal nature, fascination with his own ideas, and weakness in the face of those who would agree with his views" among his weak points. Javad Khadem, the minister of housing and urban development in his cabinet, says about Bakhtiar's distinct characteristics: "When you sat with him, you would immediately know that it was impossible for him to lie to you. You could not find anyone who would see him and not be captivated by him."[12]

Moreover, his financial generosity was also well known by those close to him as well as the public. Pari Kalantari, the secretary of Bakhtiar during his premiership who accompanied him in Paris, says: "He gave away everything he had among the Iranians. General Ja'far Shafaqat, the minister of war in his cabinet, was in dire financial straits. On the eve of the Persian New Year, Bakhtiar gave me a check and asked me to take it to him. He said, 'Do me a favor and take this check to help him. Others might humiliate him. Take this check to him as quickly as possible, so he won't be embarrassed before his wife, his children, and his grandchildren.' I went to the post office and mailed the check. Someone would have heart surgery and need help. Bakhtiar would write a check. I would get a bouquet of flowers and attach the check to the bouquet with his calling card, on which he had written, 'With wishes for your speedy recovery,' and I would give it to the patient, so they would not throw him out of the hospital. When he heard that a woman had come from Iran because of breast cancer and was hospitalized in Paris, he became very emotional and wept. He said, 'I don't know why so many Iranian women get breast cancer.' Then he wrote a check, and I went to visit the patient with a bouquet of flowers. He also helped Iranian students who were receiving no money from Iran and were in financial difficulty, and he felt happy about what he did. He said, 'I am like my mother. When she'd come home, she had nothing on under her chador, because she had given away all she had.' One day I told him, in terms of public relations, that it would be a good idea to send Christmas cards to French presidents such as Mitterrand and Chirac, or non-Iranian friends and Iranians with foreign spouses, or send cards to his former ministers to convey his best for Persian New Year. In response, he said, 'Don't collect an entourage for me where I am a stranger. Don't try to make a Hoveyda out of me!' And yet, he did all those things. He paid no attention to financial issues."[13]

• • •

Discussing the political life of Bakhtiar in the years after the revolution, or what he referred to as life in exile, was not a part of the project for this book. The reason for this, more than anything else, is the lack of availability of the necessary documents and evidence. The documents in the archives of France, which was the main center of his political activities and the organization that he had established under the name of the National Resistance Movement, have not been made available to the public. Information about his relations with Iraq, Saudi Arabia, and the Persian Gulf sheikdoms continue to remain concealed. His role and the extent of his involvement in the Nuzheh coup d'état[iv] and the why and how of his political outlook regarding the Iran-Iraq War are still unclear in many respects and require obtaining and examining the documents.

[iv] For more on the Nuzheh coup d'état, see Chapter Eight.

The materials that have been published in Iran, thus far sporadically, are not sufficient for a historical assessment. Moreover, determining their degree of accuracy and truthfulness or untruthfulness is impossible at the present time. Nevertheless, based on the available material, one can pose certain essential questions about this period in his life and leave the answers for some other time. Hopefully, these answers will be provided in the future with the publication of the documents regarding that period with the efforts of historians and will remove the curtain of ambiguity from an important period in his political life and in contemporary Iranian history.[v]

As mentioned, I have posed some of the questions regarding this period by relying on limited resources and the statements of Bakhtiar, or the statements of those close to him and his allies, in the final section of this book under the heading of "Bakhtiar in Exile," even though overall familiarity with this period of his political life and the National Resistance Movement also requires examination and investigation of evidence and documents that are inaccessible at the present time. Nevertheless, the available evidence presents a portrait of Bakhtiar that can be mentioned as a new chapter in the book of his political life, which is full of ups and downs. This time, in confrontation with the regime that ruled his homeland, he tied his efforts to gain the support of the United States and the neighbors of Iran together with the battle to overthrow the Islamic Republic, an effort that not only instigated protest by his opponents, but disbelief in a number of his defenders.

Moreover, in the years prior to the revolution, as well, we face viewpoints and ups and downs in the political life of Bakhtiar that complicate any understanding of his political character. At one time, along with and in step with religious politicians and political religious figures,

---

[v] The details of the story of the assassination attempt on and ultimate murder of Bakhtiar remain unclear in many respects. What I have written in Chapter One of this book is merely based on limited information published in a few books, reports, documents, and newspapers and does not yet convey a precise overall picture of what occurred. This important matter will become possible once we are allowed access to the documents and archives of Iran and France.

he would rise against the Shah, and at another time, he would stand against and in confrontation with them. At times during the premiership of Qavamossaltaneh, he would refer to the parliamentary elections as rubber-stamp elections, but he personally would become a candidate for the parliament; and sometimes during Amini's premiership, he would demand the holding of elections and the opening of the parliament and, at the same time, would not express any confidence in the elections. At times, alongside the leaders of the National Front, he would condemn the reforms by the Shah, which were called the "White Revolution"; at times he stood up in "admiration" of them; and finally, at times he called what he was facing a "revolution," and at times he would not consider what had occurred anything more than "sedition."[14]

Without a doubt, each of these instances presents a different and at times contradictory depiction of Bakhtiar's character and his political conduct and approach. Each of these depictions, despite their differences, has a particular meaning in delineating his political life and his place in history. In the introduction to the book, *History of the French Revolution*, by the well-known French historian Jules Michelet, Jochen Köhler makes a meaningful reference to the Dutch painter Rembrandt. In explaining a similar characteristic, quoting Michelet, he writes: "Rembrandt painted thirty self-portraits, each of which is different from others, but all of them represent his face, and despite the differences, all of them are similar and are all ultimately Rembrandt."[15]

In this sense, Bakhtiar is no different. The viewpoints of his political life present pictures that, despite their differences, are strangely similar, pictures that occasionally are not dissimilar to our past life and time. He, too, despite the differences and similarities, in the mirror of time, was born and raised in his own time, a time that has left a lasting impact on our own life and time.

• • •

The suggestion for writing this book was made to me by Mr. Bahram Shafi'i, who provided an important part of the expenses for its preparation. Ali Reza Manafzadeh translated some parts of Bakhtiar's doctoral dissertation. In analyzing this dissertation, which I have done in Chapter Three, I benefitted a great deal from his advice and knowledge. He also prepared a summary of Bakhtiar's entire doctoral dissertation, to which I have referred in the same chapter. Finding and translating Bakhtiar's educational records at Henri-IV and Louis-le-Grand high schools as well as information in the archives of the French Foreign Ministry about foreigners who served during World War II in the military of that country are also thanks to him. Finding and translating the detailed police report in the archives of the French Police regarding the assassination attempt on and ultimate murder of Bakhtiar was also carried out by him. Unfortunately, his efforts to interview Jean-Louis Bruguière, the French magistrate who was in charge of the case of Bakhtiar's murder in the French court, were without results. In addition, the difficult task of editing the first and the final drafts of the book was through his efforts. Nasser Mohajer, by searching the documents in the French Foreign Ministry and examining sixteen files about Iranian students who resided in that country, attempted to find a trace of Bakhtiar; but unfortunately, other than finding some documents related to the lives of Iranian students during WWII, nothing further was found. His continuous efforts to find the speech of Bakhtiar to the General Conference of the International Labour Organization in 1947, to which Bakhtiar makes reference in an article, also remained futile. Since seven years ago, when I began the writing of this book, Mohajer has accompanied me and I have benefitted from his guidance at every opportunity. As in the distant and near past, this time, once again, I am indebted to him for his kindness. Keyvan Dadjou made his unpublished 1986 interview with Bakhtiar about the developments that ended in the Iranian revolution available to me for use in writing this book. My interviews with France Bakhtiar, the daughter of Shapour Bakhtiar, and with Shahintaj Bakhtiar, his second wife, from whom he has a son by the name of Gudarz, helped clarify certain unclear points in his life. In my interviews with several former ministers, Bakhtiar's secretary during his premiership, and his friends and close acquaintances, I learned about certain unknown aspects of his political life. In learning about these, I am indebted more than everyone else to Mr. Mohammad Moshiri-Yazdi for his kindness. He made Bakhtiar's unpublished memoir, which is the result of two years of conversations with him, available to me, from which I benefitted greatly in writing this book. Human Bakhtiar also kindly provided an opportunity for an interview to clarify some unclear points regarding Bakhtiar's political life. Touraj Atabaki, Mansour Bonakdarian, Ali Gheissari, Amanuel Youssefi, and Hamid Zoka'i read the first draft of the book and pointed out its shortcomings. Bonak-darian, Gheissari, and Youssefi, upon reading the final draft, which still had shortcomings, once again provided guidance. Bonakdarian and Gheissari, with great kindness, shared their friendship and knowledge with me, and in the same way, Youssefi, this time as well from begin-ning to end, every time that I faced an obstacle, was my friend and supporter. I also got through my scrupulousness in the final revision of the book sheltered by the benevolent kindness of my old friend, Hamid Zoka'i. I must also add that the responsibility for all that has been stated in this book is mine alone.

Mr. Saeid Aghaei, a supporter of Bakhtiar, and several of my friends in the United States, Canada, and Europe, by pre-purchasing the original book in Persian, made its publication possible. I am grateful to all of them.

In conclusion, I must say that, considering that an important part of Bakhtiar's life was spent in France, I considered the examination of the archives of that country necessary for writing this book, so that in this way, I would gain access to more of the unknown issues about him.[vi] I was unable to do so because of my lack of familiarity with the French language at the level that I considered necessary. My hope is that historians, upon finding documents related to Bakhtiar's life in France, will make an effort to fill this gap, and by reconsidering and revising all that has been said in this book, will cast a light on other aspects of his political life, for history is kept alive through revision.

—Berlin, June 2014

[vi] For more on this topic, see Chapter Three.

[1] Ali Reza Manafzadeh, "Sarcheshmehha-ye Tahavvoli Shegarf dar Shiveh-ye Tarikhnegari (Darbareh-ye Maktab-e Annales)," *Negah-e No*, no. 28: 166; Lucien Fabvre, "Ein Historiker prüft sein Gewissen," in *Wie Geschichte geschrieben wird*, mit Beiträgen von Fernand Braudel, Natalie Zemon Davis, Lucian Febvre, Carlo Ginzburg, Jacques Le Goff, Reinhart Koeselleck, Arnaldo Momigliano (Berlin: Wagenbach Verlag, 1990), 20.

[2] *Surat-e Jalasat-e Kongereh-ye Jebheh-ye Melli*, compiled by Amir Tayerani (Tehran: Gam-e No Publishers, 2009), 216-226.

[3] *Haftehnameh-ye Iran Tribun*, "Baham beh Iran Bazmigardim: Goft-o Gu'i Vizheh ba Shapour Bakhtiar, Rahbar-e Nehzat-e Moqavemat-e Melli-ye Iran" (n.p, n.d.), 27.

[4] This writer's interview with Pari Kalantari, Paris, 14 April 2012; this writer's interview with Hamid Zonnur, 11 December 2007; this writers interview with France Bakhtiar, Washington, DC, 16 April 2008; "Man Morgh-e Tufanam," Dr. Shapour Bakhtiar, quoted from the website of the National Resistance Movement of Iran, 9. http://www.namir.info/Neuer%20Ordner/05-Spalte%20Links/Bakhtiar/16-10-10-man%20morghe%20toofanam.htm.

[5] This writer's interview with Hamid Zonnur, Paris, 11 December 2007; this writer's interview with France Bakhtiar, Washington, DC, 16 April 2008; this writer's interview with Mohammad Moshiri-Yazdi, Paris, 21 December 2008.

[6] This writer's interview with France Bakhtiar, Washington, DC, 16 April 2008; Iraj Pezeshkzad, "Bakhtiar Shifteh va Sheyda-ye Hafez." http://www.bbc.co.uk/persian/iran/2011/08/110802_l78_bakhtiar_20th_anniv_iraj_pezeshkzad.shtml.

[7] This writer's interview with France Bakhtiar, Washington, DC, 16 April 2008; this writer's interview with Hamid Zonnur, Paris, 11 December 2007.

[8] This writer's interview with Mohammad Moshiri-Yazdi, Paris, 21 December 2008.

[9] Mohammad Hoseyn San'ati, "Shapour Bakhtiar," *Faslnameh-ye Motale'at-e Tarikhi*, no. 6 (Spring 2005): 206-208.

[10] Ibid., 204-206.

[11] Ibid., 205.

[12] This writer's interview with Rahim Sharifi, Paris, 11 December 2007; this writer's interview with France Bakhtiar, Washington, DC, 16 April 2008; this writer's interview with Manuchehr Razmara, Paris, 22 February 2008; this writer's interview with Hamid Zonnur, Paris, 11 December 2007; this writer's interview with Javad Khadem, Paris, 12 December 2007.

[13] This writer's interview with Pari Kalantari, Paris, 14 April 2012.

[14] Unpublished interview of Mohammad Moshiri-Yazdi with Shapour Bakhtiar, Suresnes, France, tape 18, 25 February 1990; *Khaterat-e Shapour Bakhtiar, Nokhost Vazir-e Iran (1357)*, edited by Habib Ladjevardi, Iranian Oral History Project, Harvard University Center for Middle Eastern Studies, Bethesda, MD, 1996, 44;

Surat Jalasat-e Kongereh-ye Jepheh-ye Melli-ye, 221; Shapour Bakhtiar, *Yekrangi*, translated by Mahshid Amirshahi (Paris: Khavaran Publishers, 1982), 126; *Ettela'at*, 20 January 1979, 7; Ibid., 5 February 1979, 7; Ibid., 21 January 1979, 2; *Keyhan*, 29 January 1979, 2; Ibid., 1 February 1979, 5; Ibid., 8 February 1979, 3.

[15] Jules Michelet, *Geschichte der Französischen Revolution*, Aus dem Französischen von Richard Kühn (Frankfurt/Main: Zweitausendeins, 2009), Band I, 20-21.

Chapter One

Around the hero everything turns into a tragedy.
—Friedrich Nietzsche

Failed Assassination Attempt

The Montparnasse Cemetery, which initially was called Southern Cemetery, is located in the 14th arrondissement of Paris; and along with Montmartre, Passy, and Père Lachaise cemeteries, it is one of the most important cemeteries of Paris. With over a thousand trees, this cemetery is now one of the most important green spaces of the French capital, and it is the resting place of many famous philosophers, sociologists, playwrights, poets, writers, industrialists, motion picture actors, and painters. Like other well-known people and similar to his predecessor, Ali Amini, Shapour Bakhtiar is also buried in this cemetery. His grave and that of his assistant, Sorush Katibeh, who were murdered on 6 August 1991 in Suresnes, a suburban area near Paris, are also side-by-side in section eight of this cemetery.

From the very early days of the fall of the monarchical regime in Iran, the widespread effort that had begun for the elimination of Bakhtiar became officially finalized three months later on the order of Sheykh Sadeq Khalkhali, the religious magistrate and head of the revolution courts. In a press conference, Khalkhali mentioned Bakhtiar and another twelve "leaders and agents" of the former regime who had been sentenced to death in the revolution courts. He considered these verdicts a sign of the "revolutionary wrath of the Moslem masses," and said: "The revolution courts follow the Islamic and Iranian models, and the Western models will not be taken into consideration." Khalkhali emphasized that the above-mentioned defendants were sentenced to death alongside a number of others, and that anyone anywhere who eliminates them will not be considered a terrorist, because according to Islamic law, their blood is permissible to be shed, and "no matter where they are, their sentence is the same." According to him, no government had the right to arrest those who carried out the assassination, because they would be carrying out the verdict of the Islamic Revolution Court. In justifying this religious jurisprudential reasoning, he added: "From the perspective of religious law, it is forbidden to give food to anyone who is found guilty, and for this reason, as soon as the verdict is issued, we place such individuals in front of the firing squad… The Koran does not mention that an attorney should be assigned to defend the accused."[1]

A few days later, Ayatollah Khomeyni also in reaction to the objections of human rights organizations regarding the continual executions being carried out in Iran, confirmed Khalkhali's viewpoint and said: "If we find any prime minister who has been a prime minister at that time, such as Sharif-Emami, such as Bakhtiar, these individuals are sentenced to death. Bakhtiar admitted himself that murders occurred on his order. These individuals are murderers, and they have forced the population to murder. They are the corruptors; they are corrupt. We are doing these things in support of human rights and for this crowd that is shouting that these individuals are agents of colonialism."[2]

The statement of Ayatollah Khomeyni about Bakhtiar having issued an order to kill was not true. Bakhtiar had said that, considering the political liberties during his tenure as prime minister and the peaceful policy of his government, there is no longer any room for "violence and clashes," and, hence, the responsibility for every drop of blood that is shed belongs to those who fight the law enforcement. Even though he had opened up the doors of the prisons and freed the press from the shackles and restraints of censorship, no political prisoner or journalist rose in protest to the verdict that had been issued against Bakhtiar. His former allies in the National Front, including his fellow combatant Bazargan, who was occupying the seat of prime minister, also found it expedient to keep silent rather than to open their mouths in protest. Bazargan, likewise, found it expedient to wash his hands of the responsibility for the executions that were taking place before his eyes and to absolve himself of any wrongdoing in this connection. Apparently, Ayatollah Khomeyni, realizing this mindset in his meeting with Bazargan, also mentioned his chosen prime minister, Bazargan, and defending the rapid-fire rulings issued by the revolution courts, made an off-hand reference to his position as head of the government, lest any responsibility should become questionable before the judgment of history, or any words remain unsaid. He said: "During the entire time since this Islamic prime minister has come to office, find even one person whom they have arrested and jailed for one day or insulted without being guilty in this Revolution Court, or in the office of the prime minister, or in the military, or anywhere else in this government."[3]

As a result, the recognition of Bakhtiar as a person the shedding of whose blood was permissible and the issuance of whose death sentence had no opposition was officially finalized. In the meantime, Mohsen Rafiqdust, who drove the automobile carrying Ayatollah Khomeyni from Tehran Mehrabad Airport upon his return to Iran, assumed an important role in the elimination of Bakhtiar. Rafiqdust, who later became the minister of the Islamic Revolution Guard Corps (Sepah-e Pasdaran-e Enqelab-e Eslami) in the cabinet of Prime Minister Mir-Hoseyn Musavi and then head of the Foundation for the Downtrodden and Self-Sacrificing Disabled Veterans (Bonyad-e Mostaz'afan va Janbazan), mentions two plots that were planned separately regarding the first failed assassination attempt on Bakhtiar. One was planned by Abbas Aqa Zamani, known as Abu Sharif, the "commander of Guard Corps operations," who was an "armed struggler prior to the revolution." He states: "It was reported that Abu Sharif had dispatched another team headed by an individual by the name of Abolvafa, who had an Arabic accent because of his residence in Arab countries…to kill Bakhtiar, which unfortunately was the cause of the failure of the operation… This plot was exposed and resulted in the failure of the assassination plot."[4]

Another plot, which Rafiqdust discusses in more detail in his memoir, indicates his direct involvement in preparing and planning the assassination of Bakhtiar. He states that a person by the name of Mehdi Nezhad-Tabrizi had come to him and told him that he was prepared to carry out the "big" task, which meant the killing of Bakhtiar. Rafiqdust does not mention anything about how he became acquainted with Nezhad-Tabrizi or the date of this meeting. He only states that this meeting "took place when the hearts of the people of Iran were filled with animosity toward Bakhtiar." The past activities of Nezhad-Tabrizi also remain vague in Rafiqdust's memoir. That which is made clear in this memoir is that he was a "brother" who, after the failed assassination attempt on Bakhtiar on 18 July 1980, was arrested by French police, and after being convicted and spending a few years in prison, he went to Qom and became a seminary student. Then, with the "inheritance" from his father, he built a mosque in Isfahan and became a congregational prayer leader in order to engage in the affairs of religion and teaching Haj pilgrimage protocols to those eager to become pilgrims to the House of God in Mecca.

In the continuation of these explanations, Rafiqdust speaks about the religious decree issued by Ayatollah Gilani, a religious magistrate, regarding the killing of Bakhtiar: "Under these circumstances, consulting with others, I obtained the ruling for the revolutionary execution of Bakhtiar. I went to Ayatollah Gilani and said, 'We have a team that we want to send to execute Bakhtiar. Would you grant permission?' He said, 'Yes, I will issue the ruling,' and he wrote, 'Bakhtiar's blood is permissible to be shed.'"[5]

Rafiqdust does not mention with whom he "consulted" or which high-ranking officials of the regime knew about the plan to kill Bakhtiar. His memoir, however, indicates that after obtaining the ruling from Ayatollah Gilani, he put together a team to kill Bakhtiar. According to him, this team had five members, two Lebanese by the names of Anis al-Naqqash or Abu Mazen as well as a person by the name of Samir, who had been introduced to Rafiqdust by al-Naqqash. The three Iranian members of this team consisted of Mehdi Nezhad-Tabrizi, an individual by the name of Janab from Qom, and Mohammad Saleh-Hoseyni. The latter was a person of Iranian descent who was born in Najaf in Iraq and resided in Lebanon. Rafiqdust had become acquainted with al-Naqqash in Lebanon through Saleh-Hoseyni, who early in the revolution helped Rafiqdust in "buying weapons and ammunition." According to

Rafiqdust, "these five people formed a team and went to France to carry out the ruling of the Revolution Court concerning Bakhtiar."[6]

Referring to the plan that the "commander of the Guard Corps operations," Abbas Aqa Zamani, alias Abu Sharif, was trying to carry out but which failed from the start, in explaining the plan, the preparation of which was his own responsibility, he states: "Abu Mazen and his team had prepared everything. The revolutionary execution of Bakhtiar was to be carried out under the cover of reporting for a well-known Arabic magazine… The reporter makes an appointment with difficulty to prepare for the interview with Bakhtiar. In the first visit, he identifies the entryways and exits and the layout of the house. In the meantime, the French notice the arrival of the Iranian Abu Sharif group. Abolvafa is exposed, but they flee. The French increase the number of guards of Bakhtiar's house, and tell Bakhtiar to attach the security chain behind the door. When Abu Mazen and Nezhad-Tabrizi (in charge of the execution) go there carrying machineguns, the police intercept. In this scuffle, all the members of the team are captured, and three of them are killed. Also, the spinal cord of a woman in the building is severed. Our plot fails."[7]

French Police documents contain a comprehensive report on the assassination attempt on Bakhtiar, the details of which are as follows: "On Friday, 18 July 1980, four police officers of the Upper Seine are assigned to guard the home of Shapour Bakhtiar at the apartment of his daughter, located at 101 Bineau Boulevard in Neuilly-sur-Seine in Upper Seine. The guards, 25-year-old Philippe Jourdain in front of the building, 22-year-old Bernard Vigna in the entry hall of the building, and two other guards, 23-year-old Jean-Michel Jamme and 23-year-old Georges Marty on the second floor of the building, are standing watch.

"At 8:45, three men, all of whom appear to be around 20 years old, introduce themselves as reporters of l'Humanité newspaper, the organ of the French Communist Party. They come out of a Peugeot 505 with their equipment and engage in conversqation with the guard, Jourdain, who asks them to identify themselves to his colleague stationed in the entry hall of the building. On the request of the guard in the entry hall, they show him their press ID cards (which later are found to be forged). Bernard Vigna informs his two colleagues on the second floor of the building about the presence of the three individuals.

"The guard, Jean-Michel Jamme, comes down the stairs by himself and accompanies them to the upper floor. He has no idea that he will lose his life in doing this. The terrorists abandon their reporters' equipment in the entry hall and take Beretta handguns equipped with silencers out of their briefcases. When the guard, Jean-Michel Jamme, reaches the entry hall to the apartment, the terrorists calmly shoot him. The other guard, Bernard Vigna, also has no chance to defend himself. The shots fired at him wound him in his larynx, chest, and spine.[i]

"Everything happens in a flash. The terrorists hurry to the second floor and come face-to-face with the police guard, Georges Marty, and immediately open fire on him. When they shoot him in the scull, he collapses, they leave him to die, and go to look for Bakhtiar's apartment, when the unfortunate neighbor on the same floor, a 45-year-old woman by the name of Yvonne Stein, curious about what is going on and what all the noise is about, opens the door and asks what is happening. The terrorists also kill her immediately. Her 37-year-old sister, Viviane Stein, is also shot and wounded badly in her arm and neck.

"The terrorists, who think they have found their way to Bakhtiar's home, soon realize their mistake and go back. Finally, they are in front of the apartment they are looking for, but the door is

---

[i] On 5 February 2008, one of the police guards of Bakhtiar, Bernard Vigna, after years of physical suffering and often alone in a wheelchair, died in a poor neighborhood in a small town in the suburbs of Paris as a result of the injuries inflicted on him during the assassination attempt on Shapour Bakhtiar at the age of fifty-one, and in absolute disregard for his fate by the authorities of the country.
See: http://policehommage.blogspot.com under the heading: Jean-Michel Jamme /CDI Nannterre (92).

reinforced with steel, and this security system saves the life of Bakhtiar. The terrorists cannot enter the apartment. They steal the police guard Marty's machinegun and shoot seven rounds at the door, but to no avail.

"The sound of the firing warns the police guard, Philippe Jourdain, about what is going on and the dire situation. When he enters the entry hall of the building, horrified, he sees the body of Bernard Vigna, which is soaked in blood. Then he notices the body of Jean-Michel Jamme, and immediately with his radio he calls for backup.

"The terrorists start to escape, but when, as they are escaping, they notice Phillipe Jourdain, one of them fires at him without being able to wound him. The police guard, Phillipe Jourdain, fires at the terrorists with his machinegun and succeeds in injuring one of them in his arm and abdomen, and forces the other two to surrender by shooting at the ground.

"Jean Reillé, the high commissioner, who is patrolling in the Courbevoie neighborhood, learns about the incident from the radio in his official vehicle, rushes to the location of the incident, and along with the guard, Philippe Jourdain, takes control of the situation until another group of police officers arrives to help.

"The Anti-Gang Brigade under the command of Commissioner Robert Broussard that has arrived at the location immediately captures all three terrorists. They take them to the location of the Criminal Brigade located at 36, Quai des Orfèvres. The terrorists, who seem calm and unconcerned, are very talkative and answer the questions with self-confidence. The police then capture two other members of this commando team in their hiding place on Tuileries Street in the 5th arrondissement of Paris.

"A small group by the name of 'Guardians of Islam' that considers itself to be affiliated with the Palestine Liberation Organization assumes responsibility for this assassination attempt in a communiqué. According to that communiqué, Anis al-Naqqash, a Lebanese national and former accomplice of the well-known terrorist Carlos, announces that the assassination attempt was directed personally by Yasser Arafat, the leader of the Palestine Liberation Organization. Nezhad-Tabrizi of Iranian descent, Fawzi Mohammad El Satari a Palestinian, and two Syrians by the names of Salah Eddine El Kaara and Mohammad Janab are other members of this commando group."[8]

In his memoir, Rafiqdust regards Mohammad Janab to be an Iranian and a resident of Qom, whereas in the French Police documents, he is identified as a Syrian national. In addition, the French Police mention an Iranian, a Lebanese, a Palestinian, and two Syrians on the terrorist team, whereas Rafiqdust mentions three Iranians and two Lebanese, and he does not reveal the name of one Iranian member of the group. It appears that he either makes a mistake in explaining the nationality of the terrorists and the killing and wounding of the victims of the incident of the assassination attempt on Bakhtiar, or he is trying to conceal any trace of some of them. He also mentions the terrorists as reporters of an Arabic newspaper, whereas according to French Police documents, they identified themselves as reporters of the French newspaper, l'Humanité.

The terrorist members of the Anis al-Naqqash commando team were all captured. Four of them were sentenced to life imprisonment and one to twenty years. On 27 July 1990, however, French President François Mitterrand pardoned all of them after ten years in jail within the framework of negotiations between France and Iran.[9]

Regarding the negotiations that took place with the French authorities for the release of Anis al-Naqqash, the minister of foreign affairs of the Islamic Republic, Ali Akbar Velayati, states: "We promised them that we would use all of our influence for the release of the French hostages in Lebanon, and we actually did so; and the representative of the French Foreign Ministry promised our special envoy to do certain things for us, which included the pardoning and release of Anis al-Naqqash."[10]

The name of Anis al-Naqqash first became known to the public when OPEC ministers were taken hostage in Vienna. In November 1975, along with Ilich Ramírez Sánchez, the Venezuelan terrorist known as

Carlos the Jackal, al-Naqqash took the ministers of eleven OPEC member countries as hostages. After his arrest and trial on the charge of participation in the failed assassination attempt on Bakhtiar and spending part of his sentence in jail and his ultimate release, al-Naqqash returned to Iran, where he engaged in business and became the president of an organization called Aman Research Center.

The release of the perpetrators of the failed assassination attempt on Bakhtiar and the negotiations that are mentioned in the police report are explained in more detail in Rafiqdust's memoir. According to him, after the attack of a Lebanese guerrilla group, the members of which were friends of Anis al-Naqqash, on the French embassies in 1990 and the hijacking of a French airplane, Nicolas Lang, the representative of the French president, met with him. The topic of this meeting was apparently the attack of the Lebanese terrorists on French embassies and its connection with the jailing of Anis al-Naqqash and his accomplices. In the court, they had confessed that they had come to France to kill Bakhtiar on the order of Rafiqdust. He states: "I told the representative of the French president that we are not responsible for what has happened. If you want to prevent such incidents, release them; otherwise, their friends will again carry out other operations… These negotiations continued until Abu Mazen went on a hunger strike in prison. The French government did not by any means want him to die in prison, as he was on a severe hunger strike and was near death. They were giving him injections to keep him alive. He had said that he would stop his hunger strike if asked by a representative from Iran, in particular Rafiqdust. Even though many people told me that my name was on the list of defendants in the case and it was risky for me, after consultation with others, I decided to go. I said, 'What will be will be. This operation was carried out on my order. Now, let whatever must happen, happen.' This was during the presidency of Mr. Hashemi-Rafsanjani. I also spoke with him. And I told the representative of the French government, 'I will come and ask him to go off his hunger strike on the condition that you promise to release them.' Even though they had promised—a helicopter had even landed on the roof of the prison to take them—they changed their minds.

"Finally, to put an end to the issue, the representative of the French government suggested, 'In Iran, you have a law that if someone is innocently killed, the family of the victim is given blood money. We also have a law regarding paying damages. If you want this matter to be concluded, pay the blood money or damages for the ones who have been killed or wounded.' I agreed to it. According to their law, these damages amounted to about $500,000. Mr. Hashemi-Rafsanjani ordered the money to be paid."[11]

Continuing his explanations, Rafiqdust refers to the negotiations with the French foreign minister about the progress, of which President Mitterrand was also informed. The topic of these negotiations was the efforts of Rafiqdust to end Anis al-Naqqash's hunger strike and to obtain the promise for his release two weeks after the payment of damages. In his memoir, Rafiqdust then discusses his meeting with the French police chief and his visit to al-Naqqash in prison. He recounts: "Along with the French police chief, who was driving a late model car, we set out toward the Paris prison. I sat next to him without any knowledge of the French language. Recalling this reminds me of police movies. When we entered the prison, someone came with a large keychain, unlocked the doors one by one, and locked them behind us. I counted the doors. We arrived at the tenth door. It was different from the other doors. It resembled a clinic. We entered an area in which Anis al-Naqqash's mother was also present. We had coordinated her visit earlier... I saw Anis al-Naqqash, who was lying down on a bed. His eyes had lost their sparkle, and he did not weigh even forty kilograms. All that was left of him was skin and bones. As soon as he saw me, he told the jailors, 'Give me some vitamins.' They gave him some. We waited about half an hour until he felt a bit better. He said, 'Help me sit up.' When he did, he said, 'I won. You lost. Despite all your grandeur, you surrendered to the Islamic Republic. Now, because the representative of the Islamic Republic wants me to, I will break my hunger strike.' We were with him for an hour and then went back. They released the prisoners in two weeks, and they came to Iran."[12]

The Murder of Shapour Bakhtiar and the Trial of the Accused

One year after Anis al-Naqqash and his accomplices were released from prison on the order of François Mitterrand with the involvement of such Iranian officials as Rafiqdust, Velayati, and Hashemi-Rafsanjani, Shapour Bakhtiar and his assistant, Sorush Katibeh, were savagely murdered on 6 August 1991 in a villa where they resided in Suresnes, a Paris suburb. According to the report by Jean-Louis Bruguière, the French magistrate, to the office of the public prosecutor of that country, the murder of Bakhtiar and his assistant was a continuation of the murders of the opponents of the Iranian regime. Shahriyar Shafiq, the son of the former Shah's sister, Ashraf Pahlavi, was the first victim, who was shot to death in Paris shortly after the victory of the Islamic Revolution in Iran. After him, General Oveysi and his brother were assassinated in the capital of France. On 23 October 1990, Sirus Elahi, a member of the Derafsh Kaviyani Organization, was shot to death in the hallway of his home with several bullets. On 18 April 1991, Abdorrahman Borumand, a distinguished member and chairman of the supreme council of the National Resistance Movement, was brutally stabbed to death in the hallway of his home. On that day, he had attended a meeting in Bakhtiar's home in which Fereydun Boyer-Ahmadi, one of the murderers of Bakhtiar and Katibeh, also participated. Borumand had left the meeting early to meet, according to what he had said, with two people who had arrived from Iran. In addition to his position in Bakhtiar's political organization and being referred to as the number-two man of the National Resistance Movement, he had been a longtime friend of Bakhtiar, and his murder was an irreparable blow. Borumand was trying to organize a new effort to overcome the difficulties, in particular, the financial ones that Bakhtiar's organization was facing. An example of such difficulties is evident in the last emergency meeting of the supreme council of the National Resistance Movement, which was held to find a successor to Borumand shortly before the assassination of

Bakhtiar. Of the twenty-eight people who had been invited to that meeting, only ten people attended, one of whom was Boyer-Ahmadi and the other, Bakhtiar, who was being isolated more than ever before.[13]

Bakhtiar's secretary during his premiership, Pari Kalantari, states: "When they killed Borumand, Bakhtiar said to me, 'Why are you crying? He was killed for his country. I hope I will be killed on such a path, as well.' I remember once, when a few members of the prime minister's guards from his premiership came to Paris, and in a meeting explaining the situation of protecting him, they told me, 'His protection detail is very inadequate.' For this reason, I was worried about him. Another time, when his conversation with a person who had come from Iran lasted a long time, again I became worried about him. After it was finished, when I told him that I had been concerned for his safety, he said, 'Don't judge me by my size! I am a karate expert. You think these people can kill me?' They did kill him, in that same house."[14]

According to the police report, Bakhtiar rarely had any visitors in the final months of his life. During these months, rumors were spreading that he had serious financial problems, to the extent that he could no longer stay in the Suresnes villa. According to one of his relatives: "During the years of power, when Mr. Bakhtiar had money, baskets of flowers came during Persian New Year; but during the last New Year, not even one flower came. Bakhtiar's radio stations in Iraq and Egypt had shut down. There was no money for his publications. According to many of his close associates, in the final weeks of his life, Bakhtiar lived in severe destitution, and he was even in debt to a couple of French banks. But it was Bakhtiar personally who was suffering such a dire financial situation."[15] In this connection, Ramin Kamran, a member of the National Resistance Movement, writes about the situation of Bakhtiar and this organization: "One reason that it was managed so poorly was that Bakhtiar paid no attention to financial problems, and his excessive generosity had turned his office into a social assistance agency."[16]

Agence France-Presse reported: "On Thursday, 8 August 1991, 48 hours after their death, the bodies of Bakhtiar and his assistant were discovered at the place of their residence in Villa no. 37 on Rue Cluseret in the small town of Suresnes near Paris. The cause of death was determined to be severance of the larynx, strangulation, and numerous stab wounds, which had caused severe loss of blood. The murderers had taken two weapons, a bread knife and a butcher's knife, from the kitchen of Bakhtiar's home, which they used to carry out their assignment; and after the murders, they had left them there. Boyer-Ahmadi knew beforehand that the Portuguese couple who served at the villa were on vacation and that no one else other than Bakhtiar and Katibeh were in the house.

"With the discovery of their bodies, Fereydun Boyer-Ahmadi, Mohammad Azadi, and Ali Vakili-Rad, the last people to have visited Bakhtiar, became suspects. On 6 August at 5 PM, after going through the necessary protocols and the checking of their documents by the police, they had entered the building where Bakhtiar lived, and left that place an hour later. With the warrant for their arrests, two weeks later, at 5 AM on 21 August 1991, Vakili-Rad was arrested on the banks of Lake Leman in Geneva by the Swiss Police. The other two suspects had vanished.

"When Vakili-Rad was being arrested, he had no identification papers, but he had identified himself to the police using the name Vakili-Rad. The last time he had been seen was Wednesday morning, 14 August, when he was leaving the Windsor Hotel three hours before the police arrived there. Vakili-Rad had identified himself with a Turkish passport. A hotel computer glitch had allowed him to escape from the trap that the police had set for his arrest. On Thursday, 15 August, Geneva Police had lost track of Mohammad Azadi. A man meeting his description had spent two nights, from Tuesday 13 to Thursday 15 August, in Hotel Jean-Jacques Rousseau. On those two nights, Mohammad Azadi had been traveling with another man whose description does not match any of the sketches distributed by French authorities. Both men had identified themselves at the hotel with Iranian passports. In addition, on

Tuesday, another Iranian had reserved the room for them and said that they were supposed to come to the hotel that afternoon. The sketches that the French Interior Ministry had distributed from the beginning for finding the murderers left no doubt that the individual arrested on the banks of Lake Leman in Geneva was none other than Vakili-Rad. Three hotels in Geneva had been notified of his presence under the alias of Musa Kocer, the Turkish name on his passport, and of the presence of Mohammad Azadi, with the Turkish name of Ali Kaya, in Switzerland a week earlier.

"In the meantime, while the French officials had been notified of the presence of two suspicious individuals in Switzerland, the Parisian judge, Gille Riviére, who was in charge of the case, issued an international warrant for the arrest of Azadi and Vakili-Rad along with a request for their extradition to France. Several inspectors of the French Criminal Brigade also went to Switzerland to investigate this issue.

"Following the arrest of Vakili-Rad and numerous interrogations of him, it became clear that after committing the crime, the three suspects left Suresnes in Boyer-Ahmadi's car and had traveled to Boulogne Forest. There, Azadi and Vakili-Rad, after changing their clothes, had disposed of their bloody clothes, which were found the next day along with their torn-up Iranian passports. Then Boyer-Ahmadi drops his accomplices in front of a metro station and tells them that he will join them later. Late in the afternoon of the same day, Azadi and Vakili-Rad try, according to plan, to cross the border from France to Switzerland to meet others who were assigned to help them flee from that country. Boyer-Ahmadi goes to his rented studio apartment at 36 Avenue d'Italie in the 13th arrondissement of Paris. From there, he goes to another rented studio apartment at 112 Rue Saint-Charles in the 15th arrondissement of Paris, and then disappears. Later investigations indicated that Azadi and Vakili-Rad had gone from Paris to Lyon and then to Nancy, and on 7 August, they had presented their Turkish passports to the police at the border between France and Switzerland. The Swiss border agents send them back to France because their visas were forgeries. Four days later, they secretly cross the border and get themselves to Geneva.

"With the expansion of the investigations by the French judicial officials, Judge Riviére on 18 August 1991 assigned an international investigation committee to conduct investigations in Iran, a measure that would allow the French inspectors to travel to Tehran and pursue the investigations there. Among other things, this committee was also assigned to clarify the source of the two seemingly-legitimate Turkish and Iranian passports of Ali Vakili-Rad and Mohammad Azadi. According to a source close to the inspection team, the names on the Iranian passports could have been aliases."[17]

In an interview with the correspondent of *Paris Match*, Guy Bakhtiar, who had been responsible for protecting his father for twelve years, considering what had happened, said: "I am speaking with you not as Bakhtiar's son, but as a police officer. The police guards that were on duty at my father's villa had received instructions that were not carried out fully. The result was that an opportunity for maneuvering was provided, and the murderers took advantage of it. On that day, I left my father's villa at 3:30 in the afternoon. The three individuals arrived there at 4:30. I had, however, given the necessary instructions to the guards, the same instructions that I usually gave them. But not all these instructions were carried out… First, the commander of the guards was supposed to check the garden. This was not done. The police guards were supposed to knock on the door of the villa every day at 10 a.m. and ask my father about the people who had an appointment with him on that day. This was also not done on Wednesday morning, the day after the crime occurred. I am not saying that they could have prevented this horrible crime; but if my instructions had been followed, then everything related to the arrest of the murderers would have been different." In this interview, Bakhtiar's son had called for the cancellation of Mitterrand's visit to Iran.[18]

The murder of Bakhtiar and his secretary escalated a political controversy in France. The opposition members of the parliament strongly criticized the government, and the press and the news media, upon publishing the details of the incident, called for the cancellation of the visit of Mitterrand, the president of that country, to Iran. Addressing the prime minister, parliamentary deputy Nicole Catala said in the session of parliament: "Between 1984 and 1990, no member of the Iranian opposition was assassinated on our soil; but in October 1990, yes, only three months after Anis al-Naqqash was pardoned and released, which encouraged the clerics in Iran, a member of the opposition was murdered in the 15th arrondissement of Paris. In April 1991, another political opponent was murdered in Square Vauban. In August 1991, they stabbed Shapour Bakhtiar and his assistant to death. Shapour Bakhtiar had created hope for attaining democracy in Iran. In France, he had entrusted his life and soul to us... On the day after this murder, public opinion in France expected the Élysée Palace to announce that Mr. Mitterrand had changed his mind about traveling to Iran... But this did not happen. On the contrary, in September, we heard that Mr. Alain Vivien, the director general of the Foreign Ministry, has gone to Tehran, and on this visit, he has referred to the two crimes that occurred in Paris as 'incidents'... Last Friday, we heard that Mr. Roland Dumas, the foreign minister, wanted to sign the agreement regarding the settlement of the financial disputes between Iran and France by paying the Tehran regime seven billion francs... This indicates that Mr. Mitterrand still intends to visit Iran... Madame Prime Minister! Tell us what has happened to French honor and dignity. Should the expenses for the wishes of François Mitterrand, who wants to go to Tehran as the top leader of the country, be paid at the price of the blood of the Iranian political opponents? . . . So, do you think Anis al-Naqqash is right, who has recently said that in order for friendly relations to be established between France and Iran, another ten Bakhtiars need to be killed? . . . Madame Prime Minister! This duplicitous game cannot continue. Honor and dignity cannot be severed from diplomacy. We expect you to tell us frankly whether the president still intends to respond positively to the invitation by a terrorist regime and travel to that country? Do you still adhere to a policy of surrender coupled with weakness and disgrace?"[19]

Ali Ahani, the ambassador of the Islamic Republic in Paris, considering the accusations made regarding the role of the Islamic Republic in Bakhtiar's murder, presented a different picture of what had occurred. One day after the murder of Bakhtiar, he assured the French government that Tehran had by no means had a hand in the assassination of Bakhtiar. Issuing a statement, he said that this assassination might have been plotted by certain groups that opposed improvement of relations between Iran and France, but he did not reveal the names of such groups. The press division of the embassy also added that "the hypothesis cannot be dismissed that the murder of Shapour Bakhtiar may have stemmed from the internal quarrels and settling of accounts of various opposition groups."[20]

The trial court of the defendants accused of murdering Bakhtiar and Katibeh, following more than three years of investigations by the Justice Department of France regarding this crime, finally began its work on 2 November 1994 under heavy police protection in the Special Criminal Court in the Justice Department building of Paris. According to the bill of indictment, in this court, nine persons were to be put on trial on the charge of committing murder, assisting in committing murder, and participation in a criminal terrorist group attempting to disrupt public order in France. From among the defendants, Ali Vakili-Rad, Mas'ud Hendi, and Zeynol'abedin Sarhadi were on the defendants' platform, but the rest were fugitives. The police had tracked them as far as Turkey but had been unable to find them.

The presiding judge, seven professional judges of the special anti-terrorism court, and ninety-three witnesses were present in the courtroom. The court sessions were open; but because the defendants were charged with terrorism, the trial was held without a jury. The trial of the defendants took more than a month for examining over 8,300 pages. According to *Le Soir* newspaper, in this trial, in fact, the regime of Iran, the virtual criminal, with its government terrorism was being convicted.

Shahintaj Bakhtiar, Shapour Bakhtiar's wife, and their sons Gudarz and Guy, and Patrick and France, the other children of Bakhtiar, in addition to his grandson Turang, were in the private plaintiffs' seats in the courtroom. From Katibeh's family, no one was in the courtroom. François Rudetzki, the president of the association for helping the victims of terrorism (SOS), who had been severely injured many years earlier in a bombing, along with Antoine Espiz, the attorney of the association, were also in the court. In addition, Abdolkarim Lahiji, as the observer of the International Federation for Human Rights and former president of that federation in addition to several of the allies, colleagues, and friends of Bakhtiar were present in the court. One of them was Ms. Ladan Borumand, the daughter of Abdorrahman Borumand, the man whose murderers pulled him to the side of the elevator in the hallway of his home, and in order to prevent him from shouting, one of them covered his mouth and the other cut his jugular vein with a knife. In her testimony, Ladan Borumand stated that at least two people had told Bakhtiar that Fereydun Boyer-Ahmadi was a spy for the Islamic Republic. But, like Borumand, Bakhtiar also became the victim of "simplistic perceptiveness and simple-heartedness." One witness said that Bakhtiar had been told: "Be careful of Fereydun; he is a traitor; he is an agent." But he paid no attention. It was said that Bakhtiar had been informed that Boyer-Ahmadi's wife was a typist in the Construction Jihad (Jehad-e Sazandegi) in Yasuj, and that he was a member of the Islamic Republic Guard Corps in Yasuj. Moreover, Manuchehr Ganji, the minister of education in the cabinets of Prime Minister Hoveyda and Prime Minister Sharif-Emami, also claimed that sometime before the murder of Bakhtiar, he had been informed by a reliable source in the Islamic Republic that in August 1991, a commando team would be dispatched to Paris to assassinate "one of the four well-known opponents of the regime," Reza Pahlavi, Bakhtiar, Banisadr, or himself. Ganji had informed Reza Pahlavi and Banisadr, and with two telephone calls, he had attempted to inform Bakhtiar, but Bakhtiar apparently did not wish to speak to him and avoided conversing with him. Hence,

Ganji had to give his message to Bakhtiar's assistant. He states: "Unfortunately, Mr. Bakhtiar often behaved like that toward others."[21]

At any rate, the start of the court proceedings and the trial of the defendants along with the result of police interrogations and investigations showed that the murder plot had been planned for some time, and that preparations for it, such as preparing and forging passports and letters of invitation, and obtaining French and Swiss visas, as well as providing technical resources, had been carefully planned.

For this purpose, two passports with aliases had been issued in Iran for each murderer, and each, in their trip to France, had both of these forged passports, a passport in the name of Naser Nuriyan for Mohammad Azadi and a passport in the name of Amir Kamal-Hoseyni for Ali Vakili-Rad. Upon presenting their new passports to the French Embassy in Tehran, they requested visas. On the application form, they stated that they were going to France to purchase replacement parts for electronic equipment for the Ceefax Company. The person who introduced them to the French Embassy in Tehran was Mas'ud Hendi, one of the defendants in the case of the murders of Bakhtiar and Katibeh. Previously, Hendi had been the manager of the Voice and Vision of the Islamic Republic in Paris. After returning to Iran, he had traveled to France many times as a consultant for the Ceefax Company, and in this position, he had played a role in facilitating the issuance of visas for the murderers, who had applied for visas under the cover of trade activities. Moreover, in order to conceal the nationality of the murderers when fleeing from France, the planners of the assassination plot also prepared two forged Turkish passports for them in Istanbul.[22][iii]

All of this shows that careful planning and multilateral coordination had been carried out between the planners and perpetrators of the assassinations in Iran, France, Switzerland, and Turkey. In addition, the

---

[iii] For details of the proceedings of the court sessions and also the past record of the defendants and the testimonies of Bakhtiar's allies and colleagues, see: Pari Sekandari, *Dar Dadgah-e Mottahaman beh Qatl-e Bakhtiar*, 2nd printing (Paris: Khavaran Publishers, 2006).

visits of Boyer-Ahmadi to Germany and Austria showed that those two countries as well were also places for coordinating the advancement of this plot.

With the court proceedings and the trials in Paris, once again the issue of the murder of the last prime minister of the former regime in Iran, which was mentioned as the most important assassination in the past fifty years, occupied a special place in the mass media of that country. Considering the criticism that was made of Bakhtiar's guards, in an article, l'Humanité newspaper wrote: "The guards of Bakhtiar's villa have stated that, on the day of the murder and the following day, they had not noticed anything unusual. Guy Bakhtiar, Shapour Bakhtiar's son, stopped by his father's house, and every time he made sure that the guards were doing their duty properly. On 6 August 1991, at about 3 PM, Bakhtiar's son had given the list of those invited to Bakhtiar's home to the brigade officer, Patrick d'Chez. There were three names on the list. Those three are the ones accused of murdering him and his assistant: The first one is Boyer-Ahmadi, who was a member of the National Resistance Movement of Iran up to the day of the murders. Shapour Bakhtiar was the leader of that Movement. The second is a person by the name of Azadi, who is at large. The third is Ali Vakili-Rad, who is on trial today along with his accomplices, by the names of Mas'ud Hendi and Abedin Sarhadi.

"The police guards had performed all of their security duties regarding all three invited at 5 PM on 6 August 1991 during their entry into Bakhtiar's home, including checking their passports, searching their clothes, and having them pass through the metal detector. The team that guarded Bakhtiar consisted of a post commander, a brigade officer, and three internal security policemen (CRS). Interestingly, on 7 August, the period of the assignment of this team, that is, Squad 36 of 'Thionville,' was to end and the guard protection would become the responsibility of Squad 37 of 'Strasbourg.' The bodies were discovered by Squad 37. It might have been because of the time wasted during the changing of the guards that the police discovered the bodies so late. According to experts, Bakhtiar and his assistant were killed between 4 and 8 PM on 6 August, but their bodies were discovered about 48 hours later. What happened between 5 and 6 PM, that is, between the hour that the visitors entered and the hour that they left, in Bakhtiar's villa in Suresnes? All three policemen who were in the interrogator's office yesterday have said that all the visitors, both when they arrived and when they left, were very calm. Patrick d'Chez, the brigade officer who due to his type of assignment had been close by Bakhtiar's house, has said that during the time that the visit lasted, he neither heard any shouts nor any sound or noise. During questioning, he also expressed astonishment about the security directives. According to him, 'The police officials were not permitted to enter Bakhtiar's home. The gravel in the courtyard of Bakhtiar's house made a sound when the guards went on patrol there, and Mr. Bakhtiar complained about it. As a result, we only checked the area in front of the courtyard.' The defense attorney, referring to the statements of Guy Bakhtiar, has said in an interview with *Le Figaro* newspaper, 'Had the guards checked the entire courtyard in the afternoon on 6 August, they would have noticed Bakhtiar's body and the disarray in his office. After all, how could it be possible for the police officials not to have seen the bloodstained shirts of two of the visitors when they were leaving?' In response, the police officials have said, 'They had buttoned up their jackets all the way, and their shirt sleeves were not visible for us to notice the bloodstains.' Another question is, why had the police not become suspicious because the lights in the house were on and no one had shut the blinds? The police official had responded that this had happened frequently in the past.

"Hugh Zalmer, one of the internal security policemen, has said to the judge on 9 August 1991 that for 15 minutes, sometime between 5:30 and 6:45 PM, from where he stood watch, he saw Bakhtiar's assistant in conversation with one of the visitors, whom he had thought might have been Vakili-Rad. But because where he stood watch was 20 to 25 meters from the house, he could not hear their conversation. The only thing that he had seen was that they were smiling at each other, and perhaps this was when his accomplices were killing the last prime minister of the Shah in the parlor of his own house."[23]

In another article, under the heading of "The Suspicious Account of Bakhtiar's Murder," based on the statements of Razmara, the minister of health in his cabinet, l'Humanité newspaper wrote: "The official account about the murder of Shapour Bakhtiar leaves room for doubt. The report on the discovery of the bodies 48 hours after the crime was committed is not credible. Bakhtiar's home constantly had frequent visitors. The grocer of the neighborhood has stated that on Wednesday morning, as usual, he had placed the basket of groceries ordered by Shapour Bakhtiar's home in the courtyard of his villa home, but no one had expressed any concern that during that time, no one from Bakhtiar's house had taken the basket of groceries. Moreover, Bakhtiar's telephone after his murder was constantly busy. Considering that on Thursday at about 11 AM, Dr. Razmara had been among the first people to discover the bodies of the victims in Bakhtiar's home, he states, 'Clearly, there had been a scuffle between the victims and the criminals. At least fighting between Bakhtiar's assistant and the assailants is undeniable. How could the police guards (CRS) not have heard any sound?'"[24]

In any case, when Bakhtiar's son, Guy, who had been an inspector in the General Directorate for Internal Security of France since 1974, and who had been assigned the responsibility of protecting his father by that agency, realized that the telephone of Bakhtiar's house was constantly busy, he informed the police. But it was already too late. Bakhtiar had been soaking in blood with his throat cut on a bench in the parlor of his house since two nights earlier. The coroner announced the cause of death to be strangulation and stabbing. Bakhtiar's neck had been stabbed thirteen times with a kitchen knife. Katibeh had five large wounds to his liver, heart, and spinal column areas. He also had a large number of small wounds where they had stabbed him with a bread knife. Prior to the report of the coroner, the presiding judge had asked

Bakhtiar's wife and children to leave the session until the report was concluded. According to Lahiji: "Listening to those statements was heartrending, not only for the survivors in his family, but also for the attorneys."[25]

In the course of the trial, Vakili-Rad denied having committed murder, retracting his initial admissions. Stating that he and Azadi were supporters of Bakhtiar, he said that they had come to Paris to discuss the plot for bombing the Shiraz refinery, and that on the evening of the day before the incident, Boyer-Ahmadi had told them about the plot to kill Bakhtiar; and, fearful and concerned about his own family in Iran, Vakili-Rad had gone to Bakhtiar's house, but did not participate in the killing of Bakhtiar and Katibeh. Rather, he had merely "witnessed" it.

Finally, the court on 6 December 1994, after hearing the defense by the attorneys of the defendants and the private plaintiffs and the final defense of the defendants, declared in its ruling that the arrangements for this crime had been made in Tehran, and that it was carried out by a professional criminal terrorist network. In accordance with the ruling of the court, Ali Vakili-Rad was sentenced to life imprisonment, with the provision of serving at least eighteen years. The court sentenced Mas'ud Hendi to ten years in jail, a minimum of two-thirds of which he was required to serve. Zeynol'abedin Sarhadi, the employee of the Iranian Embassy in Berne, who was accused of having assisted Azadi and Vakili-Rad to cross the French border into Switzerland, was acquitted of all charges; however, he was expelled from France on the order of the interior minister.

With the announcement of the court ruling, in an official communiqué, the Islamic Republic regarded the acquittal ruling as proof that Sarhadi had played no role in the murders of Bakhtiar and Katibeh, proof that was not valid from the perspective of the International Federation for Human Rights. According to Lahiji, in an announcement, that federation pointed out: "Organizing such a network of professional criminals and providing the equipment and making the preparations for the entry of the criminals into France and Switzerland,

and in particular arranging their escape under the cover of authentic and forged passports with different identities, can be carried out only and indisputably by a government."[26]

Judge Bruguière wanted to extend the investigation related to Bakhtiar's murder up to the high-ranking Iranian officials who occupied the seats of power at that time. The president of France, François Mitterrand, however, had said: "This court has come to session to investigate a murder and not to put a regime on trial."[27]

After the court concluded its work, looking back at what had passed, *Le Parisien* newspaper wrote: "From the day after the murder of Bakhtiar, no one had any doubt that his murderers had received their order for this terrorist mission from an extremist Islamist in Tehran. Nevertheless, the involvement of the Iranian government in this murder has never been proven, even though his elimination benefitted a regime that knows no bounds in reacting to its political rivals. Is it not a fact that one month prior to the killing of Bakhtiar, the minister of foreign affairs of the Islamic Republic had asked France to extradite him to Tehran to be put on trial? In any case, the murder of the former prime minister of Iran resulted in the cooling of relations between Iran and France that had just begun to warm."[28] Ali Akbar Velayati, the former foreign minister of the Islamic Republic, who was a presidential candidate in 2013, without mentioning the name of Bakhtiar and his murder and pointing out that this incident had an impact on relations between Iran and France and the cancellation of Mitterrand's visit to Iran, said: "An incident was created by certain individuals who did not want to ruin things, but it ruined the business of foreign policy, and Mitterand did not come."[29]

Finally, Vakili-Rad was released from prison after eighteen years on 18 May 2010. Agence France-Presse reported that he was able to make use of a conditional release, which in accordance with the laws of that country can be implemented regarding such criminals based on certain conditions. Vakili-Rad immediately left France and returned to Iran. The order for his expulsion had been signed one day prior to his release by the interior minister. What made his release controversial was the return of Clotilde Reiss, a French national, from Iran. Reiss was a student at the University of Isfahan who had been officially charged with threatening Iran's national security. She was accused in particular of having photographed and collected information on 15 and 17 June 2009 in Isfahan in opposition to the reelection of Ahmadinezhad as president. Reiss had been arrested at the airport before leaving Iran for participating in the demonstrations following the presidential election, had been charged with espionage, and had been sentenced to 10 years in jail by the Revolution Court. French government officials denied any connection between her release and that of Vakili-Rad. Many analysts, however, believed that this was not the first time that France had engaged in such an exchange. The release of two persons accused of the murder of Kazem Rajavi in 1992, whose extradition to Switzerland the Swiss government had requested of France, was an example of the implementation of this policy. Another example was the pardoning and early release in 1980 of Anis al-Naqqash, who had been pardoned by Mitterrand, the president of France at the time. Critics were of the opinion that every time the French government has advanced this policy, it has done so "justifying it within the framework of the higher, loftier objectives of the country." According to Lahiji, the vice president of the International Federation for Human Rights at the time, contrary to the claim of the French government, the release of Vakili-Rad, more than being for judicial and legal reasons, was for political reasons. He said: "It should be noted that the period of imprisonment of which Ali Vakili-Rad was conclusively convicted in accordance with French laws ended last summer, and if he had remained in jail up to now, in terms of the judge's decision, such has been the implementation of the ruling of the French Justice Department. Since such an individual would not be allowed to remain in France after his release, and prior to his release, the order for his expulsion from France needed to be issued by the Ministry of Interior, this judge could not order his release. Hence, we can see that the release of Ali Vakili-Rad was beyond the authority of the

French judicial system and was dependent on the political decision of the French interior minister."[30]

According to the defense attorney of Clotilde Reiss, she was to leave Iran on 15 May 2010. From July 2009, Reiss had been in detention on the charge of participation in anti-government demonstrations following the presidential election in Iran. The court finally reversed the charge of espionage against her and sentenced her merely to the payment of a cash fine. This ruling was issued a few days after France announced that it would not extradite Majid Kakavand, an Iranian engineer, to the United States. This Iranian engineer had been arrested in France in March 2009 on the request of the U.S. Justice Department. The French magazine, *Le Point*, wrote: "With the release of Clotilde Reiss, the tug-of-war that had poisoned relations between Iran and France came to an end, even though these relations were sufficiently cloudy before because of Iran's nuclear energy issue and the issue of uranium enrichment in Iran. Mohammad Ali Mahdavi-Sabet, the defense attorney of Clotilde Reiss, announced on Saturday that the Revolution Court has fined Ms. Reiss 300 million *tumans* ($285,000) in cash. Mahdavi-Sabet said that following the issuance of this ruling, he has decided not to request an appeal, because he considers this ruling to be, in a way, the 'acquittal' of Ms. Reiss, especially since Ms. Reiss can leave Iran beginning tomorrow.

"The governments of Iran and France have officially denied any connection between the release of Clotilde Reiss and France's refusal to extradite Majid Kakavand to the United States. Mahmud Ahmadinezhad, however, announced on 18 December that resolving the issue of Reiss depends on 'the conduct of the leaders of France.'"[31]

On his return to Iran, Vakili-Rad was welcomed at the airport by Hasan Qashqavi, the deputy foreign minister of the Islamic Republic, and Kazem Jalali, a member of the national security committee of the parliament. In these ceremonies, Kazem Jalali referred to Vakili-Rad as a "national hero," a "hero" who along with his friends twelve years after the announcement of the decree by Ayatollah Khomeyni carried out the lightning-quick decree of the Revolution Court regarding the killing of

Bakhtiar at the hands of those he trusted, as though trust were the Achilles heel of the Bakhtiari chieftains.

[1] *Keyhan*, 13 May 1979, 1.

[2] Ibid., 17 May 1979, 2.

[3] Ibid.

[4] *Bara-ye Tarikh Miguyam: Khaterat-e Mohsen Rafiqdust*, compiled by Sa'id Allamiyan (Tehran: Sureh-ye Mehr Publishers, 2013), 129.

[5] Ibid., 128-129, 133.

[6] Ibid., 129.

[7] Ibid., 84-85, 129-130.

[8] See: http://policehommage.blogspot.com under the heading: Jean-Michel Jamme/CDI Nannterre (92).

[9] Ibid., Jean-Michel Jamme/CDI Nannterre (92).

[10] Paygah-e Khabarresani-ye Dr. Ali Akbar Velayati, 11 October 2013.

[11] *Bara-ye Tarikh Miguyam: Khaterat-e Mohsen Rafiqdust*, 130-131.

[12] Ibid., 132-133.

[13] Pari Sekandari, *Dar Dadgah-e Mottahaman beh Qatl-e Bakhtiar*, 2nd printing (Paris: Khavaran Publishers, 2006), 38-39.

[14] This writer's interview with Pari Kalantari, Paris, 24 April 2012.

[15] Sekandari, 39-40.

[16] Ramin Kamran, "Bakhtiar, Bist Sal Ba'd," *Sahand*, no. 30 (February 2012): 25-46.

[17] Reported by *Agence France-Presse* (AFP) and *Reuters*, "Swiss Arrest 1 of 3 Suspects in Bakhtiar Death," 22 August 1991.

[18] Guy Bakhtiar's interview in *Paris Match*, 29 August 1991, quoted from *Payam-e Iran*, no. 410, vol. 11 (17 November 1991): 35-40.

[19] *Journal officiel de la République française* (30 October 1991); quoted in Sekandari, *Dar Dadgah-e Mottahaman beh Qatl-e Bakhtiar*, 41-42.

[20] *Payam-e Iran*, vol. 11, no. 410 (November 1991): 27-28.

[21] Sekandari, *Dar Dadgah-e Mottahaman beh Qatl-e Bakhtiar*, 63-66, 137-146, 158-159; Abdolkarim Lahiji, "Parvandeh-ye teror-e Bakhtiar bar Asas-e Keyfarkhast-e Dadsetani-ye Paris," 4 August 2011, quoted from: http://www.bbc.co.uk/persian/iran/2011/08/110804_l10_bakhtiar_20th_anniv_lahiji; Jacques Cordy, "The Ruling of Paris Special Court, Life Imprisonment for One of Bakhtiar's Murderers," *Le Soir* (7 December 1994).

[22] Sekandari, 67-83; Lahiji, "Parvandeh-ye teror-e Bakhtiar bar Asas-e Keyfarkhast-e Dadsetani-ye Paris."

[23] Dominic Barry, "During the Murder of Bakhtiar, the Internal Security Police (CRS) Did Not Hear Anything," *l'Humanité*, 8 November 1994.

[24] Ibid., "The Suspicious Account of Bakhtiar's Murder," 16 November 1994; Lahiji, "Parvandeh-ye teror-e Bakhtiar bar Asas-e Keyfarkhast-e Dadsetani-ye Paris," quoted from:
hhtp://www.bbc.co.uk/persian/iran/2011/08/110804_110_bakhtiar_20th_anniv_lahij i.shtml.

[25] Ibid.

[26] Ibid.

[27] Quoted from France 24, 18/05/2010.

[28] "Thirty-Six Hours," *Le Parisien,* 8 July 2000.

[29] Paygah-e Khabarresani-ye Dr. Ali Akbar Velayati, 13 October 2013.

[30] Interview of Shahrokh Behzadi with Abdolkarim Lahiji, Radio France Internationale, 18 May 2010.

[31] *Le Point,* "The Quarrel Ended" (15 May 2010).

Chapter Two

What I saw there is closer to life than anything else.
—André Malraux

Bakhtiari Territories in the Passage of History

With his eyelids toward the stars, Shapour Bakhtiar opened his eyes to the world in the foothills of Mount Kalar and Mount Sabz in the village of Kunarg, which was also known as Fatehabad, named after his father, Sardar Fateh, "victorious commander." At the end of his assignment as Governor of Yazd, Sardar Fateh was living in Isfahan when for the first time he came face-to-face with his son, Shapour. In the interval, more than one year had passed since his birth. Bakhtiar states: "I had a step-uncle by the name of Sardar Jang, who was older than my father. He owned a village near the village where I was born. He sent a servant or footman to contact my father in any way he could. The former Oil Company had a telegraph office, which would charge you to send telegraphs. They sent a telegraph to Yazd informing my father that he now had a son… Sardar Jang had said to my father, 'Your name is Mohammad Reza, and for now, I have named your son Ahmad Reza.' So, for the first couple of weeks, my name was Ahmad Reza. Later, my father had told my uncle, who was older, 'Whatever you wish, but I prefer Persian names, and if you agree, we will name him Shapour or Iraj.' And I was named Shapour. For a long time, they called me Amir Shapour. Later on, when I went to Beirut, I said that I was not a prince to be called Amir and I dropped Amir from my name."[1]

The history of the Bakhtiari nomadic tribe goes back to ancient times. According to some, the Bakhtiaris are Aryan peoples who have lived since ancient times in southwestern Persia, on the two sides of the Zagros Mountain range. Now that they have become mostly village and city dwellers, the Bakhtiaris reside in the three provinces of Khuzestan, Isfahan, and Chaharmahal and Bakhtiari. Some consider them to be of the Lor lineage, although "they also have a combination of Kurdish and

Arab blood in their veins." Some scholars have linked the history of the
Bakhtiaris in the passage of time to some Assyrian tribes, or they point
out the influence of the Turks, especially the Mongols, on the political
and social organizations of the Bakhtiari tribe.[2]

With its "snow-covered precipices, rough uneven hills, mountain lakes,
horrifying floods, and deep valleys," the Bakhtiari territories have been
called the land of the brave and bravery, the land of fearless people who
have with forbearance experienced hardship and adversity, and without
any utterance of complaint and grumbling, they have treaded through
plains and hills and traversed valleys and mountain passes with meagre
provisions.[3]

Describing the people of that land in the plains and plateaus of the
slopes of the Zagros Mountains, Herodotus speaks about their bravery
and mentions the warriors and soldiers of Xerxes, a number of whom
were nomadic tribesmen. Following the changes during the Achaemenid
era, that land enjoyed security and prosperity; but centuries earlier, as
well, there had been signs of farming combined with nomadic life in
Bakhtaran and Khuzestan. The migration of the Indo-Aryan tribes and
the consequences of the wars between Elam and Assyria in the first
millennium BC created unstable governments in that region, until
finally the victory of Cyrus over the Medes in 550 BC brought an end
to the quarrels and battles of the mountain-dwelling tribes, and a new
era began in their life and time. One of the characteristics of this period
was the creation of safe roads on the slopes of the Zagros Mountains,
which began with the military victories of Cyrus and continued when
Darius became king and chose Susa as one of the capitals of the
Achaemenid Empire in 521 BC. Mention should be made that for
centuries after the disintegration of the Achaemenid Empire and the rise
to power of different ruling regimes up to now, security has had a most
fragile meaning in the life and times of tribes, to the extent that a
historian such as Kasravi finds nothing but bitter and harsh words to
describe them.[4]

We also come across descriptions of more or less the same kind regarding the Bakhtiaris in the travel diaries of European world travelers. The distinct characteristic of the Bakhtiaris, which is considered commendable to some degree, is that in order to overcome poverty, hunger, and famine, they have engaged in highway robbery and the plunder of caravans beyond the borders of the Bakhtiari territories: "Due to their extraordinary daring and boldness, these mountain-dwelling tribes have instilled tremendous fear and terror among the inhabitants of this region... These tribesmen are continually at war and engaged in hostility with one another and with the government of Persia; in addition, they are known to be notorious plunderers and highway robbers who make their living through pillaging and plundering the caravans and their cowardly neighbors who are unable to counter them. Among the human race, I have never seen any to be superior to the Bakhtiaris."[5]

With approximately 75,000 square kilometers, the Bakhtiari region is located in the south of the Zagros Mount range, a region the people of which, as long as this tribe has been there, "are never separated from the Zagros." The tribe migrates from its winter abode in July and August and from its summer abode in March and April, when the southwestern part of the Zagros becomes "hot as molten copper" and pastures dry up. In his description of the Bakhtiari region, Baharvand states that with its weak financial ability and lack of modern sciences and technology, the tribe is victim to the wrath of nature and its adversities.[6] It is as though there is no escape from a natural environment that is at times dry and hot, at times cold and freezing, and at times green and pleasant.

From ancient times, pastures and migration, as two fundamental pillars, have shaped tribal life in the Bakhtiari region. The tribe has relied on manpower that is mostly used on animal husbandry, a method of making a living concerning which Ibn Khaldun, the Tunisian historian who was one of the pioneers of sociology, in explaining the foundations of desert dwelling, when he speaks of tribal "spirit" or interdependence and cooperation, says, "The people who make their living by...raising four-legged animals, in order to find pastures and water for their animals, inevitably have to move about and search around in the desert," without this choice preventing them from attending to farming or other ways of making a living. The British historian, Ann Lambton, writes: "The Bakhtiaris provided for Khuzestan's tobacco consumption and they also exported a small amount of grains. And they sent sheep to the Isfahan market." Charles Galt, who served as the British counsel in Isfahan during World War II, speaks about herds of goats and sheep that comprised the "main capital and source of income" of the tribe. According to him, the wool and ghee of the herd, which were of significant value, were sold in the bazaars of Isfahan and Khuzestan. A significant portion of the charcoal that Isfahan needed also was supplied from the diminishing Bakhtiari forests. In the areas where the tribe had settled communities, rice and poppies were cultivated and offered to the market, along with other products, such as wheat and barley. With the discovery of oil in Khuzestan, working for the Anglo-Persian Oil Company also became an important source of income for Bakhtiari laborers.[7]

As mentioned above, the fall of the Achaemenid Empire confronted the people on the slopes of the Zagros Mountains with new developments. The military expedition of Alexander of Macedonia to Persia in 330 BC, and traveling the path that had begun following the conquest of Susa and ended in the conquest of Persepolis and the victory over Darius's army, established a new regime ruling that region. To achieve this goal, Alexander abolished the toll on traveling through the mountain-dwelling tribes, which was a concession that had belonged to them, and with a surprise invasion, he removed the obstacle on the path of the aggressors' conquests. The construction of fortified fortresses and protection of new fortifications in the occupied lands on the slopes of the Zagros Mountains was another measure for stabilizing the position of the conquerors in confrontation with the people of that region, without any of these putting a permanent end to the battles and wars or their resistance.[8]

With the growing prosperity and the population density from the days of Parthian rule, the agricultural lands on the slopes of the Zagros Mountains expanded even more during the Sasanian era. Agriculture thrived, and the creation of passageways and roads on the slopes of the valleys and the plains, which were the migration route of the tribe up to the Arab invasion, brought new meaning and dynamism to the life and times of the tribes.

Not much information is available about the occupation of the lands on the slopes of the Zagros by the Arabs and its consequences with the fall of the Sasanian Empire. We only know that during the Sasanian rule, important changes occurred in the lifestyle of the people and the texture of the land that with the passage of time came to be known as the Bakhtiari territories. The expansion of farming, the creation of roads on the route of the mountain passes and paths, and the construction of new fortresses and military fortifications that resulted in the destruction of forests were among the consequences of the changes that continued up to the time of the Atabaks. The population increase and the settling of some of the inhabitants, which also began from that period and continued to the time of the dynasties of the Safavids, the Afsharids, the Zands, the Qajars, and the Pahlavis, left lasting impacts on Bakhtiari lives, tribal structure, and land, even though up to the Safavid era, no mention is made by researchers of the Bakhtiari tribe, while the people of the Zagros region are referred to as Lors and Kurds.[9]

With the victory of the Atabaks of Lorestan over the Bakhtiari lands in the twelfth century, the power of the tribes also increased. The region of Great Lorestan and its capital city, Izaj (Malamir or Mal-e Amir), which is now called Izeh, and on the mountains of which at one time was located the sacred temple of the Parthians with hints of Greek architecture, once again encountered an increase in trade and economic prosperity. From ancient times, during the Elamite civilization and the Achaemenid era, Izaj was known for its prosperity, and with its 4,000 years of history, its name and the reputation of its grandeur extended beyond its borders. Ibn Battuta, the Moroccan world traveler, regarding his travel from Shushtar to Isfahan, mentions the forty-four Sufi monasteries that he had seen in Izeh, and the "charitable monuments" of the Atabaks. He writes: "Most of these monuments are located on high mountains that are difficult to access, on which they have built roads

through boulders and rocks. The width of these roads that are carved
and leveled into the side of the mountains is sufficient for pack animals
to climb with the cargo they carry. It takes seventeen days to travel the
length of these mountains and ten days to travel their width. The peaks
of these mountains reach the heavens, and rivers flow through them…
There is a monastery at each stopping place on these mountains, which
they call a 'school,' and when a traveler arrives there, they provide food
for him and fodder for the animal he is riding. The traveler does not
need to request these provisions; rather, the custodian of the school
drops by any newly-arrived traveler, gives him two loaves of bread, meat,
and halva, and all this is provided by donations from the Atabaks'
charitable religious endowment."[10]

Simultaneous with the Atabaks' rule, among the tribes that took up
residence on the slopes of the Zagros Mountains, we come across the
name of the Bakhtiari tribe that is divided into two main branches of
"Haft Lang" and "Chahar Lang." Each of these two branches is divided
into several clans and migration units that in the course of the passage of
time have had deep impacts on the history, culture, language, and
traditions of the tribe, to the extent that each mirrors the struggle for
power and reflects the conflicts that have played a role in shaping the
social structure of the tribe. Based on studies that have been conducted
regarding the history of these divisions, we encounter several assessments. The first one is a popular account about a tribal leader who had
two wives, from one of whom he had seven sons and from the other,
four sons. Because of the disputes that occurred after his death, the tribe
was divided into the two parts, Haft Lang and Chahar Lang. The second
hypothesis that has been considered more credible considers this division to be related to some sort of taxation system in the tribe that was
established during the Safavid rule and the reign of Shah Tahmasb. In
addition, some have considered the term "lang" to be related to the
Sanskrit term "langeh," which means "plough."[11] Even though there are
differences of opinion about the history and origin of this division,
ultimately, it seems that the term "lang" is indicative of some sort of

division and partition of pastures and agricultural lands of the tribe that has had an impact on various aspects of its life and history.[i]

From the time when the Safavid Dynasty moved its capital from Tabriz and then from Qazvin to Isfahan in 1598, the Bakhtiari tribe acquired a special place in the system of the government. In the ensuing developments, the establishment of the two main branches of Haft Lang and Chahar Lang gave a new structure to the relationship between the leaders of the tribe and the government. The duties of maintaining security, collecting taxes for the central government, and supplying soldiers and mules for the military forces were conferred on the tribal chiefs. Acquiring positions and royal decrees to govern Bakhtiari territories, they achieved such standing and power that even though all depended on the will and wish of the king, to a certain extent, such standing validated their independence in terms of how they implemented their rule over the tribe, a standing and power that each time in the illustrious name of the king was adorned with the writ and seal of the Safavid monarchs, without being coupled with kindliness.

With the reign of the Safavid king Shah Abbas I, in 1617, the position of the tribe faced a new turn. This period was coupled with a change in the natural texture of the tribal lands as a result of the elimination of the Bakhtiari forests in order to build Isfahan. The extensive albeit unsuccessful efforts of Shah Abbas to change the direction of the Karun River, to construct a dam in Kuhrang and redirect its water toward the Zayandehrud, the river in Isfahan, to bring water to the people of the capital city, which had begun from the time of Shah Tahmasb, was another attempt of this kind. With the employment of thousands of Bakhtiari people to work for wages, this project would leave a lasting impact on their lives. According to Arash Khazeni, Shah Abbas set up a new system to impose more government control and government power

---

[i] For more on the division of the two branches of the Bakhtiari tribe see: Samiya Zolfaqari, "'Lang,' 'Leng' Nist: Negahi beh Vajh-e Tasmiyeh-ye 'Haft Lang' va 'Chahar Lang' dar Taqsimbandi-ye Sakhtar-e Ejtema'i-ye Ashayer-e Bakhtiari," http://anthropology.ir/node/10552.

over the tribe. This policy was far different from the policy that was implemented during the reign of Shah Tahmasb. Even though the inefficiencies of the ruling government and the expansion of the power and independence of the tribes would impede the perpetuity and continuity of the sovereignty of the Safavid kings over the tribe, in advancing their policy, they had no other alternative but to accept this reality, a reality that more than ever before shaped the structure of the tribe during the Safavid era as an entity independent of the central government. Even the invasion by Mahmud Afghan and the plunder and destruction of the Bakhtiari territories was ultimately a temporary obstacle to the shaping of the increasing power of the tribe, a power that eventually, with the crumbling of the Safavid rule in 1731, once again escalated the rebellion and mutiny of the Bakhtiari tribe, which was reflective of the lack of security and chaos throughout the country.[12]

The reign of Nader Shah in 1735 and the rebellion of Ali Morad Khan Bakhtiari from the Chahar Lang clan was the beginning of a new development in the fate of the tribe. This development is considered the first open effort by the tribe to play a more influential role in an era that began with the overthrow of the Safavids and the rise to power of the Afshar Dynasty. The quelling of this rebellion and the killing of its leader, which brought about the forcible sedentarization of a number of the people of the tribe dispatched to Khorasan and replacing them with the Kurdish tribes of Kermanshah, shaped the developments in this period. According to Lambton, the distinct characteristic of this period in the tribal policy of Nader Shah was to expand the relocation and sedentarization of nomads and tribes. This policy pursued the objective of making the dominance over the captured territories constant and confronting the ongoing rebellions and disobedience of the tribes. Another aspect of Nader Shah's dual policy in prevailing over the tribes was to recruit their people to join the military ranks in the course of his military expedition and the conquest of Kandahar in 1738. By bestowing the titles of "sardar," or commander, and "khan," or chief, on the leader of the tribe, he enhanced the prestige of the Bakhtiaris, who were well known for their bravery and being warriors. With the death of

Nader Shah in 1747 and the return of a number of the people of the tribe from Khorasan to the slopes of the Zagros Mountains, Ali Morad Khan Bakhtiari conquered Isfahan, and declaring himself king, he ruled there for a short period of time. His short-lived rule, which with his defeat by Karim Khan Zand resulted in his being killed, ended in the forcible sedentarization of the Bakhtiari people in other territories, in their exile and imprisonment, and in the taking of the leaders of the tribe as hostages.[13]

With the fall of the Zand Dynasty and the coronation of Agha Mohammad Khan Qajar in March 1796 that would make official the rise to power of the Qajar Dynasty, Persia, with a population of five to six million people, half of which was comprised of tribes, faced new changes.[14] The policy of confrontation with the Bakhtiari tribe, however, was solidified on the basis of the same plan and perpetuation of the past since the rule of the Safavid kings and the reigns of Nader Shah of the Afshar Dynasty and Karim Khan of the Zand Dynasty. That which bestowed new meaning on this plan and perpetuated policy was the increasing competition between Russia and England, which intensified with the appearance of the first signs of weakness of the successors of Agha Mohammad Khan Qajars in overcoming the difficulties.

Against this backdrop, the strategic position of the Bakhtiari territories and the economic importance of Khuzestan left a lasting impact on the fate of the tribe. This impact, especially with the discovery of oil, gave the tribe special financial and military capability until, in the end, with the role that the tribe played in the Constitutional Revolution of 1906-1911, it eventually prepared the grounds for changes that would extend the tribe's name and fame beyond the slopes of the Zagros, and its name became kneaded together with freedom and the rule of law throughout Persia.

The death of Agha Mohammad Khan Qajar in June 1797 and the noncompliance of the Bakhtiari tribe, the open expression of which was its refusal to pay taxes to the central government, intensified the conflict and tension between the tribe and the government. In the ups and

downs of this period and the coming to power of Fathali Shah, as in the
past, the Bakhtiaris at times provided the Qajar princes or the central
government with their warriors and increased their combat capabilities,
and at times, submersed in internal feuds and disputes, they would
ignore their orders. These feuds and disputes were followed by bloody
battles, and had no other consequence but to impede tribal unity and
solidarity.[15]

This reality was reflected in the rebellion, insecurity, and disunity that
would govern the existence of the tribe during the reign of Fathali Shah
Qajar. It was then that the increased power of Mohammad Taqi Khan
Bakhtiari turned the fate of the tribe once more.

Bakhtiaris in Confrontation with the Qajar Dynasty

Mohammad Taqi Khan from the Chahar Lang clan was a grandson of
Ali Morad Khan Bakhtiari, who after the death of Nader Shah conquered Isfahan and, declaring himself king, ruled there for a short
period of time. By uniting the Bakhtiari clans, Mohammad Taqi Khan
succeeded in obtaining the allegiance of a few clans of the Bani Ka'b
Arabs in Ramhormoz and the Janaki clans, of the winter abode as his
followers. By consolidating his position within the tribe and expanding
the extent of his power, which at times went beyond the Bakhtiari
borders, in Isfahan, as well, he was considered a serious threat to Fathali
Shah and his successor, Mohammad Shah

Austen Layard, the British diplomat and archeologist, from his travel
to the Bakhtiari territories and meeting with Mohammad Taqi Khan,
remembers him as a person who hoped to open the doors to trade with
the outside world and establish peace and tranquility among the so-
called "desert-dwelling tribes." He writes: "He wanted me to talk about
the benefits of railroads and other European inventions, astronomy,
geology, and so on... He asked me to encourage British merchants and
businessmen to begin trading with the Bakhtiari people and the region
that he ruled, and he promised to personally assume the responsibility
for protecting the lives of their functionaries and the security of trans-

portation and merchandise." To Layard, who encouraged the ambitious Bakhtiari tribal chief to expand trade with the "developed and civilized" nations of the world, the tribal chief assigned the duty of speaking with British authorities on Kharg Island for expanding trade between the tribe and India. According to Layard, he declared his readiness to build a road for the transporting of foreign merchandise and cargo in the territories under his influence, which covered a vast region from the uppermost shores of the Persian Gulf and the entire plain of Khuzestan to the banks of the Shatt al-Arab.[16]

By combining his political acumen and his skill as a warrior, the Bakhtiari chief unified a significant number of the tribes and clans and refused to pay taxes to the central government. Then he conquered the cities of Ramhormoz, Shushtar, Dezful, and Behbahan to consolidate his power, to the extent that all "whether near or faraway became fearful of him." Before long, when Mohammad Taqi Khan confiscated 600,000 *tuman*s of the taxes of Fars Province, that territory became the galloping grounds of Bakhtiari horsemen, and Isfahan once again became exposed to danger. The expansion of his power and the wealth he had amassed were sufficient to intensify the anxiety and apprehension of the central government. Thus, in order to put down the "rebellion and insurgence" of the Bakhtiari chieftain and to "restore order to those territories," Fathali Shah donned the garb of battle and "set out on a journey toward Isfahan on his way to Shiraz." However, "three hours before the sun set…, he departed this world in Sa'adatabad of Isfahan." With the Shah's death, Mohammad Taqi Khan, relying on his own battle capability and financial ability, no longer placed any credible value on the power of the Qajars, especially at a time when in the heat of struggle for power among Fathali Shah's children seeking to climb atop the royal throne, everything was in disarray.[17]

In such a predicament, once again, no other choice remained but military confrontation for the survivors of the late monarch to overcome the threat of the fall of the capital city and concern over the continuation of the monarchy in the House of the Qajars. This important task was ultimately conferred on Mo'tamedoddowleh, the governor of Isfahan.

Manuchehr Khan Mo'tamedoddowleh was born to a Christian family in Georgia. Having been taken captive in childhood, he was taken away as a slave, and similar to other *khajeh*s who had converted to Islam, he was castrated. Fathali Shah had great confidence in Mo'tamedoddowleh, and "on most occasions, regarding important matters of state, he was the one the monarch consulted." About his closeness to the Shah, it is sufficient to say that "at gambling with Farmanfarma, Malekara, and others, he sat across from the late monarch and was a rival to them, and the late monarch often said, 'I am Manuchehr Khan's partner.' He already held the title of Mo'tamedoddowleh at that time, but His Majesty used to not call the princes, the people in the harem, or anyone in the ranks of those who served him by their titles. With that title, his closeness to the monarch, and his position, Manuchehr Khan was honored even to carry the ewer and basin whenever His Majesty stepped out, and Mo'tamedoddowleh was always with the Shah." He made cleverness and skillfulness combined with merit and insight based on "wisdom, good fortune, and competence" pave his way to the acquisition of status and power, to the point that he became the governor of several provinces, and finally occupied the seat of the governor of Isfahan, a most distinguished position.[18]

Simultaneously, as he was preparing an army to launch a military expedition on the Bakhtiari territories, Mo'tamedoddowleh declared his readiness to negotiate with Mohammad Taqi Khan. According to Layard, forty days of negotiations between the two in Malamir Plain did not yield the result that the trustee of the Shah was pursuing. Hence, upon his return, in a letter, he accused the Bakhtiari chieftain of disobeying government orders, refusing to pay taxes, and having secret relations with the princes who had fled to Baghdad. Another message in that letter was that, if he surrendered, he would receive a robe of honor, and while enjoying royal kindness and favor, he would remain in the position that he held. The assurance behind these promises was a letter of amnesty adorned with an oath on the Koran and an allusion to the danger that threatened Mohammad Taqi Khan's brother and son, who were being held hostage. From this point, no more than a few steps remained to the path that would end in the surrender of the Bakhtiari chieftain, steps on a path that was paved by the refusal of the functionaries of British policy to provide support for him.

It appeared that with the withdrawal of Mohammad Shah from Herat and the improvement of relations between Persia and the British government, which had some time earlier in a retaliatory step occupied Kharg Island, another policy was being pursued. In the words of Colonel Henley, the commander of the British forces on Kharg Island, the policy was something to the effect that "the war between Persia and Britain has ended and the British government can no longer politically support the Bakhtiari chieftain, but he may implement his economic plan and engage in trade with British merchants and businessmen."[19]

At any rate, in a gamble that determined the fate of the ambitious Bakhtiari chieftain, the victory belonged to the survivors of the late monarch and those he trusted. After sending Mohammad Taqi Khan to Tehran and issuing a stipend for his family, they jailed him in Niyavaran. Not long after that, he was transferred to the Tupkhaneh prison. When the reign of Nasereddin Shah began, Mohammad Taqi Khan was imprisoned in Tabriz and spent the rest of his life in incarceration. This rebellion was soon put down by the central government, and with the fall of Mohammad Taqi Khan from power, the star of fortune of the Chahar Lang clans also descended, and they never regained their past prestige and power. From that point on, the Haft Lang clans, led by Hoseynqoli Khan Bakhtiari, were the ones that attained status and glory.

Before he was appointed as Ilkhan, tribal chief, by Nasereddin Shah in 1867, Hoseynqoli Khan Bakhtiari was famed for his sharp intellect and valor. Quelling local rebellions, eliminating rivals, and establishing peace in a region that had long been subject to revolts and was unsafe had made his name synonymous with the tranquility and good fortune of his people, and worthy of unmatched esteem. For this reason, once he was able to unite the tribe for which he was considered the protector, he was first honored with the title of "Nazem Bakhtiari," and then five years later, with a royal decree, he was given the title of "General Chieftain of the Bakhtiari Tribe." Hoseynqoli Khan governed powerfully during the ensuing fifteen years in this capacity, which had been unprecedented, and by bringing order to internal tribal relations, he expanded inter-tribal and inter-clan marriages and in this way solidified their ties. Simultaneously, by reducing the current tensions and emphasizing a policy that signaled loyalty to the central government, he solidified the practice of collection of taxes and providing soldiers for the government armies as a routine arrangement, devoid of age-old suspicions. Such suspicions had once again escalated tribal rebellions, especially at the onset of Nasereddin Shah's ascent to the throne, and had left nothing of the government and its decrees but an empty name in Bakhtiari territories.

From Hoseynqoli Khan, who was somewhat of a poet, with the pen-name of "Setareh," or Star, a "notebook" is left behind in which he has recorded a number of the events that occurred in the final decade of his life. The weather, drought, hunting, marriages, as well as the issue of taxes and meetings with Nasereddin Shah and his son, Mas'ud Mirza Zelossoltan, the governor of Isfahan, are among the topics that he has written about in that *Notebook*. His account of each of these topics presents a picture of daily life as well as certain events, which helps us understand the life and times of this Bakhtiari tribal chief. He writes: "His Eminence Zelossoltan, the Shah's son, generously gifted me with Chaharmahal. I was very kind to the peasants of Chaharmahal; I was considerate, and I was successful in collecting taxes… In these few years, I brought a few teams of well diggers. God willing, with the help of the Lord of the Universe, I will have wells dug to build a few *qanat*s to supply water and irrigation in Malamir… This year, there was no spring rain in the summer abode; there is no grass; there will be serious shortages, may God protect us." The story of his meeting with the Shah and presenting gifts to him and government dignitaries, whom he seemed to regard as the key to going on pilgrimage to the House of God in Mecca and granting him salvation in this and the next world, is also worthy of note: "I intended to go on pilgrimage to holy Mecca; I had even made preparations, but government notables hindered me. Finally, The Pivot of the Universe, His Majesty, told me to go to Tehran and take my leave and go to Mecca... I went to Tehran on the eighth of the month of Zilhajjeh... Early in the morning, I went to see Mostowfiyolmamalek. The next day was the Feast of Qorban; I went to the Royal Reception... The Pivot of the Universe came. Downstairs in Shamsolemareh Palace, they placed a chair for him and he sat down. His Majesty summoned me. I went closer. He asked, 'When did you arrive? Which road did you take?' He asked about the clans; he was very kind... After three more days, the Commander-in-Chief of the Army took me to the Shah's private quarters; I was in the private quarters with His Majesty for about an hour and told him everything I had to say. He was most kind. I sent three horses and 500 gold coins as a gift to the Shah. I also sent all the dignitaries of the government horses, money, and high-quality silk and cashmere shawls. The Pivot of the Universe went hunting in Jajrud and took me and Amir Hoseyn Khan Shoja'oddowleh Quchani from Khorasan along as his retinue... Amir Hoseyn Khan and I each sent 100 gold coins to the Shah in admiration for his having shot a wild sheep."[20]

The trip of Ilkhan Bakhtiari to Tehran and his meeting with the Shah was a fruitful albeit expensive journey. On this journey that took six months, he spent "15,000 *tumans*" in "cash, silk shawls" and other gifts. In exchange, he was granted an audience with "The Pivot of the Universe" ten times and, receiving a bejeweled sword from the king, he enjoyed his "favor and kindness." A pilgrimage to the House of God and salvation in the next world was left to another opportunity, since the situation in Khuzestan, which was called Persia's Arabestan at the time, had turned chaotic, and order and the implementation of decrees, in disarray. In Dezful, "caravans were robbed every day" and "on Shushtar road, artillerymen" were killed. Hence, he was granted permission to "take his leave"; and by royal decree, he returned to Isfahan, and with a group of horsemen, he set out for Khuzestan, in order to, as he called it, restore "peace and order in Arabestan." He did so, and called on the tribal sheiks and tribal leaders to do their duty. He writes: "I sent a message and all the sheiks of Arabestan" came and "we settled all the taxes." By restoring order and collecting huge amounts of back taxes, which pleased the king, he expanded the extent of his power to the point that upon his return to Isfahan, he removed Ja'farqoli Khan, the representative of Zelossoltan in "Arabestan," from his position. Earlier, as well, by royal decree, the business of the "Qashqa'i tribe gentlemen," who had taken sanctuary in the royal stables and were exiled to Khuzestan, was "entrusted" to him. All this was indicative of the Shah's kind attention to Ilkhan Bakhtiari and his abilities. At the height of his power, with the self-confidence that stemmed from the order he had established, in the *Notebook* of his memoir, he wrote: "Thank God, I restored such order in Arabestan that the wolf and the ewe walked side by side." A telegram was also sent to the Shah, stating that "in Arabestan, never has such order" been witnessed before. Hence, the decision was made that His Royal Highness should "grant" the governorship of Arabestan to him, which he considered beneath him and did not accept; but he did point out that if the new governor were chosen upon his "humble suggestion," he would shoulder the responsibility for "Arabestan's taxes and order."[21]

The position that Hoseynqoli Khan had acquired in the tribe and the prestige that he had attained beyond the borders of Bakhtiari territories became unstable with the appointment of the Shah's paternal uncle, Farhad Mirza Mo'tamedoddowleh, as the governor of Fars Province. In 1876, relying on that position, Mo'tamedoddowleh made great strides to solidify his power, intensifying ever more the power struggle that had been going on between himself and Zelossoltan, the governor of Isfahan. Eventually, through several conspiracies and scuffles that had even extended to the capital city, this struggle for power determined the fate of Ilkhan Bakhtiari, who enjoyed the support of Zelossoltan.

The first confrontation in this arena involved the collection of taxes from the regions located within the governing authority of either Fars or Isfahan, between the Qashqa'i and Bakhtiari territories regarding the ownership of which there were disputes, especially in the fertile region of

Falard and Khan Mirza. Tax collection, however, was not possible without the political and military superiority of one over the other; and this itself had added to the ongoing tensions, opened the way to new disruptions, and again further escalated the conspiracies.

In the meantime, with the growing disputes between the two tribes and the murder and plunder that stemmed from old tribal hostilities and efforts to gain access to pastures and roads, the unrest spread; and at the peak of military clashes between the Bakhtiari and Qashqa'i tribes, the region became increasingly unstable and unsafe. This situation continued to the point that Hoseynqoli Khan granted amnesty to a number of the Qashqa'i leaders and tribesmen who had sought protection from him, and he refused to yield to the demands of Mo'tamedoddowleh to surrender them to the government of Fars. Mo'tamedoddowleh, who considered provoking the Qashqa'i tribe a means in his confrontation with Zelossoltan and Hoseynqoli Khan, sought support from the Shah and asked "His Imperial Highness" to come up with a solution regarding the position of Ilkhan Bakhtiari, since otherwise, "any leniency" would most likely result in the "sedition and riots" of tribes in the south. Mirza Yusef Mostowfiyolmamalek, the minister of interior and finance, also in a telegram to Zelossoltan, asked "His Eminence" to "admonish" Ilkhan Bakhtiari "concerning why he does not stop the Bakhtiari tribe, his own tribe," and added: "Is it not a pity for you to consent to such anarchy?" In response to Mostowfiyol-mamalek's grumbling and grievance regarding the policy that he had opted for in the dispute between Mo'tamedoddowleh and Ilkhan Bakhtiari, Zelossoltan absolved himself of any responsibility.[22]

In response to Mostowfiyolmamalek, Zelossoltan wrote: "I have repeatedly submitted that the disputes between the Bakhtiaris and Qashqa'is, or Fars and Arabestan, have nothing to do with me. Little by little, bringing up their dispute to me will cause rumors... For four years, a dispute has been ongoing between two prominent servants of the Royal Court, and no effort is being made to bring it to an end. If actually such actions have been carried out by Ilkhan, and if Mo'tamedoddowleh is telling the truth, there is no need to prolong it.

Instruct me to send a servant to fetch Ilkhan and have him punished any way you instruct me. But if he has been lied about and it has been merely out of ill intentions, why do you keep after him all the time? I am capable; why talk about weakness? Investigate the matter once and for all; if he has committed a violation, if he has blinded him, punish him, so that it will be a lesson to others. And if what they have told you is contrary to the truth, do something so this poor man can find some peace of mind and there will be no arguments and this type of telegram every day. In fact, if the matter is true and nothing has been done to remedy the situation for four years, it will make him impudent and gradually extend his reach to Isfahan and elsewhere. It is most inappropriate for him to engage in such actions. Of course, we need to try to remedy the situation."[23]

Before long, when the Bakhtiari chieftain also perceived a threat to his position, he tried to defend himself and complained to Prime Minister Mirza Hoseyn Sepahsalar, the Grand Vizier. He even wrote a letter to the Shah, and enumerating his services, he complained about the disruptive actions and provocations by Mo'tamedoddowleh and mentioned stepping aside, which was in a way for the purpose of eliminating misgivings about him and afford him immunity from punishment: "Given all these services that I have rendered, it would not please God for me to have no rest day and night due to the unkindness of His Eminence Mo'tamedoddowleh, and to be in anguish all the time. Your Majesty, The Pivot of the Universe, you will agree that I have grown old. I have served for thirty years. I no longer have the ability for such afflictions. The life of this humble servant is coming to an end. I plead with Your Majesty, The Pivot of the Universe, that for the sake of the Creator of the World and the martyrdom of the Commander of the Faithful, Imam Ali, you release this humble servant; allow me to leave and go to holy Najaf… and to pray for your long life in holy Najaf. The decision, of course, is that of The Pivot of the Universe." In a response that indicated contentment with the services of Ilkhan, the Shah dissuaded him from stepping aside and reclusion and persuaded him to continue to serve. Furthermore, right there on the margin of Hoseynqoli

Khan's letter, addressing him, he wrote, "You can rest assured of our favor with you and your children, and never think about resigning," which would be considered some sort of guarantee for his life and that of his family.[24]

However, not only did none of these decrease the conflict and tug of war between Ilkhan Bakhtiari and the Shah's uncle, but they actually increased their hostilities and intensified the fire of their disputes, to the point that Hoseynqoli Khan in January 1880, while Zelossoltan was in the capital, went to Tehran to see the Shah. As the text of his memoir indicates, on this trip, the issue of the ownership and the taxes of Falard was the topic of his conversation with the Shah. One can surmise that in the course of this conversation, they also talked about Mo'tamedoddowleh's role and all that was related to the dispute between him and Ilkhan Bakhtiari. Whatever the case may be, at the end of this same trip, when Hoseynqoli Khan was about to leave for Isfahan, the Shah "gifted" him with a bejeweled sword, and this indicated that "The Pivot of the Universe," regarding the ongoing power struggle, had made a choice other than that which his uncle expected. In May 1881, the Shah removed Mo'tamedoddowleh from governorship and appointed Zelossoltan's son, Jalaloddowleh, as the governor of Fars, a choice that undoubtedly was considered a victory and an even greater "gift" to Ilkhan Bakhtiari and his supporter, Zelossoltan.[25]

Despite all this, after the removal of Mo'tamedoddowleh, the contentment of the Shah with Hoseynqoli Khan and the support of Zelossoltan for him were short-lived. Before long, his increasing power and fame once again escalated the concerns that had existed before. Hence, the Shah dispatched two of his trusted confidants, under the pretext of taking a pilgrimage to Mecca and the purchasing of horses, to Chaharmahal and Bakhtiari and Khuzestan, but in fact in order to collect information and assess the situation. The report of those two confirmed the rumors about the power and wealth of Ilkhan Bakhtiari and the expanse of his influence within the tribe and in Khuzestan. His relationship with the British functionaries also was not risk free, from the perspective of the Shah, in terms of the survival of the Qajar rule.

Moreover, on the one hand, because of his cooperation with Zelossoltan, he was accused of preparing the grounds for pushing the crown prince, Mozaffareddin Mirza, aside, and on the other, he was suspected of cooperating with the crown prince and conspiring against Zelossoltan. Earlier on, as well, there had been talk that the Bakhtiari chieftain "nurtured in his head the desire to become king." Hence, the Shah summoned his son, Zelossoltan, and, presenting him with three notebooks that contained harsh reports about Ilkhan Bakhtiari, told him: "Today, the Qajar throne and crown are hanging by a hair. You are holding that hair, and Hoseynqoli Khan is holding a pair of very sharp scissors and wants to cut this hair. What would you, who are in charge of almost everything, say; what do you have in mind; and what is in the interest of the government?" As he claims, Zelossoltan considered all three reports "nonsense," and he refuted the accusation against Ilkhan Bakhtiari, that Bakhtiari had deceived him, and with his own "assistance," Bakhtiari was trying to engage in "great treachery against religion and state," although he emphasized that Hoseynqoli sometimes said certain things that would not be said by a "subject, servant, and devotee," and it was quite likely that if "he were not killed, much blood would be shed." Considering himself to be a suspect of accusations, he knew, "In looking for a decision contrary to that of the sultan/ One must wash his hands in his own blood," and apparently, he could see no other solution. Hence, he met in Isfahan with Ilkhan Bakhtiari, who every year returned from Khuzestan to the winter abode in Chaghakhor in the Bakhtiari region, as was his custom. Then, on the order of Nasereddin Shah, on the eve of 14 June 1882, Hoseynqoli Khan, who had been the subject of the Shah's "kindness" and "favor" not so long before, after watching the drills of soldiers in Shah Square of Isfahan, was killed in a government building. According to his son, Aliqoli Khan Bakhtiari, "the next morning, they spread the rumor in the city that Ilkhan had had a heart attack; then, with utmost respect, they carried the corpse of the late chieftain and buried him in the Mir Mausoleum of Takht-e Pulad Cemetery." His children were also arrested and jailed.[26]

Mourning the death of Ilkhan Bakhtiari, women cut off their hair, and the tribespeople, bewildered and brokenhearted, were all in tears.[27][ii] Before long, the murder of Hoseynqoli Khan intensified the disputes among his survivors, subjecting tribal unity to instability. The life and times of the Bakhtiaris no longer had any of the sign of the unity of "the late tribal chieftain's" time. This time, fighting and disunity dominated the fate of the tribe. The struggles of various Bakhtiari chieftains to occupy the positions of Ilkhan, Haj Ilkhan, and Ilbeyg further intensified the fighting and disunity.

This reality was reflected in the victory of the Qajars over the tribe and the peace of mind that the fortunate monarch had mustered for himself and his posterity at the price of the murder of Ilkhan Bakhtiari. It was, however, an ill-fated decision, the consequence of which, one generation later in the storm of the revolution, eradicated the despotic rule of the Qajar Dynasty. The participation of the Bakhtiari tribe in the constitutional movement was a clear manifestation of this reality. Aliqoli Khan Bakhtiari, whose title was Sardar As'ad, and who was the son of Ilkhan Bakhtiari and was arrested and jailed following the murder of his father, writes: "During my stay in Tehran, my mind was totally preoccupied with the thought of carrying out my intentions; in other words, I wanted to have the rule of law in Persia, and the reason for my efforts in this connection was that, because they killed the late Ilkhan and did a great deal of injustice to me and Esfandiyar Khan, I saw the heinousness of despotism. Rarely had anyone suffered such misfortune. So, I was determined to ask the people to support a government of laws, and during the period that I was in Tehran, I made a pledge with a group to eradicate despotism."[28]

By the time this process came to an end, the great developments of navigation on the Karun River, the building of the Lynch Road, and the

---

[ii] For the custom of cutting hair in the mourning ceremonies of the Bakhtiari tribe, see: Bizhan Shahmoradi, "Boridan-e Gisvan dar Sugvariha-ye Bakhtiari," *Iran Nameh*, vol. 22, nos. 3 and 4 (Autumn-Winter, 2005): 283-299.

discovery of oil on Bakhtiari territories confronted the life and existence of the tribe with astonishing changes.

Karun, Oil, and the Lynch Road

In October 1888, Nasereddin Shah, issuing a royal proclamation allowing navigation on the Karun River, made the wish that Britain had been pursuing for half a century a reality. With the start of navigation on the Karun, a path would be open that would expand British trade with the southwestern and central parts of Persia and increase the economic and political influence of Britain in Persia. In addition, the issuance of this proclamation, considering the strategic position of Khuzestan, was a concession to the British merchants for expanding trade with India and achieving a goal that in the past, despite the efforts of the functionaries of British policy in negotiations with the Persian government and the leaders of the Bakhtiari tribe, had not been within reach. The success of this effort would ultimately indicate the solidification of the British position in its rivalry with Russia in Persia.

With the opening of this navigational waterway on the Karun, the project of building a road that would connect Ahvaz to Isfahan was once again of interest to British merchants; and the Lynch brothers, who owned a shipping company on the Tigris and Euphrates rivers in Baghdad and Basra, with the support of the British government, made efforts to obtain a concession for its construction. The need for the construction of this road, which had long been noted by British tourists, merchants, and politicians, had been disregarded previously. In the past, the Persian government viewed with increasing concern the negotiations between British officials and the leaders of the tribe regarding the construction of a road that passed through Bakhtiari territories. This was such a concern that George Curzon, the well-known British politician and member of parliament who had acquired the title of "Lord" and occupied the seat as Viceroy of India, regarded the murders of Mohammad Taqi Khan Bakhtiari and Hoseynqoli Khan Bakhtiari to be the consequence of that concern. Even though the tribal leaders viewed the construction of such a road as an important step toward the prosperity of their ancestral land and the increase in their revenues and wealth, they did not consider it to be without risk. The danger stemmed from the fear of this road paving the path to the influence and intrusion by Britain and the central government over the fate of the tribe. On the other hand, England was increasingly concerned about the growing influence of tsarist Russia in Persia. This reality further intensified the efforts of the diplomatic officials of that country in their negotiations with the government of Persia and the leaders of the Bakhtiari tribe to implement and complete the project before them. Finally, with Curzon's travel to Persia in 1889 and the negotiations that took place in later years between high-ranking British officials and the plenipotentiary envoys of that country with the tribe and with the government of Persia in the ensuing years, British efforts yielded the desired results, to the point that, considering the importance of navigation on the Karun River and the Bakhtiari Road, Curzon referred to those negotiations as a diplomatic success for Britain.[29]

Considering the geographical situation of the Zagros Mountains and the Bakhtiari territories, the implementation of this project would face certain difficulties, which would not seriously hinder its progress, given the financial and technical capabilities of its planners. The main problem was to obtain the agreement of the government of Persia and the leaders of the tribe that looked suspiciously at Britain's goal, or that which Curzon mentioned as "friendly competition" with tsarist Russia. Moreover, the functionaries of British policy saw themselves in confrontation with unrest and riots that were forming in Shushtar and Ahvaz against foreigners. The highway robbery and the plunder of trade caravans in the Bakhtiari region and protest against the presence of foreigners, whose number was increasing day by day in Khuzestan with the growth in trade, had created a number of obstacles to making Britain's ambitious project a reality. Overcoming these obstacles without the cooperation of the government of Persia, and especially without reaching an agreement with the tribal leaders, was impossible. The increasing concerns of the British merchants and the Lynch brothers regarding the ongoing unrest intensified the efforts of the high-ranking officials of the government of that country in Persia for achieving the long-sought goal of signing a concession that would be agreed to by both the government and the tribal leaders. This concession would not only make one of Britain's long-sought-after goals a reality, but also, according to Henry Lynch, it would revitalize Persia and bring the Bakhtiari territories closer to civilization.[30]

In April 1897, an agreement was signed for the construction, operation, and protection of the Bakhtiari Road between the Lynch Company and Esfandiyar Khan, Mohammad Hoseyn Khan, and Aliqoli Khan Bakhtiari. One year earlier, in a meeting with the British military attaché in Tehran, in accordance with the agreement that had been signed by Foreign Minister Mirza Nasrollah Khan Moshiroddowleh and the tribal leaders, the government of Persia had granted the concession for the Bakhtiari Road to them for sixty years. Rather than giving this concession to a foreign company, the Shah preferred to grant it to the Bakhtiaris, to avoid the wrath of tsarist Russia. The third article of the concession would provide the tribal leaders with the possibility of seeking foreign investments for the construction and operation of the road.

The 435-kilometer construction of the Bakhtiari Road, which because of the contract between the Lynch brothers and the tribal leaders was also known as the Lynch Road, took nearly two years. The construction of caravanserais and bridges and providing security along the road that connected Ahvaz to Shushtar and Isfahan resulted in the expansion of trade between the Bakhtiari territories and Isfahan. The first economic consequence of this development was the collection of road maintenance tolls and taxes for the Bakhtiari khans, which increased their wealth to a level previously unknown to them. Ordinary people in remote villages could offer their products for sale in cities, and in exchange, they gained access to goods to which previously they rarely had access. Although traveling back and forth on the route of tribal treks remained the same, it did become easier, because the road was shorter. All this opened new spaces for even more changes in the lives and existence of the people affected by them.

Even though the Bakhtiari Road did not fulfil all the expectations of the Lynch Company and the wishes of the British government, it did open the way for British trade and had consequences that, in addition to economic developments, gained undeniable political importance. An important aspect of this development was making official the close relationship between the tribe and Britain in the strategic region of the Zagros Mountains and arable lands in Khuzestan. Even though this relationship and closeness had existed in the past, previously, it did not enjoy the characteristics of official relations. The sensitivity of the functionaries of British policy toward maintaining and expanding this relationship was to such an extent that in a dispute that occurred between the Bakhtiaris and the Lynch Company, they took the side of the Bakhtiaris, lest, if they did otherwise, the tribe's leanings would move toward tsarist Russia.[31] This issue, which proved to be a double-edged sword, further increased the independence of the tribe from the central government and added to the financial ability of its leaders. Even though the Bakhtiari Road on the route of the tribe's treks when it passed through valleys and plains brought the encampments closer to villages and cities and brought the cities closer to the capital, it moved the Bakhtiari khans further away from the ordinary people in the tribe. The chasm between the two was the price of the tribal leaders setting their hearts on the wealth that was a boon from the Bakhtiari Road, which moved them further away than ever before from their tribal ways and dispositions and attracted them to the comforts of urban living. With the revenues resulting from the discovery of oil this time, such comfort in the near future would allow them to taste touring and strolling in Europe, parasangs away from their tribal life.

The granting of the oil concession to D'Arcy in May 1901, which resulted in the discovery of oil seven years later in Masjed Soleyman, completely changed the fate of the tribe. This development, the expanse of which would extend beyond Bakhtiari territories and would have an astonishing impact on the future of Persia and the world, in its initial phase became the beginning of a new relationship between the tribal leaders and the British government. The weakness and inability of the central government in carrying out commitments related to the security of oil wells and their exploitation forced the functionaries of British policy to assign a special position to the Bakhtiari tribe in devising their policies in this connection. The outcome of this choice was the signing of an agreement with the Bakhtiari chiefs that gave them a share in the affairs related to the Oil Company. The establishment of a secondary company called the Bakhtiari Oil Company in March 1909 alongside the Anglo-Persian Oil Company and the transfer of three percent of its shares to the tribal leaders made this objective official.[32]

Despite all this, the great obstacle for England regarding the security of the oil regions, which had been provided at the price of granting shares to the Bakhtiari chiefs, continued to be their internal fighting of old. Such fighting, especially considering the revenues from the share of oil, intensified the disputes among the Ilkhani, Haj-Ilkhani, and Ilbeygi clans, and was reminiscent of the old rivalries between the two branches of the tribe, the Chahar Lang and the Haft Lang. These disputes, along with the clashes between the Bakhtiari tribe and its neighbors, especially in Khuzestan and in the region under the control of Sheikh Khaz'al, added to the concerns of Britain. Another problem consisted of the different interpretations and readings of the tribal leaders, on the one hand, and the Company and Britain, on the other, regarding the agreements that had been signed, to the extent that each accused the other side of breaching this or that paragraph of the agreement, especially with regard to the sale of Bakhtiari lands, the security of oil fields, and the annual share of the tribal chiefs. Moreover, the Company and Britain viewed the tribal leaders as pledge breakers and the ordinary Bakhtiaris as rebellious and disorderly. These were people who under intolerable conditions shouldered the burden of heavy labor for meager wages on polluted oil fields that would forever change the landscape of their territories. In addition, the government authorities at every opportunity declared their displeasure about the independence that they believed the representatives of the Company and the British government had in negotiations and signing agreements with the tribal leaders without informing the government of Persia. From the perspective of the government, this independence meant nothing but disregard for the right of sovereignty of Persia. Despite this fact, however, for the functionaries of British policy, the security of the oil fields in the Bakhtiari territories and protecting and expanding the British sphere of influence in Khuzestan was far too important to create a rift in its close cooperation with the leaders of the tribe. To England, the exploitation of these oil resources meant a serious blow to the economic interests of Russia in the Middle East and Asia, to such an extent that taking over the world markets by the Anglo-Persian Oil Company was indicative of the decisive role of that company in the British colonial policies in Persia and, most likely, in the Middle East.[33]

Bakhtiaris, Constitutional Movement, and Reza Shah

With the death of Mozaffareddin Shah in January 1907, when the despots had once again begun a new attempt to take back the strongholds they had lost in the ups and downs of the Persian Constitutional Revolution, the names of tribal leaders once again became household names. In the meantime, with the return of Aliqoli Khan Bakhtiari, the second Sardar As'ad, from Paris to Persia, a new round of battle against Qajar despotism began, which eventually, with the conquest of Tehran and the fall of Mohammad Ali Shah, ended in the establishment of the constitutional regime.

Sardar As'ad, who had gone to France for eye treatment following the initial proclamation regarding the Constitution and the opening of the First Parliament in October 1906, and there he had heard about the shelling of the parliament by Mohammad Ali Shah and the arrest, detention, and murder of revolutionary fighters, writes: "In Paris, I thought about once again taking steps to reestablish a parliament and made many efforts in this regard. The news that I received from the province that the Bakhtiaris were supporters of Mohammad Ali Mirza, the Shah, and that a number of them were fighting the people in Tabriz saddened me even more. Every day, through correspondences, I enticed and persuaded my brothers and cousins to serve the people and the Constitution and told them that they should not refrain from it."[34]

Hence, in April 1909, he returned to Persia, and in meeting with Sheikh Khaz'al and preparing the grounds for reconciliation with the leaders of the Qashqa'i tribe, he regained a kind of peace of mind that would lead the way for the concentration of forces and arranging for the conquest of Tehran. Interestingly, prior to leaving Europe, Sardar As'ad met with Henry Lynch, who was a supporter of the constitutional movement, and he was able, with full knowledge of the British Consulate in Tehran, to obtain a small loan from Lynch to fund the military operations of the Bakhtiaris against Mohammad Ali Shah.[iii] He also met with Charles Hardinge, the British permanent undersecretary for foreign affairs. The reason for this meeting was to have a discussion about oil and the issue of the protection of the oil wells in the Bakhtiari region. One can surmise that the developments in the constitutional movement were also discussed in this meeting. Moreover, efforts to create harmony and to eliminate the disputes among the leaders of the tribe, which would reduce their political and combative capabilities, were among other steps taken at the outset of the conquest of Tehran and confrontation with the despots.[35] These steps would make the Bakhtiari chieftain a famed leader in the Constitutional Revolution.

Sardar As'ad, the fourth son of Hoseynqoli Khan Bakhtiari, was a learned man and among the literati. He learned reading and writing Persian as a child and began learning Arabic grammar and syntax as well as the French language. Having been jailed after the murder of his father, once he was released, he served in Isfahan for a while and then acquired the rank of brigadier general and was appointed as the commander of the special guard unit of Aminossoltan, the grand vizier at the time. Accompanied by his mother, Sardar As'ad went on pilgrimage to Mecca and visited India and Egypt. He also lived in Europe for some time. In Paris, he joined the Freemasons, and after the conquest of

---

[iii] For more on British policies regarding the Constitutional Revolution, especially the role of Henry Lynch in the course of the developments that resulted in supporting the Bakhtiari tribe and the constitutionalists, see: Mansour Bonakdarian, *Britain and the Iranian Constitutional Revolution of 1906-1911: Foreign Policy, Imperialism, and Dissent* (Syracuse: Syracuse University Press, 2006).

Tehran, he became a minister. With the fall of Mohammad Ali Shah, he became a member of an assembly called the "Board of Managers" that operated like a revolutionary council and controlled the affairs of the state. He then became the Ilkhan, or chief, of the tribe, although he did not last long in that position, since he faced the rivalry of his elder brother, Najafqoli Khan Samsamossaltaneh. He then went back to live among the ordinary tribesmen, a kind of reclusive life removed from events of the day. The memento left behind from his retiring years consists of translations of a few books from English and French into Persian and a book entitled *Bakhtiari History*. In his tumultuous life of service, he is also credited with building schools for the tribe and sending students to Europe to be educated.[36] The conquest of Tehran and the occupation of the seats of power and the office of minister in a sense can be considered the payment of the blood money for the murder of Hoseynqoli Khan Bakhtiari, his father. The ensuing years were the years of the power of the Bakhtiari khans in the executive organizations and managing the affairs of the country. Aliqoli Khan, known as Sardar As'ad, became the interior minister and the minister of war, and Najafqoli Khan Samsamossaltaneh, the conqueror and governor of Isfahan, became the head of the cabinet and a minister. It was as though the change that with the opening of the Lynch Road and the discovery of oil had connected the Bakhtiari territories economically to the national and world markets had also done the same in the arena of politics with an undeniable presence, and in passing through valleys and plains to villages and cities and capturing the capital, it had given a new meaning to the place of the tribe in Persian history. The Constitutional Revolution, as far as it was related to the effective role of the Bakhtiari tribe, was the reflection of such a reality, a reality that in retribution for the murder of Ilkhan Bakhtiari invalidated the existence of Qajar despotism.

In the meantime, the fall of Ahmad Shah and the rise of Reza Khan in December 1925, as an astonishing change in Persia's government system, left a lasting impact on the life and times of the Bakhtiari tribe. Since the Safavids, this was the first time that, with the establishment of the Pahlavi regime, a non-tribal regime had governed Persia. This regime considered tribal relations to be a great obstacle to overcoming poverty and lack of safety, and to achieving constructive development and modernity in the new Persia. The national discourse that stemmed from such an approach viewed the key to opening the gates of progress and security of the society to be putting an end to the tribal way of life. Such a discourse considered ephemeral political stability and the lasting influence of foreigners as stemming from a reality the central core of which was the tribe. In this sense, the tribe symbolized chaos, plunder, disorder, and the breaking of laws, the symbol of all that had driven Persia to weakness and stagnation, to humiliation and destruction. The tribal policy of Reza Shah was structured on disarming the tribes and clans and their sedentarization on the basis of such an outlook. This policy succeeded, as far as it was pursued with the objective of creating security and putting an end to the combative ability of the tribes. On the other hand, the efforts for sedentarization and settling of the tribes in one place, which in its essential aspects was based on autocratic thinking and willful disregard for indigenous traditions, faced difficult impediments.

In advancing this policy, the tribes were called on to join in a future that would not recognize any other alternative but negation of the past. With such an alternative, violence, without having the same velocity in the passage of time, dragged the tribe from one precipice to another. The economic and cultural consequences of such a policy, along with disregard for climatic conditions and incompetent management, added to the disarray that broke the string that held the tribe together. Forced migrations at the cost of human and livestock losses in addition to the disintegration of the institutions for making a living weakened and eroded the ability of the tribe. The relocations and the imposition of unsuitable regions for the migration route escalated homelessness and poverty to the point that, during national economic crises and world economic recessions, these measures added to the hardships that the tribespeople suffered. In addition, heavy taxation, the transfer of the tribe's oil shares to the government, and the confiscation, forced sale, and exchange of the lands that were owned by the Bakhtiari khans for lands in other parts of the country diminished their financial ability. The tribal leadership positions of Ilkhan and Ilbeyg were abolished, and the Bakhtiari territories faced bureaucratic geographic change with new divisions. Another aspect of this policy was the attraction of a number of Bakhtiari khans to the new regime and the rejection of a number of others, an option that had long shaped the policy of Persian rulers in their confrontation with the tribe as an effective method. The newly-established Pahlavi regime, as well, despite breaking with the past, in this arena behaved as had those in old times. Hence, in the limbo between existence and annihilation, the meaning of what was called service and that which was called treason in the report cards of the Bakhtiari khans was uncertain, and both would result in an equally bitter end.

Ja'farqoli Khan Bakhtiari, the son of the second Sardar As'ad, was a well-known example who met such a fate. Alongside his father, he participated in the conquest of Tehran, and by quelling the counterrevolutionary forces in Azerbaijan, he rose against the supporters of Mohammad Ali Shah. With the victory of the Constitutional Revolution, alongside Yeprem Khan, he took on the dangerous duty of disarming the fighters in Atabak Park. After his father's death, Aliqoli Khan Bakhtiari, he assumed his title and became known as the third Sardar As'ad. He then became the governor of Kerman and Khorasan; and in the struggle between tradition and modernity, he rose in support of the new regime and achieved the positions of minister of post and telegraph and minister of war. Before long, by climbing to the peak of power and glory alongside Firuz, Davar, and Teymurtash, he joined the circle of those close to and trusted by Reza Shah, until at another time, with the descent of his star of fortune, he was arrested and eliminated.

In November 1933, while accompanying Reza Shah to watch horseback riding competitions and distribute prizes in Dasht-e Gorgan, Sardar As'ad was abruptly arrested, transferred to Tehran, and jailed. In addition to his arrest, a number of other Bakhtiari khans who resided in the capital were also pursued and imprisoned. Shortly afterward, the wave of arrests of the tribal khans extended to Isfahan and the Bakhtiari territories. The downfall of Sardar As'ad was attributed to misuse of bank stocks. His friendship with Teymurtash, the minister of the Royal Court, and his intervention with the Shah for his release have also been mentioned as reasons for the Shah's suspicion regarding him. There were also rumors that his relationship with England, sending weapons to the tribe, plotting an assassination attempt on the Shah, and efforts to restore Mohammad Hasan Mirza Qajar to the throne were among the reasons for his downfall.

On 2 April 1934, Sardar As'ad, the only Bakhtiari to serve as a minister during the reign of Reza Shah, after having been sentenced to life imprisonment, was murdered in Qasr Prison.[37] With his death and the sentencing of eight Bakhtiari khans to death and another twenty to life imprisonment and long-term incarceration, the latest resistance of the leaders of the tribe was quashed.

In this manner, the process that began with the rise of Reza Khan and continued with his reign as king was concluded in a wave of suppression and terror, without this process having been the sole reason for the disarray in the leadership of the tribe and the place of the tribe in the arena of Persian politics.

From the Constitutional Revolution on, a process was shaping in the Bakhtiari tribe, a distinct aspect of which was the dispute between the generation of grand old khans and junior khans who had been for the most part educated in Isfahan and Tehran. The news of social reforms and progress that had been kneaded together in the name of the Constitution turned the junior khans into passionate supporters of freedom. The education of some of them in the West and their becoming familiar with radical and social democratic views had an effect on deepening such a tendency and in its becoming widespread. In villages that belonged to old khans, the junior khans engaged in supporting the struggles of the sedentarized peasants and the negation of old values. The first indications of the shaping of class consciousness among the Bakhtiari workers of the oil industry also instigated their solidarity with the oil workers. The junior khans saw the good fortune of the Bakhtiaris not in the arena of tribal relations but in actualizing the concept of nation-hood, which was supposed to liberate the tribe and Persia from poverty and misfortune under the auspices of freedom. With the acceleration of this process, the position of the old khans, a symbol of the past, was crumbling within the tribe. This reality, however, more than being the consequence of the combat superiority of the government in its confrontation with the old khans, was the result of the resistance these khans faced from within. The discontent and the growing rivalry of the junior khans in their struggle for power against the old khans stemmed from such a reality. In addition to their demand for greater gains from the revenues of the oil shares, this reality was also indicative of their efforts to increase their financial and political power.[38] The rise of junior khans such as Sardar Fateh Bakhtiari and their role in the life and existence of the tribe symbolized such change and development.

Sardar Fateh Bakhtiari and the Junior Khans

Mohammad Reza Khan Bakhtiari, from the Haj-Ilkhani clan, who was known as Sardar Fateh, was the son-in-law of Samsamossaltaneh, the prime minister during the Constitutional Revolution, and the father of Shapour Bakhtiar. Along with Sardar As'ad, he participated in the conquest of Tehran; and in the summer of 1911, when the supporters of Mohammad Ali Shah and the opponents of constitutionalism were trying to restore Qajar dictatorship, he went to battle against them in Mazandaran. This battle prepared the grounds for an increase in Sardar Fateh's power and opened his path to government positions, and, according to Aliqoli Khan Bakhtiari, brought him and those with him "victory and triumph."[iv] He writes: "This time, the army of Mohammad Ali Mirza (the Shah) and Sho'a'ossaltaneh completely fled, and the Shah also boarded a ship and left Persia. After the dispersal of the outlaws,

---

[iv] Prior to having been granted the title of Sardar Fateh Bakhtiari, he was known as Mo'in Homayun. He was granted the title for the role he had played in the battle against the supporters of despotism in Mazandaran. Unpublished interview of Mohammad Moshiri-Yazdi with Shapour Bakhtiar, Suresnes, France, tape 1, 11 December 1988.

Sardar Fateh and Salar Bahador returned to Tehran."[39] Sardar Fateh then became the deputy governor of Isfahan, and then, governor of Yazd.

Ten years later, by participating in the establishment of an association called "Setareh-ye Bakhtiari," or Bakhtiari Star, Sardar Fateh along with the junior khans made an effort to implement reforms and change the existing conditions. The choice of the word "Star" in the name of that organization may have been a reminder of the fondness and respect of the founders of the organization for Hoseynqoli Khan, the first Bakhtiari Ilkhan, who was somewhat of a poet with the penname of "Setareh." A star was also placed next to the hammer and sickle, the scale, and the sword and the pen on the association's coat of arms, each of which symbolized the worldview of the association, reflecting its attributes, which consisted of its demand for justice, its combative spirit, and its intellectual outlook. In the eyes of the old khans and the British functionaries in Persia, this option was clear proof of the Bolshevik tendencies of that organization, and grounds for unmasking it. Bakhtiari Star, which considered itself a political party, paid special attention to the life and fate of the tribe. The creation of a "social association" for attending to important issues and the formation of "secondary associations" among the tribes for administering the affairs of their own region were among the first points that were stated in the constitution of the association. Bakhtiari Star considered the "freedom and self-rule" of the tribes with emphasis on not violating the freedom of others a fundamental principle. Only Bakhtiaris could become a member of this group, but "Persians who were eager for and supported freedom" could also become honorary members. Its constitution, which was distributed in Isfahan and the Bakhtiari territories, contained statements about "equal rights," and freedom and justice were considered two essential elements for social progress. Elementary education was mandatory for boys and girls, and similar to "public health, medicine, and doctor's visits," was free of charge for the poor. Land ownership was officially recognized, provided "democracy" was observed, and the amount of land that a person could own would be determined by the "grand association." With the assistance of the "grand association," villagers would have free access to "all types of farming equipment." Forests, pastures, religiously-endowed lands, and mines would also be subject to regulations that were supervised by the association. The members of this association would be elected "by secret, equal, direct and universal" ballots for the period of one year. The abolition of "mandatory labor" and all revenues from "free labor and slavery" were in the first paragraphs related to "land and farming" in the constitution of this political party, which was intended to refute the concessions of the old khans in the villages of the tribe. For workers, eight hours of labor per day and one day of rest per week as well as attention to the issue of child labor and the situation of women during and after pregnancy were stated demands of Bakhtiari Star. Another issue to which attention was paid in the constitution of this political party was related to the division of inheritance and women's rights. Bakhtiari Star wanted this issue to be based on Islamic laws, since if Islamic laws regarding inheritance were carried out, women would be in a better situation compared to what they were facing in the tribe. In the constitution of this association, "abolition of distinctions, ranks and titles," "mandatory military education for compulsory military service," and "development and progress of the Persian language" were considered among the "general principles," which had in fact materialized with the reign of Reza Shah. The junior khans, however, insisted on other issues beyond these. Freedom of the press and immunity from prosecution for the expression of ideas were other essential principles stated in the constitution of the association. The election of judges by the people and payment of damages to those illegally detained and convicted were solutions offered by this association for controlling autocracy and guarding security in the society.

In addition to these, Bakhtiari Star brought up viewpoints that were indicative of a specific approach to social issues. With the motto of "God, freedom, homeland," in discussing "general principles," the constitution spoke about the "separation of spiritual forces from politics," an interpretation based on the notion of separation of religion and government, which although not unprecedented in the political history of the country was very rare. Despite the hammer and sickle on its coat of arms, Bakhtiari Star's constitution presented a social democratic outlook regarding the problems and needs of the tribe. By recognizing private ownership of land and setting the wages of workers by a council comprised of the representatives of workers, employers, and the association that played an intermediary role, this viewpoint separated itself from the communist movement, without mentioning this division in the constitution of the association.[40]

Regarding how it would achieve its goals, Bakhtiari Star remained silent. Its constitution also did not mention anything about the position of the government and the role of England in Persia. Its relationship with other political parties was also unclear. It only stated: "The Bakhtiari Star Party can become united with other central associations of similar parties in other parts of Persia." Another lack of clarity in the constitution of the association was the mingling of public demands with solutions that concerned the tribe. On the one hand, tribal lineage and ancestry had a special place in the program of the association, and modernization openly was based on the good fortune of the poor; but, on the other, at times it was difficult to make any distinctions and clearly perceive which one of the demands in the constitution belonged to the tribes and which one, on a larger scale, to Persia. It was only stated: "Those who sacrifice their lives for Persia are held in respect by this party. If such people in their efforts are hurt, they can rely on this party for their own and their children's future."[41]

In spring 1929, with the increase in the disputes within the tribe and the discontent of the junior khans regarding the existing conditions, a rebellion took shape under the leadership of Ali Mardan Khan in the Bakhtiari territories that brought chaos and insecurity to the southern part of Persia. Within a short period of time, this rebellion, which initially was the consequence of the rivalry between the junior khans and the old khans and a protest against the latter's privileged position, resulted in confrontation with the government and a battle against government forces. General poverty and discontentment along with the authoritarian policies of the government intensified and expanded the riots, which were joined by indigent masses. When Sardar Eqbal, Sardar Fateh, and Sartip Khan Boyer-Ahmadi joined this rebellion, the ongoing battles expanded, resulting in a serious crisis.

Not much information is available on how Sardar Fateh joined this movement and its leadership. All we know is that, worried about what was going on, Reza Shah dispatched him and Taqi Khan Amir Jang to the Bakhtiari territories for negotiations, in order to, alongside dispatching military forces for the suppression of the rebellion, keep the door to talks and negotiations open. Without any results, this policy initially failed. Sardar Fateh joined the rebels, and after the siege on and occupation of Dehkord (Shahr-e Kord) and the fall of the Chaharmahal military barracks, Isfahan became a target and Tehran faced a threat. This time, Reza Shah sent Samsamossaltaneh Bakhtiari to negotiate with the rebels. This effort ultimately resulted in the defeat of the Bakhtiari forces in Sefid Dasht and the victory of the government forces. With the victory of the government, the junior khans who participated in the rebellion were pardoned; they were, however, put under surveillance.[42]

It seems that the fate of Bakhtiari Star was tied to the defeat of the rebellion. From then on, there was no longer any mention or sign of the association that the junior khans had established to liberate the tribe and Persia. Whatever the case, this was the last Bakhtiari rebellion during the reign of Reza Shah, which with the combination of political prudence and the military superiority of government forces ended in the defeat of the rebels, an end that five years later, in a wave of terror, resulted in the execution of Sardar Fateh and a number of tribal khans, and the murder of Sardar As'ad in prison.

Childhood and Education of Bakhtiar in Shahr-e Kord and Isfahan

Shapour Bakhtiar, the son of Sardar Fateh, opened his eyes to the world in Chaharmahal and Bakhtiari on 26 June 1914, on the threshold of World War I, when economic crisis, political disarray, and interference by foreign forces had placed Persia on the edge of an abyss. At the time when England, Russia, and the Ottomans from the south, north, and west had occupied the country, the German government made an effort to gain the support of the khans of the tribe. German emissaries encouraged the leaders of the tribe to rely on that country in order to be freed from the shackles of England and Russia. Also, the general belief was that with the defeat of Russia and England in the World War, Persia would be freed from their longtime influence. In the meantime, the famous German spy, Wilhelm Wassmuss, met and negotiated with a few leaders of the tribe, such as Bibi Maryam, Ebrahim Khan Zarghamossaltaneh, and Fathali Khan Sardar Mo'azzam. The outcome of the efforts of the German functionaries and spies in advancing this policy was the military engagement of the tribe with British forces in Qasr-e Shirin, Khuzestan, and Isfahan and its surroundings. Efforts to disrupt the oil installations in Masjed Soleyman were also placed on the agenda, which was coupled with financial aid by Germany, without having any effect on the outcome of the war.

Shapour Bakhtiar was the second child of Sardar Fateh and Naz Beygom, the daughter of Samsamossaltaneh, the prime minister during the Constitutional Revolution. Sardar Fateh and Naz Beygom, who was called Beygom, had three children, Tal'at, Shapour, and Iraj. Tal'at was two years older than Shapour, and Iraj, who was one year younger than Shapour, died in childhood of meningitis. Bakhtiar states: "Iraj was very handsome and spirited, and I—the opposite of him, who was full of life and energy—was sickly, jaundiced, and feeble… With the illness of Iraj, who was burning with fever, my mother brought every preacher, mullah, and prayer-charm fortuneteller, but to no avail. I saw with my own eyes that she did everything she could to save her child's life. You know that the Bakhtiaris are not religious fanatics. The reason for it is perhaps they have no contact with city people, who have preachers and pulpits. But they do have certain beliefs, such as respect for fire and respect for the stove, which one can see in some of the Bakhtiari customs and traditions. In any case, when my mother fell into despair and saw that she had no other choice, from the castle that we had, she walked in her bare feet for five or six kilometers to an Armenian village that had a church, and my father used to help them. She had gone there and pleaded with Jesus. I must say, even though she was a Moslem, she had pleaded with Jesus. She was so affected by Iraj's death that she herself died nine months after that. They said that she had bathed in a mountain spring and caught 'red wind' disease.ᵛ They brought a British lady doctor from Isfahan; it did no good. When my mother's condition reached this point, they put my sister Tal'at and me in a carriage and took us to the house of my uncle, my mother's brother, so we wouldn't be with her. Two or three months later when we came back, we saw that everything had changed. My mother was buried in Kunarg."[43]

Up to the age of eleven, following the death of his mother, Naz Beygom, when his grandmother took care of him and his sister Tal'at, Shapour's life was spent on learning poetry and horseback riding. His father, Sardar Fateh, had concluded that poetry is the "gateway" to Persian culture. Hence, allowing him to go horseback riding and hunt rabbits was the "reward" that his son received for learning poetry. Shapour says: "When I was eleven years old, I weighed very little, and in order to get full permission to go horseback riding, I had to memorize poems that did not have fewer than twenty couplets. If the poems were beautiful and enjoyable, I would even memorize up to thirty couplets. Sometimes, my sister and I would both memorize poems. Tal'at could memorize them quickly, but she also forgot them quickly. It would take me longer to memorize; but the poems stayed in my memory. Later on, when I went to Beirut and to France, I had not taken any Persian books with me. My only source of knowledge of language and literature was the poems that I had memorized."[44]

Bakhtiar's early exposure to Persian poetry and literature was through an in-home tutor who taught in the villages around Kunarg. He states: "My mother was still alive when a cleric with a turban and white beard showed up, and we were told that he taught our relatives in the villages around there. I learned the Persian alphabet from him. He was an old man who occasionally crushed a bit of opium the size of a mung bean

---

ᵛ Erysipelas, which is called "bad-e sorkh," or "red wind," in Persian, is an acute infection, typically with a skin rash, which usually affects different parts of the body.

and ate it with his tea. He was my and my sister's teacher for two or three years. We realized that he was not very educated and was especially stumped in calculus and geometry. That is why I took the initiative and asked my father to get us another teacher and give me permission to go to school." Sardar Fateh agreed to this request, and sent Shapour, at the age of eleven, to the School for Bakhtiaris in Shahr-e Kord. He continues: "I remember that in 1925, when I arrived in Shahr-e Kord, they had a house ready for me, where I lived with male and female servants."[45]

The School for Bakhtiaris was founded in 1914 in Shahr-e Kord, which was then called Dehkord and was considered the capital city of Chaharmahal and Bakhtiari, with the efforts of the Bakhtiari khans. According to Bakhtiar, the entire cost of this elementary school, including its land, building, and the salaries of the teachers, was provided by Aliqoli Khan Sardar As'ad. Later on, the Bakhtiari khans paid for all the expenses of the school, which charged the students a small amount in tuition. Up to then, other than a few modern schools in large cities such as Tehran, Tabriz, Isfahan, and Shiraz, in addition to those that were established by American missionaries, no such schools existed in Persian villages. The Shahr-e Kord school was the only rural school throughout Persia, and students from other Bakhtiari villages came to this school for their education. Mirza Zirak, its first principal, had studied at Darolfonun School and was familiar with modern sciences. He knew French and had translated a few books from French into Persian. Mirza Zirak, who had a close relationship with the tribal leaders, on the invitation of Sardar Ashja' Bakhtiari, had accompanied the young tribesmen who went to Europe to study, as their supervisor. On this trip, he also took his son, Ahmad, with him to study in France.[46] Later on, Ahmad became one of Shapour's friends in Paris, and upon returning to Iran, he played an influential role in the Iran Party and the National Front.

The Shahr-e Kord elementary school, and in particular its principal, Haj Aqa Janab-Nahvi, who took over the administration of the school after Mirza Zirak, played an important role in familiarizing Bakhtiar with language and literature. Bakhtiar, who at the beginning of the school year had registered in the fourth grade with the approval of the school authorities, considered the preliminary knowledge that he acquired in Persian and Arabic "owing" to Mr. Janab-Nahvi. Every day, on Mr. Janab's suggestion, he even studied Persian and Arabic with him before the classes started. He recounts: "One day, Mr. Janab asked me, 'What time do you come to school?' I replied, 'I am in school early in the morning.' He said, 'With the interest that you show in studying and given that I am a devoted friend of your father, I will be happy to come to your house and teach you Persian and Arabic for half an hour to three-quarters of an hour... You have memorized a great deal of poetry. I personally am not as versed in poetry and literature as you might wish; otherwise, I would help you with that. I will just teach you Arabic, Persian grammar, and *Kalileh and Demneh*.' And he came every day, and even without having a cup of tea, he taught me. I remember that when once he was offered a high-ranking position in the Justice Department with salary and benefits, he had said, 'My conscience is at ease in this job; that other job is in the business of judgment, and erring is always possible,' and he had declined to take the job he had been offered. When I was invited to Shahr-e Kord 30 years later, he came to see me for lunch. He was eighty-two years old. We talked, and after a while he looked at the clock and said, 'Shapour Khan, duty calls, I have to leave; I have to go and teach,' and he left. Even at that age, he was still teaching."[47]

Halfway through the school year, because of how well he had learned the subjects in the textbooks compared to his classmates, he was sent to the fifth grade. At the end of the school year, when as result of his success, "he could not contain himself," since his father wanted him to, he had to leave Shahr-e Kord and go to Isfahan. In Isfahan, he was supposed to take the sixth grade exams, and if he passed, without going through the sixth grade, he would finish his high school at Saremiyeh High School in Isfahan, and then go to Beirut and later to Paris to continue his education. Sardar Fateh was preparing this tribal chief's son for a future that, if good fortune were with him, would bring him positions such as those at the ranks of prime minister, minister, or parliamentary deputy.

At the beginning, when he left Shahr-e Kord and went to Isfahan, because he had good grades in Persian, Arabic, geography, and French language and was the top student in his class, he was permitted to take the sixth-grade exams, which was the requirement for entering high school. He had only two weeks to prepare for the exams. He did not pass all the exams, because he was weak in geometry, and according to himself, he could not calculate "the volume of a pyramid." Hence, he spent the following year at Farhang School before he could register at Saremiyeh High School.

Saremiyeh School was founded in 1921 in the Elyaran neighborhood of Isfahan by Akbar Mirza Mas'ud (Saremoddowleh), the minister of finance in the cabinet of Prime Minister Vosuqoddowleh, whose name is tied together with the 1919 Anglo-Persian Agreement. Saremoddowleh was the son of Mas'ud Mirza Zelossoltan and the grandson of Nasereddin Shah Qajar. Among the well-known principals of that school, Ziya'oddin Janab (Aqa Zia') and writer and translator Ahmad Aram should be mentioned. Jalaleddin Homa'i who taught Persian literature, Monsieur Le Poliere who taught French, and Rajabali Khan Zhimnaz who was the physical education instructor were among the famous teachers of that school. Bakhtiar states: "I do not want to judge Saremoddowleh and the many twists and turns in his life, but no school in Persia was at the same level as that school. Saremiyeh School was operated at the expense of Saremoddowleh. Of course, they collected tuition, but that was not sufficient. Saremoddowleh paid for all its expenditures."[48]

The start of Bakhtiar's education at Saremiyeh School coincided with the wedding of his sister Tal'at, the wedding of a sister to whom Bakhtiar was most devoted and whom he loved dearly, especially after the death of his mother. He recalls: "Before my sister's wedding, they came to Isfahan to buy things for her dowry. The distance between Isfahan and our village was about 130 to 140 kilometers. I figured, if I go to the wedding, it would take at least one week, and I would have to be absent from school, which would drop me from being the top or next to the top student in the class. I thought, if that happened, I would die of grief, which was all due to my youth and foolish stubbornness. The attitude that I must always be a fighter and fight was with me from that time. For this reason, despite all my love and fondness for my sister, who was closer to me than anyone else, and even though weddings meant talking, laughing, hunting, horseback riding, and having a good time, I didn't go to her wedding and I stayed, in order not to forfeit my ranking in the class."[49]

Bakhtiar received his elementary school diploma in 1927, and he studied at Saremiyeh School for three years before going to Beirut. It was at that same school where he became familiar with the poetry of the poets of the Constitutional Revolution, Aref, Eshqi, and Bahar. He did not want to remain "indifferent" to what he called injustice and oppression, and he wanted to "decisively" criticize that which ate at his soul. Hence, without having the necessary financial and technical means, he thought about publishing a newspaper. In the meantime, after organizing a student strike, which according to him was not very "rational," he was dragged into social and political issues. This, his first experience, was in confrontation with the school authorities. This experience and the exile of his father to Tehran faced him with a reality that he referred to as the dictatorship of Reza Khan: "From August 1929, my father never saw Bakhtiari country or Isfahan again, since they would not permit him to return. In Tehran, he was supposedly free, but he was under surveillance and was not permitted to leave the capital. At that time, one needed to show an ID even to go to the Tehran suburbs, like Karaj."[50]

In August 1930, Bakhtiar was sixteen years old when he went to visit his father in Tehran. This was the first time that he had left Chaharmahal and Bakhtiari and Isfahan and had come to the capital. He had heard a great deal about Tehran; but Isfahan, with that river, the Zayandehrud, with those gardens and historical buildings, such as the Justice Department building, and its greenery and freshness, for him could not be compared to the capital. In a brief explanation about this visit, he talks about the reason for the exile of his father to Tehran, which was a consequence of the rebellion in the Bakhtiari tribe; but he passes over the political views of his father and does not mention anything about the Bakhtiari Star association. The reason for this is unclear. One could surmise that Sardar Fateh, worried about the future of his son, essentially did not say anything about this matter. All that Bakhtiar says about his father is related to Sardar Fateh's character. He says about his father: "He was very healthy and quick. Both physically and mentally, he was very agile. The memory that I have, and I have worked on it, is partly hereditary and comes from him… Physically, he was short, fair skinned, with a long nose, small eyes, and blond hair and moustache… In my childhood, I can't remember ever not having seen him smiling, coupled with a sarcastic expression on his face… I might have inherited the same thing from him. He was a man who understood humor very well. Without hurting anyone, he would constantly tease people, and he enjoyed it. I never recall him doing this for any purpose other than good intentions and with a pure heart. If he wanted to make fun of someone else, he'd start by making fun of himself. But I must add that he did offend other people. He did his prayers occasionally, and he was generous and humble. But he did not like reckless behavior and laziness. He was calm and composed, and even though he neither had conventional schooling nor higher education, he tried to familiarize himself with Persian and Arabic in terms of language and history… He ate little and slept little, and after dinner, he read books or chanted prayers. Sometimes, he did that for two hours… My father mostly had a dervish-like character. He believed in the family of Imam Ali, and he believed in the knowledge and piety of Imam Ali's family. He always recited this couplet by Bahar, 'Though we suffered from oppression and injustice/ We were enlightened by Ali's family'."[51]

In the capital, Bakhtiar went to the house of Sardar Mohtasham Bakhtiari, the former governor of Isfahan, on Ala'oddowleh Street, where his father was staying. Sardar Mohtasham spent his summers in the Shemiran suburbs, and he had made his home available to Bakhtiar's father. He recounts: "I was in Tehran for two months. All that time, I went around in the city in my father's car, which had an Armenian driver during the day. My father also spent his days in the city, and he entertained invited guests, who often included the Poet Laureate Bahar. Kinfolks also came, and they were entertained in the same house of Sardar Mohtasham. Later in the afternoon, we would go to Lalehzar Street and the Tehran Bookstore, which was located near Tupkhaneh Square. The Tehran Bookstore was the hangout of a few people who were more or less the target of the wrath of Reza Shah's regime. They would sit down, talk, and drink tea. My father would ask the owner of the bookstore, who was from Azerbaijan and a friend of Taqizadeh, 'Parviz, what new books do you have?' and he often went back with his hands full. In the evening, I went to Shemiran with my father. He had rented a small building there close to Sardar Mohtasham's place, to be close together. From different wives, Sardar Mohtasham had twelve children. For the division of his lands, he had officially given my father power of attorney to settle things as he saw fit. My father often summoned Sardar Mohtasham's children, and the plan was for the elder sons to go to Europe for their education. Little by little, there were also whispers about me going to Beirut."[52]

Bakhtiar in Beirut

Bakhtiar considered the reason for his going to Beirut and studying in Lebanon to be his father's interest in "Arabism." An example of this interest was the thirty-five volumes of *al-Hilal* magazine, published in Egypt, all of which his father had read, and considered this to be the good fortune that the Creator had bestowed upon him. He was a believer in the "eloquence" and "lucidity" of the Arabs. He would say, "Other than Islam, the Arabs gave the world one thing…and that is, the diction, rhetoric, eloquence, and grammar and syntax" of the Arabic language. When he decided to send Shapour to Beirut, he sent his servant, Mr. Navvab, who was a *seyyed* and his most favorite, to accompany him. Mr. Navvab was very eager to go on pilgrimage to Karbala. Sardar Fateh told him: "Now that you are bent on going to Karbala, go with Shapour, and when Shapour goes to Beirut, you can come back." Hence, after getting his passport and receiving two letters, one from his father and the other from Teymurtash, the minister of the Royal Court, who had agreed to introduce him and be his sponsor, Bakhtiar was prepared for his journey. In those days, obtaining a passport was not easy, especially for the Bakhtiaris, not to mention the situation in which Sardar Fateh had found himself. In addition to the usual difficulties, the applicant had to prove that he had wealth or guarantee that someone would assume responsibility for his expenses for one year, lest he should leave emptyhanded and live in indigence, in which case, he would cause "embarrassment" for Persians in Europe.[53]

Before leaving for Beirut, Bakhtiar returned to the tribe to see his grandfather, Samsamossaltaneh. He remembers: "Because my mother had died, he was more affectionate toward me than his other grandchildren. In 1930, when he had come to Bakhtiari country, early in the morning, we would go for a hike. At the age of eighty-two, he would walk perhaps five kilometers. Even though he had been away from Bakhtiari territories for thirty years, he had retained his Bakhtiari character. He would put a stick across his lower back, like the Bakhtiari shepherds, and hold onto it with both hands. On these walks, he had no guards and sentinels… He wouldn't wear the required Pahlavi-style hat, and Reza Shah wouldn't say anything to him… One day when we were walking, we came to some black tents and a spring. Samsamossaltaneh said, 'Son! Go up there and find out to whom the tents and the spring belong, so we can go to them and have some yogurt beverage.' We went there and sat on the ground, and we drank some yogurt beverage from a copper bowl and went back. The hostess hadn't recognized my grandfather, something that caused her trouble. When her brother and husband arrived and saw Samsamossaltaneh and bowed to him, they started yelling at the woman for not having taken better care of us. And the poor woman got a beating, too."[54]

After this visit, Bakhtiar goes back to Isfahan and prepares to return to Tehran and for the journey to Beirut. Following the sudden illness of his grandfather, however, he is forced to postpone his journey. He recounts: "Samsamossaltaneh got sick. It was strange. He suddenly got sick. They sent for a doctor, who came from Isfahan and determined that he had to be sent to Tehran. Finally, they brought him to Isfahan, and he was put to bed in the home of one of his brothers. I used to go by his side and fan him. In the meantime, Reza Shah had also learned about it. He sent Loqmanoddowleh to Isfahan to treat him. Loqmanoddowleh came and after examining Samsamossaltaneh, said to Cheraghali, his son, 'Your father has no particular illness. He is like a lamp that is running out of kerosene. In my opinion, with the same calmness that you all have around him, you will make him content.' He passed away a few days later. It was said that he had diabetes. It was strange that the man who had conquered Isfahan returned to Isfahan and died there. When Reza Shah heard the news, he ordered Dabir A'zam, the governor of Isfahan, to have a national funeral procession for him. When the ceremonies were over, I went back to Tehran to set out for Beirut."[55]

On his return to Tehran, Bakhtiar saw his father for the last time. He relates: "When I packed up my suitcases and Mr. Navvab also did his packing, my father was unwell and he had a fever. I did not kiss him on the face. I bowed; I saw that he was crying. I also became emotional and teared up. I bowed again and left. All was ready for the journey. My cousins saw me off in three cars. In those days, it was quite impressive to see three cars taking off."[56]

Bakhtiar and Mr. Navvab spent the night in Hamadan, and from there they went to Kermanshah and then took the Khanaqin road to Baghdad and Karbala. To Bakhtiar, Baghdad, "with its bad weather, filthy hotel, and poorly-dressed people, was abominable." Later on, whenever conversations turned to Baghdad, in his recollections of that city, he would recall Ali Dashti, who had said: "I made a pledge to myself that even if I was appointed as an ambassador to Baghdad, I would not go there."[57]

On this trip, to avoid the deadly heat of the desert, Bakhtiar and his fellow traveler mostly traveled at night, until, after fulfilling the old wish of Mr. Navvab in Karbala, they arrived in Damascus and then Beirut.

For Bakhtiar, Beirut was the land of his dreams. He states: "When I headed down the mountains in Lebanon and saw the sea, I said, the Paradise they talk about is right here. It is not without reason that they call it the Promised Land." It was the place where he spent the next four years, eagerly and enthusiastically. In Beirut, he visited Nabavi, the Consul General of Persia who had replaced the father of Amir Abbas Hoveyda, who at a later time became the prime minister of Iran. Nabavi asked Bakhtiar, who wanted to register in a boarding school, about his plan and his financial resources. Bakhtiar responded that his living and educational expenses would be provided from the share of the oil revenues which would be paid monthly by the company. Hence, Nabavi provided him with guidance and introduced him to Monsieur Roche, who was in charge of student affairs.[58]

There were a few French schools in Beirut. One was a secular school that, according to the Consul General of Persia, had a higher ranking than other schools, and the others were the schools of two groups. One was the school of the American University of Beirut, and the other was the French Saint George College that was operated by the Christian order of the Jesuits. There were also a few other high schools that were operated by religious sects. Given the choices that he faced, Bakhtiar decided to register in the secular French school, because he was not inclined to go to church and be faced with religious restrictions. From the very beginning, he focused his attention on learning the French language, to the point that he even spent his weekends learning French. He states: "I even studied on Saturdays and Sundays. On Saturdays, when I left the bath, I wrapped a hairnet around my head, picked up my book, and went to the schoolyard. All the other students, with the exception of a few who had no money, were outside the school; but I stayed inside and spent the rest of the time studying French and memorizing La Fontaine. I only left the school on Sunday afternoons. At the end of the school year, when the grades were given, every course had a top prize that I would receive, along with a letter of commendation from French Prime Minister Édouard Herriot, who was the honorary principal of the school that I attended."[59]

In the summer of 1932, when the students had gone for summer break, Bakhtiar studied French with Monsieur Mandan, one of the teachers of the school. During the same break, he became familiar with a novel by Anatole France, *Le Crime de Sylvestre Bonnard*, and began to study the works of Montesquieu, Voltaire, and Rousseau. Simultaneously, according to the school's curriculum, he was supposed to learn either English or German. He opted for German, and began learning that language with a private tutor. Thus, he had no time to study Arabic, to fulfil his father's wish, although his familiarity with that language in his socializing with his Arab friends increased beyond what he had learned at Saremiyeh School in Isfahan. Bakhtiar spent his leisure time, especially during his first year in Beirut, which was coupled with "iron-clad discipline," swimming, mountain hiking, and skiing. Having decided to be a vegetarian for a couple of years, he woke up early in the morning, had his meals punctually, and went to bed on time. His discipline and "strong willpower" made him, who had been weak and feeble as a child, according to himself, a healthy and energetic young man. The same discipline prevented him, unlike other young people his age, from indulging in drinking and what he called "romantic adventures." He states: "I was so immersed in my studies that I had no time for such things. I received top grades in conduct and, contrary to my inclinations, I had established a disciplined lifestyle for myself, which I maintained until I was twenty years old. What I did is not that justifiable. Now I consider it to have been foolish."[60]

It seems that in the course of the same years, by studying books on philosophy, gradually Bakhtiar became interested in matters of religion and justice, with which his mind was preoccupied. Even though he did not adhere to religious rituals, without being forced to do so, he performed his prayers up to the age of fourteen, until in Beirut, more than ever before, he found himself face-to-face with a question that ultimately would entail negating or proving the existence of God. In other words, is the answer the acceptance of God as the Creator or is it that which religions have taught man, religions that, according to him, require some sort of readiness, some sort of submission and contentment? He states: "At the age of seventeen or eighteen, I had a notebook in which I wrote about this issue, trying to solve this problem for myself... I wanted to find evidence to either negate or prove the existence of God. In trying to prove the existence of God, however, I faced the same problem that great thinkers of the world have faced. Hence, I made an effort not to tackle the issue of Divine justice in the same way; the justice, wrath, and love that we attribute to God in fact reflects our own thinking and beliefs... How can all the crimes and atrocities that have occurred for centuries be explained? How can we explain that justice stems from the will of God, since justice specifically is by the will of humans?" With this outlook, Bakhtiar arrives at the conclusion that, regarding man's relationship with God, or what he called "telling one's secrets and needs" to the Creator, there is no need for a mediator.[61]

In June 1933, Bakhtiar completed his education in Lebanon with a full sense of "pride and triumph." Having become proficient in French and obtaining a diploma in mathematics from the French school in Beirut, he no longer saw any obstacles to continuing his education in France. The final exams had been conducted under the supervision of a committee that had come to Lebanon from France for this purpose, and the diplomas of the students had been signed by the High Cultural Commissioner of France. A few months before he completed his education in Beirut, in a letter, he asked his father to send him some money so that, in addition to the money that he had saved, he could buy a car, even though, according to himself, he understood, "What need does a student in a boarding school have for a car?" In response, Sardar Fateh wrote: "While you are there, you do not need a car. I am afraid a car will take you away from the school environment and prevent you from being successful in your final year of school." Bakhtiar, however, bought a car somehow; and as his father had predicted, he did not pass the exams and had to do remedial studying. He recounts: "I used the car only on weekends, often on Saturday afternoons. My friends and I would start going; Teymur Bakhtiar cranked, Ahmad Mirza Dara'i and Amir Abbas Hoveyda pushed the car, and I sat at the wheel, and we got the car started after a lot of effort, because the car had been sitting there outside the boarding school all week and its battery would be dead."[62]

[1] Shapour Bakhtiar, *Yekrangi*, translated by Mahshid Amirshahi (Paris: Khavaran Publishers, 1982), 21; unpublished interview of Mohammad Moshiri-Yazdi with Shapour Bakhtiar, tape 1, Suresnes, France, 11 December 1988.

[2] Charles Alexander Galt, et al, *Il-e Bakhtiari*, translated by Kaveh Bayat and Mahmud Taherahmadi (Tehran: Shirazeh Research and Publication, 2008), 15-17; Dieter Ehmann, *Bahtiyaren: Persische Bergnomaden im Wandel der Zeit* (Wiesbaden: Dr. Ludwig Reichert Verlag, 1975), 44-46.

[3] Galt, et al, *Il-e Bakhtiari*, 8; Ann Lambton, "Tarikh-e Ilat-e Iran," in *Ilat va Ashayer*, *Majmu'eh-ye Ketab-e Agah,* translated by Ali Tabrizi (Tehran: Mo'asseseh-ye Entesharat-e Agah, 1983), 216.

[4] Ehmann, *Bahtiyaren*, 36-37; Ahmad Kasravi, *Darbareh-ye Siyasat*, 2nd printing (Tehran: Daftar-e Parcham Publishers, 1945), 30.

[5] Sir Austen Henry Layard, *Safarnameh-ye Layard: Nabard-e Mirza Taqi Khan Bakhtiari ba Hokumat-e Qajariyeh*, translated by Mehrab Amiri (Tehran: Anzan Publishers, 1997), 113, 54.

[6] Sekandar Amanollahi-Baharvand, *Kuchneshini dar Iran: Pazhuheshi darbareh-ye Ashayer va Ilat* (Tehran: Agah Publishers, 2009), 48-49.

[7] Ibn Khaldun, *Moqaddameh*, vol. 1, translated by Mohammad Parvin-Gonabadi (Tehran: Bongah-e Tarjomeh va Nashr-e Ketab, 1966), 228; Lambton, "Tarikh-e Ilat-e Iran," 221; Galt, et al, *Il-e Bakhtiari*, 41-43.

[8] Ehmann, *Bahtiyaren*, 37-39.

[9] Arash Khazeni, *Tribes and Empire on the Margins of Nineteenth-Century Iran* (Seattle: University of Washington Press, 2009), 20.

[10] *Safarnameh-ye Ibn Batuteh*, vol. 1, translated by Mohammad Ali Movahhed (Tehran: Agah Publishers, 1991), 240-241.

[11] T. Firuzan, "Darbareh-ye Tarkib va Sazman-e Ilat va Ashayer-e Iran," *Ilat va Ashayer*, Majmu'eh-ye Ketab-e Agah (Tehran: Agah Publishers, 1983), 2.

[12] Mohammad Taqi Khan Hakim, *Ganj-e Danesh: Joghrafiya-ye Tarikhi-ye Shahrha-ye Iran*, edited by Dr. Mohammad Ali Sowti and Jamshid Kiyanfar (Tehran: Tehran Publishers, 1987), 71-72, 828; Khazeni, *Tribes and Empire*, 21-25, 27-29.

[13] Mohammad Mehdi Khan Astarabadi, *Tarikh-e Jahangosha-ye Naderi*, edited by Mitra Mehrabadi (Tehran: Donya-ye Ketab, 2011), 15, 322, 328-332; Khazeni, *Tribes and Empire*, 29-32; Ehmann, *Bahtiyaren*, 49-51; Hakim, *Ganj-e Danesh*, 477-478, 750-751; Lesanossaltaneh Sepehr, *Tarikh-e Bakhtiari* (Tehran: Sazman-e Shahanshahi-ye Khadamat-e Ejtema'i, 1947), 147-149.

[14] Charles Issawi (ed.), *The Economic History of Iran, 1800-1914* (Chicago: University of Chicago Press, 1971), 20.

[15] *Safarnameh-ye Rezaqoli Mirza Nayeboleyaleh, Naveh-ye Fathali Shah,* under the editorial supervision of Iraj Afshar (Tehran: Asatir Publishers, 1982), 22-25.

[16] Layard, *Safarnameh-ye Layard,* 111, 154-155.

[17] Lesanossaltaneh Sepehr, *Tarikh-e Bakhtiari,* 496-498; Mohammad Taqi Lesanolmolk Sepehr, *Nasekhottavarikh: Tarikh-e Qajariyeh az Aghaz ta Payan-e Saltanat-e Fathali Shah,* vols. 1 and 2, edited by Jamshid Kiyanfar (Tehran: Asatir Publishers, 1998), 33-34, 515-518; *Safarnameh-ye Rezaqoli Mirza Nayeboleyaleh, Naveh-ye Fathali Shah,* 2-3, 44-45; Sardar Zafar Bakhtiari, *Yaddashtha va Khaterat-e Sardar Zafar Bakhtiari* (Tehran: Yasavoli, Farhangsara Publishers, 1983), 153.

[18] Ahmad Mirza Azododdowleh, *Tarikh-e Azodi: Sharh-e Hal-e Zanan va Dokhtaran va Pesaran va Motozammen-e Si va Hasht Sal Saltanat va Navader Ahval-e Fathali Shah Qajar* (Gowhardasht, Karaj: Sarv Publishing Company, 1983), 43.

[19] Layard, *Safarnameh-ye Layard,* 150-151, 162, 174, 209; Lesanolmolk Sepehr, *Nasekhottavarikh,* 525, 722.

[20] *Ketabcheh-ye Khaterat-e Hoseynqoli Khan Ilkhani Bakhtiari,* Introduction and Notes by Ahmad Tadayyon, 1st printing (np: Mo'asseseh-ye Pazhuhesh va Motale'eh-ye Farhangi, 1994), Tarikh-e Mo'aser-e Iran, Ketab-e Sheshom, 141, 146-147, 150, 152-155, 158-159.

[21] Ibid., 156-157, 159, 176.

[22] Mas'ud Mirza Zelossoltan, *Tarikh-e Sargozasht-e Mas'udi: Zendeginameh va Khaterat-e Zelossoltan Hamrah ba Safarnameh-ye Farangestan* (Tehran: Babak Publishers, 1983), 242, 312.

[23] Mas'ud Mirza Zelossoltan, *Tarikh-e Sargozasht-e Mas'udi: Zendeginameh va Khaterat-e Zelossoltan Hamrah ba Safarnameh-ye Farangestan* (Tehran: Babak Publishers, 1983), 242, 312.

[24] Ghaffar Pur-Bakhtiar, "Qatl-e Hoseynqoli Khan, Ilkhan-e Bakhtiari va Naqsh-e Mo'tamedoddowleh, Hakem-e Fars dar An," Ganjineh-ye Asnad, *Faslnameh-ye Tahqiqat-e Tarikhi,* vol. 13, Books 3 and 4, consecutive number 25 (Autumn and Winter, 2003): 76-78.

[25] *Ketabcheh-ye Khaterat-e Hoseynqoli Khan Ilkhani Bakhtiari,* 156; Pur-Bakhtiar, "Qatl-e Hoseynqoli Khan, Ilkhan-e Bakhtiari va Naqsh-e Mo'tamedoddowleh, Hakem-e Fars dar An," Ganjineh-ye Asnad, *Faslnameh-ye Tahqiqat-e Tarikhi,* vol. 13, Books 3 and 4, consecutive number 15 (Autumn and Winter, 2003): 78-79.

[26] Ibid., 77-79; Mas'ud Mirza Zelossoltan, *Tarikh-e Sargozasht-e Mas'udi,* 241-242, 308-309, 312; Khazeni, *Tribes and Empire,* 70-73; Gene R. Garthwaite, "The Bakhtiyari Khans, the Government of Iran, and the British, 1846-1915," *International Journal of Middle East Studies* 3 (1), (January 1972): 27; *Khaterat-e E'temadossaltaneh, Ruznameh-ye Khaterat-e E'temadossaltaneh,* Introduction and Index by Iraj Afshar (Tehran: Mo'asseseh-ye Amir Kabir Publishers, 1998), 179-210; Lesanossaltaneh Sepehr, *Tarikh-e Bakhtiari,* 170.

[27] *Khaterat-e Sardar Maryam Bakhtiari, az Kudaki ta Aghaz-e Enqelab-e Mashruteh*, edited by Gholamabbas Nowruzi-Bakhtiari (Tehran: Anzan Publishers, 2003), 33.

[28] Lesanossaltaneh Sepehr, *Tarikh-e Bakhtiari*, 172.

[29] George N. Curzon, "The Karun River and the Commercial Geography of Southwest Persia," *Proceedings of the Royal Geographical Society* 12 (9) (September 1890): 514-515, 526-528; Issawi (ed.), *The Economic History of Iran*, 174-177.

[30] George N. Curzon, *Persia and the Persian Question*, vol. 1 (London: Longmans, Green, and Co., 1892), 490; Khodabakhsh Qorbanpur-Dashtaki, *Engelis va Bakhtiari, 1896-1925: Pazhuheshi dar Bab-e Monasebat-e Engelis ba Khanha-ye Bakhtiari az Aghaz-e Saltanat-e Mozaffareddin Shah ta Soqut-e Qajariyeh* (Tehran: Mo'asseseh-ye Motale'at-e Tarikh-e Iran, 2011), 140-142; Khazeni, *Tribes and Empire*, 86-91.

[31] Ibid., 104-106, 111; Garthwaite, "The Bakhtiyari Khans, the Government of Iran, and the British, 1846-1915," 31-33.

[32] Garthwaite, "The Bakhtiyari Khans, the Government of Iran, and the British, 1846-1915," *International Journal of Middle East Studies* 3 (1) (January 1972): 36.

[33] Issawi (ed.), *The Economic History of Iran*, 334.

[34] Lesanossaltaneh Sepehr, *Tarikh-e Bakhtiari*, 177-188.

[35] (United Kingdom, The National Archives) FO 248/923. "Visit of the Bakhtiari Khans to London and Conversation with Sir C. Hardinge," Louis Mallet to C.M. Marling, 6 July 1908; Mansour Bonakdarian. *Britain and the Iranian Constitutional Revolution of 1906- 1911: Foreign Policy, Imperialism, and Dissent* (Syracuse: Syracuse University Press, 2006), 176, 179; *Ketab-e Abi: Gozareshha-ye Mahramaneh-ye Vezarat-e Omur-e Kharejeh-ye Engelis dar Bareh-ye Enqelab-e Mashruteh-ye Iran az Tarikh-e Ordibehesht 1288 ta Azar1288, 20 Rabi'ossani 1327 ta 16 Ziqa'deh 1327, 11 May 1909 ta 30 November 1909*, vol. 3, edited by Ahmad Bashiri (Tehran: No Publishers, 1984), 638.

[36] A. A. Sa'idi Sirjani, "Bakhtiari, Aliqoli Khan Sardar As'ad," *Encyclopaedia Iranica*; J. P. Digard, "Golam-Hosayn Khan Shehab-al-Saltana," *Encyclopaedia Iranica*; A. H. Nava'i, "Hosaynqoli Khan" and "Ja'farqoli Khan Sardar As'ad III," *Encyclopaedia Iranica*; Mansour Bonakdarian, "India: ix. Political and Cultural Relations: Qajar Period, Early 20th Century," *Encyclopaedia Iranica*; *Ketab-e Abi*, 721; Ghaffar Pur-Bakhtiar, "Sardar As'ad Bakhtiari va Kusheshha-ye Farhangi," *Ganjineh-ye Asnad, Faslnameh-ye Tahqiqat-e Tarikhi va Motale'at-e Arshivi*, vol. 18, consecutive number 69, Daftar-e Avval (2008): 19-24.

[37] Mehdiqoli Khan Hedayat, *Khaterat va Khatarat* (Tehran: Zavvar Publishers, 1996), 403; Stephanie Cronin, *Tribal Politics in Iran: Rural Conflict and the New State, 1921-1941* (New York: Routledge, 2007), 178-184.

[38] Ibid., 72-73, 74-77.

[39] Aliqoli Khan Bakhtiari, Sardar As'ad, *Tarikh-e Bakhtiari* (Tehran: Farhangsara Publishers, 1984), 750-751.

[40] FO 371/E-13435. 5 October 1921; Cronin, *Tribal Politics in Iran*, 72-73, 74-77; Roshanak Bakhtiari, "Zendegi va Marg-e Shahid-e Bozorg-e Azadi, Khan Babakhan As'ad," in Gholamabbas Nowruzi-Bakhtiari, *Tarikh va Tamaddon-e Bakhtiari, Vizheh-ye Farhang va Honar*, vol. 1 (Tehran: Anzan Publishers, 1995), 88-89.

[41] Ibid., 90.

[42] Ja'farqoli Khan Sardar Bahador, *Khaterat-e Sardar As'ad Bakhtiari*, 2nd printing, edited by Iraj Afshar (Tehran: Asatir Publishers, 1999), 232; Sartip Mirhoseyn Yekrangiyan, *Seyri dar Tarikh-e Artesh-e Iran, az Aghaz ta Payan-e Shahrivar 1320* (Tehran: Khojasteh Publishers, 2005), 354-358, 427, 434.

[43] Bakhtiar, *Yekrangi*, 21; unpublished interview of Mohammad Moshiri-Yazdi with Shapour Bakhtiar, Suresnes, France, tape 1, 11 September 1988.

[44] Ibid., tape 3, 16 October 1988.

[45] Ibid., tape 1, 11 September 1988; tape 3, 16 October 1988.

[46] *Porseshha-ye Bipasokh dar Salha-ye Estesna'i: Khaterat-e Mohandes Ahmad Zirakzadeh*, edited by Dr. Abolhasan Ziya'-Zarifi and Dr. Khosrow Sa'idi (Tehran: Nilufar Publishers, 1997), 23-26.

[47] Unpublished interview of Mohammad Moshiri-Yazdi with Shapour Bakhtiar, Suresnes, France, tape 3, 2 October 1988.

[48] Ibid., tape 3, 2 October 1988.

[49] Ibid., tape 3, 2 October 1988.

[50] Ibid., tape 3, 2 October 1988; tape 3, 16 October 1988.

[51] Ibid., tape 1, 11 September 1988; tape 6, 23 October 1988.

[52] Ibid., tape 3, 16 October 1988.

[53] Unpublished interview of Mohammad Moshiri-Yazdi with Shapour Bakhtiar, Suresnes, France, tape 1, 11 September 1988; tape 1, 16 October 1988.

[54] Ibid., tape 3, 16 October 1988.

[55] Ibid., tape 3, 16 October 1988.

[56] Ibid., tape 3, 16 October 1988.

[57] Ibid., tape 3, 16 October 1988.

[58] Ibid., tape 3, 16 October 1988.

[59] Ibid., tape 3, 16 October 1988.

[60] Ibid., tape 3, 16 October 1988; tape 6, 6 November 1988; Bakhtiar, *Yekrangi*, 27.

[61] Unpublished interview of Mohammad Moshiri-Yazdi with Shapour Bakhtiar, Suresnes, France, tape 7, 6 November 1988.

[62] Ibid., tape 6, 23 October 1988.

Chapter Three

High School in Paris

Bakhtiar left Lebanon after four years, in November 1934, and he traveled by ship from Beirut to Alexandria and then to Marcy, and from there on the train to Paris. It was not easy for him to leave Lebanon, or in fact, Beirut. He had found that place to be a land of pleasantness and beauty comingled with French culture, a place in which, "in addition to the pleasantness of life, for the first time" he had seen "the blue sea." In a way, he considered Beirut a "second homeland," the Beirut that was called the Paris of the Middle East, and for him it was like a "waiting room" in which he was waiting, a start to finding his way into one of France's prestigious schools. He said that all he wanted was to continue his education in one of those schools, without having decided on the field in which he wished to continue his education. He was uncertain as to whether he should continue his education in natural sciences or in political science, literature, and philosophy. He only knew that he did not want to become a physician, even though he could see the potential in himself, that if he studied medicine, he would become a competent physician. Years later, when he stepped into the arena of politics, his friends would tell him facetiously: "If you had become a physician, it would have had two positive outcomes. You would have been a good physician, whereas you have become a bad politician. Secondly, you would have profited financially; what you are doing has no other outcome but losses."[1]

He had not been in Paris for long when he read in an issue of *Ettela'at* newspaper that Sardar Fateh along with seven other tribal khans had been executed on the charge of "treason against the country and armed uprising." Prior to the publication of this report, he had heard rumors about his father having had a heart attack in the temporary detention prison of the Police Department. It was not difficult for him to think that these rumors were true. He knew that after the rebellion that occurred in the tribe, his father had been under surveillance in Tehran. He had also heard in Beirut that his father had been under surveillance in Mashhad for a while and in danger of being arrested, a danger that had become a reality prior to his coming to Paris. He recounts: "Regarding the murder of my father, internally, I was stunned and worried as what would happen and what I should do. I put the newspaper into my pocket. The weather was cold. As I began walking along the Seine, I decided to go to Iran."[2]

There are vague and occasionally contradictory points in Bakhtiar's memoir regarding the date of his trip to Iran and his return to France. We only know that he had learned about his father's execution in Paris from the report in *Ettela'at* newspaper. The date of publication of this issue of *Ettela'at* newspaper is 27 November 1934. If we agree that in those years, it would have taken several weeks for a newspaper from Iran to reach France, we can surmise that Bakhtiar had learned about his father's execution in December 1934. In one place, he writes "as soon as" arriving in Paris, he had learned of this matter, and in another place he mentions this date as having been "three weeks" after his arrival. At any rate, he emphasizes that once he had learned about it, he had immediately gone back to Iran; and upon his return to France, he had faced some difficulties. These difficulties caused him to fall behind in his education in France by one year, or based on another account, "one or two years."[3] The significance of this point is that Bakhtiar relates that the start of his education in Paris began in the period when, following the news of the death of his father, he went back to Iran and then returned to France, a period of time when, after going through difficulties in connection with getting an exit permit from Iran, he returns to Paris and registers in Henri-IV High School and later in Louis-le-Grand High School. Bakhtiar's educational document at Henri-IV High School, however, indicates that in January 1935, he was a student at that school, in other words, sometime after his departure from Beirut, his arrival in Paris, and his learning about the execution of his father in November 1934. If so, Bakhtiar must have registered in Henri-IV High School before he returned to Iran; but upon learning about the death of his father, he must have abandoned his schooling just after having started, and then returned to Iran.

Henri-IV High School, one of the best-known schools in France, is located in the 5th arrondissement of Paris, near the Latin Quarters. The children of King of the French Louis Philippe I, the Archbishop of Paris André Vingt-Trois, and a number of that country's writers, politicians, and philosophers have attended this school, which was for the children of the affluent, notables, and aristocracy. Among the notable teachers of Henri-IV High School, mention must be made of writer and philosopher Henri Bergson and former President of France Georges Pompidou. Bakhtiar had also registered at this school, and makes a passing reference to Henri-IV school in his memoir.

Bakhtiar's student record (*fiche*) at Henri-IV High School shows that he was registered in that school in January 1935 for the 1934-1935 academic year.[4] His student records do not provide any information regarding a delay in registration. It is not clear how he could have been admitted in the middle of the academic year to study at such a school. Prior to being admitted to Henri-IV High School, every student is required to write down the name of the institution in which he has studied previously on a special student questionnaire. On his questionnaire, we read that Bakhtiar had been studying at the French school in Beirut. Instead of the word "French," he had written its abbreviation, "Fr," which undoubtedly meant the French school in Beirut. It appears that the person who filled out the student questionnaire incompletely was Bakhtiar himself. We can infer this from his handwriting, which is immature and most likely that of a non-European, or rather, we should say that it is the handwriting of a person who is not very accustomed to writing in the Latin alphabet of a European language. Moreover, there is an obvious grammatical error in what he had filled out. In front of the French word, "Nationalité," he has stated his nationality in the masculine case, whereas he should have written it in the feminine. In other words, he should have added an "e" at the end of the word "*Persan*" for Persian.

Another point worthy of note that we see on this questionnaire is that at the beginning of 1935, when this questionnaire was filled out, Persians in Paris had just recently started to identify themselves as "Iranians." Up to that time, they had referred to themselves as "Persian" or citizens of "Persia," which was what Europeans called them until on the order of the Foreign Ministry of the Iranian Government in December 1935, the decision was made that from then on, the ministries, government organizations, and foreign embassies in Tehran would use "Iran" and "Iranian" instead of "Persia" and "Persian."[i]

According to the information on that questionnaire, Bakhtiar registered for Basic Mathematics Level 1 courses as an "off-campus" student, that is, he was not a boarding school on-campus student under the supervision of teachers. In other words, once the class ended, he would leave the school, and similar to other off-campus students, he would not stay at the school to do his homework under the supervision of a teacher. On his student questionnaire, he had written his address in Paris as follows: Dr. Zarghami, no. 32, rue de l'Assomption, 16th arrondissement. Obviously, this apartment at that time belonged to Dr. Zarghami, possibly a close family friend of Bakhtiar or a relative.

The final point, as we see in that questionnaire, is that Shapour Bakhtiar registered at Henri-IV High School in January 1935, and he was a student at that school until 13 July of that same year, without having studied there. No reason or explanation is given on that student record sheet for his leaving that school, whereas, apparently they would write the reason for students leaving the school on the student record sheet. Why did they not write down the reason for his leaving the school and returning to Iran, which must have been his learning about the execution of his father? Was Bakhtiar reluctant to discuss this issue, did he not find it necessary to have it recorded, or did he actually leave without informing the school? At any rate, the date of his leaving the school is stated to be July 1935, that is, at the beginning of the summer break.

---

[i] For details regarding the text of the edict of Iran's Foreign Ministry, see *Ettela'at*, vol. 9, no. 2374, 25 December 1934, 3.

This means that he was officially a student of Henri-IV High School for those seven months without having attended the school. On the student questionnaire, the school also asked the students for other information, including place and date of birth, religion, father's occupation, regular series of vaccinations, telephone number, living languages that the student spoke or was familiar with, whether or not the student was on a scholarship or received educational subsidy, as well as other information that was optional for the student to write down. No such information, however, is found on Bakhtiar's records. All this indicates that immediately after registering at Henri-IV High School, Bakhtiar had returned to Iran, and upon his return, he had received his registration document for Henri-IV High School merely as an indication at the end of the academic year that he had officially been a student in that school. On the other hand, the date of his registration at the Louis-le-Grand High School is also January 1935, which means that after registering at Henri-IV High School, he had changed his mind for some reason and gone to Louis-le-Grand High School; but, apparently, after learning about his father's death, he had left that school as well and returned to Iran. The possibility also exists that immediately after registering, he had learned about his father's death, and by registering in school, he intended to go back to Iran as a student, so that he would not face any obstacle in Iran regarding his return to France.

Traveling back to Iran, Bakhtiar took a train from France to Germany, then to Poland and the Soviet Union, and from there, he took a ship to the port city of Bandar Anzali (at that time, Bandar Pahlavi). In the Soviet Union, he recounts: "I was in a very luxurious passenger coach on a train, but it did not have a toilet and water. It was a wagon from the tsar's time, which they had made for the Tsar's Royal Court. I think I was on Soviet soil for three days and nights. On the way, I ate the food I had brought with me. The waiter who brought me food knew no other language but Russian. I asked him for some soup. He did not understand what I said. I had to say it in German, and I said that I wanted 'Suppe.' Finally, he understood and said 'borsch,' and he went and brought me some cabbage borsch."[5]

After arriving in the Soviet Union, Bakhtiar went to Bandar Anzali aboard a ship, and from there he traveled to Rasht and then to Tehran. He states: "Our house was on Alborz Street…almost behind Bastion, where Amir Mofakhkham Bakhtiari's house was located. When I arrived in Tehran, I hired a droshky, put my suitcase in it, and set out for a house I had never seen before, because they had bought it while I was away. I spent that night in discomfort, because I did not know anyone. I did not know who would be there when I entered the house and with whom I should speak… When I arrived at the house, I saw that Mr. Navvab, the same man who had accompanied me up to Baghdad, was there. As soon as he saw me, he began to weep. It was exactly twelve o'clock at night. He asked, 'Have you had dinner?' I said, 'I had some tea in a teahouse on the way.' Then I asked where Bibi Maryam, my stepmother, and my stepbrother Abdolrasul were. Mr. Navvab said, 'Bibi has gone to her father's house, because her mother is sick.' This woman had suffered a great deal, because they had killed her brother Sardar As'ad, and they had also killed her son-in-law and her husband. And her son was in jail. I said to Mr. Navvab, 'Spread some bedding for me to sleep.' He came and lit the heater. There was not much to eat and drink. The house had a private courtyard and a public courtyard. The building in the private courtyard seemed nicer to me. It had two stories and was a larger space; it also had a library. I asked, 'Who lives in the private courtyard building?' Mr. Navvab said, 'Since Sardar Fateh is not there anymore, we have taken up the carpets. Not many people are there. Bibi and Abdolrasul with the maids and one cook are in the private courtyard.'"[6]

After meeting with a few Bakhtiaris who lived in Tehran, most of whom were mourning the execution of their relatives and were under surveillance, Bakhtiar tried to gain access to his father's will and to settle the issue of the inheritance. He was trying to make preparations for his return to Europe as quickly as possible. Having lived for several years in Beirut and comparing it with the stifling conditions in Tehran made living in Iran difficult, even "intolerable" to him. In particular, his eagerness to continue his education in France and his concern about the government preventing him from leaving the country added to his anxiety and impatience. His only hope under these circumstances was set on a letter he had in his hands from Esma'il Mer'at, the director of the Iranian Students Affairs Supervisory Office Abroad. Mer'at had written this letter in Paris upon the request of Bakhtiar based on the documents and the diploma he had obtained from Beirut, and he had submitted it to the Ministry of Culture. Bakhtiar went to the Ministry of Culture, and referring to that letter, he requested permission to leave the country. He states: "After a couple of months, I went to the Ministry of Culture. They said that the letter had arrived and that it would be delivered for consideration. Then I went to the security office of the Police Department. There was an officer there by the name of Capitan Meqdadi, who was very much liked by Reza Shah, since he apparently reported everything to Reza Shah every day. Even though the chief of police at the time was Ayrom, Reza Shah trusted this young man. He was an intelligent, polite, and hardworking young man. And he did not appear to be a violent man. But he was accused of having had a hand in many of the crimes. In my opinion, under the conditions of those days, he was not the kind of person to get people in trouble for no reason; he did his duty without any other regard. In the twists and turns of the predicament that I was in, I pleaded with him and told him about my situation. He said, 'Come back here in two days.' I went back in two days and found out that he had made an inquiry from the Ministry of Culture and learned that Mer'at's letter had arrived, which they had forwarded to him. He said, 'The letter has arrived, and I will make arrangements for you to get your passport.' My problem with the Police Department, however, was prolonged and I was in a state of limbo for several months. I went to the Police Department twice a week. There was a man there who was an opium addict, and every time, he said, 'What is the hurry?' I told him that I had to be back there by the start of the school year, and that if I didn't go back to France, I would fall behind one year in my education. Finally, I got through these problems and the business of the inheritance. But this going back and forth took nine months. I left for Paris in 1935, and my arrival there coincided with Mussolini's invasion of Ethiopia."[7]

Going back, Bakhtiar went on a ship from Bandar Anzali to Baku, and from there, on a train to Germany and France. In addition to Fereydun Jam, the son of the prime minister at the time, Mahmud Jam, his fellow travelers included two of the children of Prince Farmanfarma, in addition to the well-known journalist Mohammad Mas'ud, and Mr. Seyyed Hashem Vakil, who was the defense attorney of Abdolhoseyn Teymurtash and Nosratoddowleh Firuz.[ii] Before his arrival in Paris, he stopped shortly in Berlin. He recounts: "When we arrived in Berlin, Hitler was already in power… I heard his speech in the large square of the city on the radio. Until then, I had not seen such a large crowd. Two days later, Fereydun Jam, Mr. Hashem Vakil, and I took the train to Paris, and the two Farmanfarma brothers stayed in Germany. On this trip, Mr. Hashem Vakil told us his recollections about Teymurtash and Nosratoddowleh Firuz, which were very interesting. He said, 'Teymurtash was weak during the trial; but in contrast, Nosratoddowleh was very strong and bold.' Mr. Hashem Vakil added, 'My defense strategy in both of their cases was to refute the charge of treason, and to say that they had misappropriated funds. I left this route open, since if they were convicted of theft and embezzlement, they could be sentenced to a few years in prison, whereas the punishment for treason was death.' I asked him what his own view was regarding them. He said, 'I think both of them needed to be eliminated. The issue was not theft or treason. They had no evidence to prove theft or treason. Reza Shah was displeased with both of them; in fact, he was fearful. They killed Nosratoddowleh near Semnan and Teymurtash in Tehran.'"[8]

When Bakhtiar returned from Iran, he began his studies at the Louis-le-Grand public high school. Louis-le-Grand High School is located at

---

[ii] In his recollections, Bakhtiar states that he could not exactly recall whether Mohammad Mas'ud traveled with him when he went back to Iran or when he returned to France. Unpublished interview of Mohammad Moshiri-Yazdi with Shapour Bakhtiar, Suresnes, France, tape 10, 4 December 1988.

123 rue Saint-Jacques, across from the Sorbonne, the University of Paris, in the heart of the Latin Quarter. Ten percent of the students of this school, which was founded in 1563, were foreign. Registration at Louis-le-Grand High School is free and it charges no tuition. The only criterion for student admission is hard work and meeting the expectations of the school authorities. Students had to work hard at their studies and observe the school regulations. That is why this school has become a distinguished institution for training the elite of French society. The reputation of Louis-le-Grand High School is also due to the fact that student admission is not based on family name and status, although students who study there have the chance of one day becoming famous and prestigious. From Molière, Voltaire, and Baudelaire to Victor Hugo and the Marquis de Sade; from Robespierre and Régis Debray to Romain Rolland and Paul Claudel; and from Émile Durkheim and Jean-Paul Sartre to Pierre Bourdieu and Jacques Derrida, all were students in Louis-le-Grand High School. It is a school in which politicians such as Georges Pompidou, Valéry Giscard d'Estaing, Jacques Chirac, and Laurent Fabius studied. Bakhtiar, too, with his entry into Louis-le-Grand High School, enjoyed such a distinct chance and opportunity. This opportunity paved the way for him to continue his education at the Sorbonne and obtain degrees that were granted to the elite and would bring him a reputation and prestige.

Bakhtiar's school records at Louis-le-Grand High School show that he registered in the boarding school of that institution on 7 January 1935 and completed his education there in July 1936. The first document related to Bakhtiar's education at Louis-le-Grand High School includes a sheet entitled "Entrées," or "Entries." Bakhtiar's name is recorded on line 33 of this sheet, and it states the date of his entry into that school as 7 January 1936. Most likely, this sheet is from Bakhtiar's second academic year in that school. Another document indicates that from 10 October 1935, as one of the students in that boarding school, he studied in a Basic Mathematics Level 2 course. On the third sheet in Bakhtiar's educational file, Bakhtiar's nationality is recorded as Iranian, his date of birth as 2 November 1914, and his place of birth as Isfahan. Nothing is recorded about the living languages that he spoke. On the second part of this sheet, under name, home, and occupation of father, mother, or guardian, it is stated: Mr. Bakhtiar, landowner. On the next line, the address of Bakhtiar's father and mother is stated as follows: No. 9, Golbarg Street, Tehran (Iran). In the third section, under the name and home of the main contact, it is written: Mr. Zarghami, student, no. 32, rue de l'Assomption, 16th arrondissement. At the bottom of the sheet, in answer to the question of with which institution the student was affiliated prior to coming to Louis-le-Grand High School, they have written: Beirut French School. On the basis of this information, it becomes clear that he did not study at Henri-IV High School, since the name of the school that has been mentioned as the one in which he was a student prior to coming to Louis-le-Grand High School is the Beirut French School.

Considering these points, it seems that after registering at Henri-IV and Louis-le-Grand High Schools in January 1935, once Bakhtiar learned about his father's death, he went back to Iran; and when he returned to Paris, he became a student at Louis-le-Grand High School.

When Bakhtiar received his diploma from Louis-le-Grand High School, and while he was preparing himself for studying at the Sorbonne, he became interested in French poetry and literature more than ever before. His initial introduction to French literature in Beirut was through *Le Crime de Sylvestre Bonnard*, a novel by Anatole France. He then proceeded with reading works by Mauriac, Roger Martin du Gard, Charles Maurras, and later on, Sartre and Camus. The works that enchanted him more than any others were those of the renowned French poet, Paul Valéry, in which he sought "refuge," a place which in the most difficult moments of his life was the source of hope and peace of mind for him.

Enchanted by Paul Valéry

The French poet and writer, Paul Valéry, was born in 1871 in the port town of Sète in southern France. As a child, similar to other children his age in Sète, he wanted to become a navigator; but he had to have a strong background in mathematics in order to be admitted to the Naval Academy, a subject in which he did not excel. Hence, he saw no other choice but "to seek his melancholic love for the sea in literature and painting. The sea for him was the attraction of his hopes and dreams, and he would admit that at one time he had been madly in love with water and light." As a young man, he was influenced by the well-known French poet, Stéphane Mallarmé, and joined the gathering of French symbolist poets. Before long, his first poems became household words, and he was referred to as the great hope of French literature, until suddenly when his reputation had spread beyond the intellectual circles, he stopped composing and spent the following twenty years with regard to poetry, which he called the most difficult of arts, in heavy silence, an act that has been considered the start of a new age in poetic paths and ways. Upon the completion of his education in law, he left Montpellier for Paris, made his living as an employee of the Ministry of War for three years, married and became a father, and spent eight long years in a tumultuous relationship with his lover, Catherine Pozzi.[iii] Valéry then became a member of the Académie française from 1925, and in 1931, he received an honorary doctorate from the University of Oxford. Two years later, he was appointed as Chief Executive of the Mediterranean University in Nice, and in 1937, the inaugural holder of the Chair of Poetics at the Collège de France. In the 1930s, Valéry chaired the Sub-Committee on Arts and Letters at the League of Nations, which dealt with issues related to "intellectual cooperation" in the world. When Anatole France died in 1924, as his successor, Valéry was elected president of the association of writers and remained in that post for ten years.

Valéry was dignified and humble. He discounted his fame, and he relied on a pride that stemmed from intellectual aristocracy. He was

---

iii Regarding the relationship between Paul Valéry and Catherine Pozzi, see: Catherine Pozzi, *Paul Valéry, Glück, Dämonen, Verrückter: Tagebuch 1920-1928* (Frankfurt am Main: Suhrkamp, 1998).

fond of Leonardo da Vinci, Rembrandt, and Edgar Degas, and he was enchanted by Wagner's work. He was proud that his friends had shaped his character, and that Stéphane Mallarmé and André Gide were among his friends. The names of these friends along with that of Valéry himself as well as other writers and poets, such as Céline, Claudel, and Proust, are comingled with French poetry, art, and literature.

Valéry's workday began around five or five-thirty in the morning in his pajamas, with a cigarette hanging from his lipsand a cup of strong coffee, the beans of which he had roasted himself. Joyful or depressed, happy or sad, at home or traveling, nothing, not even his mother's death, could deter him from this schedule. This was a routine that for him was not a sign of deficiency in emotions and poetic nature, but a sort of refuge. The fruit of his fifty-year effort, which he recorded in more than 1,600 notebooks as "morning spiritual exercise," amounted to some 27,000 pages that were published after his death in twenty-nine thick volumes.[9]

In his younger days, Valéry had turned to mystical works. He contemplated seclusion from the world and spending the rest of his life in a monastery. In response to the question of whether or not God existed, he said: "Yes, God and Satan both exist, but within us. God is nothing but our ideal perfection, an ideal perfection that Satan is trying to steal from man." Valéry's God amazingly resembled the ideal perfection that he was trying to attain with his poetry and art, the God of beauty and the God of his dreams.[10]

For Valéry, the source of creation is attainable, and even in the complexities of his magical world, it is concealed in the transparency and clarity of his art. "What is more mysterious than clarity?" This was the question by which he would reveal the secret of the immortality of his work. He said that nothing is more attractive to him than transparency, even though he claimed that he could not find it anywhere. In response to his critics, who said that he spoke of clarity, light, and transparency while his work was most difficult and was concealed in a halo of secrets and mystery, he said: "The darkness of which they accuse me, in contrast to the darkness that exists around me, is insignificant, and it is visible. It is difficult for me to distinguish what light is before I can perceive what darkness is. True darkness should be sought in works that appear to be transparent and easily understood." Valéry considered the lowest type of literature the literature that expects of the reader the least amount of effort to understand. While being simple himself, he did not acknowledge any credibility for simple and easy truths, and he did not feel obligated to comply with that which was called public opinion. In assessing his own work, Valéry invited himself and his reader to choose an option the basis of which is doubt standing firm on a creative frame of mind: "I naturally think about a specific audience, about those who are searching without being certain that they have found what they are seeking."[11]

In the course of the occupation of Paris during World War II, in answer to a question asked by a German officer in front of the Collège de France building, "What is this building?" Valéry had said: "This is the building in which freedom of expression rules." It was in the same building that Bakhtiar became acquainted with Valéry. In two separate accounts that are slightly different, Bakhtiar recounts about how they met: "Along with two of my friends, we attended his class. Valéry was a short man with a white moustache, and he parted his hair in the middle. He was very gentle, and his eyes were blue, the color of the Mediterranean. In the first session of the course, when he came into the classroom, there were so many students that they had to stand... Valéry began to talk, and he said, 'Don't expect me to talk about things that you read in all the books and which you know better than I do. I have a peculiar outlook about everything, and I am a peculiar person, and my peculiarity has caused me a great deal of trouble. I have always been strict, whether in poetry, in prose, or in my thinking. To most other people, I appear to be a difficult man to know, whereas in my own opinion, I am a simple man and write simply.'" Apparently this characteristic attracted Bakhtiar more than ever before to Valéry's work. He observed that Valéry's "prose is clear, but understanding it is difficult." Bakhtiar would speak about Valéry's style, his scrupulousness in choosing and combining words, the harmony of the images, and the rhythm and luster of his diction, such diction that played an essential role in the creation of the texture and the shaping of his work. His praise of Valéry spoke of his familiarity with a poet whom he considered to be equal to the Persian poet Hafez. He would remark: "I prefer a book that, even if its language is not more exalted than its content, would not be less than that. This is true of Valéry's work. If the language of a book is not as worthy of praise as the ideas it offers, it is not worth reading. Valéry shuns all that is easy and all that is created without hard work and struggle."[12]

Continuing the account of his meeting with Valéry, Bakhtiar writes: "At the end of the class session, together with my friend, Cherer, who was himself a poet and painter, we went closer, to see what kind of man Valéry was. The man who from a distance appeared hard, harsh, and inaccessible treated us most cordially and unceremoniously. We accompanied him on the Metro to his home. Without a doubt, the way he spoke was neither like Cherer nor like me. He had absolutely no qualms about using colloquial words and expressions. After this meeting, Valéry came to my house several times. At that time, through a friend, I was able to buy coffee, which was one of the scarce food items during the occupation of France. Valéry would come and openly show his enjoyment in drinking the coffee."[13]

Bakhtiar's introduction to Valéry's name went back to when he was studying in Beirut; but other than knowing that Valéry's work was difficult to understand, he did not know anything else about him. He writes: "Early on, Valéry was a cause of confusion for me. When I was in the tenth grade in Beirut, on one of those smoldering hot afternoons in June, in order to get the students out of their boredom, our teacher read Valéry's poem, "Le cimetière marin." He got us so out of our boredom that we all fell asleep, or at least we pretended to fall asleep to show him that this powerful poem had not pleased us much. At that time, I promised myself never to touch Valéry's books. I broke this promise in 1940 with his La soiree avec Monsieur Teste, and I decided to read that prose text like a person who is translating a text from a foreign language into a language he knows. The precision and fineness of his prose astounded me... I wanted to find "Le cimetière marin," which had made me yawn and fall asleep. One evening in 1941, when it had become dark and the sound of the explosion of bombs could be heard near the capital city, I went to Auguste Comte Square, to the French academic press located across from the Sorbonne. I bought every one of Valéry's books that I could find and tried to discover their secrets. Valéry had once said, 'Le diplôme est l'ennemi mortel de la culture' (diplomas are the mortal enemies of culture). And all I had been doing up to that time had been merely to obtain degrees." Bakhtiar thought that he had had an education no part of which had taught him what he had learned from Valéry. That is why he said to himself: "The diplomas I have obtained are good for nothing. I need to go and learn culture. So, from 1942 to 1945, I truly spent those three years on open culture." In those years, Bakhtiar regarded all that he had acquired in the arena of culture or about impressionist and surrealist painting or symbolic poetry to be indebted to his familiarity with Valéry's work and Valéry's approach to the acquisition of knowledge. He would admit that during difficult moments in his life, he had always taken refuge in Valéry's work. He said: "The respect I have for Ferdowsi, I have for no other poet... And I do not know any writer more serious and worthy of contemplation than Montesquiou... But if I were to be exiled to an island, I would be grateful if they would give me Valéry's work and Hafez's poetry rather than the works of Ferdowsi and Montesquiou."[14]

Bakhtiar's fascination with Valéry's work and the poetry and literature that he referred to as "the soul of France" were not the only things he had stored away during his time in France, or what he would call his "backpack of educational journey." Bakhtiar did not want to devote his life to poetry alone, and he intended to also benefit from the "substantive" politics of that country during those years. In this arena, he was clearly different from his beloved poet. For Valéry, politics lacked any credibility. With a bitterly satirical outlook, he regarded politics as an art the function of which was to keep people away from that which concerned them. He said: "For me, the ancestral homeland does not become meaningful between the folds of the flag or a plot of land. My ancestral homeland consists of my thoughts and dreams, and my compatriots are those who share these thoughts with me." In contrast, Bakhtiar considered himself to be "feverish for politics" and enchanted and enamored by the homeland in which he knew "at night he could feel the stars, chest to chest with the sky, on his eyelids."[15] Nonetheless, such was destiny that, despite this difference in taste with his beloved poet and writer, the dangers that rose from the darkness that loomed over Europe had an indelible impact on the life of this young son of a Bakhtiari khan and that of his singular star of poetry.

The dangers of war tied together Valéry's life with three incidents, each of which subjected the fate of France, Europe, and Western civilization with crises and tumult. He came into this world before the blood in the Paris shelters at the end of the 1870-1871 war between Germany and France had dried. The end of World War I coincided with the period when Valéry was going through his period of obscurity, when to the disbelief and sadness of those entranced by his poetry, he underwent a long period of self-imposed silence, and, finally, World War II at the conclusion of which he left this world in hopelessness.

Even though Valéry looked at the political events of his time with cynicism, as André Gide, Jorge Borges, and T. S. Eliot said in their speeches at his funeral, he remained faithful to critical thinking to the last moment. With the inflaming of World War I, for him, Europe, this "pearl" of the earth, had reached its end. Valéry called the war the assault of the twentieth century on humanity, the assault of a civilization the distinct sign of which, in his words, was evident in the institutionalized military and economic advancements of Germany, that "iron cage" of Europe. For him, the reason for the war was not merely summed up in political and economic issues. Valéry called the war the outcome of European thinking and the disarray of modernity, "a tragedy that showed that culture is as fragile as human life." As a thinker who had called intellect his deity, at the same time, he was a staunch critic of the civilization that rose from rationalism; and in this respect, he was a protector of tradition. Unlike Gustav Mahler, the Austrian composer, however, he saw the preservation of tradition not in the benediction of ashes, but in the preservation of fire. He praised man and knowledge without forgetting for even one moment that "knowledge without conscience will have no outcome but the destruction of the soul." Valéry would ask: "What can man do?" Man who, in his words, was crucified on the cross of his own thinking. This is the question that he raised for the first time in his brilliant work, Monsieur Teste, a question that up to the moment he shut his eyes to the world "remained the most fundamental idea of his life."[16]

Bakhtiar's Doctoral Dissertation: Religion and State in the Age of Antiquity

After obtaining his diploma at Louis-le-Grand High School, Bakhtiar registered in the field of philosophy in the Law School of the Sorbonne. According to his memoir, he succeeded in passing examinations in sociology, ethics, general philosophy and logic, history, and philosophy of sciences. A year later, he registered in the field of political science at the Sorbonne, and after three years, he completed his studies with a degree in political science and a bachelor's degree in the fields of law and philosophy. He also spent another three years on his doctoral education; and he wrote his dissertation on the relationship between religion and state in antiquity. His dissertation was completed at the Sorbonne under the supervision of Professor Georges Scelle. He recounts: "I asked him about the field of general law and international law, which are related to the philosophy of law, and also asked about law itself, and requested of him to grant me the honor of allowing me to complete my dissertation with him." After agreeing to his request, Scelle told Bakhtiar: "Let me read your educational file at the Sorbonne in order to recommend a topic that would be compatible with your field." Two weeks later, he told Bakhtiar: "You have studied philosophy. Write on a topic other than things like relations between the lessor and the lessee… You are the kind of person who is not interested in working in a justice department and civil law… If you want to complete your dissertation with me, I will suggest a few topics. Go to the Sorbonne and tell them you would like to complete your dissertation here. That means that this dissertation can be defended in the fields of law and philosophy." After completing his doctoral dissertation and going back to Iran, Bakhtiar intended, if he was successful, to teach at the university, expand the topic of his dissertation, and by continuing his research in this area, publish the results.[17]

Philosophy along with poetry were the topics of interest to him. He would say: "Every field that I chose was in fact because of the philosophy of that field. I would study mathematics for the philosophy of mathematics, and I would see that mathematics means science in the European sense, not in the sense viewed in the Feyziyeh Seminary in Qom. As science advances and philosophy becomes more refined and gains depth, somewhere they connect. The idea that there is a sort of unity between science and philosophy is a part of the theories of illumination philosophers… For example, when I was doing my bachelor's degree in philosophy, it was about the comparison between science and philosophy, about how science began to grow from the time of the Chaldeans and Assyrians up to the time of the Egyptians, and then, with the manifestation of civilization in the Greek School, about how all these philosophical issues from Democrates to Pythagoras culminated and became closer to one another."[18]

Thus, with his interest in philosophy, and with the discernment of Professor Scelle, Bakhtiar decided to change the topic of his dissertation and devote himself to a topic inspired by the meaning of intellect in Valéry's work, which he termed "the potential of the intellect," in other words, the inherent ability to think. Reading the well-known book, *Matière et mémoire* by the renowned French philosopher Henri Bergson, also made him more interested in the project he had in mind. As an Iranian student, Bakhtiar made an appointment with Bergson, who lived in his neighborhood on Boulevard de Beauséjour, and went to see him. He had only a quarter of an hour to discuss with him what he had in mind. Sitting in an easy chair with a blanket over his knees and books all around him, Bergson, who was over eighty years old, welcomed him into his large parlor. Bakhtiar began their conversation with a contradiction that he thought he had found in *L'Évolution créatrice*, another book by the French philosopher.

In the meantime, the time that he was allotted went by quickly, but Bergson, despite the fact that he was suffering from rheumatism, stopped him from leaving, and asked Bakhtiar about his interests aside from philosophy. Bakhtiar mentioned law and poetry. Bergson said: "The day that you succeed in arriving at poetry and even law and ethics from philosophy, that is when you will be cultured. In the meantime, think about choosing your paths well, even if at times this seems difficult to you. Take this advice from me. After reading a work of comedy by Molière, read the text of one of Immanuel Kant's works. There is unity in spirituality. There is a way; but it has no fixed markings. Everyone must find it on his own."[19]

Research and writing about the potential of the intellect preoccupied Bakhtiar's mind for a long time, drawing him toward reading works such as those of Bergson, to the point that every now and then, he wanted to abandon everything and become, as he called it, a "rebel." Moreover, he estimated that writing such a dissertation would take him ten years; hence, in order to make a living and receive the "rest of his salary," it would be better to pursue the same topic he had chosen earlier to write his doctoral dissertation, and at the same time keep an eye open to philosophy.

Bakhtiar's 141-page dissertation, entitled "Essai sur Les rapports entre le pouvoir et la religion dans la constitution des sociétés," consists of an introduction, four chapters, a conclusion, final considerations, and a bibliography. The date of the dissertation defense is 20 November 1945, and the professors on his dissertation committee consisted of Georges Scelle, François Olivier-Martin, and Henri Levy-Bruhl. The framework of his dissertation consists of Chapter One, entitled "On the Organization of Primitive Societies"; Chapter Two, entitled "Religious Power in Semitic Groups"; and Chapters Three and Four, under the heading of "Indo-European Societies," are divided into two separate sections of "The Indo-Iranian Group" and "The Indo-European Group." Chapter

One explicates concepts such as primitive society, tribal images and myths, and power and its religious aspects. Chapter Two, which is devoted to Egypt and the Assyrian-Babylonian kingdoms, examines the issue of the Egyptian totem belief system, the divine monarchical dynasties and human monarchical dynasties in Egypt, and the concept of the divinity of the pharaoh and his rights and duties. In the continuation of this chapter, Bakhtiar studies the "religious characteristic" of the kingship of Assyria and Babylon. Chapter Three explains the castes and the social and religious organizations in Aryan India. The founding of the Achaemenid Empire and its divine character, Zoroaster and the Magi's organizations and activities, the religion of the Sassanian state, and the fall of Mazdakism after the Arab invasion of Persia comprise the other topics of this chapter. Chapter Four is devoted to ancient Greece, the characteristics of Roman religion, religious power in monarchical systems, republic and empire, the decadence of religion in the Roman state, and the rise of Christianity.

In his memoir, Bakhtiar does not mention why he chose the relationship between religion and state in the age of antiquity as the topic of his dissertation. Had he done so, this could have clarified certain other unknown aspects of his outlook and the arguments of his time, and revealed certain unclear points regarding the path that he pursued. This was an issue in which he eventually became entangled in reality, and the struggle between what he called dogmatism and social progress brought about his woeful fate. We only know that in 1938, a few years before Bakhtiar began his research on this topic, Gholamhoseyn Sadiqi, who at another time became one of the notable figures of the National Front, had also engaged in research for his doctoral dissertation at the Sorbonne. In a significant work entitled "Les mouvements religieux iraniens au IIe et IIIe siècle de l'hégire" (Iranian Religious Movements during the 9th and 10th Centuries), Sadiqi began a fruitful effort to understand the role of religion in the developments of an important period in the history of Iran.[20]

Nevertheless, Sadiqi also does not mention anything about his motivations for addressing this issue in his dissertation, an issue that preoccupied his mind as well as Bakhtiar's, and perhaps those of many others at a sensitive juncture in the destiny of a country they loved. Whatever the case maybe, the choice of a topic related to the age of antiquity and Iran's place and position in that age can be indicative of Bakhtiar's nationalism and interest in Iranian nationalism at a time when, with the reign of Reza Shah, emphasis on the history of ancient Persia had gained a special place in the public consciousness of the society and had given meaning to national identity. It is as though, despite his tribal lineage, in his doctoral dissertation, Bakhtiar seeks to give form to such a concept, especially at a time when national identity, race, and nationalism were the topic of the day and persistent issues discussed in the political and academic assemblies and circles of Iran and the Western world.

In his dissertation, Bakhtiar does not mention the amount of time he spent on writing it. His memoir is also unclear in this regard: "I studied for my doctorate for three years, and simultaneously chose what I wanted for my topic. My dissertation was in the field of general law, and the topic that I chose was the relationship between religion and politics in the age of antiquity… It was 1942, when I had a mandatory year of doctoral studies." He then adds that between 1942 and 1945, he had passed his "doctoral dissertation examination" and was busy writing his dissertation. During those years, he spent most of his time reading and examining the works of poets and writers, such as Valéry and Bergson.[21]

Hence, we can surmise that his increasing eagerness to study in an arena that he called the arena of "open culture," which was unrelated to his academic research, left him with little time and no opportunity to make use of the resources of the Sorbonne library in writing his doctoral dissertation. As he stated himself, during that interval, he sometimes was carrying out a mission for the French Resistance, or due to the difficulties of wartime, he spent most of his time with his family in Bretagne.

In the introduction to his dissertation, regarding the relationship between religion and state, Bakhtiar writes: "The battle between church and state, which at times has become quite heated in the present age, is a relatively new historical phenomenon. Humans have lived for thousands of years with harmony between, and most often the combination of, these two powers. While modern society, with its economic development, more than ever before is based on change in raw materials, ancient society, in the area that we have been able to study and discern, was managed on the basis of some sort of mysticism. Of course, neither are economic factors totally determinant in modern society, nor did mystical thinking exist in pure form in ancient societies. It would be simplistic to think that humans lived for centuries with their eyes always on the infinite. Likewise, it would be unfair to think that today the limits and bounds of our concerns are related to economic life. The truth is that in ancient societies, religious thinking penetrated all group and individual activities, and within them, they had created the social institutions with an outlook quite different from the outlook that has inspired the institutions of our society."[22]

With this assessment, Bakhtiar emphasizes that after centuries of separation of religion and political power, in their development, totalitarian ideologies had considered a sort of return to the unification these two forces. Even though this ideological tendency did not achieve its purpose, it stepped on this path and contrived a plan for the dependence of spiritual power on worldly power to devise political power devoid of any religious thought, and determined the course of its evolution. To solidify this reasoning, with a look at human societies, Bakhtiar begins with the formation of clans and studies the relationship between religion and political power in its evolutionary process: "Before growing and turning into a modern society, depending on the land on which it is located, the clan first takes the form of human groups, societies, tribes, kingdoms, and empires. The ancient global city ends with the Roman Empire in the west. Then, on the ruins of that empire, Christianity victoriously prepares itself for the establishment of the territories of the Berber Empire. With the victory of Christianity, the issue of the power of religion is raised once again. In general, a Christian citizen does not know whom to obey. Nothing is more difficult for him than returning to him that which belongs to Caesar. Primitive Christianity was not

designed for this world. Its Empyrean was not the terrestrial world...
The Christian awaited the end of the world. He awaited Resurrection
Day. But this end and Resurrection Day constantly kept him waiting.
Hence, the ties to political power that were thought to have been broken
forever needed to be restored once again."[23]

Against this backdrop, in defining "Renaissance man" and explaining
the Reformation, he points out the "critical" attitude of the Christian
faithful in examining and critiquing religious texts. This approach,
according to Bakhtiar, opened the way for the rise of the secular state,
which had no other consequence but to widen the gap that was opened
with the revolution in Europe between political power and religious
power. No longer "will any treaty and agreement reconnect the broken
ties. It seems that political power disregards the church, the worldly
power of which has become extremely limited. Nevertheless, the church
does not regard itself as defeated. It is certain that it changes and on
occasions welcomes the most courageous of reforms, without giving up
the rights that it considers indomitable and without losing hope of
dominating the state over time."[24]

In examining the developments in the Middle Ages, Bakhtiar then
discusses the emergence and flourishing of Islam and another "world-
conquering totalitarian community" that comes into existence: "The call
of Islam to the early Moslems is a call to live in this world and to this-
worldly living. Life in the next world will come in the hereafter." In
Bakhtiar's words, the organization of the Moslem community in its legal
and political details and the absence of two powers independent of each
other stem from here: "In its initial purity and simplicity, Islam has
neither a church nor a government. The Prophet and his successors
utilize totalitarian power. The simplicity and clarity of this doctrine can
be easily understood, and one can understand the resistance of the
Moslem governments for a long time to legal and social reform."
Bakhtiar considers all of this the result of "unfaltering" dogma and
"dogged and staunch" faith. It is a religion in which no sign of the
constantly recurring changes in the "stormy opportunistic" politics of
the Christian church can be seen. According to Bakhtiar, that which the

Moslem governments lost, especially with regard to "science, art, and social progress," Islam gained in terms of its "dogmatic purity and unity."[25]

The issue that Bakhtiar seems to have overlooked in his assessment is what he terms the "dogmatic purity and unity" of Islam, which is true of its beginning rather than the time of the establishment of "Moslem governments." Science, art, and social progress also are ultimately related to the period of the establishment and power of Islamic governments, and not the beginning of Islam. In his dissertation, Bakhtiar seems to compare Islam mostly with Christianity in the modern age, and he pays no attention to its history during the flourishing periods of Islamic civilization.

In the continuation of his study, Bakhtiar discusses the Persian-Aryan tribes and the Achamaenid Empire and provides an overview of Zoroaster and the teachings of the Avesta and Iranian religions, with a look at the duty of religion and the clergy during the Sassanian era. Mani and Mazdak and then the acceptance of Shi'ism as a weapon for putting up resistance against the caliphates are among the other topics examined in his doctoral dissertation that have been examined in a passing and cursory fashion. In writing his dissertation, he has paid no attention to the importance of rare indigenous written sources that are extant from ancient times. The bibliography of his dissertation shows that he has made no use of Persian sources in his research, and his reference to the Avesta is based on European sources. For instance, a work such as *Nameh-ye Tansar* (Letter of Tansar), which was published in 1932 in Tehran with the efforts and research conducted by Mojtaba Minovi and which is considered an important document for understanding the Sassanian era, has not been utilized in his research. If we assume that Bakhtiar's failure to mention *Letter of Tansar* is due to his being away from Iran, still we find no reason for his having failed to examine it in his research. The French Orientalist James Darmesteter had published this work along with its French translation in 1894 in *Journal Asiatique* published in Paris.[26] From then on, *Letter of Tansar*, due to its importance for understanding the Sassanian period, was a recognized and credible source for experts.

At the beginning of this chapter, Bakhtiar provides a definition of the term and concept of "Iran" that is not historically error free: "The term Iran is a geographical term that refers to a very vast plateau that extends much farther beyond the eastern and western borders of the country that we know by that name." What has been overlooked in this definition, leaving aside its geographical aspect, is the concept that created the meaning of the word "Iran" since the age of antiquity and transformed it into a "political unit." This concept for the first time appeared as "Iranshahr" and as a twin phenomenon of the Sassanian Empire, becoming the most important element in its ideological construction.[27] The Italian Iranologist, Gherardo Gnoli, examining Achaemenid frieze inscriptions, studied the terms Arya and Iran, which were tribal concepts during the Achaemenid era, and explains their evolution as political, ethnic, and religious concepts during the Sassanian era. Lexically, Iran means "Irha," and "Ir" is another pronunciation of "Arya."[28]

In this sense, the term "Iranshahr" as an Aryan country became common for the first time during the Sassanian era, whereas the Achaemenids never called their empire Iranshahr or Iran. Disregarding this development and the fundamental difference between the concept of Iran during the Achaemenid and Sassanian eras, and reducing it to a "geographic" term, especially in a work that studies the position of Iran in antiquity, is a significant error in Bakhtiar's doctoral dissertation. Such errors or shortcomings can also be found in other chapters of his dissertation, each of which should be examined and critiqued. The important point in his dissertation, however, is his outlook regarding the issue of religion and state, and the effect this viewpoint had on his political life.

Bakhtiar's doctoral dissertation presents to the reader a general sketch of his approach to the place of Iran in the world and the position of religion and state in antiquity. Unlike the claims of some of his defenders, this does not indicate that he was cognizant of the possibility of the dangerous predicament that many years later, when religion and state became comingled, was waiting in ambush for Iran. It seems that Bakhtiar, in keeping with the zeitgeist of the first half of the 20th century, not only failed to see any threat by the functionaries of religion, but also, in his return to Iran, he pursued his own and his country's future in being dependent on the support and cooperation of religious politicians or political religious figures such as Mehdi Bazargan and Ayatollah Seyyed Reza Zanjani.

In fact, he was preparing his doctoral dissertation at a time when religious forces and religious people did not yet have a significant presence in politics, neither in the world nor in Iran. The intellectual foundations of political Islam had not yet been completely developed and polished, and the failed attempts of clerics headed by Sheykh Fazlollah Nuri during the constitutional era had been more or less erased from memory. Similar to many Iranian intellectuals of his time, Bakhtiar had perhaps read Ahmad Kasravi's *History of the Iranian Constitution*; but most likely, similar to many of them, he had paid no attention to that historian's account of the actions of the religious movement.

In other words, his views about religion are not clear. His approach to studying the Achaemenid era and its kings, who were the manifestation of deities on earth and who ruled by their decree, is also the same. On the one hand, Bakhtiar emphasizes the role of religion in the social and political organizations of some societies, especially among the Semitic peoples, and on the other, he tries to downplay the role of religion in pre-Islamic Iranian society, and occasionally, he even attributes the strengthening of religion and religious figures in Iran to the influence of Semitic cultures on Iranian cultures. Obviously, he had not read *Karnameh-ye Ardeshir Babakan* and *Letter of Tansar*, or at least he had not dealt with them in his dissertation. In these two documents, we clearly see that religion was one of the essential pillars of ruling for the Sassanian kings as well as a political leverage in their hands.

It seems that Bakhtiar's dissertation was written under the influence of, more than anything else, the paradigm that dominated historical research in Europe in the nineteenth century. This approach to historiography intended to prove at any price the differences between the cultures of the Semitic tribes and the cultures of the Indo-European tribes, and the superiority of the Indo-European tribes over the Semitic tribes.

The point that is certain is that in explaining the place and role of religion in human societies, he has an unclear and undefined point of view. This lack of clarity that has found its way into his dissertation is the result of not only his experience as an Iranian but also the influence on his learning of the writings of some of his contemporary scholars of religion and race. Those scholars never considered that that group of religious leaders who interfered in politics openly or secretly would have a political project for taking over the reins of power. This group was particularly strengthened as a result of the unprecedented expansion of renovations and modernization during the reign of Reza Shah, and the fact that the intellectuals and the political leaders of the country distanced themselves from Islam, which they referred to as the religion of the Arabs.

In addition to these, writing about the issue of the relationship between religion and state during antiquity is a far more complex undertaking than can be carried out by a student who is still a novice in the arena of scholarly research. The expanse of the historical, cultural, and ethnic differences in the social systems of the age of antiquity confronts any scholar with numerous difficulties in terms of understanding the subject before him. An important aspect of such difficulties, in particular when Bakhtiar was doing research for his dissertation, was the scarcity of sources and the difficulty of gaining access to them. This fact would leave him no other option but to write his dissertation hastily and resort to generalities or passing references. The question, however, is, how can one explain the differences or similarities of various cultures and systems during antiquity with generalities in a dissertation that does not exceed 141 pages? He could perhaps have succeeded if instead of the goal that he had set, he had merely addressed the relationship between religion and state in Iran.

In the continuation of this study, the first question that Bakhtiar raises regarding the religious beliefs of the people of the Iranian plateau up to the emergence of Zoroaster is whether or not the Achaemenids were Zoroastrian. He writes, "Inscriptions in Bisotun and Persepolis introduce us to a dynasty that had divine rights"; and quoting Darius in those inscriptions, "All that I have accomplished has been by the grace of Ahura Mazda," he adds: "From these words that are from an inscription in Bisotun, we can infer that, first, the Achaemenid ruler considered Ahura Mazda to be the sole lord of the universe (as the rest of the inscription also verifies); second, if he was able to quell the rebellion of the usurpers, it was because 'these ambitious ones had rebelled against a power that had been established by God.' Moreover, this divinity was invisible, and they worshipped him in the form of a fire lit on an altar. The religion of the Achaemenids neither had a temple nor icons, something that was a source of great astonishment for the Greeks. This religion, if we accept Herodotus's words, was not the only religion of the empire. Alongside it was also the religion of the people, in particular, the religion of the Magi. Alas, the information that has reached us about the beliefs of the people at that time is very meagre. We know that within the gates of the empire—which according to recent scholarship were closed—people of various religions lived side by side. These religions were the creeds of the tribes and peoples that comprised the empire. Hence, if the religion of Mazda is meant to consist of the teachings of the Avesta, it seems unlikely for the Achaemenid rulers to have been the followers of this religion. There is a clear contradiction between the emphatic and repeated instructions in this sacred book and the actions of those rulers. For instance, in the religious jurisprudential section, the Avesta forbids the burial of the dead. Corpses must be placed on the 'Tower of Silence' and they must not be buried until their flesh is completely devoured by birds and animals.

"In any case, the tombs of the Achaemenid rulers near Persepolis show that their custom was contrary to the instructions in the Avesta. How is it possible for the laws of the Avesta to be implemented in a country while the kings of that country, who are the guardians of divine laws, have the right to split open the sides of boulders to build tombs for themselves? We should not, however, forget that these kings were Persian, whereas the Avesta, even if not all of it is by Zoroaster, on the whole, is a summary of the beliefs of the Medes, especially the Magi of the Medes." In the continuation of this discussion, Bakhtiar speaks of the presence and peaceful coexistence of various religions among the tribes and peoples of the Achaemenid Empire; but he believes that "the religion that the Avesta teaches was not the religion of the Achaemenid rulers."[29]

By raising the issue that the Achaemenids were not Zoroastrian, Bakhtiar bases his reasoning on the viewpoints of a specific group of Iranologists whose ideas and opinions are of value and credibility. Nevertheless, a number of scholars, such as Ernst Herzfeld, Herman Lommel, and Mary Boyce, offering relatively new opinions, considered the Achaemenids to have been Zoroastrian. One can surmise that while he was writing his dissertation, Bakhtiar was not aware of the views of those scholars who considered the Achaemenids to be Zoroastrian. But beyond this issue, in his dissertation, he has even neglected to raise such solid evidence as the sacrificing of animals to please the deities or drinking the intoxicant *haoma* during religious ceremonies (Avesta, Gathas, Yasna 32, paragraph 14), which were customary in Achaemenid creeds and were disparaged in the teachings of Zoroaster and the Gathas or old Avesta.

On the one hand, he decisively rejects the idea of the Achaemenids having been Zoroastrian, and on the other, he speaks of the undeniable influence of Zoroaster on the Achaemenid age, and he even attributes the founding of that empire in some way to the thinking of Zoroaster. He writes: "We can say this much, that apparently, the personal deeds and worldly thoughts of Zoroaster prepared the grounds for the establishment and advancement of the Achaemenid Empire."[30] Given such contradictory statements about the Achaemenids having been or not having been Zoroastrian, the reader is at a loss as to which premise or conclusion he should accept in this academic dissertation.[iv]

In his dissertation, Bakhtiar speaks about the influence of Zoroaster on the ancient beliefs of Mazda worship in Indo-European societies, and he points out the "spiritualizing" efforts of the religion of Zoroaster in establishing a monotheistic and ethical religion among the Aryans. All this, according to him, on the one hand, has been the result of contact with the "Semitic world," and, on the other, a sign of having influenced it. He writes: "Many scholars believe that Zoroaster's religious reform was the result of contact with the Semitic world, in particular with the world of the Jews who took refuge in Persia during the reign of Cyrus. The same contact can easily be used as an explanation of the influence of Iranian beliefs on the religion of the Jews. During their sojourn in Persia, Jews learned certain principles, such as the immortality of the soul and its ascension to the heavens, of which no mention is made in the books of the Torah. According to Max Müller, 'There is no doubt that the religion of the Jews, in its very ancient stages, was either totally or virtually alien to these principal beliefs.'"[31]

Still no clear answer is given to the question of whether monotheism appeared first among Persians and then it influenced Semitic religions. If we accept Bakhtiar's opinion that Persian monotheism, which was the foundation for the reform of Zoroaster's religion, was the result of contact between Persians and the Semitic world, we should be able to prove on the basis of clear historical evidence that monotheism first appeared among Semitic tribes. We know, however, that Semitic tribes, from the Hebrews to the Babylonians and Assyrians, and then the Arabs, were all similar to Indo-European tribes in that they were polytheistic. It is not clear when these tribes became monotheistic and

---

[iv] Another error in his dissertation is the issue of Zoroaster's date of birth, which, in reference to a book by the French Iranologist, R. P. Masani, or what he calls "calculations by scholars," Bakhtiar regards to be around 600 BC. Some other historians consider this date to be 558 BC. Zabih Behruz and the British Iranologist Mary Boyce, however, believe Zoroaster was born in 1768 BC.

by which tribes they were influenced. We also do not know the date of the reform of Zoroaster's religion. Was he the one who made monotheism common in the region for the first time, and did the Semitic religions follow his example, or to the contrary, was it Zoroaster who began his reform by following Semitic religions, in particular Judaism?

In the concluding observations of his dissertation, Bakhtiar gives an overview of the place of religion and state in Indo-European societies and its difference from that of Semitic societies. Explaining his reference to "total comingling of religion and power" in primitive societies, regarding the structure of the political systems that governed Aryan and Semitic tribes, he writes: "The Assyrian-Babylonian rulers, and in particular the pharaohs of Egypt, were the manifestation of deities on earth. In other words, carrying out spiritual duties was one of the highest functions of these priest-kings. For this reason, these were theocracies… Regarding the Israelites and their social organizations, suffice it to say that the Jewish prophetic mission was the highest example in a society in which separation and difference between earthly power and spiritual power was not possible, or permissible. Hence, these three Semitic tribes offer a view of religious and at the same time spiritual government.

"The certainty is that among the Aryans of all these countries, the organizations or the two earthly and spiritual powers are interconnected, and both placed in the hands of one person. In the cities of the Aryan peoples, we come across divine laws and theocracies; but their organizations have two essential differences from the organizations of the Semitic groups. Among the Semites, we are dealing with the divinity of the ruler; but we do not see anything similar among the Indo-Europeans… The difference between the pharaoh's divinity and the divinity of the Roman emperor is like night and day. In the former, they want to compensate for the virtues and services of one man by paying divine respect, while in the latter, we see the son of the deities (in the physical sense of the word). Secondly, wherever the divine shadow attribute of the political leaders in Aryan communities—which are rarely seen—has appeared, it has disappeared very quickly: The Roman emperors and Achaemenid rulers did not have spiritual duties."[32]

In Bakhtiar's opinion, the clear indication of such a difference between the structures of power in the Indo-European and Semitic societies was the status of religion and state in the Persian Empire, which was shaped for centuries, from the Achaemenid era to the Sassanian era, and continued to maintain its foundation even after the conquest of Persia by Islam. He emphasizes that even though the Achaemenid kings ruled by the will of Ahura Mazda, they never acquired a divine aspect. "We cannot say that the Achaemenid kings had spiritual duties, or that they followed—as was common in India—religiously-based laws. As a result, the government of the Achaemenid kings was theocratic and not the rule of spiritual leaders." In the continuation of his argument, Bakhtiar makes a passing reference to the Sassanian era and the power of the Zoroastrian priests up to the conquest of Persia by Islam. His passing mention of the Parthian era and its religious system is even shorter, and before it begins, it ends with statements such as, "We still do not know anything about the religion of the Parthians after Alexander's military expedition and the period of rule of the Parthians."[33]

In this assessment, as well, we find another error, an error that shows that Bakhtiar not only has no precise and overall familiarity with the topic that he claims to be studying, but also that he faces problems in understanding the preliminary concepts and their framework as well as the terminology that he employs. This problem becomes evident particularly when he contradicts himself in stating and proving the theory that he sets forth. How can one claim that the Achaemenid kings did not have spiritual duties and did not follow religious laws, but emphasize that the Achamaenid system was a theocratic one?

It seems that, despite emphasizing the essential principle that the Achaemenid kings ruled by the will of Ahura Mazda, Bakhtiar is not precisely familiar with their connection with religion and the broader concept of the relationship of religion and state in ancient Persia. This lack of knowledge should have stemmed from his lack of familiarity with the inscriptions of Darius. In the Bisotun inscription, Darius emphasizes that his kingship is a gift from Ahura Mazda. The territories that became his, payed taxes, and obeyed him or disobeyed him and were punished, everything was the will of Ahura Mazda, and it was Ahura Mazda that granted kingship to Darius. Darius' inscription emphasizes, "Urmazd is mine, and I belong to Urmazd." Furthermore, it should be kept in mind that the name Ahura Mazda has two parts, Ahura and Mazda, the first part of which means sire, leader, and ruler, and the second part means wise and sage. In the older parts of the Avesta, these two terms are often separated, and at times it is quite clear that they represent two specific concepts, as for example, in Yasna 27, section 13 (*ahu vairyo* prayer): Zoroaster performs "vahuman" tasks for "Mazda" and "kingship" for "Ahura."[34]

In fact, the Achaemenid kings considered themselves as chosen by Ahura Mazda and manifestations of his will on earth. In this sense, they supported religion and kingship, the two pillars of power, a principle that was the manifestation of the unity of religion and state for many centuries in ancient Persia and which reached its zenith with the establishment of the Sassanian Empire. That empire relied on an ideological system the foundation and principal core of which was established on the unity of religion and kingship.[35] As *Letter of Tansar* states: "And do not be surprised by my avidity and penchant in the interest of the world for the constancy of the laws of religion, for religion and state were both born from the same womb as conjoined twins, never to be separated, and each in its rectitude or corruption and its truth or falsehood is of the same constitution."[36]

Hence, we must be skeptical about Bakhtiar's statement that Persian kings did not follow a religious authority, or that they were not related to gods. It is enough to consider the position of Kartir, the Zoroastrian high priest during the reign of Bahram I, and his role in establishing and combining religion and state in the early Sassanian period for us to

become cognizant of the weakness of Bakhtiar's point of view.ᵛ Not only
has Bakhtiar disregarded the role of Kartir in his passing reference to the
Sassanian era and the Mani creed, but he has not even mentioned the
name of Kartir.

In the continuation of a segment that he entitles "From the Macedo-
nian Military Expedition to the Arab Invasion," Bakhtiar examines
religion and state during the Sassanian era. His passing reference to the
Parthian rule and all he writes about the Mani and Mazdak creeds
during the Sassanian era are cursory and hasty. He writes: "Alongside
the Zoroastrian religion with its superficiality, the religion that was the
state religion of the Sassanians, opposing sects were also formed. Here,
we need not discuss the beliefs of those sects in detail. Suffice it to say
that two of those sects, leaving aside their theoretical aspects, had
important political reverberations both within Persia and outside Persia.
One of those two heresies was Manichaeism (named after its founder,
'Mani'), which was practiced for centuries by the people of the Mediterranean and southern Russia." Other than the statement quoted, Bakhtiar expresses no further idea or statement about Mani. But even this
brief statement in a dissertation that is supposed to be about religion
and state in antiquity is not error free. He sums up the extent of Mani's
influence as being on "the people of the Mediterranean and southern
Russia," whereas Mani's religion was a global religion in every respect.
Manichaeism became a serious rival not only to Zoroastrianism in
Persia, but also to Christianity. The Central Asian Turks converted to
Manichaeism; Manichean temples were built in China; and Mani's
works were translated into Chinese. Regarding Mazdak's religion, as
well, Bakhtiar merely states: "Most bravely, he had clear communist
exigencies and strong positivist streaks. The principles of Mazdak's
beliefs were devised for earthly life, and leaving his beliefs regarding

---

ᵛ Regarding the role of Kartir at the court of the Sassanian kings, see: Ahmad Tafazzoli,
"Kartir va Siyasat-e Ettehad-e Din va Dowlat dar Dowreh-ye Sasani," *Iran Nameh*, vol
17, no. 2 (Spring 1999): 302-303; Ahmad Tafazzoli, "Chahar Katibeh-ye Kardir,
Mubad va Mosmer," *Kelk, Mahname-ye Farhangi va Honari*, no 40 (July 1993): 148-
151.

creation aside, he had formulated a social system in which sharing property and wives had been explained with utmost precision and subtlety, details that are lacking in Plato's utopic city."[37]

At the end of his dissertation, Bakhtiar describes religion as a social phenomenon from which stem ethics and politics in the ancient world. All great religions are "totalitarian" from his perspective. "From the totemic tribes to Islam, religion has always been the framework of the society and has been disposed to take hold of all the symbols of the society, to the point that, whenever its founder would give up his political privileges, human society would often be inclined to accept a new religion. But can we call a religion that gives up its rule of the city a religion?"[38]

Hence, Bakhtiar's doctoral dissertation has basic methodological flaws. He even does not find it necessary to cite sources on the basis of which he can prove his claims about Mani and Mazdak. His mistake first of all stems from his approach to the issue, in which he regards dealing with the "details of the beliefs of those sects" as unnecessary. This error is also repeated with regard to his assessment of Zoroastrianism, as he does not see "any need to discuss its details," whereas historical research is not credible if it does not pay attention "details."[vi]

Details are the foundation and backbone of historical studies. Without paying attention to the subtleties that seem minor, historical research would not get anywhere. In historical studies, one must proceed like an astrologer, with patience.

In this sense, we need perceptive eyes to identify the existence of a planet in the galaxy of history, and then prove its reality, a planet the existence of which, no matter how minor and small it is, is historically indisputable, and which explains the *raison d'être* of a system called history. In historical assessment, that which is considered to be clear

---

[vi] For more on the influence of Zoroastrianism on Manichaeism and Mazdaism, Arab tribes and Islam, as well as Buddhism, see: Ehsan Yarshater, "Moruri bar Tarikh-e Siyasi va Farhangi-ye Iran-e Pish az Eslam," *Iran Nameh*, vol. 17, no. 2 (Spring 1999): 185-213.

truth must be constantly the subject of critical assessment and revision under a new light. Such revision, which is carried out over and over again, can only bring us closer to a more or less relatively comprehensive understanding of history, when not only the basis but also the historical details are critically and scrupulously examined, each time providing us with a broader picture of our historical landscape. It is only in this case that in historical research, we get closer to a relatively comprehensive picture, a picture the broadness of which depends on the expanse of our attention to details rather than to general narratives; and all this resembles an archeological investigation that cannot be completed hastily. It is a task that seems insignificant and marginal, but for the reconstructing and discovering of the cyphers and secrets of a thousand and one points that remain concealed behind the curtain of bygone eras, it is an undeniable necessity.

Can we expect Bakhtiar to have kept all this in mind, and for that matter, at a time when he had engaged in writing his doctoral dissertation not as a historian but as a student whose family and who himself faced the unpleasant consequences of the World War? The answer to this question is not easy, even though the hastiness and occasionally unjustifiable contradictions that have found their way into his dissertation cannot be disregarded.

At any rate, ambiguities and contradictory statements are not few in Bakhtiar's doctoral dissertation. The reason may be that he is not sufficiently knowledgeable about the topic he has chosen. This very fact makes an investigation of the how and why of his interest in an issue that he labels the relationship between religion and state in antiquity difficult. In particular, the role of the functionaries of religion is not clear in his theorizing. It is not clear whether he supports the interference of religion in government and the management of the society, or he favors the separation of religion and state. We see this duality in his political relations later as well. This lack of clarity is also precisely the reason for the significant weakness of his dissertation. It is as though a clear answer to this question should be discovered not in his doctoral dissertation, but in the arena of his political struggle and the fate of his political life.

Fighting Fascism and the Statute on Jews in France

The start of World War II and the victory of the German Army over France in June 1940 changed the destiny of Bakhtiar. This change began with his opposition to Francisco Franco and his support for the Republicans of Spain and resulted in his membership in the French Army and participation in "La Résistance," the French Resistance. He writes: "When the war started, I was in Juan-les-Pins. For a long time, my mind was preoccupied with the future of the world. I had volunteered for the war of the Republicans of Spain against Franco… After the coup d'état by Franco, various organizations mobilized to collect aid, distribute fliers, and hold rallies and demonstrations in support of the Republicans and against Franco, and I joined these groups. And in the course of these activities, many times, I got into trouble and faced problems."[39] In his memoir, Bakhtiar provides no explanation about the troubles he faced and writes nothing about how he volunteered to participate in the war alongside the Republicans of Spain. He only says that he never registered in the "international brigades" that were formed in support of them. Hence, we do not know how to interpret his volunteering to participate in the Spanish Civil War without having registered in the "international brigades." All that can be inferred from his words is that his support for the Spanish Republicans did not go beyond participating in the demonstrations, distributing fliers, and collecting financial aid.

Bakhtiar also does not provide much explanation about his opposition to German Fascism, which must have been the reason for his joining the French Army and his participation in the French Resistance. We only know that his familiarity with what was happening in Germany came from the time when he studied in France. Having begun to study German in Beirut, after coming to Paris, he witnessed Nazi propaganda firsthand when he went to Germany during the summer to "practice" his German. In 1938, through the favor of a friend whose father was the editor of a German newspaper, he participated in one of the Nazi Party's "Nuremberg Rallies" that were held annually in the first week of September during the Congress of that party in Nuremberg. He writes: "I was thirty meters away from Hitler. To me, his appearance and face were not appealing. Before my eyes was an inhuman face that vehemently terrified me. Despite this, I came to believe that, in contrast to Mussolini, he actually believed in what he said." Other than this, Bakhtiar does not explain anything else about what he had witnessed in that rally. In his memoir, as well, with the exception of a few passing references, he does not say anything about the reasons for his joining the national movement of the French Resistance: "I was one among other students. I was sufficiently familiar and intimate with Europe, and in particular, with France, to understand the excitement of the young people of my age, and I felt that in the beginning, many young French people agreed with Hitler. This is a fact; but many do not wish to admit it. Fascism had to some degree appealed to the young people, and they could not imagine the atrocities that this ideology would bring about." Bakhtiar then briefly mentions the popularity of Nazi Germany in Iran, refers to his life and education in France and his marriage to his French wife, Madlaine Hevro, and considers these his justification that he had a "right" to participate in the war against Germany.[40]

Bakhtiar's references, even though in passing, indicate the fact that, in contrast to many of his compatriots, in his assessment of the Nazi regime, he made a different choice. At a time when the newly-formed Iranian nationalism, which stemmed from old animosity toward England and Russia, sought its future in cooperation with Germany and reliance on the aggressive power of that country in the world, Bakhtiar made a choice, which at the height of the popularity of Germany in Iran did not have many defenders. Bakhtiar's patriotism was incompatible with the spirit of the time in his homeland, which was overcoming backwardness and sought the key to achieving progress and construction in the authoritative policies of a powerful leader. Hence, his opposition to Fascism, and in particular his joining the French Resistance, indicated his firm belief in freedom and democracy, even though this belief would not prevent him from endorsing some of Hitler's "positive" actions, an error that was the result of a popular belief with the coming to power of the Nazi Party in Germany and had been fostered more intensely in the ensuing years. Bakhtiar states that "under the guidance and shepherding" of Hitler and his economists, unemployment was eradicated from Germany, and German engineers had succeeded for the first time in building such highways (autobahns), the existence of which became commonplace later on.[41]

Bakhtiar's view of how progress had been achieved in Germany was far from reality. The building of the first of the highways he mentions had begun in Berlin before the Nazi Party came to power and was completed in 1921. In point of fact, the Nazis expedited the construction of the highways, but they were not the originators of them. In addition, the eradication of unemployment, as far as it concerned Hitler's "services," had become possible only as a result of preparing and mobilizing for a world war. These are facts the discernment of which should not have been beyond Bakhtiar's abilities.

Issues of this kind, which seem peripheral at first glance in Bakhtiar's outlook, are indicative of more serious errors in his judgment with regard to the "Jewish question." Referring to Hitler's anti-Semitic policy, Bakhtiar writes: "I think that there exists a sort of peculiar racism among the Jews that is specific to that people and which does not rise from anywhere else or any other group. Among the people on the Mediterranean coasts and the Latin people, only the Jews consider themselves the 'chosen people.' This is Jewish thinking. These people who, as Charles de Gaulle says, 'are self-assured and domineering,' have suffered for centuries; but in their lives, they have had a very good deal. The kings of France, England, and Prussia have equally been in need of these people, while the people of those countries have been envious of them. In all European countries, the Jews comprised many minorities, and they inevitably have hastened to help one another throughout the world. Hence, they have become very competent; and they gain maximum benefit from minimum effort. And, generally speaking, in every society in which they live, they incite the envy of the people rather than their hatred."[42]

The utterance of such a statement by a person who joined the French Resistance and rose to confront the Nazi regime seems strange. Bakhtiar considered his acquisition of knowledge and information in many fields as indebted to the culture, arts, and history of France, a country that 200 years earlier, following its Revolution, had declared that Jews and Moslems are equal to Christians and enjoy equal rights, not as specific people or races, but as citizens. Hence, his disregard for such an achievement, especially in describing the characteristics of the "Jewish people," is far too acrid to be overlooked through academic criticism in proving the falsity of what he calls "Jewish thinking" or the specific character of "Latin people."

Undoubtedly, Bakhtiar's judgment about the characteristics of the "Jewish people" cannot be regarded as devoid of all truth; but is this fact true only with regard to the Jews? Are the commonly referred to characteristics of the Arabs, Persians, or black Africans and Americans devoid of all credibility? Can relying on general assessments and finding simple answers to complex questions, and for that matter within the framework of clichés and popular predispositions, pave the way to an understanding of historical truths? The Greek historian Antonis Liakos suggests a different solution for responding to this problem. In his opinion, we must try to understand how our predispositions are formed rather than trying to determine whether they are totally and indisputably "true" and "right."[43] Thus, the acrid distastefulness of Bakhtiar's approach, more than troubling our conscience due to his statements endorsing certain "positive" actions of Hitler, or his general judgments and popular predispositions regarding the "Jewish people," troubles us in terms of the silence, as evidenced by the memories that remain regarding the fate of the French Jews. In his book, *Yekrangi*, he speaks about Hitler and the "Jewish people" without any reference to the fate of the Jews who were the victims of the Nazi regime's racism in the death camps. With a cursory look at the crimes of the Vichy government in France against the Jews, we shall see that Bakhtiar's statements about the Jews are by no means justifiable.[vii]

One of the first steps by the "Free Zone" Vichy government, which came to power following the defeat of France by Germany and the declaration of a ceasefire on 22 June 1941 in the "Unoccupied Zone," concerned the Jews. With the nullifying of the anti-discrimination law in the press, and a short time later with the endorsement of a proposal called the "Statute on Jews," which was implemented in August 1940, the persecution and arrest of foreign Jews was legalized in France. Based on this proposal, which was implemented a year later regarding the French Jews, as well, the ratification by the National Assembly during the French Revolution, which regarded the Jews not as Jewish people but as French citizens with rights equal to those of other inhabitants of the country, was nullified. With this action, the Vichy government would offer a racial definition of the Jews, and based on that definition, it paved the way for trampling their national and social rights as French citizens. The next step was the creation of an internment camp for foreign Jews who resided in France, or those who had fled from Germany or the occupied territories to France.

In addition, an organization called the "Division of Jews" was administered by Theodor Dannecker, a high-ranking SS officer. This organization was affiliated with the German security police, Sicherheitsdienst, which had an office in the same neighborhood where Bakhtiar lived. From July 1942, Dannecker sent 34,000 Jews from Drancy to the Auschwitz concentration camp. In order to avoid being transferred to the camps, some Jewish families chose to commit suicide.[44]

Article 8 of the regulations that had been passed by the German occupying forces regarding the French Jews mandated that they wear a

---

[vii] At the start of World War II in September 1939, between 300,000 and 330,000 Jews lived in France. According to available figures, between the spring of 1942 and summer of 1944, at least 75,721 Jews were dispatched from France to the death camps. Hélène Berr, *Pariser Tagebuch, 1924-1944* (München: Deutscher Taschenbuch Verlag, 2011), 330.

yellow Star of David on their chest from the age of six in public. Article 9 of the same regulations prohibited their entry into theaters and cinemas, museums, libraries, athletic events, swimming pools, public parks, and cafés and restaurants. Jewish journalists, actors, and musicians were dismissed from their jobs. In offices that were operated by the Germans, Jews were not allowed to sit. In Paris, only one hospital was permitted to admit Jewish patients. Jewish patients were not even permitted to make use of ambulances. For their daily needs, the Jews were allowed to shop at stores only between the hours of three and four o'clock in the afternoon, and they were only allowed to ride in the last car on the Metro. That year, Jewish students were deprived of the right to education in certain fields, such as teaching, and Jewish professors were fired from the universities.[45]

Undoubtedly, finding an answer to the question of the extent of Bakhtiar's awareness of the existence of the extermination camps in Germany and Poland during the time when he lived in France is difficult. Even more difficult, however, is accepting that he had never heard of the Drancy camp, from which 65,000 Jews were sent to their deaths. It is difficult to accept that the firing of well-known Jewish professors such as Marc Bloch from the Sorbonne or the woeful daily life of the Jews in Paris during the occupation of France were concealed from his eyes. Astonishingly, even forty years later, when he speaks about racism and the characteristics of the Jewish people, he does not make the slightest reference to any of these events.

Bakhtiar and the French Resistance

With the start of the war, while he was still living in Juan-les-Pins, Bakhtiar decided to join the French Army. He writes: "I had made my decision. I knew that I could not remain outside these events, and everything indicated the path that I needed to follow. I wanted to join the French Army as a volunteer. To do this, I went to Nice. There, everyone gave me the run-around. They told me, 'You are a resident of Paris, apply there.' It was dumbfounding; they treated someone who was prepared to give his life for this country like that! But since I adhere to order and regulations, I returned to Paris and utilized every recourse, until finally one day an answer came from the military offices, stating, 'Register in Légion étrangère,' the Foreign Legion. This answer was not acceptable to me. I had been married to my French wife for more than a year. It was my fifth year of living in France. I was a graduate of French universities. Hence, I had the right to fight shoulder-to-shoulder with the French. Even though ultimately those in charge eventually paid attention to my reasoning, I was in a state of limbo for months, until finally I was summoned for my medical exam. At that time, I was twenty-six years old, and I was athletic. The physician deemed me fit for service… I had to wait until March 1940 to go to Orléans and join the 30th artillery regiment."[46]

As Bakhtiar states himself, after a short military training period in the anti-air artillery unit of the French military, he first served in a division called the anti-aircraft defense division, which was later named anti-air defense. Regarding the military training he was given to be dispatched to the war front, he writes: "For practice, we went to a small village near an old mill in a remote rural area. The drills were in the style of those days. So, they made us walk. The only thing we wanted to do was to take off our heavy boots and continue on the road in our bare feet… Of course, our regiment was not considered an elite regiment, but the conditions in the elite regiment were not any better either." Bakhtiar is then transferred to the 30th battalion of Fontainebleau in Moulins area near Vichy, which was the artillery center. After "about one month of frustration at being in a state of limbo," he was dispatched to behind the Maginot Line to the city of Claremont in central France; and sometime later, so as not to be taken prisoner, he was ordered by his affiliated unit to go to the Pyrenees, on the Spanish border. The plan was for him to go to Spain with a thirty-member unit. This plan did not materialize. He spent the following "tedious" two months in a remote village waiting and "walking around and exploring" the area, until finally, with the signing of the ceasefire agreement between Germany and Marshal Philippe Pétain, the head of the Vichy government of the Free Zone of France, on 22 June 1940, he returned to his French wife in Brittany.

This is basically all the information about his voluntary participation found in his memoir.

There is an archive entitled "Monitoring Foreigners" at the Document Center of the French Foreign Ministry that includes the files regarding their comings and goings, the names of those who had obtained visas from the government of France, and the files of the refugees and the detention camps for the foreigners during World War II. This archive also includes files regarding the return of the foreign Jews who resided in France to their own countries. It also contains information about the relocation of foreigners on French soil from 1941 to 1944, as well as information about foreigners who had obtained visas from the Vichy government from 1940 to 1944. There is no trace of Bakhtiar in this archive. We must assume that the information regarding Bakhtiar in the "Monitoring Foreigners" archive was totally destroyed, because in 1940 during the advancement of the German forces on French soil, a large part of this archive was destroyed. The detailed introduction to the guidebook of this archive contains a description about the destruction of 1,200 cardboard boxes of files related to monitoring foreigners, which was done on the order of the Political Office of the Ministry of Interior of France at the time. On 16 May 1940, the contents of those 1,200 boxes were set on fire in the garden of that ministry. For this reason, it is quite likely that all the information on Bakhtiar was destroyed. The possibility also exists that Bakhtiar was mentioned in the archive under an alias. But since we do not know his alias in the French Resistance, we cannot trace him in the files of this archive. Those who were active in the French Resistance usually chose an alias. Was Bakhtiar also active in that movement using an alias? If that is the case, it is unfortunate that he has not mentioned anything about his alias in the French Resistance in order for us to be able to trace him in the documents related to the wartime. Hence, all that is stated here about Bakhtiar's participation in the French Army and his membership in the French Resistance is based on information that he has stated either verbally or in writing.[47]

In 1939, when Bakhtiar had gone to the coastal city of Juan-les-Pins in southern France, he became acquainted with his future wife, Madlaine

Hevro. Before her acquaintance with Bakhtiar, Madlaine had lost her mother as a child, and her father, who had a small factory in the city of Nantes, had committed suicide as a result of bankruptcy and a dispute with his partner. Regarding how they met, Bakhtiar states: "I knew a lady who was a secretary in a British company. I became acquainted with this lady because I had given her a letter that I had received from the former Oil Company to translate. One day, I was sitting in a café with that lady; a young lady who was younger than she came in, exchanged greetings with her, and sat down. Naturally, we also exchanged greetings. Our friendship continued for two years, until we got married in early 1940." André, Madlaine's brother, arranged a small wedding for her and Bakhtiar in his home in Paris. The result of this marriage, which ended in separation several years later, was four children by the names of Guy, Viviane, Patrick, and France. France, their youngest child, was born in Abadan, when Bakhtiar worked in the Ministry of Labor and Propagation in Khuzestan. Bakhtiar relates: "One of the reasons for our marriage, aside from this lady's beauty, was the soundness of her character and temperament. She was a woman of sound character and was devoid of hypocrisy. My children also have these qualities."[48]

With the defeat of France in World War II, late in 1940, along with Madlaine and Guy, Bakhtiar went to La Baule, a city near Saint-Lazare in Brittany. The reason for this move was the situation of relative calm in La Baule. A number of his wife's relatives lived there, and in terms of availability of food items, which were expensive and scarce due to the war conditions, they did not face much hardship. Whenever Bakhtiar had a chance to return to Paris in order to use the Law School library at the Sorbonne to write his doctoral dissertation, he would bring coffee and food items, the availability of which was becoming more difficult every day, for himself and his friends. A while later, when Viviane, their second child, was born, he and his wife took up residence in a village called Saint-Nicolas-du-Pélem in Brittany. Bakhtiar considers doing this an effort to keep his family away "from both the threat of the bombings and also the shortages and rationing of food."[49]

Brittany is a peninsula in the western part of France. It is an agricultural area that was greatly damaged during World War I. Nearly twenty percent of the men who had been dispatched to the war fronts lost their lives in battle. When the war ended, a wave of migration to Paris and other large cities began, which intensified the increasing problems of Brittany. On 1 September 1939, when the danger of war became certain with the invasion of Poland by the German Army, France was also preparing itself for what was about to occur by declaring a general mobilization. Considering its geographical position and proximity to England, Brittany would play a key role for the military policymakers of France. In France's defense policy, the Maginot Line was the arena for confronting the invasion that, following the victories of the Nazi regime, was referred to as the "Blitzkrieg" (Lightning War). Behind the safety of the Maginot Line, the ensuing eight months passed in futile hopefulness and fateful expectation, such hope and expectation that in the course of six weeks reached an inauspicious end with a bitter defeat and two million prisoners of war.[50]

In the ensuing weeks and months, the rush of war refugees to Brittany escalated a widespread crisis, of which the rationing of foodstuff was one indicator. The declaration of martial law and the monitoring of mail, telegraph, and telephones as well as the railroads and public transportation were among other manifestations of the imposition of force by the Nazi regime's occupiers. Bakhtiar joined the French Resistance under these circumstances. In the course of his travels back and forth between Brittany and Paris, he met with one of his friends who was a student at the Sorbonne by the name of Félix Gaillard, who later on became the prime minister of France.[viii] In this meeting, Gaillard, who was a member of the French Resistance, asked Bakhtiar to find him a couple of

---

[viii] Félix Gaillard was born in 1919 in Paris to an affluent family. He studied at the Sorbonne, at the School of Political Science in the field of law and national economy, where he received his doctoral degree. After the occupation of France, Gaillard joined the French Resistance. In October 1957, Gaillard became the minister of economy and finance of France, and one month later, at the age of thirty-eight, he became prime minister.

apartments in Paris that were secure. Bakhtiar, who was highly influenced by Gaillard, immediately agreed to make an apartment that would meet his needs available to him. He writes: "Of course, I meant my own apartment on rue de l'Assomption. I introduced him to the doorman, whom I told that he was a friend who had no place to live, that his parents lived somewhere outside the occupied zone, and that he wanted to occasionally spend a few days in my apartment… Gaillard also had another question for and request of me. He wanted to know whether I would agree to act as a liaison between Paris and the Resistance network in Brittany. From that day on, I became his letter carrier. I would receive letters and packages from Gaillard or Fontaine, who was trusted by him, and deliver them to their destination." This was done under the circumstances when Brittany had become an important center for fighting against the German occupiers, and Bakhtiar's living in Saint-Nicolas-du-Pélem was a suitable cover for his going back and forth between Paris and Brittany. These circumstances, according to Bakhtiar, created a "new bond" between him and Gaillard.[51]

With France's surrender and the appearance of the first signs of protest and the shaping of resistance against the German occupiers, Brittany became one of the main centers of the French Resistance groups. The lower their income, the more pressure was put on the impoverished strata in terms of trying to find food and meeting their daily needs. With the rapid decline in the value of the franc and the rise in prices on the black market, hatred increased toward the occupation forces that were regarded as the cause of these conditions. Under these conditions, gradually, the number of those who joined the guerilla groups to escape forced labor increased. These people, who had left the place where they lived and would not receive food ration coupons, had no other resource but to continue fighting in the French Resistance. With the expansion of the struggle and reliance on military tactics, the impassable roads of Brittany and the Alps became safe shelters for guerillas, whose number of supporters and defenders increased day by day. In reaction to the ongoing occurrences, the German authorities knew no other recourse but suppression. Placing not the slightest credibility on the local police, they suppressed not only political actions, but also any simple criminal act, and persecuted the perpetrators.[52]

Bakhtiar writes: "One morning, when I was opening the window shutters, my eyes fell upon the metal helmets and machinegun barrels of the German soldiers glittering under the light of the morning sun. Without showing that I had seen something, I went back into the room and asked my wife to burn all the papers. All the houses were inspected, and all men between the ages of fifteen and sixty were summoned to the public park of the city in front of a small pool and fountain that was erected in the name of Saint Nicolas. We all had to show our identification papers and be interrogated. My presence there was naturally a cause for surprise. 'Are you Iranian? What are you doing here?' Explaining this was actually easy, but not for the suspicious occupiers. As a rule, in a village in Brittany, no one other than the local inhabitants was supposed to live there. At most, the presence of one or two French people from other provinces could be explained, but not a citizen of the so-called protected sovereign provinces of Iran. They would inevitably have to report this to the Command Center. There was also another person in our group by the name of Mr. Bartaran, and occasionally I would deliver letters that I received from Gaillard to him. If they could make him talk, that would be the end of me. But they could not get even one word out of him. Bartaran and his seventeen-year-old son, along with twelve other people, were later sent to the exile camp, and no one ever saw them again. Apparently, a young American by the name of Donald, who had become a French citizen, had reported to the Germans about the activities of the French Resistance in Saint-Nicolas-du-Pélem. There were all sorts of activities. For instance, once we had to hide an American soldier who had gotten stuck hanging from the church bell when he had parachuted down. We were afraid we would be exposed, because the parachutist was a black American, and you could not easily disguise him to look like everybody else. In the meantime, one of my contacts was caught by the Gestapo. True, he did not know my name, but giving them information about me was easy, something that that man never did. Had I been caught by the Gestapo, I would not necessarily have been put in front of a firing squad, but no doubt, I would have been exiled to one of the camps, similar to Mr. Bartaran. By participating in underground work, I became familiar with the rules of this game, rules that were of use to me later on in Iran, and even during Khomeyni's dictatorship."[53]

The signing of the ceasefire between Germany and France in June 1940 and the return of Bakhtiar to Paris provided him the opportunity to resume his doctoral dissertation research at the Sorbonne. In the interval, while he continued his activities in the French Resistance, traveling back and forth between Paris and Brittany, he moved his residence back in Paris to the apartment that he had made available to Gaillard for a while.

Student life in France during the occupation of that country, with the exception of a few short weeks after the illegal demonstrations at the Tomb of the Unknown Soldier, which resulted in the closing of the universities, was relatively normal, albeit not devoid of discrimination, tension, and violence. In October 1940, Jewish students were deprived of the right to study in fields such as teachers' training, and Jewish professors were dismissed and prohibited from teaching. To implement this policy, especially in regard to teaching, by firing and retiring the Jewish professors, the Vichy government welcomed this demand of the German occupiers with open arms. One month later, a list of sixty-six Jewish professors as well as professors who were "extreme enemies of Germany" was prepared in six colleges in Paris, and the decision was made that the anti-Semitic laws would be implemented most forcefully, and Jews, communists, and individuals who worked with Resistance groups would be prosecuted. Universities in France were "purged," and because of the liberal climate that dominated the student environment, the Sorbonne and in particular its School of Humanities, in which Bakhtiar studied, were put under surveillance. The next measure in advancing the policy that was imposed in the area of education was the ratification of a plan that would mandate that the universities and scientific institutions restrict their admission of Jewish students to no more than three percent, starting in the summer of 1941. In the summer of 1942, Jewish students were mandated to wear a Star of David on university campuses, as well. This order resulted in protests, and some of the non-Jewish students also wore the Star of David on their clothes in protest, which was followed by their arrests.[54]

The rule of Germany in France began with chaos and confusion. As an immediate duty, overcoming this chaos and confusion was placed on the agenda of the German Central Command at the Hotel Majestic in Paris and the Gestapo center on Avenue Foch, the neighborhood where Bakhtiar lived. The disintegration of the political system and the breaking apart of the economic fabric of the country, alongside the homelessness of the war refugees, shortages, high prices, and the Resistance that was more than ever before assuming more violent and more organized forms, confronted the German occupiers with serious obstacles to acheiving their goal.

Their first effort was to take a series of security decisions that were implemented step by step. At the end of June 1940, the decision was made that all telecommunication equipment be handed over to the security authorities. In August of the same year, assemblies, meetings, and even the moving of household furnishings were prohibited. A number of school textbooks were also banned, and motion pictures were heavily censored. From September, more than 1,000 titles, including the works of André Malraux, Arthur Koestler, André Gide, Louis Aragon, Sigmund Freud, and even Gustave Flaubert, were gathered up from bookstores, and the Nazis burned 2,200 tons of books. In the same month, taking photographs in the open air was deemed a crime. In October, lighting a fire at night became prohibited; and the owners of carrier pigeons were mandated to report the number of their pigeons to the related authorities. In November, peddlers were prohibited from selling their goods in areas near the French coasts, and fishing was allowed only upon obtaining a permit. Alongside these decisions, a committee was established to monitor paper production, in order to prevent the opponents from having access to paper for printing fliers and underground newsletters. These restrictions were later augmented with severe fines on the use of German documents, uniforms, and military insignias that were used in the operations of the French Resistance. Misuse of Red Cross signs was also subject to heavy fines. Physicians were ordered to immediately report to the security authorities all those who came to them to be treated for gunshot wounds. Changing the clocks to German time was another symbolic measure that, as a sign of a new time, as the German author, Lion Feuchtwanger, writes, made the presence of "Satan in France" official, such that in deadly silence, by cutting off the electricity and prohibiting the comings and goings at certain hours of the day and night, it would sink Paris, in darkness and horror, into a coma.[55] No mention is made of these things in Bakhtiar's memoir.

When Bakhtiar went to Brittany with his wife and children to evade the difficulties of the war and the conditions that governed Paris, he was in a dire financial situation. Regarding the past history of the financial difficulties that he had faced outside the country, he writes: "When I went to Beirut and then to France to continue my education…in order to weaken the tribe and its leaders, Reza Shah resorted to a thousand ruses and came up with some sort of excuse every day… As a result, we were not in a very enviable financial situation. In addition to the house that he had in the tribe, my father had also bought a small house in Tehran from the oil shares, and he had allocated three and a half of the six parts of it to me and two and a half to my brother. This was my inheritance from my father. During my schooling in Beirut and Paris, the only thing that I did not think about was worldly possessions. I lived on the income I had from the oil shares, even though it was not much. In 1936, the government put pressure on us that the oil shares would be taken away. My life and the continuation of my education was dependent on the oil shares, which were managed by my paternal uncle, Amir Mofakhkham Bakhtiari, who sent the money to me in France. I also had a small farm in the Bakhtiari territory that was being sold at a fraction of what it was worth to have money for my living expenses, because arrangements were made on the order of the Shah that the Bakhtiaris should not own property in that region. I received a letter one day telling me that I should give him power of attorney to sell my share to the government. I opposed it and asked the reason. He said that it was an order, and he threatened me that I was not the only one, that I had relatives in Iran who would get into trouble. Inevitably, I gave in and entrusted my heart and soul to the storm of calamity and, as Hafez says, I told myself, 'Let the flood of sorrow come and uproot the house from its foundation.' They supposedly bought the share at a price that was ridiculous. These transactions were carried out by a third party... When I went to Tehran, I heard that some people had made deals and were able to save their properties through a mediator. I was not one for things like that. I was left with only my hat in my hand."[56]

The conditions that Bakhtiar talks about, especially after the occupation of Iran in August 1941 and the disruption in the banking transactions between Iran and Europe, confronted the Iranian students in France with difficulties. During this time, Bakhtiar and his family were also facing hardship. He writes: "I lucked out. During those days, they sent me 400 pounds through the open market, which was a significant sum at that time. We lived on that money for a year and a half. Then, I advertised to teach. I gave private lessons in philosophy in a city near Saint-Lazare in Brittany. There was not one night during the time that my family and I stayed in Brittany, until 1944, when Saint-Lazare was not bombed."[57]

With the passage of one year since France was occupied, as the Resistance forces were solidifying their position, the policy of suppression also assumed more violent forms. In August 1941, a German officer was the target of an assassination and was shot and killed at a Metro station. The reaction of the German security apparatus to this assassination, which from then on was pursued by the Resistance groups as a fighting tactic, was mass arrests and execution of the elements who were caught as "saboteurs" and "terrorists" and then delivered to the firing squads. Following a decree from Hitler about avoiding "leniency" toward the opponents, the decision was made that for every German who was killed, between fifty and a hundred French prisoners of war would be executed, even if this resulted in the killing of innocent people. With the defeat of the Nazi regime on the battlefronts and the frequent bombings of the German positions on French soil by the Allies, the French Resistance, the center of which was in Burgundy and Brittany in southern France, grew even more significantly. Bakhtiar writes: "Toward the end of the war, the activities of the French Resistance in Saint-Nicolas-du-Pélem had taken on unimaginable dimensions. On one of those days when I was returning home from Saint-Brieuc after having walked 80 kilometers, I was involved in an incident that made me think that my life was over. In a café on the road, I had a cup of apple juice, and then set out on the road again. I had not walked very far yet when I saw the head of a man appear from behind an embankment, who apparently intended to kill me. He was right there in front of me, claiming that I had been seen speaking with a person they were certain was a traitor; and he said that if I did not tell him that person's name, I would have my own blood on my hands. I had neither spoken to anyone, nor had I even looked at one of the beauties of Brittany out of the corner of my eye, and I did not know how to get myself out of that predicament. Fortunately, at that very moment, one of his friends, who was older than that bully, came out from behind the bushes and ordered me to step forward. The interrogation was endless. So, I had to answer all his questions. The name Bakhtiar sounded like an Italian name to them, which apparently put me in even more danger. But since my suitcase was full of children's woolen socks, which were supposed to be unraveled and used for a different purpose, I could be forgiven from the perspective of those gentlemen, since suddenly the charge of 'treason' had been changed, and I was the 'father of a family' who was only trying to make a living. Once we arrived at that conclusion, we were able to talk in a calmer manner, and then I realized that, contrary to what I had thought before, my attackers were not 'Vichy' guerillas, but members of the French Resistance. So, having barely been able to save my life from the Gestapo, I was about to lose my life with a bullet from my fellow combatants. 'Okay, get going. If anyone stops you, say, Product 43,' he said. 'What do you mean?' I asked. 'The password.'

"That password was imprinted in my mind forever. Occasionally, during difficult moments in my life, in order to drive out gloomy thoughts from my mind, I whisper to myself, 'Product 43.'"[58]

In November 1942, with an order from Hitler for the occupation of southern France, the Vichy government that ruled the ruins of a trampled pride with a sinister reputation was drained of any credibility within a few days. The landing of the Allied forces in North Africa had confronted Germany with a new threat, which in the calculations of the functionaries of the Nazi regime left no room for the sham independence of the Vichy government. With the presence of the fresh Allied forces on the western front, this threat made Hitler resolve to quash the last signs of sham French independence that could no longer serve the military needs of the Fascist German government. From then on, in southern France, the German forces felt like they were on enemy territory. The consequence of this reality was the expansion of the operations of the French Resistance forces that were trying to set their ongoing differences of opinion aside and increase their operations and effectiveness. When it became clear that the Soviet Union would not fall to its knees in the "Blitzkrieg," French public opinion began to have serious doubts about the invincibility of the Nazi regime. In February 1943, with the defeat of the 6th Army of the German military in the battle at Stalingrad, these doubts turned into an undeniable certainty.

In June 1944, with the landing of the Allied forces in Normandy and the opening of another front on European soil, the outcome of the war was more or less clear. Two months later, Dietrich von Choltitz, the victor in the Battle of Sevastopol, who had been appointed as military commander of the German forces in Paris, by signing an agreement that made the defeat of the German Army official in France, surrendered without resistance. Within a few short weeks, in August of the same year, when he had the fate of Paris in his hands, he defied Hitler's order to bomb the bridges, destroy the city, and "flatten Paris to prevent it from falling into enemy hands." In a combination of a show of force to the people of Paris, contact with the leaders of the French Resistance, and negotiations with the Allies, Choltitz succeeded in preventing military clashes and street battles that would have resulted in the destruction of the city. In September 1944, the German forces in the fortifications on the coasts of the Atlantic Ocean faced one defeat after another. The Allies' next strategic step was to liberate Belgium and Holland. In the fall of 1944, France was liberated from Fascist domination.[59] Six months later, with the fall of Berlin in May 1945, a regime that sought to erect a government of a thousand years and had set Europe ablaze collapsed in the ashes of the ruins of the Third Reich.

In the meantime, Bakhtiar, who had resumed his research at the Sorbonne sometime earlier, defended his doctoral dissertation on 20 November 1944. He writes: "The time had gradually come for me to leave France. I would be leaving this country that had recovered its serenity. I would be taking a bit of its soul with me, in other words, the poetry and literature that had brought me such joy, which is still alive in me. My first motivator in this period of my life was Anatole France. In Beirut, on the recommendation of a teacher, I bought *Le Crime de Sylvestre Bonnard*. At the age of sixteen, I found my own self in that old sophist. I felt that in me, the irony and gravity that are a requirement for profound beliefs existed together. Later on, I found the same combination in Valéry. From then on, I continued reading the works of Anatole France. I had twenty-five volumes of his works in special editions published by Calmann-Levy in my library, which were plundered from my house."[60]

he final days of Bakhtiar before the liberation of Paris were spent in meetings with Valéry. They had lunch together several times, and Bakhtiar occasionally invited Valéry to have coffee in his apartment on rue de l'Assomption. In those days, Paris was experiencing a harsh winter. Shortages were felt everywhere, and fuel was scarce. Despite all this and despite the difficulties in getting what he needed, Valéry enjoyed a privileged position. Every Thursday, a bishop from the Académie française brought him a stick of butter, which he hid under his hat. The lovers of his work also sent him coffee and tobacco from faraway places; and Valéry, who was suffering from various illnesses, continued writing under an electric blanket, which was considered such a luxury. Bakhtiar states: "I was still in France when I heard the news of his death. I had heard that he was ill. I remember one day, it was either May or June 1945, when I was walking with him to the Metro. It was wartime, and vehicles and taxis were scarce. He said that he felt he had no energy left in him. He likened his body to a used spring, and said that his physical strength was drained."[61]

On 20 July 1945, a poet who had been called the "Marshal of Literature" during the war, precisely when freedom of expression had once again, as he said, "governed" the Collège de France, departed this world. With Valéry's death, "French poetry remained alive, but it lost its greatest representative since the days of Baudelaire and Mallarmé. He remained immortal, without having a successor." De Gaulle ordered official funeral ceremonies to be held for him in Paris. They buried his body in a cemetery beside the sea, a cemetery in his place of birth that was later named after one of his poems that expressed the meaning of existence and the secret of creation, "Le Cimetière marin."[62]

A few months after the death of his beloved poet, in the final days of December 1945, Bakhtiar went to Toulouse, south of Marcy, to return to Iran. He was leaving Paris, the city of his youth, the city that had shaped his character, the city that Mario Vargas Llosa called "the capital of world art and human fortune" before Hitler set Europe on fire.[63] Bakhtiar was one of 80 students who were returning to Iran from France after the war ended. Also, forty students from Switzerland and fifty students from Germany returned to Iran during the same time. He states: "The war had ended; nevertheless, telecommunications were not operating properly, and airlines were not available to the public. Ground travel was also problematic, since it was impossible to go through Germany. The bombings by the Allies had complicated the situation. Entering the Soviet Union was also problematic. Hence, I decided to travel by sea. The Allies had a relatively large ship with a capacity of approximately 23,000 tons, which they had captured during the war. It journeyed back and forth on the Mediterranean and went from the French ports to Beirut and Alexandria… It was a dangerous journey, because the sea had not been swept for mines, and there was the fear of the ships striking mines, although the Allies' mine sweepers had traveled this route and had returned, gathering or exploding some of the mines… There were two or three other Iranians on the ship. One of them was Hushang Samsam, my own maternal step-uncle, whom I did not know very well, and we became acquainted there. Another was one of the children of Prince Farmanfarma, whose name was Kaveh. He did not know that I was Iranian, and I did not say anything. We were in the same cabin with Kaveh Farmanfarma, and he spoke to me in French. As far as I recall, he had studied in Germany. Later on, I found out that he and Jamshid Farmanfarma had the same mother. The other person was an engineer by the name of Taqi Gorji, who had a paper-manufacturing factory in Grenoble, and yet another was a person by the name of Esma'il Sami'i. In Alexandria, alongside the Nile, I left for Cairo on a train to figure out by what means I could go to Iran. I stayed in Cairo for three days. There, I took a train, went through the Sinai Desert to Palestine, and in Gaza, I took a bus to Beirut… That was my own city."[64]

After a one-day stay in Beirut, Bakhtiar went to Baghdad. He states: "If I have not forgotten, Hushang Samsam was with me on that trip. When we arrived in Baghdad, I went to look for a vehicle to take me to Tehran. They said that I had to spend one night either in Kermanshah or Hamadan. I opted for Hamadan. They charged me about fifteen *tumans* for the fare. We drove in a Dodge convertible to Hamadan. In Hamadan, I went to Hotel de France, which was relatively clean for those days. We spent the night, and the following morning we left for Tehran, arriving in Tehran at four o'clock in the afternoon. It was early 1946. No one knew of my arrival. I took a room in a hotel called Hotel Gilan, on Ferdowsi Avenue, which was adequate." After contacting his friend, Ahmad Mirza Dara'i, Bakhtiar took a droshky to see Ahmadqoli Khan Samsam. He recounts: "Samsam was in the parliament; but on the day after my arrival in Tehran, Ahmadqoli Khan Samsam came to the hotel, and despite my objection, he grabbed my suitcase and took me to his own house. Something that caused me problems early on when I arrived was that, because of having lived in Europe for so many years, especially during the war when no one could find enough food, I had become accustomed to eating small amounts of food, and my stomach had shrunk, so to speak. In my encounter with the colorful variety of foods on Iranian tables, eating caused me certain problems."[65]

[1] Unpublished interview of Mohammad Moshiri-Yazdi with Shapour Bakhtiar, Suresnes, France, tape 3, 16 October 1988; tape 7, 6 November 1988; Shapour Bakhtiar, *Yekrangi*, translated by Mahshid Amirshahi (Paris: Khavaran Publishers, 1982), 126; *Ettela'at*, 20 January 1979, 29.

[2] Unpublished interview of Mohammad Moshiri-Yazdi with Shapour Bakhtiar, Suresnes, France, tapes 6 and 7, 6 November 1988; tape 8, 13 November 1988.

[3] Bakhtiar, *Yekrangi*, 29-30; Unpublished interview of Mohammad Moshiri-Yazdi with Shapour Bakhtiar, Suresnes, France, tapes 7, 6 November 1988; tape 8, 13 November 1988; tape 10, 4 December 1388.

[4] Bakhtiar's student record (*fiche*) at Henri-IV High School; Bakhtiar, *Yekrangi*, 30; Unpublished interview of Mohammad Moshiri-Yazdi with Shapour Bakhtiar, Suresnes, France, tape 10, 4 December 1988.

[5] Ibid., tape 8, 13 November 1988.

[6] Ibid., tape 8, 13 November 1988.

[7] Ibid., tape 10, 4 December 1988.

[8] Ibid., tape 10, 4 December 1988.

[9] Denis Bertholet, *Paul Valéry: Die Biographie* (Berlin: Insel Verlag, 2011), 34-37, 419; François Valéry, "Paul Valéry," in Carl H. Buchner und Eckhardt Köhn (Hrsg.), *Herausforderung der Moderne.Annäherung an Paul Valéry* (Frankfurt am Main: Fischer Taschenbuch Verlag, 1991), 99-111; Paul Valéry, *Cahiers/Hefte 1*, Auf der Grundlage der von Judithe Robinson besorgten französischen Ausgabe Herg von Hartmut Köhler und Jürgen Schmidt-Radefeldt, Übersetz von Markus Jakobs, Hartmut Köhler, Jürgen Schmidt-Radefeldt, Corona Schmiele, Karin Wais (Frankfurt/M: Fischer Verlag, 1987), 1, 38-39.

[10] Bertholdt, *Paul Valéry*, 96.

[11] *Paul Valéry, Werke, Band 2: Dialoge und Theater,* Herausgegeben von Karl Alfred Blühner (Frankfurt am Main: Insel Verlag, 1990), 45, 287; André Maurois, "Einführung in die Methode Paul Valérys," in Carl H. Buchner und Eckhardt Köhn (Hrsg.), *Herausforderung der Moderne. Annäherung an Paul Valéry* (Frankfurt am Main: Fischer Taschenbuch Verlag, 1991), 131-132; Carl H. Buchner und Eckhardt Köhn, "Paul Valérys *Phänomenologie* der Moderne und ihre Rezeption in Deutschland," in ebd., 9; Paul Valéry, *Briefe*, Übertragen von Wolfgang A. Peters (Wiesbaden: Insel Verlag, 1954), 221.

Ibex Publishers

English and Persian Books about Iran since 1979

Enclosed is a review copy of Hamid Shokat's *Flight Into Darkness: A Political Biography of Shapour Bakhtiar*. (ISBN 978-1-58814-186-6) translated into English by M.R. Ghanoonparvar.

Shapour Bakhtiar was the Iranian monarchy's last prime minister who served for 37 days. In 1979, after losing power to the revolution, he fled into exile in France. Shokat thoroughly researches Bakhtiar's fascinating political and personal history, including his participation in the French resistance, his work with Mosadeq in the fifties, his brief premiership, his opposition to the Iranian regime in exile and his assassination twelve years later by agents of the same government.

We would be very interested in your opinion and comments. If you have any questions, please contact us.

Post Office Box 30087 • Bethesda, MD 20824
301-718-8188 • Fax: 301-907-8707 • info@ibexpub.com
www.ibexpublishers.com

¹² François Valéry, "Paul Valéry," 107; Unpublished interview of Mohammad Moshiri-Yazdi with Shapour Bakhtiar, Suresnes, France, tape 13, 19 February 1989; Bakhtiar, *Yekrangi*, 47-48.

¹³ Ibid., 48.

¹⁴ Ibid., 40, 46-47; Unpublished interview of Mohammad Moshiri-Yazdi with Shapour Bakhtiar, Suresnes, France, tape 7, 6 November 1988; tape 13, 19 February 1989; tape 14, 5 March 1989; tape 14, 26 March 1989; Paul Valéry, *Werke. Band 7: Zur Zeitgeschichte und Politik*, Herausgegeben von Jürgen Schmidt-Radefeldt (Frankfurt am Main: Insel Verlag, 1995), 124.

¹⁵ Bakhtiar, *Yekrangi*, 21, 49; Paul Valéry, *Werke*, Band 5: *Zur Theorie und der Dichtkunst und Vermischte Gedanken*, Herausgegeben von Jürgen Schmidt-Radefeldt (Frankfurt am Main: Insel Verlag, 1991), 218; Bertholet, *Paul Valéry*, 80.

¹⁶ François Valéry, "Paul Valéry und die Politik," in Carl H. Buchner und Eckhardt Köhn (Hrsg.), *Herausforderung der Moderne. Annäherung an Paul Valéry* (Frankfurt am Main: Fischer Taschenbuch Verlag, 1991), 426; Carl H. Buchner und Eckhardt Köhn, "Paul Valérys *Phänomenologie* der Moderne und ihre Rezeption in Deutschland," ebd., 11, 13, 23; Peter Bürger, "'Ma méthode, c est moi,' Valéry und der Surrealismus," ebd., 362-363; Hans Paeschke, "Epitaph, Paul Valéry," ebd., 208; Marcel Raymond, "Paul Valéry und die Versuchung des Geistes," ebd., 268; Bertholet, *Paul Valéry*, 585; Ralph-Rainer Wuthenow, *Paul Valéry zur Einführung* (Hamburg: Junius Verlag, 1997), 33, 113; Paul Valéry, *Cahiers/ Hefte 1*, 151, 460.

¹⁷ Bakhtiar, *Yekrangi*, 30-31; unpublished interview of Mohammad Moshiri-Yazdi with Shapour Bakhtiar, Suresnes, France, tape 13, 5 February 1989; tape 15, 19 April 1989.

¹⁸ Ibid.; unpublished interview of Mohammad Moshiri-Yazdi with Shapour Bakhtiar, Suresnes, France, tape 13, 5 February 1989.

¹⁹ Bakhtiar, *Yekrangi*, 105-106.

²⁰ Gholamhoseyn Sadiqi, *Jonbeshha-ye Dini-ye Irani dar Qarnha-ye Dovvom va Sevvom-e Hejri*, edited by Yahya Mahdavi (Tehran: Pazhang Publishing Company, 1993).

²¹ Unpublished interview of Mohammad Moshiri-Yazdi with Shapour Bakhtiar, Suresnes, France, tape 13, 5 February 1989; tape 14, 26 March 1989.

²² Shapour Bakhtiar, "Essai sur Les rapports entre le pouvoir et la religion dans la constitution des sociétés" (Religion and State in Antiquity), 1.

²³ Ibid., 2.

²⁴ Ibid., 6.

²⁵ Ibid., 5.

²⁶ *Nameh-ye Tansar*, edited by Mojtaba Minovi (Tehran: Majles Print House, 1932).

²⁷ Ibid., 76.

[28] Gherardo Gnoli, *Iran als erligiöser Begriff im Mazdaismus* (Opladen: Westdeutscher Verlag, 1993), 5- 9.

[29] Bakhtiar, "Religion and State in Antiquity," 79.

[30] Ibid., 81.

[31] Ibid., 51.

[32] Ibid., 135-136.

[33] Ibid., 86.

[34] *Nameh-ye Tansar,* 8; Malandra, "Zoroaster ii, General survey," www.iranicaonline.org/articles/zoroaster-ii-general-survey.

[35] Gnoli, *Iran als erligiöser Begriff im Mazdaismus*, 14; Touraj Daryaee, *Sasanian Persia: The Rise and Fall of an Empire* (London: I.B. Tauris, 2009), 4, 20, 34, 145, 154; Fereydun Vahman, "Pishgoftar," *Iran Nameh*, vol. 17, no. 2 (Spring 1999): 180-181.

[36] *Nameh-ye Tansar,* ix.

[37] Bakhtiar, "Religion and State in Antiquity," 86.

[38] Ibid., 133.

[39] Bakhtiar, *Yekrangi*, 32-33.

[40] Ibid., 31, 33, 35, 54-65.

[41] Ibid., 34.

[42] Ibid.

[43] Antonis Liakos, "Griechenland und Europa. Im Knäuel der Krisenreaktionskräfte – Vorurteile und Richtigstellungen," *Lettre International*, 95 (Winter 2011): 20.

[44] *Die Endlösung der Judenfrage in Frankreich: deutsche Dokumente 1941-1944*, Centre de documentation juive contemporaine; (Herg.) Serge Klarsfeld Book (Paris: Klarsfeld, 1977), 45, 49.

[45] Bernd Kasten, *"Gute Franzosen": die französische Polizei und die deutsche Besatzungsmacht im besetzten Frankreich 1940-1944* (Sigmaringan: Jan Thorbecke Verlag, 1993), 101, 103, 183, 257, 262, 266, 312, 314, 317, 321, 327; *Die Endlösung der Judenfrage in Frankreich*, 13, 30, 44, 49, 58; Marc Bloch, *Die seltsame Niederlage: Frankreich 1940: Der Historiker als Zeuge* (Frankfurt am Main: Fischer, 1995), 10; Hélène Berr, *Pariser Tagebuch, 1924-1944* (München: Deutscher Taschenbuch Verlag, 2011), 104, 314-316, 320.

[46] Bakhtiar, *Yekrangi*, 35.

[47] Ibid., 35-37; unpublished interview of Mohammad Moshiri-Yazdi with Shapour Bakhtiar, Suresnes, France, tape 11, 18 December 1988; tape 12, 29 January 1988.

[48] Ibid., tape 13, 5 February 1989; telephone conversation of this author with France Bakhtiar, 1 February 2009.

[49] Unpublished interview of Mohammad Moshiri-Yazdi with Shapour Bakhtiar, Suresnes, France, tape 13, 5 February 1989; ibid., tape 13, 5 February 1989; Bakhtiar, *Yekrangi*, 40.

[50] Veronika Theil, *Die Bretagne, "a l'heure allemande"* (Dresden: Technische Universität Dresden, 2005/2006), 1-2; Eberhard Jäckel, *Frankreich in Hitlers Europa: die deutsche Frankreichpolitik im Zweiten Weltkrieg* (Stuttgart: Deutsche Verlags-Anstalt, 1966), 44.

[51] Theil, *Die Bretagne*, 4-6, 12; Bakhtiar, *Yekrangi*, 41.

[52] Kasten, *"Gute Franzosen,"* 122-127, 155, 242; Hans Umbreit, *Der Militärbefehl shaber in Frankreich, 1940-1944* (Boppard am Rhein: Harald Bolldt Verlag, 1967), 147.

[53] Bakhtiar, *Yekrangi*, 42-43.

[54] Unpublished interview of Mohammad Moshiri-Yazdi with Shapour Bakhtiar, Suresnes, France, tape 11, 18 December 1988; tape 12, 29 January 1989; Lutz Raphael, "Navigieren zwischen Anpassung und Attentismus: die Pariser Universität unter deutscher Besatzung 1940-1944," in Stefan Martens und Maurice Vaïsse (Hrsg.), *Frankreich und Deutschland im Krieg (November 1942-Herbst 1944): Okkupation, Kollaboration, Rèsistance* (Bonn: Bouvier, 2000), 701-702, 704, 706-707, 712-713, 719, 723.

[55] Kasten, *"Gute Franzosen,"* 54-55, 74; Walter Bargatzky, *Hotel Majestic: Ein Deutscher im besetzten Frankreich* (Feriburg im Breigau: Herder, 1987), 42, 57; Sabine Schutz, "'Une sale histoire': die unbewältigte Occupation bei Patrick Modiano," in Martens und Vaïsse (Hrsg.), *Frankreich und Deutschland im Krieg*, 881; Iris Radisch, *Camus: das Ideal der Einfachheit. Eine Biographie* (Reibek bei Hamburg: Rowohlt, 2013), 167; Umbreit, *Der Militärbefehlshaber in Frankreich*, 120-122; Jäckel, *Frankreich in Hitlers Europa*, 272.

[56] Unpublished interview of Mohammad Moshiri-Yazdi with Shapour Bakhtiar, Suresnes, France, tape 21, 29 July 1990.

[57] Ibid., tape 12, 29 January 1989.

[58] Bargatzky, *Hotel Majestic*, 84-85; Umbreit, *Der Militärbefehlshaber in Frankreich*, 118-119, 128, 147, 183; Kasten, *"Gute Franzosen,"* 105, 107, 223; Bakhtiar, *Yekrangi*, 43-44.

[59] Kasten, *"Gute Franzosen,"* 105, 107, 223; Umbreit, *Der Militärbefehlshaber in Frankreich*, 63, 149-150; Hans Luther, *Der französische Widerstand gegen die deutsche Besatzungsmacht und seine Bekämfung* (Tübingen: Institut für Besatzungsfragen, 1957), 62; Jäckel, *Frankreich in Hitlers Europa*, 254; Eckard Michels, "Die Stimmumg in Frankreich aus Sicht der Besatzungsbehörden, 1942-1944" in Martens und Vaïsse (Hrsg.), *Frankreich und Deutschland im Krieg*, 148; Dietrich von Choltitz, *Brennt Paris? Adolf Hitler: Tatsachenbericht des letzten deutschen Befehlshabers in Paris* (Mannheim: UNA Weltbücherei, 1950), 12, 27-30, 66, 83-84.

[60] Bakhtiar, *Yekrangi*, 45.

[61] Unpublished interview of Mohammad Moshiri-Yazdi with Shapour Bakhtiar, Suresnes, France, tape 14, 5 February 1989; Bakhtiar, *Yekrangi*, 48; Bertholdt, *Paul Valéry*, 445, 553-554.

[62] Ibid., 481, 585, 594-595, 601; Max Rychner, "Paul Valéry: Zone des Schweigens," in *Herausforerung der Moderne: Annährung an Paul Valéry*, Herg von Carl H.Buchner und Eckhardt Köhn (Frankfurt am Main: Fischer Taschenbuch Verlag, 1991), 127.

[63] Mario Vargas Llosa, *Die Wahrheit der Lügen, Essays zur Literatur* (Frankfurt am Main: Suhrkamp Verlag, 1990), 82.

[64] Unpublished interview of Mohammad Moshiri-Yazdi with Shapour Bakhtiar, Suresnes, France, tape 16, 7 January 1990.

[65] Ibid., tape 16, 7 January 1990.

Chapter Four

I am grateful to have drunk from Europe's wellsprings
and no one can force me to forget this.
—Arnold Zweig

Bakhtiar, Isfahan Department of Labor, and the 15th Parliamentary Elections

After the return of Ahmad Qavam (Qavamossaltaneh) from Moscow in March 1935 and the negotiations he had conducted with the Soviet leaders concerning the Azerbaijan issue, the government began a widespread effort to improve the situation of the workers. On the one hand, this policy was intended to implement the plan that Qavam had included in his government's program of reforms to improve the labor conditions and focus on workers' rights. On the other hand, this policy was intended to counter the increasing presence of the Tudeh Party (Hezb-e Tudeh-ye Iran) in the movement of the syndicates of the country, as well as to attempt to find an answer for confronting the increasing unrest in labor regions, especially the oil rich regions. The government's essential measures included the proposal of the Supreme Economic Council for rebuilding the national economy and creating the Supreme Council of Labor to regulate relations between the workers and employers, attending to the workers' claims, reducing work hours to forty-eight hours per week and accepting the workers' right to one day off with pay, prohibiting child labor for children under the age of twelve, and recognizing the right to establish syndicates that had been taken into consideration in the preparation and writing of the labor and social insurance law.

During this period, Shapour Bakhtiar, who had recently returned to Iran, was employed by the Ministry of Labor and Propagation. He recounts: "At that time, I had not decided on what type of work I should engage in, but I would not have minded serving in the Foreign Ministry, especially in order to be able to improve the living conditions of my wife and children, who lived in France. With this in mind, I went to the Foreign Ministry. The head of the employment office admitted me to his office. I presented my documents to him. He said that in order to be employed in the Foreign Ministry, there were three basic conditional requirements that needed to be met. First, a person who joins the Foreign Ministry should not be the son of a vegetable vendor. I explained to him that I was not a vegetable vendor's son. Second, he must have the required educational degrees. In terms of educational degrees, I had no deficiencies. Third, I was not supposed to have misguided ideas, which I suppose meant membership in the Communist Party or the Tudeh Party, and I had never pursued such thinking. Despite the fact that it was possible for me to be employed at the Foreign Ministry, given the faces that I saw there, I was disinclined to join that ministry. I picked up my documents, stuck them under my arm, and walked out of the ministry.

"In those days, Qavam was the prime minister, and the Poet Laureate Bahar, who had a cordial relationship with Ahmadqoli Khan Samsam, was the minister of culture. Bahar had asked him, 'What news do you have of the grandson of Samsamossaltaneh, the son of Sardar Fateh, who was studying in Europe? Is he not coming back to Iran?' Ahmadqoli Khan had answered, 'He has returned to Tehran and is now living in my house.' Poet Laureate Bahar had expressed his eagerness to see me, and he had asked Samsam to bring me with him to visit at his home or at the Persian Academy.

"Finally, I went to meet Bahar. He was very kind to me and asked me, 'Now that you have returned, what do you plan to do?' I said that I had gone to the Foreign Ministry. As soon as I mentioned the Foreign Ministry, he raised his voice in disapproval and said, 'Woe to that Foreign Ministry!' I added that I had not made any decision yet, and that I would get on with my life with what I had. Bahar said, 'I would like to introduce you to Qavam; but as you are aware, these days he is badly entangled in the Azerbaijan events and relations with the Soviets. So, I will introduce you to his deputy, Mozaffar Firuz, who is a friend of mine and in charge of the Ministry of Labor and Propagation, and he will definitely welcome you.' I went to see Firuz. After some discussion about my education, he asked Mr. Habibollah Nafisi, who was in the waiting room, to come in and he introduced me to him. At that time, Nafisi was the director general of Labor Affairs in the Ministry of Arts and Crafts and was about to be appointed as the deputy minister of labor and propagation. He welcomed the idea of working with me and, to be fair, his services in the creation of the Ministry of Labor and its advancement were very effective."[1]

Elsewhere, referring to how he was employed at the Ministry of Labor and Propagation, Bakhtiar offers a picture that is slightly different from what he had said in his conversations with Mohammad Moshiri-Yazdi. He writes: "I was looking for a job. There were two possibilities, either teaching at the university or being employed by the Foreign Ministry. As luck would have it, I happened to see an old friend of my father, who informed me, 'A new ministry has been established by the name of the Ministry of Labor. In the traditional ministries, everyone has occupied those positions and they will not let the young people in; but there is no rivalry and competition in the Ministry of Labor, and there is no obstacle to advancements.'"[2]

Bakhtiar does not provide any other explanation about why he was employed at the Ministry of Labor and Propagation. This choice was not compatible with his educational field. He had studied law and philosophy, and had he chosen the Ministry of Justice, it would have seemed a suitable choice. His extensive familiarity with poetry and literature would also have been more compatible with working in the Ministry of Culture, especially given that the person who introduced him to the Ministry of Labor was the Poet Laureate Bahar, the minister of culture in Qavam's cabinet. Nevertheless, Bakhtiar only viewed the university and the Foreign Ministry as possibilities. These possibilities would have been logical, since he had a doctoral degree and was proficient in French language and literature. A number of Western-educated individuals such as Mehdi Bazargan, Yadollah Sahabi, Karim Sanjabi, and Ahmad Zirakzadeh had made such a choice. Bakhtiar, however, had turned away from it. Was the actual reason for turning away from those positions, as he said, "rivalry and competition" in other departments, or "an obstacle to advancement"? Were the "traditional old" elements who, by occupying those "positions," had blocked the way to the "young people" his actual motivation for agreeing to work in the Ministry of Labor? In this case, accepting such a reality should have been difficult for Bakhtiar, a man with a rebellious nature who would not give in to any obstacle.

His close friend and colleague, Mohammad Moshiri-Yazdi, considers another reason to have affected Bakhtiar's choice. According to Moshiri-Yazdi, upon his return to Iran, Bakhtiar would have liked to be employed by the university, but his efforts to do so did not succeed. More than regarding the reason for this to be political, Moshiri-Yazdi considers it to be the influence of those who had taken over control of the teaching positions at the university. Bakhtiar also mentions somewhere that there had been opposition to his teaching at the university: "If only they had let me go to the university and teach, like Madani and many others. I tried for 18 months, through friends and acquaintances, through relatives and everyone else I knew. They said that it would be impossible to allow me to have contact with young Iranians at the university."[3] The opposition to his teaching at the university and the eighteen months that he refers to must be related to some other period, because within a short period of time after his return to Iran, without having to wait for any length of time, he was employed by the Ministry of Labor and Propagation. Moreover, it does not appear that in the early days after returning to Iran, due to opposition by the government organizations or the order of Mohammad Reza Shah, Bakhtiar would have given up teaching at the university or serving at the Foreign Ministry. The Shah's opposition to him concerns later years, at the time when due to his political activities Bakhtiar faced obstacles even to finding employment in the private sector. During the time when he had just returned to Iran, however, it was different. His statements in his book, *Yekrangi*, about his first meeting with the Shah are proof for this claim. In the course of that meeting, which according to Bakhtiar took place in the Private Palace, the two had talked about different topics, including the Shah asking him: "During all those years, what did you study in France?" He then goes on to convey:

"I explained what I had done and what degrees I had.

"'I have heard that you also fought in the French Army.' 'Yes, Your Majesty. France is a country that has broadened my vision. When the flames of war were ignited in that country, it was natural for me to help put out the fire, something that everyone does when one's neighbor's house is on fire.' The Shah repeated what I said several times. 'Absolutely, absolutely!' And then he added, 'Iran has many problems. You can serve the country, both with your education and also since you are a fighter.' It was my fate to rise against his policy."[4]

Bakhtiar's first assignment was in Isfahan. About this assignment, Moshiri-Yazdi says: "Habib Nafisi, who was the director of the Central Department of Labor in the Ministry of Arts and Crafts, considering that a large number of Iranian workers were in Isfahan, second to the number in Khuzestan, appointed Bakhtiar in 1946 as the director of the Department of Labor in Isfahan. This was the time before the Ministry of Labor existed, and the labor laws had not been ratified. Employers had a great deal of power, and there were no legislated rules and regulations to support the interests of the workers. Nafisi, the son of Mo'adaboddowleh Nafisi, who had been the guardian of the Crown Prince who later became Mohammad Reza Shah, had made some efforts to create legal benefits for the workers. At that time, during the time when the railroad was being built and the workers could be treated unfairly, only one law had been ratified to help them. Other than this, there was no protection for the workers; and we still did not have a permanent representative in the International Labour Organization. During the short time that he was the director of the Isfahan Department of Labor, Bakhtiar made a great deal of effort for the rights of workers. That period coincided with the elections for the 15th Parliament, and Bakhtiar, who had many Bakhtiari relatives there and had become popular among the workers, decided to become a candidate for the National Consultative Assembly. We know that the elections at that time were controlled by Qavam's Democrat Party of Iran (Hezb-e Demokrat-e Iran), that the candidates from the Province of Chaharmahal and Bakhtiari were most likely chosen on Qavam's order, and that, like all elections in Iran, these elections were a sham. Bakhtiar, however, acted independently. Singlehandedly, he risked everything, but despite all his hard work and the money he spent, he did not succeed. Later on, he would say, 'It was a waste.' At any rate, the tenure of Bakhtiar at the Isfahan Department of Labor did not last for more than a few months. During that time, there were workers' strikes in Abadan led by the United Central Council, and there was also unrest in Azerbaijan, and the leftists and the Tudeh Party wanted to set everything on fire in Khuzestan."[5]

Isfahan was a major labor center and, after Tehran, the most important commercial center in Iran. Almost half of all textile factories in Iran were located in Isfahan, with nearly 10,000 workers. Of this number of workers, 74 percent were men, 20 percent women, and 6 percent children. Working conditions in the textile industry in Isfahan were like in other parts of Iran in the same field. Children worked up to twelve hours per day in the textile factories. The average wage for twelve hours of work was forty *rials* and for a skilled laborer, 100 *rials*.

With Qavam becoming prime minister and with his friendly policy toward the Soviet Union and the Tudeh Party, the United Council of Workers in Isfahan gained power. On Persian New Year in 1946, there were street fights between the workers who supported and those who opposed the Tudeh Party; and more than 900 workers held a sit-in at the Telegraph Office in an effort to gain their demands. According to a U.S. Embassy report regarding the unrest, the control of the factories for all intents and purposes fell into the hands of the United Council of Workers. Those workers who refused to declare their loyalty to the Tudeh Party were fired, and in their place, workers who supported that party were employed. The owners of the factories were threatened, such that the workers would not let the owners enter the factories and nearly all of them fled to Tehran. On 6 September 1946, considering the crisis underway, Qavam sent Mozaffar Firuz, the minister of labor and propagation, to Isfahan as the head of a delegation. By declaring martial law and issuing orders for the arrest of Taqi Fadakar, the leader of the Isfahan Labor Union and representative of the Tudeh Party in the 14th Parliament, as well as a number of influential figures such as Jahanshah Samsam, the commander of Chaharmahal and Bakhtiari, Firuz succeeded in restoring calm to Isfahan.[6]

As one of the most important labor centers of Iran, Isfahan had faced labor conflicts previously as well. In March 1941, shortly after the establishment of the first organization of the Tudeh Party in that city, Isfahan labor unions began their operations, and in the summer of 1941, they had some success in regard to workers' rights. With this victory, the battles of labor unions intensified. The year 1944 in Isfahan was a year of clashes, a year of labor strikes and riots. These conditions were the result of, on the one hand, the increasing power of the Tudeh Party and the United Labor Council and, on the other, the employers' confrontation with the labor unions and their refusal to pay the workers' wages in addition to the workers being fired from the factories, all of which escalated the discontentment. In some instances, such discontentment had severe consequences, such as the occupation of factories and the confiscation of merchandise in the warehouses of the factories. The ensuing years, as well, to the extent that the situation concerned the expansion of the labor strikes, were spent in such a climate.

In April 1946, the Isfahan Labor Union instigated widespread strikes. With these strikes, the textile workers gained such important concessions as wage increases, an eight-hour workday, Fridays off with pay, and the prohibition on the firing of workers without the consent of the labor union.

With the collapse of the Azerbaijan Democrat Party (Ferqeh-ye Demokrat-e Azarbayjan) in December 1946, which resulted in enhancing Qavam's credibility and increasingly weakening the Tudeh Party, Iran's labor and syndicate movement underwent changes in its sensitive centers. The signs of such changes, which had a great impact in particular on restricting the extent of influence of the Tudeh Party, more than anywhere else could be seen in the decrease in the number of Tudeh Party members in Isfahan. In the meantime, the Democrat Party of Iran, which was founded by Qavam and was known as the Democrat Party, by relying on the popularity that the prime minister had gained following the resolution of the Azerbaijan crisis, was becoming a serious rival of the Tudeh Party. Enjoying the extensive resources of a "government" political party, the Democrat Party would not stop at any effort to push the Tudeh Party aside. Under these circumstances, the Isfahan Department of Labor under the directorship of Bakhtiar concentrated its attention more than ever before on the situation of the workers and the existing conditions in the factories.

Shortly before the arrival of the delegation of the International Labour Organization in Iran in March 1947, the British Consulate in Isfahan in a report about Bakhtiar wrote: "The Director of the Isfahan Department of Labour issued instructions for the election of factory workers' representatives to begin on March 5th. The elections took place by factories and representatives were elected in the ratio of one to every five hundred workers. The Director of Labour exercised a close personal supervision, and it was deemed necessary to publicize the fact that 'neither the Department of Labour nor the factory owners had brought the slightest influence to bear on the elections'. Women workers voted and it is claimed that this is the first time in Iran that women have been given the franchise. The result was a large majority for the members of the Workers' Syndicate of Isfahan (the Democrat Party Union), Shams Sadri, that Union's leader, being elected by two factories. But one factory, Pashmbaf, returned all members of the Tudeh Union (Shurai Muttahedi).

"Having achieved this, Dr. Shapour Bakhtiar, the Director of Labour, no doubt felt that he could face the visit of the delegation of the World Federation of Trade Unions with equanimity. The Delegation was due to visit Isfahan on March 11th, but it was not until March 18th that anything was heard of them here, and then the British Delegate, Mr. E. P. Harries, arrived alone...

"The other three delegates arrived in Isfahan on March 28th. The Director of Labour appears to have treated them the same as Mr. Harries, but the Tudeh obviously gave them a warmer welcome...

"The Delegates stayed three days in Isfahan, during which time they visited all the factories, and returned to Tehran on March 31st."[7]

One of Bakhtiar's efforts in Isfahan was to bring order to the Workers' Cooperative Fund. According to Moshiri-Yazdi, no law existed up to that time for securing workers' insurance. Only one legislative ratification had been passed during the parliamentary recess during Qavam's time, and that was based on the regulations that were devised for road construction workers during Reza Shah's reign, when a fund called the Workers' Cooperative Fund was created. In this connection, Bakhtiar states: "During the time I was in Isfahan, that fund's activities were very limited. However, a couple of issues attracted my attention. One was the hospital that the employers had built, which needed to be operated and its operation would require money that was supposed to be provided by the employers. Such aid was very limited, and each of the employers had a fund in their own factory for helping the workers, which was not much. Hence, I first made this somewhat systematic, especially in regard to the hospital. In the next step, I dealt with the funds in the factories, which was a very difficult thing to do. Neither did the funds have any regulations or supervision, nor were they based on any law. Finally, we made an arrangement for the council of each factory to have a representative, and also one representative from the employer for the operation and supervision of the fund, and the fund became somewhat regulated."[8]

Bakhtiar's efforts to secure the rights of the workers, establish calm in the work environment, and implement the law faced a great deal of opposition. Such opposition, which in his opinion stemmed more than anything else from lack of attention to the "independence of the syndicates" and violation of lawful standards, resulted in his clash with the United Workers Council, which was under the command of the Tudeh Party. Using their influence and taking advantage of their positions, the employers and the owners of the industries also were impeding the welfare programs, and they considered his presence as the director of the Isfahan Department of Labor an obstacle to their demands, to the point that, following the disputes that occurred in a factory between him and the representative of the United Workers Council, Taqi Fadakar, and once the issue was dragged into the office of the Governor General of Isfahan, Bakhtiar was summoned to Tehran. He recounts: "I felt that the military governor and the factory owners began to make provocations against me, and I reached the conclusion that there was a conspiracy going on. I went to Tehran to discuss the issue with Engineer Nafisi and told him, 'I am neither a Tudeh Party member nor do I have communist tendencies. But, while I am there, I do not agree by any means to the employers using whips in Isfahan, disrespecting the people, and violating the law. More than the workers and the employers, the law is important. If the employer is right, the worker must obey, and it is also the same conversely.' To be fair, Nafisi agreed with me."[9]

In his memoir and interviews, Bakhtiar occasionally refers in passing to his short period of assignment in Isfahan, a period that he describes as a sort of "ascetic living." Even these passing references convey viewpoints that can be considered to be a social democratic outlook regarding the struggles of the syndicates and the role of unions in the labor movement. In his statements, Bakhtiar considers the principle of the independence of the syndicates as necessary, and he discusses the disputes and clashes that occurred in the work environment between the left and the right. As the director of the Isfahan Department of Labor, he opposes the firing of workers from the factories because of their political beliefs, and he explains how he returned to work two leaders of the syndicate that opposed the Tudeh Party, and he also prevented the firing of workers who were members of the Tudeh Party: "The Tudeh Party members had expelled two people from the union. I reinstated them as workers in the factory, because the law had to be implemented, not the law of the jungle; and I also prevented the employers from firing the Tudeh Party members. If there is something that I should be proud of, it is that I tried to have neither 'hammer and cycle' in the workshops, nor 'long live the Shah.' The work environment must be healthy; it must be calm and democratic."[10]

Explaining his viewpoint, Bakhtiar on the one hand emphasizes the duties of the syndicates and their differences from the political parties, and on the other, he rises in defense of workers in political struggles. He states that the workers "can be members of various parties; they can be Catholic or, for instance, Protestant, or Moslem, or agnostic. I believe that the function of a trade union is to raise the living conditions of the workers, and the syndicates are for the practice of this philosophy of life. The same member of the syndicate, however, when there are parliamentary elections, when there are council elections, when there are presidential elections, is free to vote for anyone, any political party, or any group that he wishes. In practice, of course, workers would never come and vote for a rightwing Fascist political party; it would be unlikely. But if they were there and voted, that also, in my view, must be respected. My insistence on this issue is not merely regarding labor in Isfahan, Khuzestan, France, or anywhere else. In fact, syndicates historically were created for the welfare of workers, and for this reason, I did not want them to be contaminated with the politics of the right or the left."[11]

The start of the election campaigns for the 15th National Consultative Assembly that began in July 1947 was coupled with the activities of Ettehadiyeh-ye Sandikaha-ye Kargaran-e Iran, or the Union of Syndicates of Iranian Workers (with its acronym, ESKI). A distinct aspect of the campaign of this union, which had been established with the approval of Prime Minister Qavam under the supervision of the minister of labor and propagation, Ahmad Aramesh, was to counter the increasing influence of the Tudeh Party, especially among the workers.[12] This confrontation intensified in the competition for parliamentary seats. Relying on the statements of the military commander in Isfahan, in a report in this connection, the British Consul wrote that at the start of the elections for the 15th National Consultative Assembly, "most, if not all, had taken down the Tudeh Union signboards from their gates" and that up to this point, the Tudeh Party had not presented any candidates for participation in the elections of the 15th National Consultative Assembly.[13] On 1 December 1946, the Tudeh Party center in Isfahan was "invaded" by military troops.

Simultaneous with these developments and the clashes between Qavam's Democrat Party and the Tudeh Party in large cities and labor regions, the Tudeh Party was driven to the margins even more than before. J.W. Wall, the British Consul in Isfahan, sends a report to his government, and points out the increasing weakening of the Tudeh Party. According to him, at the height of the election campaigns for the 15th Parliament in Isfahan, the military commander in Isfahan intended to pull down the sign of the Tudeh Party from above the headquarters of that party. Under these circumstances, the leader of the Tudeh Party syndicate in Isfahan, Taqi Fadakar, had left the city and spent almost the entire month of December 1946 in Tehran. In contrast, E'zaz-Nikpey, Qavam's deputy, came to Isfahan to manage the elections, and the head of the Democrat Party, Ali Ansari, was also summoned to Tehran to discuss the arrangements for the Isfahan elections. These measures that with the strengthening of the local committees resulted in the reorganization of the Democrat Party in Isfahan, with the dismissal of certain figures such as Amirqoli Amini, who did not have a good reputation in Isfahan, paved the way for the victory of the Democrat Party in the elections of the 15th National Consultative Assembly. In the continuation of his report, the British Consul adds, to paraphrase: It appears that E'zaz-Nikpey is carrying the final list of the election candidates which has been approved by the prime minister, even though there are differences of opinion regarding the candidates of some of the rural election districts between E'zaz-Nikpey and the governor of Isfahan, on the one hand, and Qavam, on the other. Those two support the candidacy of local individuals, whereas the prime minister would like to nominate candidates for the parliamentary seats who obey his orders. The governor of Isfahan believes that the election of some of the local landlords would be less costly for the party. For example, E'zaz-Nikpey and the governor would like to have Sardar A'zam, who is not a member of the Democrat Party, as the candidate for Shahreza, whereas Qavam supports the candidacy of Mahmud, who is not very well known and whose election will be more costly. The British Consul's assessment was that the candidate for the parliamentary seat from Shahr-e Kord would be either Aqa Khan Bakhtiari or Shapour Bakhtiar. Pointing out the position and the financial resources of the election candidates, he adds that Bakhtiar is not wealthy, but he is popular among the young and the working people, and he would probably be the only candidate who would be able to get the votes in the elections by relying on his own reputation. The British Consul also mentions the differences of opinion between the Shah and Qavam regarding the electoral candidates.[14]

In his book, *Yekrangi*, Bakhtiar does not write anything about the issue of his candidacy in the elections for the 15th National Consultative Assembly. We only know that, following a meeting with Habib Nafisi in Tehran about the labor issues in his jurisdiction, and upon returning to Isfahan, he made himself a candidate for the elections of the 15th National Consultative Assembly. Bakhtiar considers having made this decision as based on the confidence he had gained regarding the possibility of his own success in the course of the elections: "A number of Isfahan and Bakhtiari acquaintances said, 'The people of Isfahan, especially the workers, are interested in you, and if you become a candidate, you can be assured that you will be elected.'" In response, Bakhtiar explained to them that in some cities, there were influential individuals who were candidates in the elections, and that Qavam had asked for E'zaz-Nikpey to become the parliamentary representative from Isfahan. He added that, in addition, he did not have the financial ability to participate in the election campaigns. Nevertheless, since the governor of Isfahan supported his candidacy and wanted him to be the representative from Chaharmahal and Bakhtiari in the parliament, Bakhtiar decided to participate in the elections: "After all, I always took risks. I went and toured the villages and saw the divisions. There were a number of other candidates, as well, one of whom was Mr. Hesamoddin Dowlatabadi, who had the support of the Royal Court and the military, and there were also two or three candidates who lacked any substance but had a lot of money, just hoping to get their names known but not wanting to be elected. For my candidacy, I needed 25,000 to 30,000 *tumans*, which I borrowed. On the first day, the government stated that complete impartiality should be observed. That was one of those His Excellency or His Royal Highness Aryamehr-type ruses that were employed in every election, and the only thing that was not at all important was the observance of impartiality."[15]

Bakhtiar's statements indicate that his decision to participate in the parliamentary elections was not merely based on the assurance given to him by "Isfahan and Bakhtiari acquaintances," or based on taking risks, as he says. Rather, another important factor influenced this decision. He states: "The governor general wrote a letter to Qavam, since he wanted me to be elected. He gave me the letter and told me to take it to Tehran myself. I went, delivered the letter, returned to Isfahan, and started working." We can infer from this statement that, alongside the factors that Bakhtiar mentions regarding his participation in the parliamentary elections, he had also used the recommendation letter from the governor general as an endorsement for his candidacy, although it is unclear as to whether he met with Qavam personally in Tehran or whether another high-ranking official had conveyed his interest in occupying a parliamentary seat to "His Excellency" the prime minister.

Regarding Bakhtiar's participation in the elections in Isfahan, the British Consul wrote about his status and that of other candidates: "There are only two other serious candidates for the three seats of the town: Hissam ud Din Daulatabadi and Doctor Shapur Bakhtiar. The former, released from prison where he was put as an enemy of Qavam us Saltaneh's regime, arrived in Isfahan about January 8th, and began to canvass vigorously. He has acquired a certain popularity through being persecuted, and though he is said to have no money, may collect a good few votes. Shapur Bakhtiar, at present Head of the Labour Department, is popular with the professional classes and the young men. He also is not rich but he may be the only candidate who could win votes on his own merits."[16]

With the start of the elections in Isfahan on 1 February 1947 and the announcement of their results, which took three weeks, E'zaz-Nikpey, Haj Habibollah Amin, and Safa Emami, who were all members of Qavam's Democrat Party, were elected as parliamentary representatives. Hesamoddin Dowlatabadi, who had withdrawn his membership from the Democrat Party and who was an independent candidate supported by the military, was defeated in the Isfahan elections. Shapour Bakhtiar and another candidate by the name of Rowghani, who had also withdrawn his membership from Qavam's Democrat Party and was supported by the military and a few clerics, received an insignificant number of votes. Aqa Khan Bakhtiari, Shapour Bakhtiar's rival, was elected as the representative of Shahr-e Kord to the parliament. In these elections, the Tudeh Party did not have much of a presence.

With the announcement of the election results, referring to Bakhtiar's personality and his defeat in the election battle, the British Consul wrote to his government: "Dr. Shapour Bakhtiar, Director of the Isfahan Department of Labour, has been transferred to Abadan. He had two blots on his copy book: he stood for election in Isfahan town in opposition to the Government candidates, (J'avais cette naiveté…he confessed), and he gave the mill-owners the impression that he was going to take the Government's propaganda about working class organization as seriously intended. He is a young man, educated in France, where he served for part of the war with French forces, talks like an idealist, and may be one, and is undoubtedly popular with that group of Isfahani young men of education but no particular wealth who are becoming increasingly disgusted with the old racket of fainéant government."[17]

With the removal of Bakhtiar as the director of the Isfahan Labor Department, this time, oil and Khuzestan were the new arena of the political life of this Bakhtiari khan offspring.

Oil and the Abadan Refinery

The Abadan Oil Refinery was the world's largest oil refinery. Regarding its importance for the British economy, it is sufficient to say that in

1945, Iran by itself produced more oil than all the Arab countries combined, and the oil-rich regions in southern Iran and the Abadan Oil Refinery operated independent of the Iranian economy. The Anglo-Iranian Oil Company had its own navy, airport, hospital, and schools, and the British community residing in Abadan with a population of 4,500 operated as a self-sufficient cultural community.[18]

Abadan became an important industrial city in the years following the D'Arcy Concession, which was signed on 28 May 1901 by Persia and William Knox D'Arcy. According to this concession, the right to the exploration, exploitation, and refining of oil throughout Persia, with the exception of five northern provinces on the border with Russia, was granted to D'Arcy for sixty years. In exchange, he would pay 16 percent of his net profits to Persia. At the end of sixty years, the ownership of all the assets of the company would be transferred to the Persian government. On 26 May 1908, the D'Arcy Oil Company discovered oil in the region of Masjed Soleyman. Shortly afterward, considering the importance of oil to replace coal for fueling the British Navy, England became interested in the exploitation of the oil reserves in southern Iran. To make use of the D'Arcy Concession, the Anglo-Persian Oil Company was established on 14 April 1909. The establishment of this company was the start of England's domination of Persian oil resources.

In 1943, the population of Abadan was 115,000 persons. In the census of that year, it was announced that 39,000 men lived in Abadan, of whom 30,000 worked for the company. The other 60,000 inhabitants of Abadan were the dependents of these workers. Ten thousand people made their living by working indirectly for the company. Nearly all workers in Abadan worked for the Oil Company. In 1946, the Oil Company had 52,000 workers. On average, they worked eight hours per day, 44.5 hours per week in winter, and 45 hours in summer. The wages of unskilled workers in Khuzestan were between 40 and 50 *rials* (equivalent to $1.30) per day. Because of the low wages, the Oil Company gave flour, granulated and lump sugar, and tea every month to certain groups of workers.[19]

In the early years after the end of World War II, the drop in the value the British pound vis-à-vis the *rial* resulted in the decrease in the real income of the workers. Even when Qavam's government ratified a bill mandating the Oil Company to pay an extra day of wages per week for the workers' day off, their level of wages continued to remain low. A comparison of these workers' wages with the amount set by the International Labour Organization for a minimum standard of living showed their meagre standard of living. The Oil Company, however, claimed that the wages it paid its workers were higher than wages in other parts of Iran. Nevertheless, the average level of wages did not increase in keeping with the increase in prices in Iran.

Elwell-Sutton, the author of *Persian Oil: A Study in Power Politics*, relying on International Labour Organization studies, shows that the general level of wages that the Oil Company paid its workers was consistently very low. In 1946, while the cost of living had increased by more than 900 percent, the minimum wage that the company paid was 14 *rials*. These conditions tangibly changed with the premiership of Qavam and the reforms that were carried out for improving the lives of the workers. In the next round, the government set the minimum wage for the Khuzestan region at 40 *rials*, an amount that raised their purchasing power almost to the level of 1936, prior to World War II. In addition, the government mandated that the Oil Company pay the workers an extra day of wages per week for the day they were off. Despite all this, compared to the increase in the cost of living, the wages still had not increased significantly. The company, of course, was correct to claim that only a small percentage of workers were paid the insignificant wages of 40 *rials*. Nevertheless, in 1949, more than 40,000 workers, that is, about ninety-five percent of them, were paid wages under 80 *rials* per day. Nowhere outside the Middle East were wages lower than in Iran. The workers' housing was not much better than their wages. A worker and his family had to live in one twelve-square-meter room. Their annual clothing ration was one set of summer clothes, one set of winter clothes, one undershirt and a pair of underpants, and four pairs of socks. A vast majority of the workers employed in the Abadan

Refinery were put to work through intermediaries, and their employment fluctuated depending on the fluctuations and needs of the Oil Company. Most were unskilled laborers who were employed as contract workers, the level of whose wages was not taken into account in the classifications and official labor statistics. They did not receive the minimum wages set by law, and since they were not included in the official labor statistics, they were not allowed to shop in the Oil Company operated stores that offered goods to the workers at lower prices. This group was also deprived of medical services in the company treatment centers, and it was constantly subject to being fired and to unemployment. The situation of these workers was such that they could always be used as a weapon against the officially-hired workers, whose fear of being fired and unemployment increased. This did not mean that the job security of officially-hired workers was much better. In 1946, the Oil Company fired more than 21 percent of its officially employed workers.

Before the start of World War II, the Oil Company needed no grace period before it could fire its workers. Occasionally, workers were suspended, and until they were employed in another job, they were paid no wages. The period of suspension could be one week or more. Another method was suspension for a few days, which was utilized for the purpose of keeping "order" and punishing "wrongdoers" and which resulted in several days of unemployment. In addition, the level of job safety conditions of the workers was very low.[20]

Another issue was the problem of open discrimination. Considering the expansion of the educational system of the country over the previous fifteen to twenty years, Iranians believed that the company should have been prepared to provide training for them, to enable them to be employed in the administrative, educational, instructive, accounting, and health services divisions. Of the 70,000 Iranian employees of the company in 1949, however, with the exception of Mostafa Fateh, who with twenty-five years of service reached the position of administrative assistant to the manager of the company, none had a chance of being appointed to the senior-level positions of the company. Other than

Fateh, only a small number of British-educated Iranians, who could be counted on the fingers of one hand, succeeded in gaining employment in minor divisions. In addition, even though the issue of the education and training of Iranians was included in the D'Arcy Concession, only a small number of Iranians were sent by the company to England for this purpose, or they were given the chance to benefit from the company's educational and training resources in Abadan. This situation changed after the end of World War II, and the company took steps to train Iranians in various fields.[21]

General discontentment was not merely due to these issues. The discrimination policy of the Oil Company was also a reason for the increasing displeasure of the workers. In this connection, the Oil Company utilized a racially biased dual policy, discriminating between the British and Iranians in addition to the Indians and Pakistanis. Similar to the Iranians, the Indians and Pakistanis also had a lower status. Moreover, the workers and white-collar employees were divided into three categories. The first category or group, "Class One," the members of which were addressed by the same term until the end of the 1930s, consisted of Europeans as well as a small number of hand-picked British-educated Iranians. The second group, "Class Two," was comprised of white-collar and technical employees at the refinery, consisting of Iranians, Indians, and Pakistanis most of whom were British-educated. Members of this group, however, were not deemed of the quality to be included in the first group. The third group, "Class Three," was divided into three groups. The first group included Indian, Pakistani, and Iranian skilled workers, and the other two groups consisted of skilled and unskilled workers, comprised solely of Iranians.[22]

The Anglo-Persian Oil Company at the beginning, that is, when it arrived in Khuzestan for the first time, faced more or less a barren desert. The company needed to build roads and bridges and provide construction and health services for its employees. These services ranged from procurement of beverages to the providing of clergy for the employees' religious needs, services which were as necessary as drilling for oil and erecting oil rigs. These were tasks that needed to be carried out in the best possible manner for the implementation of the vital and ambitious project of the exploitation, refining, and export of oil at maximum profit. Regarding whatever concerned the lives and the living of Iranian workers, however, there was no urgency. All that was needed was to provide the grounds to make the required labor force available to the company without any delay. For the managers of the company, the only concern was to advance toward their goal. There was even discrimination regarding the amount of water used. For instance, in Abadan with a population of about 150,000, the per capita amount of water was ten gallons per day, while a British employee of the company expected twice this amount for bathing twice a day. The company claimed that providing infrastructure resources for the workers was the responsibility of the Iranian government. On the contrary, the Iranian government claimed that many of the shortages in the oil-rich region of Khuzestan were created because of the presence of the company, and that the Iranian government had taken steps to provide the necessary resources to the best of its ability. Emphasizing these points, Elwell-Sutton adds: "The Iranian government was right to express dissatisfaction about receiving a small portion of the revenues of the oil industry." The Oil Company claimed that any activity outside the area under the company's ownership would be considered political activity and interference in Iran's internal affairs, which must be avoided. This claim, however, was baseless. With its expansive activities—especially in an industrially backward country—even with the best of intentions, inevitably its actions would extend to interference in the internal affairs of Iran, and in order to advance its activities, it would put pressure on the government of Iran.[23]

The non-Iranian employees of the company knew nothing of all this, and naturally, they were not expected to. They had seen nothing but a barren desert and rough, jagged hills that surrounded the oil installations from every direction. They had no access to Iranian newspapers, and they were not provided with *Journal de Téhéran*, which had been published by Ettela'at Institute in French in Tehran since 1934. The company published a daily bulletin about international issues, which rarely contained anything about Iran. In the final years, the authorities of the company made an effort to even prevent the availability of the Persian-language newspapers that were distributed among the Iranian employees of the company. There was absolute discrimination between the Iranians and the British regarding employment, housing, and the use of busses, cinemas, and recreational clubs. There was only one club, called the Golestan Club, the selected members of which included Iranians and foreigners. Dance halls, theaters, golf courses, tennis courts, and boating were all designated for the foreigners, and Iranians were not allowed to participate in any of them. Rarely would one see an Englishman socializing with Iranians, and if he did, he was considered to be a fool. Even socializing with a senior Iranian official was considered taboo. Worse than all was the status of British women who had chosen an Iranian husband in England. For this reason, they were not allowed into the gatherings and parties of the British in Khuzestan. There were a few Iranian women who had British husbands, and they were not welcomed by British women.[24]

The end of World War II and the expansion of syndicate activities brought changes to the status of oil industry workers. The Tudeh Party became active in Khuzestan, as well, and with its attempt to improve the life and the general situation of the workers, in addition to its extensive propaganda in this connection, it expanded its influence, especially among the oil industry workers. The height of this effort was the organizing of the labor strike in the Aghajari oil field on 11 May 1946, when 2,500 oil workers demanded the same concessions that were given to the textile workers in Isfahan. The Anglo-Iranian Oil Company, which initially opposed these demands and even cut off water to the workers, gave in to their demands within three weeks.

This struggle was considered a great victory for the workers. The Anglo-Iranian Oil Company not only accepted many of the demands of the striking workers, but it even agreed to pay the wages of the workers for the three weeks they were on strike. Moreover, it also consented to implement the government labor law regarding its workers. Given the status and influence of the Tudeh Party among the workers, the Oil

Company's retreat was understandable. The company had no choice but to accept the leadership of the Tudeh Party in the organizing of the workers for achieving their demands. Ignoring these demands would risk the discontentment and strikes extending to the Abadan Refinery, and would have even more dangerous consequences. The claim of the British ambassador, who said, "in fact, we can admit that at the present time, the security of the refinery and the oil fields and the safety of the British employees depend on the good will and open-mindedness of the Tudeh Party," was realistic.[25] The fact was that no measure could be implemented in Khuzestan any longer, neither by the government nor by the Oil Company, without taking into account the extent of the influence and power of the Tudeh Party.

In July 1946, following the dispute of the Tudeh Party and the United Workers Council with the central government regarding the demand to remove the governor general of Khuzestan, to release the labor leaders, to lift martial law, and to pay Friday or weekly day-off wages to workers, another strike that was much more widespread occurred in the Abadan Refinery. This strike that immediately spread to a number of production lines and services confronted Khuzestan with the largest industrial strike in the Middle East. Under those conditions, within a short time, a strike that had begun peacefully turned into violent confrontations among the Oil Company workers, the Arabs in the region, and the government forces. After three days, with the continuation of violence and street clashes, nineteen people were killed and more than 338 people were injured. To investigate and control this crisis that had rapidly become widespread, Qavam sent a delegation to Khuzestan headed by Mozaffar Firuz along with a few leaders of the Tudeh Party. The duty of this delegation was to negotiate with the leaders of the workers to prevent the continuation of the strike and to convince the Oil Company to pay attention to the demands of the workers. In its negotiations with the representatives of the workers, the delegation succeeded in restoring peace to Khuzestan.[26][i]

In December 1947, K. G. Hird, the labor attaché of the British Embassy in Tehran, made a two-week visit to the Oil Company installations in Abadan and the oil-rich regions of Aghajari and Masjed Soleyman. In a detailed report to his government, he stated the reason for this visit to be to assess the work conditions and investigate the welfare and social plans and services. Hird wanted to know whether the criticism aimed at the Anglo-Iranian Oil Company was based on solid evidence, and if so, what suggestions could be made to improve the work conditions. In his investigation of the conditions, Hird examined the issues of housing, education, health services, and work hours, as well as the roles of the Tudeh Party, the company, the central government, and the local authorities. Referring to the 115,000 population of Abadan, the major part of which was directly or indirectly affiliated with the company, he criticized the Iranian government for lack of attention to such infrastructure services as building roads, schools, and hospitals; and he refuted the claim that such work was supposed to be the responsibility of the company, a task that, in his opinion, was the responsibility of the Iranian government, pointing out that should the company carry it out, the result would be a flood of people coming to Abadan from other parts of the country. Based on the detailed plan of the Ministry of Labor and Propagation regarding the minimum wage, maximum hours of work, and vacations and holidays of workers, he emphasized that in all these areas, the workers employed by the company were better off than what the labor law had stated. Hird regarded the quality of the Oil Company workers to be at a high level, and added that prior to the increase in the unrest in Khuzestan and the establishment of the labor union by the Tudeh Party, they did not have any chance to express their discontentment. Regarding the issue of the workers' housing, he assessed

---

[i] Based on a report by the U.S. military attaché in Tehran, Habib Ladjevardi states the number of those killed to be fifty and those injured to be 165 persons. See: Ladjevardi, *Labor Unions and Autocracy in Iran*, p. 129.

their new houses as excellent, although he emphasized that, as a first
step, their numbers needed to be increased rapidly and then their quality
improved. The labor attaché of the British Embassy considered the
health services offered by the company and the workers' wages, if they
become ill or injured on the job, to be compatible with Iranian laws,
even though in referring to the example of the Masjed Soleyman
Hospital, he also added that despite the fact that a large number of
hospital beds were empty, ordinary patients were not allowed to use
them since the hospital beds were for employees and workers affiliated
with the company. Hird confirmed that the criticism made in the past
about the existence of discrimination between the Europeans and
Iranians had not been without grounds. The company, however,
intended to advance a clear policy based on lack of discrimination. To
him, the issue of education in Abadan was better than in other parts of
Iran, and every worker who wanted to become literate was able to
benefit from such resources. Hird considered the high rate of illiteracy
among the workers to be the result of their lack of interest in becoming
literate and lack of awareness of the available resources. Emphasizing
what he called Iranian standards, the labor attaché of the British Embassy in Tehran assessed the company to be a good employer, an
employer that before becoming exemplary in this regard had to prevent
further criticism. Regarding 12 instances, which he enumerated in
detail, Hird called the attention of the company to engaging in reform
measures. Despite his insightful observations, however, since he considered the Anglo-Iranian Oil Company to be an organization independent
of the British government, he considered the recommendations and
advice offered by the British government not to be a priority in its
implemented policy. From the perspective of the company, relations
with the government of Iran were more important than paying attention
to a policy offered by the functionaries of the British government for
confronting the ongoing crisis.[27]

Bakhtiar as the Director of the Khuzestan Department of Labor

Bakhtiar's second assignment was in Khuzestan. At the height of the unrests that within a short period of time ended in the largest labor strike in the oil-rich regions of southern Iran, this time, as the deputy minister of labor and propagation, Habib Nafisi appointed Bakhtiar as the director of the Khuzestan Department of Labor. The root causes of the unrests were the problems of making a living and low wages, as well as numerous instances of chaos and confusion that the oil industry workers faced throughout Khuzestan. The British Consul in Isfahan wrote about the appointment of Bakhtiar as the director of the Khuzestan Department of Labor and his dispatch to Abadan in June 1947: "He is an energetic and well-meaning official, and may find the atmosphere of Abadan more congenial than that of Isfahan, there the mill-owners closed their ranks against his efforts at labour reform." Also, in the same connection, referring to the failed effort of Bakhtiar in trying to obtain a seat in the 15th National Consultative Assembly, the British Foreign Office regarded the reason for his transfer from Isfahan to Khuzestan to be the result of his active efforts to implement the labor law, efforts that, according to the documents of the Foreign Office, were faced with the opposition of factory owners who succeeded in preparing the grounds for his transfer from Isfahan.[28]

Regarding his assignment in Khuzestan, emphasizing the power of the Tudeh Party and the strike that had occurred in the oil-rich regions, Bakhtiar refers to his meeting with Minister of Labor and Propagation Ahmad Ramesh and his deputy, Habib Nafisi. In that meeting, the unrests in Khuzestan and the issue of the strike in the oil-rich regions that were indicative of crisis conditions as well as the influence of the Tudeh Party among the workers were discussed.

During the 1947 Persian New Year holiday, when Bakhtiar had gone to Tehran, upon his return to Isfahan, he received a telegram from Nafisi asking him to immediately go to Abadan for an assignment that was related to the ongoing problems in the labor environment of Khuzestan. Bakhtiar states: "I went to Khuzestan. When I went there and saw the problems firsthand, I realized that there we were not dealing with Iran at all. The Oil Company was despotically autonomous. At least one could say 'be quiet' to some old-fashioned rich merchant from Isfahan or to a factory owner in Qazvin. In those places, there was state or government rule; but there in Abadan, the city had been built for the Oil Company. If not for the Oil Company, there would not have been any Abadan, and the Oil Company, well, it was taking away all of Iran's resources and wealth, and, of course, it gave a bit of it to Iran. The wages were very low. Of course, the Tudeh Party and the United Workers Council had done some work there, but it was not in order to raise the standard of living of the workers, it was to have a base for the power that was supporting them. I am not saying that they did not help to serve the workers through all those phases, but the main 'idea' was not to serve a successful Iranian syndicate. The problem stemmed from elsewhere."[29]

After a short stay in Abadan, Bakhtiar returned to Tehran for discussions with Aramesh and Nafisi, and he presented a report about the consequences of the strike in the oil-rich regions and the power of the Tudeh Party. In the course of this meeting, given the "popularity" that he had gained in Isfahan, they asked him to accept the position of director of the Khuzestan Department of Labor in order to find a way to "calm the situation." Bakhtiar spoke of certain stipulations before he would accept the position. He asked that the Anglo-Iranian Oil Company not have the right to fire the workers, an issue that should be subject to investigation and the opinion of the responsible official in the Ministry of Labor and Propagation. Also, after the elections of the labor councils, the Oil Company should not have the right to fire the members of the councils without notification and the opinion of the Workers Arbitration Committee. In addition, the project of the construction of housing for workers who lived in "shantytowns" should be completed. Until the construction of the housing project is completed, the water needs of the "shantytowns" should be provided by the Oil Company, and the Oil Company officials should reconsider the workers' wages. Regarding the success of the measures, a number of which he included in his stipulations for accepting his position of responsibility in Khuzestan, Bakhtiar states: "When two years and four months later, in September 1949, I wanted, that is, they forced me, to leave Abadan, 6,000 workers came to the airport to see me off, and the refinery was closed. This happened for the first time ever without foreign provocation, whether British or Russian."[30]

Bakhtiar's negotiations with Nafisi in Tehran were fruitful. He states: "Nafisi said, 'Tomorrow, along with His Excellency the minister, we shall have a meeting with the president of the Oil Company. If they are willing to agree, you can go.' On the following day, once the meeting had taken place, Nafisi said, 'In the presence of the minister of labor, I told the president of the company that Bakhtiar is our last arrow in the quiver, and if he promises to cooperate, we would send him to Abadan.' Then he added, 'With the situation that we saw in Abadan, this assignment will not be easy.' A couple of days later, I went to the ministry. I learned that in the meeting that was held, the president of the company and Linden, who was in charge of public relations, were present… I saw that the gentlemen had held some preliminary discussions. I also spoke a bit and said that I would go to Abadan from right there."[31]

The policy that Bakhtiar pursued during his tenure in Isfahan and Abadan was based on the independence of the labor syndicates, or what he called the "principle of syndicates." As he stated, he did not view the political opinions of the workers as the basis for elections or the criterion for viewing the correctness or incorrectness of the policy that the labor syndicate would pursue. The criterion was only and solely the votes of the workers in the election of the workshop council and the representative that was elected on the basis of democratic standards. He stated: "Any person who has the majority of votes in the ballot box of the workshop, he is the representative. Now, even if he is a Tudeh Party member, let it be so… Whether the leader is Taqi Fadakar, or Mr. X from the Third Force (Niruy-e Sevvom), or the gang of Khalil Maleki, or the gang of Mr. Baqa'i, it makes no difference to me."[32]

Bakhtiar's first effort in Khuzestan was to establish the workshop councils. This measure was considered an important step toward regulating democratic relationships between the worker and the employee. The basis for this policy that had been shaped in May 1946 with devising the labor law by the Qavam government in practice faced difficulties and incited opposition. The employers were not in favor of workers' organizations, and the distrust of the workers in the government also played a role in all this. The same reality would cause Bakhtiar's effort to investigate the workers' complaints and improve their situation, an important aspect of which was the creation of the workshop councils, to face impediments. For example, British Foreign Office documents indicate that Mostafa Fateh, the assistant general manager of the Oil Company, when Bakhtiar wanted to go to Masjed Soleyman to create the workshop councils, had considered "no necessity" for this action. This resulted in a reprimand of Fateh by the general manager of the Oil Company.[33]

In January 1948, the employees of the Anglo-Iranian Oil Company established the Central Council of Labor Unions. Yusef Eftekhari, a union leader, had extensive experience in the syndicate movement. This union, which had a publication called *Ranjbar*, in the beginning ignited some hope, especially among the opponents of the Tudeh Party, without succeeding in becoming a serious rival to the United Workers Council. According to the documents of the British Foreign Office, Eftekhari blamed the "failure" of the union on lack of support by the Oil Company, and Mostafa Fateh in particular. Fateh, however, attributed Eftekhari's failure to form a new union to the jealousy and machinations of Dr. Bakhtiar, the local representative of the Ministry of Labor and Propagation, who had independently set out to organize the factory's councils among the workers.[34]

When the Oil Company workers engaged in establishing the Central Council of Labor Unions of Khuzestan, Bakhtiar welcomed this step. As the director of the Khuzestan Department of Labor, he officially recognized that organization, which considered itself as merely a workers' union devoid of politics. In contrast, Bakhtiar opposed the registration of the "Trade Syndicate of Confectioners and Teahouse Owners," which in his opinion was not for "guild purposes" but had been established for political aims. He also refused to legally recognize the strike by the Zahmatkeshan (Toilers) Party in Ahvaz and the elections of the Glycerin-Manufacturing Factory, which were held to fulfill the wishes of Mozaffar Baqa'i-Kermani. He states: "Mr. Baqa'i made a lot of illegitimate requests of me, and these requests involved his trying to impose a bunch of professional knife-wielding thugs that he had at his disposal as the representatives of the factory, and I would not agree to it." His refusal to submit to such requests resulted in the parliamentary representative, Shams Qanatabadi, calling him the "spy of bloodthirsty British imperialism" and his being attacked by Baqa'i-Kermani and *Shahed* newspaper, who accused him of cooperation with the functionaries of the Oil Company and England.[35]

With such an approach toward syndicate issues and their relationship with the government and political parties, Bakhtiar made himself distinctly separate from the extremist tendencies of the right and the left. He considered disregard for the law as one of the essential difficulties of his tenure of service in Isfahan and Khuzestan. He stated: "We are not accustomed to respecting the law. We either bully others or we are bullied. I wanted to inculcate firsthand to the workers in Isfahan and Khuzestan that in the long run, it is in our best interests to accept the rule of law; otherwise, today you have more power, and tomorrow, I will."[36] He created the conditions in which, in regard to disputes between the worker and the employer, the employer would not be the only one to make a decision; rather, decisions would be made within a group comprised of the representatives of the concerned parties, in other words, the worker, the employer, and the representative of the Ministry of Labor. This plan was implemented with the establishment of the Arbitration Council that headed the workshop councils.

Undoubtedly, one reason for Bakhtiar's success in the position he had gained in the Ministry of Labor and Propagation in Isfahan and Abadan was his friendship with Habib Nafisi. As the president of government factories, Nafisi was favored by Qavam, and during the time that he served in the Ministry of Arts and Crafts and later in the Ministry of Labor and Propagation, he did certain things in support of the workers and their rights. Later on, as the deputy minister of labor and propagation, he intended to turn that ministry into an institution for supporting the workers. Nafisi supported the view that workers unions must be "apolitical" and "independent," and at the same time, he defended the workers' right to strike as one of their most basic rights. In the course of the strike by 4,500 brick-kiln workers, which occurred in August/September 1947 in protest to the decrease in their wages, he defended their right to strike. With this action, which was an unprecedented change in Iran's labor movement, he officially recognized the points that had become law for the first time during the premiership of Qavam as one of their most fundamental rights, even though by doing so, he was fulfilling one of the demands of the Tudeh Party syndicates that opposed the decrease in wages. These efforts were indicative of Nafisi's support for the rights of the workers when he was the deputy minister in the Ministry of Arts and Crafts and later the Ministry of Labor and Propagation, and showed that he supported efforts to improve the living conditions of the workers. In advancing this policy, which meant confrontation with the employers and being accused of going along with the Tudeh Party, Bakhtiar cooperated with Nafisi. On another occasion, when Bakhtiar assumed the directorship of the Khuzestan Department of Labor, he retained Abbas Garman, a member of the Tudeh Party in whose honesty and competence he believed, as his own colleague in the position he held. This action also provided the grounds for his being accused of weakness and, at times, cooperation with the Tudeh Party. In response to Emad Fatemi, the governor general of Khuzestan, who had called his attention to this point, Bakhtiar said of Garman that he "is an honest and sincere person. Even if he is a member of the Tudeh Party, he will do his work properly, and there is no room for concern. I know that he will neither betray his country nor his party, nor the organization in which he works... If ever it is proven that he has committed treason, or even caused disruption, I believe that he should be dismissed. But if every employee that I hire is a suspect for whatever reason, that is not proper… I have a free hand in choosing my colleagues, and I am responsible for their actions." And he threatened that, otherwise, he would go back to Tehran.[37]

The period that Bakhtiar served in Isfahan and Abadan, when he had already become the director of the Khuzestan Department of Labor, should be considered an important chapter in his political life. He regards this chapter as his period of "political training." It was during the same period that Bakhtiar, relying on the possibilities provided in the labor law of Qavam's government regarding workers' rights, persistently defended their rights and pursued the efforts to improve their harsh living conditions. Nevertheless, in trying to achieve this goal, he faced serious obstacles. General poverty, the employers' disregard for the most basic material needs of the workers, interference by the Oil Company, and the corruption that dominated the bureaucratic system were his main obstacles. Overcoming these difficulties would not be possible without the friendship and support of Nafisi. Regarding his relationship with Nafisi and the first term of his service in Khuzestan from the Persian New Year in the spring of 1947 to fall of 1949, he told Moshiri-Yazdi: "I was hesitant to accept that position. I doubted whether when my children came there to that hot region, they would be able to *adapter* themselves, as the French call it, to those conditions. Moreover, confrontation with the British Oil Company was not an easy task. Nevertheless, because of Nafisi's kind regard for me, I accepted the position."[38]

There exist in the British National Archives documents that detail Bakhtiar's difficulties in advancing his programs. A report regarding the concerns of the British authorities about the "activities of Dr. Bakhtiar," which was prepared in Abadan, states: "Bakhtiar is considered by our Management in Iran to be carrying out in an able manner the very difficult task of reconciling the conflicting claims of five separate elements, namely employers, an awakening labour force, a Union virtually Government sponsored, the vote-seeing Government group to which Bakhtiar owes his job and the requirements of ill-drafted and muddled legislation.

"Although in these circumstances it is inevitable that he should occasionally speak out of turn, he has not caused our Management any serious embarrassment. Indeed, they maintain that they seldom fail to persuade him to adopt a correct point of view over major matters and that he maintains a close personal contact with them.

"It would seem, therefore, that such apprehensions as we had following on the report referred to are not in this case justified and that Bakhtiar is serving conflicting interests in as satisfactory a manner as possible under difficult conditions. Our Management also feels satisfied as to his personal probity."[39]

In addition, in another document, references are made to Bakhtiar's period of service in Khuzestan and his efforts to improve the work conditions and create calm in the factories. This document mentions Bakhtiar as an honest individual and staunch nationalist who considers himself to be anti-communist. Moreover, it emphasizes that, on the whole, he has a good relationship with the Oil Company. In another report, Bakhtiar is mentioned as an individual who has a relationship with the Tudeh Party, and more than representing the government policy, his views are in harmony with those of the Tudeh Party.[40]

On the other hand, the British authorities in at least one instance were of the opinion that the main purpose in Bakhtiar's actions was more than anything else directed toward pushing the labor unions aside and taking charge of the affairs of the workers himself: Bakhtiar "in a press conference in December 1946 stated most decisively that his department has no interest in any union, and he would prefer to take charge of all the affairs of the workers. This might be only out of personal bias. There are indications, however, that a number of other officials here, who believe they have rid themselves of the crafty Tudeh Party, avoid even replacing it with a tame guard dog. The factory owners, of course, encourage this attitude."[41]

In addition to the difficulties that Bakhtiar faced in advancing his views as the director of the Khuzestan Department of Labor, there were also other obstacles. The complete implementation of a progressive labor law was not possible in the absence of democratic political parties and syndicates and a culture developed on such a backdrop. Social-democratic values would also not fall into place in an environment based on a traditional system, and the Tudeh Party, despite its undeniable efforts in the interest of the disadvantaged in the society and the promotion of the labor movement, had distanced itself from a social-democratic approach more than ever before, leaning more and more toward military-style thinking and deeds, the foundation of which was the whip. On the other hand, the conservative political parties and forces also, in their efforts to protect their own interests and gain as much profit as possible, regarded any effort toward improving the conditions of the indigent as a sign of devotion to a global pivot, and endlessly fearing the threat of communism, they relied on the old tradition of despotism. This reality also played a role in the way unions and syndicate battles were shaped as a leverage for advancing the goals of the political parties. A distinct aspect of the reason for the establishment of the Union of Syndicates of Iranian Workers (ESKI) on the initiative of the Ministry of Labor and Propagation was to counter the United Workers Council affiliated with the Tudeh Party. The United Workers Council also was an instrument in the hands of the Tudeh Party for advancing a policy the fluctuations of which, more than depending on the guild and professional needs of workers, was dependent on calculations that pursued political party tactics. Detailing aspects of his work in Abadan, Bakhtiar provides a noteworthy description of the situation: "In Abadan, there were three basic organizations. One was the Anglo-Iranian Oil Company that exploited the workers. The second was the one who waited in ambush to exploit the workers in its own interest; and the other consisted of right-wing elements who opposed any expansion of the freedom of the syndicates. I was like the village head. My major preoccupation was to replace the influence of the Tudeh Party with social-democratic standards… This task took one and a half years."[42]

In August 1947, when Nafisi headed the Iranian delegation to the International Labour Organization in Geneva, Bakhtiar accompanied him to Switzerland as Iran's representative and participated in its affiliated conference, which concerned the issues of the oil workers. On this trip, in the course of discussions, he called the attention of the company's officials and those in charge of British labor relations to the problems of the Oil Company workers, especially with regard to housing. Upon his return to Iran, Bakhtiar implemented the project of the construction of housing for the workers of the shantytown of Abadan, which was in a dire state. Also, under the conditions that the workers did not even have enough water for bathing, he instructed the Oil Company to provide them with water twice a day, in the morning and in the afternoon, and to give one block of ice to each household. Another beneficial step that he took was his efforts to have water pipes installed in the shantytown workers' neighborhood and prevent the role that intermediaries played in the distribution of rations. He assigned this task to the workshop council and to the representative elected by the workers.[43]

Regarding his assignment for the establishment of the workshop councils in Masjed Soleyman, Bakhtiar states: "Despite the fact that efforts had been made for the workers to regard the government and the Ministry of Labor as the authority for investigating their complaints, I heard the workers with my own ears cursing and insulting the Ministry of Labor and its agents. My first step was to try to neutralize the skepticism and insults; and I tried to gain the workers' trust by attending to their problems... I thought I would go to that area first and begin my measures with the creation of labor councils. And I did this. Of course, parallel to these efforts, I went to where the workers lived in the afternoons and evenings. They had heard my name, but they did not recognize me. The older workers had heard my father's name... Finally, after making an appearance in Masjed Soleyman, I was able to have free workshop councils elections, and when the news of what I had accomplished reached the administrators of the Oil Company that such a thing could be done, I received a commendation letter from the Ministry of Labor. Then I tried to implement this plan in Abadan. It was a difficult task. Neither were there any bylaws, nor was this possible, because the classification of the workers of various units was not easy... We could not create just one council for 14,000 refinery workers. We divided them... We set up one council for the oil workers and one council for each of the other sections, for instance, for construction, shipping, and bussing. There was a lot of serious opposition in other places, because the workers' foremen had a lot of influence among the workers, and they had figured out that with the creation of the councils, they would be out of business... It took us six months until we were able to create the labor councils. Then I went and suggested to the company authorities that the distribution of the groceries that were given to the workers be handled under the supervision of the labor councils. This supervision by the representatives of the councils in the distribution of groceries that significantly helped their welfare and comfort was effective and prevented misuse."[44]

In the meantime, the British authorities, who were closely monitoring the developments in the labor movement in Khuzestan, in a report on Bakhtiar's activities for organizing the workers, wrote: "Dr. Shapour Bakhtiar, local representative of the Ministry of Labour and Propaganda, was successful in organizing factory councils amongst the tribal workers of M.I.S. and Haft Khel [sic]. A large percentage of the labourers took part in the elections to the councils which were carried out in complete fairness and to the satisfaction of all concerned. He was unable to carry out his programme of forming similar bodies in other Fields...but intends to do so in due course. He returned 2nd September to Abadan, where he has since been endeavouring to organise factory councils. He commenced by calling a general meeting of the Electrical Department with a view to electing a representative to the Council, but the workers, prompted by their Tudeh foremen, heckled him at the meeting and refused to vote. He is now trying to gain the support of the foremen before addressing the workers again."[45]

Bakhtiar, Candidate for the 16ᵗʰ National Consultative Assembly Elections

With the premiership of Mohammad Sa'ed in November 1948 and the announcement of the decree for the preparations of the 16ᵗʰ National Consultative Assembly elections, Bakhtiar became a candidate in these elections. His popularity and influence among the workers in Khuzestan, in particular in Abadan and Masjed Soleyman where many of them were Bakhtiaris, had provided the opportunity for him to pave the way, through victory in the elections, for his effective impact on the destiny of the country and achieving the goals he had before him. The main obstacle to Bakhtiar's occupying a parliamentary representative seat, however, was the situation and position of the election candidates in Iran. Interference by the Shah, the government, and the influential elements in addition to the wheeling and dealing that dominated the election climate would not leave any chance for anyone to enter the parliament without relying on the leverages of power. The capital city was the only place where the grounds for passage through such obstacles existed, to a certain degree. Even reliance on his history and credibility due to the old ethnic and tribal relations among the Bakhtiaris alone would not guarantee Bakhtiar's chances for victory in the elections.

Bakhtiar's rival in this election battle was Dr. Abdolhoseyn Raji, the director of the Oil Company Health Department, who had close ties with Manuchehr Eqbal, the interior minister in Sa'ed's cabinet, who later on became a minister in Eqbal's cabinet. The Anglo-Iranian Oil Company, without openly interfering in the elections, was also an ally and supporter of Raji in this election battle. Moshiri-Yazdi observes: "As a man who had lived and was educated in Europe, Bakhtiar believed in assemblies and rallies, and the rallies that had been carried out by the workers in support of his candidacy in the elections with his consent had been coupled with some tension. This was the first time that disruptions had occurred in support of a man in the Abadan Refinery electoral district, which were considered unprecedented as such. This by no means pleased the Oil Company and its native functionaries."[46]

Moshiri-Yazdi, who a while after the appointment of Bakhtiar in Khuzestan had replaced a person by the name of Mo'tamedi as the director of the Isfahan Department of Labor, states about the issue of Bakhtiar's participation in the elections that resulted in his removal from the position of director of the Khuzestan Department of Labor: "It had not yet been six months since I had been working in the Isfahan Department of Labor when I received a telegram from the capital saying that I should immediately go to Tehran. That night, I traveled to Tehran in a government car, and the following day I went to the office of the minister of labor, Gholamhoseyn Foruhar.

"It was in fall of 1949. Foruhar asked me if I knew Shapour Bakhtiar. I said yes, and Foruhar precisely made the following statement, 'That gentleman has been disobedient, and I want you to replace him.' Being fond of Bakhtiar and having a lot of respect for him, I kept silent. Reading my silence as a sign of my fondness for Bakhtiar, Foruhar added, 'Of course, this Mr. Bakhtiar has not committed any violation; he has even worked very well, but becoming a parliamentary deputy has nothing to do with being the director of the Department of Labor. As a result, there have been such disturbances that the president of the Oil Company and the minister of finance, Mr. Hazhir, have called on the telephone and said that the workers' disturbances will cause a drop in production. In the government cabinet meeting, as well, which was held in the presence of His Majesty, the issue was discussed, and he said, who is this little young man? Fire him!' In the end, Foruhar said, 'Mr. Moshiri, before you leave, you must also meet with the chief of staff of the army, Mr. Razmara. I will call him right away.' And he called and made an appointment for me.

"On the following day, I went to the Military Command Headquarters on Sevvom Esfand Street, which was in the old Officers Club building. This was the first and last time that I saw Razmara. He admitted me and said very politely, 'You are aware that this Mr. Bakhtiar has caused a great deal of disturbance in Khuzestan. I would like to give you the assignment to go to Khuzestan.' I was at a loss as to why this assignment had to be from the military. Razmara said, 'Because, due to the disturbances, martial law has been declared there.' In the meantime, he summoned his adjutant and said, 'Send a coded telegram right away to Colonel Mo'inpur, the military commander there, to let him know that Moshiri is coming to be the Khuzestan director of the Department of Labor. If Shapour Bakhtiar disobeys, ask Mr. Moshiri's opinion and arrest Bakhtiar in accordance with Article 5 of Martial Law.' And then he said goodbye to me.

"After this meeting, I went to Bakhtiar's office in the Department of Labor in Abadan. I told him, 'Mr. Bakhtiar, I have come here, and I am on assignment. If you do not agree, I will go back. But I would like you to know that they will send some unsavory person in my place who would not approve of you. This is not Hyde Park in London, so that anyone can stand there and freely express his political views. When I was leaving Tehran, they told me that the Shah, Sa'ed, the chief of staff of the army, and so on and so forth, all are against you. You will not succeed on your own. My wish was that you would, but you will not. This is not the time in which you can achieve what you have in mind.' Bakhtiar said, 'This is unfortunate. You know that I am an obstinate man, and I am steadfast in my beliefs.' On the other hand, he knew he had no choice.

"After all, Bakhtiar saw that resistance would be futile. So, I went and saw him off at the airport, and he returned to Tehran on the same airplane on which I had come to Khuzestan. Before leaving for Tehran, he let me have his residence, which belonged to the Oil Company. I remember that in Khuzestan, when I met with Colonel Mo'inpur, who happened to be a relative of mine, regarding Bakhtiar's participation in the elections, he said, 'I must be fair. If the elections are free, Bakhtiar will be elected; but in today's world in Iran, no one can become a parliamentary deputy on his own; he will not get anywhere.' And Bakhtiar's case was no exception.

"Bakhtiar left for Tehran and immediately went to see Foruhar. Apparently, Foruhar was impolite to him, and this was too much for Bakhtiar. He was not an ordinary employee, to submit to disrespect.

Bakhtiar later told me that Foruhar had said to him, 'Have you become an outlaw rebel, sir?' He said, 'As soon as I heard that, I slapped him, the minister of labor, on his face and left his office.'"[47]

Regarding the meeting of Bakhtiar and Minister of Labor Foruhar, and all that had happened, Moshiri-Yazdi adds: "Following this incident, they fired Bakhtiar from the Ministry of Labor and Propagation. They even wanted to fabricate a false financial embezzlement case against him, a person who was the embodiment of truthfulness and honesty. They sent an agent by the name of Malekniya from the Ministry of Finance to Khuzestan to investigate this matter. I told Malekniya, who fortunately was an honest man, 'The more I look into it, the more I see that Bakhtiar has not committed any violation.' It seemed to me that Malekniya had also reached the same conclusion.

"The truth was that Bakhtiar was a khan, a tribal chief, and if he saw that a worker was in a dire situation and the laws would not allow helping him, he would order that the worker be paid something from the cooperative fund. In other words, some instances had occurred in which perhaps his action had been carried out without regard for the legal procedures.

"In any case, Malekniya wrote a favorable report in my presence about this. Later, the whole story was dragged to the Royal Court, to Shokuholmolk, who was the head of the Special Office of the Royal Court, and it was decided that Shokuholmolk should investigate the matter. Shokuholmolk, who was a reasonable man and Western-educated, gave his opinion in favor of Bakhtiar, who fortunately emerged from this predicament unscathed. Later, Foruhar was let go, and in the next cabinet, Sa'ed did not become prime minister."[48]

In his memoir, Bakhtiar considers the reason for the involvement of Shokuholmolk in the incident that had occurred to be a letter that he had written to the Shah to have the charges against him dismissed: "When I came to Tehran, Engineer Nafisi said, 'They intend to fabricate a case against you. I believe that you should write a letter to the Shah.' I asked him, 'What should I write, and why should I write it? I will only write a letter and request an investigation.' I wrote the letter and Mr. Nafisi made some revisions, and we sent it through one of my relatives to Mr. Shokuholmolk... A few days later, I received a telephone call and was told to go and see Shokuholmolk in the Marble Palace on Kakh Square on a certain day and hour. In my letter, I had written that they should appoint a committee, not for my sake, but for the sake the other young Dr. Bakhtiars who would come later, so that they would not have to face such individuals and receive such mistreatment for their good services."[49]

In his book, *Yekrangi*, in which he also discusses his period of service in Abadan, Bakhtiar does not mention anything about his participation in the 16th Parliament elections and his efforts to gain a seat in that parliament. He merely states that because of the popularity he had gained among the workers, he was the target of accusations, including having engaged in dangerous actions such as countering the interests of the Anglo-Iranian Oil Company, an action because of which he had to leave Abadan, escorted to the airport by a colonel, and inevitably return to Tehran. He considered the support of "6,000" workers who had come to the airport to see him off a source of "encouragement and heart-warming validation," and said that he could see clearly that "in social issues, good intentions and firm resolve can be fruitful." His other efforts, however, in trying to improve the situation of the workers in Khuzestan, and the issue of his candidacy in the parliamentary elections, resulted in clouding his relationship with the government: "When I arrived in Tehran, they informed me that the Shah had developed an unfavorable opinion of me, not to mention Princess Ashraf's opinion. The officers who were in charge of the affairs considered me to be an active member of the Tudeh Party, whereas I have never had communist inclinations and, specifically, Tudeh Party tendencies. My business with the minister of labor led to squabbling, and in the middle of our arguing, I told him, 'This country will either be saved by encouraging those who have patriotic and democratic sentiments, or it will be cast to the wind by the likes of you.' It goes without saying that I immediately joined the circle of the unemployed. This unemployment, however, did not last long. A new era of demands for freedom and anti-British reactions had begun. Seven months later, I was returned to the ministry, and this time they gave me the position of 'director general,' in other words, the highest position the young people of my generation could achieve."[50]

A little more than one year after the 19 August 1953 coup d'état, the American Embassy in Tehran prepared a report about Bakhtiar's period of service in the Khuzestan Department of Labor and his participation in the elections of the 16th Parliament. The content of this report, which had apparently been written on the basis of the statements of a "reliable Iranian source," states: "According to a reliable Iranian source in the NIOC, Dr. Bakhtiar's activities as Labor Officer in Khuzistan were almost entirely devoted to strengthening his political position. Bakhtiar was attempting to obtain election to the 16th Majlis as Deputy from Khuzistan. In order to build himself up with the laborers he would do such things as presenting benefit checks from the Laborers' Welfare Fund to each laborer personally, pointing out, 'It is I the honest Bakhtiar who give you this check; the money would never come to you if the matter were left to the Government', etc. The source remarked that this was hardly fair as Bakhtiar was in a position to hand out the checks only because of his Government appointment and all the work of preparing the checks was done by the AIOC Administrative staff.

"The source added that when it became clear that Dr. Raji might win the Majlis seat coveted by Bakhtiar unless the latter obtained the votes of outlying Khoramshahr, Andimeshk, etc., Bakhtiar took extreme measures. He instigated bus company laborers who were being laid off as surplus by the AIOC with the authorization of the Ministry of Labor, and finally brought on a strike in which the laborers lay down in the roads in front of the busses.

"The source also remarked that Bakhtiar took in Bakhtiari tribesmen who visited Abadan. Bakhtiar's French wife allegedly found it most irksome to have about fifty Bakhtiari tribesmen sleeping in her front room every few days. However Bakhtiar apparently kept tight control over her refusing to permit her to dance, or even attend local entertainments. During the Mosadeq regime she returned to France for a time.

"According to the source Bakhtiar is a poor administrator, as well as a political opportunist. The source explained how Bakhtiar would go over the head of Dr. Fateh, Assistant Manager of the Refinery, who was responsible for assisting in making Company policy. Bakhtiar would also call Fateh in the presence of a complaining workman suggesting immediate action to meet the laborer's desire. Fateh could not of course take action on such individual cases and this would give Bakhtiar an opportunity to insist on action and leave the worker with the impression that it was Fateh and the company who were resisting the righteous demands of the worker and the sincere efforts of Bakhtiar.

"The source described Bakhtiar as a man with well developed theoretical ideas on politics who never forgot political matters for a moment. A real intriguer was the source's epithet for Bakhtiar."[51]

Bakhtiar's family life during his assignment in Khuzestan, glimpses of which are pointed out in the report of the American Embassy in Tehran, faced some difficulties. Bakhtiar considers the reason for these difficulties, which eventually resulted in his separation from his wife, to be his political and social activities. Despite all his love and affection for his wife and children, these activities always caused him to be in a different "state and mood." About his marriage and his separation from his wife, he told Moshiri-Yazdi in a conversation: "When I sit in judgment, I realize that I was not a good husband... I must add that she also had some faults, and she did not manage our life and living the way I wanted. But not only was I not an ideal husband, I was not even a good husband, because I was interested in things that had taken over my mind and my emotions. I had deprived myself of my tranquility by my own hands. When a person deprives himself of tranquility, it indicates that he is interested in something else, and it is that interest that has now kept you and me in exile. My wife had a very good heart, was very good natured and very beautiful, and she loved her children. She was not highly educated, and in terms of knowledge and education, I was superior to her… At the end of the War, when I came back to Iran, after a short while, she came to Iran with our three children, and our fourth child, France, was born in Abadan. We did not have a calm life. In Abadan, I rarely had time to see our children. No one ever saw me with my wife at a party, because I did not go to parties, and she would not either, because she did not know what to talk about with other people in a party… Financially, as well, I was in a bad situation. I had fallen down from very high up… An average person can put up with average circumstances, as I used to, but what was her fault? She had thought we would have a comfortable and worry-free life in Iran; but, unfortunately, it did not work out. And then, political struggle regularly threw me in prison, and this was very hard for her… This was our married life, when I was either in the war, in prison, or a wanderer…

"When I arrived in Iran, one of my real estate properties was left with two plots of land, which they had sold, one plot for 60,000 *tuman*s and the other for 30,000 *tuman*s… I was left with about 110,000 *tuman*s… At that time, I neither had a house nor any income. There was also a small amount of my father's mementos, like carpets and rugs, which we gradually sold to meet our daily expenses. In fact, with my particular mood, I looked at these things as fortuitous… Had it not been for being an offspring of a tribal chief and what the people and relatives expected, I could live on what I had, or even less. I had no choice, being born to notables creates responsibilities… It is very difficult for a person who has previously had wealth and affluence to become emptyhanded… My problem was that I had to keep my cheeks rosy by slapping myself on the face. I had never been one for luxury, gambling, smoking opium, and such. I also opposed extravagant living; but I wanted my life to appear respectable on the surface. I tried to maintain this mental balance all my life… In Abadan, I had a government-owned house and a salary of 1,200 *tuman*s. It was not too bad; we had a simple life. I did not care for formalities and parties. I was not interested in other types of entertainment either. So, I carried the burden of the living expenditures of myself and my family with the salary I had. But having a wife and four children was expensive… We had to go on with our lives by borrowing.

Even when we had a house built for us, it was with borrowed money. Up to the time that I became prime minister, we had lived in that house for twenty years, fourteen years of which the house was mortgaged. Nevertheless, when we separated, she was not insisting on separating; but I saw that I was not good for her. In 1956 and 1957, I managed to send the children to Europe somehow, and the other two, who were young, I sent to Jeanne d'Arc School, the French boarding school in Tehran. Three or four years after our separation, my wife married a Frenchman who worked in Iran. They stayed in Iran for a few years and then moved to Beirut for three years and then left for France. When her husband passed away, she became very depressed. She had a pension, and the children and I put some money together and placed her in a reputable boardinghouse where she lived a quiet and respectable life."[52]

The sale of the lands of Bakhtiar's family was in line with a policy that the Iranian government implemented by passing the bill on "exchanging the lands of the tribal leaders" in the parliament in 1932. The implementation of this plan, the objective of which was to disperse the tribes and decrease their economic and political capability, advanced the mandatory sale, confiscation, and exchange of such property with lands in other parts of Iran. This policy was implemented in regard to the heirs of executed tribal leaders. Iranian government documents make reference to the issue of the sale of property left from Bakhtiar's father. The supervision and involvement of the government in the way this measure was carried out can be perceived in a letter written by Hoseyn Jeddi, Bakhtiar's family attorney, to the Isfahan Department of Finance about settling the situation of those lands: "Please issue instructions to inform the official Property Registration Office about the situation of the aforementioned lands, so that they can be transacted." A report by the Isfahan Office of the Governor in August 1938 indicates that that office granted permission for the sale of the "entire farm in Bagh Cheshmeh and four-sixths of the farm in Ramazanabad by the representative and attorney of the heirs of the late Mohammad Reza Bakhtiar (Sardar Fateh)" to three buyers who had been identified.[53]

Bakhtiar, Deputy Minister of Labor

In August 1952, Dr. Afshar, a professor at the University of Tehran, was removed as the deputy minister of labor and Bakhtiar was appointed to that position. Not much information is available about this appointment. Bakhtiar also does not provide any clear explanation in this regard. Recalling the period of his service at the Ministry of Labor and Propagation, he merely writes: "After four and a half years of service, I had reached the position of director general, and in Mosaddeq's second cabinet, the position of deputy minister in that ministry was conferred on me. I was first transferred to Khuzestan. I could now call my family to come to Iran from Paris. Our fourth child was born in Abadan, a girl we named France, in order for that country and the writer who has that name to always be with us… This is how my political training began. But before joining Mosaddeq's cabinet, I gained another type of experience. The management of two industrial complexes under the chaotic conditions that were the result of the tumult of the communists was conferred on me. Similar to the time when I was in Abadan, I concentrated my efforts on replacing the Leninist policy with a social democratic policy. In other words, I made an effort to guarantee individual and collective freedoms. I especially believed that the freedom of membership in political parties and political groups and syndicates had to be protected. At the same time, I would point out the syndicate and political party responsibilities and commitments. For instance, assembling and rallying during work and even writing slogans on the factory walls were prohibited. I encouraged the heads of the establishments to maintain absolute impartiality."[54]

Regarding how Bakhtiar was appointed to the position of deputy minister of labor, Fereydun Amir-Ebrahimi speaks about the role that Ebrahim Alemi played in this connection: "Dr. Alemi, a member of the Iran Party and the minister of labor, had prepared a report as a proposal for the labor law. Mosaddeq studied that report carefully and asked, 'Who prepared this report?' Alemi said, 'This was prepared by a young man by the name of Bakhtiar, who has come from Abadan.' Mosaddeq said, 'Issue a letter of appointment for him right away appointing him as deputy minister of labor, and ask him to prepare the draft of the labor law.'" To the extent that it relates to preparing the draft of the labor law, Bakhtiar offers a different narrative. Confirming his role in writing the draft of this law, he mentions the cooperation of Ahmad Zirakzadeh and Shamsoddin Jazayeri.[55]

The issue of the attention Mosaddeq paid to Bakhtiar can also be seen in a report prepared by the officials of the American Embassy in Tehran about Bakhtiar's reputation among the workers and Mosaddeq's positive opinion of him. According to that report, Bakhtiar "is popular with the working class. During a recent visit to Isfahan, over 2,000 workers from the textile industry turned out to greet him. Workers' delegations often ask to see him, rather than the minister, when visiting the Ministry of Labor. Even the prime minister tends to by-pass the minister and consult Bakhtiar when he wants to be informed on labor affairs. He is considered to be one of the best persons on labor matters and exerts influence among the workers."[56]

The star of Bakhtiar's fortune shone against such a backdrop, and for that matter, at a time when someone like Amir-Teymur Kalali, who did not know much about labor issues, was the minister of labor in Mosaddeq's cabinet. This fact alone shows that Bakhtiar's outlook regarding the labor policies of Mosaddeq's government was critical. He believed that one cannot say that "during Mosaddeq's time, labor organizations made progress in terms of guild-related or other issues," or claim that in regard to "political party and political organizations, astonishing advancements" were made.[57]

Furthermore, in his negative assessment of the situation, Bakhtiar stepped further, and in an interview about Mosaddeq's lack of familiarity with labor issues and current developments in the world, he presented the following picture, stating that Mosaddeq "was not a man who, as you might think, knew about the current issues of the world. After serving as a deputy in the 4th Parliament, in other words, around 1926 or 1927, up to the time that Reza Shah left, he was housebound.

It was as though he was totally unaware of these developments in the world and the issues in the world between the two World Wars, and paid no attention to labor issues or even sociological, political party, and such issues. Dr. Mosaddeq never wanted to be, or perhaps was unable to be, a political teacher for the Iranian people, as an organizational and political party person. Because of his past and the reasonable statements that he had made under difficult conditions, Mosaddeq always knew the emotional force of the people of Iran, the people always respected him, and he always had predominance over the people's sentiments. But he never converted this potential force into action. Neither was he very interested, nor was he perhaps the man for it, nor those on the front line... Mosaddeq essentially paid no attention to labor issues, in the sense that you have in mind in your question."[58]

The officials of the American Embassy in Tehran also, in a report about the conditions that were dominant in the Ministry of Labor during Mosaddeq's term, labeled the appointments that were made "confusion and chaos" in the administration of the affairs. Referring to the dismissal of Afshar and the appointment of Bakhtiar to the position of deputy minister in that ministry, they regarded Afshar as an incompetent individual unfamiliar with labor issues. In contrast, they described Bakhtiar as industrious and active. Nonetheless, this assessment did not prevent the American Embassy from declaring its unhappiness with his appointment in that position, because despite his statements about his fondness for moderate socialist philosophy, he was attracted to leftist policies.[59]

In January 1952, Bakhtiar nominated himself for the elections of the 17th National Consultative Assembly. These elections, which this time were held at the height of the unrest and tug of war between the government and its opponents, were cancelled on the order of Mosaddeq, who saw no hope of victory in them before they would be concluded. With this action, Bakhtiar was once again deprived of becoming a representative and occupying a parliamentary seat.

Since the fall of the government of Qavam in July 1952 and the development of differences of opinion between Mosaddeq and Ayatollah
Kashani, one of whom was prime minister and the other, the speaker of
the parliament, each of whom considered himself the unrivalled leader
in fighting England, new developments were underway. With the
support of the Tudeh Party for Mosaddeq, these developments intensified the anxiety and concerns of the followers of Kashani, to the point
that Baqa'i, who had turned away from supporting Mosaddeq and had
become one of his staunch opponents, would not lose any opportunity
to condemn whatever in his belief indicated the support and cooperation of the Tudeh Party for the government. A distinct aspect of this
opposition was the status of Bakhtiar as the deputy minister of labor,
which was the target of fearless attacks in *Shahed* newspaper, the organ
of the Toilers Party of Iran: "This Mr. Bakhtiar, who is in fact the
embodiment of the 'oil-Tudeh Party,' most impudently in the factories
of Tehran and provincial cities has placed the fate of the patriotic
workers in the hands of the treasonous Tudeh Party members, and does
not stop at anything to strengthen them and to threaten and put
pressure on the struggling workers and toilers. The Ministry of Labor,
which is supposed to be the protector of the interests of the workers and
toilers and prevent their unjust treatment and the violation of their
rights, has unfortunately today become an instrument for the victory of
the traitors and an agent for the domination of the gang of foreign spies
over the noble workers of Iran. His Excellency Dr. Mosaddeq probably
has been and is aware who these noble workers are who are subjected to
the treacherous lashes of His Excellency the deputy minister, and how
they have offered their lives for the victory of the struggle of the Iranian
people and walked courageously on the battlefields of the sacred national jihad. And he has undoubtedly not forgotten that he personally
had made promises to the Iranian people, the deprived Iranian people,
which did at least not include the promoting of the status of the likes of
Dr. Shapour Bakhtiar and Dr. Fallah… Otherwise, if these lions, who
are the captives of the likes of Dr. Bakhtiar, raise a hand, neither will
there be left any chance for these perpetrators of corruption, nor an ally

to carry their banner of worshipping the foreigners." Furthermore, *Shahed* newspaper accused the Abadan Department of Labor and "ill-reputed" Bakhtiar of disregarding the complaints of the workers about the violation of their rights and their unjust treatment and, "as in the past, continuing their old policy of backing and supporting the ruling employers class," a practice that on the day of "revenge" will have a "dangerous and dire" consequence for these "wolves in human clothing."[60]

Against such a backdrop, at the height of the disputes between the followers of Kashani and the supporters of Mosaddeq, *Shahed* newspaper in an article entitled "The Past is the Key to the Discovery of the Truth," referring to what it called the "evidence of espionage" regarding Bakhtiar, once again attacked the head of the government. Referring to Mosaddeq's speech in the 14th Parliament regarding his opposition to the elimination of the "ban on the prosecution" of those who are known for "ill repute" or those who were "deserving of punishment" because of their actions, the author of the article wrote: "Today, Dr. Mosaddeq works with a group the members of which have supposedly done no wrong in this country and are supposedly not at all known for 'ill repute.' For instance, his deputy minister of labor, Dr. Shapour Bakhtiar, has supposedly never been a spy for England, and Dr. Mosaddeq has supposedly not placed the evidence of his espionage on the desk of the International Court, and he supposedly does not deserve any punishment."[61]

These accusations, the sharp edge of which was pointed at Bakhtiar, were in reference to documents that were said to have been discovered in June 1951 in the house of Richard Sedan, and which intensified the rapid developments based on the tension and confrontation between Iran and England. Even though these developments created even more rumors, they indeed conveyed the expanse of the interferences by the functionaries of British policies in Iran, and in particular regarding the issue of oil.

On 25 June 1951, Sedan, the British representative of the Oil Company in Iran, when vacating the building of the office for publications and communications of that company on Naderi Street in Tehran, transported some important documents to his house. Six days later, Police Department and Justice Department officials, who had learned about this transfer, went to his house on Hafez Street and confiscated the documents. With the publication of the news regarding this incident, rumors spread that the discovered documents contain evidence that some Iranian notables and politicians had had secret relations with British high-ranking officials, especially with the functionaries of the former Anglo-Iranian Oil Company. One month later, with the ratification of a special law, a committee was formed to investigate this matter, and the prosecutor general of the country was instructed that if any documents were discovered among those found in Sedan's house that were indicative of crime in accordance with Iranian laws, they should be submitted to the proper court for investigation and prosecution. In addition, a decision was made that evidence regarding "illegitimate" relations between Iranians and the British government, even if not a prosecutable crime, should be discussed by the minister of justice before the National Consultative Assembly. Finally, after the investigations were conducted, the investigative committee published a 350-page report informing the public that the confiscated documents did not contain any proof of criminal action by any person. Apparently, sometime prior to vacating the building of the company in Tehran, the British officials had either destroyed or taken the important documents out of Iran. Nevertheless, there was also evidence of clear interference by the officials of the former Oil Company in political affairs in Iran. The company contacting the representatives of the parliament, the senators, and the former ministers; efforts to remove the opponents of British policy from their positions in the official organizations of the country; and financial support for newspapers to publish bogus reports on members of the National Front being the instruments and on the payroll of the company, these were all documents that based on materials found in Sedan's house indicated clear interference by the Oil

Company and the creation of tension, distrust, and crisis in the political climate of the country. It was even said that the company provided financial support to some of the leftist newspapers to publish harshly-toned articles against the United States, to deter that country from aiding Iran.[62]

In the meantime, ill-intentionally referring to the documents obtained from Sedan's house, along with the baseless claim that Mosaddeq had presented Bakhtiar's espionage documents to the International Court of Justice in The Hague, *Shahed* newspaper stated: "Some of the most ignoble flagrant mercenaries of England have been appointed to high positions, and they even participate in the government cabinet meetings." According to the open letter of *Shahed* newspaper addressed to the prime minister, in the course of the dispute between the government of Iran and England, Mosaddeq had presented the evidence of their treason to the United Nation's Security Council![63]

The claim by Baqa'i and *Shahed* newspaper was baseless. Even though Mosaddeq in a speech in October 1951 in the Security Council mentioned that "the former company had established a government in Iran, and this shadow government had gradually overshadowed Iran's independence," and added, "We proved that the company has interfered in all political, economic, and social ranks of Iran," he did not present to that council any document as a sign of proving "treason" by any person. In his speech at the International Court of Justice in The Hague in June 1952, he once again emphasized the same points and said that he had "numerous documents" at his disposal that indicate "serious interference by the Anglo-Iranian Oil Company in the internal affairs" of Iran, but since he did not want to get off the subject, in keeping with the wish of the court, he would not present them.[64]

Hence, clearly, all that had been said by the government's opponents about the evidence of "treason" and "espionage" by Bakhtiar for the Anglo-Iranian Oil Company was unfounded. Mosaddeq's sensitivity in preventing interference by the functionaries of British policy in the affairs of the country and the appointment of Bakhtiar to the position of deputy minister of labor during his administration were considered solid evidence regarding the prime minister's trust in Bakhtiar.

At any rate, in the continuation of these disputes, when the National Consultative Assembly placed the assessment of the performance of Mosaddeq's government on its agenda, Bakhtiar's name came up once again. This time, two representatives, Shams Qanatabadi and Ali Akbar Bina, targeted attacks at him. To refute all the accusations against him, Bakhtiar tried to respond by publishing a letter in the *Tehran Post*. Defending the role he had played during his tenure in Khuzestan and his participation in Iran's delegation to the conference of the International Labour Organization in Geneva, regarding his dispute with former Minister of Labor Foruhar and the former Anglo-Iranian Oil Company, he wrote: "At that time, when Mr. Gholamhoseyn Foruhar fired me from my position on the charge of defending the representative of the oil workers, Mr. Mohammadi, on that day when thousands of oil workers in the south went on strike in support of me despite the bayonets of martial law at the time, and the government of Sa'ed dispatched me to Tehran under arrest, at that time, freedom or dictatorship was not an issue for Mr. Bina and the likes of him. But His Excellency Mosaddeq knew me from that time, and knew that my struggles in Isfahan and Khuzestan were a prelude to the movement of the suffering classes. Moreover, Mr. Bina can take a look at the documents that were given to one of the parliamentary representatives and see how the former company in its report, which is available in the office of the National Oil Company, expresses its opinion about me, and how worried they were about my influence and popularity among the workers in the south and their request that I be replaced, and how Mr. Norgraft had explicitly told Mr. Nakha'i, 'As long as we (the former Oil Company) are in Khuzestan, we shall not allow Dr. Bakhtiar to reside in Khuzestan, even for an hour.' So, it has not been without reason that, despite the God-pleasing, so to speak, reminders of Mr. Qanatabadi and Mr. Baqa'i, I have remained in my position and Dr. Mosaddeq has endorsed me."[65]

Four months after Bakhtiar was appointed as deputy minister of labor during the administration of Mosaddeq, we find a confidential report about his character and views prepared by the officials of the American Embassy in Tehran. This report mentions Bakhtiar's history, education, and family issues in passing and is more comprehensive regarding his activities and political views. According to this report, Bakhtiar is thoroughly French in terms of culture and thinking, which is due to his education in that country. He does not have a good opinion of American policy in Iran, and he believes that it must pursue a policy independent of England regarding Iran. In Bakhtiar's words, American policy in Iran has been a "tool" of British policy. He defends the Marshall Plan, but he opposes Iran's participation in regional pacts such as NATO, believing Iran must retain its neutrality. Bakhtiar has a friendly temperament and gets along with others. He became nationally known first between 1946 and 1948, especially due to his participation in a strike against the Oil Company in Khuzestan, and in the course of his activities as the director of the Khuzestan Department of Labor, he gained popularity among the oil workers. By standing up to the Oil Company, Bakhtiar was accused of having incited the strike. He was a candidate in the elections for the 16th Parliament in 1948, and it was said that not only was he not opposed by the Tudeh Party, but that party supported him. Nevertheless, he was defeated, because, according to claims, England and the Oil Company opposed him. This time, in December 1951, he is an official candidate of the Iran Party in Khuzestan, running against Ali Omid of the Tudeh Party and Abbas Mazda of the Kargar (Labor) Party. Bakhtiar considers himself to be a socialist of the French syndicalist school, a socialism which in his opinion means control and ownership of the industries by the government. At the present time, he is one of the most active members of the Iran Party and is affiliated with the left faction of that party. Bakhtiar has been compared with Karim Sanjabi and Ahmad Zirakzadeh. This left faction was prepared in the past to cooperate with the Tudeh Party, provided it served its interests. Bakhtiar is a determined person who does not hesitate to take extremist positions to achieve his goal. Under the current conditions, even though there are no indications about him being a communist or a member of the Tudeh Party, he must be viewed as someone who is prepared to cooperate with the Tudeh Party in the arena of Iranian politics and labor issues.[66]

Even though the assessment of Bakhtiar's personality and views by the American Embassy in Tehran is not devoid of harsh and petulant accusations, as far as it concerns his approach toward the Tudeh Party, it more or less expresses the same points expressed by his opponents, such as Baqa'i and Shahed newspaper, about him.

---

[1] Unpublished interview of Mohammad Moshiri-Yazdi with Shapour Bakhtiar, Suresnes, France, tape 16, 7 January 1990.

[2] Shapour Bakhtiar, *Yekrangi*, translated by Mahshid Amirshahi (Paris: Khavaran Publishers, 1982), 126; *Ettela'at*, 20 January 1979, 60.

[3] This writer's telephone conversation with Mohammad Moshiri-Yazdi, 25 March 2009; *Khaterat-e Shapour Bakhtiar, Nokhost Vazir-e Iran (1357)*, edited by Habib Ladjevardi, Iranian Oral History Project, Harvard University Center for Middle Eastern Studies, Bethesda, MD, 1996, 199.

[4] Bakhtiar, *Yekrangi*, 39-40.

[5] This author's interview with Mohammad Moshiri-Yazdi, Paris, 21 February 2008.

[6] Habib Ladjevardi, *Labor Unions and Autocracy in Iran* (Syracuse: Syracuse University Press, 1985), 149, 166-167; Baqer Aqeli, *Ruzshomar-e Tarikh-e Iran az Mashruteh ta Enqelab-e Eslami*, vol. 1 (Tehran: Goftar Publishers, 1993), 396.

[7] TNA 371/62008/E3361. J.W. Wall, British Consulate, Isfahan, 31 March 1947.

[8] Unpublished interview of Mohammad Moshiri-Yazdi with Shapour Bakhtiar, Suresnes, France, tape 19, 4 March 1990.

[9] Ibid., tape 18, 25 February 1990.

[10] *Khaterat-e Shapour Bakhtiar, Nokhost Vazir-e Iran (1357)*, 22.

[11] Ibid., 26.

[12] Ahmad Aramesh, *Khaterat-e Siyasi*, edited by Gholamhoseyn Mirza-Saleh (Tehran: Danesh Publishers, 1990), 171-173.

[13] FO 371/62008/490. J.W. Wall, British Consulate, Isfahan, 31 December 1946.

[14] Ibid.; 371/62008/E490. J.W. Wall, British Consulate, Isfahan, 31 December 1946.

[15] Unpublished interview of Mohammad Moshiri-Yazdi with Shapour Bakhtiar, Suresnes, France, tape 18, 25 February 1990.

[16] FO 371/62008/E1692. J.W. Wall, British Consulate, Isfahan, 31 January 1947.

[17] Ibid.; 371/62008/E4296. J.W. Wall, British Consulate, Isfahan, 30 April 1947.

[18] William Roger Louis, *The British Empire in the Middle East, 1945-1951: Arab Nationalism, the United States, and Postwar Imperialism* (Oxford: Clarendon Press, 1984), 8-9.

[19] Habib Ladjevardi, *Labor Unions and Autocracy in Iran*, 118-119.

[20] L.P. Elwell-Sutton, *Persian Oil: A Study in Power Politics* (London: Lawrence and Wishart Ltd, 1955), 88-90; Norman Kemp, *Abadan: A First-hand Account of the Persian Oil Crisis* (London: Allen Wingate, 1953), 46-47.

[21] Elwell-Sutton, 92-93; Kemp, 44.

[22] Elwell-Sutton, *Persian Oil*, 92.

[23] Ibid., 93-94, 98-100.

[24] Ibid., 100-103.

[25] FO 371/E-5134/401/34. Le Rougetel to Bevin, Tehran, 29 May 1946.

[26] Ervand Abrahamian, *Iran Between Two Revolutions* (Princeton: Princeton University Press, 1982), 364-365.

[27] FO 371/61984. K.J. Hird, British Embassy, Tehran, 31 December 1946; Carlo Morelli, *The Angelo-Iranian Oil Company 1945-54: Government Business relationship in conflict?*, 11. http://74.125.95.132/search?q=cach:B8n6seOiFL8J:www.dundee.ac.uk/econman/dis ...

[28] FO 371/62008/E5512, 25 June 1947; British Documents on Foreign Affairs, Part IV, April-December 1946, 296.

[29] Unpublished interview of Mohammad Moshiri-Yazdi with Shapour Bakhtiar, Suresnes, France, tape 19, 4 March 1990; *Khaterat-e Shapour Bakhtiar, Nokhost Vazir-e Iran (1357)*, 24-25.

[30] Ibid., 25.

[31] Unpublished interview of Mohammad Moshiri-Yazdi with Shapour Bakhtiar, Suresnes, France, tape 19, 4 March 1990.

[32] *Khaterat-e Shapour Bakhtiar, Nokhost Vazir-e Iran (1357)*, 30-31.

[33] FO 371/62044. E 7254. 17 August 1947.

[34] Ibid.; 371/62044. E 7254. 1 July-September 1947.

[35] *Rejal-e Asr-e Pahlavi, Shapour Bakhtiar beh Revayat-e Asnad-e SAVAK*, vol. 24 (Tehran: Center for the Examination of Historical Documents of the Ministry of Information, 2011), 39-40; *Khaterat-e Shapour Bakhtiar, Nokhost Vazir-e Iran (1357)*, 30.

[36] Ibid., 16.

[37] Ibid., 29-30; unpublished interview of Mohammad Moshiri-Yazdi with Shapour Bakhtiar, Suresnes, France, tape 20, 11 March 1990, 1 April 1990.

[38] This writer's interview with Mohammad Moshiri-Yazdi, Paris, 21 February 2008.

[39] FO 371/68738. E 9422. 1 July 1947.

[40] British Documents on Foreign Affairs, Part IV, April-December 1946, 296; ibid., Persia: Quarterly Report, July-September 1947, Creswell to Bevin, 118.

[41] FO 371/62008. E 490/490/34. Isfahan Diary for 1946, 12 December 1946.

[42] Bakhtiar, *Yekrangi*, 60-61.

43 This writer's interview with Rahim Sharifi, Paris, 11 December 2007; this writer's interview with Mohammad Moshiri-Yazdi, Paris, 21 February 2008.

44 Unpublished interview of Mohammad Moshiri-Yazdi with Shapour Bakhtiar, Suresnes, France, tape 19, 4 March 1990.

45 FO 371/62044. July-September 1947.

46 This writer's interview with Mohammad Moshiri-Yazdi, Paris, 21 February 2008.

47 Ibid., 21 February 2008.

48 Ibid., 21 February 2008.

49 Unpublished interview of Mohammad Moshiri-Yazdi with Shapour Bakhtiar, Suresnes, France, tape 20, 1 April 1990.

50 Bakhtiar, *Yekrangi*, 60-61.

51 (United States, Digital National Security Archive), (DNSA): From R.H. Bushner RHB, 29 September 1954.

52 Unpublished interview of Mohammad Moshiri-Yazdi with Shapour Bakhtiar, Suresnes, France, tape 19, 5 February 1989; ibid., tape 21, 22 January 1988.

53 Nafiseh Va'ez (Shahrestani), *Siyasat-e Ashayeri-ye Dowlat-e Pahlavi-ye Avval* (Tehran: Tarikh Publisher, 2009), 299-306.

54 Bakhtiar, *Yekrangi*, 60-61.

55 This writer's interview with Fereydun Amir-Ebrahimi, London, 12 November 2007; *Rejal-e Asr-e Pahlavi, Shapour Bakhtiar beh Revayat-e Asnad-e SAVAK*, 40.

56 (DNSA): Confidential Biographic Data, Tehran, 10 November 1952.

57 *Khaterat-e Shapour Bakhtiar, Nokhost Vazir-e Iran (1357)*, 9-10.

58 Ibid., 27-28.

59 Ladjevardi, *Labor Unions and Autocracy in Iran*, 190-191.

60 *Shahed*, no. 919, 22 April 1953, 1-4; ibid., no. 917, 29 April 1953, 3.

61 Ibid., no. 919, 22 April 1953, 1-3.

62 Mohammad Ali Movahhed, *Khab-e Ashofteh-ye Naft, Dr. Mosaddeq va Nehzat-e Melli-ye Iran*, vol. 1 (Tehran: Karnameh Publishers, 2005), 176-177; Mostafa Alam, *Naft, Qodrat, va Osul, Peyamadha-ye Kudeta-ye 28 Mordad*, translated by Gholam-hoseyn Salehyar (Tehran: Chapakhsh Publishers, 1998), 197-201.

63 *Shahed*, no. 919, 22 April 1953, 1-3.

64 *Panj Daheh pas az Kudeta Asnad Sokhan Miguyand*, vol. 1, research and translation by Dr. Ahmad Ali Raja'i and Mahin Soruri (Raja'i) (Tehran: Qalam Publishers, 2004), 831, 858, 874.

65 *Rejal-e Asr-e Pahlavi, Shapour Bakhtiar beh Revayat-e Asnad-e SAVAK*, 41.

66 (DNSA): Confidential Biographic Data, Tehran, 10 November 1952.

Chapter Five

It will not be tolerable for the Iranian people to halt or to shut down the implementation of the Constitution, which contains the religious and national rights of the Moslem people of Iran and the rights of freedom and is the result of the efforts the two Grand Seyyeds, God's mercy upon them... No doubt exists that at this time, the preservation of the true religion and the protection of independence and freedom is not possible except by creating national unity and the true constitutional government which has been abolished for many years.
—Allahyar Saleh

Bakhtiar and the Iran Party

In October 1949, when Bakhtiar was serving in Khuzestan, he became a member of the Iran Party (Hezb-e Iran). This action brought a new change to his political life, which had always undergone harsh ups and downs. From the very beginning, he attracted the attention of the party leaders, and with his membership in the central committee of the Young People's Organization (Sazman-e Javanan) and the leadership of this organization, he played an important role in setting its policies, to the point that in 1955, by solidifying his position in the party, he was elected as a member of the central committee of the Iran Party, and alongside the well-known figures of the National Front, he assumed an important position of responsibility in that organization. At the time when he agreed to become prime minister, in January 1979, he was the secretary general of the Iran Party. The executive committee of the Iran Party removed him from all political party positions once he accepted this responsibility and left the final decision about him to the next plenum of the party. For the same reason, Bakhtiar was expelled from the National Front.

Among the political parties that had an impact on the political fate of the country after September 1941 and the forced abdication of Reza

Shah, the Iran Party had a special place. Later on, this party had an impact on the political developments of the country as the most organized group in the National Front of Iran. A number of the leaders of this party, such as Allahyar Saleh, Karim Sanjabi, Kazem Hasibi, and Shapour Bakhtiar, left lasting marks on sensitive events such as the Azerbaijan crisis and the formation of Qavam's coalition cabinet, the founding of the National Front of Iran and the nationalization of the oil industry, the formation of the Second National Front, the political developments during the premiership of Ali Amini and the opening up of the political climate of the country between 1960 and 1963, and finally, in the course of the collapse of the monarchical regime in February 1979.

With the fall of Mosaddeq's government in August 1953 and the increasing expanse of political restrictions, along with the widening of the stifling climate, the velocity of which had accelerated in the final years of Mohammad Reza Shah's reign, no opportunity was left for the activities of the Iran Party, which insisted on lawful struggle. In the course of these years until the start of the developments that eventually ended in the 1979 Islamic Revolution, with the exception of the period of the premiership of Ali Amini, no distinct sign of the Iran Party was visible on the political landscape of the country. These conditions rapidly changed with the start of the political unrest in the final years and months of the Shah's government, and once again, the names of a number of the leaders of the Iran Party, who had at one time been on the frontlines of the National Front and had fought at the side of Mosaddeq, were on everyone's lips. This period, the distinct characteristics of which were the absence of organized political parties, the lack of programs, and the day-by-day increasing political incidents, confronted the Iran Party with serious problems.

In such a climate, the active members and the leaders of the party, more than acting on the basis of political party policy and plans and preparing a targeted program and project to confront the crisis that was dragging the society into chaos and revolution, based their fate on individual reputation and competence. Such reputation and competence was merely based on a recollection that remained in the memory of a specific stratum in the society and stemmed from the sound reputation of the name of Mosaddeq and the struggles of the National Front in the distant past as well as more recent years.

There is a lack of clarity about the precise date of the formation of the Iran Party as the main group of the National Front, and the available documents and evidence also do not provide us with the precise date of the establishment of this party, even though the announcements and articles recorded in the documents related to that period indicate that the Iran Party must have been established after the elections of the 14th National Consultative Assembly, which were held in autumn 1943 by a group of the activists in the election headquarters of Engineer Farivar and Dr. Mosaddeq.[1]

The original members of the Iran Party were comprised mainly of "nationalist personalities who initially created the Association of Engineers (Kanun-e Mohandesin) to address their guild-related and professional concerns, and after a while, due to their political inclinations and the favorable climate in the wake of September 1941, they established this party. The main members of the party were a number of academics and engineers, the most distinguished of whom were Engineer Ahmad Hami, Engineer Gholamali Farivar, Engineer Kazem Hasibi, Dr. Abdollah Mo'azzami, Engineer Abbas Gozidehpur, Engineer Ahmad Zirakzadeh, Morteza Mosavvar-Rahmani, Dr. Safi Asfiya, Mohsen Khajehnuri, and Jahangir Haqshenas. Later on, Allahyar Saleh, Karim Sanjabi, and Abolfazl Qasemi joined that party."[2]

Regarding the way the Iran Party was established, the idea of the creation of which had been discussed a few days after the announcement of the results of the elections of the 14th National Consultative Assembly, Ahmad Zirakzadeh writes: "In the meeting of the founders of the party, who consisted of about twenty people..., the initial discussion was about the name of the party. The party's name is of significant importance, because the name itself can represent the main beliefs and the basis of the ideology of the party. It can be a pleasing popular slogan that can easily be remembered and its utterance can manifest certain beliefs and ideas in one's mind. In industrial and democratic countries, the name of the party expresses the ideological foundation of the party, and terms such as radical, liberal, democratic, republican, socialist, and even religious adjectives are used in such names. We were, however, quite cognizant that such words would be alien to a large number of people in Iran's environment; hence, they would not have the necessary psychological impact. Words such as motherland and homeland seemed to us to be too elementary and trite. Hence, we chose the name Iran, which was both general and also without any coloration."[3]

In a discussion about the way the Iran Party was formed, mention should be made of the Association of Engineers, which was established in early 1942. A significant number of the influential members of that association, such as Gholamali Farivar, later on assumed an active role in the establishment of the Iran Party. Other figures, such as Mehdi Bazargan, also shared in the creation of the Association of Engineers and were involved in the activities of the Iran Party, even though they did not become members of that party. Seyyed Morteza Moshir also mentions the role of the engineers in the establishment of the Iran Party and writes: "In 1943 or 1944, with the assistance of a number of engineers and other high-ranking educated people, we established the Iran Party and began our activities."[4] Up to this point, the most important action of the Association of Engineers was the organizing of the largest strike, held in May 1943 sometime after the forced abdication of Reza Shah. The reason for the strike was to protest the situation of the salaries and administrative status of the engineers.

One of the characteristics of the Iran Party was its support for Mosaddeq in the course of the shaping of the oil industry nationalization movement and its participation in the National Front. This support continued during the premiership of Mosaddeq, as well, and nearly all the leaders of the party were members of the cabinet. Despite the fact that this party had a central organization in addition to offices in some provincial cities as well as a labor organization and a trade organization in the bazaar, however, this party did not have much of a base among the masses. Lacking a base among the masses, and on the other hand, the participation of the leaders of the party in government organizations and membership in Mosaddeq's cabinet, caused it to be known among its opponents as the "Pawnbrokers Party," in the sense that the Iran Party, more than anything else, was the instrument for advancing the objectives of the notable elite in the parliament and the government, a political party that, with an eclectic interpretation of Islam and socialism, had attracted a number of the young enthusiastic intellectuals who supported social reforms. The Iran Party supported land distribution, economic development, and a government formed on a backdrop of democratic conditions. Efforts toward efficiency and vitality in the bureaucratic system of the country was also one of the main objectives of this party.[5]

References made by Bakhtiar's friends and supporters regarding the manner and the date of his membership in the Iran Party, despite some differences, share certain points. About the way he became acquainted with Shapour Bakhtiar and his membership in the Iran Party, Zirakzadeh writes: "I think it was in 1934 when I saw Bakhtiar for the first time in Paris. He had just arrived in Paris and I was about to leave… He spoke French well… He had an extensive vocabulary, and I, who claimed to know French well, liked this in him, and perhaps he also was fond of me for the same reason. Moreover, we both considered ourselves to be socialists. As a result, we clicked from the first time we met, and for the short time that we were in Paris together, despite the differences in our educational and social environments, we still saw each other a great deal. But I soon left Paris, and we were not in touch anymore. In 1946 or 1947, in the cabinet in which I think Aramesh was the minister of labor, one day I went to see Engineer Habibollah Nafisi, who was the deputy minister in that ministry, and he told me that I should get to know a young man who had just returned from Europe. He made a telephone call and Mr. Shapour Bakhtiar entered the office…

"In our very first meeting, I suggested to him that he become a member of the Iran Party, but I cannot exactly remember when he actually became a member of the party. I know that he was the director of the Department of Labor in Abadan for a while, and he held a similar position in Isfahan, as well, but I remember him mostly from 1949 and onward, when he participated in some of the party district offices and gave speeches; and in the second government of Dr. Mosaddeq, he became the deputy minister of labor after 21 July 1952. But during all that time, until the 19 August 1953 coup d'état, he did not play an important role in the party, and even if he was a distinguished member, he was not one of the leaders."[6i]

Bakhtiar mentions the date of becoming a member of the Iran Party to be in September 1949 and states that he was introduced to the party by Zirakzadeh and Haqshenas, or by Saleh, and received a membership card. Pointing out that he had no role in the establishment of the Iran Party and that he was not involved with the developments that led to the coalition with the Tudeh Party and its consequences, he adds: "I wanted to see which party would be close to my own thinking and beliefs and to join it... And the reason for this was my acquaintance with some of these friends and the respect I had for their friendship and their virtues."[7]

Fereydun Amir-Ebrahimi, who had been a member of the Iran Party since 1944 and was in training as a petrochemical engineer at the Abadan Refinery, regarding Bakhtiar's membership in that party, refers to his assignment in Abadan: "In summer 1949, my sister's husband, Hasan Mo'inpur, was the Military Governor of Abadan; he had a party at his house to which I was also invited. Mo'inpur told me, 'Come, let me introduce you to someone whose head is screwed on pretty much to the left, like yours,' and he introduced me to Shapour Bakhtiar. He shook my hand and said, 'I am Shapour Bakhtiar, not Shah-pur, to mean Prince Bakhtiar.' He always stressed this point. This was the

---

[i] Sanjabi believes that Bakhtiar became a member of the Iran Party "during Mosaddeq's time," which seems to mean during the premiership of Mosaddeq. See: Karim Sanjabi, *Omidha va Naomidiha (Khaterat-e Siyasi)* (London: Jebheh-ye Melliyun-e Iran Publishers, 2007), 196.

beginning of my friendship with Bakhtiar. Our conversation led to political issues and the Iran Party. I asked him, 'Don't you want to join the Iran Party?' Bakhtiar responded, 'I will join the next time I come to Tehran.'" Amir-Ebrahimi adds that he was the one who introduced Bakhtiar to the Iran Party and provided him with a membership form. According to him, Bakhtiar spoke at the meeting of the central committee and was admitted as a member of the party with a majority of votes.[8]

Thus, it is clear that Bakhtiar played no role in the establishment of the Iran Party and the early years of its activities. In the first congress of the party as well, a number of the documents and ratifications of which are available, no mention of Bakhtiar's name can be seen. This was the case until the fourth congress of the party, which was held in December 1951 in Tehran. In that interval, although he had been involved in political party activities for some time, his name does not appear among those of the members of the central committee, the supreme oversight committee, or the adjudication committee of the party, which were the central core and leadership of that party. This was the period when the Iran Party had left behind the difficulties of its early years, when several of its members were among the influential members of the National Front and allies of Mosaddeq, and when it had an impact on the political developments in the country. In the meantime, in its program and policy, the party spoke about the necessity of "Iran's absolute political and economic freedom and decisive and serious struggle against colonialism, feudalism, capitalism, and any type of colonization and subjugation," and expressed its demand for the "establishment of socialism."[9]

Reminiscing about those years, Rahim Sharifi states: "Bakhtiar was an enthusiastic young man, and the young people in the party wanted him to be in charge of the Young People's Organization of the party. For this reason, they came to me, and since I was a member of the central committee, I proposed him for that position. From then on, Bakhtiar was in charge of the Young People's Organization and responsible for the young people's journal of the party, which was called *Javanan-e Sosiyalist*."[10]

The central committee of the party in the meantime decided to establish educational courses called "advanced political party courses" to raise the level of knowledge of the party members. A program was also devised for the participants with the same purpose, which included explanations about issues such as "basic principles of the great policies of the world, political party training, and leadership virtues." Examples of these lessons included "the Soviet Revolution, the French Revolution, short courses on the economy, the Constitution, explanations about the history and beliefs of political parties of Iran and the world, detailed discussions of political party beliefs, the history and organizations of the Iran Party, and facts to know about Iran's history and geography." The list of "professors" who were chosen to teach these political party courses includes Bakhtiar's name as well: "Respected Fellow Party Member, Dr. Bakhtiar. In order to raise the level of the social and political party knowledge of the members, a course is intended to be established. Since a part of these lessons will be conferred on Your Excellency, please come to the office of the party to prepare for the launching of the course and arranging its syllabus at 7 pm on Tuesday, 8 July. Secretary General of the Iran Party, Engineer Ahmad Zirakzadeh."[11]

The Program and Constitution of the Iran Party

The fifth congress of the Iran Party was held in Tehran in early January 1953 and planned its program for the following year as "the year of heroic struggle of the Iran Party against feudalism." Also, in ratifying a resolution, the congress declared its overall support for the struggle that was underway under the leadership of Mosaddeq regarding the issue of oil: "At this time, when the people of Iran are in the final stage of their battle against their old foreign enemy, any opposition to our national hero, Dr. Mosaddeq, is tantamount to treason and the undermining of national unity. We the representatives of the fifth congress of the Iran Party who have assembled from various parts of the country in Tehran hereby declare our support for the continuation of His Excellency's government, and request of the honorable members of the parliament to realize the sensitivity of the occasion and by ratifying the authority of the government, to neutralize the treacherous plot of the enemies." In the course of the continuation of the work of the congress, Karim Sanjabi was elected as the secretary general, and Kazem Hasibi, Ahmad Zirakzadeh, Asghar Gitibin, Abolfazl Qasemi, Rahim Sharifi, and several others were elected to leadership positions in other executive organizations of the party. Shapour Bakhtiar was also elected as a member of the central committee of the Young People's Organization of the party. From then on, his name was placed side by side with the well-known names of the party, such as Sanjabi, Zirakzadeh, Hasibi, Parsa, and Bayani, and mentioned as someone who had spent half of his life in "a free environment and civilization on studying modern social thought," to the point that the organ of the Young People's Organization in the course of the elections for the 17th National Consultative Assembly in 1953 wrote about Bakhtiar in that term: "Our courageous fellow party member went to Abadan and was most warmly welcomed by the patriotic workers of Abadan. Had the elections not been halted in Abadan, the success of our dear friend would have been certain. It is with such confidence that, should the future elections begin, the true candidate of the suffering laborers of the oil-rich regions does not deem it necessary to travel to that province... As acknowledged by friends and enemies—if he had any principled enemies—our learned fellow party member is the most serious, industrious, and compassionate deputy of a ministry that for a long time has seen many occupants in that seat. Now, like a brilliant star, he shines in the sky of the national movement, and it is hoped that he will have a positive impact on the administrative organizations of the country in the interest of the deprived classes of the society, of whom he is one of their staunchest supporters, and add to the proud accomplishments of the Iran Party."[12]

Bakhtiar was gradually becoming one of the influential figures who played a role in shaping the views of the Iran Party. This is evidenced in an article written in opposition to him on the danger of the "Pawnbrokers Agency of the Iran Party," which states: "Sheltered by a few honest and valuable individuals are a large number of fraudulent traitors. Any person who registers in that agency is given an influential position. Dr.

Fallah is also a member of that party, and his secret enquête number, or membership application number, is 139. For the same reason, Dr. Engineer Hasibi defended him in the parliament. Dr. Shapour Bakhtiar, the honorable deputy minister of labor, is also a member of the committee on writing and interpreting the beliefs of the agency, and his enquête number is 418."[13]

The Iran Party had established the basis for its political, economic, and social activities and ideology on three principles: "Protection of the absolute independence of the country and support for democratic principles, the establishment of social justice and efforts to improve the material situation of the people through paying attention to agriculture and industry and use of all the rich resources of the country, the refinement of ethics, the propagation of culture, and securing public health." By publishing a statement in defense of "democracy, independence, and freedom," this party declared its opposition to "dictatorship by individuals and minorities who sacrifice the demands of the majority for those of an individual or a minority." It also condemned "dictatorship of a majority that impedes the expression of the demands of the minority." It stated: "Where there is no democracy, independence will not last. Where there is no independence, a democratic government will never materialize. The independence of nondemocratic governments will not perpetuate, since in such governments, progress and advancement do not exist for individuals, and these two reasons keep people discontented and weak… Lack of people's contentment always threatens the ruling class, and a government that has no domestic support will be forced to rely on foreigners to maintain its rule, sacrificing the country's independence for the survival of its rule. Hence, a nation that does not have a democratic government will not have independence, and, on the other hand, a nation that is dominated by foreign governments will never be able to make its government democratic, since a democratic government pursues the wishes of its people, whereas the duty of dependent governments is to carry out the orders and instructions of the foreign government. A government that relies on foreigners must take foreign interests and wishes into consideration, in which case, it cannot be democratic."[14]

An examination of other evidence, documents and statements that are available regarding the ideology and program of the Iran Party shows that this organization, as a group that had organized a number of the intellectuals and educated people within itself, was a nationalist group that adhered to the foundations of the regime of constitutional monarchy and emphasized socialist ideas and thoughts, the type of socialism based on independence, freedom, and lack of dependence on world powers; and it insisted on social democratic principles. Regarding the formation of the Iran Party in the early years of its activities and the positions of other political parties and groups, Bakhtiar states: "When the Iran Party was established, I was a student in Europe... It was made up of individuals who were mostly educated in France... At that time, the Iran Party consisted of a group of the elite and chosen individuals who had studied in Europe or a number of people who had gathered around them, since they sympathized with them and because of the way they thought... The people that I knew, and I say that they were social democrats and nationalists, they gathered around the Iran Party. More radical individuals and some who later became very patriotic gathered around the Tudeh Party. Because of the very precise political training that they were given, and since their leaders had experienced imprisonment, and one should not deny the very clear presence and support for them by the Soviet Union, a number of Iranian intellectuals had also gathered around the Tudeh Party... Regarding the Iran Party, I can say that it represented the thinking of the people who were mostly petit bourgeois intellectuals with nationalist tendencies. They wanted Iran's freedom and independence, but they did not have the experience and orderly and cohesive organization that the Tudeh Party had. For this reason, the Iran Party never became the party of the masses of the people. In terms of quality, patriotism, and democratic attitude, this group had a higher social status than the type of organization that could attract the so-called poor classes of the people."[15]

The description offered by Bakhtiar regarding the position and view-points of the Iran Party is based on the realities of the life of that organization, even though in each of its members we see contradictions and sometimes confusion in their political plan and program as well as their social opinions and beliefs. We find an example of such contradictions and confusion in an article by Abolqasem Zirakzadeh entitled "The Iran Party and Social Classes," published in the organ of that organization, in which he states: "The Iran Party basically repudiates the existence of social classes in the form that they exist in some European and American countries, and in Iran, it only recognizes one class, which is the same downtrodden and stunted people of Iran. The Iran Party believes that the people of Iran are divided into two parts. One group is comprised of nearly a hundred percent of the Iranian society and lacks any right to live, and in contrast to them, there is a small group of people whose number does not exceed a few thousand and who have taken possession of the fruits of the labor of 15 million of the Iranian people. The Iran Party does not consider this group of a few thousand people to be a social class, and it essentially does not count them as the Iranian people... The Iran Party relies on this mass of 15 million people who are all in one social class, which can be called the deprived class... It is the same deprived class that is the backing of the Iran Party."[16]

To justify his reasoning, the author of the abovementioned article refers to the small number of Iranian workers, whose number he considers to be 100,000, and addresses the hardships that essentially existed in determining and describing various social classes, especially in the formation of classes in Iran. Pointing out the differences between Iran and advanced industrial societies and their effect on the formation of social classes is an issue to which attention was paid in order to avoid generalizations and cliché interpretations in the party's plan and program, without any of these intending to prove the correctness of the outlook that the Iran Party offered about the formation of social classes and the concept of nation and its rights. A strange example of such an outlook can be found in the opposition of the Iran Party to a "recommendation" made by Qavam's government for the signing of an agreement with the Azerbaijan Democrat Party regarding the teaching of the Turkish language in Azerbaijan schools. According to the functionaries of the Iran Party, no measure would be more effective for dividing Iran than "recommendations regarding the use of the languages of the minorities, such as Arabic, Kurdish, Turkish, and so on."[17]

Another issue concerned the requirements for membership in the Iran Party. Applicants were required to be Iranian and Moslem, and not "to be known for moral corruption and treason to the country." Other conditions included not being a member other political parties or groups and being at least eighteen years of age.[18] The constitution of the party does not provide any explanation about being "known for moral corruption and treason to the country." Had "moral corruption" and "treason to the country" by the applicant for membership in the Iran Party been contingent upon proof in a proper court, one could perhaps express an opinion about this paragraph more easily, but such a statement, with the flexible and ambiguous term of being "known" for one charge or another, especially with regard to membership in the party, is indicative of lack of clarity in this connection. The second paragraph of the requirements for membership, in other words, for the applicant to be a Moslem, is similar, and it could be viewed as indicating discrimination among individuals who were Iranian nationals and wanted to become a member of the party without being Moslem. It is not clear why a party that repudiated various class differences and interests among the people of Iran would discriminate between Moslem and non-Moslem Iranians.

Later on, in its first congress, which was held in April 1948 in Tehran, by changing a paragraph in its constitution, the Iran Party amended its requirements for membership as follows: "Anyone who accepts the ideology of the Iran Party and meets the following requirements may become a member of the Iran Party: (a) being Iranian and a subject of the Iranian government; (b) being a Moslem or a Zoroastrian; (c) having a good past record."[19]

In his memoir, enumerating the views of the Iran Party and the split that occurred in it, regarding the requirements for membership in the party, Karim Sanjabi states: "The Iran Party, which was active in the Islamic society of Iran, was cognizant that one basic pillar of our identity is being Islamic. We did not, however, believe that a non-Moslem Iranian could not participate in the party, and several Zoroastrians were members of our party; and we saw no impediment to Zoroastrians, Armenian Christians, or any other Iranians in terms of their religious beliefs becoming members of the party. We all, however, had respect for Islamic principles."[20] This claim about the requirements for membership in the Iran Party, however, is true only regarding Moslem and Zoroastrian Iranians, and not the followers of other religions. To prove his claim, which contradicts the ratified constitution in the first congress of the party, Sanjabi makes no reference to this or any other ratification to verify the accuracy of his statements.

Regarding the way the Iran Party was established, another issue must also be pointed out. Shortly after the creation of the party, several personalities such as Allahyar Saleh as well as the Forest Party (Hezb-e Jangal), which was active in Gilan, joined that party; but the most important coalition that took place was when the Motherland Party (Hezb-e Mihan) joined it. Following the splits that had occurred in it, the Motherland Party was becoming weaker. Sanjabi, the leader of the Motherland Party, considers the reason for joining the Iran Party to be the shared positions and ideals as well as the "unpleasant financial situation" of the Motherland Party: "We issued instructions for all of our branches in the provinces to join the Iran Party, and a group of the members of the Motherland Party became members of the committee and council of the Iran Party, including myself, who became a member of the committee of the Iran Party from that time."[21]

An important point in the political program of the Iran Party was support for workers and peasants and the struggle for social justice and fair distribution of wealth. In its program, the Iran Party considered this possible by increasing the share of labor proportionate to the share of capital and regarded its implementation as a way to prevent exploitation.

Propagation of culture, refinement of ethics, and attention to public health were considered other grounds for advancing the goals of the party. The Motherland Party also had limitations on the "ownership of farmland" and "strengthening" the farmers among the principles of its constitution. The constitution of that party also emphasized that "order in production and fairness in the distribution of wealth" must be the basis for the Iranian economy. The Motherland Party considered its goal to be the creation of "a great Iran" based on "strong party rule" that had the support of the people. The notion of the "refinement of ethics" in the program of the Iran Party also existed in more detail in the constitution of the Motherland Party: "The true principles of religious faith that strengthen the foundations of ethics and piety must be propagated, and religion must be cleansed of the superstitious and delusory beliefs with which it is intermingled."[22] The requirement for membership in the Motherland Party echoes similar sentiments: "Article 62. An applicant who is accepted as a member of the party must take an oath of loyalty to the ideology of the Motherland Party." The text of the oath is as follows: "I ask Almighty God as my witness and swear on the holy Koran and the sacred flag of Iran to be loyal to the ideology of the party and to perform the duties that are conferred on me within the boundaries of the regulations of the party most honestly, seriously, and with effort and belief, and to strive for the advancement of the ideology of the party."[23] This was the outlook of Sanjabi and the Motherland Party when they joined the Iran Party.

With a cursory look at the constitutions, programs, and ratifications of the Iran Party and the Motherland Party, which announced their unification in April 1946 in a published statement, we come across important issues regarding two essential points in the views of both parties about social justice and the issue of religion.

Concerning social justice, the program of the Iran Party in connection with the distribution of wealth and its support for the rights of workers and farmers, more than being based on an analysis of Iran's political and economic situation, was based on generalities and hasty assessments. In the statements and ratifications of the Iran Party and the Motherland

Party, we do not find any explanation about how the programs of the party can begin and be carried out, especially given the chaotic situation of the Iranian economy. The truth is that both parties, incapable of preparing and offering a comprehensive plan for the step-by-step advancement of extensive economic reforms, had based their plans for improving the situation of the poor in the society on taciturn and malleable slogans and phrases, such as "breaking asunder the front of money, force, and treason," to the point that, ultimately, despite their ambitious claims, they did not offer any solution to move beyond backwardness and to what was called the "government of welfare." The Iran Party emphasized the necessity of improving the condition of the laborers and the propagation of culture, and it considered itself the supporter of some sort of socialism that was remote from Russian Marxism and could be achieved in a democratic environment. Such socialism, however, more than anything else, relied on hopes and wishes that, despite avoiding dependence on the Soviet Union, at times in speeches and reasoning was a repetition of the same issues for which the Tudeh Party was considered to be the proselytizer and propagator.

Considering the increasing influence of the Tudeh Party among the intellectuals and workers in the society, socialism was viewed as a very important alternative from the perspective of that party. The Iran Party, however, was entangled in the coils of such moral considerations as "piety" and "nobility," and it disregarded the element of secularity as one of the major guideposts of such socialism. It was perhaps for this reason that Mehdi Bazargan was often invited as a speaker to explain his views about "spirituality and moral piety" to the members of the party.

Accordingly, Ahmad Zirakzadeh, one of the founders and the chief editor of *Jebheh-ye Azadi* journal, the central organ of the party, would "open the congress in the glorious name of God," and Allahyar Saleh, emphasizing that he had "always been a true socialist" and would continue to be, in the course of the first congress of the party said: "I seek assistance from God and ask God to grant me success in uttering all that I have in my heart."[24]

Other contradictions can also be found in the program of the Iran
Party in regard to the path and policy it pursued. At times, distinguished
personalities of the party such as Allahyar Saleh considered respect for
the Constitution and its implementation the solution to many of the
problems of the country and insisted on the principles of constitutionalism, and at times the central committee of the party by publishing a
resolution would demand the "establishment of special national courts
with the right to issue the final verdict for the arrest and the prevention
of the flight of all suspicious individuals and their urgent trials," a
measure that was intended to "save the homeland," and warned that if
no attention is paid to the matter, this time, the party would "take direct
steps by any means possible."[25]

The issue of religion and the role of the religious in the society were
among the issues that were of special importance in the approach of the
Iran Party to the ongoing developments. In this arena, the picture that
Saleh presented of constitutionalism was worthy of great pause. In
August 1961, in an affirming response to the letter of Ayatollah Behbahani who was persuading the National Front to avoid holding a demon-
stration for the reopening of the parliament, addressing him, he wrote:
"You will agree that it will not be tolerable for the Iranian people to halt
or to shut down the implementation of the Constitution, which contains the religious and national rights of the Moslem people of Iran and
the rights of freedom and is the result of the efforts the two Grand
Seyyeds, God's mercy upon them... No doubt exists that at this time,
the preservation of the true religion and the protection of independence
and freedom is not possible except by creating national unity and the
true constitutional government which has been abolished for many
years."[26]

But did the Constitution only contain "the religious and national
rights of the Moslem people," and was it the result of the efforts of the
"two Grand Seyyeds," and did the efforts of others, from Seyyed Hasan
Taqizadeh and Mohammad Ali Khan Tarbiyat to the members of the
secret associations, the businessmen and bazaar merchants, the well-
known intellectuals, and the secular reformists, or the Armenian and

Georgian revolutionaries, not have anything to do with it? Was disregarding the efforts of those who sacrificed their lives with a secular viewpoint on the path of the Constitution and freedom acceptable, and was such a definition of the Constitution, and for that matter from the mouth of a person who called himself a socialist, realistic?

In the same vein, shortly after the forced abdication of Reza Shah, when the clerics were dreaming about retaking their lost strongholds, Allahyar Saleh had begun a new attack on secular rights and values. In an article entitled "How Can Social Justice be Established in Iran?" he wrote: "Before anything beneficial is done in Iran, we must try to reform the ruling power and refine the ethics of those who implement the law and other people in the country; and doing so by observing the principles and common arrangements is a very difficult task and will require a very long time, for which we might not have the opportunity, given the current situation of the world. Nevertheless, it is the duty of the religiously faithful speakers and writers of the society, such as Mr. Rashed and others, not to stop preaching and giving advice, and to lead the people toward God's commandments and the true Islamic teachings. By the will of God, perhaps once again a path to saving this country might be found."[27] It was as though for Saleh, the cure to the ailment was only in the capable hands of the proselytizers of religion and by their preaching and advice, those who by the will of God were given the duty of guiding the people to achieve social justice. Parenthetically, some thirty-five years after the publication of the abovementioned article, on 1 April 1979, leaning on the arm of his old National Front fellow combatant, Daryush Foruhar, Saleh participated in the fateful referendum that would make the rule of the clerics and the functionaries of religion official in Iran, the rule of those who regarded themselves to be the representatives of "God's commandments and the true Islamic teachings," and who would take the reins of power with the cooperation of the supporters and followers of Mosaddeq and the support of the Tudeh Party.

In June 1946, after the Iran Party held its elections, the political group of the central committee of the party, comprised of Saleh, Farivar,

Sanjabi, Zirakzadeh, and Sadeqi, took over its leadership and the opponents of the coalition with the Tudeh Party were expelled. In his memoir, regarding the split in the Iran Party, Sanjabi states: "Mr. Nakhshab along with a group of his friends, such as Hoseyn Razi, Dr. Sami, Habibollah Peyman, and others, perhaps about sixty or seventy people, came and joined the Iran Party... At that time, they had a great deal of contact with Ayatollah Kashani, and they presented themselves as being very religious... Nakhshab's supporters used religion, which no one opposed or objected to, as a pretext and began to create disputes within the party, and finally, they left the party."[28] In his memoir, Hoseyn Makki writes about himself and Arsalan Khal'atbari, Mohsen Khajehnuri, and Mosavvar-Rahmani leaving the party and states that the reason for leaving was the coalition of the Iran Party with the Tudeh Party.[29] Rasul Mehraban writes: "The coalition of the Iran Party and the Tudeh Party of Iran caused supporting and opposing arguments within the party, and a large group resigned from the party. The well-known figures who were expelled from the party by the order of the central committee included Dr. Shamseddin Jazayeri, Hoseyn Makki, Arsalan Khal'atbari, and Engineer Mehdi Bazargan.[ii] The central committee of the party also issued an announcement expelling Ali Reza Saheb, Farajollah Baghi, Mohammad Nakhshab, Zarrabi, and Ja'far Shahidi from the party. Sadeqi, a member of the central committee of the political group, also resigned."[30]

Coalition with the Tudeh Party and the Azerbaijan Issue

One month later, with the publication of the six-point announcement about the coalition between the Iran Party and the Tudeh Party, the efforts that had been made since sometime earlier for close cooperation between the two parties came to fruition. This was a step the preparations for which were made in the negotiations and with the coordina-

---

[ii] Although Mehdi Bazargan confirms having cooperated with the Iran Party, he denies having been a member of that party. See: *Shast Sal Khedmat va Moqavemat, Khaterat-e Bazargan, Goft-o Gu ba Sarhang Golamreza Nejati* (Tehran: Khadamat-e Farhangi-ye Rasa, 1996), 198-199; Sanjabi, *Omidha va Naomidiha*, 198-199.

tion among the Association of Engineers, or the Central Council of Engineers, and its technical employees regarding a coalition and had resulted in the establishment of the workers and toilers unions in May 1946. Shortly afterward, the Azerbaijan Democrat Party, the Kurdestan Democrat Party, the Socialist Party, and the central committee of the Forest Party also joined this coalition, which was called the Coalition Front of Freedom Parties (Jebheh-ye Mo'talef-e Ahzab-e Azadikhah).

The most important effect of the formation of the Coalition Front of Freedom Parties on the policy of the Iran Party was its support for the Azerbaijan Democrat Party and the coalition government of Qavam. Attending a banquet that the Tudeh Party had arranged for the delegation of the Azerbaijan Democrat Party in Tehran, representing the central committee of the Iran Party, in his speech, Allahyar Saleh said: "The progressive Iran Party from the very beginning has embraced the Azerbaijan movement with much joy and hope. Our joy and hope was because of our confidence in those who managed this movement. Now, no more than a year later, we see that our expression of trust and confidence was not for naught... When our freedom-seeking comrades in Azerbaijan began the movement and said that they intended to carry out reforms, we were confident, because this was uttered by individuals such as Mr. Ja'far Pishehvari, who has spent all his life on the path of freedom, and has never in his life uttered a word in exaggeration. The same is true of his other comrades... So, we were right to trust such individuals. They banned opium and established a university. They eliminated embezzlement and bribery, and created safety and security throughout Azerbaijan. Today, Azerbaijan is one of the safest parts of the country. Mr. Padegan as well as other leaders of the Azerbaijan Democrat Party are examples and models of patriotism, bravery, and piety. A number of the enemies of freedom tried to create certain misunderstandings regarding the inclinations of the Azerbaijan Democrat Party in the eyes of the supporters of freedom and the world. It serves them right that when the pro-freedom government under the premiership of His Eminence Mr. Qavamossaltaneh came to power and extended a hand of friendship to all of them, they shook that hand most sincerely and showed the beloved head of the government and the people of Iran that Azerbaijan wants the progress, independence, and territorial integrity of Iran. I conclude my words with the following mottos. Long live His Eminence Mr. Qavamossaltaneh, the beloved leader of the Democrat Party of Iran and the honorable head of the government. Long live the Azerbaijan Democrat Party. Let the Coalition Front of Freedom Parties be everlastingly and progressive."[31]

One of the basic problems of the Iran Party in its defense of the Azerbaijan Democrat Party was the latter's dependence on the Soviet Union and objections to this issue in the political circles. This fact, especially after the unrests that had occurred in Fars, would force the Iran Party to find some justification for its policy.

In the second half of August 1946, with the publication of the statement of the "Resistance Movement of the South," a new chapter opened in the rapid ongoing developments. Sometime after the signing of the agreement between Firuz and Pishehvari, the representatives of the central government and the Azerbaijan Democrat Party, on 4 April 1946, the Arabs in Khuzestan also demanded autonomy. In addition, the leaders of the Bakhtiari tribe signed an agreement and announced their opposition to the policy of Qavam's government regarding the Tudeh Party. They were of the opinion that a similar agreement to the one that had been signed between the central government and the Azerbaijan Democrat Party needed to also be implemented in the south. The leaders of the Fars tribes also demanded the expulsion of the Tudeh Party ministers from Qavam's cabinet, an increase in the number of representatives from Fars Province in the National Consultative Assembly, and the government's attention to the development and increase in the budget for the implementation of the infrastructural, cultural, and health-related projects of Fars Province. Before long, Bushehr, Kazerun, Abadeh, and a number of the coastal cities in the south were occupied by the tribes, and Shiraz was on the verge of collapse.

The crisis situation of the country that had assumed widespread dimensions with the rebellion in the south pushed the Azerbaijan issue to the top of the list of current problems. Expressions of opinion by the leaders of the Iran Party and the various positions taken by the organs of that party about the issue showed the high degree of its sensitivity. In its published articles, *Jebheh*, the organ of the Iran Party, regarded the issue of Soviet support for the Azerbaijan Democrat Party to be completely different from all that was occurring in Fars, and emphasized that the Soviets' aid to the Azerbaijan Democrat Party should not be considered the same as the British aid to the Qashqa'i tribe. Rather, one needed to take the nature of such assistance into consideration before making a judgment. Another reckoning by the Iran Party was based on the general belief and common conjecture that in the course of the Constitutional Revolution, the constitutionalists had benefitted from the financial and military assistance of England. Hence, should one stop praise of constitutionalism and the memory of those who lost their lives for it? Thus, the relationship with and receiving aid from a foreign government should not be the criterion for judging a social movement; rather, one must look at its nature.

For the Iran Party, the difference between the events in Azerbaijan and the occurrences in Fars was a fundamental difference, indicative of a policy "one part of which relied on the masses, and the other on the landowners and influential individuals." In addition, "one part moved people toward progress and strength, and the other kept them in misfortune, poverty, and opium addiction." The Iran Party referred to the leaders of the Azerbaijan Democrat Party as "freedom fighters and old strugglers," most of whom were people of "virtue and knowledge" in whose "honesty and integrity" not even the enemies of the movement had any doubt. In contrast, the leaders of events in Fars were from among those who "up to yesterday were the source of insecurity, murder, plunder, and poverty" of their own people. Thus, the party announced that from the beginning of the creation of the "Azerbaijan movement," it had pursued a policy of support for it: "Our policy regarding Azerbaijan has been to try with all our might to link this movement to other freedom movements and establish strong ties between a democratic Azerbaijan and other parts of Iran."[32]

In December 1946, once the Soviet Union had withdrawn its support, the Azerbaijan Democrat Party collapsed without any significant resistance to the military forces of the central government. Shortly before that, by reshuffling his cabinet, Qavam had dismissed the Tudeh Party ministers. The efforts of Allahyar Saleh, who served as the minister of justice in the coalition cabinet, representing the Iran Party, to mediate between Qavam and the Tudeh Party ministers failed.

With the reshuffling of the cabinet followed by the collapse of the Azerbaijan Democrat Party, which meant a clear turn to the right in government policy, rumors spread that Qavam's goal in forming the coalition cabinet had been to deceive his allies and sacrifice them. Even though this policy as part of a set of other initiatives ultimately had achieved its goal by resolving the Azerbaijan crisis, it inflicted a harsh blow to the prestige and credibility of the Tudeh Party and the Iran Party. The difference was that, while the Tudeh Party was criticized for having participated in Qavam's cabinet, the Iran Party was in principle called to account for its participation in the Coalition Front of Freedom Parties. In a look at the past, assessing the events that had occurred in this connection, Zirakzadeh wrote: "At any rate, the coalition caused a lot of problems, the worst of which was dragging us into the Azerbaijan Democrat Party story. We were forced to claim that the Azerbaijan Democrat Party was not a local political party, that its ideas and beliefs were a prelude to the struggle against despotism and for helping all the people of Iran. We said that the Azerbaijan Democrat Party was by no means trying to partition Azerbaijan from Iran... We continue to consider the Azerbaijan Democrat Party the vanguard of the freedom fighters of Iran and its operations a prelude to the establishment of true democracy throughout Iran, and declare its local aspect to be tactical and temporary."[33]

Following the collapse of the coalition cabinet and the policy that Qavam pursued in his confrontation with the left, the cautious criticism of Qavam by the Iran Party also intensified. With the approaching elections of the 15th National Consultative Assembly in 1946 and the clear interferences by Qavam's Democrat Party in the elections, the

Tudeh Party and the Iran Party distanced themselves from him more than ever before. The use of extensive government resources for specifying certain individuals as candidates for the election and exerting influence in the voting districts pushed the cautious criticisms into open clashes and confrontation between Qavam's "government party" and his allies of yesterday, to the point that the issue of refusing to participate in the elections in protest to interferences by the government was discussed and debated in the party and its publications. The leadership of the Iran Party, however, while objecting to everything that was happening, insisted on the need for participation in the elections in order to protect the rights of the people.

Simultaneous with the start of the election campaigns in order to mobilize public opinion and encourage the people to participate in the elections, efforts were also made to make use of legal resources by meeting with government officials and the Central Election Oversight Association. In these efforts, the process of the elections in Tehran and the provincial cities was considered to be a violation of the law and disregard for the rights of the people, and demands were made for immediate revision. In its election campaign, the Iran Party announced that, despite all the restrictions imposed and the disruptions by the government, it would not give up identifying its candidates in Tehran and the provincial cities in its fight to occupy the parliamentary seats. Allahyar Saleh, the former minister of justice; Ahmad Zirakzadeh, university professor and editor of *Jebheh* newspaper, the central organ of the Iran Party; Gholamali Farivar, the former parliamentary representative; and Karim Sanjabi, university professor, were the candidates of the party for the 15th Parliamentary elections.

In April 1948, the first congress of the Iran Party was held in Tehran and examined the issue of the coalition. By presenting the report of the central committee to the representatives in the congress, Zirakzadeh, the secretary of the central committee, criticized the coalition. Other speakers such as Karim Sanjabi, a member of the central committee, and Mohammad Tavassoli, the secretary of the congress, who later on after the Islamic Revolution became the Mayor of Tehran, rose in criticism of the coalition with the Azerbaijan Democrat Party and assessed it as an improper action. As the president of the central committee of the party, Saleh criticized this policy, and referring to his enthusiastic speech at the banquet that the Tudeh Party had arranged to welcome the members of the delegation of the Azerbaijan Democrat Party to Tehran, he said: "We brought the representatives of Azerbaijan, so that they would not talk about autonomy and about the nation of Azerbaijan, and told them that if they truly want freedom and reforms, they should want them for all the people of Iran, and it was because of our persistent and repeated reminders that they modified their ways. In an official meeting, Dr. Javid (a member of the delegation of the Azerbaijan Democrat Party for negotiations with the central government), with tearful eyes, stood up and said, 'We have taken an oath on the holy Koran to sacrifice for the independence and freedom of Iran.' If I expressed certain statements when the Azerbaijan representatives were our guests that have been misused by our enemies and opponents, they were because of the expression of such sentiments. Later, however, contrary to what we anticipated, the situation was revealed, and I realized my great mistake. I offered to my political party comrades that with an official communiqué Saleh be expelled from the party on the charge of being the original cause of the coalition. I believed that mistakes require punishment. For the survival of the Iran Party, I considered being sacrificed to be necessary, and I offered myself. To protect its dignity, France sacrificed its great general, Marshal Pétain, and such a sacrifice was necessary for the Iran Party. But our party comrades did not accept my offer."[34]

Saleh's reasoning to justify the coalition and the policy that the Iran Party pursued regarding the Azerbaijan Democrat Party does not seem sound. In the same vein, the role that he believed the Iran Party played in modifying the policies of the Azerbaijan Democrat Party is not realistic. Any modification in the policies of the Azerbaijan Democrat Party, more than anything else, was the result of Soviet pressure on the leader of that party to go along with the central government in addition to the diplomatic efforts of Qavam in the way he confronted the Azerbaijan crisis. Naturally, from a more general perspective, any success in making that party retreat from its demand of autonomy or modifying anything that was in conflict with Iran's interests should be included in the report card and records of the Iran Party. As one of the parties that participated in Qavam's government, the Iran Party shared in both its victories and its defeats, and the resolving of the Azerbaijan crisis was considered a great victory for it. In a more scrutinizing look, however, it must be pointed out that the avoidance of the leaders of the Azerbaijan Democrat Party in insisting on the issue of the autonomy of Azerbaijan was not due to the efforts of the Iran Party, but the outcome of Qavam's diplomacy and Soviet intervention to convince the leaders in Azerbaijan to go along with the government, a policy that had been advanced in particular in the course of the negotiations of the central government with the representatives of the Azerbaijan Democrat Party in Tehran and Tabriz, and the agreement that was ultimately signed between Qavam and Soviet Ambassador Ivan Sadchikov in March 1946. In his speech at the congress, Saleh kept silent regarding this issue; but more important than that was his reasoning about the Iran Party's trust in the Azerbaijan Democrat Party and the justification of his own behavior, a simpleminded trust in the oath of Salamollah Javid on the Koran, which apparently had resulted in his being misled about the main goal of the Azerbaijan Democrat Party and the policy it pursued.

Firstly, from the perspective of Javid and a number of other leaders of the Azerbaijan Democrat Party, sacrificing for "Iran's independence and freedom" was not in contradiction with the autonomy of Azerbaijan, such that it would impede his taking an oath on the Koran. More important was Saleh's simplemindedness in trusting the promise that Javid had given him with such an oath. All the policies of the Azerbaijan Democrat Party indicated that, as an instrument in the hands of Moscow, they served to advance Soviet policy, and they hoped to partition Azerbaijan from Iran with a thousand and one ruses. Lack of attention to this fact, especially by reliance on Javid's oath, was tantamount to lack of attention to the alphabet of political struggle. In fact, in order to evaluate the approach of Saleh to politics in more general terms, one must emphasize a more fundamental point. With a moral and religious

Sardar Fateh, Mohammad Reza
Khan Bakhtiari, Shapour's father.

Photograph of a young Bakhtiar
with his cousin Teymour. Shapour
is standing on the very right.
Teymour is on the top left. Other
two persons are not identified.

Family photo: Shapour Bakhtiar and Madlaine
Hevro (middle row) France, (front row, left to right)
Viviane, Patrick, and Guy.

Shapour Bakhtiar during his years as a student in
Paris.

The apartment on Rue de L'Assompton in the sixteenth arrondissement of Paris where Bakhtiar lived during his student days.

Bakhtiar and members of the Iran Party.

Bakhtiar with members of the National Front.

Group photo from a meeting of the National Front. In addition to Bakhtiar, Alahyar Saleh, Kazem Hasibi, Karim Sanjabi can be seen.

Bakhtiar at the memorial service in Ahmadabad after the passing of Mosadeq.

Group photo at a meeting of the Second National Front. Among the persons in the picture: Karim Sanjabi, Gholam-Hossein Sadighi, Mehdi Azar, Shapour Bakhtiar, Mohammad Ali Keshavarz Sadr, Ebrahim Karimabadi, Ghasem Ghani, Hasan Shamshiri, Darioush Forouhar and Abdol-Ali Adib Boroumand.

Bakhtiar and members of the Iran Party. Asghar Parsa, Dr. Bijan and Mohammad-Ali Khonji are in this photograph taken in 1949.

Bakhtiar in the National Consultative Assembly January 1979.

Press conference on January 6, 1979 at Bakhtiar's residence in the Farmanieh neighborhood of Tehran. He presented his cabinet to the Shah the next day.

Niavaran Palace, January 7, 1979. Bakhtiar presents his cabinet to the Shah.

Niavaran Palace, January 7, 1979. Bakhtiar presents his cabinet to the Shah.

Speaking to the parliament after being confirmed as prime minister.

Bakhtiar posing with a photograph of former prime minister, Mohammad Mosadeq.

Probably taken outside his residence in the Farmanieh neigborhood of Tehran.

Shaking hands with one of his security detail outside his residence.

January 16, 1979. Bakhtiar escorts the Shah and queen on their final departure from Iran.

From left to right, Mohammad Moshiri-Yazdi, Shapour Bakhtiar, Abbas-Gholi Bakhtiar and Amir-Reza Il-Beygi.

Bakhtiar with British member of parliament and leader of the Liberal Party, David Steel and Roy Jenkins, British labour politician,who at that time was President of the European Commission.

Bakhtiar in his residential villa in Suresnes, a Paris suburb.

Bakhtiar's second wife, Shahintaj escorted by his son, Giv at Bakhtiar's grave site at Montparnasse Cemetery in Paris.

Bakhtiar with three of his children.

Photograph of Bakhtiar, taken a few days before his assassination.

Bakhtiar's grave at Montparnasse Cemetery, Paris.

reference, Saleh was justifying an error, which ultimately required secular reasoning. Saleh's error was that his assessment of the true nature of the Azerbaijan Democrat Party should have been made through an evaluation of the specific policies of that party and the reaction of the Iran Party. Instead, however, he raised the issue of Javid's oath on the Koran, and by relying on the religious sentiments of the representatives in the congress, he assessed the error, which more than anything else required another type of analysis and examination based on recognized secular criteria in politics. Saleh's mention of the point that "mistakes require punishment" was also devoid of any earnestness, since he said that "for the survival of the Iran Party," he was ready to be "sacrificed," whereas if an error had been committed and a mistake made, speaking about "sacrifice" would be meaningless; rather, as the president of the central committee of the party, he would have to accept responsibility for everything that had occurred under his watch. All his reasoning and conclusions indicate that instead of accepting responsibility for the "mistake" he had admitted to making, to which in any case he confessed, he was trying to gain sympathy for himself, and for that matter, by relying on the religious sentiments of the representatives in the congress, representatives whose silence in reaction to the issues that Saleh raised indicated that they apparently followed that same path.

At any rate, the participation of the Iran Party in Qavam's cabinet was recorded as a negative experience in the history of that party, whereas this action was of special significance as an important experience in the age of constitutionalism. Participation in a coalition cabinet, despite all its weaknesses and deficiencies, meant the acceptance of the principle that democracy is not possible without cooperation and collaboration among the social parties, and for that matter, parties that are ready to agree on a shared program, parties that while retaining their independence and emphasizing their differences are willing to fight for the implementation of a specific program. The affirmative response of the Iran Party and the Tudeh Party to Qavam's invitation to participate in the coalition cabinet meant their understanding of this fact.

Insisting on the differences in the views of the Iran Party and those of
the Tudeh Party and Qavam's Democrat Party, in his memoir,
Zirakzadeh points to an example of such cooperation: "Qavamossaltaneh's coalition cabinet, in which Allahyar Saleh participated on behalf of
the Iran Party, and in particular the joining of Qavamossaltaneh's
Democrat Party to that coalition, made our existence as a party separate
from that of the Tudeh Party more clear day by day, particularly since
our approach to the events and our interpretation of them were not the
same as those of the Tudeh Party. We neither insisted on praising His
Eminence (Qavamossaltaneh), nor did we engage in hyperbole in
supporting the Azerbaijan Democrat Party, as did the Tudeh Party. We
protested the arrests, even the arrests of our opponents, such as Seyyed
Ziya'oddin Tabataba'i and Jamal Emami, and when they were done
autocratically and without trials, we referred to them as evidence of the
absence of the implementation of justice. We continually supported Dr.
Mosaddeq and his opposition to the oil concession, and we supported
his efforts in preventing any concession to foreigners."[35]

In the meantime, trying to turn away from a fragile coalition with
Qavam's Democrat Party and the Azerbaijan Democrat Party, the Iran
Party was pursuing a new policy. At this interval, with his membership
in the party, Bakhtiar began to solidify his position in the Young
People's Organization. Years later, about the coalition and the "damages" to the Iran Party because of it, he said: "When I joined the party
in 1949, that woeful story of the coalition with the Tudeh Party had
occurred, and after a while, there had been a separation and the Iran
Party no longer had any relationship with the Tudeh Party. I should also
point out that that coalition was with the provocation of Mr. Farivar,
who later became Mr. Khomeyni's ambassador to Bern and is now a
wanderer somewhere in southern France, by taking advantage of the
weakness of Mr. Sanjabi and the lack of knowledge of Mr. Allahyar
Saleh, since these three were the signatories to the coalition document
and the operators of the Iran Party. This inflicted great damage to the
Iran Party, which happened before I had joined the party. I say this
from the perspective that it greatly weakened the party's nationalist

label… Then, one of those gentlemen, Mr. Saleh, according to friends, went and cried and said that he wanted to be punished; Mr. Sanjabi stepped aside for a while; and Mr. Farivar from that day on was not in the Iran Party anymore, not in the National Front, and occasionally flirted with the Tudeh Party members, and also occasionally, as we saw, flirted with Amini and became a minister in his cabinet. So, when I joined, the Iran Party was on the decline, and they would not give any promises to anyone there. I wanted to make use of this luxury ship that was moving on the tumultuous ocean of Iran. I tried to turn it back to the social democratic state that it used to have and put it in motion, without making any claim that we were very weak in terms of the strength of the organization. I joined the Iran Party in 1949, and a while later, in about six months, I became the president of the Young People's Organization."[36]

Bakhtiar and the Young People's Organization of the Iran Party

The Young People's Organization of the party, of the central committee of which Bakhtiar was a member, had set its goal as "fighting on the path of establishing socialism," with the motto, "the socialism of the Iran Party will guarantee the prosperity of the people of Iran," regarded the only path to rescue the society from poverty and injustice to be moderation and independence. That organization considered itself a follower of the French school of socialism, and in contrast to Russian socialism, it emphasized civilization, culture, freedom, and social justice. "Neither the so-called socialist Soviet Union nor the plundering force of the United States and England will be able to free our nation. Rather, only the struggle of the justice-seeking young people of our nation will bring a prosperous life to our country."[37]

On this basis, the organ of that organization, *Javanan-e Sosiyalist*, by publishing a series of articles explaining the structure and the political and organizational programs of conservative, progressive, and revolutionary political parties, critiqued the weak and strong points of the conservative and revolutionary parties and defended the European socialist parties. The latter were described as parties that included the principle of struggle for both freedom and social justice together in their political program, and defended change through social reforms. In planning the future socialist society, the Young People's Organization recognized private ownership, without disregarding the role of the government in the economy. The extent of this plan, however, went so far as to not only include the ownership of the underground resources by the government, but also the nationalization of bus and telephone companies.[38]

Undoubtedly, the familiarity of a number of the leaders of the party and its Young People's Organization, such as Zirakzadeh, Sanjabi, Bayani, and Bakhtiar, who had received their education in France, played a role in this choice. It was, however, as though none of these would prevent that organization, in announcing its views and assessments or in the articles it published, from sometimes emphasizing issues that were rooted in another approach. Fighting for what they called pouring the foundation of "national rule," they spoke about the victory of the "angel Ahura Mazda" over the "demon Ahriman" and seasoned mental confusion and eclecticism with taking an "oath" on "Almighty God and the tri-colored socialist flag of Iran." Displaying such an understanding of the concept that the party called socialism, they claimed that under the conditions when "no more than a few small steps until the political party government, the freedom of the people, and the establishment of the socialist regime" remain, "the people of Iran will not allow themselves to once again be dominated by the rule of the aristocracy or the clerics, both of whom are the obedient servants of dictatorship." Regarding women's freedom, the Young People's Organization of the Iran Party, on the one hand, attacked the ignorance and darkness and the "illegitimate" ideas "in the name of religion" that prevent the involvement of women in their own destiny, and on the other, it claimed that "no religion has been as considerate of women as Islam." At times, it defended moderation and reforms and regarded them as the "sole" path to overcoming the hardships, and at times it regarded uprising as "the only solution for improving the condition of the country and the people," considering any other alternative to be tantamount to compromise and misguidance; and finally it would claim that in establishing freedom and social justice, "no religious law is as close to socialism as the laws of Islam." Hence, as Hafez says, until the demon departs and the angel arrives, the party offered its congratulations on the "auspicious Feast of Ghadir-e Khom to all Moslems, especially the Iranian Moslem brothers," and spoke about "blood" and "honor," or it wrote about Ali, the Imam of the Shi'ites, that "socialist leader of the world," stating, "if you are a Moslem, if you claim to follow the school of Ali, you must act on all his instructions. Fight, and let your shroud be stained by blood rather than the stain of disgrace," since "the stain of disgrace must be washed with blood."[39] Thus, let the establishment of the promised paradise, the mudbrick of culture and civilization, be solidly in place on the main pole of the tent of religion, and what they called the school of French socialism, in a mingling of faith and knowledge, bring about the victory of Ahura Mazda over Ahriman.

With such an understanding, the writers of *Javanan-e Sosiyalist* regarded that organization to be "vast and powerful," stating that like "hardened steel" it had employed its ability in supporting the government of Mosaddeq and the "establishment of socialism," and in walking in step with the people of Iran, it had made the "disposing of the leftover waste of reactionaries and colonialism" the target of its unyielding struggle. In its journal, the organization propagated the viewpoint that the government of Mosaddeq played the role of an intermediary in the coming to power of the future democratic socialist regime, a government that like "a heavy tractor, gradually levels and paves the uneven road of Iran for the future socialist government."[40]

In July 1953 when Mosaddeq's ability to confront the ongoing crisis was waning more than ever before, in an article addressed to "political party comrades," *Javanan-e Sosiyalist* wrote: "Every moment that our nation gets closer to the final victory, and every day that the beliefs of our powerful socialist party become more widespread, the more the recognized and disgraced enemies of the nation, the feudal lords and those who see their annihilation in the victory of the people, conspire and fight with all their power against our party, the only stronghold of freedom. Now, in all the cities and villages, all the farms and factories of the country, from Chabsaku and Lotfabad to Kut Abdollah and Kerend and Shaqachi, everywhere, the great force that is the Iranian people have risen up under the socialist flag of our party and engaged in battling the highway robbers of the society and major landlords and those who have most vilely usurped the natural and social riches, and the people are fighting them most vehemently." Presenting such a picture, especially regarding the position of the party in villages and the spreading of socialist beliefs in the Iranian society, was far from reality, in particular for proving the "goodness" and "authenticity" of a political party that claimed that the "rebellious" young people of the homeland with their "unmatched and dazzling power" and their "warm blood" had erected its proud flag, "waving above the most remote parts of Iran."[41]

On the threshold of the coup d'état, when Mosaddeq as prime minister was preparing for a referendum and closing the parliament, in an editorial entitled "The Referendum Is the Only Solution to the Problems of the National Movement of Iran," Zirakzadeh wrote about the need to dissolve the 17th Parliament: "The 17th Parliament was uncooperative with a government that, in the heat of the greatest of the national battles of Iran, was engaged in fighting the foreigners, and neutralized the actions of the government by various means... Those who in the 17th Parliament fought against the national movement of Iran and created problems on the path of the actions of its leader were betraying the wishes of those in whose names they had entered the parliament, and were treading a path contrary to theirs... Hence, they served no other purpose but to cause disruption for the national movement of Iran and deviation from the mission the people have assigned to them. Thus, whenever a parliament assumes such a posture, it must be dissolved. The way these gentlemen acted in the parliament was so insulting to constitutionalism and harmful to the democratic regime that, even if they had not deviated from the path of the movement, the existence of the 17th Parliament was a threat to constitutionalism, and its dissolution seemed logical."[42]

Three days after the publication of this editorial, on 3 August 1953, by holding a most undemocratic referendum that was unprecedented in the history of the Constitution, backed by the support of the masses, Mosaddeq removed the parliament that he saw as an impediment to his policies. A country that had from ancient times sought tranquility and security in entrusting power to victorious statesmen once again found itself in the vicious circle of a mentality contaminated by despotism. This time, in the utterances of the functionaries of the National Front, there was no sign of respect for and oversight of the law and the place of the parliament in a constitutional regime in which "the law is for the people, not the people for the law." But what was there to fear for those who claimed to support moderation in a climate in which threats and intimidation ruled and who had chosen another option, an option that despite the warning of some of the allies of Mosaddeq did not create the slightest hesitation in the decree of "the incorruptible vanguard and leader of the people of Iran" to eradicate the parliament? The situation reached the point that the operators of *Javanan-e Sosiyalist* and support-ers of the "French socialist school" were forced, in their lightning-fast and violent judgment, to call a referendum that had no place in the Constitution, the rescue of what they called the "national movement," and for that matter, at a time when Bakhtiar, with his place in the leadership of the Young People's Organization of the party, played an influential role in determining its policies: "A referendum is the most brutal and most courageous national and democratic weapon. A refer-endum shows that the cleaver of public will is always ready and prepared to chop off a contaminated and treasonous hand, any hand that intends to violate our sacred beliefs and democracy and conspires against the people as a parliamentary representative; that cleaver shall sever without mercy such disruptive hands and dispose of them."[43]

With such an outlook, when with the dissolution of the parliament no sign remained of constitutionalism but its name, Bakhtiar was invited to attend a meeting at the Iran Party club "for an urgent matter."[44] In a brief announcement that was published for this purpose, the reasons for this meeting, the date of which was announced to be 17 August 1953, were not mentioned, even though the way the invitation was made and the way the meeting was held as well as the presence of such others as Ahmad Zirakzadeh, Aliqoli Bayani, and Mohammad Mokri, who were among the distinguished members of the Iran Party, was indicative of the importance of that meeting. And all this indicated that Bakhtiar in those fateful days before the fall of Mosaddeq's government had joined the circle of the influential members of the Iran Party, and that he had achieved great success in solidifying his position in that party.

¹ *Hezb-e Iran, Majmu'eh'i az Asnad va Bayaniyehha 1323-1332*, compiled by Mas'ud Kuhestaninezhad (Tehran: Shirazeh Publishers, 2000), 1-2.
² *Asnadi az Ahzab-e Siyasi-ye Iran (Hezb-e Iran, Hezb-e Sa'adat-e Melli-ye Iran)*, "Moqaddameh" (Office of the Vice President for Management and Information Dissemination), 5.
³ *Porseshha-ye Bipasokh dar Salha-ye Estesna'i: Khaterat-e Mohandes Ahmad Zirakzadeh*, edited by Dr. Abolhasan Ziya'-Zarifi and Dr. Khosrow Sa'idi (Tehran: Nilufar Publishers, 1997), 79-80.
⁴ *Khaterati az Allahyar Saleh*, edited by Seyyed Morteza Moshir (Tehran: Mehrandish Publishers, 2003), 219.
⁵ Leonard Binder, *Iran: Political Development in a Changing Society* (Berkeley: University of California Press, 1962), 210.
⁶ *Porseshha-ye Bipasokh dar Salha-ye Estesna'i*, 207-208.
⁷ Unpublished interview of Mohammad Moshiri-Yazdi with Shapour Bakhtiar, Suresnes, France, tape 21, 22 July 1990; *Khaterat-e Shapour Bakhtiar, Nokhost Vazir-e Iran (1357)*, edited by Habib Ladjevardi, Iranian Oral History Project, Harvard University Center for Middle Eastern Studies, Bethesda, MD, 1996, 16-17.
⁸ This writer's interview with Fereydun Amir-Ebrahimi, London, 12 November 2007.
⁹ *Javanan-e Iran*, no. 9, 15 December 1951, 1; ibid., no. 27, 24 May 1952, 1-2, quoted from *Hezb-e Iran*, 253, 270.
¹⁰ This writer's interview with Rahim Sharifi, Paris, 11 December 2007.
¹¹ Ibid., no. 4, 29 November 1952, quoted from *Hezb-e Iran*, 277-278; *Rejal-e Asr-e Pahlavi, Shapour Bakhtiar beh Revayat-e Asnad-e SAVAK*, vol. 24 (Tehran: Center for the Examination of Historical Documents of the Ministry of Information, 2011), 1.
¹² *Javanan-e Sosiyalist*, no. 2, vol. 3, 26 June 1953, 1, 4; ibid., no. 9, vol. 1, 14 August 1953, 1, 4.
¹³ *Khorush-e Jebheh*, no. 36, 8 February 1953, 1, quoted from *Hezb-e Iran*, 294.
¹⁴ *Jebheh*, no. 3, 28 November 1945, 4; *Asnadi az Ahzab-e Siyasi dar Iran (Hezb-e Iran, Hezb-e Sa'adat-e Melli)*, 12, 14-16.
¹⁵ *Khaterat-e Shapour Bakhtiar, Nokhost Vazir-e Iran (1357)*, 13-16.

[16] *Jebheh*, no. 124, 12 April 1946, 1-4.

[17] Ibid., vol. 1, no 58, 11 December 1945, 1.

[18] Ibid., vol I, no. 25, 28 November 1945, 4.

[19] *Hezb-e Iran*, 222.

[20] Karim Sanjabi, *Omidha va Naomidiha (Khaterat-e Siyasi)* (London: Jebheh-ye Melliyun-e Iran Publishers, 2007), 189-199.

[21] *Jebheh*, vol. 1, no. 118, 5 April 1946, 1; Sanjabi, *Omidha va Naomidiha*, 71-72.

[22] *Jebheh*, vol. 1, no. 25, 28 November 1945, 4; *Maramnameh-ye Hezb-e Mihan, Jarideh-ye Iran-e Ma*, no. 156, 25 June 1944, quoted from *Hezb-e Iran*, 344.

[23] *Iran-e Ma*, no. 162, 2 July 1944, 3, quoted from *Hezb-e Iran, Majmu'eh'i az Asnad va Bayaniyehha 1322-1323*, 339.

[24] *Javanan-e Iran*, no. 7, 27 May 1948, 1-2, quoted from *Hezb-e Iran*, 250; *Jebheh*, no. 354, 26 April 1948, 1-3, quoted from *Hezb-e Iran*, 202.

[25] *Jebheh*, no. 354, 24 May 1948, 1-3; ibid., vol. 1, no. 52, 3 January 1946, 1.

[26] Iraj Afshar, *Parvandeh-ye Saleh (dar bareh-ye Allahyar Saleh)* (Tehran: Abi Publishers, 2005), 88-89.

[27] Ibid., 227.

[28] *Jebheh*, vol. 1, no. 183, 21 June 1946, 1.

[29] Hoseyn Makki, *Khaterat-e Siyasi* (Tehran: Elmi Publishers, 1989), 19.

[30] Rasul Mehraban, *Barrasi-ye Mokhtasar-e Ahzab-e Borzhuazi-ye Melli-ye Iran dar Moqabeleh ba Jonbesh-e Kargari va Enqelabi-ye Iran* (Tehran: Peyk-e Iran Publishers, 1980), 30.

[31] *Jebheh*, vol. 1, no. 233, 29 August 1946, 1-2.

[32] Ibid., no. 258, 30 September 1946, 4.

[33] *Porseshha-ye Bipasokh dar Salha-ye Estesna'i*, 102, 107.

[34] *Jebheh*, no. 354, 27 May 1948, 1-3, 202-204.

[35] *Porseshha-ye Bipasokh dar Salha-ye Estesna'i*, 107.

[36] *Khaterat-e Shapour Bakhtiar, Nokhost Vazir-e Iran (1357)*, 17-18.

[37] *Javanan-e Sosiyalist*, vol. 3, no. 1, 19 June 1953, 1, 3.

[38] Ibid., vol. 3, no. 2, 26 June 1953, 1, 4.

[39] *Jebheh*, vol. 1, no. 7, 31 July 1953, 1, 4; ibid., vol. 2, no. 298, 21 November 1946, 4; ibid., vol. 1, no. 53, 4 January 1946, 1; ibid., vol. 1, no. 41, 21 December 1945, 1; ibid., vol. 1, no. 153, 17 May 1946, 1; ibid., vol. 1, no 292, 13 November 1946, 1; ibid., vol. 3, no. 2, 3 July 1953, 1-4; ibid., vol. 1, no. 9, 26 June 1953, 1, 4.

[40] Ibid., vol. 3, no. 1, 19 June 1953, 1, 3; ibid., vol. 3, no. 2, 26 June 1953, 1-4.

[41] Ibid., vol. 3, no. 2, 3 July 1953, 1-3; ibid., vol. 3, no. 2, 3 July 1953, 1-4.

[42] Ibid., vol. 1, no. 7, 31 July 1953, 1, 4.

[43] Ibid., vol. 1, no. 8, 7 August 1953, 1, 4.

[44] Ibid., vol. 1, no. 9, 14 August 1953, 3.

Chapter Six

*The crisis had begun some time ago, when seemingly at
the height of success, in fact, I had everything except my
poetic ability, which I had lost.*
—Johannes Robert Becher

Bakhtiar and the National Resistance Movement

In the latter days of August 1953, when Mosaddeq, a number of the
cabinet members, and the leaders of the National Front were in detention or lived in hiding, while the government of Zahedi was trying to
solidify its gains, an announcement entitled "The Movement Continues" called on the people to put up resistance to the coup d'état government. This effort within a short period of time resulted in the
establishment of the "National Resistance Movement" (Nehzat-e
Moqavemat-e Melli), and it placed at the top of its agenda the organizing of the struggle against the government and the reinstating of the lost
rights of the so-called national movement.

Various assessments have been made about how the National Resistance Movement was formed and its founders, who acted clandestinely.
Despite their differences, in their main accounts, these assessments share
a number of points. According to what has been said in this connection,
the first meeting for the purpose of creating such an organization
comprised of political personages and parties for organizing the "National Resistance Movement" was held a few days after the coup d'état at
the home of Ayatollah Seyyed Reza Musavi-Zanjani in Tehran. Ayatollah Zanjani, who had a long history of struggle against the Pahlavi
regime, rose in opposition to the ban on veiling during Reza Shah's
reign. He was the shining light of the nationalists and a staunch supporter of Mosaddeq. Zanjani, by founding the National Resistance
Movement and the Seminarians Committee of Tehran (Hey'at-e
Elmiyeh-ye Tehran), sided with the supporters of the National Front.
Along with Mehdi Bazargan and Ayatollah Taleqani, Zanjani partici-

pated in the establishment of the Freedom Movement of Iran (Nehzat-e Azadi-ye Iran). In the winter of 1962, he was elected to the congress of the National Front as a member of the central council of that organization, but he preferred not to have an official executive role, since he believed that he could play a more effective role in his position as a cleric. In this position, during the riots on 5 June 1963, Zanjani played an essential role in recruiting thugs such as Tayyeb Haj-Reza'i to the ranks of the opponents of the government.[i] He supported the activities of Ali Shari'ati and the Ershad Religious Center, and on the threshold of the Islamic Revolution, with a group of likeminded people, he established the "Human Rights Committee" (Komiteh-ye Dafa' az Hoquq-e Bashar) and the "Association for the Defense of Freedom" (Jam'iyat-e Defa' az Azadi). Zanjani was among the prominent clerics who accompanied Motahhari and Beheshti to the Tehran Mehrabad Airport to welcome Ayatollah Khomeyni when he returned to Iran in February 1979.[1]

According to a published report about how the National Resistance Movement was established, "the leadership was able in the first half of September 1953 to form the central committee of the National Resistance Movement with the participation of the representatives of the Seminarians Committee, the bazaar merchants, and the nationalist parties (Iran Party, Third Force, People of Iran Party), and with the opinion of the advisory committee, prepare and devise its program of struggle." Regarding the process of the formation of the National Resistance Movement, Yadollah Sahabi writes: "The day after 19 August 1953…Engineer Bazargan and I, worried at seeing the situation of Mosaddeq's house and the revengeful behavior of the perpetrators of the coup d'état, made an appointment together to go to the home of the late Haj Seyyed Zanjani for news. The next day, we went to Mr. Zanjani's house; we saw that Dr. Mo'azzami and a few other acquaintances were present. Dr. Mo'azzami was an experienced struggler who was first active in the Iran Party and then independently. In Mr. Zanjani's house,

---

[i] For more on this topic, see Chapter Seven.

we started discussing the events and incidents that had occurred, exchanged news, and the discussion led to what would happen to the country and what had to be done. The issues of the fate of the home-land, independence, and freedom were raised. Finally, we all came to the conclusion that we needed to wait for now and follow the news. We could not think of another solution. Just getting the news and being informed about the political events became a motivator, and despite the watchful eyes of martial law, the meetings continued. It was decided that the news from reliable sources should be gathered in an organized form, and that the people should be informed about the actual true news as much as possible, so that lies and rumors would not misguide them. For this purpose, a simple collaboration was created. Other people came, too, and everyone took charge of some part of the task. Among the people who actively participated in these meetings was Shapour Bakhtiar. He said, 'We need to establish an association that in an organized fashion stands against despotism, and like the French who fought against the German Army secretly and were called the Resistance, we should call our group, resistance.' This idea was agreed to, and the word 'national' was also added to it as a sign of its demand for inde-pendence. Thus, the group was called the 'National Resistance Move-ment.' Of course, others also continued the struggle in other parts of the city or in other provincial cities, and flyers were also distributed with the slogan, 'The Movement Continues,' which had brought some hope to the people. And even though the movement worked in secret, it had gained a reputation. Of course, the main operator among the groups was Ayatollah Zanjani; and most of the meetings were held at his home."[2]

Shapour Bakhtiar, in the first congress of the National Front, which was held in 1962 in Tehran, in a speech about how the National Resistance Movement was established and his role in its creation, also mentions Ayatollah Zanjani as the main figure in the National Resis-tance Movement: "On 24 August 1953, Ayatollah Zanjani sent some-one to me, and I went to meet him; and from that time, my relationship with him and the National Resistance Movement began. As far as I recall, Messrs. Mehdi Bazargan and Asghar Parsa were also in the central committee of the National Resistance Movement."[3] In that speech, Bakhtiar does not reveal the name of the person whose duty it was to take him to meet Ayatollah Zanjani. Years later, however, in an interview, he mentions Mehdi Bazargan as the person with that assignment: "Mr. Bazargan called me and told me, I will come to your house and we will go to Farhang Street together and have an 'orange party.' This is exactly what he said. I said, 'Please come, and I will also be ready.' He came in a taxi to the door of my house, and we drove to Farhang Street, to an alleyway somewhere in the middle of Farhang Street, which I remember was one-way. He said, 'This is the home of Ayatollah Zanjani.' I said, 'I met him once in Dr. Mosaddeq's office.' He said, 'He is the one.' The foundation of the National Resistance Movement was established there." In the same interview, he mentions himself, Mehdi Bazargan, and Ayatollah Zanjani as the founders of that organization.[4] In a different context, Bakhtiar states: "I believe that along with Engineer Bazargan and the late Ayatollah Zanjani, we were the first three. I heard no talk about Mr. Sanjabi there, since apparently he was in hiding at the time, and neither in a major way about Dr. Azar, whose political activities were essentially very limited."[5]

According to Bazargan, however, the first nucleus of the National Resistance Movement was formed by Ayatollah Zanjani, Rahim Ata'i, Abbas Radniya, and Naser Sadrolhefazi, and while Gholamhoseyn Sadiqi emphasizes the key role of Ayatollah Zanjani in the establishment of the National Resistance Movement, Ayatollah Zanjani mentioned himself as the founder of that movement.[6]

In the course of several secret meetings at the home of Ayatollah Zanjani, that group invited the personages and representatives of the political parties and groups to join them for discussions and exchange of views. Bazargan states: "A few days later, they invited me and a few of our friends, including Dr. Yadollah Sahabi, Dr. Shapour Bakhtiar, Fathollah Banisadr, and Hoseyn Shah-Hoseyni, for membership and cooperation. The name of the National Resistance Movement was proposed by Dr. Shapour Bakhtiar due to his familiarity with the

French Resistance in World War II against the German occupiers."[7] Shah-Hoseyni, on the other hand, states that the choice of the name of the National Resistance Movement for the organization was proposed by Naser Sadrolhefazi.[8]

In other assessments about the establishment of the National Resistance Movement, Seyyed Mahmud Taleqani, Haj Seyyed Reza Firuzabadi, and Hojjat ol-Eslam Haj-Seyyed-Javadi, the representative from Qazvin, have been mentioned as the founders of that organization. Asghar Gitibin as the representative of the Iran Party, Mohammad Nakhshab from the People of Iran Party (Hezb-e Mardom-e Iran), and Mohammad Ali Khonji from the Third Force participated in the National Resistance Movement. Ayatollah Zanjani, Abdollah Mo'azzami, Mehdi Bazargan, Abbas Radniya, Hoseyn Shah-Hoseyni, Abbas Sami'i, Rahim and Mansur Ata'i, and Hasan Nazih were mentioned as members of the "central cadre" of this organization.[9][ii]

With a look at the families, professions, and political history of the founders and the influential members of the National Resistance Movement, we see that most of them had religious roots, and that from the very beginning the bazaar had influence in that organization. Chehabi writes that in terms of organizing, the bazaar was the backbone of the National Resistance Movement. Regarding the role of the bazaar merchants, he mentions the financial assistance by such merchants as Shamshiri, Qasemiyeh, and Anvari to the National Resistance Movement. The key role of individuals such as Rahim Ata'i, Mehdi Bazargan's nephew, in the National Resistance Movement and the joining of Ezzatollah Sahabi, Kazem Sami, Taher Ahmadzadeh, as well as Mohammad Taqi and Ali Shari'ati in Mashhad in this movement reveal other aspects of the origins and political history of this group, all of which shows the influence of religion in that organization. With the

---

[ii] Hasan Nazih joined the National Resistance Movement a few weeks later. See: Houchang E. Chehabi, *Iranian Politics and Religious Modernism: The Liberation Movement of Iran under the Shah and Khomeini* (Ithaca, New York: Cornell University Press, 1990), 128-129.

victory of the Islamic Revolution, with the exception of Bakhtiar, a number of those active in the National Resistance Movement reached high government positions. Bazargan became the prime minister of the provisional government, Abbas Amir-Entezam the government spokesman and deputy prime minister, Yadollah Sahabi the minister without portfolio, Sadegh Ghotbzadeh and Ebrahim Yazdi the foreign minister, Mostafa Chamran the defense minister, Kazem Sami the minister of health, Hasan Nazih the head of the National Iranian Oil Company, Ezzatollah Sahabi the head of the Plan and Budget Organization, Hoseyn Shah-Hoseyni the head of the Physical Education Organization and the National Olympic Committee of the Islamic Republic of Iran, and Ayatollah Mahmud Taleqani the Friday prayer leader of Tehran and chairman of the Islamic Revolution Council. Also, Habibollah Peyman became a member of the Islamic Revolution Council.[10]

In its assessment of its own history in the early weeks and months after the coup d'état, the National Resistance Movement also makes a meaningful reference to the role of the bazaar and the university: "Those places where they have not yet removed the banner of independence and dignity from above them, two environments that on the surface are at two opposite poles of our society, but as a result of authenticity, the unity of the words, and the miracle of the rightfulness of the movement, raised their voices as a unified environment. On the one hand, the bazaar, which is the center of business and the gathering place of free men who have not donned the chains of regulations and the captivity of employment, with a five-day public protest, angered the government people and brought hope to the country. On the other side, the independent environment of the university, the center of education, full of enthusiastic young people who have neither been shackled by official regulations nor concerned about making a living for their families, started protest after protest, to the point that three of their beloved friends were killed in the hallway of the Technical College."[11]

In examining the history of the National Resistance Movement, mention must be made of a significant number of young people who, with a history of membership in the Islamic student associations, were active in that organization. Ebrahim Yazdi, Mostafa Chamran, and Ezzatollah Sahabi were a few distinguished examples of Islamists who joined the National Resistance Movement, individuals who following the victory of the Islamic Revolution were granted positions as ministers, or the head of the Plan and Budget Organization in the cabinet of Mehdi Bazargan. Mohammad Ali Khonji, Mas'ud Hejazi, and Daryush Foruhar along with Bakhtiar can also be counted among the non-religious personalities of the National Resistance Movement, even though this group had far less power and influence than such figures as Mohammad Nakhshab. It was mostly political viewpoints based on religious inclinations that had an impact on the politics of the National Resistance Movement.

In the publication of the second announcement of the secret committee of the National Resistance Movement on 29 August 1953, the general guidelines of the viewpoints of that organization regarding the struggle ahead were stated as follows:

"Continuation of the National Movement and restoration of independence and national government.

"Struggle against any foreign colonialism, whether red or black.

"Struggle against puppet foreign governments and agents of corruption."

Accordingly, and considering the preparations that it had made to attract political personages, forces, and parties, as well as codification of the strategy of the struggle, by examining and analyzing the reasons for the past defeat and the path ahead in confrontation with the government, the National Resistance Movement published a statement announcing its viewpoints. The main points of the statement consisted of efforts to create an organization "suitable to the historical situation of the society" for the purpose of the "formation and cohesiveness of forces," and readiness for fighting the regime at an appropriate time. Confrontation with the "efforts of the regime in suppressing the structure of people's resistance"; exposing the conspiracies of the government apparatus in trying "to make the goals of the national resistance prior to the coup d'état and those of the National Resistance Movement after the coup d'état seem the same as those of the Tudeh Party"; countering the ratification of the Consortium Agreement in the parliament through organizing demonstrations, strikes, and other forms of struggle; and finally, "thwarting the propaganda of the governments of the United States and England in connection with making the regime of the coup d'état appear legitimate and popular in the eyes of the world" were other points raised in explaining the future policy of the National Resistance Movement.[12][iii]

Struggle against Zahedi's Government and the Arrest of Bakhtiar

The first organized step by the National Resistance Movement was a call for demonstrations against the Zahedi government. The "Grey Revenge Committee" (Komiteh-ye Enteqam-e Kabud), affiliated with the National Resistance Movement, by publishing an announcement entitled "We Sound the Alarm Bell," wrote: "More than one month has passed since the coming to power of the government of the thugs and hooligans headed by Zahedi, the agent of the United States and British imperialism. During this period, the illegitimate government of Zahedi, with the assistance of the boot-wearing soldiers of Reza Khan and the pupils of the school of autocracy, has not stopped at any disgrace and treason. They dispatch to prisons the free men who had risen up for liberty and freedom. Zahedi, a graduate of the espionage school of England, imagines that through force and dictatorship, he would be able to stop the people from national struggle; the Shah, the original perpetrator of anti-national conspiracies, deceives the people by sham religiosity… Beloved Mosaddeq, in the course of three years of sleeplessness, contemplation, and travel weariness, gained the greatest proud victories

---

[iii] The first announcement, which was signed by Ayatollahs Rasuli, Razavi-Qomi, and Zanjani in connection with the issue of the reopening of the bazaar after consultation with a number of bazaar merchants, was published before the return of the Shah to the country. See: *Safahati az Tarikh-e Mo'aser-e Iran: Asnad-e Nehzat-e Moqavemat-e Melli*, vol. 5, compiled by Nehzat-e Azadi-ye Iran (Tehran: Nehzat-e Azadi-ye Iran, 1984), 256-257.

for the Iranian people. Now Zahedi, this political clown, after several years wants to return the people to square one. Fellow countrymen, let us be alert to neutralize Zahedi's conspiracies. For this purpose, we must organize our forces on one front. And we will also sacrifice our lives to our last drop of blood."[13]

By publishing an announcement, the leaders of the National Resistance Movement protested against the restrictions that existed on the path to advancing the election campaigns. These restrictions, however, were nothing new, and the opponents faced serious problems from the very beginning in trying to have their voices of protest heard, problems an example of which Shapour Bakhtiar has described in an interview as follows: He and Mehdi Bazargan had hired a taxi to distribute announcements, tossing the flyers out of the taxi window as it was moving, and in order for the driver not to recognize them and find out what they intended to do, they conversed in French. According to Bakhtiar, Bazargan objected to the taxi driver listening to music on the radio.[14iv]

With the call by the National Resistance Movement for demonstrations, on 8 October 1953, the bazaar was closed, and in various parts of Tehran, following the closing of classes, university students engaged in demonstrations. Even though these demonstrations were not widely welcomed by the people, they were an alarm bell to the government, and in the propaganda of the National Resistance Movement, they were a sign of the efforts of the opposition forces to continue the struggle.

The next activity in connection with organizing demonstrations and general closures came on 12 November 1953, which this time took

---

[iv] Regarding his outlook about music, Bazargan writes: "Joyful singing and music and other enjoyable entertainment that causes temporary artificial happiness and makes a person forget the problems and suffering are said to ameliorate tiredness and tedium and prepare a person for life. But we must ask if all tedium and suffering are bad. If there were no pain and no need in the world, would it result in any action and order? By sedating the pains and killing the very valuable sensing mechanisms that are given to man for this purpose, would the society move toward expediency and perfection, or toward decadence?" Mehdi Bazargan, *Eshq va Parastesh ya Termodinamik-e Ensan*, 3rd printing (Houston, Texas: Daftar-e Pakhsh-e Ketab, 1979), 197.

place in coordination with the Tudeh Party. The National Resistance Movement wanted to have the bazaar, the government offices, the University of Tehran, and the schools closed. The closing of factories and bus lines was conferred on the Tudeh Party. According to a report published by the National Resistance Movement in this connection, by not following the previously-made agreement and suddenly changing the program and the date of the demonstrations and general closures, the Tudeh Party created obstacles to the successful overall execution of these efforts. Nevertheless, the bazaar and the university were closed, and demonstrations were held in front of the bazaar. In response, the Zahedi government arrested a large number of people and jailed and exiled a group of the bazaar merchants and several of the clerics.

Hence, within less than three months, the battle of the opposition for effective and continuous confrontation with the regime came to a fateful end. This confrontation should have not only inflicted a deadly blow to the government of Zahedi, but from the perspective of the Tudeh Party, it should have been the harbinger of cooperation between the two main factions of the opposition. The National Resistance Movement, however, was not inclined in the least to form a joint front with the Tudeh Party, and at every opportunity, rejected the invitation of that party for the formation of such a front against despotism by referring to the Tudeh Party's policies regarding the government of Mosaddeq. Another reason for the need for such a policy was based on the viewpoint that the nationalists had seen nothing but "incarceration, suffering, torture, and execution" from their coalition with the communists in other countries. "Hence, since it is an error to test the tested, and according to His Holiness the Revered Messenger of God, 'a believer should not be stung twice from the same hole,' the National Resistance Movement does not accept this invitation for the second time, and does not consider coalition with that party even against the current common enemy to be in the interest of the people of Iran."[15]

About the formation of the National Resistance Movement, we should note that from the very beginning, Mosaddeq was in "regular" contact with the central committee of this organization through his children,

Ahmad and Gholamhoseyn, as well as his grandson, Hedayatollah Matin-Daftari. Nosratollah Amini, the mayor of Tehran during Mosaddeq's administration, who was among a small number of people who had contact with Mosaddeq in Ahmadabad, was working with Ayatollah Zanjani. Along with Shamshiri and Anvari, two merchants who were supporters of the National Front, he was active in supplying financial aid for the printing of the announcements and the publications of the National Resistance Movement. Despite all this, in the course of the formation of this movement, the top tier leaders of the National Front had no role. During those dire days, they were either in detention or in hiding, and moreover, it would have been too far-fetched to expect them to have the readiness to join a secret underground movement. In fact, with the exception of Shapour Bakhtiar, who had gained some experience during World War II in secret operations in the course of cooperating with the French Resistance, others had no experience in this area. This arena from old times belonged to the leftists and some religious groups, whereas the nationalists, except for a few, wittingly or unwittngly, had had no experience with it.

The unrests at the University of Tehran, which had expanded in the course of protests to the visit of Richard Nixon, the Vice President of the United States, to Iran and had reached their peak after three students were killed on 7 December 1953, were followed by a wave of violence and suppression. These unrests, especially on the threshold of the Senate and National Consultative Assembly elections that were about to be held with the goal of normalizing the conditions of the country and legitimizing the position of Zahedi's government, would provide a good opportunity for the National Resistance Movement to rise through a lawful channel in confrontation with the regime. Taking advantage of this opportunity and participating in the elections that were to be held in a non-democratic climate would also, however, have had the dangerous consequence that the National Resistance Movement would affirm the legitimacy that the regime was trying to gain, a legitimacy that not only with the despotic rule that governed but also considering the continuation of martial law was not legal, and would make the holding of any election on the basis of the current laws of the country lawfully invalid.

For this reason, a number of "religious scholars, prominent figures, and university professors affiliated with the National Resistance Movement," by publishing an open letter to the Ministry of Interior, announced that prior to the start of the second term of the Senate, considering "the independence and grandeur of the country and the prestigious status of the legislative branch," and also emphasizing that the government had announced that the elections would be free, formed the "Association for Securing Free Elections." The government, however, prevented oversight by this association in the course of the elections, and the tabulation of the votes had been carried out with supervision by the people and only with the help of the military and police forces, to the point that disruptions of the efforts to form associations and the detention and exile of the opponents had drained the elections of true meaning. They emphasized that this time, on the threshold of the elections for the 18th National Consultative Assembly, they demanded securing the right for election campaigns with the goal of holding free elections, securing freedom of expression and freedom to hold rallies, and the revocation of martial law in accordance with the note to the 23 January 1951 law. The authors of the open letter considered participation in the elections, especially given "the current situation of the country, the duty of every honorable Iranian," and a right granted to them by the Constitution. This right could not be utilized "without securing safety and freedom," as the four points had expressed explicitly in the open letter, and "without observing the aforementioned points, any election held would be annulled, and the ratifications of a parliament with this type of elections without freedom would be considered worthless and invalid by the people of Iran."[16]

By publishing another announcement, which had this time been signed by a number of them, including Ayatollah Reza Zanjani, Ali Akbar Dehkhoda, Allahyar Saleh, Abdollah Mo'azzami, Seyyed Mohammad Ali Angaji, Haj Seyyed Reza Firuzabadi, Seyyed Baqer Jalali-Musavi, as well as university professors Dr. Kamal Janab, Asadollah Bizhan, and Mohammad Qarib, pointing out "the heinous actions and the fraud" committed in the course of the second term Senate and National Consultative Assembly elections in the provincial cities, the authors of the open letter called on the people of Tehran to participate in the elections: "At the present, as well, the national movement relies on and is supported by the grace of God and then, you, the combative brave people of Tehran… We ask you, for the prosperity of the nation and the country, to participate in the elections with utmost equanimity and implement your national right of sovereignty. Encourage and invite your friends, acquaintances, and close and distant relatives to vote and elect honest, noble, faithful, Moslem, and patriotic individuals and those who have been tested for their political piety as their representatives… It is hoped, by the grace of God Almighty, the undiminishing power of the nation, the unity and unanimity of words, and the courageous efforts of you, the self-sacrificing people of Tehran, that the true representatives of the nation will enter the parliament and serve on the path of the prosperity of the people. Strive courageously; God will support and help you."[17] The tone and the manner of expression and reasoning of the authors of this letter were also indicative of a non-secular approach based strongly on rooted religious standards.

We see another example of the policy of the National Resistance Movement in the opposition of the Mashhad branch of that organization to the issue of the elections. In contrast to the advocates of participation in the elections of the 18th Parliament, they supported the boycotting of the elections; and even though theirs was also a non-secular approach, it was clearly based on theology and religious values. The supporters of an election boycott "emphatically instructed all freedom fighters of the honorable lineage of students of religious sciences as well as merchants, businessmen, craftsmen, workers, university students, pre-collegiate students, and white-collar employees" to avoid participation in the Mashhad elections, the list of parliamentary representatives of which had been chosen ahead of time, in order to "avoid, at these sensitive moments and during the sacred national and religious jihad, doing something for which they would be deemed responsible by history and, like the people of Kufa, be subjected to the cursing and hatred of future generations."[18]

In the course of these developments that were followed by the prosecution and detention of the opponents, Bakhtiar, who also had been arrested during the third week of February 1954 on the charge of "activities in opposition to the government and inciting authors to write harmful and insulting articles against the Royal Court," was released after one month. According to the Second Division of the Military Command, he was released upon pledging that from then on, he would not take any step in opposition to the government and the interests of the country. Another report indicates that for some time prior to his arrest, Bakhtiar had been under surveillance. In that report, which was prepared by General Dadsetan, the military commander of Tehran city region, addressed to Prime Minister Zahedi, reference was made to Bakhtiar's efforts to collect financial aid for the National Resistance Movement and his opposition to the government. At the end of his report about Bakhtiar, General Dadsetan had entreated the prime minister: "I request that instructions be issued to notify this Governor's Office of Your Excellency's decision." We can surmise that Bakhtiar's history in the Ministry of Labor and his kinship with Brigadier General Teymur Bakhtiar, the commander of the Second Armored Division, and with Sorayya Esfandiyari, the Shah's wife, would have impeded the military commander's ability to make a decision about him before obtaining instructions from the prime minister, especially since during the first days after the fall of Mosaddeq's government, Zahedi had asked Bakhtiar to join his cabinet as the minister of labor. According to Moshiri-Yazdi: "It was three or four days after the 19 August 1953 coup d'état. One day we were sitting with Bakhtiar in the home of his stepbrother, Abdolrasul Bakhtiar, who is a dignified and enlightened man, on Zahiroleslam Street, talking about all sorts of things. The house servant came and informed us that Mr. Amir Hoseyn Khan Ilkhan Zafar-Bakhtiar had come for a visit. I knew Ilkhan from the time when he was the governor of Yazd. He was Bakhtiar's paternal cousin, whose sister, Forugh Zafar-Bakhtiar, was the lady-in-waiting to the Queen, or, as the French say, '*dame d'honneur*'. Later on, Ilkhan became a senator, and in the end, he died in a traffic accident on Karaj Road. With his arrival, I did not want to be a burden. I got up and said that I was leaving. Bakhtiar kindly said, 'No have a seat,' and I sat down.

"Ilkhan came in, paid his respects, and sat down in the parlor. Again, I asked for permission to leave. You know that among the Bakhtiaris, age is very important. When someone is older, the younger people show a great deal of respect for him. Bakhtiar said, 'You know Mr. Moshiri; he is not a stranger.' Ilkhan Zafar said, 'No, he is not a stranger. Why do you want to leave? Have a seat.' I sat down. After exchanging pleasantries, Ilkhan turned to Bakhtiar and said very politely, 'Shapour Khan, why did you leave your job? I have come here on behalf of General Zahedi. You are a nominee for the Ministry of Labor. I have come to tell you that you are going to be the minister of labor.' In response, Bakhtiar said most respectfully, 'Your Excellency, I am most grateful for your kindness. I have made a pledge with Mosaddeq, a covenant. I cannot work with his successors who are certainly his opponents.' Ilkhan said, 'You are a relative of the Queen of the country, and you cannot do this.' Bakhtiar said, 'Despite this, give me permission; let there be one person in the Bakhtiari tribe who would not listen to advice. He might benefit the country one day.' Then, Mr. Ilkhan Zafar began to say things like, 'you are not behaving properly, you must come and be a colleague,' and the meeting came to an end. Today, Bakhtiar is no longer with us, but what I said is the actual real incident that I witnessed."[19v]

In the course of his detention, during his interrogations in response to the charges made against him because of his opposition to Zahedi's government regarding the issues of oil, foreign policy, and the elections, Bakhtiar rose in his own defense and wrote on the interrogation docu-

---

[v] In his recollections, as well, Bakhtiar mentions that he did not accept the offer of membership in Zahedi's cabinet. Unpublished interview of Mohammad Moshiri-Yazdi with Shapour Bakhtiar, Suresnes, France, tape 21, 29 July 1990.

ment that in the constitutional system, according to the Constitution and its supplements, "certain freedoms and rights have been foreseen for the people of Iran," and that on the basis of these rights regarding which he had "always wished for their implementation," he is free to have ideas and a viewpoint contrary to the government at the time: "I believe that this government is ruling over the people contrary to the wishes of the majority of the people, and the people of every class and ideology have expressed their distrust and discontentment whenever they have been able to do so." He admitted to having known Lieutenant Mosharrafolmolk and Captain Sadeqi, members of the officers' organization of the Tudeh Party, but rejected the charge of having cooperated with that organization. Bakhtiar also expressed lack of knowledge about the publication of "*Rah-e Mosaddeq*" and the existence of a committee called the "Revenge Committee" in the National Resistance Movement. Finally, he submitted a note to the officials of the military governor's office and stated, "Until now, I have never done anything in violation of the law and the interests of the country," and he pledged that from then on, as well, he would "respect all the laws and regulations of the country."[20]

After he was released, Bakhtiar went into hiding for a while, and then moved to a house on Forsat Street that belonged to Shahrokh Firuz, the son of Nosratoddowleh Firuz. Firuz writes: "One day, Gholamhoseyn Mosaddeq came to my mother's house unexpectedly. We were still there, busy with moving furnishings. He pulled me aside and said, 'Shapour Bakhtiar needs a place to live. He is now in hiding somewhere where he might be exposed. Since you are moving to the house in the Farmaniyeh suburb, if possible, let him use your house in the city.' I immediately agreed to what he asked for and gave him the key to the house. I also had the movers work faster… The house in the city had two rooms, which I immediately made available to Shapour Bakhtiar. To avoid any suspicion, I made the place look like a business company, since I had obtained a permit for it a long time before but had not used it. I set a salary of about 500 *tumans* per month for Dr. Bakhtiar. I hired him with the explanation that he was the translator of the company."

Bakhtiar's release did not last long. Six months later, when he was arrested again in September 1954 and interrogated, in response to why he was continuing to oppose the government despite his promise to the military governor, he wrote: "Firstly, I have not been involved in any sort of activity against the interests of the country, and this was all I promised in February. Moreover, criticizing and expressing opinion about the government in a constitutional regime is the right of all people, and in particular, the educated."[21]

Finally, Bakhtiar was put on trial in a military court in June 1955 and sentenced to three years in prison. The charges against him were more or less the same as those made during the interrogations and that had been argued in the primary and appeals courts. Contesting the charges against him, he referred to the content of the Constitution, and regarding the charge of having insulted the monarch, he said: "The monarch is exempt from responsibility. Hence, if someone has insulted the government, it is not an insult to the monarchy and the Shah personally... A person who forces His Majesty the Shah to accept responsibility is either a wise enemy or an ignorant friend. What we fanatical or misguided or extremist nationalists would like to have is a king like the king of England, regarding whom, when the sailors on a warship that is sinking deep into the ocean, without expecting any reward or high position, shout out, 'Long live the King.'"[22]

The Plot to Kill Prime Minister Zahedi and the Consortium Agreement

In October 1953, Mehdi Bazargan and Ezzatollah Sahabi attended a secret meeting with Navvab-Safavi, the leader of the Self-Sacrificing Devotees of Islam (Feda'iyan-e Eslam), and Khalil Tahmasebi, the murderer of former Prime Minister Ali Razmara, who had been pardoned during the administration of Mosaddeq. About this meeting, Sahabi writes: "Discussions were about the perpetrators of the coup d'état, General Zahedi, Iran's dependence on England and the United States, and the ongoing moral corruption and debauchery. Mostly, Engineer Bazargan and Navvab-Safavi talked, and Khalil and I kept silent. We saw that the two sides had a lot of ideas in common. Finally, Navvab-Safavi turned to Engineer Bazargan and said, 'We understand what our duty is. You must help us. We will introduce one of our members to you. You somehow hire him as a gardener or laborer for the Qeytariyeh Garden, and leave the rest to us' (he meant the assassination of Zahedi). At that time, the coup d'état prime minister, Zahedi, was staying in the Qeytariyeh Garden, and that was his command center, so to speak." Continuing to recount the details of that meeting, Ezzatollah Sahabi then discusses Bazargan raising of the issue of the assassination of Zahedi in the meeting of the central committee of the National Resistance Movement, and the opposition to it. This opposition, however, did not mean the leaders of the Freedom Movement's severance of relations with the Devotees of Islam. Two years later, Ayatollah Taleqani, a distinguished member of the National Resistance Movement, hid Navvab-Safavi, who was wanted by the authorities for an assassination attempt on Prime Minister Ala', in his house. Sahabi writes: "One morning shorty after my release from prison, Mr. Taleqani contacted me and asked me to go and see him. I went to Mr. Taleqani's house... After I arrived, Mr. Taleqani spoke a bit about the current situation. Then he talked about the Devotees of Islam and their situation... Mr. Taleqani asked me to contact Bazargan and other leaders of the National Resistance Movement and ask them to prepare a safe hiding place for the Devotees of Islam... Then Mr. Taleqani asked me, 'Would you like to meet Navvab-Safavi?' When I said that I would, he took me to the building on the other side of the courtyard. There, I saw the late Navvab-Safavi, Khalil Tahmasebi, Seyyed Mohammad Vahedi, Mohammad Mehdi Abd-e Khoda'i, as well as four or five other supporters of Navvab-Safavi sitting there, reading the Koran. Khalil was reciting the Ashura prayers, weeping. The mood of the gathering was peculiar, as though it were the gathering of the companions of the Sire of the Martyrs, Imam Hoseyn, on the eve of Ashura." In conclusion, Sahabi writes about having been "emotionally touched" by Navvab-Safavi; he made an effort to shelter and hide him. With the arrest of Navvab-Safavi by the agents of the military governor, his efforts failed.[23]

Just before the Persian New Year in March 1954, elections in Tehran were held under undemocratic conditions. The National Resistance Movement nominated twelve well-known personages, such as Mo'azzami, Sanjabi, Hasibi, Saleh, Shayegan, and Zirakzadeh, for the Tehran elections of the 18th National Consultative Assembly. None of these candidates were elected to the parliament. In its election campaign organizations, the government on the one hand had guaranteed free elections, and on the other, it had blocked the way to the participation of its opponents in the election campaign.

Simultaneous with these developments, a delegation comprised of the representatives of the Consortium arrived in Tehran in April 1954 for negotiations and writing the oil agreement. These negotiations lasted five weeks, and finally, on 21 September of the same year, the oil bill was presented to the National Consultative Assembly, a parliament that had been formed in an undemocratic climate and had started its work around mid-March 1954, without the election candidates of the National Resistance Movement having been elected to it.

For this reason, in May 1954, upon assessing the developments in the country in the previous nine months, the National Resistance Movement published a statement explaining its views and the future process of struggle in opposition to the government. This statement, comprised of eight points, provided the general outline of the main areas of the movement's policy and program. In its first paragraph, Mosaddeq was considered the legal prime minister and Zahedi a traitor to the national interests, who had been assigned by foreigners to pave the way for their domination of Iranian politics and the economy once again. The third point of the statement recognized the National Resistance Movement as "an authentic national movement stemming from the people's opinions and will," one that had nothing to rely on "but the approval of Almighty God and the undiminishing power of the nation" and that "rejected any ideas and beliefs that are contrary to the sacred religion of Islam and love of the homeland." According to other contents of the statement, the elections of the second term of the Senate and the 18th term of the National Consultative Assembly had been carried out under martial law, in violation of the articles of the Constitution, and because of the deprivation of individual and social freedoms, they did not express the votes and opinions of the people. Hence, their decisions were also considered lacking any credibility in public opinion. The statement declared that any agreement regarding the oil issue, if it "is contrary to the text and the spirit of the law ratified in March 1951 and the nine-article law ratified in May 1951, is null and void, and those who act on, sign, and ratify such an agreement must be condemned to the most severe of punishments on the charge of treason to the homeland."[24]

Another issue was the role of the Shah in the events of the country: "His Majesty, the King of Kings, by discharging Dr. Mohammad Mosaddeq, the legal prime minister of Iran, from office has exceeded his authority and has acted in violation of the Constitution and the interests of the country and the nation." The Shah must "reign and not rule"; otherwise, according to Mosaddeq, "the beloved leader of the nation," in the "sessions of the illegal court," the result will be nothing but to move the government of "constitutional monarchy toward absolute despotism." The other paragraphs of the statement, which were about the future of Iran in regard to domestic and foreign policy, contained the following points: "The foundation of order in the society is based on social piety and justice as well as individual liberties in accordance with the spirit of the Constitution and the Universal Declaration of Human Rights." Other points included efforts to "increase production forces and strengthen the structural ability of the general economy," raise the standard of living of the people especially that of the poor, extend social insurance to all, along with observing the principle of impartiality, "protecting and solidifying the complete economic and political independence and territorial integrity," countering "colonialist avaricious intentions," supporting independence movements, and "observing absolute neutrality in international disputes." In conclusion, the statement declared its opposition to Iran's participation in "political and military blocs with either the East or the West."[25]

The eight-point statement of the central committee of the National Resistance Movement regarding an assessment of the political situation and the future perspective and prospects of the struggle ahead was also important from a different perspective: "The illegal usurping government of Zahedi, with all its military power and the financial aid and support by colonialist governments, has been unable to implement any of the objectives for which it has been placed in the seat of power, because it has faced the vehement opposition, protest, and resistance of the people of Iran at every step … such that today, on its nine-month report card, it sees nothing but failure and disgrace in the face of the people inside and outside the country and the strong hatred and disgust of the people of Iran."[26]

One dare say that none of these statements contained the slightest sign of a realistic outlook or an analysis firmly based on the ongoing realities in the country. By overthrowing Mosaddeq, returning the Shah to Iran, and suppressing the opposition, Zahedi had been able to solidify his position. Establishing the court for the trial of Mosaddeq, establishing diplomatic relations with England, holding the elections of the two houses of parliament, and preparing for the signing of the Consortium Agreement were other examples of his success recorded on the report card of Zahedi's government. Iran had transitioned from unrest and chaos to peace and security, and economic stability had replaced recession and crisis in the financial sector. Even though this stability and security had been created at the high price of sacrificing democratic freedoms, which would have an unpleasant impact on the history of Iran, they could not be denied. Rather than an analysis based on perceptible reality, the statement declared that in every arena, the government of Zahedi "has faced the vehement opposition, protest, and resistance of the people of Iran." But what widespread "opposition, protest, and resistance"? The authors of the statement should have admitted that "the brave and combative people of Iran" had not achieved "tangible results" in their goals, and had not "succeeded in overthrowing the government of Zahedi"; but it was as though the expression of this fact served merely to fill the page, since the statement was immediately made: "The fact is clear to everyone that in the struggles of nations, time is not much of a factor, and since Zahedi's apparatus, from the start of the treasonous 19 August coup d'état until now, has retreated in front of the people, it will eventually fail and, defeated and vanquished, leave the scene of struggle."[27]

From the very start of the unofficial negotiations about the oil issue, especially after the arrival of the representatives of the Consortium in Tehran, the National Resistance Movement focused its attention more than ever before on the ongoing negotiations. The central committee of that organization, in a letter addressed to Ali Amini and other members of the Iranian delegation assigned to negotiate with the representatives of the Consortium, warned them to avoid signing any agreement that was contrary to the law on the nationalization of the oil industry. In the same connection, efforts were also made to gain the support of a larger number of national figures to protest against the signing of the agreement that was being prepared with the Oil Consortium. These efforts resulted in the sending of a written protest by "Islamic and national personages of the country against the Consortium Agreement" to the two houses of parliament, the National Consultative Assembly and the Senate, which had a significant impact from the perspective of publicity. The important aspect of the text of this protest was the vast spectrum of the signatories that not only was comprised of the founders and influential members of the National Resistance Movement, but also included a number of the distinguished personalities of the country who were not affiliated with any organization or political party.

The text of the protest first discussed the former Oil Company and "the nullified concession that it had obtained through intrigues and resorting to illegal instruments" and condemned all that had been done within fifty years by the "colonialists" and their "cronies" in establishing the business of "dictatorship," and said that all this effort was with the goal of "eventually wearing out, exhausting, making helpless and despairing, and annihilating the nation." However, it said, "the will of Almighty God, the conditions of the time, the world events, and the alertness of the Iranian nation and the suffering people of this country neutralized their sinister plot ... until finally, with the courageous efforts of the representatives, the nation carried out its will to nationalize the oil industry throughout Iran." The written protest, which was addressed to "the two sacred houses of parliament," discussed the developments that occurred following the nationalization of the oil industry, and mentioned the obstacles created on its path. Amidst all this, however, was the sensitive point of the cursory mention of the 19 August 1953 coup d'état: "After disruptions, restrictions, and the creation of domestic and foreign political and financial problems, with the support of the united and allied lines of the courageous and brave nation on the path of the fulfillment of the national wishes and the implementation of the laws on the nationalization of the oil industry, the government of Iran made a most staunch effort, and the nation as well stood and advanced in the face of all deprivations and various pressures, increasing its steadfastness and tenacity. The old rival that had received a blow, however, did not fall, and with the prelude of the 28 February events and finally the unfortunate 19 August 1953 incident, regarding the perpetrators of which you already know, it impeded the activity and service of the national government; another government came to power; and by forming a rubberstamp parliament, it achieved its objectives and wishes with the continuation of the previous conditions and arrangements."[28] The point worthy of note is that no mention is made throughout the written protest of Zahedi or of Mosaddeq.

Referring to the coup d'état as an "unfortunate" incident and avoiding the mention of Mosaddeq's name was not a simple matter. The entire existence and the foundation of the National Resistance Movement were tied to these two, and passing over them, especially in a written document as sensitive as this, was something worthy of much contemplation. It appears that in order to achieve the more important goal of gaining the support of the parliament, the signatories of the written protest meant to avoid any expression of opinion that would risk undermining such a goal, perhaps hoping to convince the parliamentary representatives to refrain from ratifying an agreement contrary to what they considered to be in the interests of the Iranian people in connection with the issue of the oil industry. In its expression and its content, the written protest was devoid of the customary slogans and quarrelsome harsh words and the customary settling of accounts. It was a text in which the authors had made an effort to concentrate on the principle of relying on sound reasoning, not only in the legal and technical arenas, but also politically, without disregarding the essentials and sacrificing their beliefs for an unprincipled compromise.

Under such circumstances, even though in its diction and reasoning the written protest took the side of caution and indicated thoughtful consideration, it was characterized by an undeniable frankness, an explicit frankness that seemed uncompromising in its assessment of the details of the agreement that was about to be ratified, and regarded that agreement to be "in violation of the laws on the nationalization of the oil industry in Iran and contrary to the right of sovereignty, freedom, and independence." On the same basis, since its "stipulations and the manner of its signing, ratification, and exchange" did not "stem" from and were not the "result of the will of the Iranian people," the parliamentary deputies were asked to refrain from ratifying it, since its text was an explicit negation of the national interests, and hence invalidated and devoid of any official value.

Moreover, the expanse and the wide diversity of the personalities that signed it added to its importance. Among them were the names of notable figures such as the former speaker of the National Consultative Assembly, Abdollah Mo'azzami; the former minister of finance, justice, and interior and Iran's ambassador to the United States, Allahyar Saleh; the former minister of justice and Iran's former minister plenipotentiary in Belgium, Shamsoddin Amir-Ala'i; the former minister of agriculture, Ahmad Ata'i; the former mayor of Tehran, Nosratollah Amini; the former minister of labor, Shapour Bakhtiar; the former chairman of the board of directors of the former Oil Company, Mehdi Bazargan; the former director general of Iran's roads and former chairman of the Supreme Council of Railroads, Hasan Shaqaqi; the former president of the Insurance Company, Abdolhoseyn Daneshpur; as well as a number of former parliamentary deputies, university professors, Justice Department attorneys, and religious scholars and clerics, such as Ayatollah Reza Zanjani, Haj Seyyed Reza Firuzabadi, Seyyed Ja'far Gharavi, and Seyyed

Mahmud Taleqani. The signatories to the written protest included Ali
Akbar Dehkhoda, Khalil Maleki, Mohammad Ali Khonji, Mohammad
Nakhshab, and Ali Asghar Gitibin, each of whom commanded high
esteem in one arena or another.[29][vi]

Religion and Politics in the National Resistance Movement

When we examine the views of the National Resistance Movement or
the texts of its announcements, we often see a religious approach to
political issues. In contrast, in its "Charter of National Unity"
(Manshur-e Vahdat-e Melli), not only is there no hint of a religious
approach, but, rather, it deliberates on "political independence," "the
right to sovereignty," and "the inalienable rights of all members of the
human family (according to the Declaration of Human Rights and the
League of Nations Covenant)." Regarding the organization itself,
however, the requirements for membership and entry into probationary
branches consisted of signing a written oath in which, while the applicant declared his loyalty to "the independence and prosperity of the
homeland and the freedom and preeminence of the nation" and made
an effort for its "growth and development," the oath contained a clear
emphasis on religious principles and moral issues based on non-secular
values: "I swear by omnipotent God and my social conscience and my
mother's honor and my own honor to act in accordance with righteous-
ness and truth and to always respect the untampered Constitution that
guarantees the independence and is the secret of the survival of Iran."
The organizational bylaws of the National Resistance Movement
emphatically mandated that the organizational chapters recite verses

---

[vi] Following the publication of that text, twelve professors were expelled from the
university, and some who were government employees were suspended. Ali Akbar
Siyasi, the president of the University of Tehran, did not sign the letters of suspension
of the expelled professors. Six months later, on 11 September 1954, *Sepid-o Siyah*
magazine wrote that the Shah had agreed to the reinstatement of the professors and the
continuation of their service. For more details, see: *Shast Sal Khedmat va Moqavemat,
Khaterat-e Mohandes Mehdi Bazargan dar Goft-o Gu ba Sarhang Golamreza Nejati*
(Tehran: Khadamat-e Farhangi-ye Rasa, 1996), 325-327.

from the Koran for three minutes prior to raising questions, offering political analyses, or the presentation of reports in their sessions.[30]

Accordingly, the instructional publication of the National Resistance Movement regarded the 19 August 1953 coup d'état to be an incident that was carried out "by the hands of the ungodly treacherous domestic agents" and caused the nation to go into "religious mourning." The same publication emphasized: "Omniscient God, by making the duty of defense and jihad mandatory, and as the noble Koranic verse states, 'if God had not repelled some men by others, the earth would have been corrupted,' has made the task of repelling corruption in the world and preventing oppression the responsibility of the people themselves, and He has made it a means for correction and gaining reward, and on the Day of Judgment, not only will the oppressor be punished, but the oppressed will be called to account and punished as to why he has failed to defend his right and assisted the oppressor in his practice of oppression." The instructional publication of the National Resistance Movement called on the "brave faithful men" to accept the truth that "the sole solution and the religious, national, and conscientious duty of everyone is uprising and action, action and uprising with attention to the truth, reliance on God, and organizing in the National Resistance Movement," because: "God's will, that is the course of nature and society, always assists the oppressed people who fight. As the Koran states, 'How many a little company hath overcome a mighty host by God's leave! God is with the steadfast' (II: 249)." And "the fruitful sapling grows from the ground of bravery and vengefulness." In the conclusion of an article about the history of the National Resistance Movement, this publication, which was published with the signatures of the core nucleus of this organization, wrote: "We hope that with the guidance and affirmation of God that always encompasses the suffering who fight on the path of Truth, and with the cooperation and self-sacrifice of our beloved compatriots, we will take firm steps in achieving the three goals of the movement, to cleanse our sacred country from the filth of corruption and oppression, to expel the foreigners, and to dispose of their domestic cronies. We are certain that we shall succeed, and our dignity, which is true dignity, will become victorious. 'Verily, those in the party of God are the successful' (LVIII: 22)."[31]

Shortly before the arrival of Richard Nixon in Iran in December 1953, an announcement entitled "The People Will Take Revenge" was published by the National Resistance Movement that also in its wording and content indicated an approach mixed with religious beliefs in confrontation with the government: "Once again, a bunch of ungodly good-for-nothings have taken advantage of these few days of temporary stifling dictatorship, displaying their excessive spitefulness and wicked nature, attacking the people… How moronic and shortsighted are those who imagine that these servants of money and coercion, these worshipers of this world who are the feeble tools of their own concupiscence, would be able to stand against men of faith and possessors of belief to keep that cardboard organization and hollow apparatus standing… We declare at this very moment that the National Resistance Movement of Iran has already created an organized system to record on the blacklist, without any errors and omissions, the names of these treasonous functionaries who receive salaries from the treasury of the people and under these conditions, with torture and fabrication of charges, engage in the most heinous atrocities against the people, so that on the day of the uprising that will liberate the Iranian people, these traitors to the homeland will be hanged from the gallows in public squares."[32]

Based on all that was said, it appears that the religious approach that from the beginning had a special place in the outlook and attitude of the National Resistance Movement, within a short period of time, became dominant and official as the prevailing tendency in the views and principles of that organization. From the very beginning, considering the class structure and the political history of its founders, with the exception of Bakhtiar, this reality was not too unexpected, although we also see no sign of criticism of the religious approach of the National Resistance Movement to political issues on the part of Bakhtiar.

With the ratification of the Consortium Agreement, the differences of opinion that existed from the very beginning in the National Resistance

Movement peaked, resulting in the confrontation of two powerful factions within that organization. The faction represented by Allahyar Saleh, Shapour Bakhtiar, and a number of other influential members of the Iran Party had reached the conclusion that, given the support of the West and the revenues from the sale of oil, the regime's position had solidified. The other faction, of which Bazargan and Ata'i were well-known members, heedless of this reality, condemned any and every compromise, and by solidifying its position, was gaining the upper hand in determining the policies of that organization. In the continuation of this trend, Bazargan was elected to membership in the central committee of the National Resistance Movement, and according to Ezzatollah Sahabi, he also assumed responsibility for the publications and publicity committee, which played an undeniable role in advancing the policies of that organization. This was the time when the religious approach dominated the thinking and the opinions of the National Resistance Movement more than ever before, an approach that played a role in its closeness to an extremist group such as the Devotees of Islam and its notorious leader, Navvab-Safavi.

Simultaneous with the aforementioned statement that included the main outline of the views, positions, and political assessments of that organization regarding the situation, an open letter signed by the National Resistance Movement addressed to Ayatollah Borujerdi was also published in May 1954. That letter called the "blessed attention" of the eminent Ayatollah Borujerdi, "the Grand Source of Emulation," who was considered "the refuge and sanctuary of Moslems," to the "dire consequences of the current situation," and called on "the Grand Leader of Moslems, may your great shadow extend," to, "before the opportunity is lost, with the help of the people, find a solution to that usurping government and reinstate the national government." The open letter of the National Resistance Movement addressed to Ayatollah Borujerdi contained important points, each of which indicated a religious approach to the events in the society. That letter demanded the involvement of the clerics in the political developments of the country. In its beginning, where it discussed the history and the role of the clerics in social developments, the open letter mentioned the Constitutional Revolution, a revolution that, according to the authors of the open letter, resulted in the success of the oppressed Moslem people of Iran, "under the guidance of the grand religious scholars and revered religious sources of emulation of the constitutional era, as mandated by the Koranic law of 'God enjoins you toward justice,' and with the intention of impeding oppression and injustice and implementing justice and fairness, with the most tremendous valuable efforts and enduring great hardships and suffering, and by offering their property and lives," in changing the government of despotism to constitutionalism and establishing the national government centered around the Constitution and its supplements.[33]

According to the content of this open letter, the constitutional strugglers had deemed "the blessed beings of the grand religious scholars in every age until the advent of the Imam of the Age, the possessor of religious law, to be the protectors and overseers of the Constitution," such that the representatives of the people with absolute freedom, "based on their religious duty and observance of the interests and requirements of the time," would implement their timely decisions for the prosperity of the people. And this, "with the endeavors and the efforts of the grand religious scholars of the constitutional era," provided the grounds for proclaiming that "the people of this Islamic country have the right to vote and express their opinions freely, and have the right to legitimate involvement in the affairs of their country, while their lives, property, homes, reputation, and dignity remain protected." Instead, however, the current generation faced the reality in which "the people's religious faith, reputation, honor, and property were violated and attacked, and among them, the religious scholars were placed under even more restrictions and pressure than other classes."[34]

By emphasizing such assessments of the role of the clerics in the constitutional government and the duty conferred on them to guide "the oppressed Moslem people," the open letter referred to the "martyrdom of Modarres" and the incident of the Gowharshad Mosque in "the holy city of Mashhad" during the reign of Reza Shah, pointed out the consequences of Zahedi's government, and requested of the clergy not to allow an opportunity for misuse by foreign enemies, so that "the dignity and rights of Moslems would not be ruined and toyed with by foreigners more than they already have been."[35]

In the conclusion of its open letter to Ayatollah Borujerdi, the National Resistance Movement made this emphatic statement: "Hence, in accordance with our religious duty, conscience, opinion, and the need to protect Islamic honor, and if only for the chastity of one Moslem and for stopping the hands of the usurping government that interferes in the interests of foreigners and in violation of all national rights and dignity, and in order for a Moslem nation not to be under the influence and colonial domination of foreigners in accordance with the noble Koranic verse, 'God will not give the infidels any way of success against the faithful' (IV: 141), we find it necessary to call to your blessed attention the dire consequences of the current situation. We believe that, due to the fondness of Your Great Reverence for and influence in the Moslem society of Iran, it is a religious obligation for the Grand Source of Emulation, who is the refuge and sanctuary of the Moslems of this country, before this opportunity is lost, with the help of the people, to try to find a solution, to expel this usurping government, and to reinstate the national government, in order not to leave any opportunity for misuse by foreign enemies, and in particular, not to once again have a situation in which, similar to the twenty years of Reza Shah's reign, the performance of religious observances and duties becomes prohibited and the religious scholars and clerics become the targets of murder, incarceration, torture, disrespect, pressure, and restrictions."[36] This was also a facetious wile of history, that a servant of religion, a famed cleric such as Borujerdi who was known for avoiding politics, was asked to step into the arena and, with his impactful involvement, to perform the historic duty of a person such as Bakhtiar, who after years of studying in Europe spoke about respect for the law and the teachings of socialism.

All that I have quoted shows a chaotic picture and is a clear indication of the religious approach to constitutionalism and the political developments in the distant and recent past, and all these issues were raised while Bakhtiar and a number of other renowned figures of the National Front were members of the National Resistance Movement. In the ensuing years, as well, without the slightest revision and reconsideration, they recalled that period as a golden page in their political report card and records. Only when he was interrogated on the charge of cooperating with an extremist group, the National Resistance Movement, did Bakhtiar criticize the policy and the ways of that organization. Other than this, however, he never spoke a word in criticizing, revising, or reconsidering those views that would indicate his critical outlook regarding an organization that was a mixture of religion and politics, and displayed the dominance of religious politicians or political religious figures over that organization's ideology and behavior.

In November of 1957, when he was interrogated in the Office of the Military Governor, Bakhtiar once again expressed lack of knowledge about the existence of a committee called the "Revenge Committee" that published announcements under the same name, and he called it contrary to his own "philosophical, religious, and political party beliefs." He also expressed his opposition to the Tudeh Party, stating that he was a "Moslem" and had "strong religious beliefs." In the course of his interrogation, he referred to his and the Iran Party's disagreement with the "extremist views" of the National Resistance Movement, and discussed the difference in the "method and mode of thinking" of the Iran Party and the National Resistance Movement that resulted in the separation of the two organizations: "We do not agree to secret societies and underground operations. I have essentially not seen any announcement signed by the National Resistance Movement, whether about oil or any other issue, for more than a year... Our school of thought (that of the Iran Party) cannot be compared with that of the National Resistance Movement, about which I do not have sufficient information. There may be patriotic people in that organization; but certainly (and because the Iran Party severed its contact with it three years ago), there may be suspicious and audacious individuals among them; and I keep saying that the Iran Party's ideology is not the same as that of the members of the movement... Since a long time ago up to now, I have had and have no contact with the members of the movement, and I am totally removed from political activity. I have not seen any of the movement's publications since a year ago, and they have not been sent to me. I have, however, heard from my political party comrades that these publications contain very offensive language, and contrary to expectations, the constitutional monarch was insulted. I and all those who think like me oppose such methods; and we consider cursing and insults as a sign of weakness in politics."[37]

In none of these statements is there any indication of criticism of the religious approach of the National Resistance Movement, which was the basis for its ontological existence. If discussing the political dogma of that organization would not have a place in the course of the interrogations by the military governor, in the ensuing years, when there were discussions about criticism and reconsideration, such a discussion would have been considered an inevitable necessity. Bakhtiar's statements meant ultimately nothing but mild criticism of the "extremist views" and "extremist" actions of the National Resistance Movement, or what he termed disrespect to the monarch, or "heinous and insulting" phrases, mild criticism of such pretenders as Bazargan, Sahabi, and Taleqani, who, prostrating on the prayer rug, plotted the assassination of a prime minister and sheltered other perpetrators of assassination under the auspices of the Koran and the kindness of the Creator in their own hearth and home.

Bakhtiar and the American Embassy

Simultaneous with the clashes and the start of the increase in the disputes that faced the National Resistance Movement, on 26 November 1953, Bakhtiar contacted the American Embassy in Tehran. This contact, the preparations for which had been made earlier in a telephone conversation and a short meeting in the office of the second secretary of the embassy, was to discuss his political positions and views about the government of Zahedi, the details of which are reported in two documents of the United States National Security Archive, which indicate: During this meeting, explaining his views, Bakhtiar said that he was chosen by a "certain organization" for the assignment of establishing contact with the American Embassy. He said that his duty was to explain the general positions of the organization. Moreover, he wished to know whether both sides considered it beneficial for the embassy to have a conversation with the prominent member of the "certain organization."[38]

According to the report by the representative of the embassy, "it appears that the 'certain organization' mentioned by Bakhtiar was the growing faction in the Iran Party of which he was an active member, and on the recommendation of which he had participated in the government of Mosaddeq. Bakhtiar called this group the 'true nationalists,' and regarding their goals, he said that they consider themselves to be loyal to Mosaddeq. In his opinion, even though Mosaddeq might have made certain mistakes, he continues to dominate the sentiments of 80% of the people of Iran. Bakhtiar attributed Mosaddeq's mistakes mostly to his advisors, especially Fatemi, and said that Hasibi, as well, made incorrect recommendations to Mosaddeq."[39]

The second point in Bakhtiar's statements was opposition to the Tudeh Party, an opposition that "in his opinion, should be done constructively, rather than through suppressing measures." The final point recorded regarding Bakhtiar's first meeting with the American Embassy in Tehran "is the lack of opposition of the group to Zahedi, even though in the opinion of Bakhtiar, there is the concern that Zahedi's government might become more fascist than ever before, rather than democratic." Bakhtiar also made the point that he thought "Zahedi's government is a fascist government at the present time." He added: "On 12 November 1953, using tanks and machineguns, the government prevented the people's demonstrations, and arrested 12,000 people throughout the country as Tudeh Party members, people many of whom were arrested unjustly, or they were teenagers who had been the target of the Tudeh Party propaganda, or those who after release expressed their strong hatred for the government. In Bakhtiar's opinion, the government is comprised of a set of the most corrupt personalities, something that has been unprecedented in Iran." In conclusion, he declared his readiness for talking about the positions of his group with the American officials of the embassy in another meeting.[40]

The next meeting was held on 1 December 1953 at the home of the second secretary of the American Embassy in Tehran. The first secretary of the American Embassy also participated in that meeting. According to the embassy's "Memorandum of Conversation," during this meeting, Bakhtiar explained the positions of the Iran Party, or that portion of it that he represented, as follows: "Opposition to the Tudeh and Unwillingness to Cooperate with it Directly. Dr. Bakhtiar admitted that the Iran Party and the Tudeh had many short-run objectives in common and that neither party could be expected to stand in the way of the other's attempt to achieve these objectives. This did not imply cooperation, however, either tactically or in principle... He spoke of having received a Tudeh member in his home within the past few days for a discussion of current affairs." In their assessment of Bakhtiar's statements, the American officials point out that he considers himself to be a "social democrat," and "his opposition to the Tudeh and Communism appears genuine." The memorandum continues: "Dr. Bakhtiar's opposition to the Tudeh seems to be based largely on the conviction that the Tudeh is an anti-national force dominated by a foreign power." Nevertheless, referring to his period of service as the deputy minister of labor in Khuzestan, the embassy officials believe that he "did not very effectively resist Communist infiltration of the ministry and the labor movement."[41]

Regarding Bakhtiar's opinion about the role of the Shah, this report states that he "argues that the Shah's role is purely representational or protocolaire. He declared that the Shah had no right to 'flee' on August 16; it was the duty of the King to face the country's problems on the spot even at the risk of his life." Bakhtiar did not conceal his hatred of Reza Shah, "beside whom Hitler was an angel." In his opinion and that of other Iran Party figures, "not even the most nationalist government could survive in Iran without the active friendship of one of the three great powers. Cooperation with the British had proved 'disastrous' and cooperation with the U.S.S.R. would mean 'no country.' The support of the United States represented Iran's only hope for relative independence." He made "only implied criticisms" of current American policy in Iran and said that, like "many younger Iranians, he thinks of late President Roosevelt as the man of the century." Bakhtiar added that he considers Iran at the present time to be occupied by "Fascists." In his opinion, "Iran nationalists may have to wait 5 to even 10 years for the wheels to turn in their favor... France had to wait 5 years for her deliverance from her German Fascist occupiers."

Bakhtiar called the reestablishment of diplomatic relations with the United Kingdom "a return to 'the former pattern' of British interference in internal Iranian affairs." He believes that "the oil dispute must be solved in a manner which offers the British no opportunity to control the oil industry." Bakhtiar said that a "commercially equitable" settlement would be one that guarantees "Iran an income equaling a 50-50 profit sharing arrangement." He strongly believes that "the great virtue of his party and of Dr. Mosadeq's government was its freedom from corruption and the new men it brought to office." According to Bakhtiar, "of Mosadeq's ministers, only Fatemi was personally dishonest. The personal dishonesty of the men around him—particularly Amidi-Nuri and Dowlatabadi—was Zahedi's greatest fault." According to him, "the British liked to have dishonest men in power, as they were easier to influence."[42]

Bakhtiar's discussion with the officials of the American Embassy in Tehran, especially within a short time after the coup d'état, was not a simple matter. Undoubtedly, in and of itself, this action—had it been exposed—would have been unacceptable for Mosaddeq, or for the extremist faction of the National Resistance Movement. This meeting can be considered, more than anything else, a sign of two different approaches in the outlooks and assessments that were taking shape in the two major factions of the National Resistance Movement, sooner or later impeding the continuation of its activities as one group. Given the solidified position of the regime, Bakhtiar had apparently come to the conclusion that he had to find a way to get through the crisis the opposition was facing, a path that could not be traversed by denying the existing reality. He and the faction he represented can be considered as representing the moderate faction in the National Resistance Movement. Considering the lost opportunities and the policy that the United States was pursuing in its support for Zahedi, from the beginning, this faction did not have much of a chance. So low were its chances that with the dominance of the extremist group in the National Resistance Movement, which was under the influence of religious viewpoints, the moderate faction was losing ground more than ever before and was being driven to the margins.

The End of the National Resistance Movement

From the 19 August 1953 coup d'état on, efforts had been made to hold demonstrations and strikes and to draw the people into the struggle against the government. With the increasing stabilization of the regime, such efforts more or less either failed or remained without results, without creating any tangible outcomes. On occasions such as the anniversary of the 21 July 1952 demonstrations that resulted in the reinstatement of Mosaddeq as prime minister, the 19 August 1953 coup d'état, the passing of the nationalization of the oil industry legislation on 15 March 1951, and other historic events that in some way revived the memory of the struggle, the National Resistance Movement hoped to persuade the people to stand against and resist the regime. With the passage of time, however, it was having less and less success. A clear example of this was its call for widespread demonstrations on 21 July 1954.

Under such conditions, more than any persistent efforts to prepare and organize the struggle against the regime, there was talk about the actions that were indicative of the inability of those who instigated them to engage in effective resistance in confrontation with the regime. On Persian New Year in March 1954, the central nucleus of the National Resistance Movement "emphatically recommended to all honorable patriotic Iranians" to "devote traditional New Year exchanges of visits seriously to their own close families and relatives, to avoid attending official New Year celebrations and decorating, and to refrain from sending New Year cards or telegrams to anyone, and instead of New Year's greetings, to express condolences, to give each other lessons on resistance and spreading the struggle, and to call on each other to organize and unite." Referring to the incarceration of Mosaddeq, it stated: "Our beloved is in the enemy's shackles and chains; be fair, leave your greetings for happier occasions. 'O you who believe! Endure, outdo all others in endurance, be prepared, and observe your duty to God, in order that you may succeed' (III: 200)."[43]

The unfavorable situation of the National Resistance Movement escalated many discussions about the difficult circumstances that it faced. Bakhtiar considers the reasons for the failure of the National Resistance Movement to consist of the coup d'état, martial law, and the prosecution and exile of the opponents of the government, which in his opinion "was a fascist dictatorial regime in the fullest sense of the word," and emphasizes that the security organization (SAVAK), "had the duty of not allowing even one independent authentic national force to be formed."[44]

If we disregard the inadequacy of Bakhtiar's description of the nature of the coup d'état government and consider the phrase "fascist dictatorial regime in the fullest sense of the word" to mean merely suppressive, we still will not find an explanation of the incorrect assessment that he offers regarding the reasons for the failure of the National Resistance Movement. Martial law and the arrest, exile, and elimination of opponents cannot be considered the only reasons for the failure of that organization. These factors existed from the very beginning, all of which, for Bakhtiar and the founders of the National Resistance Movement, were essentially considered the raison d'être of that organization. Had it been otherwise, there would have remained no other reason for the establishment of the National Resistance Movement. Bakhtiar considered the same reasons that necessitated the creation of that organization as the reasons for its failure, without being prepared to mention the internal factors that caused that failure, which from a critical perspective would have brought about a fate different from failure.

The coup d'état government undoubtedly played an important role in the failure of the National Resistance Movement; but one cannot look for the reasons behind that failure merely in the suppressive policy that was implemented by the government without mentioning the internal factors. Bakhtiar's insistence on the role of SAVAK in the failure of the National Resistance Movement seems erroneous. SAVAK was established in 1956, when nothing but a name remained of the National Resistance Movement.

In terms of devising policy, organizing, and organizational structure, as well, the National Resistance Movement faced serious obstacles. Differences of opinion about the position of the government and how to confront it was one such obstacle. Since the coup d'état, especially after the signing of the Consortium Agreement, from a fragile position, the regime had reached the stage of consolidating and solidifying its positions, and had forced the entire opposition that lacked the support of the masses of the people into an unfavorable situation. The reflection of this reality in the policies of the National Resistance Movement was the increasing support for the faction within the National Front that evaluated the regime as being stabilized, and offered a different policy for confronting it, a policy that relied mostly on leniency, caution, and moderation rather than the policy of violence and rebellion that would shape its legitimacy at the price of disregarding dogged social realities. This tendency can be seen in the positions of some of the leaders of the nationalist forces, such as Allahyar Saleh and Karim Sanjabi, who in their attacks against the regime criticized the government and did not mention the Shah and the role he played. In contrast, Khonji and Hejazi condemned Khalil Maleki for compromising with the regime and accused him of treason, an outlook that eventually resulted in a split in the Third Force and had a negative effect on the stability of the National Front and its role in the National Resistance Movement, to the extent that with the increase in the differences in outlooks, the Iran Party and the People of Iran Party considered the regime to be stable and left the National Resistance Movement.

Mehdi Bazargan regards personal disputes, splits and disunity, internal factionalisms, insults, accusations, and even disruptions along with factors such as lack of attention to the principle of "keeping secrets" in clandestine political operations as other factors contributing to the failure of the National Resistance Movement: "At the beginning, almost all the political parties and nationalist groups warmly welcomed the invitation of the movement and expressed their readiness for cooperation with the movement. Unfortunately, in practice, however, they did not cooperate with the National Resistance Movement as expected, and they were unable to play a significant role in carrying out the plans for struggle against the coup d'état regime. In fact, the university, the bazaar, and the business people in Tehran were the main and major force behind the National Resistance Movement, not the political parties. Lack of cooperation by the political parties reached such a point that after 21 July 1954, the National Resistance Movement committees met without the representatives of the political parties in attendance."[45][vii]

In addition, there existed serious obstacles to organizing and to organizational structure. In this case, as well, as one of the active members of the National Resistance Movement pointed out: "Because of the intensity of the government presence and operations, and in particular the Office of the Military Governor, it was not possible to assemble and plan for organizing extensively, and the methods of search and suppression by the intelligence and military officials had eliminated the necessary conditions for the creation and survival of a specific permanent organization."[46] This reality, however, apparently did not prevent this organization from misjudging its capabilities. The organizations of the National Resistance Movement included its central committee, executive committee, the four committees (Tehran organization, provincial cities organization, financial organization, and publicity organization),

---

[vii] In addition to the tactical problems of the National Resistance Movement, Katouzian considers the issue of personalities and their personal conflicts also as having had an impact on the disintegration of that organization. See: Mohammad Ali Homayoun Katouzian, *Mosaddeq va Nabard-e Qodrat*, translated by Ahmad Tadayyon, 2nd printing (Tehran: Mo'asseseh-ye Khadamat-e Farhangi-ye Rasa, 1993), 381-382.

and the seven Tehran organizations (workers, farmers, university, schools, government departments, neighborhoods, and bazaar organizations). Each one of these organizations had its own separate branches and committees as well as its own organizational structure, organizing committee, chairman, and spokesman, and each was responsible for carrying out certain specific and complicated duties for its own branch as well as the central committee. In terms of organization, there was an "organizational and cooperation executive committee" comprised of five main subcommittees, each of which had separate duties, the details of which had been specified paragraph by paragraph regarding organizing and organizational structures, similar to other activities of the National Resistance Movement. The weekly newspaper organ was supposed to publish precise statistics of the affiliated organizations and archive them in an orderly fashion in order for faithful, active, unidentified members to "infiltrate other political parties and corruptive publications," so as to "in accordance with the plan, take maximum propaganda advantage of the slightest opportunity, such as high prices of bread, shortages of busses, foreign borrowing, and so on, as well as corruption by deviant individuals currently in charge, and by explaining and understanding the causes of each instance, come to inevitable conclusions, and impregnate and inevitably prepare the nation more than ever before for a government of the people by the people."[47]

In contrast to these organizational principles, the execution of which was contingent on carefully observing secrecy and struggle under the conditions that governed the Iranian society, there was also the fact that not the slightest possibility existed for the implementation of many of these organizational principles and precepts, and, considering the dictatorial circumstances and the limited capabilities of the National Resistance Movement, their materialization was far from expectation, a fact that was not reflected in the devising of policies and the picture that the organization presented of itself. Not only in regard to correctly understanding the conditions and the possibilities for fighting the government, but also in regard to comprehending its own position and ability, the National Resistance Movement did not have much potential.

A look at the manner of publication and distribution of *Rah-e Mosad-deq*, the organ of that organization, shows the limitations and insignificant resources of the National Resistance Movement in connection with its propaganda activities: "*Rah-e Mosaddeq* was published secretly as the organ of the National Resistance Movement from 1953 on, and it was distributed through the committees and branches of the National Resistance Movement and affiliated organizations and political parties. In the beginning, this organ was published with a few pages in half-page, or compact size, and later when because of the dominance and surveillance by the Office of the Military Governor and other security agencies of the coup d'état government, it was no longer possible to continue in that form, copies of the newspaper were inevitably made on a mimeograph machine and distributed. From early 1954 to mid-1955, for about a year and a half, considering the practical problems, eight printed issues were published irregularly; but after that, when access to printing presses was not possible, from June 1955 when the publication of the organ was done with mimeographs, we tried to publish two issues a month... We did not use a specific location for typing the stencil sheets and making multiple copies on a mimeograph machine, since that would increase the chances of discovery by the officials of the Police Department and the Governor's Office. For this purpose, we used different locations, including the room above Abbas Sami'i's store on Amir Kabir Street, which was mostly used for typing, and a reputable furniture store on what was called Shahabad Street, as well as the homes of some of the branch members. On several occasions, Haj Mohammad Anvari made two orchards available to us, one very large orchard in Karaj and several times his own orchard in Shemiran, past Dezashib around the Farmaniyeh neighborhood, which had a building and all sorts of equipment and resources."[48]

It seems that with the increasing differences of opinion in the National Resistance Movement and the withdrawal of some of the political parties and personalities, the Islamic approach, which had been more pronounced from the very beginning, became dominant. By publishing an announcement in April 1956 regarding the elections of the 19th

National Consultative Assembly, while protesting the arrests of a number of its leaders, the central committee of the National Resistance Movement mentioned Ayatollah Zanjani, who was a cleric, as the "religious and political leader of the people of Iran." The word "leader," however, was a title used for Mosaddeq, the attribution of which to Zanjani, especially not only as the "religious leader" but also as the "political leader," was a meaningful turn from the perspective of the functionaries of the National Resistance Movement, a turn that, even though as usual it spoke about "Mosaddeq's path," conferred their combative leadership on another personality, so that "in pursuing the statement of the leading light of Moslems and the leader of Shi'ites, His Holiness Ali ibn Abi-Taleb, 'Life in abjectness is death, and death with dignity is life,'" they carried on their combat against the apparatus of the government, a struggle that would "continue under the rays of the religion of Mohammad, peace upon him, and the help of Almighty God to secure independence, freedom, the implementation of the right of national sovereignty, and taking charge of our own destiny."[49]

In April 1955, with Zahedi stepping aside and Hoseyn Ala' becoming prime minister, no tangible change occurred in the policies of the National Resistance Movement. The reaction of the leaders of this Movement to this removal was an announcement entitled "Let Us be Alert to this Conspiracy." To them, the removal of Zahedi and the coming to office of Ala', which was followed by the release of some of the nationalist leaders from prison, had been done "in line with the foreign policy and only with the goal of deceiving the movement." Even speaking about giving the position of minister of finance or minister of justice to Allahyar Saleh was considered nothing less than a conspiracy. According to a report that was published in July 1956 by the National Resistance Movement, "Arsalan Khal'atbari and Dr. Jazayeri came to a meeting with the leaders of the movement, paved the way for compromise and reconciliation with the Royal Court, and in exchange for the eight-point statement by the movement..., they quoted the Shah's statement, 'Ask them to remove the first article regarding support for Dr. Mosaddeq, and ask me for the implementation of the rest of the articles.' Obviously, even making this promise was merely to deceive the people and the movement."[50]

With the publication of the announcement, "Let us be Alert to this Conspiracy," which meant nothing but negation of negotiations and talks with the government, no path was left to compromise and reconciliation, which had no chance from the very start. The response of the regime to the policy that the National Resistance Movement pursued was nothing but arrests and exiles. The ensuing weeks and months went by in a climate without any conversation between the government and the opposition, a climate in which a number of the activists and leaders of the National Resistance Movement, such as Ayatollah Zanjani, Mehdi Bazargan, Rahim Ata'i, Yadollah and Ezzatollah Sahabi, Taher Ahmadzadeh, and Mohammad Taqi and Ali Shari'ati, were arrested and jailed. The following years during which Bakhtiar and a number of other leaders of the National Front were arrested and imprisoned came to an end in the same way.

[1] Mehdi Abolhasani-Taraqqi, "Naqsh-e Ayatollah Haj Seyyed Reza Zanjani dar Tahavvolat-e Siyasi-Ejtema'i-ye Iran, 1272-1362," MA thesis on the history of Islamic Iran, Ministry of Science, Humanity Research and Technology Center, Cultural Studies, History Research Center, 2003, 62-66; Kiyan Katuziyan (Haj-Seyyed-Javadi), *Az Sepideh ta Sham* (Tehran: Abi Publishers, 2002), 55; *Namehha, Zendeginameh, Asnad va Namehha-ye Ayatollah Haj Seyyed Reza Zanjani*, edited by Behruz Tayerani, 2nd printing (Tehran: Samadiyeh Publishers, 2009), 22-23, 27.
[2] *Yadnameh-ye Yadollah Sahabi*, compiled by Mohammad Torkaman, The Cultural Foundation of Engineer Mehdi Bazargan (Tehran: Qalam Publishers, 1998), 356-363.
[3] *Surat Jalasat-e Kongereh-ye Jebheh-ye Melli-ye Iran*, compiled by Amir Tayerani (Tehran: Gam-e No Publishers, 2009), 221.
[4] Ibid., 221-222.
[5] *Khaterat-e Shapour Bakhtiar, Nokhost Vazir-e Iran (1357)*, edited by Habib Ladjevardi, Iranian Oral History Project, Harvard University Center for Middle Eastern Studies, Bethesda, MD, 1996, 34-35.
[6] *Surat Jalasat-e Kongereh-ye Jebheh-ye Melli-ye Iran*, 360-361; *Namehha, Zendeginameh, Asnad va Namehha-ye Ayatollah Haj Seyyed Reza Zanjani*, 30-31, 40-41.
[7] *Shast Sal Khedmat va Moqavemat, Khaterat-e Mehdi Bazargan dar Goft-o Gu ba Sarhang Golamreza Nejati* (Tehran: Khadamat-e Farhangi-ye Rasa, 1996), 306-307.

[8] Vahid Mirzadeh, *Tadavom-e Hayat-e Siyasi dar Ekhtenaq, Tarikh-e Shafahi-ye Nehzat-e Moqavemat-e Melli* (Tehran: Selk Publishers, 2000), 102.

[9] Rasul Mehraban, *Barrasi-ye Tarikh-e Mokhtasar-e Ahzab-e Borzhuvazi-ye Melli-ye Iran dar Moqabeleh ba Jonbesh-e Kargari va Enqelabi-ye Iran* (Tehran: Peyk-e Iran Publishers, 1980), 32-33.

[10] Houchang E. Chehabi, *Iranian Politics and Religious Modernism: The Liberation Movement of Iran under the Shah and Khomeini* (Ithaca, New York: Cornell University Press, 1990), 93, 129-130; Mirzadeh, *Tadavom-e Hayat-e Siyasi dar Ekhtenaq: Tarikh-e Shafahi-ye Nehzat-e Moqavemat-e Melli*, 16, 26, 37, 70-71, 130, 132, 179.

[11] *Safahati az Tarikh-e Mo'aser-e Iran: Asnad-e Nehzat-e Moqavemat-e Melli*, vol. 5, compiled by Nehzat-e Azadi-ye Iran (Tehran: Nehzat-e Azadi-ye Iran, 1984), 86.

[12] Bazargan, *Shast Sal Khedmat va Moqavemat*, 307-308.

[13] *Safahati az Tarikh-e Mo'aser-e Iran: Asnad-e Nehzat-e Moqavemat-e Melli*, vol. 2, compiled by Nehzat-e Azadi-ye Iran (Tehran: Nehzat-e Azadi-ye Iran, 1984), 507-508.

[14] Chehabi, *Iranian Politics and Religious Modernism*, 135.

[15] *Hadis-e Moqavemat: Asnad-e Nehzat-e Moqavemat-e Melli-ye Iran*, vol. 1, compiled by Nehzat-e Moqavemat-e Melli-ye Iran (Tehran: Nehzat-e Moqavemat-e Melli-ye Iran, 1984), 16.

[16] Ibid., 72-74.

[17] Ibid., 69-71.

[18] Ibid., 91-92.

[19] *Rejal-e Asr-e Pahlavi, Shapour Bakhtiar beh Revayat-e Asnad-e SAVAK*, vol. 24 (Tehran: Center for the Examination of Historical Documents of the Ministry of Information, 2011), 7-8; this author's interview with Mohammad Moshiri-Yazdi, Paris, 21 February 2007.

[20] *Rejal-e Asr-e Pahlavi, Shapour Bakhtiar beh Revayat-e Asnad-e SAVAK*, 12-16, 19.

[21] Shahrokh Firuz, *Zir-e Sayeh-ye Alborz* (Washington, DC: Mage Publishers, 2011), 444-445; *Rejal-e Asr-e Pahlavi, Shapour Bakhtiar beh Revayat-e Asnad-e SAVAK*, 27.

[22] Ibid., 113-114.

[23] Ezzatollah Sahabi, *Nim Qarn Khatereh va Tajrebeh: Khaterat-e Mohandes Ezzatollah Sahabi az Dowran-e Kudaki ta Enqelab-e 57*, vol. 1 (Tehran: Farhang-e Saba Publishers, 2007), 102-104.

[24] *Hadis-e Moqavemat*, vol. 1, 144-147.

[25] Ibid.

[26] Ibid.

[27] Ibid., 144-145.

[28] Ibid., 144-147.

[29] *Hadis-e Moqavemat*, vol. 2, 59-61; ibid., vol. 1, 251-255.

[30] Gholamhoseyn Mosaddeq, *Dar Kenar-e Pedaram: Khaterat-e Dr. Gholamhoseyn Mosaddeq*, compiled and edited by Sarhang Gholamreza Nejati (Tehran: Rasa Cultural

Services Institute, 1990), 161; *Safahati az Tarikh-e Mo'aser-e Iran: Asnad-e Nehzat-e Moqavemat-e Melli*, vol. 5, 4, 15, 26; Mirzadeh, *Tadavom-e Hayat-e Siyasi dar Ekhtenaq*, 105-106.

[31] Ibid., 81, 91.

[32] *Safahati az Tarikh-e Mo'aser-e Iran: Asnad-e Nehzat-e Moqavemat-e Melli*, vol. 5, 21-22, 32-33.

[33] Ibid., vol. 2, 27-30.

[34] Ibid.

[35] Ibid.

[36] Ibid.

[37] *Rejal-e Asr-e Pahlavi, Shapour Bakhtiar beh Revayat-e Asnad-e SAVAK*, 127-131.

[38] (DNSA): Memorandum of Conversation, American Embassy, Tehran, 27 November 1953.

[39] Ibid.

[40] Ibid.

[41] Ibid.

[42] Ibid.

[43] *Safahati az Tarikh-e Mo'aser-e Iran: Asnad-e Nehzat-e Moqavemat-e Melli*, vol. 2, 702.

[44] *Khaterat-e Shapour Bakhtiar, Nokhost Vazir-e Iran (1357)*, 36.

[45] Bazargan, *Shast Sal Khedmat va Moqavemat*, 308-310.

[46] *Khaterat-e Mas'ud Hejazi: Ruydadha va Davari, 1329-1339* (Tehran: Nilufar Publishers, 1996), 192.

[47] *Safahati az Tarikh-e Mo'aser-e Iran*, vol. 5, 10, 21.

[48] *Hejazi: Ruydadha va Davari*, 204.

[49] *Hadis-e Moqavemat*, vol. 2, 580-582.

[50] *Safahati az Tarikh-e Mo'aser-e Iran*, vol. 5, 288-289.

Chapter Seven

*If the situation advances as it is, the National Front as a
political force will be eliminated, and instead of being
the headquarters of the strugglers of Iran's national
movement, it will be turned into an abandoned temple
the most faithful devotees of which will only attend each
other's funeral ceremonies and nod as a sign of being acquaintances, and in regret.*
—Khalil Maleki

Bakhtiar in the Stronghold of the University of Tehran

The resumption of activities of the nationalists, which had begun with
the private meetings of the National Front's leaders and influential
figures in the summer of 1960 and had resulted in the formation of the
Second National Front, would open an important chapter in the history
of that organization. Bakhtiar along with Saleh, Sadiqi, Sanjabi, and
other leaders were among the 30 nationalists who, in signing a brief
statement, informed the public about the start of these activities in the
name of the supreme council of the National Front. With this step, a
force of which nothing visible had remained other than its name once
again announced its active presence on the political scene and in the
arena of the struggle for power. The announcement by the Shah in the
summer of 1960 that the elections for the 20th Parliament would be free
not only was an implicit admission of the fact that the previous elections
had not been free, but it also would provide an opportunity for the
National Front to announce its willingness to participate in the election
campaigns. The submission of a letter signed by Sadiqi, Bazargan,
Bakhtiar, and Keshavarz-Sadr to Atabaki, the interior minister in
Manuchehr Eqbal's cabinet, requesting free elections and the candidacy
of Allahyar Saleh as a representative to the National Consultative
Assembly from Kashan were examples of the start of such activities. In
the meantime, through the mediation of General Abdollah Hedayat, the
Shah invited Sanjabi to the Royal Court for negotiations. In response,

emphasizing the belief of the National Front in the law and the principles of constitutionalism, Sanjabi raised the issue of the need for free
elections and freedom for political activities, and regarding a meeting
with the Shah, said to General Hedayat: "If His Majesty generally agrees
with what I say, an audience would be proper; otherwise, it would be
cause for the further displeasure of His Majesty." Simultaneously, Khalil
Maleki was also invited to the Royal Court for a meeting and discussions with the Shah about national issues. He discussed this matter with
Sanjabi, and after obtaining his agreement, he went to meet the Shah.
Failing to realize the importance of the opportunity that had been
offered, Sanjabi said: "Naturally, the main purpose of such meetings and
invitations was to separate and disunite us."[1]

With the resignation of Eqbal and the premiership of Ja'far Sharif-
Emami in the summer of 1960, the activities of Bakhtiar and the
nationalists also expanded as much as possible and resulted in a sit-in in
the Senate. Asghar Parsa, the spokesman of the National Front, says:
"Along with a number of our nationalist comrades, we decided to have a
sit-in in the Senate and demand free elections, in the same way that
Mosaddeq began the national movement with a sit-in in support of free
elections." Referring to the names of the well-known members of the
National Front who participated in the sit-in, Parsa mentions Sanjabi
and Bakhtiar as the liaisons between the people and academics and the
sit-in participants: "The students held demonstrations in support of the
sit-in, and the police got into scuffles with them. Dr. Sanjabi and
Shapour Bakhtiar came to report to us about the demonstrations. They
stayed there, and our sit-in turned into detention, and we were in
detention for two months in the Senate building." In a similar description of what had happened, Sanjabi also points out that he and Bakhtiar
were wounded in the course of the attacks by the police on the student
demonstrations in support of the sit-in in the Senate.[2]

The University of Tehran was the main center and constant arena for
the National Front's confrontation with the government. In the absence
of cohesive and permanent political parties and organizations, this arena
placed the student demands, which always had a political hue, at the

center of the ongoing events and developments. Under these conditions, considering the weak position of the government and the opening up of the political climate, a committee called the "Inter-Political Parties Committee" (Komiteh-ye Beyn-e Ahzab), comprised of students affiliated with the political parties that supported the National Front, was formed and assumed the task of directing the students' battles. *Payam-e Daneshju*, the organ of the student organization of the National Front, also as the connecting link among the students, played an effective role in the organization and coordination of their struggle. The responsibility for the relationship between the National Front and the students committee was conferred on Bakhtiar. As a member of the supreme council of the National Front, this opportunity allowed Bakhtiar to benefit from a great deal of capability and resources with which to advance his beliefs. Hamid Zonnur, who was a member of the University of Tehran committee and has written about the formation and the activities of the student committee,[3] says in this connection: "This committee met once a week in the office of the Hamun Construction Company on Qavamossaltaneh Street, which belonged to Bakhtiar and two of his colleagues.[i] In these meetings, he provided the members of the committee with the decisions of the supreme council of the National Front. Bakhtiar was a steadfast person, and he was fearless. The young people supported him. He really unified the university." According to Zonnur: "In these meetings, political and organizational issues and future plans were discussed and decisions were made. In this way, there was constant contact between the university and the executive committee of the National Front; hence, the political activities of the university and the decisions of the executive committee were totally coordinated."[4]

---

[i] In a SAVAK report, the location of the Hamun Company is mentioned to be on Stalin Street, Zartoshtiha Alleyway, in Tehran. See: *Jebheh-ye Melli beh Revayat-e SAVAK* (Tehran: Markaz-e Barrasi-ye Asnad-e Tarikhi-ye Vezarat-e Ettela'at, 2000), 220.

The first effort in the multifaceted struggle that was made under the leadership of the University of Tehran committee affiliated with the National Front occurred on 7 December 1960. With organized preparations, the widespread demonstrations on the university campus were unprecedented. This combative challenge, which was followed by the closing of the University of Tehran, resulted in the arrest of the leadership of the committee as well as a number of students. The reaction of the university students to the arrests was a strike and sit-in for several days and nights at the university. In the continuation of this struggle, the leaders of the National Front decided that the sit-in should end, a decision that was announced to the students by Bakhtiar. Among the leaders of the National Front, Bakhtiar was the only one who opposed this decision, but since the decision had been made, as the liaison between the National Front and the students committee, he felt obliged to convey to them this decision, to which the students objected. Bakhtiar's reasoning in his opposition to ending the sit-in was that its continuation, even if for only one more night, would result in "sufficient international exposure." In his memoir, he does not offer any other reason for his opposition to the decision of the other members of the National Front leadership. Lotfollah Meysami, who participated in the student sit-in, referring to the difficult situation of the students in the cold winter weather in the building of the College of Literature where the students held the sit-in, the heat registers of which had been shut off, as well as other restrictions imposed with the university under siege by the law enforcement and police forces, states about the reason that Bakhtiar offered for ending the sit-in: "One night, all the students gathered in one area, when we saw Shapour Bakhtiar had come to the college. Bakhtiar made a speech and asked the students to end the sit-in. He said, 'Tomorrow, we have an important event and we must go to Ark Mosque for demonstrations.' As I recall, the Association of Seminary Clerics (Jame'ah-ye Elmiyeh-ye Ruhaniyun) had announced that there would be ceremonies at Ark Mosque. The Association of Seminary Clerics was comprised of Ayatollah Taleqani, Mr. Sadreddin Balaghi, Ayatollah Zanjani, and other clerics who supported Mosaddeq. The ceremonies were supposed to be on the occasion of the anniversary of the birth of the Imam of the Age, on 15 Sha'ban of the Islamic lunar calendar, or some such occasion. That evening, Bakhtiar said that the students should end the sit-in and go there. These statements resulted in disputes among the students. Some said that we should continue the sit-in, and some opposed it... The morning after the evening when Bakhtiar spoke, the sit-in for all intents and purposes ended."[5]

The student sit-in and its end was a topic of discussion for a long time in the political circles and among the groups within the National Front. In a report, SAVAK also discussed the difference of opinion that had occurred in this connection between Bakhtiar and other leaders of the National Front. In that report, SAVAK emphasized that Bakhtiar supported the continuation of the strike, and that this policy of his pitted him against the leaders of the National Front.[ii] The SAVAK report states: "Dr. Bakhtiar has said, 'I was against this action, but a number of people including Dr. Karim Sanjabi, Ebrahim Karimabadi, and Asghar Gitibin, based on available reports that a number of the sit-in participants were girls, and that in addition, the number of students was continuously decreasing, decided that I should go personally to the university and end the students' sit-in, and I did so.'"[6]

With the status that he had gained at the University of Tehran, from the very beginning, Bakhtiar tried to prevent the influence of the Tudeh Party members in determining the policies of the university committee affiliated with the National Front. In contrast, based on a tradition that Comintern (Communist International) had made common in communist parties, the Tudeh Party used infiltration in the political parties and democratic organizations to serve its policies, and the weapon of organizing played a very important role in advancing this policy. Since the Tudeh Party was considered an illegal organization and was deprived of

---

[ii] Homayoun Katouzian refutes the claim that Bakhtiar conveyed the decision to end the sit-in to the students despite his own wishes. See: Mohammad Ali Homayoun Katouzian, *Mosaddeq va Nabard-e Qodrat*, translated by Ahmad Tadayyon, 2nd printing (Tehran: Mo'asseseh-ye Khadamat-e Farhangi-ye Rasa, 1993), 406.

openly having organizations, this policy was an effective tool for its supporters to somehow have an impact on the ongoing developments. Such impact, however, was not possible except by concealing everything linked to the name of the Tudeh Party.

For Bakhtiar, as well, the concept of organizing was especially important. He believed that disregarding the issue of organizing would result in nothing but the repetition of the bitter experience of 19 August 1953. He insisted on this viewpoint, and he was not afraid that in his effort to create a solid organization, he would be charged with using a "dictatorial" approach. He said: "If we place no importance on organizing in the National Front, we will go nowhere else but where we ended up on 19 August… Regarding the steps taken which have resulted in charging us with dictatorship, I need to explain. The organization of the university is the first and most important stronghold of the National Front. If this stronghold is taken away from us, the National Front will be eliminated in Tehran, the consequence of which will be the annihilation of the National Front in the provinces." He gave the assurance that "the university is fully at the disposal of the National Front," and in response to "suspicious" individuals who had said that he had turned the university into a "garrison," he agreed, and said: "This place will be the garrison of the National Front."[7]

With the responsibility he had in the election oversight committee of the National Front congress, Bakhtiar prevented the candidacy of some of the active members of the student movement, such as Bizhan Jazani, as representative to the congress that was held in autumn of 1963. Justifying his reasoning for advancing a policy that he considered an impediment to infiltration by the Tudeh Party, he said: "Regarding a person who used to say that he opposed the National Front, we cannot cut off his head or expel him from the university, but we can tell him, sir, you are not a Moslem, so you are not allowed to go to Mecca. I am giving you a religious analogy. Let me be religious for once. It is clear that a number of Tudeh Party supporters…wanted to enter the National Front and make it implode. When I was in charge, I would say, go ahead and apply for membership in the National Front, and we will examine and evaluate your enquête, or membership application, within two months… All the efforts of SAVAK and the Shah's instructions at that juncture were to prove that there were individuals with a Tudeh Party background among the students and the leaders of the National Front, to say that they were Tudeh Party members, and to take them to the Americans and say, 'Aha, aha, you see, see! You can't have another 19 August every day. You are ruining everything by your own hands.' Knowing this, I tried not to even admit one of them into the National Front… Bizhan Jazani…came to me one day and said, 'Sir, why don't you accept us into the National Front?' I asked, 'Did you apply?' He said, yes. I asked, when? He said, 'Fifteen days ago.' I said, 'We can inform you of our decision within two months, but if you want to go to the branch of the National Front, you can go there. We are not going to give you a permanent membership card until you get some training and we decide whether or not it is the right thing for us to give you a membership card.' A number of them were there, and they said that everybody who was in the university had to vote, and in some colleges, the Tudeh Party members won the elections. In some colleges, of course, very few of them, but with their being organized, we could not stand up to them. We said, 'Sir, these elections are for the National Front. A National Front candidate must be a member of the National Front.' …It was not important for us whether some Hasan was elected or some Hoseyn. It was enough for the candidate to be loyal to the National Front."[8]

It is worth asking what Bakhtiar's motivation was in doing so. Did he want to halt the storm of the Shah's vengefulness regarding the Tudeh Party, which had been declared illegal on the charge of having had a hand in the assassination plot on the Shah's life in the winter of 1949? Was he trying to bring the ship of the National Front in the midst of the stormy waves of accusations and slander of the "threat of communism" in Iran, which caused concern for the United States, to the safe shore of struggle within the framework of lawful standards? Undoubtedly, being placed alongside an illegal group, and for that matter, the Tudeh Party, was not risk free. If that were the case, why in the course of all those years did Bakhtiar and the National Front not try to take a step toward revealing the truth about the assassination attempt on the Shah that resulted in the Tudeh Party being banned and which continues to remain a dark spot in Iran's contemporary history? It was an attempt on the life of a "fortunate young" king who, due to his reconsideration of some of the rulings passed by his father regarding the clerics, was given the title of "protector of Islam" and was subject to the kindness and favor of the eminent seminary scholars for many years.

It appears that for the National Front, participation in demonstrations such as the anniversary of the Imam of the Age and cooperation with the Association of Seminary Clerics, or those who were called combative pro-Mosaddeq clerics, was far more important than pushing aside the curtain that covered dark historic events and lifting the ban on the Tudeh Party. In fact, as far as it concerned confrontation with the Tudeh Party or fighting communism, it did not matter that the person who had made the assassination attempt on the Shah on 4 February 1949 had gone to the University of Tehran where that attempt took place with the press pass of *Parcham-e Eslam* (Banner of Islam) newspaper. The important point for the National Front was respect for the status of a famous cleric by the name of Ayatollah Kashani, who was referred to by the nationalists as the "revered leader," and whose presence, they said, "motivates unity of the word, inspires hope, and is the effective factor for lasting independence and strengthening the foundations of constitutionalism."[9] He was a famous cleric and one of the founders of the National Front, who during the administration of Mosaddeq occupied the seat of speaker of the National Consultative Assembly, and for that matter, at a time when the Tudeh Party continued to be banned.

Even in the ensuing years, as far as it concerned the ban on the Tudeh Party, the National Front insisted on the same policy. Concerning the beliefs of the National Front regarding the freedom of political parties, suffice it to say that even in the political resolution of its first congress, in which it addressed individual and social rights and freedoms, it only demanded the freedom of "authentic national" parties, as though the hidden secret of such a resolution, which had been embellished with emphasis on the need for the adherence to the Constitution and the Universal Declaration of Human Rights, meant nothing but opposition to the freedom of the Tudeh Party. Even though the resolution emphasized the necessity of the "elimination of censorship of the press, illegal pressure on printing houses, and prohibition of assemblies and political parties," it did not disregard declaring that such a demand includes only assemblies and political parties regarding the authenticity of which no doubt exists.[10] It was as though the hidden secret of "authenticity" from the perspective of the National Front became meaningful not only in its battle against communism, but in marring the concept of freedom.

Bakhtiar and the Rally of the National Front in Jalaliyeh

The rapid developments that with the removal of Zahedi and the inability of Ala', Eqbal, and Sharif-Emami had confronted the post-coup d'état governments with failure finally opened a new landscape in the horizon of Iranian politics with the appointment of Ali Amini as prime minister in May 1961, a prospect that increased hope for achieving freedom and reforms and passing beyond crisis, and simultaneously escalated the unrest. The ambitious prime minister of Iran at the height of this development had arrived "on the wings of crisis."[11]

Amini was born in 1905 in Tehran. He was of Qajar Dynasty lineage, the grandson of both Mozaffareddin Shah and Mirza Ali Khan Ami-noddowleh, Iran's reformist grand vizier. Amini had his early education in the Roshdiyeh and Darolfonun Schools; and after studying law in France, he returned to Iran with a doctoral degree. From the very beginning, he intended to become the prime minister some day, like his grandfather, to keep this position within his family. Amini considered his mother, Ashrafolmoluk (Fakhroddowleh), the daughter of Mozaffareddin Shah, as the person who encouraged him to attain fame and power.[iii] After returning from France, he worked in the Ministries of

---

[iii] Amini's mother, Ashrafolmoluk, was a well-known, highly regarded lady in praise of whom the famous constitutionalist cleric, Seyyed Hasan Modarres, had said, though in

Justice and Finance. It was there that he became familiar with the ins and outs of government bureaucracy and in particular gained experience in economic and financial affairs, until finally, as deputy prime minister, he joined the cabinet of Ahmad Qavam, the paternal uncle of his wife. He then became a minister in the cabinets of Ali Mansur and Mohammad Mosaddeq, and the minister of finance in the cabinet of Fazlollah Zahedi, when he assumed the grave responsibility of negotiating with the representatives of oil companies, a task that stained his name with bitter accusations as the signatory to the Oil Consortium Agreement. This caused him to face certain limitations in regard to support by the National Front. His appointment as prime minister was also attributed to having been by the will and wish of the United States, even though this was not considered to be an obstacle to gaining public support.

With the victory of John Kennedy in the United States presidential election in 1960, the speculations had gained strength that from then on, social liberties, reforms, and fighting corruption would be the central focus of that country's foreign policy in the Third World. The appointment of Amini as prime minister, after stepping down as Iran's ambassador to the United States, was deemed to be a reflection of that policy. The reality of these circumstances caused the National Front to consider the grounds to be more suitable than ever before for participating in the political process and having an impactful involvement in the country's developments, and all that without forgetting the past and, according to Bakhtiar, without trying to "endorse" Amini's government. Amini, however, had no fear of the aforementioned accusations, since he regarded himself to be a "realistic" politician, and considered politics to be "devoid of fear of fame and infamy." About his past, he said: "At the time when the Consortium Agreement was being discussed in the parliament, I said candidly that we had made our best effort and that it was not an agreement that was compatible with the ideals and wishes of

---

patriarchal terms: "There is only one man in the Qajar family, and she is Lady Fakhroddowleh."

the Iranian people, but nothing better was possible under the current circumstances. If I wanted to have national popularity or was afraid of accepting responsibility, I would certainly have stepped aside. In fact, Ayatollah Seyyed Abolqasem Kashani, who was fond of me, called me several times and said, 'Since I am fond of you, I am telling you to resign, because your life and dignity are in jeopardy.' I responded, 'I am grateful, but when I got involved in this task, it was to solve a problem in which my country was entangled, and I cannot leave the battleground now. You know well that I had no personal interest in the matter, except that I am doing my duty with regard to the people and my country. Of course, after ill-intentioned sentiments subside, history will judge that I rendered a service; otherwise, shirking one's responsibility is easy.'"[12]

The first reaction of the National Front to the appointment of Amini, who was assigned to form a cabinet in early May 1961, was based on reasoning that the nationalists had offered about the previous governments, as well, which is that they were illegal. Hence, the supreme council of the National Front, in a published announcement, declared the parliamentary elections null and void and the government approved by it, illegal. On 9 May 1961, only one day after the announcement of the supreme council of the National Front, upon Amini's request, the Shah dissolved both houses of parliament, an action that gained the widespread support of the people, given the manner in which the elections were conducted and the widespread fraud. The text of the edict emphasized that, considering the increasing difficulties of the country and the need for fundamental efforts to improve the affairs, the government is mandated to amend the election law and "take steps to hold new elections." With the publication of the edict, the National Front declared in an announcement that, in accordance with the Constitution, the reason for dissolving the parliament must be mentioned, the new elections must be held within one month, and both houses of parliament must resume their work within two months.[13]

About the dissolution of the two houses of parliament, which meant the implementation of an important demand of the National Front, years later, Bakhtiar said: "Mr. Amini had dissolved the parliament.

Now, whether or not a person dissolves the parliament makes no difference. Such parliaments do not represent the people. I mean, none of them did. But we were happy that it was dissolved, because we said that in accordance with the law, when he dissolved the parliament, he was obliged to hold elections again after a little while, and in that climate, we would have certainly won. The other reason that neither he nor the Shah wanted this to be done was that the National Front would win the elections, and it was not necessary to win a majority. When you have a force outside that supports you…every government has to count on such a force."[14]

From the very beginning, the issue of holding the elections and re-opening the parliament became the topic of one of the serious disputes between the National Front and the government. The leaders of the National Front had also made the issue of holding free elections the main focus of their policy during Sharif-Emami's premiership, and with a sit-in in the Senate, they had centered their activities on this demand. This was a demand based on the Constitution, which regarded a parliament elected by the votes of the people as a guarantee of the implementation of the principles of constitutionalism and the establishment of democratic liberties. There was, however, another reality that stemmed from the increasing concern of Amini about holding the elections. He was facing the risk that such an election prior to reforming the election law would provide the Shah and the large landowners the opportunity to win the seats in the parliament, thus neutralizing his efforts to achieve deep social reforms, and alongside the ongoing conspiracies against his government, they would also prevent the implementation of his programs in the parliament. These were the obligations and considerations in regard to how to devise policy and how to advance in the ongoing power struggle that in the ensuing months created endless tension and eventually deadlocks in the relationship between the National Front and the government. This issue had also not remained concealed from Julius Holmes, the American Ambassador in Tehran, and the State Department officials of that country. According to their assessment, the possibility existed that the Shah would in the near future give in to the pressure to hold free elections, not that he wanted the elections for their own sake, but, rather, to use the elections as a tool to be able to control Amini, or even get rid of him.[15]

This fact had focused Amini's attention more than ever before on cooperating with and gaining the support of the National Front for his policies. In an interview, the details of which are recorded in documents of the United States National Security Archive, Bakhtiar says in this connection: "Ali Amini, Prime Minister, had appointed a small group of his friends to talk with representatives of the NF about cooperation between the NF and the government. Bakhtiar did not feel that any significant progress would be made."[16]

In the latter part of May 1960, the news of the arrests of a number of high-ranking military commanders and the consent of the government for the National Front to hold a rally on Jalaliyeh Square of Tehran were indicative of extensive developments that within a short period of time after Amini came to power were a sign of change in the interest of the forces that supported reforms. The publication of the news of the establishment of the Freedom Front (Nehzat-e Azadi) in the press and the printing of Mosaddeq's photograph in the newspapers of the capital city were also actual events that were far from expectations, actual events that would place land distribution and the abolition of large land ownership, fighting corruption in government organizations, support for domestic producers, decrease in the cost of living, and emphasis on law and security in the society at the top of the government's programs.

Regarding the National Front's rally, which became known as "Mit-ing-e Jalaliyeh" (Rally at Jalaliyeh, which is now Laleh Park), as an important factor in destroying the relationship between the nationalists and the government, the statements of the leaders of the National Front, especially about the preparations for that rally, contain unclear and sometimes contradictory points that make a final assessment about it difficult. All we know is that Amini's consent to the holding of the rally, especially shortly after he was appointed as prime minister, was a very difficult step. Cognizant of the Shah's sensitivity about the ongoing developments, he had asked the leaders of the National Front to postpone the rally for a few days, until the return of the Shah from Norway, a request that was not accepted, and despite his own inclination, Amini agreed to it while the Shah was abroad.[17]

According to Mehdi Azar, a member of the executive committee of the National Front, in the course of deciding about the rally and about speakers and the topic of the speeches, the decision was made that Sanjabi and Sadiqi be chosen as speakers, and that the topics of the speeches be "only about the ideology of the National Front, its demand for a lawful government, and also mentioning the government's illegal treatment of the National Front and other freedom fighting parties. In particular, it was decided that nothing should be said and no names should be mentioned in connection with the oil issue, its nationalization by Dr. Mosaddeq, and the National Front's support for him." According to Azar, in the same meeting, which was held to make preparations for the rally, or in another one, the name of Shapour Bakhtiar was also added to the list of speakers, on his own request, with the emphasis that the topic of the speech remain confined to whatever had been determined before. Sanjabi and Bazargan, also in criticizing Bakhtiar's speech, mention more or less the same points. Sanjabi states that they were not supposed to speak about "provocative" and "damaging" issues, and Bazargan recounts the decision of the supreme council of the National Front that "speakers must not speak about the foreign policy of the government, the Consortium Agreement, or CENTO" (the Central Treaty Organization). According to him, "Mosaddeq's name was also not supposed to be mentioned."[18]

Bakhtiar, however, presents a different picture of the preliminary work done to prepare for the National Front rally. He states that they sat down together and he said: "I will make some general criticism of the government, Sanjabi should talk about freedom, and Sadiqi about the law, or the other way around. Neither did I see a line of their speech, nor did they see a line of mine." In addition, considering the criticism made of his speech for discussing the oil issue or the Consortium,

Bakhtiar denies having said a word on these topics. Another point worthy of note is that, according to *Payam-e Daneshju*, the publication of the students committee of the University of Tehran affiliated with the National Front, just prior to the holding of the rally on Jalaliyeh Square, certain important changes had been made in the executive committee, changes on the basis of which Sanjabi had been elected as the president and Bakhtiar, as the general manager of the organization. Azar, Khalili, and Keshavarz-Sadr were other members of the leadership of this organization, and Saleh was no longer a member of the executive committee.[19]

In the afternoon of 18 May 1961, Jalaliyeh Square was filled with a crowd of people who had gathered to listen to the speeches of the leaders of the National Front. The first speaker, Sanjabi, harshly criticized the past governments and demanded the holding of elections. He called the text of the edict for the dissolving the two houses of parliament and evading the announcement of the date of the next elections a violation of the explicit text of the Constitution, and quoting Article 48 of the Constitution regarding the dissolving of the parliament, which emphasized that "in any instance that the two houses of parliament or one of them should be dissolved by Imperial Command, the reason for the dissolution must be mentioned in the same command, and at the same time, orders shall be given for the holding of new elections. The new elections must begin within one month from the date of the issuance of the edict, and the new parliament or two new houses of the parliament must be in session within three months of that date," he called the attention of the government to observing the articles of the Constitution and to constitutionalism. The focal point of Sadiqi's speech, also similar to that of Sanjabi, was the issue of holding the elections. Explaining the crisis conditions of the country, he called the previous governments "lawbreakers" and spoke about "misfortune" and "the horrendous and horrifying spiritual poverty" of the society, as well as the need for "the freedom of expression and the freedom of the press."[20]

The final speaker of the Jalaliyeh Square rally, Bakhtiar, offering a comprehensive picture regarding various issues, explained the policy of the National Front on domestic issues, the economic and cultural situation, the judiciary of the country, oil, and Iran's position in international treaties. At the beginning of his fervent speech, he criticized the past governments that had dragged the country to "absolute bankruptcy, despite hundreds of millions of dollars in oil revenues and hundreds of millions of dollars in back-breaking loans, by the force of bayonets, incarceration, exile, torture, and misguiding propaganda"; and addressing Amini's government, he said: "The articles of the Constitution and the rights of the people of Iran are the foundation of social order. In the name of whatever is expedient today, the rights that have been explicitly stated in the Constitution must not be toyed with, and individual and social freedoms must not be trampled with sophistry and bogus verbosity." Up to this point, his emphasis in criticizing the past governments and the government of Amini in connection with postponing the elections was more or less based on the same points to which attention had been paid in the speeches of Sanjabi and Sadiqi, although in expressing these points, theirs were not toned as harshly and bitterly as Bakhtiar's words. Sanjabi even criticized the text of the edict on the dissolving of the two houses of parliament that had been signed by the Shah, and without mentioning his name, he spoke of the "lack of good intentions" of those who prepared the edict. Even though he referred to Amini as a person who "has no support among the people," and saw in the prospects for the future no other end but the "negation of his experiment," he also left open a small window for coming to an understanding and said: "We are of the same mind as those who have diagnosed Iran's condition as being dangerous... Now, are they asking what the remedy is? The only remedy is to sincerely, non-hypocritically, truthfully, honestly, and compassionately turn to the nation and return its sovereignty to it." Sadiqi also left the past to the past, and without being condescending or bowing and surrendering, looked to the future, and addressing Amini, said: "Others sat straight and spoke crookedly; sit crookedly and speak straight."[21]

Bakhtiar, however, in the continuation of his speech, emphasized issues of a different kind. Now that as a member of the executive committee, he had climbed to the sensitive position of general manager of the organizations of the National Front, he called the University of Tehran and the Abadan Refinery the "thinking brain and capable arm" of the Iranian people, and by doing so, made a reference, although vague and concealed, to his distinguished role in those two "unconquerable" strongholds of the National Front. This was a reference to his position and the authority in charge of student affairs of the National Front at the University of Tehran, and a reminder about his services at the Abadan Refinery, when he was on assignment in Khuzestan. In the name of the National Front, he promised "to punish without mercy, most carefully, and severely all individuals who in the past recent years have taken undue advantage of their positions and have committed violations of the treasury of the people or the Constitution and the human rights declarations." Bakhtiar spoke about mandatory training, the concentration of all forces on the creation of heavy industries, and organizing the society on the basis of the absence of class differences and said: "The National Front has planned extensive in-depth programs for managing modern Iran, which it will implement if it comes to power. In the economic affairs, parallel to production and development, it will necessarily and mandatorily insure all members of the society against poverty, ignorance, unemployment, and illness." This was a claim that, considering the depth of Iran's economic and financial crisis, even if it was not for public deception, stemmed from lack of awareness of the harsh realities, the disregarding of which would have no other result but the provocation of public sentiments, appeasement, and boasting about the capabilities of the nationalists to overcome the crisis and build a promising future. In this sense, Bakhtiar's error was not in raising these demands as a long-term plan, but in suggesting that, from his point of view, the National Front was capable of achieving all those feats within a short period of time.

To Bakhtiar, the foreign policy of the National Front was to avoid "participation in hostile blocs and military pacts," which suggested the need to stay out of any policy that helped the Cold War, and recognized this as a distinct aspect of an independent Iran on the world stage.[iv] This was a suggestion that meant opposition to Iran's remaining a member of CENTO.

Bakhtiar then mentioned Mosaddeq's role in the nationalization of the oil industry, and in doing so, he discussed an issue which, alongside the issue of foreign policy and Iran's membership in CENTO, was supposed to be avoided by the speakers. Contrary to Bazargan's statement, the mentioning of Mosaddeq's name was apparently allowed, and it could not be criticized by other leaders of the National Front, since Sanjabi and Sadiqi had also mentioned his name. Their reference to Mosaddeq's name, however, was only and solely to his participation in the parliament and the election law, not in the context of the issue of oil and the Consortium. Even though Bakhtiar had also refrained from speaking "one word" about the Consortium, speaking about Mosaddeq's role in the nationalization of the oil industry went beyond the references made by Sanjabi and Sadiqi to Mosaddeq's name.

At the end of his speech, Bakhtiar also made a brief reference to past mistakes: "The collective leadership of our National Front of Iran will deter us from making some of the technical and tactical errors of the past."[22] Even though this issue is mentioned in passing, Bakhtiar's courage in his reference to this issue was worthy of much contemplation. Even though he reduced the strategic mistakes of the National Front during the administration of Mosaddeq to "technical and tactical errors," emphasizing the phrase "collective leadership" as a deterrent factor to the repetition of errors meant nothing but a criticism of

---

[iv] Bakhtiar's outlook in this connection had been shaped by the Bandung Conference which was held in 1955. In that conference, the leaders of India, Egypt, and Indonesia raised the concept of establishing an assembly by the name of Non-Aligned countries. In 1961, the first conference of the leaders of this group was held in Belgrade with the participation of Yugoslavia's President Josip Broz Titi, Ghana's president Kwame Nkrumah, India's Prime Minister Jawaharlal Nehru, Egypt's President Gamal Abdel Nasser, and Indonesia's President Sukarno. The Non-Aligned Movement holds a conference once every three years and it has more than 120 member countries.

Mosaddeq, who at one time as the man in charge was called the un-matched leader of the National Front, in charge of mistakes that in the error-concealing words of Bakhtiar were apparently secondary and could be disregarded.

With the ratification of the resolution of the rally, which Daryush Foruhar read, the first gathering of the National Front, which had been welcomed by various groups of people, was concluded. What had occurred in Jalaliyeh Square, however, indicated a different conclusion, an end that was indicative of the disarray in the position of the national-ists in understanding the necessities and limitations that could shatter the reforms that, after a difficult beginning, were taking the first steps on a path that had been paved by the premiership of Amini. Heedless of the opportunity that had been provided, not by relying on a widespread movement, but in the wake of a profound crisis and with the support of the United States, the National Front rose in confrontation with a reality that in the end had no fate but the autocracy and dictatorship of the Shah. The memories and the contradictory and sometimes confused statements of the leaders of the National Front about how the Jalaliyeh Square rally was held, despite the differences in speaking about a historic event, are crystal clear about one point, and that is that the preparations for that gathering were coupled with indescribable confusion. About that gathering, Azar speaks of the agreement on avoiding mentioning the role of Mosaddeq in the oil nationalization issue, Sanjabi about the "provocative" and "damaging" points in Bakhtiar's speech, and Bazargan about the issue of silence regarding the "foreign policy of the govern-ment, the Consortium Agreement, and CENTO," and states: "They should not have talked about Mosaddeq, whereas not only Bakhtiar, but Sanjabi and Sadiqi as well, although from a different perspective, mentioned Mosaddeq." The resolution of the rally emphasized that "devising of an independent Iranian foreign policy and a measured and progressive plan" in various "economic, political, social, and administra-tive areas is a part of the plan of the National Front of Iran," although what was of prime importance to them was the holding of free elections and guaranteeing the freedoms explicitly stated in the Constitution and the International Declaration of Human Rights.[23]

If that was the case, then why was it necessary for Bakhtiar to raise all those issues and, in careless judgment, to speak of the National Front's commitment, not to the trial, but to the "punishment without mercy" of those who violated the rights of the nation, and for that matter, without any trial? On the basis of which study and the assessment of which financial and economic capability were the masses of the people going to be insured against "poverty, ignorance, unemployment, and illness" if the National Front came to power, and in which congress, assembly, or meeting was such a decision made? Even though at the height of the Cold War, considering that support for the "Non-Aligned Movement" was defensible and thus meaningful, at a time when not much had passed since the propaganda and military threats of the Soviet Union on the northern borders and when the United States in advancing its foreign policy found overcoming economic crisis and implementation of political reforms in Iran necessary, what could be the meaning of speaking about "an independent Iranian foreign policy"? If we agree that the emphasis of the rally's resolution on determining the foreign policy and devising plans for various social areas in the society was not of primary importance under those conditions, and if we agree that this was an effort to reduce the tension that Bakhtiar created by emphasizing those points, the question remains: Why was no attention paid to this issue prior to his speech? Bakhtiar claimed that the topics of the speeches were supposed to be about the law, freedom, and criticism of the government; if so, what was the reason for addressing topics that were not supposed to be discussed? In his speech, he regarded unity and "being of one heart and one tongue" to be the superior characteristic of the leaders of the National Front as true leaders of the people. How was it then that, despite the joint decision that was made about the rally and the topics of the speeches between him and Sanjabi and Sadiqi, neither had Bakhtiar seen "one line" of their speeches nor had they seen one line of his? Why was Saleh, who was not one of the speakers, in the rally and on the speech platform? Apparently, Saleh more than others became "upset and depressed" by Bakhtiar's "autocratic" speech, and Sadiqi, expressing his discontentment about Bakhtiar's speech, had said that those statements were his "personal views." Was all this not another sign of the confusion in the organization's position, which cannot be called anything other than a "suspended coalition?"[v] It was a suspended coalition since, according to Azar's claim, Bakhtiar's name was placed alongside the names of Sanjabi and Sadiqi on his own suggestion, and because he was "young and seeking to make a name for himself."[24] No matter the answer to this question, undoubtedly, the rally in Jalaliyeh Square and its consequences were of much greater value than to come to such an end, a fateful end the impact of which on the future of the National Front and possibly the people of Iran can be considered to be more important than the personal views of a person who was "young and seeking to make a name for himself."

One day after the rally, Hasan Arsanjani, the minister of agriculture and a powerful man in the cabinet, in a meeting with Sanjabi, told him: "Make no mistake, the Shah is very powerful; and if you get into a fight with Amini, you will strengthen the Shah."[25] Sanjabi and the National Front, however, never fully understood the meaning of those few words, words that at a different time determined the sad fate of the reforms in Iran. It was as though Arsanjani's warning was a fateful message the resonance of which had already been lost in the turmoil and commotion in Jalaliyeh Square, in the climate of errors and injudicious deeds of the leaders of the National Front. Standing up to Amini meant standing up against a process that from the very beginning was subject to the risk of disruptive actions by the Shah and the Royal Court. The forces that could not tolerate profound and lasting social reforms did not lose any chance to carry on what Sanjabi had already called Amini's "false experiment," an opportunity the loss of which, aided by the cheering

---

[v] For more on the choice of "suspended coalition" in the organizational and political structure of the National Front, see: Ahmad Banijamali, *Ashub: Motale'eh'i dar Zendegi va Shakhsiyat-e Dr. Mohammad Mosaddeq* (Tehran: Ney Publishers, 2007), 279-280.

and jubilant dancing of the nationalists, came to a culmination within a short period of time.

In the meantime, apparently worried about the negative reaction of the United States to the incidents in the rally in Jalaliyeh Square, Bakhtiar tried to clarify the views of the National Front about current issues and the future, the details of which have been recorded in the United States National Security Archive. In a long interview with a "competent American observer," he explained: "Incidentally, *Kayhan International* greatly exaggerated my statements at the Jalaliyeh Stadium meeting in May, saying 'Front Demands Neutrality.' I did comment on the desire of the people for an independent policy for Iran, and I did refer to Nehru, but it was not as indicated by that newspaper." Bakhtiar added: "For example, some students have recently been outspoken about CENTO, and I have had to quiet them and calm them down. Such extreme ideas must be controlled or they lead to chaos. Naturally, I feel that CENTO is not beneficial to Iran. If it is constituted an automatic guarantee, like NATO, it would be of more value. I see CENTO, however, as being primarily a British device whereby they can maintain their pressure here—their political pressure… If I should be prime minister, I would get out of CENTO, within a day, a month, or a year, depending on the circumstances."[26]

Bakhtiar further added: "We must have neutralism in the Middle East, so that between the East and the West there will be a series of neutral and independent states. Total neutrality is, of course, impossible… Basically, Iran has a traditional tie with the West which cannot be simply erased… Basically, the people of Iran, prior to August 1953, had more love and respect for the United States than for any other country. You had done many things to help us, and we appreciated it. But August 1953 was a severe blow to American prestige here. Since then, American prestige has gone down. You have spent over a billion dollars here, only to be less loved for it. I am not sorry for the billion dollars that you have given us; I am only sorry that it has gone to the wrong places and the wrong uses, and that you have suffered as a result. But in the last few years, we have sensed that perhaps the United States is coming to recognize its error. Perhaps the loss of the past few years can be recovered. I am not just speaking of Iranian interests here, but the best interests of Iran and the United States and the best interests of humanity as well."[27]

Then discussing the United States policy in connection with the current developments in Iran, Bakhtiar said: "We have felt that the half-freedoms that have been given to the NF are not unrelated to the new American policy. So the people look with some favor on the United States. Our government cannot do anything by itself, only with your help. If our feeling is right, then it would be unwise for the United States to help bring back a military dictatorship. General Fazlollah Zahedi was our Fulgencio Batista. There is much talk of a *coup de plalais* these days. If such a thing would occur, it would be so clear to the people that they would rebel on the first day. Only democratic reforms can clear the way for a good future for Iran. Any person or group that is so inclined, if it should understand that it has the moral and material support of the Americans, and if the Americans believe that the country can really be reformed, that group could accomplish the task. United States support would have the greatest possible effect on any such person's motions. But this must not be accomplished at the cost of servility."[28]

Regarding the bilateral pact with the United States, Bakhtiar said: "The bilateral pact with the United States is our guarantee against aggression, and neither Turkey nor Pakistan has any voice in it. I consent in maintaining this agreement. I would not mind having a similar one with the Soviets, but if they do not offer one, that is all right." Regarding Soviet aid, he said: "I have not been in a position to witness first hand a Soviet aid program anywhere. But I believe that if such a program could be completely without conditions and it did not pave the way for penetration into our political life, a truly national government could not refuse Soviet offers of aid. But this can be very dangerous, because they might use their aid program for political purposes, making sudden and unwanted pressures. The Iron Curtain could come down quickly over Iran, and raising it would be difficult, indeed... The Soviets could overcome Iran in two ways. First, by direct aggression, about which we could do little. Second, by penetration. The only way to prevent this is to give satisfaction to national sentiments, and to follow up with a serious program of economic reform and development. The people can live on slogans for a while, but then there must be some accomplishments." Considering Iran's long common border with the Soviets, Bakhtiar emphasized: "We cannot ignore them, and we must do what we can to develop a reasonable relationship with them...to have them neutral in Iran, and grant us a non-aggression pact." He called the policy that the Shah followed in connection with the Soviet Union "shortsighted." In Bakhtiar's opinion as expressed to the "competent American observer," the government and the Shah were "very foolish...when they tried to blackmail you with all that business about a non-aggression pact with the Soviets."[29]

In this interview, which began with a discussion about economic issues, Bakhtiar spoke about the necessity of building a steel mill for the development of the Iranian industries and added: "We are backward, but we are not without sources of wealth. Foreign aid is essential and is desirable if well spent, and in the right places. It is not good, however, if its purpose is merely to keep a government in power, as has been in the past few years. This is not good from the standpoint of the Americans either... A government that is truly popular can well use foreign aid, but a government that remains only because it receives foreign aid cannot." Regarding foreign advisors, he said: "We need them. We have to have them. They are no threat to our national pride if they are good advisors doing for us what we cannot do for ourselves. They are like a doctor who comes to treat a man who is not well. It is, of course, ideal for us to employ Iranians in all such technical and professional positions, but this is not possible now. We do not have enough properly trained Iranians."[30]

The issue of oil and the Consortium was another part of Bakhtiar's interview with the American official. In his opinion: "The consortium agreement was signed against the will of the people." However, he emphasized: "Such an agreement, had it been concluded by the Mossadeq government, would not have been so unpopular." According to him: "Even a much more desirable agreement, completed by the then government, could never be popular." Bakhtiar added: "But we have many other problems, serious and important problems, to solve before attacking this one." Stating that the conditions of time and place must be taken into consideration in the policy that must ultimately be devised in regard to the Consortium, and that any revision should be through discussions and negotiations, not hasty and sudden measures, he added: "One of the students at the University of Tehran was saying 'Death to the consortium,' and we expelled him."[31]

Referring to the position and the policies of the National Front, Bakhtiar said: "There are many groups and ideologies in the NF, and our great weakness is that we must accept a kind of average of the sentiments and beliefs that they hold. We have common goals, but we are lacking any kind of general ideologies. For example, we have religious figures in the NF who could not tolerate talk of women's equality with men, or even of the principles expressed in the Declaration of Human Rights… And on the other hand, we have many feudal landlords who will not hear any talk about land reform. And so it goes. We must not be thought of as a party, strictly speaking, but as a front in the European sense, a group of different groups and individuals who have joined together for the accomplishment of certain specific goals… Our weakness comes from the lack of solidifying ideology."[32]

Bakhtiar then discussed the issue of leadership and the factional divisions within the National Front and said about Mosaddeq: "Mossadeq himself is not, and can no longer be, an effective leader. At best he can serve only as a kind of spiritual figure. He is greatly loved by the people, of course, but he is finished, in terms of actual politics. I cannot say who might be the man chosen to be a prime minister from the NF, because that is up to the Shah, by law. But I presume that Saleh would have the best chance of being selected."[33]

In the continuation of this interview, Bakhtiar addressed the necessity of gradually reducing the number of people in the military and ensuring that they are well trained and well equipped to defend the borders of the country. Free elections, his opposition to the Tudeh Party, the inability of Amini's government, and the nationalists' lack of confidence in the Shah were among other topics that he discussed. Bakhtiar defended the principle that the Shah must reign, and not rule, and said: "Essentially, we must retain the monarchy... We are not yet ready to have a republic."[34]

In the meantime, the ensuing months passed with the squabbles between the National Front and the government of Amini over the date for holding the elections. In the latter days of August 1961, the negotiations that had been held with the participation of the prime minister and the leaders of the National Front for finding a way to settle their differences failed. The arrests and release of a large number of students of the University of Tehran of Tehran and the leaders of the National Front during a gathering of the nationalists on the anniversary of the incident on 21 July 1952, which occurred shortly prior to the failure of the negotiations, seemed a new effort that increased the hope for reaching an understanding, an effort the failure of which resulted in even more tensions between the opposition and the government. From then on, the demand for the dismissal of Amini was tied together with the motto for free elections, and his position, which had faced increasing problems and interruptions by the Royal Court and conservative elements following the Jalaliyeh Square rally, was confronted with new difficulties. Perhaps aware of this difficult position and the increasing isolation of Amini, the Shah declared his "dissatisfaction" to the American officials about the prime minister having had no other supporter but him.[35]

The National Front and the Incident at the University of Tehran

On 21 January 1962, with the unprecedented raid of the antiriot forces on the University of Tehran, the last fragile ties between the National Front and the government of Amini were broken. Since a month earlier, signs of unrest could be seen in the University of Tehran due to the students' efforts to show solidarity with a few students from Darolfonun

High School who had been expelled because of political activity, and also in protest to the termination of financial aid to the first-year students of the Teacher Training College. A few days prior to these incidents, the executive committee of the National Front, in a meeting in which Bakhtiar also participated, decided to hold demonstrations at the University of Tehran in order to show solidarity with the expelled pre-collegiate students and to support the demands of the Teacher Training College freshmen. The task of making preparations for these demonstrations was conferred on the Young People's Organization and the student committee of the National Front.

By closing down the classes on 21 January 1962 and shouting slogans such as "the movement will continue until the death of the dictators," the implicit meaning of which went beyond solidarity with the students of Darolfonun and the Teachers Training College, the University of Tehran students began a march on the university campus. Apparently due to rumors, there were also certain concerns: "From the circles in the bazaar and other sources, news had been received that certain groups intended to turn the 21 January demonstrations into demonstrations far larger than an ordinary protest gathering. Even apparently in some branches, a number of cable pieces and clubs had been distributed in preparation for the following day. It was strongly suspected that Dr. Khonji's group along with some of his supporters, such as Dr. Mas'ud Hejazi and Ahmad Salamatiyan, who was in charge of the young people's committee of the National Front, were involved in this plan. This issue and the issue that other interested groups might take advantage of these events were openly discussed in the students committee and with Dr. Sanjabi. Nevertheless, considering the existing differences of opinion, in practice, other than Sanjabi appointing Banisadr as the person in charge of maintaining order in the next day's demonstrations, no other specific plan or guidelines were offered... In the meantime, considering the extensive presence of the law enforcement forces and the resulting clashes, the number of demonstrators began to decrease. One group left the campus through the east and north gates, and those in another group who had been injured, after receiving emergency care, were delivered to the city's clinics and hospitals. Hence, around 11:00 a.m., a total of only about 300 demonstrators were still there. Nevertheless, around 11:30 a.m., the paratroopers along with the Police Academy and Gendarmerie forces suddenly rushed into the campus through the doors and from in between the fence rails, and in a savage raid, assaulted and beat whoever they found on their way. According to one of the eyewitnesses, 'the police and the law enforcement forces…beat the female students with the intention of killing them. They ripped their clothes off and tossed them on the lawn. The students took shelter inside the buildings of the colleges. The police broke the windows and, shouting savagely, stormed into the buildings. The students took shelter in the classrooms. The police chased them, threw them out of the classrooms, and beat and wounded them. The furnishings in the buildings were all broken. They even pulled out the university employees, who had been hiding in some corner during the demonstrations, one by one, and beat them.' Even though the government announced the number of wounded as 120 students and 96 law enforcement personnel, the actual number of those injured (or at least the student portion of them) was far beyond these numbers. Such violence had been unprecedented."[36]

Amini assessed the incident at the University of Tehran, which on the following day resulted in demonstrations and clashes between the law enforcement officials and the opponents, as a pre-organized conspiracy, one that by creating turmoil and riots and escalating the unrest was indicative of a widespread plot, the main goal of which was to topple the government. He identified the feudal landlords and the extremist elements of the National Front as responsible for the university incident and issued an order for the arrest of a number of people affiliated with the Royal Court and the leaders of the National Front. Amini also asked the Shah to agree to the arrest of Teymur Bakhtiar, the head of SAVAK, as the main perpetrator of the riots and turmoil that had occurred. The Shah did not agree to this request; but he did send Teymur Bakhtiar to the United States. Also, on the order of the government, a three-member committee called the "Investigation Committee Assigned to

Examine the 21 January 1962 Incident" was formed for investigating the incidents that had occurred at the university. After a few months, that committee prepared a report on the university incident, according to which, evidence showed that the issue of solidarity for the expelled students and the issue of financial aid to the students of the Teachers Training College essentially had been unrelated to how the demonstrations were held and to its slogans, which were political. Moreover, all three expelled students had registered in other high schools, and refraining from the payment of financial aid to the students of the Teachers Training College was based on the bylaws of the Ministry of Culture regarding the independence of the Teachers Training College and was legally justifiable. Accordingly, "because of its opposition to the government, the executive committee of the National Front has used the insignificant and settled issue of a few expelled students who were already studying in other schools, and the request of financial aid by the students of the Teachers Training College, which was not rational and legal considering the background of this issue, as a pretext to organize demonstrations at the university and in schools in order to display its power, to express opposition, and to impose its demands." In addition, according to that report, the executive committee of the National Front had been negligent, and in particular, Sanjabi had neglected his grave responsibility as a professor in the College of Law, the head of the executive committee, and the person in charge of the university's student office affiliated with the National Front. When the students went to his home to "receive instructions" just prior to the demonstrations, neglectful of the duty conferred on him, he had failed to take any steps to outline and regulate the program for the ensuing demonstrations and the provocations. Under such sensitive conditions, the fate of 14,000 students and a larger number of pre-collegiate students had been "entrusted to a few inexperienced students, among whom, unfortunately, no consensus existed, each having his own plan, and the result was what we witnessed." The report of the investigation committee also strongly criticized the roles of Mas'ud Hejazi, as the person in charge of the Young People's Organization of the National Front, and his colleagues, such as Ahmad Salamatiyan, as the liaison between the Young People's Organization and the National Front. In the course of the 21 January demonstrations, Salamatiyan had played "an extraordinarily influential role, was more active than others, and prior to the entry of the law enforcement forces, he was the one who encouraged the students to go toward the University Club and, according to him, destroy that nest of spies." Harshly criticizing Mohammad Derakhshesh, the minister of culture, Ahmad Farhad, the president of the University of Tehran, and the deans of the colleges, the report of the investigation committee strongly criticized the officials in charge of maintaining order and discipline at the university, and reprimanded the law enforcement forces for their violent actions. The report also contained some vague references to the role of Teymur Bakhtiar, a few individuals close to the Royal Court, and some "influential clerics" who, by "organizing gatherings, delivering speeches, and publishing announcements and statements, have used the issue of the elections as a pretext for vehement attacks on the government, and for actions with the intention of creating a coalition of the opponents and preparing the grounds for toppling the government," although in this connection, either no "irrefutable evidence of their complicity" had been found, or their direct involvement in the university incident was an issue that would become clear in the future, with the trial of individuals under prosecution.[37]

The University of Tehran incident instigated other reactions, as well, that are worthy of contemplation. Bizhan Jazani, one of the leaders of the student movement, assessed the 21 January 1962 incident to be the result of the concerted thinking of Khonji and Hejazi, two influential members of the National Front, as well as the opponents of Amini. In his words, as a result: "The expelling of a few students from the schools in Tehran became a pretext for demonstrations and a general strike." Criticizing what he calls the "strategic mistake" of the leadership of the National Front in their confrontation with Amini, regarding the university incident, Khalil Maleki said: "After all these mistakes one after another, did we try to correct our policy? It was clear that if things continued as they were, the result would be a catastrophe, and unfortunately, that is precisely what happened. Once again, because of demonstrations on a specific day (the day that the agents of the reactionaries and feudal landlords assumed would be their victory day, and they had also already decided on their own government cabinet), we became involved in an issue we did not know about, and the 21 January university catastrophe occurred. Strangely enough, informed individuals, who had figured out the conspiracies behind the scene, had warned the leaders of the National Front, and even the government, in its own interests, tried to stop the National Front forces from becoming involved in the interest of the feudal landlords, which would mean the fall of the government. Despite all this, the leadership of the National Front, with astounding insistence, sent thousands of students to be beaten by whips, bayonets, and billy clubs, and what it gained was a few hundred wounded people, the long closure of the university, and a more stifling climate."[38]

In the meantime, the National Front also formed a committee for examining the university incident, a committee about which Jazani says, "its members were manifestations of incompetence and conservatism," and its inquiries "never clarified anything." With the passage of time, Saleh called the occurrence at the university a "horrible crime," a crime that, according to Saleh, the ruling group had committed to break asunder the "organizational and political power" of the nationalists and to justify "its shameful acts" by "making a series of unjust accusations and charging the sacred movement" of connection to the groups on the right and left. Sanjabi, as well, without any reconsideration and revision, regarded the policy of the National Front in connection with the university event as one of the "proud accomplishments" of the nationalists, and up to the end of his life, did not express any doubts about its "authenticity."[39]

In this process, Amini's government, which at the height of the crisis faced numerous difficulties, shortcomings, and disruptions, collapsed.

Bakhtiar and the Negotiations of the National Front and the Ruling Power

With the fall of Amini's government and the appointment of Asadollah Alam as prime minister in July 1962, the possibilities still existed for the participation of the National Front in the current developments of the country. Alam's invitation to Saleh for negotiations, which took place on the order of the Shah, indicated that the new government wanted the resumption of the talks that had failed during Amini's administration. The readiness of the central council of the National Front to accept this invitation also showed that there were still possibilities for talks and negotiations about the current issues of the country. These negotiations, which also failed, were held from September 1962 in three rounds between the prime minister and the representatives of the National Front, alternatively at the homes of Alam and Saleh. Even though the negotiations were not official, the results were made available to the public with the publication of an announcement by the National Front in December 1962. Mehdi Azar, a member of the central council of the National Front, who accompanied Saleh to participate in the first round of the negotiations, years later wrote about the meetings: "Alam expressed the Shah's interest in the National Front of Iran, especially his respect for the late Saleh, and said that His Imperial Majesty has said several times that the gentlemen of the National Front are 'assets,' and as a result of their past services, they have gained fame and prestige among the people of Iran and abroad. He has also said that we should make more use of their credibility, experience, and competence in government services. Also, whenever he has consulted about a tutor for His Highness the Crown Prince, everyone has made suggestions, and in the end, everyone has voted in favor of Mr. Saleh. His Majesty has said, 'He is fine, but he might not agree to it. In any case, someone needs to speak with him.' Expressing his gratitude for the Shah's 'interest and favor,' Saleh regarded the acceptance of 'serving and responsibility' as very 'difficult' because of the conditions of the country, and added, 'The National Front or any other organization that wants to accept responsibility and form a government must inevitably take such matters into consideration and think of prudent answers in order to be able to accomplish something and serve; otherwise, that government would not be able to do anything, and the end would be what it is now.'"[40]

The next round of negotiations, which this time were at Saleh's invitation, ended without any results. At the beginning of the session, without mentioning the National Front's name, Alam emphasized the point that, if a few were arrested in the middle of the night and executed, nothing would happen. Thus far, as well, it had been only royal "kindness and affection" that had impeded such actions. On the other hand, His Majesty did not want the type of constitutional monarchy that the National Front demanded. The reason for that was an experience in another era that determined the fate of Ahmad Shah, the last Qajar king. This time, such a fate, the deposing of the Shah, was prevented only by the "uprising of the people" on 19 August 1953, and "His Imperial Majesty who had left" returned to the country. Alam added: "Despite all this, the government is prepared to appoint a few of the selected members of the National Front to such positions as governor general, ambassador, and senator, positions other than minister. Appointment as minister, although there is no problem with it, is with the consideration that not much time has passed since the current government has come to office, and changing and shuffling its members will not be expedient or pleasant. In addition, the government will leave the elections for the National Consultative Assembly and the Senate to the National Front in Tabriz, Isfahan, Yazd, Mashhad, and Tehran, so that the gentlemen themselves or a few of their friends and like-minded members who wish, will become candidates in the elections of the aforementioned cities, and the ones who get enough votes will become representatives in the National Consultative Assembly or the Senate." Saleh responded that "the National Front was not formed for acquiring positions and being selected as representatives in the National Consultative Assembly or the Senate," and he demanded a "legal government" and the "improvement of the country's situation by the proper implementation of the Constitution and free elections throughout Iran, that is all." Accordingly, he rejected Alam's offer for participation in the elections of the two houses of parliament and government positions, ranks, and services as suggested. The final meeting also was concluded with the presentation of a written text to Alam that contained three points about the National Front's stipulations for participating in the elections, or its readiness for "appointment to the positions and services that the government offered." The full implementation of the Constitution, free elections throughout the country, and the monarch's refraining from interfering in affairs that, in accordance with the Constitution, were exclusively within the jurisdiction of the government were the stipulations that Saleh offered the prime minister, with the approval of the central council of the National Front. With these stipulations, if "His Majesty agrees to in writing and signs it, the National front will be ready to be of service."[41]

Undoubtedly, the proposed stipulations of the National Front, which were based on the articles and the content of the Constitution, were irrefutably credible; but the implementation of political reforms and the ongoing power struggle required other considerations, especially in confrontation with a monarch who had not long before dismissed a reformist prime minister; and by getting through a crisis that was unprecedented since Mosaddeq's administration, he had overcome a grave problem. Understanding this fact was itself one of the requirements for taking the upper hand in the power struggle, achieving social reforms, and creating change in the political arena. These were considerations disregard for which would render any effort for compromise and settlement devoid of credibility and the result of any talk and negotiation, null and void before it began.

Had the Shah been determined to accept the Constitution in all its aspects and give up interfering in affairs that were only and solely related to the government, why would he any longer need to enter into negotiations and talks with the National Front, and for that matter, by giving a written guarantee and signing a text that had been unilaterally prepared by the nationalists? It seemed that for the leaders of the National Front, lack of attention to the experience they had had regarding the administration of Amini had resulted in a lost opportunity, of the importance of which they were negligent, this time, in the course of negotiations and talks with Alam. This fact, in the words of Zirakzadeh, a member of the central council of the National Front, about whatever determined the fate of that organization, means: "This Front now creates incidents; rather, it pursues incidents. It does not create incidents itself. Instead, sometimes it shows a reaction to certain events and publishes rather harsh announcements here and there, and each time, faces more restrictions."[42]

By participating in the elections and acquiring seats in the parliament, by making use of legal resources, the National Front would have gained the ability to engage in impactful participation in the destiny of the country and, by offering a codified program, gained the support of the people. Such support could have, in the next step, opened the way to future successes and prepared the grounds for changes that were demanded by those who claimed to support reforms and defended the Constitution. Undoubtedly, the chance of this process moving forward depended on other factors, such as the balance of the political forces, the extent of the weakness and power of the government, the United States policy, as well as the role of the people, which would have ultimately determined the failure or victory of such an experiment. It would have been an experiment that, even if it had no results, would have provided the opportunity for the nationalists to offer a constructive plan for overcoming the ongoing hardships and would have thereby played the role expected of any responsible opposition. By turning away from this option, rather than offering an alternative to what the government had stated, the National Front continued to speak about the principles of the law and the need for reforms without being prepared for compromise in order to have its demands implemented. The doomed fate of such an approach was nothing other than being driven from the text to the margins, and in the arena of the confrontation of forces that had no respect for the law and reforms, not being able to play any role but that of a spectator.

At any rate, such was the case. By standing up against Amini, had the National Front not interpreted compromise to mean surrender and settlement to mean expedient thinking, and for that matter, merely to gain a good reputation, could it not have faced an alternative to Alam? It was also unaware that its obstinate response to Alam's offer was the same kind of negligence, as well, such negligence that in a vicious circle had no other sinister result but the administrations of Hoveyda and Sharif-Emami, nor any other destructive consequences but those of Bazargan and Banisadr.

In his reconsideration of the policy of the leaders of the National Front, which he regarded as a lost "historic opportunity," Khalil Maleki wrote in this connection: "In those days, the market of absolute nihilism was thriving; and the leaders of the movement, as in the past, were not even public deceivers; rather, they were fully and totally infatuated with the public. Unfortunately, the leaders of the National Front in practice showed that they were not men who become consciously involved in political currents and take advantage of opportunities with prudence and promptness. They showed that their goal was merely to be loved, not to take social action and engage in service that results in love and respect in history. They held to their positions in the comfortable stronghold of nihilism."[43]

In spring of 1963, a few months after a large number of well-known and active nationalists were arrested, and when the leaders of the National Front were in prison, the regime once again took a new step toward negotiations with them. First, they transferred Saleh, Sadiqi, Sanjabi, Azar, Bakhtiar, and Keshavarz-Sadr from the Police Department prison to Qezel Qal'eh Prison, and from there, to the prison office that had a few rooms and bathrooms. Prior to that, they had facilitated certain things, such as bringing the prisoners food from their homes and allowing their family members to visit them, which according to Sanjabi indicated a type of "moderate treatment of and reconciliation with" the prisoners, showing that the "Royal Court and the government were trying to arrive at some sort of reconciliation with the National Front." According to him, the main topic in these negotiations was for "the National Front to express loyalty and respect for the monarchy, and for the government to officially recognize the National Front and allow it to be freely active, to some degree." Referring to the process of the negotiations, Sanjabi remembers General Hasan Pakravan, the head of the Organization of National Intelligence and Security, who had "extremely good suspicions" and says: "They turned the thing more or less into an agreement, and their intention was to release us and allow us some degree of freedom, but it was not clear to what degree… They were going to allow us to have a club, and to have a newspaper, but regarding the elections, they would by no means agree to hold the elections again or allow us to participate in them. It was clear that they wanted to drag us behind them and somehow whitewash the whole thing. That is why in such an ambiguous situation, with the suspicion and doubt and differences of opinion that existed among our colleagues, Mr. Saleh declared an end to the negotiations… When Mr. Saleh declared in that meeting that we would not continue the negotiations any longer, the only person who strongly objected was Dr. Shapour Bakhtiar… He very much supported the idea of the negotiations reaching some result."[44]

In examining the reasons for the failure of these negotiations despite the agreement that had been made about the principles, Sanjabi refers to important points in Pakravan's statements: "One day, Pakravan came to see Saleh when Dr. Sadiqi and I were also there. He told us, 'Do not imagine that the talks we have had and the results that might be gained were accomplished easily and without any reluctance. No, you, for what you want to do, and we, for getting results, have many big opponents and enemies. There are many people who go to the Shah and express their opposition to these talks." In the continuation of his statements, Pakravan mentions what Ne'matollah Nasiri, the chief of police, and others told the Shah about the dangers that letting the National Front be free would cause for the regime: "They tell the Shah that letting the National Front be free is like opening a window to a place with no air. If that window opens, suddenly all the people and all public opinion will notice the National Front, and they will expand so much and gain such power that we can no longer control them. They had really frightened the Shah and made him hesitant."[45]

Despite this warning, the negotiations that offered the possibility of creating an opening in Iran's political climate were unwisely forced to fail. Continuing his assessment of the reasons for the failure of the negotiations, Sanjabi once again refers to the conditions that the National Front faced: "There were also differences of opinion among our friends regarding these negotiations. Mr. Saleh gathered a group of those who were in the Qezel Qal'eh Prison, told them about the negotiations, and asked for opinions. Most of them had extremist views and said that they were absolutely trying to dupe us, and we should not give in to such a compromise."[46] Bazargan and Parsa also in their memoirs discuss the process of the negotiations and the stipulations that were offered by the government. These stipulations are different in one sensitive point from what Sanjabi had said, and that involves the participation of the National Front in the next round of the parliamentary elections and the appointment of the nationalists to a few positions in the cabinet. While in the first negotiations that took place between Alam and Saleh, the government would only accept the candidacy of nominees of the National Front for the parliament merely in a few cities and postponed the issue of membership in the cabinet to an uncertain future by stating that "not much time has passed since the current government has come to office, and changing and shuffling its members will not be expedient or pleasant," this time, such an obstacle did not exist, provided the six points of the reforms that had been put to a referendum on 26 January 1963 would be endorsed by the National Front.[47] The main aspects of these reforms consisted of land reform, the right to vote for women, and sending members of the Literacy Corps to the villages to fight illiteracy.

Without discussing the government proposal regarding the National Front's participation in the elections, the spokesman of the nationalists, Parsa, also refers to the report about the negotiations with the representative of the government that Saleh presented to the executive committee of the National Front in his presence: "In Qezel Qal'eh Prison, one day, Sergeant Saqi came and said, 'Mr. Saleh would like to meet with the gentlemen who are members of the executive committee.' We went to Mr. Saleh, who was in a room separate from the cell blocks. Mr.

Saleh said, 'Before we were incarcerated, Mr. Asadollah Alam came twice to my house and met with me, and now Mr. San'atizadeh-Kermani has brought a message from him that His Majesty has agreed to have a few members of the National Front be in the existing cabinet, provided they would not oppose the status of the monarch and the authority of the Shah.'" According to Parsa, Saleh had made his response to the prime minister contingent on "the opinion of the executive committee and the central council of the National Front."[48]

The government's negotiation with the leaders of the National Front caused serious differences of opinion and disputes among them this time. According to Parsa, among the members of the executive committee, Khalili and Bakhtiar supported the negotiations of the leaders of the National Front with the government and participation in the cabinet, and Saleh, Sadiqi, and Sanjabi were among the opponents. Bazargan, Foruhar, Keshavarz-Sadr, and a few other well-known nationalists also declared their explicit opposition to any type of negotiations. Emphasizing what he calls the struggle principles of the National Front, in a statement in opposition to the offer of participation in the cabinet, a statement that was supported by Saleh, Parsa himself said: "Our struggle is about principles. To become ministers, if we wanted to, there were other ways… Our path, with all these incarcerations and hardships that we suffer, is toward the freedom of the people; otherwise, to reach high positions, other ways existed. I think that if we accept such an offer, we would be betraying the young people and freedom fighters in Iran." Without his name being on the list of candidates for ministerial positions, in protest to Parsa's opinion, Bakhtiar said: "Sir, is Parsa France's Robespierre, who decides whether or not he wants to? Some may want to."[49]

The First Congress of the National Front and the Issue of Women

Eventually, the negotiations that had begun with the leaders of the National Front in September 1962, shortly after Alam came to power, and once again were resumed in May 1963, a few months after they were jailed, ended in their eventual failure. During this interval, after the first round of negotiations that took place between Alam and the National Front in Tehran, which had no result, the first congress of that organization began its work from 25 December 1962 at the home of Haj Hasan Qasemiyeh, a member of the central council of the National Front, in Tehran. Before starting the agenda, Allahyar Saleh, the chairman of the congress, asked the representatives for a moment of silence for the "happiness of the souls" of those who had "sacrificed" their lives on the path of freedom and constitutionalism, and to recite the prayer for the dead. Continuing his speech, Saleh said: "On the occasion of this auspicious holiday, which is the greatest religious holiday of the Islamic world, I would like to humbly request of His Eminence Ayatollah Taleqani to enlighten us for a few minutes with his spiritual words of wisdom."[50]

Seyyed Mahmud Taleqani, a founding member of the Freedom Front, began his speech, which was intermingled with the loud sound of the religious salutations of the audience, with the recitation of some verses from the Koran. On the occasion of the anniversary of the day that the Messenger of God was appointed as Prophet, regarding the "great significance" of that day and "the impact of that great uprising on rational, social, intellectual, and scientific developments," he said: "What would the world be like if this mission did not exist in the world and this wave of movement had not been created from the Hira Cave in the middle of the peninsula, and from the peninsula to beyond the peninsula, and from there in the course of history? And this is a proud accomplishment of Islam, which no other nation, no other tribe possesses."[51] In the continuation of his speech, he explained five instructions from the Koran, which he called the requirement for victory of "every movement, every uprising, every struggle," and added: "I hope we will all, with absolute sincerity on this great day, which is the day of the appointment of the Prophet, and is the day of the mission and the source of uprising and delegation and motivation, be able to perform our great duty and responsibility to this Shi'ite Moslem nation that has passed its test in Islam and in its own history, and on that day to come, we will be able to congratulate everyone. In other words, by the blessing of such an uprising, the entire nation, the future generations, and history will all benefit, God willing… Greetings upon you and God's mercy and blessings."[52]

The choice of the anniversary of the appointment of the Prophet for the commencement of the congress and inviting Taleqani, the congregational prayer leader of Hedayat Mosque, to recite verses from the Koran and to explain the "divinity" of the Creator in the course of the commencement of the first meeting of their congress were all telling signs of everything, telling signs of a reality that would rediscover its meaning in the resonance of the recitation of the prayer for the dead and the sound of the religious salutations uttered by religious politicians and political religious figures. Yet this was only the beginning. With the offering of congratulations by Saleh, the chairman of the congress, on the occasion of the anniversary of "the birth of His Holiness Imam Hoseyn," this beginning also came to a similar end: "The day of the commencement of the congress coincided with the greatest feast of the Islamic world, that is, the day the revered Prophet was appointed as the Messenger of God; and today, when we hope the congress will be concluded and will, God willing, be completely successful, coincides with the feast of the birthday of the greatest struggler and the greatest freedom fighter of all history, and we regard this auspicious day to be most prosperous and blissful, and we hope that all the members and fighters of the National Front take a lesson from the manner of this Imam."[53]

In line with the same outlook, Haj Mahmud Maniyan, the representative of the bazaar committee of the National Front, presented the short message of the bazaar merchants, which began with "in the name of God" to the congress. Declaring a moment of silence in memory of "the self-sacrificing devotee of the homeland, the late Shamshiri," he asked the representatives to recite the prayer for the dead for his "triumphant soul."[54] Another speaker, Taher Ahmadzadeh, the representative of the Province of Khorasan, with reference to a Koranic verse, spoke about the characteristics of the resolute leader who has faith in victory, who like the Prophet of Islam "stands most courageously on the crossroads and guides the thirsty people to the refreshing spring of cool water and says:

This is the way, o thirsty ones, go ahead and drink of that crystal clear water." In discussing and delineating the political guidelines of the National Front, he regarded socialism, or what he imagined to be socialism, as the only solution: "Whenever it is carried out by authentic, compassionate, and informed leaders, the result will be the severance of hostile foreign domination over the national economy." Ahmadzadeh considered accomplishing this "historic mission" to be the "responsibility" conferred on the National Front. In the conclusion of his long speech, which received praise from Saleh, he "asked God's forgiveness" for the souls of three "deceased" members of the National Front, and then reciting another "noble verse" from the Koran, he asked the faithful to have patience in order to achieve "victory and salvation."[55]

In the same vein, Jalaleddin Ayatollahzadeh-Shirazi, the representative from Fars Province, spoke of "hadith and reported sayings from the Prophet and imams" and of "the key to the Seven Heavens" and "the wing of the locust." He spoke about the imams and the prophets, of the holy Islamic lunar months of Moharram and Safar, and about the Karbala incident and the piety and faith of a faithful that is as steadfast as a mountain and even more so, since "bits and pieces can be chopped off from a mountain, but nothing can change the faithful." In his detailed explanations, which were devoted to the caliphate of the first imam of the Shi'ites, that "greatest freedom fighter of the human community," and "his revered spouse" Fatemeh Zahra, he said: "We are the followers of a religious sect of which Imam Ali ibn Abitaleb is the leader... The sword that Ali drew on the day of the Battle of Kheybar and which descended on the head of Marhab was more valuable that most religious battles."[56]

In such religious mourning ceremonies, current issues of the day were not ignored either. In contrast to Ahmadzadeh, who had spoken about socialism and had regarded the delineation of policy as having priority over all else, the representative from the Province of Fars looked at this matter from a different perspective, postponing the codification of the programs to some day after victory: "Without a discussion of class struggle, we must first make the thesis of fighting the government of colonialism and dictatorship our motto, and given the severe discontentment that governs all classes, we must draw the classes toward ourselves, and recruit forces from among the people. We should not create the notion that we have special interests in mind for ourselves. On the day that, God willing, we will be able to topple this Ahriman of corruption, then we will prepare a progressive plan for the government of the National Front and follow it, with the help of God."[57]

With the start of the work of the congress, the question of how the National Front should approach the issue of women and their right to vote and participate in the elections, which the regime had raised, was among the important topics. Worthy of note was that from 170 representatives in the congress, only Homa Darabi and Parvaneh Foruhar were representatives of women in the congress. Regarding the speech of Homa Darabi at the congress, only a brief report is available: "Ms. Homa Darabi, the representative of women in the congress…made a speech about the status of women in Islam and Islam's support for women's rights, and she also thanked the congress and the National Front for admitting women into their ranks." No reference other than this is made to her speech. Concerning Parvaneh Foruhar, as well, no information exists other than that she participated in the congress as a representative of women.[58] According to the report on the minutes of the meetings of the congress, the recorded voice tape of the sixth session of the congress was not available. Hence, the text of the speech of Homa Darabi and the negotiations and discussions of that session were not published. What was published was a brief report on the speech of Homa Darabi about the problems of women and a brief mention of the speech of Aziz Dadehbeygi, one of the representatives of the students of the University of Tehran.[59]

According to Mehdi Azar, a founding member of the central council of the National Front, the presence of women at the congress caused objections by two of the participating clerics, who left the congress "because the representatives of the women's committee were not wearing veils but only simple headscarves… On the suggestion of the gentlemen clerics who stayed, it was decided that women should sit on one side of the room, so that they would not be very much within the field of vision of men, who were not religiously allowed to look at them."[60]

During the ratification of the charter of the National Front regarding women's rights, Ahmadzadeh said that granting them the right to vote under the rule of colonialist regimes is nothing more than "false maneuvers for public deception." He asked the representatives of the congress: "Considering the current conditions of the country and the recent events, about which you are informed, replace the term 'women's movement' and add the words 'based on Islamic standards and the Constitution' in that article of the charter that is about women."[61]

The emphasis by the representative from Khorasan on the "conditions of the country" and "recent events" was nothing but an affirmation of the opposition of the clergy to women's right to vote. Three months prior to the congress of the National Front, the government cabinet, on 6 October 1962, by ratifying a bill regarding the swearing-in protocols of the representatives of the regional and provincial associations as well as the right to vote for women, had placed these two issues on its agenda. The government considered this bill to be a step toward securing the rights of the religious minorities and women. Since the stipulation of the representatives being Moslems had not been mentioned in the bill, it would be enough for them to take an oath on a "sacred divine book" rather than only on the Koran. The government decision in both cases was confronted with the harsh reaction of the clerics and sources of emulation, and eventually, because of their threats, the government was forced to retreat. The publication of the announcement addressed to the high-ranking clerics of the country about the ratification not being implemented clearly showed the official defeat of the government regarding these issues.[vi]

[vi] For more on the telegram by Prime Minister Asadollah Alam to the sources of emulation of the Qom Seminary dated 13 November 1962 regarding the revocation of the government bill, see: Ali Davani, *Nehzat-e Ruhaniyun-e Iran*, vol. 3 (Tehran: Bonyad-e Farhangi-ye Imam Reza Publishers, 1981), 106.

The silence of Bakhtiar and other leaders of the National Front in reaction to the statements of Ahmadzadeh at the congress and also to what Homa Darabi had called "Islam's support for women's rights" clearly revealed that hand-in-hand with the clerics, the nationalists opposed women's right to vote. Asghar Parsa, a member of the central council and the spokesman of the National Front, justified this opposition based on the requirement of adhering to the Constitution and emphasizing the "Koran and Islamic standards," as follows: "One of the principles of the National Front is that all its actions are within the framework of the Constitution... I do not oppose the opinion of the congress regarding the issue of women, and since in my opinion, it is an effort to acquire what has already been acquired and also, since I have no opposition to adding, in accordance with Islamic standards (Audience: That is correct)... That which contains all issues, in the opinion of we Moslems, is the Clear Book. 'Naught is there anything wet or dry but that which is recorded in the Clear Book'" (VI: 59). Abolhasan Banisadr, also in affirmation of Parsa's statements, displayed his pleasure and said that if there was any "concern regarding women, His Excellency Mr. Parsa set everyone's mind at ease."[62]

If the statements of Ahmadzadeh and Parsa about women's rights and the necessity of conforming to the Koranic principles and Islamic standards were regarded to be in reference to a religious principle, the emphasis on the Constitution in this case seemingly would perhaps suggest that they also paid attention to secular principles. The reality, however, was otherwise. Article 5 of the regulations ratified by the first National Consultative Assembly deprived women—alongside lunatics, those intentionally gone bankrupt, and those who were legally punished on the charge of committing murder and theft—of the right to vote and to be elected. Regarding election bylaws, that article, which was dated 10 July 1909, states: "Persons who are absolutely deprived of the right to vote: (1) women; (2) retarded persons and those under religious guardianship; (3) foreign nationals; (4) persons whose relinquishment of orthodox Islam has been proven in the presence of a fully-qualified religious magistrate; (5) persons under 20 years of age; (6) those who have intentionally gone bankrupt; (7) those who have been subject to punishment by Islamic law for committing murder or theft or other violations and those known for committing murder, theft, and other crimes who have not religiously been acquitted; (8) members in active service in the Army and Navy."[63]

Hence, emphasis on the principles of the election bylaws in the Constitution regarding women's rights in practice had no other meaning but a negation of their indisputable rights, a meaning that in the statements of the nationalists turned reference to that document into a weapon for advancing a goal that, in their clear collaboration with the clerics, left nothing about the matter ambiguous. The National Front tied its emphasis on Islamic standards regarding women's rights to its referring to the Constitution, and instead of supporting the positive step by the government in this arena, it endorsed the clerics' assault on women's rights. While the clerics emphasized the religious impediments for their opposition to women's right to vote, and for their reasoning, posed the question, "Are men free such that women should be free?" the nationalists also used the same words in their opposition to this indisputable right of women. With this approach in the congress, the functionaries of the National Front used such statements as the "moral and intellectual nurturing of women and strengthening the foundations of family life" as a pretext for their opposition to the right of women to vote; and the Freedom Front, under the leadership of Bazargan and Taleqani, warned "the honorable sisters and intellectual ladies" not to be deceived by the propaganda of the regime, since by raising the issue of women's right to vote, the government intends "to advance a few more steps the plan of toying with our religious and national honor, an issue that is the wish of colonialism and that guarantees the perpetuation and expansion of riding the backs of the people."[64]

With such an approach regarding the women's issue, Bazargan and the leaders of the Freedom Movement began an overall effort in the congress to protect what they called "religious and national honor." This effort, which was supported by a strong faction in the National Front, was also reflected in the ratifications of the congress. With the outlook that he had espoused previously regarding this issue, Bazargan considered men to be "superior" to women, and granted the "honor" to women that, in accordance with the will of the Creator, insofar as concerns procreation and the affairs of children, they should become "partners" of men. He writes: "The superiority of man over woman became apparent from the fact that the former became the lover and the latter the beloved. Man has learned the lesson of self-sacrifice in the school of love, has sought union, and then has begun to struggle, to be trained, and to evolve to provide comfort for the woman. But neither has the kind Creator deprived womankind of His kindness. He has granted her motherly love, in order to make sacrifices for her children, and she has been granted the honor of being his partner in the building and advancement of offspring."[65]

  Another example of the nationalists' attitude regarding the role and duties of women in the family is recorded in the memoir of Ali Shayegan, one of the leaders of the National Front: "On Saturday, 26 November 1949, I arrived home at 12:30. My wife still was not there; a quarter of an hour later, she called from her grandmother's house telling me that she was not coming home for lunch and that she wanted to take care of her paternal aunt, who had fainted and was sick. I was sorry that Ms. Qodrat, my wife's aunt, was sick, and angry that my wife had not come home. These sentiments caused me that evening to speak in detail about the duties of a wife and mother to her husband and children… After 7:00, I spoke to my wife for a while about the fact that religiously and customarily, her primary duty was to take care of me and our children, and then if she is able to, she can attend to the needs of others, that she must not spend the time that she should spend on us in worrying about and taking care of others. Of course, I repeatedly told her that I did not mean that she should be unmindful of relatives, and even others. On the contrary, she should do whatever she could in this regard; but a woman's duty is first to her husband and then to her children, and taking care of and attending to their needs is a mandatory religious obligation, whereas attending to the needs of relatives and others is a recommended religious obligation."[66]

In any case, the outlook of the nationalists regarding the issue of women's right to vote, which had a special place in the propaganda of the regime, was one of the important issues of the congress. Such propaganda, which was offered under the cover of propaganda sensationalism and clamor and reduced their effectiveness in the climate of dictatorship and despotism, was not without its effect on the tendency to disregard the positive step by the regime toward granting women the right to vote. However, admitting this fact should not negate the importance of such a step. Insofar as the official laws of the country were concerned in connection with having certain rights equal to those of men, women having the right to vote was not only defendable, but also, on the basis of weakening the restrictions that had deprived Iranian women for many years of their indisputable rights, it was an unquestionable necessity. On the other hand, the National Front dismissed the importance of women benefitting from the right to vote based on the reasoning that, due to the existence of the dictatorship that governed, men's right to vote was also a sham. Accordingly, however, men having the right to vote should have been dismissed, and likewise, the entire government, the parliament, and the judiciary organizations as well that operated under the domination of dictatorship should have been regarded as meaningless until such time as a democratic regime could be established. Even so, such was not the case for Bakhtiar and the National Front. Based on the same regime and social agreements, the National Front wanted free elections, but elections in which only men had the right to participate. In this sense, the opposition to women's right to vote, to participate in the provincial and regional councils elections, and more significantly, in the elections of the National Consultative Assembly and the Senate, under the pretext that men were also not free, stemmed from a different source. Regarding the issue of women's right to vote, this outlook was rooted in the way the nationalists confronted the Shah's government, from a backward and most likely a reactionary perspective. This fact was reflected not only in the announcements and statements of a number of the functionaries of the National Front, such as Ahmadzadeh, Parsa, and Banisadr, but also in the political resolution of the first congress of the nationalists. In that resolution, where in addressing issues related to "hygiene'" the congress discussed the issue of the young people and the establishment of organizations for providing them with "training in the spirit of cooperation" and respect for "virtue and piety," it also marginally addressed the issue of women: "In the modern society of Iran, sufficient attention must be paid to the rights of the family and the important position of this primary social unit. The rights of women must be protected while observing Islamic standards, and the rights of children and issues related to the economic life and judicial affairs of children are among the issues that require appropriate new laws. In the reconstruction of the modern Iranian society, by observing Islamic standards, women must perform their social and national responsibilities shoulder to shoulder with men. Women must create the necessary organizations for the moral and intellectual development of women and for strengthening the foundations of the family, and step by step with the advancement of women in other societies, especially in Islamic societies, advance on the path of progress and development."[67]

Here there was no longer any mention of the Constitution. Regarding the rights of women, this time the nationalists entirely emphasized the necessity of observing Islamic standards, and no word or statement can be found to have been uttered by Bakhtiar in refutation of this outlook in the report that has been recorded about the sessions of that congress.

In fact, the statements about the "moral and intellectual development" of women as an auxiliary to the "rights of children" and "strengthening the foundations of the family" were more revealing than anything left unsaid concerning the attitude of the National Front regarding the issue of women, or what was referred to as the barrier between what was and was not religiously sanctioned in connection with women. It was as though in the private courtyard and the public courtyard of this traditional Iranian house and the structure of such a mentality, the National Front was unveiling its true, veiled inclinations regarding the issue of women, as though speaking about the role of women in the "reconstruction" of the society and playing their "social and national duty" had no purpose other than to fill in the blank pages. It was a fine conclusion, as Banisadr had said, to eliminate the "concern" of the gentlemen, and for that matter, under the auspices of "observing Islamic standards." Such was the viewpoint of the congress of the National Front regarding women, the distinct symbol of which was considered to be their "advancement," "progress," and "development," especially in "Islamic countries." To be more disgraceful was impossible.

The National Front, Organizational Issues, and the White Revolution

The issue of the organizational structure and the differences of opinion about the requirements for membership in the National Front were among other important issues of the congress. These differences of opinion, which had begun with the establishment of the National Front and continued in the ensuing years, in the course of the congress, continued over the issue of the membership of the Freedom Front and various assessments of the concepts of political party and front by the representatives. These differences of opinion were the cause of endless disputes that eventually resulted in several splits in and the ultimate disintegration of that organization. An important aspect of these differences of opinion could also be seen in Mosaddeq's message to the congress and his emphasis on the need for revisions in its constitution. Mosaddeq supported the faction that considered the National Front as an organization comprised of member political parties and associations and wanted the central council of the National Front, as the leading organization, to be comprised of the representatives of member political parties and associations. In contrast to his view, he saw himself confronted with a strong faction that considered the National Front to be a collection of political parties and associations as well as individuals who either were or were not members of a political party, and offered other solutions for overcoming the difficulties in connection with organizational structure. A number of notable figures of the National Front, such as Bakhtiar, Foruhar, and Zirakzadeh, supported the first faction, and a number of others, such as Saleh, Sanjabi, and Hejazi, defended the second,[vii] without either side achieving the desired result in terms of a structure that would meet the organizational needs of the National Front. The proposed idea of inviting individuals to become members would confront the National Front with the risk of young people who were infatuated with the Tudeh Party and the Soviet Union infiltrating that organization. In contrast, the supporters of the idea of inviting the political parties faced another impediment, which was the membership of the Association of Socialists (Jame'ah-ye Sosialistha) and the Freedom Movement as two strong groups in the National Front, two groups that, due to their influence among the intellectuals and the bazaar, were considered serious rivals for the powerful leaders or those who were waiting in ambush to gain power in the National Front. So serious was this threat that the request of one group for membership in the congress was ignored without being responded to, and the decision about the membership of the other was postponed to an unspecified future date.

The fact was that the inherent organizational difficulties of the National Front themselves mirrored a structure that was rooted in the lineage and history, in the torn-asunder binding threads, of an incongruous coalition. Daryush Foruhar set his hopes for the survival of such a coalition on "Divine support"; Sadiqi understood it as a "national reformist movement"; and Hejazi regarded it as a "revolutionary" group that intended to "eliminate the existing social relations" and replace them with "other relations," and for that matter, under the organizational leadership of the National Front, in which, according to him, "all the people of Iran" were called members.[68]

In such intellectual chaos, mental confusion, and instability of action, principled differences of opinion were drained of their meaningful content, and everything occurred in an environment saturated with nods and gestures or common and customary pleasantries, and for that matter, the type of pleasantries the source of which should be sought in

---

[vii] For more about the views of these two factions, see: Rahbani, "Nokhostin Kongereh-ye Jebheh-ye Melli-ye Iran (Dey 1341)," *Jahan-e Ketab*, nos. 251-252, vols. 1 and 2 (Farvardin-Ordibehesht 1389)," 38-44.

the history and tradition of the National Front. Bakhtiar sought assistance from "Lord God Almighty" to carry out the grave responsibilities—as dictated by his conscience—that were conferred on him in the congress. He considered all the "gentlemen" as possessing "piety and faith," and regarded Sanjabi as the "noblest and most genuine individual" that he knew. And if there was any difference of opinion, the cause and source of it was SAVAK. He would plead with Abolfazl Qasemi on the "freshly blood-soaked shrouds of martyrs" not to allow those with certain known dispositions to be on the "frontline of the National Front." Hasan Habibi in devising the proposals of the congress about the oil issue regarded the opinion of Kazem Hasibi to be aptly correct, because he was an "expert" and "most respected by the great leader." And in this matter, there was nothing to fear if there was any shortcoming, since it would be "put in order" under his own supervision and would undoubtedly be accepted by the "gentlemen." Bazargan spoke with his Azerbaijani "frankness and truthfulness," a characteristic that he did not know whether to call a "fault" or a "virtue." After all, he accepted differences in opinions and preferences, but he did not think the congress was the place for "disputes." He would add: "If we have erred, place our heads on a rock and chop them off with an axe." At the peak of arguments, as though once again calling on the "frankness and truthfulness" of which he had spoken to bear witness, pointing imperceptibly to the verse from the Koran with which they had adorned the congress hall, he would say that upon seeing this verse: "I say to myself, there are no differences of opinion among us!" Sanjabi, who considered Ayatollah Taleqani to be the source of "pride" for the nation, in one session of the congress, considered giving a speech a sort of "individual" responsibility and "religious duty," and in another session, he had no time for it, because he would be "traveling" shortly. Saleh spoke of his "ailment," and left the speaking to Keshavarz-Sadr who, from the perspective of "respect" for others, considered himself to be "more insignificant, lower, and more humble" than everyone else and addressed Saleh as "sir, elder, and as having priority over" himself. Thus, he would take the Creator as his witness that he did not want to have an "impact," just being "obedient" would suffice. Sadiqi considered himself to be a "very minor and humble member of the National Front," a member whose "mistakes" might exceed "his good deeds," and finally, Hashem Sabbaghiyan regarded the participation of a few pre-collegiate students in the congress as the "best" sign of democracy in the organizations of the National Front. As the representative of the Young People's Organization, despite all his "fondness" for the "unity" of the people of Iran, he did not think it was "prudent" to deliver his entire speech, which was from a "personal" point of view, thus he recited a poem and ended the discussions.[69]

Three weeks after the conclusion of the congress, when Sanjabi had returned from his travels and Saleh's ailment had improved, the National Front was confronted with the six-point plan of Mohammad Reza Shah, which had been put to a referendum on 26 January 1963. This plan, which became known as the "White Revolution," as the most important event in the history of Iran in the years after the coup d'état, had an astonishing impact on the structure of the society and its future developments, an impact that played an essential role in shaping the 5 June 1963 uprising, as a beginning of the fall of the monarchical regime and the victory of the Islamic Revolution in Iran.

In reaction to the "White Revolution," the National Front, by publishing an announcement, enumerated the disarray and problems in the country and, protesting against the ruling despotism, regarded the referendum for the ratification of the Shah's six-point plan as unlawful. The significant point in the announcement was that, in accordance with the Constitution, the king has a position of non-partisan functions, and his interference in the affairs related to the laws of the country is a clear violation of the articles of the Constitution. In addition, the holding of a referendum in the absence of political and social freedoms was protested by the National Front and regarded as another reason for the invalidity of the referendum.

The National Front's assessment and terming the referendum unlawful contained some contradictions. Paragraph four of the announcement emphasized that "the referendum can only represent the opinion of the people if it is held in a lawful environment and all individual and social freedoms are observed."[70]

Such a claim could be refuted, since a referendum in principle had basically not been projected in the Constitution, such that its being held in a "lawful environment and all individual and social freedoms are observed" should be regarded as legitimate. The absence of political freedom ultimately was another reason given for terming the referendum invalid without in essence creating any change in the inherent illegality of an action in violation of the Constitution. What made the referendum unlawful was the holding of the referendum itself, regardless of whether it was held in a politically stifling environment or a democratic one. Neither the Shah nor the head of the government had permission to ask the people to participate in a referendum and change the laws of the country by a nationwide public vote. By considering referendums to be lawful under free legal conditions, the National Front affirmed the legality of the violation of the Constitution, in which no mention was made of the permissibility of changing the laws of the country. Such an error would also disarm the National Front in that it had not found a political response for countering the reforms by the regime. This error stemmed from the history and tradition of the nationalists and had posed a threat to the foundations of the constitutional system in the not too distant past with Mosaddeq's action of holding a referendum.

On 3 August 1953, by holding a most undemocratic referendum, in which the people's votes were supposed to be the backing for its legitimacy, Mosaddeq dissolved the parliament. Since the Constitutional Revolution, this was the first time that a head of government, through a referendum, had removed from his path a parliament that he considered to be an impediment to the implementation of his programs. Not only was this referendum a violation of democratic principles in the way it was conducted, but its foundations were in contradiction to the Constitution. With the announcement that it published in opposition to the 26 January 1963 referendum, by referring to Mosaddeq's referendum and comparing it to the referendum by the Shah, the National Front once again endorsed Mosaddeq's decision to hold a referendum for dissolving the parliament, and praised its "brilliant results." Mosaddeq's referendum was an action that not only his staunch opponents but even a number of his supporters, such as Sadiqi, Sanjabi, and Majdzadeh-Kermani, had warned him against.

Sadiqi states: "When a decision was being made to dissolve the parliament, His Excellency was also told that in the absence of the parliament, the Shah might dismiss the government and appoint another prime minister. Dr. Mosaddeq, however, did not consider such an action by the Shah to be likely."[71] Sanjabi had also warned Mosaddeq against the referendum: "It was a on a Thursday. At 12:30 in the afternoon, I left the parliament and went directly to meet with Mosaddeq. I saw that he was absolutely angry and frustrated. He said to me, 'Sir, we must shut down the parliament.' I asked, 'Why shut it down?' He said, 'This parliament is opposed to us and will not let us do our work. We must shut it down with a nationwide public vote.' I said, 'Mr. Prime Minister, I do not agree with your opinion.'"[72] Parsa reports the opposition of Majdzadeh-Kermani to holding the referendum and Mosaddeq's reaction as follows: "Then the issue of the referendum came up. Dr. Mosaddeq summoned the representatives for one whole day, and as an introduction to his statements, he said, 'You gentlemen should know that laws are for the sake of the people, not the people for the laws, and the will of the people is above any law.' Then he said, 'I am going to hold a referendum to dissolve the parliament.' And he said the reason for it was, 'We do not have a majority in the parliament. It is true that when the people of the minority faction speak, some of them vote in support of you, but that is not what is at the bottom of their hearts. And the reason for it is quite obvious. When the leaning of the parliament was asked for on 21 July, forty people voted for Qavamossaltaneh. This shows that you do not have a majority. Hence, this parliament will strike again when the time comes. That is why I will dissolve the parliament and will hold a referendum.' One of our comrades, the late Majdzadeh-Kermani, who was an attorney and a truly good man as well

as a member of our faction, said, 'Sir, the Constitution does not mention anything about referendum.' Dr. Mosaddeq turned to him and
said, 'Who do you think voted for the Constitution?' Majdzadeh-
Kermani said, 'The people.' Dr. Mosaddeq replied, 'And now the same
people will vote to have a referendum.' …After these discussions, we left
that place and thought that in order not to have a parliament that would
vote against Mosaddeq, the best way was for us to resign, to have a
parliament that did not have a quorum and would never be able to have
a session. We, the members of the National Front faction, held a
meeting in the parliament, prepared the text of our resignations, and
after the meeting, as the representative of the faction, I read it for the
reporters.'"[73]

If Mohammad Reza Shah's plan in holding a referendum was considered an imposition of rule outside the boundaries of relations in a
parliamentary system, Mosaddeq's emphasis on the vote of the general
public to dissolve the parliament was also of the same nature. One of
them in a position of non-partisan functions sought the good fortune of
his people—the prosperity and good fortune of a people who, as though
in the vicious circle of history, were experiencing no other reality but
lack of attention to and respect for the law—in advancing his authoritative goals, and the other, in a position of responsibility, considered
himself the leader of the people, such that in their name he assumed that
the validity of the parliament and the law meant nothing.

Years later, Asghar Parsa, the spokesman and member of the executive
committee of the National Front, recounting confusing memories in
which no indication of reconsideration and revision is detectable,
revealed what was happening on the verge of the holding of the referendum for the "White Revolution," exposing the thinking that was
another sign of the continuation of the foolish policy of the nationalists
regarding social developments. He states: "Well, we opposed the
referendum. We supported land reform in principle, but we opposed
this White Revolution, which was prescribed by the Americans. What I
am saying is not like releasing gas from my stomach, like some so-called
gentlemen do. The evidence has been published abroad that this project

was imposed by the Americans in order for the Shah to carry out certain reforms. The Shah carried out the reforms, but they were planned in the United States. We decided to write a statement about the referendum that the Shah intended to hold. There were three or four of us, including the late Khonji, who sat down together and wrote it. Afterward, since I was supposed to approve the text and present it, they gave me the text of the statement again at home. As I was editing some parts of it, I realized that the usual slogans of the Iran Party, such as 'long live Iran' or 'Iran forever,' were no longer appropriate and sufficient under those circumstances, and that after all, in that statement, we needed to have a slogan that was a response to the referendum. That was why I added at the end, 'Yes to reforms, no to autocracy,' and sent it for publication and distribution."[74]

After that, Parsa recounts his meeting with Zirakzadeh and Khalili, members of the central council of the National Front, and the demonstrations that the students held in opposition to the referendum in front of the University of Tehran: "When we arrived in front of the university, I saw that the students had written the slogan that I had written at the end of the announcement, 'Yes to reforms, no to autocracy,' in big letters on a piece of cloth and displayed it at the university. I told Zirakzadeh, 'I did what I was supposed to do. Now I am happy; let the regime do any damned thing it wants to do. My objective was to transmit this idea and slogan to the young people, and that was done.'"[75]

If we take a look at the confrontation of the National Front with the governments of Amini and Alam, if we look carefully at the process of the work of its congress and take the statements of Parsa seriously, we can see how the nationalists lost a historic opportunity to take advantage of the situation. Standing in opposition to the opportunity that had been created in the political environment, the National Front not only cast to the wind the sole serious possibility of taking the initiative to create fundamental changes in the political climate of Iran, but also in that congress, where there was also an opportunity for critiquing the past mistakes, a chance for reconsideration and revision, it refused to take another look at its policy. This opportunity, which was created ten years after the coup d'état, had placed the nationalists in a special position for holding a congress in that climate of fleeting freedoms in order to play a constructive role in the ongoing destiny-making developments.

Instead, the National Front utilized all of its ability to advance a policy that displayed their incompetence due to their disregard for the provided possibilities and their indecision because of their blind and uncompromising opposition, a policy that had no other result but Parsa's vengeful expression of joy. The assertions of the spokesman of the National Front about the preparations for the statement of the nationalists in response to the 26 January 1963 referendum expressed the reality or the fact that they lacked a plan and were unprepared to respond to that historic moment's requirements as well as future developments. Parsa had realized that the Shah's six-point reforms were far too important to be countered perpetually by the tedious slogans of "long live Iran" or "Iran forever." Hence, instead of critical support for those six-point reforms or offering a comprehensive plan as an alternative to what was put to a vote in the referendum, the only solution he found was to create a new slogan, and for that matter, because what occurred was what the United States "wanted," as though if it had not been what the United States wanted, the functionaries of the National Front would have found the courage to openly rise in support of their leader, or to hold a meeting or a conference, and, lost in the tumult and commotion of the resonance of the loud prayers for the dead and the chants of religious salutations, would have talked about the coup d'état and dictatorship, about the reforms and revolution.

Bakhtiar and the Contention between the National Front's Leadership and Mosaddeq

With the conclusion of the congress, the old differences of opinion that had a long history in the National Front continued as before. Individual rivalries and contentions among personalities and among political parties—and for that matter, political parties of which no sign was left but a name—had confronted every decision and measure with deadlocks. The disarray regarding plans and programs and the lack of harmony in how to counter the reforms that were initiated by the regime had deprived Bakhtiar and the nationalists, who claimed to support reforms, of any stratagem. In their up-side-down approach to the future, inaction had replaced dynamism, and stagnation had supplanted change. They sought their credibility merely in the tiresome repetition of past "glorious accomplishments," to the point that, ultimately, with the escalation of the disputes about its organizational structure, no longer able to play any role in the ongoing developments of the country following the fall of Amini's government and the fiasco of the negotiations with Alam, the National Front faced an impasse and eventually, disintegration. The pronounced aspect of these disputes concerned the requirement for membership in the National Front. Mosaddeq wanted the Second National Front to be an organization made up of political parties. This outlook was quite different from what he had previously considered to be the solution. In the past, Mosaddeq had not placed much importance on the role of political parties in the political developments in the society. As he stated, he "did not pay attention to the philosophy and ideology of political parties," but rather, he regarded "gathering individuals together" as the effective weapon for advancing political goals. This time, however, in his message to the congress, he had asked for a revision of the organization's constitution, and he had risen in opposition to the faction that regarded individual as well as political party membership in the National Front to be the solution for overcoming the difficulties; but this faction would not agree to the solution offered by the unmatched leader of the National Front, and offered a different solution.

In the meantime, when Mosaddeq realized that Bakhtiar and the central council of the National Front were not paying attention to his proposed solution regarding the structure of the organization, in a letter addressed to the Executive Committee of the Organizations of the National Front in Europe (Hey'at-e Ejra'iyeh-ye Sazmanha-ye Jebheh-ye Melli dar Orupa), he wrote: "The National Front must be regarded as the center of the political parties of the country, all of which believe in one principle, which is the independence and freedom of the country. If the political parties and associations do not participate in the National Front, it will become what it has become now, and the supporters of the National Front will only consist of a few people that the organization has elected for the formation of the council. The National Front must not quarrel about the eligibility of political parties and associations... If you look at the ideological statement of a political party, you shall see that numerous reasons have been the cause of its creation; otherwise, individuals would not agree to participate in an association, and if it is dissolved, there would no longer exist an ideology for a group to gather together, in which case, those who want to have the National Front are the same individuals who have been elected due to their history and being recognizable, and who will be unable to take one step in its defense... I never wanted to interfere in the affairs of the organization of the National Front from where I am in this prison without knowing what is going on anywhere. I was asked to send a message, but they did not pay any attention to it, and they changed the form of the National Front into something that will not be capable of doing anything. The split that occurred and caused a number of people to be prosecuted was the result of the operations of the National Front."[76]

Mosaddeq's harsh words to the central council of the National Front regarding its organizational structure were far too clear to take seriously his false humility in his statement that he did not intend to interfere in the affairs of the National Front. The content of the letter addressed to the Executive Committee of the Organizations of the National Front in Europe indicated that he not only knew about the current develop-ments, but also, by supporting the issue of the membership of the Freedom Movement in the National Front, he declared his opposition to the faction that impeded the ratification of his proposal. Just before the holding of the congress, in a letter endorsing the establishment of the Freedom Movement as a group that had comingled religion and politics, Mosaddeq regarded discussions about the "eligibility" of that organization not to be within the purview of the National Front, and he called the dispute that had occurred a split. More importantly, in his strange judgment, he considered the arrests of the leaders of the Freedom Movement to be the result of the decisions of the congress that had postponed the issue of the membership of that organization to sometime in the future.[77]

Mosaddeq's letter addressed to the Executive Committee of the Organizations of the National Front in Europe and its distribution in Tehran was a clear sign of the growing differences of opinion between Mosaddeq, on the one hand, and Bakhtiar and other leaders of the nationalists, on the other. The first reaction of the executive committee and the board of directors of the central council of the National Front to that letter was the writing of a detailed response to Mosaddeq about the political developments in the previous four years and their effect on the activities of the National Front.

As usual and based on the common and customary pleasantries, Bakhtiar and the leaders of the National Front began their letter by declaring their delight that the "exalted leader," despite all the hardships, had at every opportunity been concerned about guiding the "fighters on the path of justice" and had not deprived them of his "guidance and advice," although they emphasized that for more than ten years, "the national movement" had been deprived of "the joy of the leadership and wise guidance of its leader," who also had been kept away from the possibility of contact with the nation and the nationalists. This reality had made him unable "to have access to authentic and precise information through proper channels." It was as though all the pleasantries and praise for the advice and guidance of the "exalted leader" were meant merely to tell him that he knew nothing about was going on. Emphasis on the first article of the organization's constitution ratified by the congress about the organizational structure of the National Front as a group comprised of member political parties, individuals, associations, and unions; the process of the formation of the Freedom Movement and the ensuing disputes; along with measures to drag the National Front into internal fighting and creation of crisis were among the reasons that were stated to prove the erroneousness of Mosaddeq's views. With the expression of these points, it seemed there was no longer any secret to hide. Bakhtiar and the leaders of the National Front were accusing Mosaddeq of not only being uninformed about the ongoing developments, but by raising certain points contrary to the ratifications of the congress and standing up against its elected central council, he was also taking steps toward the destruction of the National Front: "Such is inferred from your noble missive that the manner of the activities and organizational policy of the National Front and even the composition of the central council of the National Front of Iran are not acceptable and pleasing to Your Excellency. Considering the principle that the central council of the National Front cannot take any step contrary to its own beliefs and contrary to the ratifications of the congress that is the originator of this council, and considering that countering the views of Your Excellency, who is the leader of the nation and the movement, is not in the interest of the country and the nation, and the central council of the National Front by no means and under no circumstances would submit to such confrontation and contention, if Your Excellency still continues to hold your views in light of the aforementioned written explanations, the result might be the disintegration of the organizations of the National Front, and under the conditions that a huge wave of opposing sentiments has spread to all strata of the society, undoubtedly, the ruling apparatus will be overjoyed at the disintegration of an organization that is capable of occupying all the positions in the interest of the nation."[78]

From this point on, there was no return. In the harsh exchange of accusations, Mosaddeq considered the action of the ruling regime in arresting the leaders of the Freedom Movement to be the consequence of the opposition of the congress to the membership of that organization, and Bakhtiar and the other leaders of the National Front regarded Mosaddeq as the cause of the disintegration of the National Front and the delight of the regime. With the continuation of the letters that were exchanged, by criticizing the dominant policy of the leadership, Mosaddeq enumerated his reasons about why and how the National Front "had not been able to take the smallest steps toward the interests of the country" because it paid no attention to his views. He called the organization's constitution and bylaws ratified by its congress "a few useless sheets of paper," and regarded the composition of the central council, with the membership of "a few of those better than us people" in it, a suspicious group. The central council, as well, by expressing "its devotion to and sincere prayers for" him, spoke about his "noble letter" and pointed out that His Eminence "has frequently clearly stated a lack of cognizance of the events outside" his confines, and thus stressed that he was unaware of the ongoing developments.[79]

In the meantime, the central council of the National Front in another letter in response to Mosaddeq explained its views and wrote: "Considering that Your Excellency, who is the leader of the national movement, has explicitly negated the composition of the council and its bylaws, and considering that we do not find the views of the revered leader to be in the interest of the movement, the country, and the nation, and given that the members who believe in the present organizational basis of the National Front would like to be excused from membership in other types of organizations, if the explanations offered in the previously submitted letter as well as this letter are not accepted, the continuation of this council will be beyond our abilities."[80]

Hence, with the stepping down of Saleh from the position of chairmanship of the executive committee in May 1964, the Second National Front, of which merely a name remained, approached disintegration. In a letter to Mosaddeq, Saleh mentioned the reason for his resignation to be his "ailment." Mosaddeq's efforts to return him and his request about preparing a constitution that would be "for the good of the society" and "acceptable to everyone" were fruitless because of his "severe illness and recent exhausting problems," as Saleh said in his response to Mosaddeq. Regarding the constitution, Saleh's brief answer was undeniably frank: "Concerning the issue of amending the constitution of the National Front, which you had mentioned again, the answer is as was presented to you in the official letters of the executive committee and the central council of the National Front, and I cannot add anything to it. I wish Your Honor good health."[81]

Interstingly, however, in the final meeting of the central council of the National Front that was held in May 1964, Saleh stated the reason for his resignation as the chairman of the executive committee to be the unfavorable political conditions and his wanting to "avoid" opposing Mosaddeq: "Because of the uprising of a group of the people on 5 June of last year, SAVAK is tightening the noose of pressure and strangulation on the order of the Shah day by day, and we are in a situation in which even our place of getting together to eat lunch outside the city is being put under siege by the gendarmes, and there remains no room to breathe; hence, it is not possible to follow the directives of His Excellency Mr. Mosaddeq, to open the door of the National Front to various groups and to have widespread activity, which makes the continuation of our work impossible under these conditions. In order to avoid disobeying our revered leader's instructions, I shall resign from the chairmanship of the executive committee, and I request of the honorable council to elect my successor."[82]

A look at the developments that eventually resulted in the disintegration of the Second National Front indicates that that organization had found no answer to counter what Mosaddeq had stated. Mosaddeq did not consider the constitution and the bylaws ratified by the congress to be "for the good of the society," and he had called the central council, with "a few of those better than us people" in it, a suspicious group and had totally discredited it. In addition, his judgment about the National Front not having been able in the course of those years to take "the smallest steps toward the interests of this country" would completely discredit that organization before it accomplished anything. His demand that Saleh prepare a constitution that was "acceptable to everyone" was also a violation of democratic standards. As the chairman of the executive committee, Saleh was not in a position that would allow him to write a new constitution. Such an undertaking was within the authority of the congress and not the executive committee and the central council, nor the gentlemen for whose "success" Mosaddeq was asking God.

On the other side, the leaders of the National Front regarded Mosaddeq's solutions as an indication of his being unaware of the ongoing developments and his being removed from the arena of current politics, without having the boldness to stand up against what he proposed and to defend the rights and the duties that the congress had conferred on them. Ultimately, considering that they did not regard "countering the views of the revered leader in the interest of the country and the nation," they resigned, as though they placed no credibility not only on his opinions and beliefs, but also on that upon which they themselves had insisted.

Among them, Bakhtiar was the only one who had the ability to openly confront Mosaddeq. Although in the course of the congress he engaged in the customary pleasantries and spoke about the greatness of Mosaddeq and his intellectual prevalence, similar to the prevalence of Damavand Peak over the "mountains, valleys, and plains," he also raised certain important points, points which the other leaders of the National Front did not have the courage to mention, except in private and in secrecy. Bakhtiar believed that the reason for the failure of the National Front on 19 August 1953 was lack of attention to the organizational problem. He said that Mosaddeq "relied on our sentiments, but he did not rely on the forces," and he mentioned Mosaddeq's lack of attention in the past to this important matter. According to Bakhtiar, this time, the reality of this issue had opened the way to that "revered leader" to understand "certain important points" as a result of "continuous incarceration and having free time" to think. Emphasizing that "most people mistakenly think that our National Front today is the same as it was at his time," he spoke about a new era in which Mosaddeq was considered to be "on the same level" as Amir Kabir, a time when he had been elevated from being a "political figure to an intellectual presence," as though all those tedious compliments were for nothing but to bestow the arena of intellectuality on Mosaddeq and the arena of politics on those who contemplated another solution for overcoming the increasing difficulties of the National Front.[83]

Later on, recounting Mosaddeq's role in those years, Bakhtiar said: "He had thought that in his old age, they wanted to set him aside… He was unhappy, since from 1953 on, Mosaddeq was never the leader of

the National Resistance Front, so that he could criticize them… Dr.
Mosaddeq was not very much interested in organizing, and he did not
have much ability in that regard. And then, they had filled his ears
enough about the members he was suspicious about… In my opinion,
in the course of those events, he should not have ordered us and said,
'do this, and don't do that.' Those who were in contact with Mosaddeq,
after the congress, 'incited' him against the National Front. He was
never prepared to create a political party or an organized force… He
exaggerated…a bit…saying, 'I am the leader of the National Front as
long as I am alive'… Sometimes his attitude really made you fed up…
Mosaddeq should have rolled up his sleeves and, based on his own views
and mine, done some organizing. The people were mesmerized by him.
He could have done this…especially during the nationalization of the
oil industry. Or he should have, of his own accord, done like Napoleon
Bonaparte said, which is that, after all, one should leave the scene at the
end of his life beautifully. He should have just left… Once he had
played his role in an event, he should have said, 'I have done my work,
gentlemen.' Mosaddeq was not very much interested in organizing, and
he did not have much ability in that regard. And then, they had filled
his ears enough about the members he was suspicious about."[84]

In Bakhtiar's statements about Mosaddeq, there was undeniable
frankness. Even though such frankness was unprecedented, with the
passage of years after Mosaddeq had passed away, it still left one point
ambiguous. Considering what Bakhtiar said, was Mosaddeq's suspicion
baseless, or were there certain signs that indicated an overall effort to
accomplish such a measure? Indeed, who were those who had incited the
suspicion in Mosaddeq that they were going to set him aside, and to
what extent was this suspicion based on solid evidence? At any rate,
Bakhtiar himself was the target of the accusation. Bazargan states: "From
the very beginning, after the 19 August coup d'état, the 'thesis' of the
national movement minus Mosaddeq had been discussed. The major
faction of the leadership of the Iran Party welcomed this thesis. Dr.
Shapour Bakhtiar, one of the active leaders of the Iran Party at that
time, said in a private meeting, 'Mosaddeq was Iran's Gandhi; now that

Gandhi has left, we have gone to Nehru. Allahyar Saleh is Iran's Nehru!' With this justification, without expressing any opposition to Mosaddeq, the gentlemen insisted that the name of Mosaddeq, who was in prison, should not be mentioned. Their reasoning was that the regime and the Shah personally were sensitive to Mosaddeq, and that his name should not be mentioned. And they claimed that they were not only followers of Mosaddeq but also did not want his name mentioned."[85]

Considering Bakhtiar's negotiations with the officials of the American Embassy in Tehran, which took place three months after the coup d'état, at the start of the activities of the National Resistance Movement, this assessment was quite meaningful, especially since in the course of these negotiations, while declaring his loyalty to Mosaddeq, he also mentioned his "mistakes." In Bakhtiar's opinion, these mistakes were more than anyone else those of Mosaddeq's advisors, especially Fatemi. According to Bakhtiar, Hasibi also had made misguided recommendations to Mosaddeq.[86]

Up to this point, still there was no open talk about setting Mosaddeq aside, even though there was evidence indicating efforts to implement this grave task. Ten years later, however, at the height of the power struggle between Mosaddeq and his followers, new developments were underway, developments that were indicative of the increasing concerns of Mosaddeq as the unmatched leader of the National Front, as though these concerns made him determined, considering the lack of attention of the leaders of the National Front to his proposals, not to allow anyone to decide on who the leader and his successor would be as long as he were alive: "If this is done while I am alive, no one will obey him, and regarding afterwards, the position of leader is not hereditary, such that someone might want to appoint a leader for when he has passed away. The appointment of the leader is an indisputable right of the Iranian people, who will in practice choose whomever they consider to be worthy to be the leader, in other words, one who obeys them. Hence, anyone who serves the beloved homeland is in practice the leader."[87] All this showed that despite all his concerns, Mosaddeq would not allow the slightest doubt that he was the leader of the National Front for life, and more importantly, that of the people of Iran for life. This position, for which being worthy, as far as it concerned the leaders of the National Front, was not determined by the votes of the congress, "in practice" could be attained in another arena, which, in Mosaddeq's words, was bestowed in the course of meaningful procedures such as "service to the beloved homeland"!

In this sense, the expression of opinion by Bakhtiar that Mosaddeq felt his position as the leader of the National Front was being threatened was not without reason. Heedless of the protocols that he inevitably had to observe as a member of the executive committee of the National Front, in practice, he was stepping on the path of putting Mosaddeq, whom in the congress he had placed on the same level as Amir Kabir, aside.

After Saleh resigned from the central committee of the Iran Party and the central council of the National Front, Bakhtiar immediately contacted the American Embassy in Tehran. According to the embassy report, his statements about the situation of the National Front after Saleh's resignation were as follows: "Allahyar Saleh has sent a letter to the Iran Party Central Council and formally resigned from the Iran Party Central Council. Saleh stated that he is very tired, old, sick and has decided to withdraw from any political activity… Shapur Bakhtiar said that with Saleh inactive, he will remain at the head of the Iran Party and bring it up to strength and try to make it a disciplined group. Bakhtiar said that he would not oppose Dr. Mosadeq, the symbol of the nationalist movement, but would try to use him and his programs to his own benefit. Bakhtiar described Mosadeq as a massive egotist, who cannot agree that the National Front (NF) be put into the hands of any one man, other than himself. Bakhtiar said that other than the removal of the NF conservative leadership, nothing practical has come out of Mosadeq's recent suggestions. Therefore, it is up to the younger NF leaders to take the lead in reforming the NF, of course deferring to Mosadeq as a matter of form. Bakhtiar said that he will use persons like Dariush Foruhar but they will not take control of the nationalist movement… Bakhtiar said that the NF ties with the religious community are better than with the Army, but if the NF could get a good leader and organization, the young officers who are discontent with the government would side with the nationalists. He said that the NF has contact with the Freedom Movement of Iran (FMI) and the religious leaders through Ayatollah Zanjani. At the present time the NF plans to use Zanjani as a mediator of the nationalist forces… The NF will work openly since if it tried to work clandestinely, the government would identify the NF with the Tudeh Party as a clandestine party and put the NF members in jail. The NF will not try to keep its plans secret since several NF people are in the pay of the government. Bakhtiar said that he and other NF leaders think that Khonji is a SAVAK agent or at least has contact with SAVAK."[88]

In another report, the American Embassy had emphasized that according to Bakhtiar, "Mohammad Mossadeq was passé as a leader, but would always symbolize the nationalist spirit of the country. He said if he were appointed prime minister, his first act would be to pay his personal respects to Mossadeq at his village. Mossadeq belonged to another era, and would have no active role in running the country again."[89]

A few months after the disintegration of the Second National Front, the central council of that organization in a meeting in November 1963, by granting full authority to Saleh as the chairman of the executive committee elected by the congress, began a fateful effort to prevent its doomed end, which was the atonement for its numerous transgressions. What became known as the policy of "patience and waiting" or "silence and calm" was the outcome of this meeting, a policy that Saleh proposed as the only solution, given the situation in which the National Front found itself. He considered this decision to be the result of the realization that the regime, by gaining international support, in "appearance" has claimed to have carried out reforms, the mission of the implementation of which was supposed to be the responsibility of the National Front. This time, he called on the nationalists to be "realistic" and to be "patient and steadfast," lest otherwise, the National Front would be declared illegal.[90]

In that meeting, Saleh's efforts to justify the policy that was called "patience and waiting" were fruitful, and the policy was endorsed by the leaders of the National Front, although with the formation of the new executive committee, he did not succeed in taking an effective step in regard to solving the organizational problem or finding a way to get through the crisis by offering a codified plan and program. According to Sanjabi, this meeting was held "at the time when the National Front was about to be shut down… Hence, they thought to give some authority for now to Mr. Saleh to see what would happen, and what organization those with new ideas might create. For now, Saleh would be a leader until later, if necessary, when they would ask others as well. In that meeting, a number of people began denigrating a great deal… They attacked Mr. Saleh and were very disrespectful, and the meeting ended."[91]

The gist of Sanjabi's words suggests that the leaders of the National Front had not found a way to have effective involvement in the political developments, and by losing the opportunities that were provided, they knew no other way but to wait. This was a situation that, considering "the leadership cadre's indecisiveness and lack of frankness regarding the principles," Abolfazl Qasemi had described as follows: "Our policy is like that of the snail. Every once in a while, we get out of our shell, make an appearance, and then go back into the shell and, for a while, like animals, hibernate."[92]

Bakhtiar was one of those who supported granting authority to Saleh. He found this choice effective only when it was coupled with devising a clear and active policy. About that meeting and granting Saleh authority, he said: "Granting authority to a leader for a definite amount of time and for specific purposes is something that might be quite logical, and I have no objection to it… If you have a plan for struggle, offer it, and we will grant you a vote of confidence… Saleh said, 'No, first vote, then I will think about it and find a solution.' This, I would not agree to, and I strongly opposed it… After a while, we had some harsh words for the first time. I told him, 'Mr. Saleh, for eighteen years and the years after Mosaddeq, you considered yourself to be his successor, and we wasted a lot of our time and the time of the people of Iran. I cannot promise you political cooperation any longer. I will remain a member of the Iran Party and of the National Front, but in meetings where you want to talk about being silent and quiet, I am no longer prepared to cooperate. In my opinion, you must offer a positive plan and tell us for what reason, when, and how you will do it.' Two or three other people accompanied me, and we left the meeting, and I never saw Mr. Saleh again, to the end of his life... I was not at all against granting him extraordinary authority in order for him to do something, not to give him authority to sit in his house and become a recluse, like a dervish, like Dervish Saleh Ali Shah. I told him, 'You are a pious person. I have no doubt about your piety and honesty, but this attitude is not acceptable in political struggle. If it becomes necessary for us to start the struggle again tomorrow and go to jail for it, well, we will go to jail. We will stay and fight.' This was the difference between my temperament and nature and that of those gentlemen... In my opinion, the indecisiveness, the personality, and the lack of seeing things clearly caused the National Front to end. Some of these gentlemen wanted to keep their doctor's offices open, and to occasionally drop by the meetings. And they often came two hours late and stayed for fifteen minutes and said, 'I was a minister in Mosaddeq's cabinet, and this is enough for me to be one of the first-tier leaders.'"[93]

In light of these developments, it was perhaps for this reason that according to a document in the US National Security Archive, sometime after the disintegration of the Second National Front, in January 1964, Bakhtiar began to think about establishing a political party comprised of the young cadres and leaders of the National Front, such as Daryush Foruhar, Hoseyn Mahdavi, Abdolrahman Borumand, and Hedayatollah Matin-Daftari. Within a short period of time, however, he changed his mind about that plan and decided to remain in the National Front and reorganize it with a new policy, and take over its leadership.[94]

The National Front and the 5 June 1963 Uprising

On 5 June 1963, when the National Front was waning more quickly than ever before, certain developments the grounds for which had begun with the opposition of religious notable seminary scholars and clerics to the elections of provincial and regional councils, and were formed with their confrontation to the "White Revolution," turned into a full-fledged rebellion. Since July 1952, from the time that Ayatollah Kashani had called on the masses of the people to disobey the government and had driven Qavam from his seat of premiership and his efforts to regain power, this was the first time that another well-known cleric had called on the masses to disobey the regime and to rebel and riot, disobedience and rebellion that eventually came to fruition with the fall of the monarchical regime and the victory of the Islamic Revolution in February 1979.

The first measure after the 26 January 1963 referendum was the refusal by the clerics and religious sources of emulation to perform congregational prayers and religious ceremonies and to preach during the fasting month of Ramazan. The one-month silence of the functionaries of religion in protest against the government up to the first day after that month, which was the day when the Fetr Feast is celebrated, and the performance of prayers on that day with the participation of grand ayatollahs in the city of Qom instigated a new round of protests against the regime. During this round, by publishing an announcement declaring a prohibition on celebrating the Persian New Year on the first day of spring in 1963, Ayatollah Khomeyni called on the clerics to confront the regime. In that announcement, he called the attention of the "honorable high-ranking religious scholars and clerics" to the threat against Islam by the regime and asked them to declare a prohibition on celebrating the Persian New Year and instead to "go into mourning and offer condolences to the Imam of the Age, may God hasten his advent" and inform the "Moslem nation of the calamities inflicted on Islam and Moslems."[95]

Sometime later, publishing another announcement, this time addressed to the people, Ayatollah Khomeyni wrote: "The ruling regime in Iran transgressed against the sacred laws of Islam and transgressed against the indisputable laws of the Koran. Moslem women's honor is exposed to violation, and the despotic regime with ratifications that are contrary to religious law intends to disgrace the chaste women and humiliate the people of Iran. The despotic regime intends to ratify and implement the equality of men and women, in other words, it wants to trample on the obligatory laws of Islam and the holy Koran. This means that it intends to take eighteen-year-old girls into compulsory military service and drag them into barracks; it means that, by the force of bayonets, it intends to take the chaste Moslem girls to the centers of debauchery. Foreigners have targeted the Koran and the clerics. At the hands of these types of governments, foreign hands intend to eliminate the Koran and trample on us, the clerics... I declare this Persian New Year a day of mourning for the Moslem community, in order to alert the Moslems of the threat against the Koran and the country of the Koran. I declare a warning to the despotic regime. I swear by God Almighty that I am worried about a black revolution, a revolution from below... I think the solution is for this despotic government to be removed on the charge of transgression of the laws of Islam and violation of the Constitution and be replaced by a government that adheres to the laws of Islam and is sympathetic to the people of Iran." In conclusion, emphasizing that he has performed his present "duty," and that if he remains alive, he will perform his next duty, Ayatollah Khomeyni asked God "to save the holy Koran and the honor of Moslems from the evil of foreigners."[96]

With the publication of this announcement, the sessions of mourning on the anniversary of the "martyrdom of Imam Ja'far Sadeq" became scenes of confrontation with the government, and in the early days of spring 1963, resulted in clashes between the religious seminary students of the Feyziyeh Seminary in Qom and security forces. Several people were killed in Qom and Tabriz, and a number of people were wounded.

The rapid developments that had escalated the ongoing tensions with the ceremonies commemorating the fortieth day after the Feyziyeh Seminary clashes also brought unrest and disturbances to Kerman, Isfahan, and several other cities. In the Islamic lunar month of Moharram, which coincided with June 1963, Ayatollah Khomeyni asked the leaders of the mourning processions to speak about the "calamities" inflicted on Islam, and of "religious jurisprudence, religious faith, and the supporters of religious law" in their self-flagellation chants, and at a time when religion was threatened, to learn self-sacrifice on the path of the "revival of religious law" from the "Sire of the Oppressed, Imam Hoseyn."[97]

Meanwhile, the dispatching of the shroud wearers from Varamin to Tehran was reminiscent of the time when, in July 1952, Ayatollah Kashani had issued a decree for the shroud wearers of Kermanshah to go to the capital city to overthrow Qavam's government, reminiscent of the time when in the words of Ayatollah Kashani, because of a "treacherous" element like Qavam, beloved Islam was threatened, and the sacred religion was exposed to attack by foreigners and separation from politics. This time, by the time Tehran became aware, religious mourning sessions were being held in religious centers and mosques filled with people. The members of the National Front, the Freedom Movement, and several Islamic groups assembled in protest to the government in Haj Abolfath Mosque, and the university and religious seminary students gathered in Hedayat Mosque, the name of which was tied together with the name of its prayer leader, Seyyed Mahmud Taleqani. Coalition societies and mourning procession groups began their march in front of Haj Abolfazl Mosque on Rey Street heading toward the northern part of the city, and gradually the number of marchers increased, from Amin Hozur Intersection to Sarcheshmeh Intersection and Baharestan Square, from Mokhberoddowleh neighborhood to Shahabad, and from Pahlavi to Takht-e Jamshid Streets. Tupkhaneh Square and 24 Esfand Square to the bazaar and the university were all witness to the expansion of the demonstrations. On the day of Ashura, the anniversary of the martyrdom of Imam Hoseyn, Tehran was under the exclusive occupation of the followers of the "Sire of the Oppressed" and the promoters of the "revival of religious law."

On the evening of Ashura, when the Feyziyeh Seminary and the court-yard of the shrine of Her Holiness Ma'sumeh in Qom were packed with crowds of people, Ayatollah Khomeyni, in a fiery speech the content and the expression of which was unprecedented, addressed to the Shah, said: "I advise you, oh Mr. Shah, oh Your Excellency the Shah, I advise you to stop these actions and policies. I do not wish that, if one day your masters decide that you should leave, the people will be grateful for it. I do not want you to become like your father... If they dictate to you and hand it to you, think about it. Why do you speak without reflection? Are the clerics defiled animals? If they are defiled animals, why does this entire nation kiss their hands? Why do people bless themselves with the water the clerics drink? Are we defiled animals? ...Are the clerics and Islam black reactionaries? But you, black reactionary, made a white revolution? You started a white revolution? What white revolution? Why do you want to deceive the people so much? Why do you threaten the people so much? Mr. Shah! Maybe your masters want to present you as a Jew, so that I would say that you are an infidel, to kick you out of Iran and decide what to do with you."[98]

In the course of the developments that led to the 5 June 1963 rebellion, the leaders of the National Front were in prison. With the information they received here and there in prison, they began discussions about publishing an announcement in protest against the regime that had engaged in suppressing the rebellion. Without any conclusions, these discussions failed. According to Bazargan, the text of the announcement was supposed to be prepared in protest against the government and published with the signatures of the members of the supreme council of the National Front. The majority of the members of the supreme council of the National Front, most of whom were in prison, agreed to the publication of such a text. Saleh, who was among the supporters of this action, left the decision regarding its publication to the vote of the executive committee. Of the seven members of the executive committee, four opposed and three supported the publication of the announcement. Finally, after long arguments and debates, the issue of the publication of an announcement condemning the regime was left without any results. The supporters of the publication of the announcement regarded the suppression of the people and the arrests of the clerics the reason behind the need for that action, and the opponents raised the issue of not being informed about the conditions outside prison in support of their argument. In the reports and memoirs of the leaders of the National Front, no mention is made of the details of the argument that occurred in prison for or against the publication of the announcement. The point that is certain is that neither did the supporters of the publication of the announcement consider the necessity of supporting Ayatollah Khomeyni the reason for this action, nor did the opponents, in justifying their opinion, speak of opposition to his views. Outside prison, to the extent that it was related to the policy of the National Front regarding the 5 June rebellion, we face the same situation. Shamsoddin Amir'ala'i, a member of the central council of the National Front, who served as the minister of national economy and the minister of justice in the cabinet of Mosaddeq and who became Iran's ambassador to France after the Islamic Revolution, in his memoir recounts the differences of opinion that existed outside prison among the nationalists regarding the 5 June rebellion. According to him, those differences caused them to be unable to reach a consensus in this connection. He writes: "At that time, those who were of the same mind as I was in the National Front and had not been arrested told me verbally and in writing, reminding me that in accordance with Article 17 of the constitution of the National Front, I and others were obliged to hold the meetings of the provisional executive committee of the National Front and follow up on our measure... Hence, a few sessions were held that coincided with the 5 June events. Those events were discussed in one of those sessions, and there were many discussions. With the votes of the other members, I presided over the sessions... In one of those sessions in which there were differences of opinion, I prepared the minutes to be printed and distributed; but because of the differences of opinion, they were not distributed, and I was saddened."[viii] Other than this, no information about the policy of the leaders of the National Front in reaction to the 5 June riots is available. We only know that Bakhtiar was among the opponents, and Sadiqi, who supported the publication of that text, in protest to the opposition to that policy, had said that after he was released from prison, he would no longer work with the National Front. Years later, in his book, *Yekrangi*, explaining the reason for his opposition to the occurrences on 5 June 1963, Bakhtiar wrote: "The National Front did not support Khomeyni's movement. I played a role in that decision. I did not by any means want to link myself to the type of thinking that was at odds with the progress and development that we extolled, such as more land for farmers and more rights for women. With four votes to three votes, we decided not to support Khomeyni by any means."[99]

Bakhtiar's reasoning regarding what he calls "Khomeyni's movement" is far from reality. In the policies of the National Front or the documents of its congress, not only is there no sign of "extolling" the progress and development that Bakhtiar talks about, but there are clear indications that the National Front had declared its opposition to the regime's reforms at every opportunity. In the report of the congress, the executive committee of the National Front called land reform a device for diverting public opinion from the "national anti-colonial struggle" and regarded it as "a fresh coat of paint on the rusted apparatus" of the regime. About women's rights, as well, it raised the issue of the need to observe "Islamic standards" against granting the right to vote to them, which was included in the regime's plan. If we consider Bakhtiar's opposition and the vote of the executive committee in prison as evidence of the lack of support of the leaders of the National Front for Ayatollah Khomeyni, we must also accept the fact that the reason for

---

[viii] For more regarding the text of the unpublished announcement of the National Front about the 5 June 1963 riots, see: Shamsoddin Amir'ala'i, *Mojahedan va Shahidan-e Rah-e Azadi* (Tehran: Dehkhoda Publishers, 1979), 549-550.

this action, more than representing the negation of his rebellious views, is an indication of the lack of knowledge of the leaders of the National Front about the ongoing events outside prison, not to mention the fact that a strong group in the executive committee and the central council of the National Front was pursuing a policy other than the policy that Bakhtiar and some others supported.

In the course of the developments that began with the opposition of the clerics to the bill on the elections of the provincial and regional councils and the "White Revolution" and which resulted in the violent events of June 1963, the National Front did not express the slightest opposition to the views of the clerics regarding the reforms by the regime. With the release of the leaders of the National Front from prison, which occurred shortly after the 5 June riots, as well, no sign can be seen of any inquiry and investigation into the true nature of what drove the clerics, and Ayatollah Khomeyni in particular, to confrontation with the regime. The National Front had a chance for another fifteen years to present its assessment of what Bakhtiar referred to as "Khomeyni's movement" to the public for its judgment, and to critique and reexamine the rebellion that was staged as a final rehearsal for the Islamic Revolution. The effective participation of the National Front in that revolution was indicative that such negligence, more than stemming from the inherent weakness and instability of the nationalists who were sitting in ambush to gain power, was indicative of their cooperation and collaboration with the clerics. The way they opposed the reforms by the regime, the ratifications of the National Front congress, and the participation of a number of the members of the National Front in the 5 June incidents are further evidence of this reality.

In addition to all this, the point that more than anything verifies this fact is the relationship of Hoseyn Shah-Hoseyni, who was in charge of the bazaar organizations of the National Front, with such infamous thug leaders as Tayyeb and Esma'il Haj-Reza'i, whose names are synonymous with the June 1963 riots, a relationship another aspect of which is revealed, in Shah-Hoseyni's words, in the cooperation between "roughnecks, hoodlums, and gang leaders" and the clerics. In an interview about the history of this relationship and his friendship with Esma'il Haj-Reza'i, he said: "The devout and shrewd clerics, with their charming speeches and behavior, attracted the masses of the people who had religious zeal and sentiments. Mr. Seyyed Mehdi Lalezari was also able to establish a religious group like that of Ansar ol-Abbas (greetings to him) and others around Tehran, in which Haj Esma'il Haj-Reza'i was a permanent member. The father of Dr. Haddad-Adel, Haj Reza Haddad, whose name is now given to Saffari Street around Khorasan Square, was one of the followers of Haj Esma'il Haj-Reza'i... The reason for my acquaintance with Haj Esma'il was that I was a close friend of Haj Hasan Melli, the owner of the Melli Rice and Kebob Shop in the Sarcheshmeh neighborhood of Tehran. That place was a hangout for my work and political activities, and that is why we called it Melli (National) Rice and Kebob Shop. In fact, his actual name was Hasan Naderkhani. Haj Hasan had made a pilgrimage to Mecca, and he had been the so-called pilgrimage caravan guide of these people. Through Haj Hasan, I became friends with his friends, including Haj Esma'il, and they liked the way I spoke and behaved, and they sometimes consulted with me in these affairs... One of the services of Haj Esma'il Haj-Reza'i that was very important and showed the religious zeal and honor of that man is that, for the first time during the Shah's rule, the people of Tehran decorated all the way from 24 Esfand Square to the end of the Pepsi Cola neighborhood with lights for the birthday of the Imam of the Age, may God hasten his advent, on the 15th of the month of Sha'ban. On the recommendation of Mr. Seyyed Mehdi, Haj Esma'il Haj-Reza'i paid for all the lighting decorations and the celebrations... This goes back to before 1961, when the buying and selling and drinking of Pepsi Cola—because of its ties to that misguided sect of Baha'is and spending some of its revenues on fighting the religious beliefs of Shi'ites—had been religiously prohibited by sources of emulation. Haj Esma'il made an effort and, given his status as a neighborhood strongman, he organized a magnificent religious rally against the Baha'is. Haj Esma'il also played a major role in the construction of the Saheb al-Zaman Mosque. Haj Esma'il, of course, was in contact with Ayatollah

Khomeyni and was devoted to him, but the relationship was not at the level of, for instance, having a coalition group with the late Imam Khomeyni. I think the reason for his arrest during the 5 June 1963 riots was his fighting against the Baha'is in connection with Pepsi Cola and the construction of the Saheb al-Zaman Mosque... Haj Esma'il's contact with the clerics was mainly through the late Lalehzari. He and his friends had rotating sessions on Friday eves with Mr. Seyyed Mehdi Lalehzari, in which I also participated. We were fifty to sixty people; every Friday eve, we went to someone's house and recited the Komeyl prayer and wept. When the prayer was over, we got up and left. Or on Friday mornings, we went to Ebn-e Babuyeh Shrine. We first performed a Friday full-body ablution in the Ebn-e Babuyeh Bathhouse that had a hot water reservoir, and from there we went to the Shrine of His Holiness Abdolazim on pilgrimage, and then went back to the same house."[100]

Shah-Hoseyni's collaboration with Tayyeb Haj-Reza'i, who was initially one of the hoodlums who supported the Shah, was also based on the same type of relationships that had shaped his friendship and collaboration with Esma'il Haj-Reza'i. Shah-Hoseyni's statements about this collaboration indicate that Ayatollah Zanjani, the founder of the National Resistance Movement, who among the well-known clerics was considered a shining light of the National Front, played an important role in the creation of such a relationship and recruiting Tayyeb to the ranks of the opponents of the regime, to the point that Tayyeb became a follower of Ayatollah Khomeyni, and in praising Tayyeb, Ayatollah Khomeyni called him the "servant of Imam Hoseyn," and tried to save his life when he was sentenced to be executed.[ix]

[ix] For more on the opinion of Ayatollah Khomeyni about Tayyeb and his efforts to save him from execution, see: Mehdi Eraqi, *Nagoftehha: Khaterat-e Shahid Haj Mehdi Eraqi*, edited by Mahmud Moqaddasi, Mas'ud Dehshur, and Hamid Reza Shirazi (Paris: Mo'sseseh-ye Khadamat-e Farhangi-ye Rasa, 1987; Tehran: 1991), 175-176, 190-191.

About the start of his relationship with Tayyeb, Shah-Hoseyni states: "One day, Ayatollah Zanjani, who was working with the National Resistance Movement, summoned me and said, 'Mr. Shah-Hoseyni!' I said, 'Yes.' He said, 'Go and tell these friends of yours that doing political work in such a society in which the government makes use of a bunch of hoodlums, prostitutes, and knife-wielders to break up and disperse the people cannot get anywhere with a bunch of educated young people wearing ties or dignified and religious bazaar merchants. It requires a bunch of roughnecks and strongmen to be able to stand up to the hooligans and murderers, and if necessary, resort to their knives. Through one channel, I am working on Tayyeb and his friend Qasem Samavarsaz...' I said, 'Sir, this is beneath you, to have contact with such people.' He said, 'It is none of your business. It is my business.' Gradually, it got to a point that when we had rallies, these people did not bother us anymore." In continuing to recount this relationship, Shah-Hoseyni mentions the arrests of Tayyeb and Qasem Samavarsaz on the charge of writing hot checks and the efforts of Ayatollah Zanjani and Ahmad Sadr-Haj-Seyyed-Javadi for their release.[101]

Ahmad Sadr-Haj-Seyyed-Javadi was a member of the executive committee of the Freedom Movement and the Tehran prosecutor at that time. Shortly before the fall of the monarchical regime, he became a member of the Revolution Council, and in the cabinet of Bazargan, he was the minister of interior. Shah-Hoseyni recounts: "We received a message that Tayyeb had been jailed and that we should do something. I informed Mr. Zanjani about the message, and he said that he would come up with a solution. At that time, Mr. Sadr-Haj-Seyyed-Javadi was the Tehran prosecutor, and he was a friend of Engineers Bazargan, Hasibi, and others. One day, Mr. Zanjani sent someone after Mr. Ahmad Sadr-Haj-Seyyed-Javadi. When he came, Mr. Zanjani asked him, 'Can you do something for me?' In response to Mr. Sadr-Haj-Seyyed-Javadi, who asked what it was he wanted him to do, Mr. Zanjani said, 'Rescue Tayyeb and his friend from these people, so that they can figure out that the regime is not loyal to them, and that even if needed, it will kill them'... I was in the Sarcheshmeh neighborhood 10 days

later when Mr. Sadr-Haj-Seyyed-Javadi called me and said, 'Come to
the prosecutor's office; I will release both of them today.' At four o'clock
in the afternoon, both of them were released from the Justice Department prison.

"In any case, we went to Mr. Zanjani's house at four o'clock, and at
five o'clock, both Tayyeb and his friend Qasem Samavarsaz entered Mr.
Zanjani's house together... When they entered, they started to kiss the
doors and the walls and then dropped in front of Mr. Zanjani and
kissed his hands and feet. Mr. Zanjani said, 'No, this is not necessary, go
and learn to behave yourselves!'"[102]

Two weeks after Tayyeb was released, when the leaders of the National
Front were preparing for the rally in Jalaliyeh Square, Shah-Hoseyni
arranged a meeting between Tayyeb and Allahyar Saleh, the chairman of
the central council of the National Front. Not much information is
available about the details of that meeting, which took place at the home
of Saleh, other than, according to Shah-Hoseyni, at the end of the
meeting, Tayyeb and those who accompanied him expressed their
"regrets for their past actions, all stood up and kissed Saleh's hand, and
each paid his respects and left."[103] Shah-Hoseyni also refers to the
relationship between Sanjabi and Abdollah Koromi, also known as
Abdollah the Butcher. He mentions Abdollah Koromi as one of the
supporters of Mosaddeq who wanted to stab Sha'ban Ja'fari, also known
as Sha'ban the Brainless, to death. Shah-Hoseyni has also mentioned
Abdollah the Butcher as one of the "zealous and devoted athletes and
champions" of Tehran. On the days of Tasu'a and Ashura (10 and 11
December 1978) before the Islamic Revolution, along with several other
traditional athletes, he was the bodyguard of Ayatollah Taleqani,
Bazargan, Sanjabi, and Sahabi.[104]

Regarding the friendship of Shah-Hoseyni with Tayyeb and Esma'il
Haj-Reza'i, who were arrested as the perpetrators of the 5 June 1963
incidents and were put on trial and executed, not much more information is available other than what Shah-Hoseyni has provided. The point
that is certain is that, considering the role that Shah-Hoseyni played as

the liaison between Tayyeb and Ayatollah Zanjani and Saleh, one can surmise that whatever has been said about the National Front having been completely unaware of the shaping of the developments that resulted in the 5 June rebellion is not based on solid evidence. Whatever the truth, Shah-Hoseyni, the instigator of the meeting between Saleh with Tayyeb and Qasem Samavarsaz, participated in the congress of the National Front and was elected as a member of its central council. This shows that his relationship with well-known thugs such as Tayyeb and Esma'il Haj-Reza'i, who played a symbolic role in the 5 June rebellion, was not an impediment to his becoming a representative at the congress and his rise to such a distinguished position as membership in the central council of the National Front, especially at a time when Saleh as the chairman of that organization knew about that relationship.

Shah-Hoseyni, a member of the central council and the person responsible for the bazaar organizations of the National Front, who describes himself as being enamored by the hoodlums, "sly imposters," and "chivalrous thugs," was a follower of Ayatollah Kashani in his youth. After the 1953 coup d'état, he was one of the founders of the National Resistance Movement and became the executor of Gholamreza Takhti's will. When Ayatollah Khomeyni was returning to Iran in 1979, Shah-Hoseyni was a member of the welcoming committee, as the representative of the National Front. With the victory of the Islamic Revolution, as a deputy minister, he was appointed president of the Physical Education Organization and the National Olympic Committee of Iran in the provisional government of Bazargan. With the formation of the Fifth National Front in 1994, Shah-Hoseyni was elected as a member of the executive committee of that organization. He is now a member of the Board of Trustees of Ahmadabad "Fortress," the tomb of Mosaddeq.

---

[1] Rasul Mehraban, *Barrasi-ye Mokhtasar-e Ahzab-e Borzhuazi-ye Melli-ye Iran dar Moqabeleh ba Jonbesh-e Kargari va Enqelabi-ye Iran* (Tehran: Peyk-e Iran Publishers, 1980), 51; Karim Sanjabi, *Omidha va Naomidiha (Khaterat-e Siyasi)* (London: Jebheh-ye Melliyun-e Iran Publishers, 2007), 205.

[2] Asghar Parsa, *Farzand-e Khesal-e Khishtan*, compiled by Ali Parsa (Tehran: Ney Publishers, 2009), 147-148; Sanjabi, *Omidha va Naomidiha*, 207.

³ Hamid Zonnur, "Negahi beh Jonbesh-e Daneshju'i-ye Salha-ye 1339-1342 Khorshidi dar Iran," quoted from *Tajrebeh-ye Mosaddeq dar Cheshmandaz-e Ayandeh-ye Iran*, Proceedings of the Conference on "Tajrebeh-ye Mosaddeq dar Cheshmandaz-e Ayandeh-ye Iran," edited by Houshang Keshavarz-Sadr and Hamid Akbari (Bethesda, MD: Ibex Publishers, 2005), 311-331.

⁴ This writer's interview with Hamid Zonnur, Paris, 11 December 2007.

⁵ Ibid., *Khaterat-e Shapour Bakhtiar, Nokhost Vazir-e Iran (1357)*, edited by Habib Ladjevardi, Iranian Oral History Project, Harvard University Center for Middle Eastern Studies, Bethesda, MD, 1996, 50-52; Emadoddin Baqi, *Jonbesh-e Daneshjui'i-ye Iran az Aghaz ta Enqelab-e Eslami*, vol. 1 (Tehran: Jame'ah-ye Iranian Publishers, 2000), 59-60.

⁶ *Jebheh-ye Melli beh Revayat-e SAVAK* (Tehran: Markaz-e Barrasi-ye Asnad-e Tarikhi-ye Vezarat-e Ettela'at, 2000), 115-116.

⁷ *Surat Jalasat-e Kongereh-ye Jebheh-ye Melli-ye Iran*, compiled by Amir Tayerani (Tehran: Gam-e No Publishers, 2009), 218, 224, 228.

⁸ *Khaterat-e Shapour Bakhtiar, Nokhost Vazir-e Iran (1357)*, 31-32.

⁹ *A'in-e Eslam*, no. 4, vol. 7 (17 June 1950): 3, 38.

¹⁰ *Surat Jalasat-e Kongereh-ye Jebheh-ye Melli-ye Iran*, 535.

¹¹ Iraj Amini, *Bar Bal-e Bohran: Zendegi-ye Siyasi-ye Ali Amini* (Tehran: Mahi Publications, 2009), 34-35.

¹² Abdolhoseyn Azarang, "Ali Amini va Rishehha-ye Shekast-e Eslahat," *Bokhara, Majalleh-ye Farhangi va Honari*, no. 55 (November 2006): 108-114.

¹³ *Keyhan*, 10 May 1961, 1-4.

¹⁴ *Khaterat-e Shapour Bakhtiar, Nokhost Vazir-e Iran (1357)*, 44.

¹⁵ Foreign Relations of the United States, FRUS: 1961-1963; Iran, United States Government Printing Office, Washington, DC, 1998, 304.

¹⁶ (DNSA) Interview with Shapour Bakhtiar, Report NO. WIT-5579, 3 July 1961.

¹⁷ Amini, *Bar Bal-e Bohran*, 229-300.

¹⁸ Iraj Afshar, *Parvandeh-ye Saleh (dar bareh-ye Allahyar Saleh)* (Tehran: Abi Publishers, 2005), 88-89; Azar, 139-140; Sanjabi, *Omidha va Naomidiha*, 210; Mehdi Bazargan, *Shast Sal Khedmat va Moqavemat, Khaterat-e Bazargan, Goft-o Gu ba Sarhang Golamreza Nejati* (Tehran: Khadamat-e Farhangi-ye Rasa, 1996), 355-356.

¹⁹ *Khaterat-e Shapour Bakhtiar, Nokhost Vazir-e Iran (1357)*, 54; *Payam-e Daneshju*, no. 10 (April/May 1961): 1.

²⁰ *Keyhan*, 20 May 1961, 13-14.

²¹ Ibid.

²² Ibid.

²³ Ibid., 13.

[24] Afshar, *Parvandeh-ye Saleh*, 140-141; Gholamreza Nejati, *Tarikh-e Siyasi-e Bist-o Panj Saleh-ye Iran (az Kudeta ta Enqelab)* (Tehran: Mo'asseseh-ye Khadamat-e Farhangi-ye Rasa, 1992), 178.

[25] Sanjabi, *Omidha va Naomidiha*, 211-212.

[26] (DNSA) Interview with Shapour Bakhtiar, Report NO. WIT-5579, 3 July 1961.

[27] Ibid.

[28] Ibid.

[29] Ibid.

[30] Ibid.

[31] Ibid.

[32] Ibid.

[33] Ibid.

[34] Ibid.

[35] FRUS: Memorandum from Robert W. Komer of the National Security Council Staff to President Kennedy, Washington, 4 August 1961, 1961-1963, Vol: XVII, 213.

[36] Kaveh Bayat, "Daneshgah-e Tehran, Avval-e Bahman 1340," *Goft-o Gu, Fasl-nameh-ye Farhangi va Ejtema'i*, no. 5 (Autumn 1994): 48-50.

[37] *Asnad-e Jonbesh-e Daneshju'i dar Iran (1329-1357), Majmu'eh-ye Asnad-e Tarikhi*, vol. 1, compiled and edited by Deputy President's Office of Management and Information Services (Tehran: Printing and Publication Organization of the Ministry of Islamic Culture and Guidance, 2001), 152-187.

[38] Bizhan Jazani, *Tarikh-e Si Saleh: Tarh-e Jame'ahshenasi va Mabani-ye Esteratezhi-ye Jonbesh-e Enqelabi-ye Khalq-e Iran* (np: np, nd), 129; Khalil Maleki, *Khaterat-e Siyasi*, (Europe: Kushesh baray-e Pishbord-e Nehzat-e Melli-ye Iran, 1981), 144.

[39] Jazani, *Tarikh-e Si Saleh*, 129; *Surat Jalasat-e Kongereh-ye Jebheh-ye Melli-ye Iran*, 64; Sanjabi, *Omidha va Naomidiha*, 220-221.

[40] Afshar, *Parvandeh-ye Saleh*, 151-152.

[41] Ibid., 152-155.

[42] *Porseshha-ye Bipasokh dar Salha-ye Estesna'i: Khaterat-e Mohandes Ahmad Zirakzadeh*, edited by Dr. Abolhasan Ziya'-Zarifi and Dr. Khosrow Sa'idi (Tehran: Nilufar Publishers, 1997), 197.

[43] Amir Pishdad and Mohammad Ali Homayoun Katouzian, *Namehha-ye Khalil Maleki* (Tehran: Markaz Publishers, 2002), 65-78.

[44] Sanjabi, *Omidha va Naomidiha*, 229-233.

[45] Ibid., 231.

[46] Ibid.

[47] Bazargan, *Shast Sal Khedmat va Moqavemat*, 391.

[48] Parsa, *Farzand-e Khesal-e Khishtan*, 175-178.

[49] Ibid., 177.

[50] *Surat Jalasat-e Kongereh-ye Jebheh-ye Melli-ye Iran*, 28-29.

[51] Ibid., 29.

[52] Ibid., 31-32.

[53] Ibid., 351-352.

[54] Ibid., 38-39.

[55] Ibid., 141-144.

[56] Ibid., 177-179.

[57] Ibid., 188.

[58] Ibid., 245.

[59] Majid Rahbani, "Hezb ya Jebheh: Nokhostin Kongereh-ye Jebheh-ye Melli-ye Iran (Dey 1341)," *Jahan-e Ketab*, nos. 251-252, vols. 1 and 2 (Farvardin-Ordibehesht 1389): 38-44.

[60] Mehdi Azar, "Beh Yadbud-e Allahyar Saleh" in Afshar, *Parvandeh-ye Saleh (dar bareh-ye Allahyar Saleh)* (Tehran: Abi Publishers, 2005), 142-143.

[61] *Surat Jalasat-e Kongereh-ye Jebheh-ye Melli-ye Iran*, 314.

[62] Ibid., 323, 342.

[63] http://www.sdil.ac.ir/index.aspx?PID=211&CaseID=117680.

[64] "Dowlat az Hayahu-ye Entekhabat-e Anjomanha-ye Eyalati Cheh Khiyali Darad?" announcement of the Freedom Front, Tehran, November 1962, quoted from Seyyed Hamid Ruhani (Ziyarati), *Barrasi va Tahlili az Nehzat-e Imam Khomeyni* (Qom: Daftar-e Entesharat-e Eslami, 1982), 166.

[65] Mehdi Bazargan, *Eshq va Parastesh ya Termodinamik-e Ensan*, 3rd printing (Houston: Daftar-e Pakhsh-e Ketab, 1979), 197.

[66] Seyyed Ali Shayegan, *Zendeginameh-ye Siyasi: Neveshtehha va Sokhanraniha*, vol. 1, compiled by Ahmad Shayegan (Tehran: Agah Publishers, 2006), 203-204.

[67] *Surat Jalasat-e Kongereh-ye Jebheh-ye Melli-ye Iran*, 525.

[68] Ibid., 390, 424, 444.

[69] Ibid., 47, 216-230, 260, 262, 346-347, 370-371, 373, 389, 435-436, 438, 445, 464-466, 475.

[70] *Yadnameh-ye Ostad Dr. Gholamhoseyn Sadiqi*, compiled and edited by Dr. Parviz Varjavand (Tehran: Chapakhsh Publishers, 1993), 549.

[71] Ibid., 151.

[72] Sanjabi, *Omidha va Naomidiha*, 134.

[73] Parsa, *Farzand-e Khesal-e Khishtan*, 125-126.

[74] Ibid., 161-163.

[75] Ibid., 163.

[76] Gholamreza Nejati, *Mosaddeq: Salha-ye Mobarezeh va Moqavemat*, vol. 2 (Tehran: Mo'asseseh-ye Khadamat-e Farhangi-ye Rasa, 1997), 401-402.

[77] Ibid.

[78] Ibid., 406-415.

[79] Ibid., 415, 418-419, 422, 430, 434.

[80] Ibid., 419-422.

[81] Afshar, *Parvandeh-ye Saleh*, 418; Nejati, *Mosaddeq: Salha-ye Mobarezeh va Moqavemat*, 432.

[82] Quoted from *Yadnameh-ye Ostad Dr. Gholamhoseyn Sadiqi*, 55.

[83] *Surat Jalasat-e Kongereh-ye Jebheh-ye Melli-ye Iran*, 224, 228.

[84] *Khaterat-e Shapour Bakhtiar, Nokhost Vazir-e Iran (1357)*, 67-70.

[85] Bazargan, *Shast Sal Khedmat va Moqavemat*, 395.

[86] (DNSA) Memorandum of Conversation, American Embassy, Tehran, 27 November 1953.

[87] Nejati, *Mosaddeq: Salha-ye Mobarezeh va Moqavemat*, 402.

[88] (DNSA) Memorandum: Comments of National Front Leader, Shapur Bakhtiar, P-223/64, 16 May 1964.

[89] (DNSA) Memorandum: Comments of Shapur Bakhtiar, Report No. WIT-5552, References WIT-5530, 20 June 1961.

[90] Nejati, *Mosaddeq: Salha-ye Mobarezeh va Moqavemat*, 394-400.

[91] Sanjabi, *Omidha va Naomidiha*, 244.

[92] *Surat Jalasat-e Kongereh-ye Jebheh-ye Melli-ye Iran*, 255.

[93] *Khaterat-e Shapour Bakhtiar, Nokhost Vazir-e Iran (1357)*, 78-81.

[94] (US National Security Archive) NSA. Memorandum of Conversation. Participants: Dr. Hossein Mahdavy, National Front Leader; William G. Miller, Second Secretary of Embassy, Tehran, January 28, 1964; ibid., Confidential, Ni Foreign Dissem. Views of Shapur Bakhtiar, Tehran, February 25, 1964.

[95] Javad Mansuri, *Tarikh-e Qiyam-e 15 Khordad beh Revayat-e Asnad*, vol. 1 (Tehran: Markaz-e Asnad-e Enqelab-e Eslami, 1998), 545.

[96] Ibid., 546.

[97] Ibid., 620-621.

[98] Seyyed Hamid Ruhani (Ziyarati), *Barrasi va Tahlili az Nehzat-e Imam Khomeyni* (Tehran: Rah-e Emam Publishers, 1986), 231.

[99] Bakhtiar, *Yekrangi*, 126.

[100] "Az Ayyari ta Lompenism," interview with Hoseyn Shah-Hoseyni about Sha'ban Ja'fari and Tayyeb Haj-Reza'i by Ali Abolhasani (Manzar), *Faslnameh-ye Takhassosi-ye Tarikh-e Mo'aser-e Iran*, no. 26 (Summer 2004): 202-203, 205-208.

[101] Ibid., 205-208.

[102] Ibid., 208-211; Mehdi Eraqi, *Nagoftehha: Khaterat-e Shahid Haj Mehdi Eraqi*, edited by Mahmud Moqaddasi, Mas'ud Dehshur, and Hamid Reza Shirazi (Paris: Mo'asseseh-ye Khadamat-e Farhangi-ye Rasa, 1987; Tehran: 1991), 71.

[103] *Faslnameh-ye Takhassosi-ye Tarikh-e Mo'aser-e Iran*, no. 26 (Summer 2004): 208-211.

[104] Vahid Mirzadeh, *Tadavom-e Hayat-e Siyasi dar Ekhtenaq, Tarikh-e Shafahi-ye Nehzat-e Moqavemat-e Melli* (Tehran: Selk Publishers, 2000), 116-117, 139-142.

Chapter Eight

In every generation, no more than 10 individuals can be found who are afraid to say something contrary to the truth, whereas in every generation, we can find thousands, even millions of individuals who fear that by saying something, they shall be left alone, even if that which they say is truth itself.
—Søren Kierkegaard

The Open Letter of Sanjabi, Bakhtiar, and Foruhar to the Shah

The publication of the open letter of Sanjabi, Bakhtiar, and Foruhar to "His Imperial Majesty, the King of Kings" on 12 June 1977 was the declaration of the discernable presence of the National Front in the changes and developments that eventually led to the fall of the monarchical regime and the victory of the Islamic Revolution in Iran. Since the days of the administrations of Amini and Alam, this was the first time that the leaders of the nationalists, relishing what was termed an "open political climate," once again stepped into the arena of politics and the struggle for power. In that interval, Iran had gone through an important period, becoming a powerful force in the region. The consequences of the land reform, the uprooting of the villagers from villages, the growth and expansion of urban living, economic prosperity, relative welfare, and the widening of class gaps, along with the Shah's autocratic rule and the increasing political repression, were distinctly emblematic of this period. Having left behind the coronation ceremonies, the 2,500th year of the foundation of the Imperial State of Iran, the establishment of the Rastakhiz (Resurgence) Party, and the start of the guerrilla movement, the political climate of the country was undergoing change in every arena.

Under these conditions, with the appearance of some signs of economic crisis and general discontentment, Iran was becoming the scene of social unrest, to the point that with the election of Jimmy Carter as the President of the United States and his human rights policy, the opponents of the regime became more hopeful than ever before of gaining freedom. This was the climate in which the open letter of the leaders of the National Front was written.

Fearlessly criticizing the existing "crisis condition," as they termed it, the authors of the letter viewed Iran in all political and cultural arenas as facing a crisis. Hence, in the assessment of the authors of the letter, the rising prices; the high cost of groceries and housing; the destruction of agriculture, animal husbandry, and newly-established national industries; the spread of corruption and prostitution; and the disregard for individual and social freedoms had placed the country on the "edge of the precipice," conditions that with the imposition of police tactics, "exaggerations, propaganda, and imposition of celebrations," escalated general hopelessness and discontentment and the exit of capital from the country and placed the society at an impasse. This situation was the consequence of mismanagement and was regarded to be in clear violation of the explicit text of the Constitution and the Universal Declaration of Human Rights. According to the open letter, contrary to the Constitution, the management of the country had "assumed an individual and despotic aspect in the arrangement of the monarchical regime."

In describing the crisis condition of the country, the open letter also refers to the guerilla struggle and the "rebellion" of young people who "willingly volunteer for prison, torture, and death, engaging in actions that the ruling regime calls terrorism and treason, but they call it self-sacrifice and honor." This reference more or less indicated a coming to an understanding with those who had risen against the regime in an armed struggle, without this understanding either meaning approval or disapproval of the path that they had chosen.

With reference to the Constitution and its supplement, which regarded the Shah as not having a position of responsibility, the signatories of the open letter demanded that he "end his authoritarian rule, conform to the principles of constitutionalism, restore the rights of the people, and truly respect the Constitution." Other demands that were emphasized included the "revocation of the one-party system, freedom of the press and assemblies, the release of political prisoners and political exiles, and the instituting of a government based on the vote of the majority of the elected representatives of the country itself, thus regarding the Shah as responsible for administering the country in accordance with the Constitution."

Referring to the Shah's statement at Harvard University a few years earlier, with utterances such as "respect for individual dignity and freedom" and "humans are not the servants of government, but the government is the servant of the people in the country," in their letter, Sanjabi, Bakhtiar, and Foruhar called his attention to another statement that he had "recently made in Holy Mashhad," declaring that "problems cannot be solved by guns; rather, corruption can be fought through social struggle." From the perspective of the leaders of the National Front, this political turnabout was a positive sign. However, "succeeding in it was only possible by seeking the sincere cooperation of all the people's forces in a free and lawful environment, and with respect for human dignity."[1]

The insistence of the leaders of the National Front in their open letter was in fact focused on old issues such as the principles of constitutionalism, observing the law, social liberties, and the authority of the king, which comprised the basic views of the nationalists. In addition to these, however, the open letter contained another meaningful point that, from the perspective of its authors, considering the grave situation of the country, stemmed from a sense of "national and religious duty to God and the creatures of God."

The leaders of the nationalists tied secular demands together with religion and religious laws and spoke about God's creatures at a time when there was, as yet, no mention of religion and no sign of the functionaries of religion in the social demands of that day. Perhaps if the leaders of the National Front had left religion to the religious and the world to the worldly, if they had not adorned what was completely of a secular nature with the garb befitting the religious, and if they had not paved the way for religion to enter into the arena of politics, Iran would have had a different fate. But they did otherwise; and in confrontation with a king who, whatever else he was, was not an enemy of religion and religiosity, they chose another option. They had confronted a king who in the not-too-distant past had adorned his modernizing reforms with justifications of the same sort. In his book, *Enqelab-e Sefid* (White Revolution), which must be considered his modernization manifesto, Mohammad Reza Shah used the "advice" of a religious leader to prove the correctness of his reforms. He wrote: "In his famous letter to Malek Ashtar fourteen centuries ago, His Holiness Ali, greetings upon him, recommended, 'Always maintain justice such that it would include both the privileged and the masses, and in doing so, give priority to the majority, since the discontentment of the masses neutralizes the contentment of the privileged few, whereas the discontentment of the privileged few will cause no harm to the contentment and happiness of the majority.' In other words, if the general public is happy with you, the discontentment of a few will have no effect, and conversely, the happiness of these few will never prevent the effects of the discontentment of the public."[2]

In their memoirs, Bakhtiar and Sanjabi mention the roles of Bazargan and Foruhar in the writing of the open letter, which is considered the start of the resumption of the activities of the National Front. As far as it relates to Sanjabi, the letter was written by Bazargan, and Sanjabi made some changes and corrections in the text. According to Sanjabi, the letter was supposed to have been signed by a large number of people, but some, due to being "conservative and cautious," were not prepared to sign it, and some others who were willing to sign the letter were not well-known individuals. Hence, the decision was made to publish the open letter with only a few signatures. This decision was opposed by Bazargan, because he wanted a larger number of well-known figures as well as some who were affiliated with the Freedom Movement to sign the letter. Bakhtiar and Sanjabi were opposed to this idea. Sanjabi believed that that there were people in the organizations and political party members of the National Front who, even if they were not regarded as having "priority" over the members of the Freedom Movement, were not at a lower level. Hence, either they would have "to think about a large number of signatures, or if they were going to be limited, there needed to be some rules and restrictions." Bakhtiar states that since the letter was addressed to the Shah, the signatories had to be from among the "leaders" who would be recognized by the Shah. Bakhtiar did not see any problem in having Bazargan and Sahabi sign the letter on behalf of the Freedom Movement, and himself and Sanjabi on behalf of the National Front. Sanjabi had also expressed his agreement to adding the signatures of others, such as Yadollah Sahabi and Hasan Nazih, who were members of the Freedom Movement, in addition to Bazargan; but Bazargan continued to insist on his own opinion, and in addition to the ones mentioned, he wanted to add the signatures of Hashem Sabbaghi-yan and a few others, a request that was not agreed to by the leaders of the National Front. Hence, finally, the open letter was published with the signatures of Sanjabi, Bakhtiar, and Foruhar, a letter in the writing of which, according to Bakhtiar, Bazargan was "very much" involved, but, "unfortunately," he did not sign it.[3]

If we accept the explanations of Sanjabi and Bakhtiar about the decisive role of Bazargan in preparing the open letter to the Shah, and track his ideas in the content of the letter in which secular demands are comingled with religion and religiosity, then the strongest reason for regret is the signature of Bakhtiar at the bottom of such a text. In inspiring the content of that letter, which was going to be signed by the leaders of the National Front, Bazargan had essentially achieved his goal. Years earlier, referring to a "noble" verse from the Koran with which they had adorned the hall of the National Front congress, he had said that he saw no "difference of opinion" between himself and those "gentlemen" of the National Front, and he ultimately wanted to impose more influence over the codification of the National Front policy. This time, as well, was no different. By wishing to add the names of a number of religious politicians to an open letter to the Shah, he wanted a greater share for himself and his supporters and likeminded people; and within a short period of time, he would achieve the actualization of what was called the "national and religious duty before God and the creatures of God."

The open letter of the leaders of the National Front was published when no more than one month had passed since the resignation of Amir Abbas Hoveyda, the prime minister who had occupied the seat of premiership for nearly thirteen years. In the meantime, the Iranian society was undergoing rapid developments. With the fall of the cabinets of Jamshid Amuzgar, Ja'far Sharif-Emami, and Gholamreza Azhari, finally, the door was opened to the administration of Shapour Bakhtiar. During that time, by holding alternating meetings at the homes of its leaders, the National Front began its efforts to expand its activities and organize for the struggle ahead. These efforts finally resulted in a meeting on 31 October 1977 with the participation of seven leaders of the National Front at Bakhtiar's home. According to a report prepared by SAVAK about this meeting, the participants reached an agreement that from then on, by coordinating their future activities, they would advance their struggle under the name of the "Union of the National Front Forces" (Ettehad-e Niruha-ye Jebheh-ye Melli).[4] The importance of this meeting was in particular due to the fact that their previous meetings to end the differences of opinion and create harmony in organizational relations among the various factions of the National Front had reached no result.

Three weeks after this meeting, which was an important step regarding the manner of regulating the organizational relationships for creating harmony in the activities of the nationalists, by inviting the people to a rally on 22 November 1977, the National Front began new preparations for confrontation with the regime. This rally, which was held following the open letter of Sanjabi, Bakhtiar, and Foruhar, was considered the first open confrontation with the regime. The location of the rally was the garden of a member of the Nation of Iran Party (Hezb-e Mellat-e Iran) by the name of Hoseyn Golzar-Moqaddam on Karaj Road, around Karavansara Sangi. The selection of that day for the rally by the National Front was a meaningful one. In the announcement that was distributed in the bazaar, the people were invited to participate in ceremonies on the Feast of Qorban! This invitation was successful, and according to the SAVAK report, in addition to the leaders of the political parties affiliated with the National Front, more than a thousand people attended the rally.

In the afternoon of that day, the supporters of the regime and SAVAK agents came to the location of the rally in several busses, and breaking the tables, chairs, tape recorder, microphones, and furnishings in the garden, they attacked the participants with stones and bricks. The cars parked outside around the garden were also attacked by individuals wearing Rastakhiz Party armbands. According to Daryush Foruhar, who had filed a complaint to the local gendarmerie to investigate this incident, in the course of this pre-organized raid, more than 300 people were severely injured and transferred to Aban Hospital. In a report that it prepared in this connection, among the injured, SAVAK mentions the names of such individuals as Daryush Foruhar, Kazem Hasibi, Abolfazl Qasemi, Mehrdad Arfa'zadeh, Fathollah Banisadr, and Shapour Bakhtiar, whose arm had been broken.[5]

Simultaneous with these developments and the appearance of the first signs of protest by the intellectuals and political and social figures in the society, the Shah's regime was facing increasing difficulties in the international arena in connection with the issue of the violation of human rights in Iran. International human rights organizations accused Iran of basic violations of these rights and demanded the investigation of the situation of political prisoners.

Against such a backdrop, with the political unrest that within a short period of time resulted in the expansion of the protest movement by the people, the leaders of the National Front and the Freedom Movement and well-known clerics, or in a broader sense, all the opposition forces, found the situation favorable for their involvement in determining the fate of the country as much as possible. These conditions, especially with the presence of Ayatollah Khomeyni in Paris, who had come to France on 7 October 1978 from his exile in Iraq after a short stay in Kuwait, gave the ongoing struggle in Iran new meaning and depth.

Although this event played an important role in determining the direction of the people's protest movement, there was still a long way to go before the victory of the clerics, or the particular faction represented by Ayatollah Khomeyni. On the other hand, the appearance of the first windows to freedom had revived the memory of the National Front from the recent and distant past in the minds of the public. The invitation to Sanjabi to participate in the Socialist International Congress in Canada, in particular before the arrival of Ayatollah Khomeyni in Paris and Sanjabi's name becoming known once again, was another sign of this reality. Simultaneous with the increasing isolation of the Shah's regime, not only for the people, but also for a powerful force in the West, the National Front was considered an important alternative in the power struggle in Iran. The invitation to the leader of the National Front to that congress meant official recognition of that reality.

The National Front and the Disarming of the Secular Forces

In November 1978, when Sanjabi was traveling to Canada to participate in the Socialist International Congress held in Vancouver, in the course of a short visit to Paris, he met and conversed with Ayatollah Khomeyni. At the end of his visit to Paris, he submitted a handwritten letter containing three points and delivered by Abolhasan Banisadr to the "world revered source of emulation of the Shi'ites."[i] The National Front, in an announcement that was published "in the name of God" and addressed to "our compatriots," about how this letter, which it called an announcement, had been prepared, wrote that the announcement "was issued after the last meeting of His Eminence Grand Ayatollah Khomeyni, the revered world source of emulation of the Shi'ites, and farewell to His Eminence, by Mr. Sanjabi, the leader of the National Front." It also stated: "The text of this announcement was agreed to by Grand Ayatollah Khomeyni prior to its issuance." A segment of

---

[i] Ebrahim Yazdi believes that Haj Mahmud Maniyan, an old member of the National Front who accompanied Sanjabi to Paris, was the carrier of the letter to Ayatollah Khomeyni. See: Ebrahim Yazdi, *Akherin Talashha dar Akherin Ruzha: Matalebi Nagofteh Piramun-e Enqelab-e Eslami-ye Iran* (Tehran: Qalam Publishers, 1984), 32.

Sanjabi's announcement, which began with "In the name of the Almighty" and bore the Islamic lunar date of 4 Zihajjeh 1398 inscribed above the Persian solar calendar date of 14 Aban 1357, or 5 November 1978, was as follows:

"(1) Because of its continuous violations of the Constitution, imposition of oppression and injustice, propagation of corruption, and submission to the policies of foreigners, the present monarchy of Iran is devoid of legal and religious foundation. (2) With the existence of the unlawful monarchical regime, the national Islamic movement of Iran cannot agree to any form of government. (3) The national government of Iran must be determined on the basis of Islamic standards, democracy, and independence, by the vote of all the people." According to Sanjabi, after reading the letter, Ayatollah Khomeyni had added the word "independence" to the third point.[6]

In addition to the handwritten letter that would have an indisputable effect on the political developments, the way it was prepared was also worthy of contemplation. Before preparing that letter, in the first hour of his arrival in Paris, by publishing an announcement that was prepared by Ahmad Salamatiyan and made available to the mass media, Sanjabi had canceled his travel plans to Canada and his participation in the Socialist International Congress under the "pretext" of the British foreign minister's support for the dictatorial regime that ruled the country. Bakhtiar considers Mahmud Maniyan and, in particular, Ahmad Salamatiyan to have been those who encouraged Sanjabi to cancel his travel plans to Canada and participate in the Socialist International Congress. According to Bakhtiar, on the way from the airport to the city, Salamatiyan had convinced Sanjabi that, because of the participation of the representative from Israel, it was not expedient for him to go to Canada, since Sanjabi's participation would anger Ayatollah Khomeyni.[7]

Later on, considering the arguments that occurred about the text of the three-point letter and its impact on the fate of the National Front and the Iranian Revolution, he said that when "they say I was pressured by Mr. Khomeyni and those around him to issue that famous three-point letter, it is an absolute falsehood…" He continued: "I personally found it necessary to clarify the position of the politicians and the National Front in the Iranian revolutionary movement. And the comrades who were around me endorsed this idea. For instance, a couple of nights later, we were guests for dinner at the home of Hoseyn Mahdavi, and there were some people such as Salamatiyan, Banisadr, and two or three others. Dr. Mokri was also with me every day. He also prepared some ideas. I set all of them aside. On the evening when we were in Mahdavi's home and they had spread the supper cloth on the floor, I asked for paper, picked up a pen, wrote those three points slowly, and read it right there for the comrades, who all approved of it."[8]

After preparing the handwritten text, in his last meeting with Ayatollah Khomeyni, he "requested" of him that, because of the need for unity and cooperation between the political groups, in a joint meeting, he provide "guidance for him and Bazargan, who was in Paris." Furthermore: "He also personally contacted Bazargan and told him, 'Mr. Khomeyni kindly agreed for us to visit him tomorrow to provide us with guidance and advice.'" Bazargan, who had met and conversed separately with Ayatollah Khomeyni, without finding such a meeting necessary, returned to Iran.

Sanjabi's final step before returning to Iran was to ask Ayatollah Khomeyni's permission regarding the public announcement of the three-point letter. He states: "I asked His Eminence, 'Sir, should this announcement of mine that you approved and are keeping remain hidden and a secret, or can I publish it and announce my opinion?' He said, 'No, sir; announce it right here in Paris. And when you go to Tehran, announce it there, as well.' When I left him, I went to another courtyard, which was the place where his followers gathered. There was a crowd of seminary students, clerics…bazaar merchants, and so on there. We sat in a rather large hall there, and I read the text of the announcement in the presence of that crowd. They all chanted, 'God is great,' applauded me, and wished me a long life."[9]

The submission of the three-point text of Sanjabi to Ayatollah Khomeyni, which in a way made the disarming of the secular group vis-à-vis the clerics official, was another chapter in the cooperation between the nationalists and the religious forces. This chapter began with the establishment of the National Front; it was shaped in the collaboration of Ayatollah Kashani and his followers in the course of the nationalization of the oil industry; and it had come to fruition with the overthrow of Qavam in July 1952, until once again, it became visible in the events that resulted in the fall of Amini and the 5 June 1963 rebellion; and finally in the Islamic Revolution of 1979, it left behind a destiny-making consequence. The three-point announcement of Sanjabi, which marked the beginning of such an end, however, should not have surprised anyone. From old times when he occupied the seat of minister of culture in Mosaddeq's cabinet, Sanjabi believed that Islam and "Islamic movements" had a special place in social struggles. He considered "Islamic teachings" to be the antidote to "disgrace, poverty, and ignorance." From his perspective, lack of attention to such teaching had caused the period of the "progress, development, science, literature, order, justice, wealth, and supremacy," of "Islamic civilization," to come to an end. In illustrating the sunset of those "prosperous" days, he spoke about "ungratefulness for Divine gifts," and in describing the policy of the enemies of Islam, he mentioned the destructive role of the "Europeans." Even so, in Sanjabi's words, with awareness of past mistakes and "repentance and asking forgiveness" before "the Court of Divine Justice," the new days of "salvation and happiness" were ahead. These days, by the will of "the Creator," would open the path of the "Islamic nations" to uprising for "gaining freedom" in the battle with an enemy called the "Occident."[10]

In this manner, the leader of an organization whose name in our unfortunate historical conscience had been attached to moderation and civility, to the guarding of the Constitution and constitutional traditions, when freedom and reforms seemed achievable, turned away from all that he had sought for many years, such that this time, sitting at a banquet of foolishness that rarely had been matched, he washed his hands of constitutionalism and everything he had spoken about up to then.

In any case, if we look carefully, we see that in the past, at other opportunities such as those during the administrations of Amini and Alam, as well, when the door to moderation and civility was opened, the National Front acted the same. It did so to the extent that during Amini's time, when with the support of the United States and because of the weakness of Mohammad Reza Shah, the path to social freedoms had been paved, it squandered such an opportunity. During Alam's premiership, as well, in the name of the Constitution and law and freedom, it saw participation in the elections of the two houses of the parliament and the acceptance of government positions of service as possible only if the Shah, by signing a three-point document, were to agree to comply with the Constitution; and then, in the strange turn of history, when once again the door to law and freedom was being opened, by signing another three-point document that invalidated the Constitution, it opened the way to the power of religion and religious functionaries.

Sanjabi's three-point announcement and the impact it left behind on the power struggle and the shaping of the oncoming developments was a subject of debate for a long time in political circles. The fact that Ayatollah Khomeyni held onto the original copy of the document that was being made available to the public was another indication of the fact that he and those around him did not imagine that the National Front would surrender that easily. Bakhtiar, as well, later on when he went to Paris, regarded that announcement to be the effective reason for the defeat of the National Front, an announcement that, according to him, had been prepared and published on the personal decision of Sanjabi.

The manner in which the text of the announcement was prepared and Bakhtiar's opinion in this connection leave no room for doubt that the preparation of that text and its publication were the result of Sanjabi's decision. This, however, does not change the fact that the announcement was published in the name of the National Front, and in this sense, it was considered to be the position of that organization in public

opinion. Moreover, no one openly stood up to challenge that announcement, and the collective silence in this regard left no doubt or
suspicion about its content having been merely the position of one of
the leaders of the National Front. Hence, reducing it to a "personal"
decision, considering its consequences, not only fails to tell the whole
truth, but, ultimately, it is further evidence of the chaotic situation and
the collapsing organization of the National Front at the dawn of the
Islamic Revolution.

During those destiny-making days, how was it possible, as the leader of
the National Front, to go and visit Ayatollah Khomeyni without having
prepared a plan and program for negotiations and expect the desired
outcome? The memoirs of Sanjabi, Bakhtiar, and several other functionaries of the nationalists indicate that not only did no plan or program
exist, but also, no preparations had been made other than the procurement of money and "foreign exchange currency" for staying in a hotel
that would be fitting of the "status" of the leader of the National Front.
Bakhtiar even reduces the reason for the visit of the leader of the National Front to Paris to a marginal issue, such as attending a gathering of
some of his supporters in that city, which he calls the "cohorts and
cronies" of Sanjabi, and such trivial matters as Sanjabi's knowledge of
the French language, or his wife's interest in shopping in Paris stores,[11]
whereas the story went beyond all this. He further states that the
meeting of Sanjabi with Ayatollah Khomeyni in Paris was not based on
the decision of the central council of the National Front. Moreover, no
discussions took place among the leaders of the National Front in this
regard, and no minutes of any such session exist. Bakhtiar claims that
prior to Sanjabi's departure for Paris, Bakhtiar had emphasized that if
Sanjabi decided to meet with Ayatollah Khomeyni, such a meeting
should be only to become acquainted with his views.[12]

Upon his departure for Paris, in an interview with the correspondent
of *Ettela'at* newspaper, in response to a question about his reason for
participating in the Socialist International Congress in Canada, Sanjabi
said that he intended at "the beginning of this trip, to go to Paris and
meet with Grand Ayatollah Khomeyni, the world leader of Shi'ites." He

added: "In that meeting, I will once again emphasize the cooperation of the National Front of Iran in the brave struggles of our nation alongside Iran's progressive clerics." In another interview, which was again about his trip, Sanjabi emphasized: "I am going to Paris, because under the present conditions, this is the most important step that is necessary for determining our future policy... I will go to Paris to meet with the revered leader of Shi'ites. Of course, His Eminence is informed about the course of the struggles of our nation; but there might be some minor points that need to be mentioned, and it is also necessary for us to listen to his important and decisive viewpoints in person... We will go to meet the revered source of emulation to coordinate the struggles. Such coordination already exists in regard to many issues. The progressive clerics have always been at the side of freedom-loving and popular forces. This is our history. It is our Shi'ite sect that recommends the principles of freedom." At the end of this interview, when the discussion turned to plans and policy, Sanjabi added that he would like to "postpone talking about the future of the political struggles of the National Front to later."[13]

Based on all that was said, the meeting of Sanjabi with Ayatollah Khomeyni in Paris was not a "personal" and marginal issue, but a prearranged plan without the slightest preparation by the leaders of the National Front. In fact, what remained in the margins was the level of reaction of the National Front to the consequences of such a meeting. Sanjabi also mentions in his memoir that after the publication of the text of the communiqué and his return to Iran, he did not face any objection from Bakhtiar or the leaders of the National Front.[14]

It seems that, despite the displeasure regarding the text of the communiqué, Bakhtiar preferred to forego any open objection, and in a private conversation, he would only say: "The National Front must stand on its own feet." However, relying on its own power and capability would have been effective only if coupled with a plan and program based on democratic goals, a plan and program different from the demands that were made by the clerics, the Freedom Movement, and the anti-democratic groups in their confrontation with the monarchical regime.

From the time of the publication of the open letter of Sanjabi, Bakhtiar, and Foruhar to the Shah in June 1977 until just prior to Sanjabi's trip to Paris in December 1978, in other words, during the interval when such high-circulation newspapers as *Keyhan* and *Ettela'at* would devote daily numerous pages to interviews with the leaders of the nationalists, by discussing its views and policies among the people, the National Front would have had the opportunity to mobilize public opinion in support of all that it had demanded for many years. Such an opportunity, however, as in the past, rather than being utilized to organize and coordinate the secular forces in the arenas of theory and practice, was used to provide cooperation and coordination with the clerics and "revered" sources of emulation, or to praise what was referred to as the "principles of freedom" in Shi'ism. Such was the practice, to the extent that Sanjabi, as the leader and secretary of the executive committee of the National Front, would state that any talk about the policy and the form of political struggle should be "postponed" to another opportunity and an unclear future. On the other hand, even though Bakhtiar regarded "religious dictatorship" to be more dangerous than any other type of dictatorship, he preferred to avoid confrontation with Ayatollah Khomeyni. According to a report prepared by SAVAK about a National Front meeting, in a gathering, he said in this connection: "Explicit and open opposition to Khomeyni under the current conditions will result in the disintegration and ineffectiveness of the National Front's force that is taking shape. The National Front considers itself the last arrow in the quiver for rescuing the homeland, and we must make an effort not to squander this arrow and make it ineffective... Considering the existing conditions and realizing the fact that it cannot rise in open opposition and perceivable resistance to Khomeyni, the leadership of the National Front has inevitably decided to appear to show support for him in order to weaken his forces and consolidate its own position."[15]

Bakhtiar emphasized that there was debate indicating differences of opinion about the content of Sanjabi's announcement. "Fearing excommunication," however, the organization decided to publish that text. Another justification by Bakhtiar was that the National Front of Iran in that announcement "had not agreed to accept several essential points from Khomeyni, such as regime change and declaration of a republic or an Islamic government."[16]

Before long, Bakhtiar found himself facing another reality. He considered the National Front to be the "last arrow in the quiver" for rescuing Iran, which had to be used at a "suitable opportunity"; but the course of events showed that confrontation with Ayatollah Khomeyni required a different plan and program than offering adulation and condescension, or what Bakhtiar called a "suitable opportunity." He and the National Front, nonetheless, lost such an opportunity to form a powerful alternative vis-à-vis the clerics who were sitting in ambush to take power, a unique opportunity the loss of which had no other echo than that of a shot in the dark.

Bakhtiar's Endeavor to Gain Power

Shortly before Sanjabi's departure for Paris, by contacting Jamshid Amuzgar, the former prime minister, Bakhtiar tried to directly communicate the views of the National Front to the Shah. He told Amuzgar: "The country is in a dangerous crisis. The people have no confidence in Sharif-Emami. After Black Friday, the situation has become more critical and the country is rapidly going down the slope toward collapsing. Every day that Sharif-Emami's premiership continues, the situation will become worse. We have come to you so that, to save the country, you will tell His Majesty that, before it is too late, he must dismiss Sharif-Emami and transfer the government to the National Front. We might be able to find a solution to this crisis."[17]

This first effort of Bakhtiar to contact the Shah was arranged by his friend, Manuchehr Razmara, the well-known physician who was acquainted with Ahmad Qoreyshi, the Dean of the College of Economic and Political Sciences of National University and chairman of the executive committee of the Rastakhiz Party. Qoreyshi was a friend of Amuzgar, whom he had informed about the request of Bakhtiar and

Razmara to meet with Amuzgar. This meeting took place on 26 October 1978 with the participation of Amuzgar, Bakhtiar, Razmara, and Qoreyshi at the home of Amuzgar in the Tehran suburb of Tajrish. At the beginning of the meeting with Amuzgar, Bakhtiar explained that because Sanjabi had a meeting with Ayatollah Shari'atmadari in Qom, he was unable to join them.[18]

Amuzgar, who informed the Shah about the meeting and what had happened, was faced with the Shah's concern that "they want to establish a republic in Iran, and now they want me to carry out this plot by my own hand." He writes that he said to the Shah, "If you permit me, I would like to ask a question in this connection." He then adds: "Without a pause, he said, 'Go ahead and ask.'" Amuzgar immediately discusses with Bakhtiar the Shah's concern about the establishment of a republic. Bakhtiar responds: "In the National Front, we are twenty-two or twenty-three people. I cannot speak on behalf of everyone. I will discuss this issue tomorrow when we have a general meeting and let you know about the outcome." Bakhtiar's response, which was delivered to Amuzgar two days later, was as follows: "The National Front does not oppose monarchy. We want to have the responsibility for the government and running the country, so that perhaps we would be able to eliminate this dangerous crisis… We are prepared to announce our view about supporting the monarchy openly, explicitly, and clearly." Amuzgar informs the Shah about Bakhtiar's opinion. He writes: "I asked for an audience and delivered Bakhtiar's response precisely to the Shah. The Shah's face, which was frowny those days, became a bit cheerful. For some minutes, he talked about various things, and in the end, he said, 'Very well. Ask them who their candidate is for premiership.' I took my leave and immediately contacted Bakhtiar. I felt he was indescribably exhilarated when he heard what the Shah had said. Exited, he told me, 'I think we will suggest Allahyar Saleh, but the decision must be everyone's. We did not think His Majesty would make a decision so quickly. Now the problem is that Sanjabi and Bazargan have gone to Paris and London, and without their presence, we cannot make a decision. I will try to contact them so that they return immediately.'"

According to what Amuzgar writes, when the Shah learned about Bakhtiar's opinion regarding the candidate that the National Front had in mind for premiership: "He was really elated upon hearing Saleh's name and said, 'Very well. Tell them to let us know as soon as possible.' Two or three days passed without any news." This time, it was the Shah who asked Amuzgar about the reason for the delay in the National Front's response. Amuzgar writes: "I had no answer. I felt that he was upset. I told him that I would pursue the matter. I called Bakhtiar immediately and told him, 'You have placed me in a very uncomfortable situation. It was you who came to me. It was you who asked me to deliver your message. Now that the Shah has agreed to your proposal, you keep saying, if only and maybe, and you have made me feel like you are pulling the rug out from under me." Then, explaining the conversation between him and Bakhtiar, Amuzgar mentions Bakhtiar's having become "upset" about what had happened and quotes him: "You have no idea about the problems I am facing. Contacting Sanjabi and Bazargan is very difficult. They often are not at the place they are staying. In the past two or three days, I have tried frequently to contact them. Finally, I spoke to Sanjabi today. He said he has some business there, and that he will come back to Tehran when he is done." According to Amuzgar, Bakhtiar, who was able to contact Sanjabi on the following day, tells Amuzgar that Sanjabi's "business is done, but he cannot find a seat on any airline destined for Tehran." Amuzgar had been surprised by what Bakhtiar had told him. He writes: "Immediately, as though I was inspired, I told him, 'We will send the government's airplane to bring him.' Overjoyed, he said, 'I will let him know.' After this conversation, it dawned on me that I had made a promise without being authorized and without permission. I called the palace immediately and told His Majesty about it. He said, 'You did well. Set the date for departure in order to send the airplane.' I contacted Bakhtiar again and told him what the Shah had said. Two or three more days passed and there was no news. I was frustrated. I called Bakhtiar and asked him what had happened. His response was, 'Mr. Amuzgar, I do not know what is going on, but Sanjabi and Bazargan are not prepared to return

and have a discussion. I am very sorry.' It was at this point that I realized
that a wide gap had been created among old friends and allies that
would be to the detriment of all of them... Most upset, I told His
Majesty about it. He said, 'I told you that they have something else in
mind.'"[19]

In any case, the rest of the story, as Amuzgar writes bitterly, was an
open secret: "Perhaps this negligence by the National Front resulted in
the coming to power of the military government and the ensuing
events." Such were the consequences that following Sharif-Emami's
resignation and the coming to power of the incompetent government of
Azhari, the depth and breadth of the crisis assumed a new velocity, and
the National Front, by turning away from a unique alternative that was
provided for overcoming the difficulties, squandered another opportunity, an opportunity that in the book and report card of the National
Front indicated the nationalists' negligence in both recent and distant
history.

One month before this meeting with Amuzgar, in a secret location in
Tehran, which is mentioned in the United States National Security
Archive as the "Iran-Sokna" apartments, Bakhtiar met with John
Stempel, the Political Officer of the American Embassy in Tehran. The
details of this meeting, which was held on Bakhtiar's request, contain
important points about his outlook regarding Iran's conditions, the
National Front, the Freedom Movement, and the issue of political
freedom during the administration of Sharif-Emami. At the start, he
emphasized: "It was important to have contacts with the Americans even
if they would not agree on many things." Bakhtiar added: "It was
important for the Americans to realize that the opposition has no
confidence in the Shah." In response to the question of the Political
Officer of the American Embassy about the National Front's participation in parliamentary elections the following year, Bakhtiar replied:
"This would not be possible unless there was freedom to discuss problems and to organize." He said: "We need six months of freedom, not
extreme freedom, but at least the right to meet and organize...if this is
not done, leadership of the opposition would pass to fanatics." Bakhtiar

considered "Martial Law unnecessary because it hindered the organizational process and it was not really necessary to maintain public order."
In the continuation of his conversation with the Political Officer of the
American Embassy about the National Front, he described that organization as "a group of pretty independent people," and said that "he and
Dr. Karim Sanjabi and Dariush Forouhar had not advocated violence
and cooperation with religious fanatics." Bakhtiar regarded Bazargan
and his group as a faction that "had cooperated fully with religious
individuals associated with Khomeini and Shariatmadari." According to
him: "Bazargan mixed politics and religion, and negotiations with his
group had fallen apart because he had allowed his friends to push him
toward the religious group." Bakhtiar added: "The Front would make
common cause with any organizations except the Communists and the
Free Masons." In explaining his assessment of the Free Masons, he
emphasized that the Iranian Free Masons "were not like the Free
Masons he respected in America and France." Bakhtiar thought that
"the reconstituted National Front could make common cause with more
moderate religious elements and that this was the only hope to develop a
massive following for social democracy."[20]

In addition, Bakhtiar mentioned: "Certain changes might be possible
under Sharif-Emami. Eventually the Shah's whole system had to be
dismantled. Parviz Sabeti had to be removed from SAVAK because he is
associated with torture and foul dealings." He thought "it was important
to work with the present parliament to get free speech and free assembly." He added: "If the social democrats do not triumph, Iran, and by
extension America, will be faced with a choice between dictatorship and
Communism."[21]

In Bakhtiar's outlook and his assessment of the conditions and the
situation of the political forces, considering what had been termed an
"open political climate," there were also issues that were removed from
reality. Undoubtedly, the conditions that he, or the National Front,
faced during the administration of Sharif-Emami were far removed from
the establishment of political freedoms. The Iranian society, however,
from the fall of Hoveyda to the coming to power of Amuzgar and

Sharif-Emami, had undergone changes in the political arena that could not have been believed a few months earlier, changes such as Bakhtiar's secret meeting with the Political Officer of the American Embassy in Tehran. Up to a few months earlier, neither Bakhtiar nor any official of the embassy would have agreed to such a meeting, not even behind closed doors and in secret. And then Bakhtiar, under such conditions, spoke about the hypothesis that if the National Front were reconstituted, this and that would happen. The course of the events, however, showed that in the arena of the confrontation with the forces that Bakhtiar called "backward," the conditions would not advance in the interest of what he referred to as "social democracy."

Three weeks after that meeting, in another meeting that this time was held at the embassy with the participation of John Stempel, the Political Officer of the American Embassy in Tehran, along with Congressman Stephen Solarz and a friend of the congressman, Bakhtiar provided a broader view of his perspectives. He spoke of the Shah as an "absolute monarch" who had for many years "presided over a corrupt regime" and "had created no political institutions." He acknowledged that many had supported the Shah, but it was not so easy to do so now: "Intellectuals did not support the Shah because of lack of freedom. Merchants thought the ruling family had enriched itself and religious leaders were disappointed at the lack of attention given to religious matters. The National Front seeks a democratic solution. It wants a constitutional monarchy if the Shah will seriously utilize the constitution and accept limits on his power." He also said: "The recently established free press remained to be proven in practice… the National Front was very wary of participating in elections unless they are totally free. If they were not, the Front would abstain." He described the National Front's opposition to the Shah as basically "secular," but "in alliance with religious leaders." According to Bakhtiar, the Shah could not continue a foreign policy because "he has no base in the nation." He thought that "the National Front offered the only alternative to today's corrupt regime or to a Soviet takeover."[22]

Regarding the issue of oil and the Persian Gulf, Bakhtiar emphasized that in his opinion, "oil sales were purely business" and "no government in Iran could afford not to sell its oil." He added that "the Front would not block sales of oil to Israel" and that "U. S. fears that Persian Gulf oil would fall into the hands of foreign powers were easily placate[d]." In response to a question from Solarz as to what the United States should do, Bakhtiar said: "It should stop supporting the Shah... If the U.S. would stop its military and political support, the Shah would obviously fail." Considering the ongoing events in Iran, in conclusion, he added: "The month of December (Islamic month of Moharram) would probably see some large demonstrations particularly on the high holy days, tenth and eleventh of Moharram (Dec. 12-13)."[23]

The third meeting took place on 22 October 1978 at Bakhtiar's home with the participation of John Stempel and Gregory Perett, political officers of the American Embassy in Tehran. In this meeting, he "expressed great concern over the near future of Iran in light of pervasive civil unrest." The report continues: "While he also looks ahead to the elections, he said they will not matter if the government cannot defuse the present combination of strikes and agitation." He regarded the following month to be critical and added: "If troublemakers such as the Tudeh Party cannot be brought under control, the Soviets will infiltrate the country, especially in the north and west, and the Baluchis may also move against the integrity of Iran." In the religious forces, he saw hopeful signs, and said that the representatives of the National Front as well as Bazargan and Minatchi—whom he was careful to separate from the National Front—were in contact with Ayatollah Khomeyni in Paris. Bakhtiar was pleased that Bazargan and Minatchi had said that the reforms should come under the Shah. He added: "The mullahs cannot rule Iran. Khomeini, meanwhile, has shown new flexibility... In Paris, he meets many Iranians who have studied in the West." Bakhtiar felt: "Khomeini's move to France broadened the Ayatollah's horizon a bit... He has not changed fundamentally, but he now attacks the Tudeh Party, a position he did not take previously." In addition, Ayatollah Khomeyni has "dropped his insistence of two or three months ago on an

Islamic government. He speaks instead of the need for Islamic justice. Nonetheless, Khomeini's personal hatred toward the Shah still dominates other factors." Bakhtiar spoke about the incompetence of Sharif-Emami's government to find "a way out of the immediate crisis, which Bakhtiar repeatedly said he desperately wants." He then added: "The Shah does show a certain new mellowness, but the Cabinet is riddled with untrustworthy men. Five ministers are ex-Tudeh Party members and six or seven are Freemasons, including Sharif-Emami, the leader of the Iranian masons. Foroughi and Amin[i] are also Freemasons; Bakhtiari [sic] had forgotten the other names... Moreover, the government was hopelessly involved in the very corruption it was supposedly stamping out." He added: "As head of the Pahlavi Foundation, Sharif-Emami made a fortune selling confiscated land... Former Minister of Agriculture Rouhani confiscated land under a nationalization act."[24]

Bakhtiar spoke about cooperation with the government and the difficulties that existed. In his view: "The National Front will cooperate, but only under strict conditions. In the first place, the Shah must apply the Constitution 'with material guarantees.' He must acknowledge that he will reign without ruling, and he must admit, albeit indirectly, that he has been in the wrong. The Government, not the Shah, must be responsible for national policy, although the Shah may 'supervise.' He must promote prosecution of all corrupt public figures... 'especially Hoveyda,' for he is the symbol of the entire corrupt system." Bakhtiar added: "An unblemished, purely transitional government should come into being to run the elections." In the continuation of these discussions with the political officers of the embassy, Bakhtiar speculated about the mechanics of the election and about the number of seats that the Tudeh Party and the National Front would win. Bakhtiar supported the candidacy of the religious figures in Tehran, Mashhad, and Qom, and the secular candidates from industrial cities such as Isfahan. He himself had in mind to run in the south, in Abadan, Ahvaz, or Isfahan.[25]

All this is indicative of Bakhtiar's increasing concerns regarding the developments that had brought Iran to the verge of riots and rebellion. Even though in the course of these conversations he had a negative assessment of the view of Bazargan, who comingled religion and politics, more than regarding it as stemming from his ideology and political history, he attributed it to the influence of those around him. His view of Ayatollah Khomeyni and what he called his change of mind about an Islamic government was also too naïve to be taken seriously. This was an outlook the measuring criterion for which stemmed from the battle between the nationalists and communism in the recent and distant past, from the time when the good and the bad of each option became meaningful in the National Front's outlook regarding the Tudeh Party. And all this was a sign of disregarding the reality that, at the peak of crisis and tumult, when everything took on the color and odor of religion, he still considered the Tudeh Party as a serious threat, or the result of a conspiratorial mindset that made simpleminded judgments about the political past of this or that cabinet minister, or speculations about the votes for this or that political organization in the forthcoming elections.

One could also surmise that the other focus of Bakhtiar's statements about the danger of the Tudeh Party was with the objective of gaining the support of the United States for the National Front as the only alternative given the crisis conditions of Iran. Concerns about the danger of the Tudeh Party and communism in Iran always had a certain place in devising American policy, and this time was no different. It was as though, with such a calculation, Bakhtiar sat in conversation with the officials of the embassy, such that instead of discussing more essential issues, this had become the approach to the topic of the open and secret talks with this or that representative or functionary of American policy.

In the meantime, when he apparently had lost all hope regarding the National Front, Bakhtiar engaged in a new effort, which were it to come to fruition would mean that he would take charge of the affairs of the country. This time, he contacted Reza Qotbi, the former president of Iranian National Radio and Television, who was the maternal cousin of Queen Farah Pahlavi (Diba). Qotbi's mother, Ms. Louise Qotbi, was the daughter of Samsamossaltaneh Bakhtiari, the prime minister during the constitutional era and Shapour Bakhtiar's grandfather.

To achieve the goal that he had in mind, in late November 1978, for the first time, he met with the Queen at the home of her aunt, Louise Qotbi, in order for the Queen to prepare the grounds for his meeting with the Shah.[ii] The choice of the location of the meeting was suggested by Farah Pahlavi, and the Shah was informed about it. Bakhtiar also wanted the release from prison of Sanjabi, who had been arrested at Mehrabad Airport upon his return to Iran after his trip to Paris and meeting with Ayatollah Khomeyni. Farah Pahlavi discussed this meeting with the Shah, and the Shah ordered Naser Moqaddam, the chief of SAVAK, to release Sanjabi. Moqaddam naturally knew about the Queen's meeting with Bakhtiar. According to the Queen, sometime later, Moqaddam and Gholamali Oveysi, the military governor of Tehran, had gone to her and called her attention to the fact that the critical situation in Tehran required the Shah to dismiss Azhari, who had had a heart attack on 22 December 1978, and appoint a "new" prime minister. In that conversation, they mentioned Bakhtiar, who had declared his readiness for this position. Qotbi, as well, in a conversation with Moqaddam had referred to Bakhtiar as a courageous person who, even though he held a grudge against the Pahlavi family, respects the Constitution and the monarchy.[26]

Thus, at the height of the unrest, when Sanjabi had refused to accept responsibility, by being placed in the small circle of nominees for premiership such as Entezam, the nominee for forming a coalition cabinet of the National Front and the Pen-Iranist Party, or Amini, Sadiqi, Pezeshkpur, and Baqa'i, there were only a few steps to the seat of premiership for Bakhtiar.

[ii] Hushang Nahavandi thinks that this meeting took place in September 1978, which does not seem to be correct. He writes: "That meeting lasted for six hours. The owner of the house later said that she had vacated the house of servants for six hours, but the conversations were shorter and continued for two and a half hours… At least one more meeting took place a few days later." See: Hushang Nahavandi, *Akherin Ruzha: Payan-e Saltanat va Dargozasht-e Shah*, 2nd printing, translated by Behruz Sur-Esrafil and Maryam Seyhun (Los Angeles: Sherkat-e Ketab, 2005), 310-311.

Premiership

At sunset on a December day in 1978, General Naser Moqaddam took Bakhtiar to Niyavaran Palace for a conversation with the Shah. This was the first meeting between the two of them in 25 years. In response to the Shah's observation that he still looked young and had not aged, pointing out the Shah's support for the previous governments and his own situation, Bakhtiar said: "Even if I have not reached the winter of my life, undoubtedly, I have begun its autumn. This hall in which I have been granted an audience has heard many total lies. Would Your Majesty wish me to follow the customary ways of the past, or would you permit me to express the facts, even if they are bitter? If Your Majesty does not wish to hear honest statements, I will take my leave. I will be at your service whenever you summon me, but always for the purpose of expressing my thoughts sincerely about the future of Iran." The Shah asked Bakhtiar to tell him the facts, and he listened patiently. Bakhtiar said: "Your father killed my father, and you imprisoned me. I should not have any sense of loyalty to your family. I believe, however, that at least for another 50 years, Iran will not be ready to have a democratic republic. And once it has the readiness, a parliamentary monarchy will meet this expectation. Now, at the present moment, our primary duty should be to put an end to this savagery." The issue of the Shah's traveling abroad was not discussed explicitly in this conversation. Apparently, the Shah made a passing reference to this issue, and Bakhtiar expressed hope that the Shah would stay at least until the parliament gave him a vote of confidence.[27]

In the course of the second meeting ten days later, the Shah asked Bakhtiar for his opinion about forming a government, and shortly after, when Bakhtiar had just returned from the palace, in a telephone conversation, the Shah assigned him to form a cabinet. On the following day, Bakhtiar went once again to meet with the Shah, stating that he would accept the offer with five stipulations, consisting of freedom of the press, dissolution of SAVAK, release of political prisoners, transfer of the property of the Pahlavi Foundation to the government, and elimination of the Imperial Commission, which according to him "interfered in all the internal affairs of the government like another government." Bakhtiar then made two more stipulations: that he would be responsible for selecting the ministers, and that the Shah must leave the country. He writes: "The first five suggestions were accepted without any discussion or even comment. Regarding the selection of minsters, the Shah said, 'Give me a list of your proposed names and I will give you my opinion.'" Bakhtiar provided the Shah with the list and promised himself that if the Shah decided "to impose an ill-qualified person on the cabinet," he would not accept him. At the end of this meeting, the Shah brought up the subject of leaving the country and said that he intended to go abroad. The Shah writes that Bakhtiar's wish was that, prior to the Shah's traveling abroad on vacation, "a Royal Regency Council should be established and obtain a vote of confidence from both houses of the parliament." He continues: "I accepted this stipulation."[28]

Thus, the issue of the Shah's traveling abroad was raised for the first time in the conversation between Bakhtiar and the Shah. Bakhtiar writes: "About two months, or even one and a half months, before that, I would not have made such a request from the Shah; but the fever was so high and the climate was so turbulent that I thought it was necessary for the Shah to be away. Moreover, I insisted on having a free hand in running the country, based on the principles to which I always adhered. The presence of the Shah would undoubtedly impede these principles. If I would succeed in establishing relative order in the country, the Shah would immediately use the common intrigues to disrupt my work, or he would use this or that minister in the cabinet to reinstitute his supervision of those who carried out the affairs. Once again, 'he would divide to rule.' This was Iran's problem, and this was precisely the problem of His Majesty personally. Since I am determined to speak nothing but the truth, I admit that I did not make this request from the Shah willingly and from the bottom of my heart. My loyalty to the Shah was complete, not because of personal fondness for him, but rather, because of the principles that I believe in and which conformed to my inherent fidelity. More than anything else, however, I feared intrigues."[29]

It seems that Bakhtiar's fear of what he referred to as the Shah's "intrigues" stemmed from the experience of 19 August 1953, which had set his fate and that of the Shah and the country on a different course. Precisely twenty-five years earlier, in an interview with the officials of the American Embassy in Tehran, Bakhtiar raised the same issue. In the course of that conversation, explaining his views regarding the Tudeh Party, the government of Zahedi, the importance of political freedom, and the role of major powers in Iran, he said that "the Shah's role is purely representational or *protocolaire*" and that "the Shah had no right to 'flee' on August 16; it was the duty of the King to face the country's problems on the spot even at the risk of his life."[30]

This time, Bakhtiar was looking at the past experiences from a different perspective. In contrast to Sadiqi, who regarded the stipulation for accepting a position of responsibility that the Shah should remain in Iran and confront the clerics who were sitting in ambush to gain power, Bakhtiar supported the Shah's departure from the country. Nevertheless, despite fundamental differences, both had their hearts set on the other one's success. In meeting with the Shah, when the discussion turned to the premiership of Sadiqi, Bakhtiar described him as a "patriotic, intelligent, and very noble" personality, and he declared his readiness to provide "every kind of assistance" to the government that he would form.[iii] Sadiqi, as well, in his first reaction to the premiership of Bakhtiar, when he was facing a wave of threats, accusations, and slander by his old fellow combatants, said: "Dr. Shapour Bakhtiar, as I know him, possesses two major characteristics that distinguish him from many of the national leaders. He is so courageous that, under these conditions, when everyone is thinking about becoming a hero and gaining popularity, he steps into the arena... Bakhtiar has had the courage to step into the arena, and our duty and that of all the national leaders is to assist

---

[iii] According to a report available in the United States Security Archive, Bakhtiar would not agree to participate in a cabinet headed by Sadiqi. NSA, Department of State, Confidential, An: 0780529-1005 12539 221513Z. E.O.12065: GDS 12/22/84 (Stempel, John D.) Tehran, 22 December 1978.

him. The country must be rescued. We are not talking just about the person of Bakhtiar, the National Front, me, or even His Majesty the Shah; rather, we are talking about the country, the preservation and protection of which is our responsibility."[31] Sadiqi looked at his friends and fellow combatants, at his life and time, in this way.

The issue of whether the Shah should stay or leave the country was a key issue. Sadiqi, the distinguished candidate for the position of prime minister, had rejected the departure of the Shah. In the course of several meetings with the Shah, he had asked him to stay in Iran, but leave Tehran. According to Hushang Nahavandi, who was informed about the developments in the Royal Court, Sadiqi had suggested to the Shah that he go to the Bandar Abbas Naval Base at the Strait of Hormuz. He regarded the Shah's remaining in Iran to be the guarantee of maintaining the army's unity and was worried that with the departure of the Shah from Iran, the military might refuse to obey the government. A report by the British Ambassador in Tehran, Anthony Parsons, indicates that the Shah, from at least 31 October 1978, had been thinking about leaving the country.[32] With Sadiqi's failure to get the Shah to agree and gain the support of the National Front that had risen in opposition to his premiership, others such as Mozaffar Baqa'i-Kermani stepped into the arena. Bakhtiar considers the opposition by the National Front, in particular by Sanjabi and Foruhar, the reason for the withdrawal of Sadiqi and his rejection of the Shah's offer of the position of prime minister.[33]

Baqa'i, one of the well-known politicians of the period of the nationalization of the oil industry and the leader of the Toilers Party of Iran, who thought that he still had a place in the sphere of Iranian politics, was one of the staunch opponents to the departure of the Shah from the country. Even though his name was not on the tip of everyone's tongue as one of the candidates for premiership, according to Hushang Nahavandi, notable figures such as Daryush Shirvani, the influential representative from Tehran in the parliament; Ardeshir Zahedi, Iran's Ambassador to the United States; and Amir-Hoseyn Rabi'i, the Commander of the Air Force, were among his enthusiastic supporters for this position.

Nahavandi writes that Baqa'i's suggestion was for the Shah to remain in Iran but leave Tehran and go to the Vahdati Military Base in Hamadan. His plan for putting an end to the unrest was to obtain emergency authority from both houses of parliament, and to arrest 4,000 opponents on the basis of martial law regulations. He thought that by restoring calm to the country and holding free elections, in the next step, gradually, the time for the release of those detained would come. Baqa'i, who had been one of Bakhtiar's staunch opponents for a long time, had cautioned the Shah against the appointment of Bakhtiar as prime minister.[34]

In his last meeting with the Shah, when Baqa'i had gone to the Royal Court to find a solution to confront the ongoing crisis, he remembers the Shah's jaundiced face and his eyes that had lost their sparkle, and he recounts: "The Shah said, 'Well, in your opinion, who can take control of this situation?' I said, 'Someone who is as strong as Qavamossaltaneh.' This was the only time that the Shah's eyes lit up. The name shook him. I am not sure whether he liked or disliked it, but it shook him."[35] A few days after this meeting, Bakhtiar had become prime minister. Quoting Bakhtiar, Sirus Amuzgar states that George Brown, the former British Foreign Secretary and a Labour Party leader, had told him that in a meeting with the Shah, he tried to convince the Shah to choose Bakhtiar as prime minister. British Foreign Office documents also show that Baron or Lord George-Brown knew about Bakhtiar's candidacy for prime minister and that he had spoken to Parsons, the British Ambassador in Iran, about Bakhtiar.[36]

The reason that Bakhtiar accepted the position of prime minister, to the extent that it was related to his personality and individual characteristics, has been occasionally considered to be related to his ambitiousness. He had considered himself deserving of such a position for many years, and during the premiership of Amini, in a conversation with an official of the American Embassy in Tehran, he had spoken about the subject openly. Without any false humility, Bakhtiar considered ambition "the engine of a political man." Hence, he saw no need to refute such a characteristic, nor to consider it incorrect. Nevertheless, he regarded his decision to accept a position of responsibility under those critical conditions as stemming from another reason. In addition to individual and political inclinations and achieving a position for which he had been struggling for many years, he regarded his increasing concern over the future of Iran as the main reason for this decision. He writes: "The truth is that the problem was no longer the problem of the person of the Shah. It was not even the issue of the Constitution. The issue was Iran, the existence of Iran, above and beyond all else!"[37]

Various views have been expressed about the possibility of his success and his assessment of the situation. Some of his close associates state that when Bakhtiar became prime minister, he did not consider the chance of his success as more than one or two percent. His own opinion in this connection is different. He states: "As for myself personally, the issue was not my chances. For me, the issue was to serve the country after twenty-five years. If an occasion is found after twenty-five years for a person to bring this idea to reality, this belief, in my opinion, amounts to a duty from which he should not shirk. Shirking one's responsibility under difficult conditions is very easy, but what is difficult is to stand and be resistant. For this reason, I never calculated any percentages or computed what percent and which percent."[38]

Because of his individual and familial potential, Bakhtiar had the opportunity to relinquish his beliefs and achieve political ambitions. His kinship with Sorayya Esfandiyari, the Shah's wife at the time, and Teymur Bakhtiar, the head of SAVAK, each was a privilege that could pave the way for his ascent to the peak of fame and power. Because of his political beliefs, however, he turned away from all these. In the early days after the fall of Mosaddeq's cabinet, in August 1953, he did not give any consideration to the offer of membership in Zahedi's cabinet, and when he saw that he could acquire power in the National Front, despite all their former differences of opinion, he nominated Allahyar Saleh for the position of prime minister. Given another opportunity, he made every effort to ensure the premiership of Sanjabi, and when Sadiqi's name was talked about by many for that position, he spoke well of him to the Shah. Finally, when he saw the existence of his country in danger, he stepped into the arena as a fearless leader, and with a courage that stemmed from his self-confidence and tribal lineage, like a "storm petrel," he hastened in the direction of an ill-fated battle, a storm petrel flying into darkness.[iv]

Years before rising in confrontation with Ayatollah Khomeyni, about the characteristics of political leaders, Bakhtiar had said at the National Front congress: "My dear friends and experienced politicians who are present here have frequently reminded me that frankness and courage are the second and third principal characteristics of a political man. I believe that courage and frankness, despite all their many disadvantages, will some day be fruitful. Such investment will result in loss at the beginning; but gradually and over time, in the same way that time is in the interest of the truth, they will some day yield fruit. The problem is that some people in all stages of their lives pursue a comfortable and peaceful social situation and at the same time prefer residence in Paradise to all alternatives of life. I, however, since 1936, when I was active against Franco and his dictatorship in the student organization affiliated with human rights and fought Fascism and Hitler's dictatorship, essentially cannot be in the second line on the field of battle... Basically, some people are born to command and some to obey, and that is their inherent nature. As one politician said, Marshal Pétain was the greatest military man in the world, but as a deputy commander. A man like General de Gaulle, who was two ranks lower than Pétain, however, was a man who was born to be a commander... Of course, all of you gentlemen possess piety and faith, and you are virtuous... But piety, nobility, and faith are not sufficient... Have you ever heard anyone say

---

[iv] In his first radio message on 6 January 1979, Bakhtiar seasoned his statements with a couplet from a poem, "Storm Petrol" (Morgh-e Tufan), by the contemporary poet, Golamali Ra'di-Azarakhshi, with a hint at his own character: "I am a storm petrel, I do not fear storms / I am a wave, not a wave that flees from the sea." From then on, his supporters and detractors, either in praising or denigrating him, referred to him as the "storm petrel." Moshiri-Yazdi says that at one time, he had recited this poem to Bakhtiar, who had said: "This poem describes me; it describes how I feel today." This writer's interview with Mohammad Moshiri-Yazdi, Paris, 21 February 2008.

that Churchill, or de Gaulle, or Roosevelt were noble men? However, those same individuals were saviors of their own countries. In contrast, the late Mostowfiyolmamalek was a noble, faithful, and free-spirited man, but he was not a combatant. Chamberlain was also like him. In any case, every country needs pious and patriotic individuals; but such pious and patriotic individuals will not bring this ship to shore. A number of strong and determined individuals are necessary."[39]

A few weeks before he became prime minister, in a conversation with Parsons, the British Ambassador in Tehran, Bakhtiar expressed hope that the influence of Ayatollah Khomeyni was diminishing, because the people would gradually figure out that he was trying to take revenge on the Shah. In the same conversation, pointing out that the National Front was deeply against an "Islamic republic" and would not make any unnecessary concession to the clerics, Bakhtiar emphasized that with the selection of the new prime minister, the strikes and the discontent of the journalists and students would calm down.[40]

The Formation of Bakhtiar's Cabinet and the Government Program

Simultaneous with the announcement of the news of Bakhtiar's assignment to form a government cabinet, the central council of the National Front informed the public in a published announcement that its organization "cannot agree to any composition of government, with the existence of the unlawful monarchical regime." By "strongly condemning" Bakhtiar's decision, the central council emphasized that his assignment to form a government had been without organizational "discipline," and was "by no means" in conformity with the "ideal and organizational ratifications" of the National Front, and on this basis, he was expelled from membership in the National Front.

Shortly before the publication of this statement, in a fervent announcement that was prepared in the name of God and addressed to the compatriots, with a discussion about the current developments and the issue of the premiership of Bakhtiar that was about to occur, the National Front wrote: "If the unlawful monarchical regime up to yesterday demanded blood bowl by bowl, today it runs its ship on a lake of blood. That which we had been spared thus far in this field of blood was the striking blow of betrayal, which descended into the heart of the nation like a poisonous dagger, and as dictated by the genuineness of our movement, increased steadfastness in those affiliated with our foundationally strong path." In this announcement, as a sign of "empathy and commiseration with the grand family of martyrs" and "its profound hatred of the compromising traitors," the National Front declared 7 January 1979, on which Bakhtiar's cabinet was introduced, as a day of "national mourning" and called on the people to go on an "absolute and total" strike. Even "shopkeepers and salesmen who provided the daily needs of the people" were asked to join this strike.[41]

Citing the monarchical regime as being unlawful as the reason for expelling Bakhtiar from the National Front lacked any credibility. Based on the Constitution of the constitutional monarchy and its supplement, that regime was not unlawful in principle to warrant Bakhtiar's removal from membership in the National Front due to his acceptance of the position of prime minister. The so-called nonconformity of Bakhtiar's decision to the "ideal and organizational ratifications" of the National Front was also contrary to the truth. From the distant past to recent years, that organization had continuously demanded free elections and the coming to power of a government that relied on the rule of law. This demand in the not-too-distant past had been made even in the open letter of the leaders of the National Front to the Shah, and with the offer of premiership to Sanjabi, Sadiqi, and then Bakhtiar, it seemed legitimate and attainable. Furthermore, in the announcement of the central council of the National Front regarding the expulsion of Bakhtiar, the point worthy of contemplation was the issue of violating organizational discipline in his accepting the assignment to form a government. The National Front conditioned the acceptance of any position higher than director general in the government organizations on obtaining permission from the organizational authorities. Bakhtiar's decision, however, was not in contradiction to the "ideal and organizational ratifications" of the National Front. Moreover, before Bakhtiar deviated from organizational discipline, by submitting the three-point letter to Ayatollah Khomeyni, Sanjabi had politically violated the policy and ratifications of the National Front's congress. In addition, Sanjabi, Foruhar, Ahmadzadeh, Ardalan, Mobashsheri, and Shah-Hoseyni within a short period after that, by accepting ministerial and deputy ministerial positions in the cabinet of Bazargan without obtaining permission from organizational authorities, had violated organizational "discipline."[v]

All this aside, the issue of the unlawfulness of the monarchical system had not been ratified in any assembly, meeting, or congress of the National Front to warrant the central council of the National Front basing its decision regarding the expulsion of Bakhtiar on such a ratification. Even beyond all this, according to the same Constitution to which the nationalists considered themselves loyal, the monarchy was called "a Divine gift." Such a "gift" was a memento of the religious-scholar clerics at the dawn of the constitutional era, which required reconsideration, similar to some other articles of the Constitution. Why, then, did an organization such as the National Front, which adorned the top of every announcement and communiqué with the name of the Creator, call this Divine "gift" unlawful? Ultimately, the reality was that, with their widespread participation in marches and demonstrations, the people had demanded the removal and "death" of an autocratic king who had violated the oath of upholding the Constitution and who, at the height of weakness, sought the only solution to save his crown and throne in adhering to the articles of the Constitution, entrusting the government to the National Front, and leaving the country. In confronting such a reality, instead of leaving every option about the future of the regime to an assembly elected by the vote of the people, the functionaries of the National Front called the monarchical regime unlawful. Looking back at

---

[v] For more regarding the constitution and bylaws of the National Front, see: *Surat Jalasat-e Kongereh-ye Jebheh-ye Melli-ye Iran*, compiled by Amir Tayerani (Tehran: Gam-e No Publishers, 2009), 495-512.

the history of the Constitution in confronting monarchical despotism, another alternative existed.

Seventy years earlier, without submitting to despotism, the leaders of the constitutional movement deposed a king who had opened artillery fire on the parliament and taken refuge under a foreign flag, and placed his son, who was a minor, on the royal throne. Without even contemplating such an alternative, however, in their compromise with the clerics, and in the name of an organization that considered itself the heir to the tradition of constitutionalism and the rule of law, the leaders of the National Front gave in to another option and followed a different path.

On 6 January 1979, before forming his cabinet and introducing the members of the government cabinet, in an interview with the correspondent of *Ettela'at* newspaper, Bakhtiar discussed his views about the sensitive issues of the country. In that interview, he spoke about the critical situation of the society, "corruption, autocracy, and the decadent practices of the rulers" in the previous twenty-five years, and regarded his most important duty to be ensuring the "calming of the conditions of the country, the implementation of the demands of the people, and the creation of a national democracy based on socialism." Among his other duties were "modification of wealth, fighting corruption, and the speedy trial and punishment of the traitors to the national interests," along with "solving the issue of oil and signing an agreement for its export on the basis of an independent policy, and solving the economic problems that had placed the country on the verge of bankruptcy." He emphasized that "dissolving SAVAK, releasing political prisoners, and granting the rightful freedoms of the Iranian people on the basis of the Constitution and the Universal Declaration of Human Rights" were at the top of the agenda of his government.

In that interview, Bakhtiar devoted an important aspect of his statements to explaining the situation of the country, the general public discontentment, and his reason for accepting the position of prime minister under the critical conditions. About the policy that the leaders of the National Front were pursuing, he said: "Because of the extraordinary public excitement and the revolution, the people who had made a revolution most sincerely became confused, and all the fundamental demands that were necessary to be met under special conditions were summed up in one thing, without paying attention to other issues and points. The situation went even so far that opposition to the Constitution attracted the attention of the national leaders as a factor for becoming a hero, whereas the Constitution, which was gained with the blood of thousands of Iranians, is not a bad thing in and of itself; rather, failure to implement it had turned it into its current form." Then, in explaining his views about Mosaddeq, Bakhtiar called him his "intellectual guru," and regarding the duty he had taken on to form a government, he added that under those conditions, accepting a position of responsibility for a person who had a history of fighting Fascism and despotism for thirty years was not easy. Considering the danger that threatened "the independence of our country and the foundations of the existence of our nation," he said: "The loss of my popular image is not a problem. I have not gained this popular image for the next world; rather, this popular image had to be useful sometime, and when would it be more suitable than today when none of the national leaders are prepared to risk their popular image… Hence, when I was faced with either accepting a position of responsibility or protecting my national popular image, I considered accepting the position of responsibility my conscientious, ethical, and human duty… Whereas, had there been even one ray of hope, like many of my friends, I would have preferred to spend these few remaining days of my life in comfort and tranquility, and to live benefitting from my national image, and as some say, become a hero." He regarded any delay in finding a way to overcome the ongoing difficulties a danger that would result in "the killing of a large group of people, the destruction of all the social institutions, complete bankruptcy, and ultimately a dangerous and catastrophic uprising," which, with the reaction of the military forces, most likely would confront the country with civil war and partition.[42]

Simultaneous with this press interview, the Iran Party published an announcement removing Bakhtiar, who was the secretary general of that party, from all his political party positions. The decision of the plenum of the party was based on the "acceptance of the actual reality that the composition of the great and widespread revolution of Islamic Iran" that "is inspired by the directives of the great leader of the clerics, Grand Ayatollah Khomeyni" and the three-point announcement of Sanjabi in Paris. Refuting any sort of "grouping" and "factionalism" within the National Front, the Iran Party emphasized that Bakhtiar had accepted a position of responsibility without having been given any assignment, and that "he will be removed from all positions that he had held in the party," and "the final decision about his membership" would be postponed to "the next plenum of the party."[43]

In the afternoon of the same day, in another press conference that he had arranged at his home with a large number of reporters and representatives of domestic and foreign media, Bakhtiar answered their questions. He first spoke about the Shah's traveling abroad, and said: "His Majesty's traveling abroad is due to his wishing to rest and for treatment, and obviously, if he travels, in accordance with the indisputable articles of the Constitution, the establishment of the Royal Regency Council is necessary." He once again provided the reporters with a general outline of his policies about restoring calm to the country, the role of the military in a democratic regime, the revocation of martial law, freedom of political parties and the press, and the release of political prisoners. Fighting administrative corruption, the trial of those who had violated the rights of the nation, not selling oil to Israel and South Africa, support for Palestine, and peace in the region were among the other political issues that, from his perspective, built the foundations for creating "a democratic society based on social justice and the principles of democratic socialism."[44]

In his press conference, this time Bakhtiar also paid special attention to his opponents. He called Sanjabi his "fellow combatant," and stating that he still considered himself a member of the National Front, he expressed hope that his work would be such that in the following year, the National Front would move toward him and he toward the National Front. Regarding the clerics, his views were no different. Bakhtiar said: "I have the utmost respect for all grand ayatollahs, Grand Ayatollah Khomeyni and Grand Ayatollah Shari'atmadari. This stems from my heartfelt faith in the progressive religion of Islam, and I do not think anyone can have the slightest doubt about my faith. I am trying to negotiate with and gain the support of the revered grand ayatollahs and clerics, who were the leaders of the revolution of the nation." He spoke about Ayatollah Khomeyni as a "highly esteemed" Iranian who could, like other Iranians, return to the country, and obviously, the government would take steps in that regard.

The harsh response of Bakhtiar's "fellow combatants," or those he had called "highly esteemed" clerics and, according to him, "leaders of the revolution of the nation," was not too unexpected. Ayatollah Khomeyni referred to Bakhtiar's government as an unlawful government and called on the people to disobey it. The National Front, as well, in a call for a "total strike" wrote: "A politician who had been toying with the people's beliefs for many years in the role of the savior of an unlawful regime that has dragged Iran into the current dark days and placed it on the edge of a precipice came into the arena with a bagful of deception. Fortunately, the embryo of this shameless compromise had not yet completely formed when vigilant Iranians in cities and villages with their unmatched solidarity revealed their hatred, and the highly revered leader of the national revolution, which has taken substance from lofty Islamic teachings, also today, by sending a message, put a complete stop to all the confusion and declared that obedience to this apparatus is the same as obedience to the Tyrant and is religiously forbidden, and with his wise guidance, rejected the delusion that there will be any leniency on the path of those who with lame legs claim the leadership of the national movement."[45]

Bakhtiar's effort in the press conference to neutralize the obstacles that the opponents had placed in his way was an effort that was doomed to fail from the start, especially since this effort had been made with the futile hope in which he sought his success in getting along with them.

Bakhtiar still considered himself a member of the National Front, especially at a time when his fellow combatants in such a front, hand in hand with Ayatollah Khomeyni, or those who were called "progressive clerics," were speaking of another solution. His approach to the clerics at the beginning of his premiership was also similar. In enumerating the reasons that had prepared the grounds for "the revolution and national uprising," Bakhtiar mentioned "constant insults by the rulers to the religion and highly revered religious scholars" and said: "With the rulers' disregard for the clerics and propagation of corruption, they toyed with the principles of Islam and Shi'ism in such a way that anyone in the clerics' place would also rebel. Those religious leaders are most magnanimous who still tolerate it." Considering it his duty to restore calm to the country and to establish the principles of constitutionalism, simultaneously, he mentioned efforts for advancing the revolution and implementing the "progressive principles of Islam," and on this path, he had his "hopeful eyes" set on the support of the clerics, which he considered to be "self-evident," the support of clerics who, according to him, were "pioneers" in the constitutional movement and were now on the "frontline of the revolution."

One can surmise that Bakhtiar's bowing to the opponents may have stemmed from his awareness of the fact that he knew he was alone. Release from the isolation in compromise with Sanjabi and the clerics represented by Ayatollah Khomeyni was not achievable. He had come to the arena with a plan that was in clear contradiction to the demands of the National Front and the clerics. The path to Bakhtiar's success—if there was any hope for success—went through revealing and highlighting such a contradiction. He spoke of constitutionalism, the Constitution, and a regime based on the principles of democratic socialism; and Ayatollah Khomeyni, of what was religiously allowed or forbidden, of the Tyrant, and of Islamic government; and the leaders of the National Front, of "Shi'ism's principles of freedom" and "lofty Islamic teachings." The courage that Bakhtiar had displayed in accepting the position of prime minister and discussing his goals and political program would only bear fruit if he did not fear open confrontation with their approach, rather than in bowing, moderation, or even further having one's hopeful eyes set on the support and solidarity of those who with the weapon of religion and praise for the functionaries of religion had come to the arena. These were self-evident issues; and Bakhtiar, despite all his fearlessness and risking of what he called his national popular image, had disregarded the self-evident, and for that matter, he was trying to be opportunistic within a brief opportunity.

Nevertheless, his failure to understand this fact was not the only consequence of his opportunism, political tactics, or his desperation and isolation, a desperation and isolation that were themselves the consequence of his awareness that the masses of the people did not support him and his program. Bakhtiar's bowing to the leaders of the National Front and the clerics in his first press conference at the beginning of his administration was indicative of a longstanding behavior in his political career. Despite all the struggles, he had spent his life alongside religious politicians and political religious figures, and at the height of the crisis, as well, he continued to insist on all that he had done, setting his hopeful eyes on their support and solidarity. This hopefulness, however, was a mixture of gullibility and loyalty, most likely stemming from his tribal lineage.

The increasing difficulties that Bakhtiar faced on a daily basis, in addition to the political turbulence, widespread strikes and demonstrations, and general discontentment, also included the question of how to confront Ayatollah Khomeyni and the issue of his return to the country. Before making any decision in this regard, Bakhtiar faced the problem of making his government official and the difficulty of forming a cabinet. Even though it was formed within a short period of time and in a crisis situation, in terms of its credibility and the experience of its members, it was a competent cabinet. In this cabinet, the reputable military figure, General Fereydun Jam, was the nominee for the Ministry of Defense; Ahmad Mirfendereski, an experience diplomat, was designated for the Foreign Ministry; and Yahya Sadeq-Vaziri, for the Ministry of Justice. Dr. Manuchehr Razmara, a famous physician and the brother of former Prime Minister General Haj Ali Razmara, was in charge of the Ministry of Health and Welfare. The journalist Dr. Sirus Amuzgar, as the advisor to the prime minister and head of the Ministry of Information and Tourism, had the delicate responsibility of negotiating with the representatives of the press and radio and television and ending their strike. The members of the cabinet of ministers included individuals with a long history of government administration and service, such as Dr. Abbasqoli Bakhtiar, Dr. Rostam Pirasteh, Dr. Mohammad Amin Riyahi, Dr. Manuchehr Kazemi, Dr. Mohammad Ali Nabegh, Lotfali Samimi, and Manuchehr Ariyana. Javad Khadem, a former member of the International Confederation of Iranian Students, was in charge of the Ministry of Housing and Urban Development; and Mohammad Moshiri-Yazdi, Bakhtiar's old friend, was deputy prime minister. Bakhtiar himself managed the Ministry of Interior, since Bazargan had rejected his offer for that ministry; and Ahmad Sadr-Haj-Seyyed-Javadi had excused himself from accepting the position of minister of justice in the cabinet with "embarrassment," stating, "I have a religious obligation and should be exempted." Ahmad and Gholam-hoseyn Mosaddeq, the sons of the former Iranian prime minister, had also rejected Bakhtiar's offer to join the cabinet.[46] In addition, the withdrawal of Fereydun Jam and the resignation of Yahya Sadeq-Vaziri, who were two of the most important personalities in the cabinet, was a heavy defeat for Bakhtiar's government. Jam withdrew before the cabinet was formed because the Shah was unhappy with that choice, and in his place, General Ja'far Shafaqat joined the cabinet as the minister of defense. The resignation of Sadeq-Vaziri occurred with the departure of the Shah from Iran on 16 January 1979.[47]

According to Sirus Amuzgar, on the day that he presented his cabinet to the Shah in Niyavaran Palace, Bakhtiar told his ministers: "The point to which all of us must pay attention is that His Majesty is the king of the country and we must be most respectful." He continues: "Lotfollah Samimi asked, 'Do you mean we should also kiss his hand?' Dr. Bakhtiar said, 'That is up to you.' When we were leaving Bakhtiar's house, the house servant, who was all in tears, following the tradition of when someone is about to leave on a trip, poured a bowl of water behind us on the ground for us to have a safe journey. Razmara, who had become very emotionally touched by the servant's act of compassion, took out a 20-*tuman* banknote and handed it to the servant, who with tearful eyes said, 'No, Sir; the days of tipping games are over.' I felt my eyes also tearing up." In a heavy air of anxiety and silence, the ministers traveled the distance between Bakhtiar's house in the Farmaniyeh neighborhood to the Niyavaran Palace, which was surrounded by the tanks and armed-to-the-teeth soldiers of the Royal Guard. The anxiety was the sign of the heavy burden and the uncertain future of the ministers, most of whom had met each other just a few days earlier. According to Amuzgar, in these ceremonies, none of the ministers were wearing the customary official uniforms, and the minister of the Royal Court did not place much importance on the cabinet ministers standing in a specific order in accordance with official protocol and being introduced to the Shah. He sates: "It was the first time that I had seen the interior of Niyavaran Palace. It was not even one-tenth as luxurious as I had imagined it to be. It was a large hall in which apparently the official ceremonies were supposed to be held. On the right, there were a few rooms, and on the left, a window that opened toward the garden... Dr. Bakhtiar walked straight to the Shah, and we were led into a room near the entrance to the hall with a few sofas and chairs, two tables, and a window facing the city. I collapsed on one of the sofas. The borrowed suit that I wore and the borrowed tie on my neck looked appalling on me, and I do not know why I was so sleepy. Sadeq-Vaziri, the minister of justice, was looking out the window and seemed deep in thought. Wearing a well-made black suit and brand new shoes, Manuchehr Ariyana was pacing back and forth in the middle of the room. Mirfendereski was sitting on a chair next to the table, with his hand resting on it, and seemed quite calm to me. Abbasqoli Bakhtiar and Kazemi were chatting at the other end of the room, and it was obvious that neither was listening to what the other said. Dr. Riyahi was standing in front of the only painting in the room, pretending to be studying it carefully. Mohammad Moshiri-Yazdi was sitting on a couch and was leafing through the papers in a file on his lap. Pirasteh, Khadem, and Samimi were arguing, and Razmara was looking with curiosity through the crack of the door. After a long wait, the reason for which no one knew those days, finally, they informed us that the ceremonies were about to begin. Everyone was called into the hall, and we stood in line. The Shah, accompanied by several others, entered the hall, and Bakhtiar went forward to welcome him, and then, together with the Shah, they walked toward us. Dr. Bakhtiar introduced the ministers, and the Shah shook their hands and said a few words to each. When the introductions were done, the Shah went to the end of the line and gestured for a microphone to be brought to speak to us. No one followed the Shah's order. The Shah asked for a microphone again a few moments later, without any movement or reaction to his order. The scene was painfully depressing. When the Shah asked for a microphone the third time and no one moved, Dr. Bakhtiar reacted, walked quickly toward the hallway, asked the official who was either out of it or daydreaming to bring the Shah a microphone, and he stood there until his order was carried out. Suddenly, in my eyes, Dr. Bakhtiar became a bigger man than whatever he had been. It was no longer important whether he lost or succeeded. History will never forget his name."[48]

What Amuzgar describes is the bitter end of a king who at one time not too far back had spoken about the "revolution of the Shah and the people," and now, upon hearing the "sound of the revolution," he could not find a device to convey his message to the members of the cabinet, a cabinet the ministers of which, despite individual capabilities for gaining the support of the people and confronting a mass of difficulties, had no other choice but anxiety and waiting.

In the continuation of his recollections, Amuzgar refers to the Shah's statements in which he had said that he was tired and he had to travel abroad, since he needed rest and medical care. In conclusion, he writes: "In the hallway of the palace, Dr. Bakhtiar stopped before the exit. We also stopped. He said, 'We will all first go to the prime minister's office and hold a cabinet meeting; from there, the gentlemen will each go to their own ministries.' Fourteen people facing the massive, calamitous problems of one country!"[49]

On the Seat of Grand Vizier

The Prime Minister's Palace was located in a complex of palaces the largest of which, the Marmar or the Marble Palace, was built during Reza Shah's time. It was said that he did not wish to live in Golestan Palace, which was a reminder of the Qajar kings, and he therefore had the Marble Palace built. The office and the sleeping quarters of Reza Shah were in this palace. Later on, the Queen Mother; Mohammad Reza Pahlavi, the Crown Prince at the time; and other children of the king had several other palaces built around the Marble Palace. The palace of Ashraf Pahlavi, the Shah's sister, was located between Kakh Street and Heshmatoddowleh Street, which the government bought. The central building of that palace was named the Private Palace, which later became the prime minister's center of operations. The office of the prime minister was on the first floor. The government cabinet meetings were held on Mondays every week on the ground floor of this building, in a hall named Mansur Hall after Prime Minister Hasan Ali Mansur was assassinated in 1965, and the prime minister would have an audience with the Shah at 2:00 p.m. on the same day. (Because of the critical conditions during Bakhtiar's administration, the meetings of the government cabinet were not held on a specific day, as in the past. The prime minister's audience with the Shah also did not take place as in the past for the same reason.)[50] There was also a room with a table and a couple of chairs next to the hall in which, after the cabinet session ended, any minister who had anything in particular to discuss with the prime minister would meet with him. Later on, the government bought the palace of Shams Pahlavi, the Shah's other sister, and after repairs and decoration, converted it into the Entertainment Palace. The sleeping quarters of former Prime Minister Amir Abbas Hoveyda was in that building. The Private Palace that overlooked the Entertainment Palace was where high-ranking guests stayed.[vi]

[vi] The Marble Palace is one of the historic palaces in Tehran, the building of which was constructed on the order of Reza Shah. This palace was initially used as Reza Shah's place of work, and until prior to the national treasury law, the national jewels of Iran

Later on, during Hoveyda's administration, a large building was also constructed alongside Firuz Alleyway near Pasteur Street; the alleyway was named Firuz because that was the last name of the Farmanfarma family that had donated part of the land surrounding the Marble Palace to Reza Shah. This building, which was also called the "glass building," was located next to the Private Palace and housed the offices of the prime minister and his deputies and employees. The prime minister's office is the same building in which, in the bombing on 30 August 1981, President Mohammad Ali Raja'i, Prime Minister Mohammad Javad Bahonar, and several members of the government of the Islamic Republic were killed. Moshiri-Yazdi, who was Bakhtiar's deputy during his thirty-seven-day administration, states: "My office was the same room in which Raja'i and Bahonar were killed. With the fall of Bakhtiar's government, Bazargan, who succeeded him, ran the affairs of the new government from my office, because he did not want to govern from the prime minister's office in the Private Palace, which once had belonged to Ashraf Pahlavi and which he considered 'religiously defiled.' Such were his beliefs." Moshiri-Yazdi adds: "In a message he had sent me, Bazargan asked me to continue in my position. In response, also attaching my resignation, I wrote, 'I worked with Bakhtiar and I will take my leave with him.' And then, I sarcastically concluded my resignation letter addressed to Bazargan with a couplet by Qa'ani, 'Behold the nobility of my tavern, o friend / that when it falls into ruins, it becomes the house of God.'"[51]

Bakhtiar's secretary, Pari Kalantari, states: "A few days after he became prime minister, he still would not come to the Private Palace, as though he wanted to run the affairs of the country from his home, like Mosaddeq. The prime minister's guard service, however, called his attention to the issue that it was not the right thing to do in terms of security. So, he

---

were transferred from Golestan Palace to this palace and stored in its basement. In the early years of Mohammad Reza Shah's reign, this palace was used as the official office of the Shah and the place for meetings and audiences. The Shah and Princess Fawzia of Egypt, the Shah's first wife, lived in this palace. The Shah's betrothal to Farah Pahlavi, his last wife, also took place in this palace.

changed his mind and came to the prime minister's office. The custom
was that when a new prime minister came to office, the employees of the
prime minister's office stood in line in the hallway and were introduced
to the prime minister. Bakhtiar, however, was not familiar with this
custom, and the introduction ceremony was not carried out. So, one
day, I just went to his office and introduced myself. The first thing that
he said was, 'I am a member of the boards of directors of two companies
in Isfahan. Because I have become prime minister, please write a letter to
each and tell them that I am resigning from the board of directors.' He
then added, 'I have a small suitcase with a couple of suits. Tell the guard
to put these somewhere.' I realized that he did not know what he should
do with his suitcase. I said, 'There is a palace next to the Prime Minister's Palace, which is the prime minister's residence. They will take the
suitcase there. And if you wish, you can spend the night there.' There
was also a room next to the prime minister's office in which he could
rest if he wished to rest in the afternoon. Hoveyda also used to take a
nap there in the afternoons. Early on, he rested in the same small room
next to the prime minister's office, and he also slept there for a few
nights.

"Every morning, Bakhtiar came to the Prime Minister's Palace from
the Entertainment Palace at about eight o'clock or 8:30. These two
buildings were just a few minutes apart. He often had lunch there with a
couple of other people. In the evening, at about nine o'clock, a few of
his friends or children would come to have dinner together. If he had an
appointment with his daughter France and something had come up, he
would tell me, 'My France will be coming here; tell her I will be late.'
He often worked until nine or ten o'clock at night in the office, and he
did the same on Fridays and holidays. On those days, he went from the
Prime Minister's Palace to the Entertainment Palace, and because he
liked to walk, he walked around in the garden.

"During his administration, several representatives of clerics who were
supporters of Shari'atmadari and Khomeyni came to see him, and some
members of the National Front met him in the prime minister's office;
but since he had been expelled from the National Front, they did not

want anyone to find out that they had a relationship with him. Once someone, whose name I have forgotten, called the prime minister's office and said, 'Tell Mr. Prime Minister that I have 6,000 cavalrymen ready, and that I am prepared to make them available to His Honor.' Bakhtiar said, 'I do not want 6,000 cavalrymen, I want six active people, so the majority would not be silent.' When he heard that upon the Shah's departure, they had taken his pictures down in the prime minister's office, he was enraged and said, 'I will not give permission to take the pictures of the king down, unless they take my corpse out of here. I received my premiership appointment decree from the king, and as long as the Constitution is in place, his picture shall remain.' He also had a large photograph of Mosaddeq in his office."[52]

According to Moshiri-Yazdi, the Bakhtiar government was more or less his own government. The closures and agitations had spread everywhere, and in fact there was not much opportunity. Some ministries had no ministers and the hope for success, especially with Khomeyni's return to Iran, was diminishing. In this interval, the government cabinet held five sessions in the thirty-seven-day administration of Bakhtiar to attend to the ongoing work.[53]

Sirus Amuzgar states: "At the beginning, despite the rumors about the employees of ministries going on strike or the possibility of preventing the ministers from going to their offices, we were more or less making progress in our work; but gradually, when the strikes became widespread, the work of the ministers became more difficult." The resignation of Fereydun Jam, the nominee for the Ministry of Defense, before he even began his work, was a severe blow. The resignations of Seyyed Jalal Tehrani, the chairman of the Royal Regency Council, and Yahya Sadeq-Vaziri, the minister of justice, were other blows that would seriously damage the credibility of the prime minister. Jam, a reputable military officer on whom Bakhtiar had set his hopes for coordinating the military forces and having them follow government orders, when he was resigning, said to the deputy prime minister with tearful eyes: "Mr. Moshiri, I need to be excused. I have a child who is sick and who is probably not going to survive. I cannot accept the position." And he had withdrawn. Possibly, in addition to the Shah's opposition to him as a nominee, his child's illness was another reason for his withdrawal. Sadeq-Vaziri did not even muster the courage to come face-to-face with the prime minister; he had asked Moshiri-Yazdi to deliver his resignation to Bakhtiar. Moshiri-Yazdi states: "Sadeq-Vaziri was an honorable man. He even participated in a couple of cabinet meetings. One day, he called and said, 'Mr. Moshiri, there is something I would like to tell you. I do not have the ability to manage the Ministry of Justice. I am incapable of it. That is why I want to resign, and I am embarrassed to say so to Mr. Bakhtiar. Allow me to send you my resignation letter and you deliver it to the prime minister.' Bakhtiar said that it was fine and that one of the senior deputy ministers in that ministry should take charge of the Ministry of Justice."[54]

Under the most difficult of circumstances, Bakhtiar was in control of his nerves. One night, when as a result of the strikes the electricity to the Prime Minister's Palace had been cut off and the building and the surrounding streets were engulfed in darkness and silence, laughing and smiling as though nothing had happened, he had maintained his composure. Looking for matches to light a kerosene lamp, he was reassuring those around him and joking with Colonel Ebrahim Zargham, his office administrator and the husband of his paternal cousin, who instead of matches was handing him his weapon. One day, in response to Ayatollah Khomeyni who had said that Bakhtiar had a desert temperament, Bakhtiar said: "He himself has a desert temperament; I have a mountain temperament." From the Prime Minister's Palace, he sent a message to Sanjabi that he should not sacrifice the National Front for Ayatollah Khomeyni. He promised to hold free elections, to create a Constituents' Assembly, and to accept whatever the outcome. In the course of a conversation with Haj Maniyan, who wanted him and the National Front to reconcile, he said: "Haji, go tell your friends to stop these games. I will get the Shah to resign and hold free elections. Even if the outcome is a republic, so be it. Whoever wins, let them, but not from Khomeyni's side. They should let the situation calm down and let the people go back to their work."[55]

Sirus Amuzgar states: "Occasionally, Bakhtiar would say things that he did not truly believe. For instance, he spoke about a republic, whereas he was a tribal man and believed that the only regime that was beneficial for Iran was a monarchy, albeit a constitutional monarchy. He was a tribal man, and he regarded monarchy as the symbol of the country. Occasionally, however, when he was in Iran, he talked about a republic, and that was to buy time. There was a reason for saying what he said; he wanted to disarm the opponents."[56]

The first obstacle for Bakhtiar after receiving the decree for premiership was to obtain a vote of confidence from the parliament. When he was presenting the government program to the parliament and introducing the cabinet ministers, referring to the "corruption and incompetence" of past governments, he spoke about an international conspiracy for the "weakening" and "aggression on the existence and sovereignty" of Iran. Bakhtiar emphasized that his government would "respect the spirit and the letter of the Constitution that has an unbreakable tie to Islam," and that he would make an effort to prepare the grounds for "cooperation between the government and the spiritual realm, such that the grand ayatollahs have oversight of the execution of the affairs by the government." In his speech, he spoke about striving on the path of "the principles of the goals of the National Front," and considered his government to be "the indisputable outcome of a revolution" that was created since "two years ago to eliminate continuous violations and indescribable atrocities" in the country. Bakhtiar called himself a responsible prime minister who would "observe all the parliamentary traditions and individual and social freedoms," and by dissolving SAVAK, releasing political prisoners, and "rapidly putting on trial the plunderers and violators of the nation's rights," he would strive to establish social and political freedom on the basis of the Constitution and the Universal Declaration of Human Rights. According to him, these trials would be carried out either by existing courts or by preparing and offering new laws and establishing "national courts" with special authority.

In conclusion, emphasizing that he had accepted that position of responsibility in order to establish order and advance the program that he presented to the parliament, he refuted the claim by those who called his government a "reactionary government of suppression" and said: "I have become the heir to particular circumstances in the creation of which I had no involvement whatsoever. I have become an heir to a country in tumult and a chaotic system in which in the past 25 years I had no role but that of being imprisoned, being exiled, and being confined to sitting at home. Had the situation been as it was a few years ago, undoubtedly, I would not have been invited to become prime minister… I will continue on the same path that I have been on for the past 25 years, and I will respect the Constitution. For me, however, the Constitution is not the Constitution that has been implemented in the past few years. I must also prepare for the independence of the judicial branch, the independence of the legislative branch, and the dynamism and at the same time irreproachability of the executive branch, in order to be able to solve the current economic and diverse problems of the country."[57]

Confrontation with Ayatollah Khomeyni

With the introduction of the cabinet and obtaining the vote of confidence from the parliament, the issue of the return of Ayatollah Khomeyni to the country as one of the main difficulties of Bakhtiar's administration was placed on the agenda of the government. Before he was appointed prime minister, he had regarded the exile of Ayatollah Khomeyni in November 1963 to be an action "in violation of the Constitution and liberties in human societies." The reason for the exile of Ayatollah Khomeyni was that on 26 October 1963, in a harsh speech, he rose in opposition to the capitulation bill that extended diplomatic immunity to American military personnel and which had been passed by the parliament. In a published announcement, he also spoke about the conspiracy of the regime to eliminate Islam and the influence of the clerics, and attacked England, the United States, and the Soviet Union. In reaction, the regime engaged in security measures in Qom and

Tehran, arrested Ayatollah Khomeyni, and exiled him to Turkey on 4 November 1963.[vii] Bakhtiar's assessment was apparently in reference to Article 14 of the Constitution, which stated: "No Persian can be exiled from the country, or prevented from residing in any part thereof, or compelled to reside in any specified part thereof, save in such cases as the law may explicitly determine." Bakhtiar had added that the responsibility for the exile of Ayatollah Khomeyni belonged to "the governments that violated the principles of the Constitution and democratic freedoms and in opposition to public opinion, exiled him from the country and prevented him from residing in any part thereof." According to him, Ayatollah Khomeyni had the right to reside freely in any part of Iran or outside Iran that he wished. Hence, if the government at the time in fact considered itself to be the implementer of the Constitution, its duty was "to take steps for his return, as demanded by public opinion."[58] Three months after making these points in *Ettela'at* newspaper, when in January 1979 he occupied the position of prime minister, Bakhtiar saw himself confronted with what he called public opinion, or the democratic rights of Ayatollah Khomeyni.

Bakhtiar's first unofficial attempt to contact Ayatollah Khomeyni was on 9 December 1978, simultaneous with the preparations for forming a cabinet. When he was inviting Manuchehr Razmara to join his cabinet, he asked Razmara, who was temporarily in Paris, to go to Neauphle-le-Château to meet with Ayatollah Khomeyni. About this meeting, Razmara says: "On 29 December 1978, when I was in Paris to see my wife and children for New Year's celebrations, Bakhtiar called me and asked me to immediately return to Iran, since he was forming his cabinet and I would be a member of the cabinet. In the same telephone conversation, Bakhtiar suggested to me that I should go to Neauphle-le-Château and see Khomeyni. He said, 'If you can, go and see what this

---

[vii] On 21 January 1964, Prime Minister Hasan Ali Mansur, during whose administration the capitulation bill to extend immunity to American military personnel had passed, was the target of an assassination attempt by Mohammad Bokhara'i, a member of the Devotees of Islam, and passed away in the hospital a few days later.

old man says.' I went to Neauphle-le-Château on 30 December. I saw that a number of people had come in several busses from throughout Europe to see Khomeyni, and the French police and gendarmes were monitoring the situation.

"Khomeyni's residence in Neauphle-le-Château had two sections. One section was a garden with an apple tree, under which he sat and performed his prayers, and the other section farther down was an ordinary, one can say tiny, house in which he resided. There was also a narrow alleyway between the garden and the house. I realized that, given the crowd of people who had come to see Khomeyni, I would have to wait for days. I wondered what I should do. I went to the garden and saw that Yazdi and Banisadr were holding a news conference. I also heard from a French reporter who knew me that Ramsey Clark, the former Attorney General of the United States, was also there. Right there, I saw a comely cleric, whom they addressed as Ayatollah Eshraqi and said that he was Khomeyni's son-in-law. I remembered that when we lived in the Sarcheshmeh neighborhood, across from our house was an Office of Record's branch, the director of which was someone by the name of Eshraqi, and he took care of my father's business transaction records. I walked up to him, introduced myself, and said, 'Since I am going back to Iran tonight, before I left, I wanted to have an audience with His Eminence Ayatollah Khomeyni.' He asked, 'How are you related to the late Amir Tuman, Colonel Mohammad Khan Razmara?' I said, 'I am his youngest child.' He praised my father and was very respectful. He had also heard that I would be a member of Bakhtiar's cabinet. He asked me to wait. After 10 minutes, he came back and took me to Khomeyni's residence. When I entered, Sadeq Qotbzadeh, Ebrahim Yazdi, Hadi Ghaffari, the retired General Satvati, who opposed the Shah, and Farhang Qasemi the son of Abolfazl Qasemi, who was a member of the National Front's central council, also came and sat down. After the customary greetings, I said to Ayatollah Khomeyni, 'Your Eminence, tonight I am supposed to return to Iran. The conditions are chaotic and the country has reached the edge of a precipice. The Shah is most likely to leave the country. I would like to know the views and instructions of Your Eminence.' Khomeyni thought about it and said, 'I have given all my instructions. There is nothing to worry about concerning the country, and the plan for there is an Islamic republic, not a word less and not a word more.' I said, 'Very well. In the meantime, under these conditions, the Shah will leave the country, and you shall come back. The situation, however, is critical, and the country needs to have someone in charge.' Again he said, 'I have given all the answers and instructions. There is nothing to worry about.' In the meantime, he asked me, 'How are you related to the late General Razmara?' I said, 'I am his youngest brother.' Khomeyni said, 'One of your brothers did a great service to Islam.' He meant my brother General Hoseyn Ali Razmara, the head of the Geographic Division of the Military Headquarters, who invented a Mecca-direction locating compass. I said, 'Since I am going to Tehran, if you wish, I will send you a Mecca-direction locating compass.' He said, 'That is not necessary,' making me understand that he was coming to Iran himself. I asked, 'What will happen to the military?' He responded, 'Don't worry, I have also made arrangements for the military. There is nothing to worry about.' He did not say anything about Bakhtiar. Only, when he said that Iran will be an Islamic republic, he made a statement that still rings in my ears. He said, 'I have given my instructions. Islamic republic, not a word less and not a word more. Anyone who decides to stand against it would be committing a cardinal sin that cannot be forgiven.' He then held his hand out for me to kiss, which I did not. At that point, he stood up and left the room for prayers.

"Before I left Neauphle-le-Château and went back to Paris, Ayatollah Eshraqi asked me to take Banisadr with me. Thus, accompanied by him and Farhang Qasemi, I went back to Paris. On the way, Banisadr and I had a heated argument, because he attacked Bakhtiar, saying that he was wrong and accusing him of being a traitor.

"When I arrived in Paris, I immediately contacted Bakhtiar by telephone and told him, 'Your friends have stabbed you on the back. They expelled you from the National Front, and here I see Ramsey Clark and the Americans involved. This old man is not a normal person. When I saw his eyes, I saw that they were not normal. He said these things to me about an Islamic republic and the military, and I think the situation is out of hand.' In response, in that peculiar accent of his, with which he always called me Manachehr, he said, 'Manachehr, if it had not been out of hand, no one would have come to you and me for a solution. We must be men and accept responsibility under these conditions!' I said, 'I will be at your service tomorrow,' and returned to Iran."[59]

Concerning the choice of Bakhtiar as prime minister, Parsons, the British Ambassador in Tehran, quoting Amir Khosrow Afshar, the Iranian foreign minister in the cabinet of Azhari, states: "Afshar said that, when the Shah had told him this, he had expressed doubt whether Bakhtiar could succeed in forming a cabinet or restoring calm to the country. The Shah had thrown his hands in the air saying 'Who else is there?'"[60]

Once his administration was in place, this time as prime minister, facing the problem of Ayatollah Khomeyni's return to Iran, Bakhtiar wrote a letter addressed to him in an attempt to find a way to get through the crisis. In that letter, which began with "To Your Honorable Eminence Grand Ayatollah Seyyed Ruhollah Khomeyni," Bakhtiar addressed him as "the great spiritual leader" and "revered Islamic leader." Bakhtiar emphasized that the program of his government was the same as the wishes of "your holiness and other strugglers on the path of justice and freedom" and that if a "reasonable deadline is provided," with "Divine help due to the sacred breath of your holiness and the prayers of all those who wish the good of this country," those wishes would be fulfilled.[61]

In addition to the customary adulations, such as Ayatollah Khomeyni's "sagacious insight and well-wishing sincere intentions" for the "good fortune" of the people of Iran, the letter contained other points, which in two essential instances conveyed a clear message. In that letter, Bakhtiar called the attention of Ayatollah Khomeyni to the issue that, due to the critical conditions of the country, "the return of your precious being would cause certain agitations and disruptions" and could deter the government from continuing its program. Hence, he was asked to postpone his return. He also emphasized that if Ayatollah Khomeyni, upon returning to Iran, were to engage in forming a political organization that would be incompatible with the Constitution of the country, he would place the government in a "difficult and dangerous" position, the responsibility for which Bakhtiar could not accept. Not only in political terms but also in theoretical terms, the content of the letter was saturated with religious phrases and values. Nevertheless, the letter suggested his intention to stand in confrontation with Ayatollah Khomeyni. In the conclusion of the letter, he asked Ayatollah Khomeyni to allow any change in the political system of the country to occur peacefully and calmly, and on the basis of democratic traditions, since otherwise, the fear is that Iran "after a quarter century of the dominance of absolute autocracy and savagery and general and inclusive corruption will once again become entangled in a more profound and greater calamity."[62]

According to Javad Khadem, that letter was written by Aliqoli Bayani, Bakhtiar's old friend, who was familiar with religious matters. The letter was carried to Paris by Reza Marzban, Bakhtiar's friend and colleague. Ayatollah Khomeyni received the letter, but he refused to meet with Marzban.[63]

Bakhtiar, who had not obtained any results from sending that letter and continued to find himself confronted with Ayatollah Khomeyni's plan to return to Iran, once again made a new effort. This effort consisted, on the one hand, of closing the airport and preventing his return, and, on the other, a plan that Bakhtiar had made in negotiations with Bazargan and Amir-Entezam to travel to Paris personally to meet with Ayatollah Khomeyni. For this purpose, in the latter part of January 1979, a short text was prepared by Moshiri-Yazdi addressed to Ayatollah Khomeyni. Moshiri-Yazdi states: "The decision was made that before it was sent to Paris, the text should be reviewed by Montazeri, Motahhari, Beheshti, and Bazargan, so that if they approved of it, it would be telegrammed to Paris. After discussions that took place among us, the liaison for which was Ehsan Naraqi, I wrote a polite letter addressed to

Khomeyni in the presence of Naraqi and Bakhtiar. The text of that letter, which was published in high-circulation newspapers, was as follows, 'As a patriotic Iranian who considers myself a small part of this great national and Islamic movement and uprising, and sincerely believes that the guidance and leadership of His Eminence Grand Ayatollah Khomeyni and his opinion can solve our problems today and guarantee the stability and security of the country, I have decided to personally travel to Paris within the next forty-eight hours in hopes of attaining the honor of seeing you and presenting a report on the particular conditions of the country and my efforts, in order to receive your blessing and obtain your opinion about the future of the country.' When I read the letter to Bakhtiar, he said, 'What is this phrase, Grand Ayatollah, which you have written?' He crossed it out. I said, 'Permit me to leave the word, Grand. Let us not be obstinate, and solve the problem.' Naraqi also said, 'Leave the word, Grand, where it is.' Finally, Bakhtiar consented.

"In addition, there was an important point in the letter that was requested of Bakhtiar by Beheshti, that he should state in his letter to Khomeyni that he was going to Paris to 'obtain instructions,' to which Bakhtiar did not agree, and the letter stated that he would go to Paris to 'obtain opinion.'

"I remember, it was a Friday. Bakhtiar said, 'I will go and talk to this cleric; maybe something can be done.' An hour passed, and after lunch, they brought the good news that they had contacted Khomeyni and he had agreed to see Bakhtiar. You know that up to then, he had insisted that Bakhtiar must resign before he came. Now, apparently, he had agreed to meet with him as prime minister. So, I gave instructions for preparing the airplane and the passport for Bakhtiar. It was decided that the minister of health, Razmara, would also accompany Bakhtiar on this trip."[64]

Concerning the reason for his choice of a travel companion, Bakhtiar had told Razmara: "You have previously gone and met with Khomeyni. Secondly, you have treated most of these clerics; you have been their physician, and they are familiar with you. But before leaving, you need to take a letter to Beheshti, who is Khomeyni's representative. After he reads the letter, a courier is supposed to deliver it to Paris." Then Bakhtiar had asked him to read the letter. Razmara states: "I read the letter. I saw that it had been written in very polite language. Then Bakhtiar took the letter, put it in an envelope, sealed it, and I went with the driver and a person who was an acquaintance of Beheshti to his house, which I guess was behind the Ershad Religious Center. It was an ordinary, relatively respectable apartment with its reception room on the ground floor, which was full of books in English, French, and German. Beheshti came in, and they brought us tea. He was not a preacher and pulpit type of cleric. He looked comely and intelligent. I said that I was assigned by the prime minister to give him a letter, since I was supposed to accompany Bakhtiar to meet with Ayatollah Khomeyni. Beheshti, who knew the whole story, took the letter, began to read it, and after a while said thoughtfully, 'Doctor, to me it seems unlikely that Ayatollah Khomeyni would accept this letter.' I said, 'I am assigned to give you this letter, which is supposed to be sent with a courier to Ayatollah Khomeyni, and for us to leave for Paris tomorrow.' Beheshti said, 'Doctor, why go there? Ayatollah Khomeyni will be coming soon.' Then, in response to my having mentioned the dangerous situation of the country, he said, 'Do not worry, all aspects have been taken into consideration, and everything will be in order. Mr. Bakhtiar should resign and then be appointed as the Ayatollah's prime minister.' I said, 'This is not within my authority, but if you ask for my personal opinion, Dr. Bakhtiar is not the kind of person to resign. What he has in mind from meeting with Ayatollah Khomeyni is to solve the problems of the country and for the Ayatollah to return to Iran with utmost respect.' Then I asked, 'What will be the situation of the military?' Beheshti said, 'Do not worry, we have also clarified the situation of the military.' That was all.

"My meeting with him lasted more than an hour. Before saying good-bye, he said, 'Let me tell you, we have a great deal of respect for you. Come and resign, and become appointed as the Ayatollah's minister of health.' I answered, 'I came with Bakhtiar, and I shall stay with Bakhtiar to the last moment,' and I left Beheshti's home."[65]

Considering Bakhtiar's hopes concerning his meeting with Ayatollah Khomeyni, about the fate of that letter, Moshiri-Yazdi states: "I will never forget it. When I wrote the letter and we sent it to Beheshti, it was one of the most comfortable nights that I slept. We had become hopeful that there might be an opening; but on the following day, the news came that Khomeyni had changed his mind, and that he would consent to meet with Bakhtiar only if, like Seyyed Jalal Tehrani, the chairman of the Royal Regency Council, he would resign. Apparently, Banisadr had urged him to change his mind." Mohammad Ja'fari, the editor and director of *Enqelab-e Eslami* newspaper, also speaks about Banisadr's role in the cancellation of the meeting. He writes: "Mr. Banisadr told Ferdowsipur, 'If Bakhtiar is received by His Eminence, His Eminence is the one who will lose and go, and Bakhtiar, the one who will win and stay… The movement that has begun is not going to turn around and go backward. His Eminence should not be worried about it. The storm is on its way, and it is moving to get results… Tell His Eminence that he is a religious source of emulation and that he cannot change his mind every moment. After all, would the people not say, what kind of source of emulation is he if he changes his mind from one moment to the next? His Eminence is not a political player; he is a religious source of emulation."[66]

Manuchehr Razmara considers Mehdi Bazargan, Mohammad Beheshti, Sadeq Qotbzadeh, and Ebrahim Yazdi as the supporters, and Abolhasan Banisadr, Ayatollah Montazeri, Ahmad Khomeyni, and Hadi Ghaffari as the opponents of the meeting between Bakhtiar and Ayatollah Khomeyni. In addition to Banisadr, Bakhtiar also mentions the roles of Sanjabi and his wife as well as Parvaneh and Daryush Foruhar in convincing Ayatollah Khomeyni to cancel his plan to meet with him.[67]

Simultaneous with the publication of the news of the cancellation of Bakhtiar's trip to Paris, an announcement by Ayatollah Khomeyni addressed to the "Hojjat ol-Eslams (clerics) of Tehran and other cities" was issued. The announcement stated: "All that has been mentioned about my consent to meet with Shapour Bakhtiar in the position of prime minister is false; rather, I will not consent to meet with him unless he resigns, because I do not consider him to be a legitimate prime minister. You gentlemen, notify the people that a conspiracy is underway, and not to be deceived by the ongoing affairs. I have had no understanding with Bakhtiar, and all that he has said previously about a conversation between us is an absolute lie. The people must maintain their position and be watchful regarding the conspiracies."[68] From this point on, as far as it concerned the return of Ayatollah Khomeyni, Bakhtiar could see no other option but to accept public opinion, or what he called the democratic rights of Ayatollah Khomeyni.

What must be done with Ayatollah Khomeyni? This was the important question regarding the return of the leader of the Islamic movement and how to confront him, not only for Bakhtiar, but also for the Council of Military Commanders (Showra-ye Farmandehan-e Artesh), to which all of them needed to find an answer. Bakhtiar and the military leaders were determined to prevent the return of Ayatollah Khomeyni. In their consultations about this issue, they could see no solution other than a political alternative. Neither the downing of the airplane in the sky over Iran nor its forced landing in a remote area, which had been discussed in the meeting of the Council of Military Commanders, was considered a solution to the problem. Efforts to postpone the return of Ayatollah Khomeyni had also failed. The success of these efforts was tied to the organizing of demonstrations on 25 January 1979 by the defenders of the Constitution in support of Bakhtiar's government. The hope was that these demonstrations would bring the so-called "silent majority" to the scene, and by the time Ayatollah Khomeyni returned, it would gradually become a cohesive force against the opponents of the government. Bakhtiar's failed attempt to negotiate with Ayatollah Khomeyni as well as to postpone his return to Iran resulted in the failure of this plan, in the success of which little hope had been invested.

The consequence of the failure intensified the tension between the high-ranking military officials and Bakhtiar. On the one hand, Bakhtiar mentioned loyalty to the Constitution, and on the other, he spoke of the possibility of a referendum and changing the regime. Even though the military leaders regarded him as a determined and fearless personality, they increasingly viewed what was ahead for him with uncertainty. On the one hand, they hoped for his success, because the Shah had called on the high-ranking military personnel to support him, and on the other, they saw his government as a buffer between the military and the people, in the sense that Bakhtiar's failure meant nothing for them but accepting a responsibility for which they were unprepared. With the departure of the Shah from the country, this responsibility would bring about a nightmare beyond belief.

On 4 January 1979, the visit to Iran of General Robert Huyser, the deputy commander in chief of the United States European Command, the goal of which was to assess the situation of the military and gain its support for Bakhtiar's government, confronted the high-ranking military officials with a new problem. Huyser's mission from the very start seemed suspicious. The Shah, Bakhtiar, and the military commanders had not been informed about his visit ahead of time, something that was contrary to the official protocols and most unusual, although with the ending of the strike by the press, all that had been concealed was obvious from the start.

Huyser's visit was taking place when the leaders of the United States, England, France, and Germany at the Guadeloupe Conference, increasingly worried about the developments in Iran and the situation in the Middle East, were withdrawing their open support for the Shah. The exaggerated response to this decision escalated the speculations in public opinion that the Shah's fate had been determined in Guadeloupe, and that he had to leave Iran. William Sullivan, the United States Ambassador in Tehran, who was a supporter of removing the Shah and of the military cooperating with the opponents of Bakhtiar, was unhappy about Huyser's visit to Iran. Along with a number of other United States foreign policy officials, he not only saw no reason for the Shah to remain in power, but also, more than ever before, imagined a future for Iran that with the coming to power of a moderate Islamic government would act in the direction of protecting the interests of the West. This would be a government that, while maintaining the military as a stronghold against communism, could also contain Soviet expansionism in a sensitive region of the Middle East. Bazargan and Minachi were among the Iranian functionaries for advancing such an option. Hand in hand with the advisors and those close to Ayatollah Khomeyni, the Freedom Movement, and the National Front, these political functionaries would turn the clerics who were waiting in ambush to come to power and the leader of the Islamic movement into an acceptable alternative for the leaders of the military, the people, and world public opinion.

In the meantime, what added to the distrust and doubt of the Shah, the military leaders, and Bakhtiar were the unclear points and contradictions that dominated the U.S. policy about the ongoing events in Iran. President Jimmy Carter, National Security Advisor Zbigniew Brzezinski, and Secretary of State Cyrus Vance each offered a picture of the United States policy that would have no other consequence than the escalation of the difficulties and the creation of increasing concerns. Huyser, as well, who apparently had come to Iran to put an end to the confusion and to choose a clear policy in gaining the support of the military for the Bakhtiar government, was no different. This issue is reflected in a British Foreign Office document. In this connection, in an available report, the lack of clarity and the contradictory policies of the United States indicate that at times the United States did not support the formation of a military government, and at times, it asserts that the United States supports either the formation of a military government or a coalition cabinet.[69] Abbas Qarahbaghi, the commander-in-chief of the army, points out that Huyser had asked him to meet with Bazargan and Beheshti, and without Qarahbaghi asking for it, he had given him Minachi's telephone number. Describing the details of the second meeting of the Council of Military Commanders, which was held with the participation of Huyser, Qarahbaghi writes: "I told the brigadier generals, as you see, up to now, General Huyser has told us that the United States government supports the Bakhtiar government and that to establish calm in the country, it was necessary for the military to support Mr. Bakhtiar; but now that we have made our suggestions and offered our reasoning about how this support must be provided in practice, in response to our demands, he suggests meetings with the representatives of Khomeyni and the opponents. Obviously, they do not believe in what they say, and they do not know themselves what they want and what they have in mind. Could they want both sides? The commanders and generals affirmed my statements. We were all astounded and upset. I said that I would convey the issue to His Majesty, and the session ended… When I had an audience after this meeting, I reported the discussions as usual to His Majesty. When I said that Huyser had suggested that I should meet with Engineer Bazargan and Dr. Beheshti, he was dumbfounded and said, 'That is very strange! What does this mean? What is it that they want?'"[70]

The Return of Ayatollah Khomeyni to Iran and Bakhtiar's Doomed Effort

Shortly before the return of the leader of the Islamic movement to Iran, in a published "announcement of glad tidings," the National Front regarded him as the manifestation of the nation's ideals: a man whose being was law and freedom, and whose existence, the memory of suffering and the good news of liberation; a man who was the symbol of the freedom of the faithful human being and the enemy of corruption, falsehood, and suppression, the glory of whose worshipping of the truth could not be inscribed by the pen; a man with the blessed voice of liberation and the pleasant sound of the harmony of independence, in whose body flowed every drop of the blood of those who had suffered pain, and from whose heart dripped the drops of the blood of martyrs; the sun of the East's keepsake in the West, a sun that only came once from the West to the East, and it was just for him to be safe from the evil eyes of the enemies.[71] On 1 February 1979, the functionaries of the National Front went to welcome Ayatollah Khomeyni with such an announcement of glad tidings.

Years earlier, upon the return of Ayatollah Kashani from exile in Lebanon, Mosaddeq and other leaders of the National Front had gone to

Mehrabad Airport to welcome another well-known cleric after publishing an announcement of glad tidings of the same type. They had called Kashani "a revered leader" whose name, among the names of the "bravest" children of Iran, was considered, like a proud symbol, "the effective buttress of piety, virtue, purity, and free spiritedness," a leader who was "the source of the harmony of voices, the means for hope, and an effective factor for the perpetuation of independence and the strengthening of the foundations of constitutionalism," and who was coming to once again, under the auspices of "Divine affirmation and the sincere assistance of all Moslems and self-sacrificers for the motherland," actualize one of the "indisputable principles of the sacred religion of Islam, that is, the victory of truth over falsehood."[72]

The return of Ayatollah Khomeyni to Iran, which was followed shortly thereafter by the establishment of the Revolution Council and Bazargan's provisional government, made Bakhtiar's position more unstable than ever before. These developments, which had gained velocity with the resignations of Seyyed Jalal Tehrani and Abdolhoseyn Aliyabadi from the Royal Regency Council, were another blow to the prestige and credibility of the government, which with the resignations of Javad Shahrestani, the Mayor of Tehran, and a number of parliamentary deputies was indicative of the fragility of the executive and legislative organizations of the country. The publication of the news of lack of support by such grand ayatollahs as Shari'atmadari, Golpayegani, Mar'ashi-Najafi, and Ruhani for the government of Bakhtiar, who claimed that they supported him with their silence, was a new blow and indicative of Bakhtiar's isolation from the high-ranking clerics. In a published announcement, they emphasized: "The issue is neither the current government nor similar governments; rather, we are expressing our opinion about the essence of the issue and the entire existing regime, and demand the establishment of a just Islamic regime in place of the former despotism and dictatorship."[73] This would be a regime that, with its potential, had attracted and enamored not only the religious scholars and clerics and those close to and the followers of Ayatollah Khomeyni, but also the Tudeh Party, the People's Feda'i Guerrillas, the People's

Mojahedin, and a number of well-known intellectuals and writers, including Simin Daneshvar, Ali Asghar Haj-Seyyed-Javadi, Abdolkarim Lahiji, Naser Pakdaman, Baqer Parham, Reza Baraheni, and Gholamhoseyn Sa'edi.

In the meantime, Bazargan referred to Ayatollah Khomeyni as the Imam Hoseyn of the age, and spoke about the will of the people and "God's decree" that was expressed "through the religious sources of emulation and religious magistrates." He was happy that he had attained his "old wish," for which he had fought for forty years, the wish that in his words, with the fusion of "religion and science," would result in the establishment of an Islamic republic, a regime the example and model of which he sought "during the ten-year period of the prophetic mission and political leadership of the Messenger of God (peace be upon him) in Medina, and the five-year imamate of Ali (greetings to him) in Kufa." Banisadr asked everyone to only follow the strategy of "Islamic unity and an Islamic government," so that this time the movement that "began with Islam would end in an Islamic government," lest the historical experience of the Constitutional Revolution be repeated. That Constitutional Revolution, according to the revered leader, had followed a deviant path and "continued outside Islam and against Islam." Banisadr's old concern was about Ayatollah Khomeyni losing control of the "task at hand." Hence, he constantly warned him against "issuing a religious edict that would exempt people from the performance of their duty." His Eminence had to be "careful," and the religious scholars and clerics "should continue, united and in union, to take advantage of every opportunity…so that when the time is right, they can finish the job." His other constant concern was lest the "dastardly intellectual types," and for that matter, the "Western-educated ones," would find a footing among the people. Since "the dog of one ordinary religious seminary student" was worth "a thousand of those doctors and engineers." At times, he was "worried" that women might get the right to vote, and at other times, he did not find a problem with or object to "women's education and schooling, provided all religious standards were observed." Simin Daneshvar, the first president of the Association of

Iranian Writers, a pioneer among Iranian women writers, and the author of such novels as *Savushun*, regarded Ayatollah Khomeyni to be, in a word, the "truth," a man who "came to the battlefield with words and books, and with such weapons gained victory over an unrivaled arsenal, doing what no one else could," a man who was "the manifestation of a new history, new environment, and new ethics." Ali Asghar Haj-Seyyed-Javadi, a well-known opponent of the Shah's regime, spoke about "the unity of the word, the phrase used by Imam Khomeyni at the moment of his arrival in Iran," as the "secret of victory." He spoke about experienced SAVAK agents among the "very close colleagues" of Bakhtiar in the government, and accused him of killing innocent people. Lahiji, a legal scholar and one of the founders of the Iranian Society for the Defense of Freedom and Human Rights (Jam'iyat-e Irani-ye Defa' az Azadi va Hoquq-e Bashar), called on everyone to "preserve the spiritual and humane content of the revolution."[viii] Pakdaman, a member of the provisional Secretariat Committee of Iranian Academics, spoke about the "value" that "the great leader of the revolution, Ayatollah Khomeyni," placed on the universities. Like a pioneer on his way to "purging" the universities, he spoke of the necessity of "academic cleansing," which he termed the same as "purging and reconstruction," the negation of "the defiled," and moving toward "purities," a demand that in the words of Pakdaman, was affirmed by Talegani's interpretation of the "Glorious Word of God." Parham, a famed translator and sociologist, regarded Ayatollah Khomeyni to be "the manifestation of spirituality of the Iranian soul, the genuineness of the profound cultural values of this nation, and the embodiment of Shi'ite beliefs." Baraheni, a poet and influential literary critic, rose to cleanse the "revered religious scholars of Islam" of the accusations and slander by "world capitalism and its defiled ally, Zionism," and he called Bakhtiar an agent of

---

[viii] Pointing out that a number of people had no respect for freedom, in an admonishing article, Lahiji felt the need to remind them that the Islamic Republic meant "a regime that considers man the viceroy and trustee of God on earth" and "a regime that negates the domination of human beings by an individual, stratum, or class. It is a regime that values human rights and dignity." *Keyhan*, no. 10687, 19 April 1979, 6.

American imperialism and the "most illegitimate and unlawful" prime minister in Iranian history. Sa'edi, writer, playwright, and the creator of the script for the acclaimed film, *The Cow*, presented Ayatollah Khomeyni as the "great fighter and the staunch combatant for freedom," and Bakhtiar as the "irresolute" politician affiliated with the Shah and the United States. Ne'mat Mirzadeh, "the poet of the masses," composed poetry about "Imam Khomeyni," and the humorist Hadi Khorsandi, using obscene and mangled words, contaminated Bakhtiar's name and past history heinously. And this was just a start, and merely a small sample. By the time Ayatollah Khomeyni referred to Bakhtiar as a debaucher and a usurper, and Taleqani, speaking of disbelievers and jihad, regarded him as more of an infidel than any infidel, other steps had to be taken.[74] They were the steps that paved the way for the unity of the nationalists, the religious forces, and the leftist groups for overthrowing Bakhtiar, and they were reminiscent of another time and experience. That experience, in July 1952 with the fall of Prime Minister Qavam, resulted in the "unity of the words" of the allies of Mosaddeq, the followers of Ayatollah Kashani, and the devotees of the Tudeh Party, and had come to fruition in the comingling of religion and politics as a victorious alternative.

At that time, Qavam, who was the captain of the ship of a different policy, in his historic communiqué, referring to Mosaddeq, Kashani, and the Shah, wrote: "In the same way that I despise public deception in political affairs, I am also disgusted by hypocrisy and imposters in religious issues. Those who under the pretext of fighting red extremists have strengthened black reactionaries have also inflicted a severe blow on freedom and have wasted the hard work of the founders of the Constitution since half a century ago. While I revere the sacred teachings of Islam, I will keep religion removed from politics and will prevent the spreading of superstition and retrogressive beliefs." By negating the viewpoint that strengthened "black reactionaries" against "red extremists," he delineated the reality that comprised the essence of politics during the reign of Mohammad Reza Shah. With this choice, Qavam determined his own fate as well. In a conversation with Arsanjani, he said about Ayatollah Kashani and the role of the clerics: "I am neither Razmara nor Mosaddeq, to be considerate of Kashani and the likes of him, or to believe in making use of the clerics for the affairs of the country… My heartfelt intention is that religion must be separated from politics. A cleric must do his own duty as a cleric. Why should he meddle in the business of the governor of some city, the head of customs, or elections in some region?"[75]

At the height of the crisis, Bakhtiar looked upon the ongoing events from a similar perspective. Like Qavam, he also could not tolerate the clamor of the crowd and was unafraid of being called an agent of foreigners, since he knew that in the rapid turning of the wheel of politics, history needs the truth, and truth requires courage. Hence, similar to Qavam, in an unequal battle, he went into hand-to-hand combat with the clerics, was called a usurper and an infidel, and was trounced. These were two similar battles, in one of which Ayatollah Kashani threatened Qavam and in the other, Ayatollah Khomeyni threatened Bakhtiar with a declaration of holy war. Each battle called on the masses to disobey the government and asked the people to cry out "God is great" from the rooftops and recite the Koran for the soul of the martyrs. Thus, religion was intertwined with politics and politics, with the "holy" verses of the Koran, the message of which for the defeated prime ministers of Iran was nothing less than religious retribution. It was as though in retribution for the foolishness and disregard for previous experiments and trials, this time, within shooting range of another incident, history would arrive at a sinister fateful repetition, a repetition that would sacrifice freedom and thought for what Bakhtiar had called the "absolutely unknown."

At every opportunity, Bakhtiar made an effort to find answers to people's questions. Emphasizing the necessity of preserving the Constitution, he left the nature of the future regime to the choice of the people's representatives in the parliament, and for the justification of his position regarding the acceptance of premiership, he said: "They say that I received the decree for my appointment from him (the Shah). I can respond by saying that the likes of Dr. Mosaddeq, Mostowfiyolmamalek, and many others who were greater than I did the same. All the prime ministers from the National Front, all these gentlemen, honorable judges, many of them received the same type of decree. I cannot see why when this decree reached my hands, its value decreased, or it was deemed to be despicable… All the freedoms that civilized nations have, including the freedom of the press and expression, the freedom of assembly, and respect for individual and social rights, are also observed in Iran… I am aware that the nation under the domination of a dictatorial regime over the course of many years cannot be receptive to a free environment easily… Anarchy and disorder could pave the way for dictatorship… It is quite possible that the new dictator would be more terrifying than the old dictator… The people have the right to express their opinion in a calm environment democratically with the formation of political parties. The votes of these people must be respected, and I will be the first person to bow to their vote… Eighteen months ago, we fought to gain a place for our political party. Eighteen months ago, we fought for the establishment of the National Front. Why do these leaders not engage in political party activities within the framework of the Constitution? Many of the same people demanded compliance with the Constitution 18 months ago, but now that these principles are being implemented by me, again, they cry out and draw the people out into the streets…instead of taking advantage of the existing freedoms and thinking about establishing political parties… Without political parties, democracy will absolutely not exist; and when there are no political parties or there is only a single political party, dictatorship will be established in the country. These gentlemen said that the Shah must leave, that political prisoners should be released, and that the press must be free. I did all that; but now all that is going on is due to personal grudges and the settling of private accounts. In the four weeks of my administration, I have done many things that had not been done in the past fifty years, and I will still stay and fight, even if I become the victim of dictatorship and oppression by the other side. I fought the oppression by the Shah; I will also fight the oppression by this side… In addition to various dangers that threaten us, the country will return to a dark period of dictatorship and feudalism... I warn my beloved compatriots loudly that from this moment on, any drop of blood that is spilled in this country, given all the freedoms that have been provided and the peaceful approach of the government, will be the responsibility of those individuals who conspire and challenge the law enforcement forces to fight them. With all the freedoms today, there is no longer any room for violence and clashes."[76]

Speaking to domestic and foreign reporters, Bakhtiar also mentioned the issue of trying to meet with Ayatollah Khomeyni and the letter that he had written to him and said: "The gist of the letter was that I, not as prime minister but as an ordinary citizen, would go to Paris and, as two Iranians, we would have a discussion. Later, however, I read in newspapers that the stipulation for the discussions was that I resign as prime minister. Apparently, there had been differences of opinion between him and those around him. Hence, I will not go to Paris... I am not going to resign, but I am prepared for negotiations... The rumors about my resignation and abandoning the stronghold of the Constitution and moving toward the absolutely unknown are baseless. The damage and harm that in the past six months has been inflicted on the national economy as a result of strikes and slowdowns is greater than what criminals and thieves have done to this country in the past fifteen years. I support democracy, but will never submit to terrorism. We have had twenty-five years of terrorism, and that is enough. Any member of Ayatollah Khomeyni's provisional government who decides to enter any ministry will be arrested... We will not replace an old dictatorship with a dictatorship of new forces... If they establish an Islamic state in the city of Qom, I will let them do so freely, in which case, we will have a small Vatican. But the establishment of an actual government will never be allowed... I will agree for them to go to Qom and create a Vatican. And I will build a wall around Qom for them. All my life, I have struggled for democracy; and regarding the principles of my beliefs, I would neither compromise with Ayatollah Khomeyni, nor anyone else... If he wants to create a state in Qom, we will allow it. It will be interesting, and we will also have a small Vatican. No one knows what an Islamic republic is, and if a person were to check the sources about it, he would begin to tremble from fear. Neither does he accept the plurality of political parties, nor does he accept democracy. He wants the clerics to carry on God's law. All begins and ends there."[77]

At any rate, dreaming about the establishment of a lost constitutional system, with fearless frankness, Bakhtiar pointed out the realities and the disarray, and he spoke of security, law, freedom, and reforms. In the first step, by dissolving SAVAK, with the freedom of the press, and by releasing the political prisoners, he wanted to fulfill some of the people's old demands; but, in his doomed effort, he did not have the good fortune of opening a path for them and showing the way to their good fortune and better days. At the height of the unrest, when the masses of the people and the educated elite sought the secret to their peace and security in unequivocal, uncomplicated answers to their difficult and complex questions, he did not overlook any effort to speak with them about all that he regarded as knowledge and wisdom. The people, however, had become accustomed to a different language, a language that in its expression and reasoning was symbolically different from the tone and structure of Bakhtiar's language. For Bakhtiar, that language was the language of castigation, the language of curses, damnation, and animosity. He believed that it was a language that exerted a toll on freedom, and in its illusive chants, it was the unbroken bewitching spell of foolishness, a language that knew no other alternative but good and evil, service and treason, and angel and devil. This was the language of Fridays, the language of black Fridays.

In such an environment, the words and language of Bakhtiar, with its absolute frankness, would not get anywhere vis-à-vis the language that had replaced knowledge and understanding with faith. Describing the characteristics of such a language, the philosopher and art critic, Boris Groys, emphasizes how a faithful person remains immune to any idea other than his own by relying on his unwavering faith. Another aspect of such a mindset, in Groys' opinion, is the understanding of the fact that this language does not merely provide immunity to common sense and knowledge; rather, more than that, it is a metamorphosed language, the language of stagnation. Hence, reducing the differences between the two by saying that one is the language of faith and the other the language of knowledge would only state half the truth. Even though on the surface, both seem to use the same instrument to express their views, they speak in two different "languages." In fact, the basis is not a common language, but the space that the two languages "share." Describing the difference between the language of faith and the language of knowledge, the well-known philosopher Ludwig Wittgenstein refers to the language of the days of the week and the language of Sundays, and he speaks of the futility of comparing the living, dynamic language of weekdays with the language of the church. It is a type of futility the goal of which is a comparison between the dynamic language of weekdays and the language of Sundays, since on Sundays, language is devoid of thought, motion, and life.[78] The immunity of such a language to criticism or to a viewpoint other than that which it recognizes stems from such a difference, from belief in a fate that God's will has determined for his servants. Thus, adorning ceremonies that they call revolution, they can speak of the necessity of freedom of expression while simultaneously depriving themselves of freedom of thought and placing their fate in the powerful hands of the chosen few who have no respect for freedom, or for thought.

The Fall of the Cabinet

The evening of Friday, 9 February 1979 marked the swift onset of a tumult of historic magnitude. On that evening, severe fighting occurred between the Air Force lower-rank and noncommissioned officers and the members of the Imperial Immortal Guard in the Dushan Tapeh Air Force Training Center near Tehran. The reason for this was the rebroadcast of the video of Ayatollah Khomeyni's return to Iran on television on the order of Bakhtiar. Upon his return to Iran, in response to a reporter who had asked him what his feelings were, Ayatollah Khomeyni had answered: "Nothing." Sirus Amuzgar, the counseling minister and head of the Ministry of Information and Tourism in Bakhtiar's cabinet, states: "We thought that the people becoming aware of what Khomeyni had said would damage his credibility."[79] The showing of the video, however, resulted in the expression of sentiments in support of Khomeyni on the part of the lower-ranking Air Force personnel and the reaction of the members of the Imperial Guard, and ultimately their confrontation. In the meantime, a large crowd shouting "God is great" rose in support of the Air Force personnel, and a number of the people in that crowd gained access to the arsenal depot. That same evening, some units of the Imperial Immortal Guard set out from other parts of Tehran for Dushan Tapeh to suppress the Air Force personnel. On the following day, with the spreading of these incidents to the surroundings of the Dushan Tapeh barracks as well as to other parts of the city, the police precincts and military barracks were attacked by certain groups of people who had armed themselves. Finally, toward the end of the night, the Imperial Immortal Guard, in the continuation of a heated battle, was forced to retreat.

In the morning of the same day, on the order of Bakhtiar, General Rahimi, the military governor of Tehran, by extending the martial law hours from 4:30 in the afternoon to 5:00 a.m., had tried to prevent the collapse of the police precincts and military barracks. In the meantime, with armed people barricading themselves in strongholds in various parts of the city and the continuation of clashes, some sensitive centers fell into the hands of the opponents of the government. The capital of the country as well as other large cities had transformed into scenes of a full-fledged war.

On the following day, 10 February 1979, holding a National Security Council meeting, Bakhtiar called for immediate measures to confront the riots and the fall of the government and military centers; and he also issued an order to bomb the arsenal and machinegun manufacturing plant. He had asked the military personnel in charge to distribute flyers and announce on loudspeakers that the people should disperse from that area; otherwise, the Air Force personnel and those who had come to support them would be suppressed, in order to prevent light weapons and munitions from falling into the hands of the people. Badreh'i, the commander of the military forces, refused to carry out Bakhtiar's order.

After the fall of the regime, in the course of interrogations, General Mehdi Rahimi and General Amir-Hoseyn Rabi'i said emphatically that Bakhtiar had ordered them to bomb the arsenal area, but they had refused to do so. Qarahbaghi refutes the claim that Bakhtiar had issued the written order for the bombing of the machinegun manufacturing plant.[80]

At midnight on the same evening, Bakhtiar telephoned Amuzgar, his cabinet minister, to immediately go and see him. He had decided to have a number of people arrested, and for this reason, he told Amuzgar to go to the Radio and Television Organization at five o'clock the next morning. One week prior to the incident at the Dushan Tapeh barracks, Bakhtiar had informed Amuzgar and Razmara that a list of opponents had been prepared who would be arrested soon. According to Razmara, in addition to himself and Amuzgar, Foreign Minister Mirfendereski had also been informed about this list. The list, which had been prepared by Gholamali Oveysi, the former military governor of Tehran, with the cooperation of General Rahimi and several others, initially included nearly a thousand people, which was later reduced to 440 or 460 people. With the departure of Oveysi from Iran, the list was given to Rahimi, the new military governor of Tehran. Bakhtiar had assigned General Changiz Voshmgir, the acting commander of the Ground Forces, to go to Kish Island and prepare a place for the detention of those on the list.[81]

Amuzgar states: "Bakhtiar wanted to take a serious military step. He changed the hours of martial law and banned traffic from 8:00 p.m. to 4:30 p.m., and this was his greatest mistake. He realized his mistake, and later he constantly repeated that he had made a mistake. If he had not done this and martial law had remained as it was, from 8:00 p.m., the military would have had the chance to arrest the opponents whose names were on the list. With the changing of the hours of martial law, however, and the reaction of Khomeyni and Bazargan, which was to call on the people to disobey, the plan failed."

In a published announcement, Ayatollah Khomeyni wrote: "Today's announcement of martial law is a ruse and in violation of religious law, and the people should not pay attention to it by any means." The provisional government as well in its announcement no. 1, which was published with the signature of "Prime Minister Mehdi Bazargan," wrote: "The report on the radio at 1400 hours today about the prohibition on comings and goings in the city of Tehran from 4:30 p.m. is a conspiracy against the victory of the Islamic Revolution of the people, and it is unacceptable. May the government of justice of the Islamic Republic be established!"[82]

Amuzgar continues: "In any case, that day, the car that was supposed to come and take me to the television department did not come. So, I went on foot and arrived there at about 7:00 a.m. That afternoon, Bakhtiar was supposed to meet with Bazargan at the home of Senator Jafrudi. At about 11:00 a.m., Qarahbaghi called me and said that he had sent an announcement to the radio department to be read on the radio, but they refused to agree to it. He asked me to issue orders to have that announcement, which was about the neutrality of the military, read on the radio. I told him that I would not agree for that announcement to be read, since it would result in disturbances in the city. Moreover, he was going to meet with Bakhtiar and he could raise the issue with him. Qarahbaghi said angrily, 'If you do not give the order to read this announcement, I will send tanks to the television station.' I told him that this had nothing to do with me and that I needed to ask the prime minister. We exchanged some more harsh words, and I resisted his demand. At about 12:15 p.m. I called Bakhtiar and explained what had happened. I told him that I had resisted Qarahbaghi's demand. Bakhtiar said, 'The country is lost; have them read it.' A little later, the people were informed about the neutrality of the military. In the interval, everyone had left the television department, and other than me, no one remained in the Ministry of Information."[83]

In the morning of 11 February 1979, the text of the announcement of the neutrality of the military was approved in the meeting of the Council of Military Commanders after two hours of discussions. The text that was signed by 22 high-ranking military officers marked the end of the work of Bakhtiar's cabinet, and its downfall.[ix] He had spent the previous night after the meeting of the National Security Council with Khadem and Samimi, who were ministers in his cabinet; Reza Marzban, the courier of his letter to Ayatollah Khomeyni in Paris; and his guards. His secretary, Pari Kalantari, who had stayed in the prime minister's office that night because of the martial law and prohibition on comings and goings, states: "In the morning, Bakhtiar came to the prime minister's office at eight. I went to his office. He asked, 'Did you rest well?' I said, 'The sound of machinegun fire really scared me. How about you?' Bakhtiar said, 'You know that I am a tribal man, and I am not afraid of the sound of guns and cannons. The phone calls one after another did not let me sleep.' And then, in his particular polite manner, he added, 'I forgot to tell you to write in your notebook that at 8:30 or 9:00, General Qarahbaghi is coming to see me.' Obviously, this appointment had been made the night before, when they had the National Security Council meeting in the prime minister's office. Otherwise, I would have been informed about it and would have written it in the prime minister's appointment book."[84]

In the meantime, Moshiri-Yazdi came from his office in the Prime Minister's Palace to Bakhtiar's office. He recounts that he told Bakhtiar: "Nili, the head of the prime minister's guards, said a few minutes ago, 'There is a lot of unrest. The security of the prime minister and his life are in danger.' Upon hearing this, Bakhtiar stood up and opened the window of his office that faced the garden. We could hear the clamor of the crowd outside. He then turned to me, and emphasizing the word 'Yazdi' (suggesting the popular notion in Iran that people from Yazd are scaredy-cats), with a smile that displayed calmness, he said, 'Moshiri-Yazdi, it looks like you are scared.' He then shut the window, and as he

---

[ix] According to Sharifi, a person close to Bakhtiar, General Shafaqat, the minister of defense in Bakhtiar's cabinet, who had signed the text of the neutrality of the military leaders, changed his mind and crossed out his signature. This writer's interview with Rahim Sharifi, 1 February 2014.

was returning to his desk, he added, 'You can leave. I still have some work to do.' This was our last meeting in the Prime Minister's Palace. I left the place after that short conversation."[85]

Pari Kalantari recounts: "That afternoon, the prime minister was supposed to meet Engineer Bazargan and Dr. Siyasi at Senator Jafrudi's home, and I knew that the times of his appointments had all changed. Nevertheless, because I had given appointment times to a few people, I asked him for permission to contact those who had appointments and to ask the ones who were close by to come. I spoke to a couple of them. I remember that on that day, Khodadad Farmanfarma'iyan and Amin Alimard came to see the prime minister. Qarahbaghi, however, did not come. No matter how many times I called, he would not answer, and his aide also said that he was not available. Finally, Bakhtiar said, 'Madame, please find out whether Qarahbaghi is alive or dead.' But still, there was no news. So, I told Mr. Ra'ufi, the Prime Minister's Palace chef, to prepare lunch for the prime minister. Ra'ufi asked, 'What would you like me to make, Madame?' I said, 'Is there not a piece of meat in this Prime Minister's Palace? Just make something.' In the meantime, Qarahbaghi finally called. I said, 'We tried to find you all day, since this morning, but we could not find you.' Contrary to his usual demeanor, this time he said angrily, 'Get me on line with the prime minister.' I connected him to Bakhtiar's phone, and a little later, the call was finished. We heard that because of the events, Bakhtiar did not finish his lunch and left the Prime Minister's Palace in a hurry. I am not sure. He usually ate very little. Or maybe because he was so shocked by speaking to Qarahbaghi that he lost his appetite. I remember that they had given visiting time on Monday to Ms. Majidi and Ms. Ruhani, the wives of two former ministers who were in prison. I went to his office to have him verify his next day's schedule. I saw him standing there, angry. His paternal cousin, Abbasqoli Bakhtiar, was standing next to him. I asked, 'Have you confirmed tomorrow's schedule?' Bakhtiar said, 'We still have time; we will talk about it later.' In the meantime, Colonel Nili called and said, 'Tell Mr. Prime Minister that I called and asked for a helicopter, but they would not send it. Please ask the prime minister to contact Qarahbaghi himself.' I figured out that Bakhtiar had asked for a helicopter. I had to call Qarahbaghi again. Bakhtiar spoke to Qarahbaghi, and then I heard the helicopter. On that day, this was the only thing that Qarahbaghi did for him. What I want to say is that before that, there was no helicopter at the Prime Minister's Palace to take Bakhtiar.[x]

"In the meantime, Mr. Afshar came to my office and said, 'Mr. Prime Minister is leaving.' I went down the stairs quickly and rushed toward him. At the entrance to the garden, he saw me. I asked, 'Are you leaving, Sir?' He said, 'When I leave, you leave, too.' I asked, 'Are you coming tomorrow?' He responded, 'If I do, I will call you.' And I always waited for the day when he would call me. Now I could hear people's voices, the sound of pounding on the door of the Prime Minister's Palace, and I saw Colonel Nili trying to stop the crowd from rushing in. Finally, they came in and took over the Prime Minister's Palace. In the meantime, as I was leaving the place, I saw Khadem and Marzban next to a store that was known as the Royal Court store. They were also leaving the Prime Minister's Palace.[xi]

"At three o'clock in the afternoon, I was at home when General Rahimi, the military governor of Tehran, called. I asked, 'Where are you?' In a voice in which I could feel kindness and concern, he said, 'I am somewhere in the south of the city. No one is with me.' He asked about Bakhtiar. Then, Javad Sa'id, the speaker of the National Consultative Assembly, called and asked, 'Where is the prime minister?' I said, 'He left.' Sa'id said, 'The dictatorship of the crown has left, and the dictatorship of the turban has arrived.'"[86]

---

[x] In his memoir, Qarahbaghi verifies Bakhtiar's request for a helicopter. See: Abbas Qarahbaghi, *E'terafat-e Zheneral: Khaterat-e Arteshbod Abbas Qarahbaghii, Akherin Ra'is-e Setad-e Bozorg Arteshdaran va Ozv-e Showra-ye Saltanat (Mordad-Bahman 57)* (Tehran: Ney Publishers, 1987), 369-370.

[xi] Khadem recounts that in addition to himself and Reza Marzban, Hushang Mo'inzadeh, the "security man" of the Prime Minister's Palace, was also at the palace on that day. This writer's interview with Javad Khadem, Paris, 12 December 2007.

Ayatollah Khomeyni and the Refah School

Ten days before Bakhtiar's cabinet fell, after Ayatollah Khomeyni returned to Iran and gave a speech at Behesht-e Zahra Cemetery, he visited the One Thousand Bed Hospital. From there, he went to the home of the son of his brother, Ayatollah Pasandideh, and close to midnight, he went to the Refah School. Hashemi-Rafsanjani called the Refah School the "identity card of the revolution" and considered it the "memento of a lifetime of jihad, struggle, and torture." According to him, whoever worked at this school was a person who had a "significant share" in the revolution.

The history of the Refah School began with the failure of the 5 June 1963 rebellion and the trial and execution of the perpetrators of the assassination of Hasan Ali Mansur, the prime minister at the time, in January 1965. According to Haj Mehdi Shafiq, one of the founders of the Islamic Coalition Committee (Hey'at-e Mo'talefeh-ye Eslami), when political struggle against the regime had no result and the opponents were arrested and imprisoned, the decision was made that after their release, another path should be followed, and to fight the Shah's regime, "investments" should be made in cultural matters. For this purpose, in meetings with the participation of Ayatollahs Motahhari, Beheshti, and Hashemi-Rafsanjani, as well as Raja'i, Bahonar, Rafiqdust, and several businessmen and merchants from the bazaar, the decision was made to create a school, cultural center, and foundation.

The first effective step for this purpose was taken by Hashemi-Rafsanjani. Contacting some of the bazaar merchants, he asked them to provide financial support for starting the school and cultural center, and he succeeded in collecting a significant sum from Haj Hoseyn Akhavan-Farshchi, a well-known carpet seller in the bazaar, and from several other merchants.

In early 1967, with the collected funds, 3,000 square meters of land with an old house were purchased on Iran Street, on Mostajab Alleyway, behind the former building of the National Consultative Assembly. What was special about the school was that "it was mostly built with the religious funds from 'sahm-e Imam,' or tithes." Haj Mehdi Shafiq adds: "After the procurement of the land and location, the next step was the naming of the school. The name 'Refah' was chosen after a great deal of discussion and exchanges of opinion. Then, another issue was raised regarding whether it should be a boys' school or a girls' school. Following much discussion, and considering the unfavorable condition of girls' schools and the unhappiness of religious families in sending their daughters to government schools, the decision was made for this high school to be for girls, so that in this way it would provide a new opportunity and chance for the families who did not want to have their daughters register in government high schools." The responsibility of obtaining the permit for establishing the school was conferred on Beheshti, Raja'i, and Bahonar, all three of whom worked for the Ministry of Education. They were members of the Board of Trustees and the "actual educational architects and custodians of this school," and were responsible for managing the cultural affairs as well. The principal of the elementary school was Raf'at Afzar, a member of the People's Mojahedin Organization, and the principal of the high school was Puran Bazargan, another member of the same organization and the wife of Mohammad Hanifnezhad, the leader of the People's Mojahedin Organization. A number of the teachers of the school were also members of that same organization.[87]

Shortly before the return of Ayatollah Khomeyni to Iran, when he was contacted regarding the place of residence of the leader of the revolution, Ayatollah Khomeyni chose the Refah School. Ali Danesh-Monfared, a member of the Freedom Movement and a member of the administration of the Refah School, who after the victory of the Islamic Revolution became a member of the Command Council of the Islamic Revolution Guard Corps, the governor of Fars, and a parliamentary representative, during the return of Ayatollah Khomeyni to Iran was a member of the central welcoming committee. He states: "The first and most important issue that needed to be specified was the place and location of the welcoming committee... For this reason, His Eminence Imam Khomeyni was contacted in Paris through his son, Haj Ahmad, to inquire about his opinion concerning the location of the welcoming committee. The Imam offered certain criteria, stating that the headquarters of the Imam (the welcoming committee) should be in a populated area of Tehran and the center of the struggle, not in the neighborhoods in northern Tehran or away from the Tehran city center; it should not belong to any specific person or owner; and it should be a popular public place. Naturally, it could not be a government location, either; and the type of activities of that center needed to be in keeping with the goals of the Islamic movement. Considering the criteria offered by the Imam, several places were suggested to him, including Alavi School. Ultimately, His Eminence chose the Refah School for the initial phase as his first place of residence after coming back from Paris, because firstly, the Refah School was located on Iran Street, near Baharestan Square, which was in the heart of Tehran and one of the best neighborhoods; secondly, it did not belong to any specific person, and it had been established by a group of such religious and informed personalities as Ayatollah Hashemi-Rafsanjani and a number of faithful and struggling people of the bazaar as the Refah Cooperative Institute; and thirdly, the activities of this center were educational and Islamic and nurturing grounds for the great Islamic movement under the leadership of the Imam.

"Considering these criteria, even though the Refah Girls' School did not have an acceptable large courtyard and other facilities, in terms of further requirements, it was compatible with the Imam's views, and the Imam chose that location for his headquarters and informed us about it. Immediately after the Refah School was chosen for the headquarters of His Eminence, the welcoming committee began its activities. Although this committee was for welcoming the Imam, in fact, it was the center for the great Islamic Revolution."[88]

With the return of the leader of the Islamic Revolution to Iran, for security reasons, the decision was made to transfer the place of his residence to the Alavi School, near the Refah School. The Alavi School was larger and could better serve for people's visits and the meetings of Ayatollah Khomeyni. Nevertheless, the Refah School continued to remain the command center of the revolution, and the meetings of the Revolution Council were held there. The office of Bazargan, the prime minister chosen by Ayatollah Khomeyni, who in accordance with the principle of the government regime of the guardianship of religious jurisconsult acquired his legitimacy on 4 February 1979 by an edict from the spiritual leader, was initially in one of the classrooms of Refah School.[89]

The text of the edict for the appointment of Bazargan as prime minister was as follows: "On the suggestion of the Revolution Council, in accordance with the right of religious law...and due to trust in your solid faith in the sacred ideology of Islam, ...I assign Your Excellency to form the provisional government in order for you to make arrangements for the running of the affairs of the country, and in particular, holding a referendum" in regard to "changing the political regime of the country into an Islamic Republic, forming the founding assembly comprised of officials elected by the people for the ratification of the Constitution of the new regime, and the election of the new assembly of the representatives of the people on the basis of the new Constitution."[90]

With the fall of the monarchy, the confiscated weapons were handed over to the officials at the Refah School, and they were stored in the basement of the school. Confiscated gold, jewelry, and cash were also delivered there, and the leaders of the regime of the Shah and those who had been arrested in the name of the revolution were put under surveillance and imprisoned in the classrooms. The Refah School also became the headquarters of the committees that were created in the course of the revolution. Manuchehr Khosrowdad, the commander of the Air Force of the Ground Forces; Mehdi Rahimi, the military governor of Tehran; Reza Naji, the military governor of Isfahan; and Ne'matollah Nasiri, the former head of SAVAK, were detained in one of the classrooms of the school that was allocated for military personnel, and they were executed by firing squad on the order of Sadeq Khalkhali, the religious magistrate and head of the revolution courts. Prime Minister Hoveyda and the head of SAVAK, Moqaddam, were also imprisoned in the Refah School prior to being sentenced to death. Regarding the executions at the Refah School, Mohsen Rafiqdust, a member of the Islamic Coalition group, the board of trustees of the Refah School, and the welcoming committee of Ayatollah Khomeyni, who became the minister of the Islamic Guard Corps in Mirhoseyn Musavi's cabinet and then head of the Foundation for the Downtrodden and Self-Sacrificing Disabled Veterans, states: "Starting from 11 February 1979, almost all the leaders of the regime were gradually arrested. We immediately converted a few classrooms on the third floor of the Refah School to prison cells; we did not have anywhere else... We did not put Hoveyda in the room with the others, we kept him in another room... They brought Khosrowdad, Naji, and Nasiri on the same day. We took them to the room for the military personnel... Then there was a discussion about what to do with them. Mr. Khalkhali held a trial and sentenced Naji, Khosrowdad, Rahimi, and Nasiri to death. We had two arsenals, which were under my charge. They received a few Uzi submachineguns from me to execute them. They took them to the roof. In that confusion, if the guys had been at all careless, they could have killed one another, because they had them standing in the middle and were firing at them from both sides."[91]

In this manner, within six months after the fall of the regime of the Shah and the establishment of the revolution courts, a number of the leaders of the military and high-ranking officers of the three branches, the Police Department, and the Gendarmerie; military governors; heads of prisons; SAVAK chiefs, officials, and torturers; minor officers and commissioned officers; ministers; representatives and speakers of the two houses of the parliament; and former Prime Minister Hoveyda were executed by firing squad. The names of Gholamreza Nikpey, the mayor of Tehran, and Parviz Nikkhah, as the theoretician of the regime, were also on the list of those who were executed. Amnesty International announced the number of those executed from the beginning of the revolution to August 1979 as 438 people.[92] Bakhtiar, however, fled the peril, and despite the rumors about him having committed suicide or having been arrested in the early moments and days following the fall of the monarchical regime, he hid in a safe place.

Bakhtiar in Hiding

According to his family and those close to him, on 11 February 1979, after leaving the Prime Minister's Palace, Bakhtiar went from the Officers' College by helicopter to the Eshratabad Barracks, and from there to the ISB building at the corner of Hakim and Kordestan Streets, to the home of an acquaintance. The doorman of the building recognized him, and the owner of the residence had warned Bakhtiar that that place was not safe. Hence, he had to go to the home of one of his relatives for a few days. Bakhtiar's nephew, Human Bakhtiar, states: "I was in Lorestan during those days until they called me and asked me to go back to Tehran. When I arrived and I saw Bakhtiar, I was astonished. I did not expect to see him under those conditions. He had picked up Trotsky's book, *My Life*, from the bookshelf and was reading it. On that night and the following days, I did not see any sign of worry on his face."[93]

In the meantime, Senator Kazem Jafrudi, mindful of the danger that Bakhtiar faced, prepared a new place for him with one of his friends. Bakhtiar stayed there until he left Iran in July 1979. In his memoir, he makes a passing reference to the time he was in hiding and writes: "I changed the place where I was staying, and I went to a house where I did not know how long I would have to live. My isolation took nearly six months, and during that time, I never stepped outside. My reasoning was that if I went to a friend's house, I would soon cause suspicion, that I would endanger my friends, and I would not be safe either. In the homes of relatives, it would be even more dangerous. Hence, I took refuge in the home of acquaintances. My hosts, those noble and very kind people, in order to prevent any possibility of my being exposed, let go of their servants. The owner of the house, his wife, and his daughter and son-in-law did all the housework while I stayed there. I am naturally a recluse. Hence, that situation was not too intolerable for me... My room was adjacent to a revolution court. All day and night, I was listening to my own trial. The warrant for my arrest was issued, and the charges against me were numerous. This was undoubtedly the most difficult period of my life, but it did not shake my beliefs."[94]

During the time that Bakhtiar was in hiding, his daughter, France; his son-in-law, Kiyumars Mokhateb-Rafi'i; and Mehrnush Bakhtiar, a close relative, went to see him a few times. Mehrdad Bakhtiar, Mehrnush Bakhtiar's husband, preferred not to know his hiding place, because he was worried that he would be arrested and would be unable to withstand torture and would reveal his hiding place.[xii] Hence, it would be better for him not to know where he was hiding. France Bakhtiar says: "I went to see my father a few times. I was very careful, and changed cars on route. My father lived in a small upstairs room that had a window toward the alleyway. Sometimes he went downstairs, but he would go back to his room if he heard the doorbell. He spent most of his time reading books and listening to the radio. I remember that he said once he heard gunfire in the alleyway, and a bullet had been shot through the window and hit the wall, which he showed us, four or five centimeters above the bed." Once, when members of the neighborhood Islamic Revolution Committee had entered the house in which he was hiding, the son-in-law of the owner of the house hurriedly asked him not to turn on the light in his room. Bakhtiar, who did not want to be captured in his pajamas, stood up calmly, put on his suit, and in the darkness, searched inside the drawer of the wardrobe for a tie that would match his blue suit. By touching the fabric of the ties, he wanted to find the tie that he liked. In his recollections, he considered himself among those who "react swiftly to ordinary incidents of life, and keep their calm under exceptional circumstances." What "tormented him" more than the "death threat that he faced every day" was his realization that "some people were still slaves to their own illusions."[95]

France Bakhtiar says: "About my father, I never had the feeling that he was afraid of being captured. He was mostly worried that if he were captured, they would insult and disrespect him. He was, of course, worried about the owner of the house, and he was tormented when he

---

[xii] The names of Mehrnush and Mehrdad Bakhtiar are aliases.

heard about the executions one after another. The incarceration of the ministers of his cabinet, Abbasqoli Bakhtiar in particular, upset him." In the course of one of these meetings, he gave a tape, which he had recorded addressing the people of Iran on the occasion of the Islamic Republic referendum in March 1979, to his daughter France to make available to foreign news agencies.[96] Later on, after he left Iran, he distributed another tape informing the people of his views.

In his first message, Bakhtiar made reference to being "secluded and away" from the people, as though more than having the people in mind, he wanted to suggest to the rulers at the time that he had left Iran, perhaps hoping to ward off the danger that was waiting in ambush on his path and possibly render it ineffectual. In that message, referring to the arrival of the Persian New Year, he stated: "This New Year could have been the most auspicious of Iran's past twenty-five years. This New Year could have arrived in a free and safe environment devoid of concerns, and it could have made all of us, Moslems, Christians, Zoroastrians, and Jews, dance after years of oppression, united and brothers, despite differences of opinion, hopeful for the future." The "chaotic" conditions and the "indecision" in the country showed that, unfortunately, this was not the case. Then, with a look at the past, he discussed the reasons for accepting the responsibility of premiership and the later developments, and for the first time confirmed that the stipulation of the Shah leaving the country was one of the conditions for his acceptance of the position of prime minister. Bakhtiar, on the one hand, said that this issue "complicated" his relationship with the military and the law enforcement forces, and on the other, it had occurred without any "important actual clashes and reactions" between him and the military. Seemingly, the secret of this message was hidden in the fact that Bakhtiar was implicitly admitting that the issue of the Shah's departure and the stipulation that he had made for accepting the position, considering its effect on the fate of the military, had had an undeniable impact on his life, on the process of the revolution, and on the future of the country, a secret the revealing of which Bakhtiar postponed to another opportunity.[97]

In addition, he raised the issue of the return of Ayatollah Khomeyni to Iran alongside demands such as "selection of the cabinet ministers without interference by the Royal Court, return to democracy and the rule of law, and determining the type of government in a calm and free environment" as some of the conditions he had set for accepting that position of responsibility,[98] whereas neither the issue of the return of Ayatollah Khomeyni nor the future of the regime were among the preconditions for starting his administration, not to mention why he felt the need to raise those issues in his message.

Moreover, Bakhtiar made reference to his failed attempt to meet with Ayatollah Khomeyni in Paris. He considered the reason for the failed attempt to be obstructions created by a faction of the National Front and a few "imbalanced pseudo clerics" who prevented his meeting with Ayatollah Khomeyni, whom in his message he referred to as "His Honor." Presenting a dark picture of the situation of the country, Bakhtiar stated: "Oppression, a country in disarray, and a crumbled economy, as well as force and bullying by a group who have replaced the former ones can be seen everywhere. We changed a corrupt dictatorship into a dictatorship coupled with chaos, and all of this with the hope for an Islamic Republic… Now, what will this Islamic Republic be like, and how will it respond to our problems and calamities? …No one can clearly tell what this republic will be and its characteristics… So, you want the people to go and vote for an absolute unknown or not at all, and there is no other way? Dear sisters and brothers, I will not vote for such a republic, because I consider it incompatible with the advancement of the society, the pride of the country, economic prosperity, and the implementation of human rights."[99]

In his first message to the people, Bakhtiar emphasized that the movement of the Iranian people for freedom did not begin in 1963, and that he himself was in prison in those years for the fifth time. He was proud that following the 1953 coup d'état, despite the many possibilities that he had at his disposal, he did not choose any other path but that of Mosaddeq. He stated: "I followed the path of Mosaddeq, and I will not deviate from that path. Now, whether I had a desert or a mountain nature, I did not yield. But, as far as I know, every prime minister is appointed by the king or the president of that country, and he is approved by the representatives of the people. I received an appointment decree from the same king that gave Mosaddeq his." He said that such prominent people as Amir Kabir, Moshiroddowleh, Mostowfiyolmamalek, and Forughi received their premiership appointment decrees from the kings, and among them, he spoke of such a "prominent figure" as Qavamossaltaneh. Mentioning Qavam alongside Amir Kabir and Mosaddeq, especially by a person who considered himself to be a follower of the "path of Mosaddeq," was an uncommon outlook that added a special characteristic to his personality in comparison to individuals such as Fatemi, or Sanjabi and Hasibi.[100] Previously, as well, when he was presenting his cabinet to the Parliament, by mentioning "national courts," he revived the memory of Qavam in the public's minds. In July 1952, Qavam, too, by publishing the historic announcement, "the captain has a different policy," had threatened his opponents with establishing "revolutionary courts."

In conclusion, Bakhtiar also spoke about a futile expectation, that Ayatollah Khomeyni, upon returning to Iran, "as a personality beyond politics and planning, would gather a number of those who struggled against the corrupt dictatorial regime and say, 'I want you to drive away corrupt, false, flattering, and such individuals from the government; convict and punish the criminals; ensure individual and social liberties; abolish laws contrary to Islam; and pursue an independent Iranian policy.'" Ayatollah Khomeyni, however, actually did all that. Is it not true that within a short period of time, to the extent that it was related to "corrupt, false, and flattering" individuals, the punishment of "criminals," and the revocation of "laws contrary to Islam," Ayatollah Khomeyni had actualized the demands that Bakhtiar made in his Persian New Year message? Had he not appointed individuals such as Bazargan, Sahabi, Sanjabi, Foruhar, and a number of others to the cabinet in which the leaders of the Freedom Movement and the National Front were its distinguished members? Were these individuals not the very people who had fought alongside and in step with Bakhtiar "for many long years against the corrupt dictatorial government"? Were these not the same "gentlemen" whom he considered "pious and faithful" or had mentioned as the "noblest and most genuine" persons he knew? Apparently, his entrusting things related to the spiritual realm to Ayatollah Khomeyni and matters in the sphere of politics to others was an indication that his political life, despite all his fearlessness, had continued to be shaped in the limbo of the weakness and simplemindedness that was rooted in the lineage and history of the National Front. Confused in theory and practice, his was a lineage and history that had become meaningful in terms of bowing and surrendering to clerics of the type of Zanjani and Taleqani or Ayatollah Kashani and Ayatollah Khomeyni, to the point that, despite all his abilities, seemingly he knew no other way but to merely chant his prayers for the good fortune of the people whose love he had in his heart. This time, it was he who took refuge to the realm of spirituality, and in his Persian New Year message, he entrusted the people to God, and with sincerity of heart, he "prayed" for the future of his homeland, for the freedom of the men and women of his country, and for the proud waving of the flag of Iran, in hopes that "the prayers of those with *fidelity* will be answered."[101]

In July 1979, with a French passport in the name of Francois Boivin, which the French government had provided for him, Bakhtiar left Iran. His exit from Iran was arranged in Tehran by Michel Poniatowski, the former interior minister of France. Bakhtiar's son, Guy, and his older daughter, Viviane, knew about the preparations for his exit from Iran.[xiii] Bakhtiar writes: "A number of brave individuals helped me. I needed a foreign passport with an alias, and a goatee. Neither was I supposed to have anything Iranian in my suitcase, nor any labels of Iranian tailors on my clothing.

[xiii] The American political scientist, Mark Gasiorowski, quoting Khadem, the minister of housing and urban development in Bakhtiar's cabinet, writes that Israel helped Bakhtiar in his exit from Iran. See: Mark Gasiorowski, "The Nushih Plot and Iranian Politics," *International Journal of Middle East Studies*, no. 31 (2002): 663.

"In the morning one day, I went to the airport. Thanks to the goatee and dark sunglasses, I looked somewhat different. The person who accompanied me entered the airport with a first class ticket and my suitcase and got the suitcase through. I stayed in the car until the time of the departure of the airplane was announced, within fifteen minutes. Then I immediately tossed my jacket over my shoulder and entered the terminal like a businessman in a hurry. The line of Iranian travelers was long, but there were only seven or eight people standing in the foreign travelers' line. I only came face to face with a policeman, who neither paid any attention to my face nor to my passport. I did not have to wait in the Transit Room for long, and I got on the bus that drove toward the airplane...

"I took a window seat. I still had my dark sunglasses on. I opened the *Le Monde* newspaper on my lap and placed my passport on it. My back was toward the door from which the passengers entered. I just looked out the window calmly and pretended that the comings and goings of the airline employees had attracted my attention. The quiet sound of the door which was closed by the stewardess was beautiful music to my ears... I stared at the clouds and asked for champagne. The hostess brought it, and I sipped it most calmly... No one knew about the day I would arrive in Paris. When I arrived in Paris, I called my children to come take me home."[102]

Bakhtiar in Exile

After leaving Iran, Bakhtiar engaged in an all-out effort to overthrow the Islamic Republic. This effort, which began with his participation in the failed Nuzheh coup d'état and continued with the founding of an organization called the National Resistance Movement, was a new chapter in his political life. On 6 August 1991, however, with Bakhtiar's murder, this chapter came to a bitter and tragic end.

The Nuzheh coup d'état, the general plan of which had been prepared after the revolution in Iran on the initiative of a number of military officers and civilians who opposed the Islamic government, was defeated on 9 July 1980 with the arrest, trial, and execution of most of its perpetrators. It also resulted in the purging of the military.[103]

The Nuzheh coup d'état must be regarded as Bakhtiar's most important political act in opposition to the regime of the Islamic Republic, and his last significant effort to return to power. Since the failure of the Nuzheh coup d'état, neither he nor the National Resistance Movement, which was formed in Paris in August 1980, were able to engage in serious action against the Islamic Republic.

To achieve the objective he had in mind, Bakhtiar opted for cooperation with Iraq and receiving financial assistance from that country, as well as Saudi Arabia and the Persian Gulf sheikdoms. According to Shahintaj Bakhtiar, the "financial assistance from the king of Saudi Arabia, Fahd bin Abdulaziz, and Sheikh Zayed bin Sultan, the emir of Abu Dhabi and founder of the United Arab Emirates, was provided through the efforts of Gerald Ford, the former U.S. President, and one of the oil partners of George Bush (the father), who later on became the president of the United States. Ford and Bush's partner in a meeting with Bakhtiar, which took place in Paris, met and discussed the issue of receiving assistance from Saudi Arabia and the Persian Gulf sheikdoms."[104][xiv] Regarding Bakhtiar's relationship with American officials, France Bakhtiar states: "In a visit to the United States in 1982, my father met and had unofficial discussions with Barry Goldwater, the well-known American senator and 1964 presidential candidate of that country, in Washington, D.C."[105] Sirus Amuzgar and Javad Khadem also verify Bakhtiar's receiving financial assistance from Iraq, Saudi Arabia, and the Persian Gulf sheikdoms. Both of them also mention assistance to Bakhtiar from several Iranian "sources," such as Ashraf Pahlavi. According to Khadem, "Asraf Pahlavi's assistance was not done in her own name."[106]

[xiv] "When Bakhtiar traveled to Saudi Arabia to receive financial assistance, to appease the Saudi rulers, despite his own wishes, he went on Haj pilgrimage." This writer's interview with Human Bakhtiar, Washington, D.C., 18 April 2008.

This choice opened a new chapter in the chronology and history of a personality the pages of whose political notebook and report card had been turned with patriotism and nationalism. Even though Bakhtiar continuously declared his opposition to Iraq's military aggression on Iran, he was never able to offer clear solid evidence that would clear him of the accusation that he had agreed with or encouraged Iraq to invade Iran. He said: "I believe that Iraq should not have invaded Iran... I repeat, between Saddam and Khomeyni, I choose Saddam. But regarding Iran and Iraq, I would never become involved in a discussion. Naturally, Iran is my homeland, and I consider Iran to be above any other place. In the war between Saddam and Khomeyni, the guilty one is Mr. Khomeyni, because he is the one who wants to export his false revolution. He wanted to start a Shi'ite-Sunni war... Before this war, I was fully in agreement with Iraq, and I believed that Mr. Khomeyni was a destructive element for the entire region. I believe the same now. Now, as well, it is only the West that still supports Mr. Khomeyni; otherwise, the countries in the region do not agree with his remaining... No Iranian can agree to Iraq's invasion of Iran... As far as I know, if an acceptable regime other than Khomeyni's comes to power in Iran, Iraq will rapidly withdraw from Iranian soil. This is my opinion about Iraq. A country such as Iraq can never imagine taking over Iran. But if Mr. Khomeyni stays in Iran, the danger exists for Iraq's government to be toppled, and as a result, Saudi Arabia, Egypt, and other countries will become unstable. So, all of them inevitably need to remedy the situation before it occurs."[107]

But was it not true that the "remedy of the situation" that Bakhtiar mentions found its meaning in the military invasion of Iran by Iraq? The picture that he drew about the threat of the Islamic Republic for Islamic countries had many supporters, especially in the diplomatic circles of the West. Bakhtiar, however, was not speaking as a political analyst, but as a political leader, and in this arena, his word meant nothing but a justification of the full-fledged war of Iraq against Iran. As a nationalist politician, he felt it was his duty to regard Iran as "above" everything and keep it safe from danger, and simultaneously place the "guilt" of the warmongering of Saddam, in his belief, on the shoulders of those who, with a "false" revolution and igniting a "Shi'ite-Sunni war," had paved the way for aggression on his homeland.

Shahintaj Bakhtiar states: "Shortly before the invasion of Iran by Iraq, the ambassador of that country in France called Bakhtiar on the telephone and informed him about it. The ambassador thought that the news would make him happy, whereas that was not the case. He immediately traveled in a small rented airplane, the pilot of which was Iranian, to Iraq to make Saddam Hussein reverse his decision. My husband told Saddam, 'The people of Iran are patriotic; and if this happens, they will support Khomeyni.' But Saddam did not agree to it, and from then on, they were no longer on speaking terms. When he came back from Baghdad, he was upset for several days."[108] Other than these statements, no more information is available about the why and how of Bakhtiar's relationship with Iraq, or what occurred in the aforementioned meeting and his other meetings with Saddam and other leaders of that country after Bakhtiar left Iran.

Bakhtiar's relationship with the United States, as well, was peculiar and different from what it had been in the past. An example of this relationship can be found in the confidential report of a security official of that country with whom Bakhtiar met in Paris in October 1979. A U. S. National Security Archive document states in this connection: "This was Bakhtiar's message to us. He has started an organization with chump change, and if he does not get financial support and practical advice from the United States, he will not get anywhere. He is still in the planning phase, but he expects all the details to be clarified within about five months. Then he would like to come to the United States for direct talks and directly negotiate with the U.S. government about the future of the movement and his country. He said confidentially to 'F1' that if he does not receive American assistance, he might seek help from the Persian Gulf Arab countries."[109]

In the past, Bakhtiar had frequently had discussions and negotiations with the American Embassy and American officials. This time, however, by relying on the United States and seeking to obtain financial assistance from that country in his battle against the Islamic Republic, his efforts were of a different sort. Bakhtiar had made this effort for several reasons that had serious proponents among the political circles and his supporters in the National Resistance Movement. His opponents, however, considered this behavior to be a decisive break with a tradition to which he considered he was adhering. In that tradition, the name of the United States in the historical conscience of the National Front, and perhaps the people, had been synonymous with trampling on Iran's independence in the 19 August 1953 coup d'état.

Critiquing the policy that Bakhtiar pursued in regard to the Islamic Republic after he left Iran, Sirus Amuzgar states: "I must say that, in fact, the problem was with Bakhtiar's strategy. He wanted a coup d'état, and I said that it could not be done. Of course, he usually consulted me. Sometimes, the officers also consulted me as to whether or not to join the Nuzheh coup d'état. I told them if they loved their country, they should do it, and they did, and most of them were executed. For this, my conscience bothers me. Another point is about the second coup d'état that they were pursuing, after the Nuzheh coup d'état, and they were preparing for it. I think this was four or five years after the revolution. It had already become clear that this policy was not right." Amuzgar also opposed some aspects of the publication and publicity policy of Bakhtiar and the National Resistance Movement, especially the creation of a radio station on Iraqi soil.[110]

Regarding the creation of a radio station in Baghdad, Amuzgar states: "It was either October or November 1980. I did not want Bakhtiar's voice to be transmitted to Iran from Iraq, and I made every effort not to have the location of the radio station be in Baghdad. I had considered three other places for this purpose; one was in Nicosia in Cypress, another in Beirut in Lebanon, and the other, in Sicily in Italy. We had also thought about Cairo, and finally that location was provided. For this purpose, we had negotiations with a few people who could facilitate what we had in mind. It was clear that a radio transmitter in Cypress would not be possible without the consent of the United States. Nevertheless, in Paris, we contacted the deputy prime minister of that country. That meeting took place in the apartment of an Iranian friend in the 15th arrondissement in Paris. The deputy prime minister introduced us to a person with the alias of Jones from Sicily. We knew that Sicily was controlled by the Mafia, and that Jones was playing the role of an intermediary. He put us in touch with a French citizen by the name of Michel. Michel was about 35 years old, dark complexioned, with a round face and dark brown hair. The topic of discussion with Michel, who had also introduced himself to us with an alias, was about the technical preparations and, for instance, that the station had to be located on a mountain, and so on. In the meantime, Michel gathered up the papers that were on the table and said, 'This is all childish; let us talk seriously a bit.' And he added, 'I will kill Khomeyni for $5 million. And you can pay me after Khomeyni is killed.' It was obvious that Michel was talking on behalf of the Mafia. I asked, 'What if you kill Khomeyni and we do not pay you?' He said, 'We are not worried, you will pay.' I said, 'The decision about this is beyond my authority, I need to ask.' He agreed. After leaving the meeting, I contacted Bakhtiar over a public telephone. Since I did not want to tell him about the matter on the phone, I told him that I needed to discuss an important issue. I went to see him and explained the story. I pointed out that they were prepared to receive the money after they had killed Khomeyni. When Bakhtiar heard all I had to say, he jumped up angrily and said, 'What are you talking about? Do you think that I would pay to have an Iranian killed, and for that matter, by a murderer? We have differences of opinion; but these differences and enmities are between us. We are doing all these things in order to have compliance with the laws. Then you expect me to pay a Mafia member to kill Khomeyni? Do not talk about this anymore, not to anyone.' And thus, the issue was put to rest. Shortly after that meeting, in late December 1980, Michel was killed in a gunfight, which was reported in the French newspaper, *France Soir*."[111]

Javad Khadem, the former cabinet minister who, in contrast to Amuzgar, was among the serious supporters of the Nuzheh coup d'état, also criticized Bakhtiar's policy. He states: "Even after the Nuzheh coup d'état, there was a chance to fix things, but not by trying something different every day, like a drowning man. When the Nuzheh coup d'état failed, you no longer needed to follow the same path. Counterrevolutionaries can only succeed in the short term, not in the long term. It has been like that everywhere. When you do not succeed, you need to stop and come up with a different plan. But once a person starts on a path, it is very difficult for him to allow himself to admit that he will not succeed. I supported the Nuzheh coup d'état, and I am not criticizing it, because in political struggle, the possibility of the success of the counterrevolutionaries exists. But my criticism was about afterwards. What was done after the Nuzheh coup d'état to overthrow the regime was wrong. You know, a person who gambles at the gambling table might not think that he will lose, but he will lose sometimes. Politics is also a gamble. If you continue, sometimes the result is losses one after another and complete defeat. The fact is that Bakhtiar had become desperate. He thought time was running out. In fact, I must say that what happened to him—although not in human terms but in political terms—was the best win and victory. He could have continued, and things could have become worse and worse. Historical determinism forced him to a point that he could not even gamble anymore. The gamble of politics impeded him."[112] Amuzgar and Khadem both separated from Bakhtiar and the National Resistance Movement after a while.[xv]

Bakhtiar's failure in the arena of politics, in the arena of organizing and organization, is also undeniable. The National Resistance Movement was made up of an incongruent group. A few of Bakhtiar's cabinet

---

[xv] From among Bakhtiar's cabinet ministers, the fate of Amuzgar, as far as it concerns his profession, is more interesting than that of others. Having gone from being a journalist, in the position of advisor to the prime minister, and the head of the Ministry of Information and Tourism, a position in which he was responsible for the media and in charge of negotiations with his striking colleagues, after the revolution and his release from prison, he joined the National Resistance Movement in Paris. After breaking away from that organization, Amuzgar opened a dry cleaning shop in Paris, and after a while, turned to selling newspapers. For years now, he has owned a newspaper store in Paris.

ministers, this or that high-ranking employee of the former regime in the Foreign Ministry, former officers of the monarchical regime, individuals from the tribe, and those who with the exception of a few had no experience in fighting for freedom and democracy were the main members of that organization. A distinguished example was Iraj Pezeshkzad, the well-known humorist and author of the popular novel, *My Uncle Napoleon*, a former administrator of the Foreign Ministry, who was fired after the revolution. He joined Bakhtiar's organization in Paris, and was the editor-in-chief of the organ of that organization, *Qiyam-e Iran*. Pezeshkzad, who called himself "the offspring of the nation," after the fall of the monarchy, in justification of his service at the Foreign Ministry, spoke about "hardship and indigence" and that he had to make a "dervish-like" living! In an article about his dismissal from the Foreign Ministry, addressing Sanjabi, the foreign minister of Bazargan's cabinet, he wrote: "Since you carry the dignified and proud title of the leader of the National Front and you are a memento of my beloved old man, the immortal Dr. Mosaddeq, and on the other hand, you were appointed by the great leader of today's Iranian revolution, I forgive you." In that article, Pezeshkzad wrote: "My membership in the Foreign Ministry, if I do not say it happened out of a mishap, was at least due to an incident. Everyone has to make a meagre living somewhere. If writing could have provided for this dervish-like living—which I have never wanted, nor have I had anything but—without enslaving my pen, I would have left this seemingly calm and clean but internally contaminated palace… My pen has labored in fighting corruption, defilement, and oppression. My main job was not at the Foreign Ministry. I have been serving the nation, and I am not embarrassed before my employer." And thus he concluded his "tedious" service in that ministry.[113] In addition to having been the editor-in-chief of *Qiyam-e Iran* and the author of several books and dozens of articles, he also has a book entitled *Cheeky Kids International* (Internasiyonal-e Bacheh Porruha)!

A number of Bakhtiar's colleagues stood by his side once again, either due to the mishap or out of friendship or fulfillment of their promises. Some would have perhaps, under normal circumstances, prepared themselves to step aside and leave the arena to others, to those whom Mirfendereski, the foreign minister in Bakhtiar's cabinet, called the "young wolves" in the ranks of the National Resistance Movement. Not long before, some of them had been among the opponents of the Shah, and now, along with the supporters of the former regime, they found themselves at the side of their enemies of yesterday and their allies of today. This was a group that had a bagful of experience and history in the struggle, a history that at one time was considered a source of pride, but now, with a critical reconsideration of that history, more than being considered a source of pride, at times was the source of such despair and despondence that it impeded the way to the past ability and dynamism and novel and constructive solutions for the future. In addition, the formation of the National Resistance Council and the presence of its leaders, Mas'ud Rajavi and Banisadr, in Paris as an alternative to the Islamic Republic more than ever before drove Bakhtiar and the National Resistance Movement to the margins. Before long, the Western governments and their allies accepted the sovereignty of the Islamic Republic as an undeniable reality. The consequence of this approach left a negative impact on the position of Bakhtiar and the organization that he had established.

Now, with the solidification of the Islamic Republic, the passage of time for the National Resistance Movement would find meaning in hopelessly counting the anniversaries of a revolution that was called "sedition" in their escape from reality, and more than ever before, time passed with meetings and rivalries and in the tedious recounting of the memories of bygone days, in disregarding the reality that since the Russian Bolshevik Revolution in October 1917, it seemed to have become a principle rule in the trend of the successful revolutions in the world that no opposition in exile would have the ability to overthrow the government formed by a revolution.

The fact is that the National Resistance Movement, more than being an alternative for confronting the regime that rose from the Islamic Revolution, was an organization that found meaning only and solely due to the credibility of the name and personality of Bakhtiar. He was a matchless leader and messenger, who with his financial abilities ulti-mately, for his followers who called him "Khan," in exile was considered a shelter or a tangible abode, or the savior and the symbol of hope and a future most unattainable, to the point that the renowned novelist Mahshid Amirshahi, who at one time had raised her lone voice in support of Bakhtiar, wrote about the organization that he had estab-lished: "The Movement was more and more resembling Noah's ark day by day, and it needed to have all sorts of animals in it."[114]

At any rate, in the early years, Bakhtiar had continued to maintain his hopes for returning to Iran. He said: "I consider being here as tempo-rary, a short wait, and nothing more. I cannot imagine remaining in exile for many long years and being unable to return to Iran. I wait; therefore, I have not surrendered to exile to feel its pain, to suffer depression, despair, and despondence." According to Sirus Amuzgar, however: "He had gradually lost hope of returning to Iran, even though he would not say so. He felt that he had grown old; he had lost hope."[115]

Explaining the conditions in which Bakhtiar lived in the final months of his life in terms of finances, Mohammad Moshiri-Yazdi recounts the efforts of the French government to have him leave the country: "Two or three months before he was murdered, I was in his home one eve-ning. Referring to his bad financial situation, he said, 'There is also another problem, the French Foreign Ministry has asked me to leave this country because of political considerations. I need to think about going to an African country.'"[116]

His wife, Shahintaj Bakhtiar, is unaware of the efforts of the French government to have Bakhtiar leave that country. She says: "The fact is that in the final years, my husband had become discouraged about the people and the opposition. In the past, he considered the people of Iran to be peace-loving and intelligent. He used to say, if they are given freedom, Iran can become one of the most advanced countries in the world. But he gradually changed his opinion. He said, 'I did not know the extent to which selfishness and superstition had infiltrated them.' In fact, he no longer saw any hope for returning to Iran. He said, 'Before anything else, the people must learn a great deal about democracy and superstitious beliefs. I worked so hard, and it did not get anywhere. My life has come to an end. The young people must get involved, and I should be a consultant, so that in this way I will step aside.' In the final years, he had also become physically weak. Several cancer tumors had appeared in his intestines, and he had surgery in the fall of 1987 in the Rothschild Hospital in the 12th arrondissement in Paris. As far as I know, other than me and Razmara, who was a physician and a close friend of his, no one knew about it. We visited him every day without anyone finding out, until he recovered and was released from the hospital.[xvi]

"Toward the end, he was in a very bad financial situation. He wanted to sell the Suresnes villa that was in the name of his son, Patrick, and leave France. He had decided to go to Réunion Island in the Indian Ocean, which belongs to France. He said, 'I might be able to teach at the university there.' I told him that it was too far away, and since I had studied in the United States and was familiar with its culture, I suggested that we go to the United States. He did not agree, and he said, 'Either we go to Réunion or to Quebec in Canada, since its language is French.'"[117]

Bakhtiar's sentiments about the people in his final days were also echoed by his paternal cousin, Abbasqoli Bakhtiar, who served as the minister of commerce, industries, and mines of his cabinet, in the final months of his life in 2008. Suffering from a stroke and Alzheimer's and having lost almost all his memory, he expressed himself in the following statement: "All that has happened is the fault of the people." And then he recited the following verse: "Dust on my head from sorrow, the soil of the homeland is gone, what dust should I throw on my head?"[118]

Pari Kalantari, Bakhtiar's secretary during his administration, who worked with his organization in Paris, says: "Toward the end, he was in

---

[xvi] According to Manuchehr Razmara, Bakhtiar's son, Giv, also knew about his illness and treatment, but due to security considerations, he would not go to the hospital to see him. This writer's interview with Razmara, Paris, 31 January 2014.

a very bad financial situation. We vacated the office of the National
Resistance Movement on Boulevard Raspail, the rent for which had not
been paid for several months. Everything had been cut off. The only
thing that worked was the telephone, which they also cut off. Last time
that he called me, the telephone went dead. We had no money to turn
the lights on. We had no money for the servant's Metro fare. Bakhtiar
wanted to go and live with his son. He had said, 'Since I am moving, I
have a carpet and a painting that I want to give to Ms. Kalantari.'" It is
reported that one month after Bakhtiar's murder, his son, Guy, had said
in the house of his paternal uncle, Abdolrasul Bakhtiar: "If they had not
killed my father, he would not have had enough money to live on this
month."[119]

[1] *Jebheh-ye Melli beh Revayat-e Asnad-e SAVAK* (Tehran: Markaz-e Barrasi-ye Asnad-e
Tarikhi-ye Vezarat-e Ettela'at, 2000), 429-430.
[2] Mohammad Reza Shah, *Enqelab-e Sefid* (n.p.: n.p., n.d.), 5.
[3] Karim Sanjabi, *Omidha va Naomidiha (Khaterat-e Siyasi)* (London: Jebheh-ye
Melliyun-e Iran Publishers, 2007), 281-282; Mehdi Bazargan, *Enqelab-e Iran dar Do
Harekat* (Tehran: Bazargan Publishers, 1984), 27 *Khaterat-e Shapour Bakhtiar, Nokhost
Vazir-e Iran (1357)*, edited by Habib Ladjevardi, Iranian Oral History Project,
Harvard University Center for Middle Eastern Studies, Bethesda, MD, 1996, 82-84.
[4] *Rejal-e Asr-e Pahlavi, Jebheh-ye Melli beh Revayat-e SAVAK* (Tehran: Markaz-e
Barrasi-ye Asnad-e Tarikhi-ye Vezarat-e Ettela'at, 2000), 240-241.
[5] Ibid., 240-247.
[6] *Rejal-e Asr-e Pahlavi: Jebheh-ye Melli beh Revayat-e SAVAK*: 278; Sanjabi, *Omidha va
Naomidiha*, 292, 299.
[7] Unpublished interview of Keyvan Dadjou with Shapour Bakhtiar, Suresnes, France,
tape 2, 1 October 1986; Shapour Bakhtiar, *Yekrangi*, translated by Mahshid Amirshahi
(Paris: Khavaran Publishers, 1982), 126; *Ettela'at*, 20 January 1979 136-137.
[8] Sanjabi, *Omidha va Naomidiha*, 292, 296.
[9] Ibid., 300.333
[10] *Mozakerat-e Majles-e Showra-ye Melli, Dowreh-ye Hefdahom*, vol. 7, no. 2277, session
42, 27 November 1952, 1-2.
[11] This writer's interview with Abdolkarim Anvari, tape 1, London, 13 November
2007; unpublished interview of Keyvan Dadjou with Shapour Bakhtiar, Suresnes,
France, tape 2, 1 October 1986.
[12] Unpublished interview of Keyvan Dadjou with Shapour Bakhtiar, Suresnes, France,
tape 2, 1 October 1986.

[13] *Ettela'at,* 23 October 1978, 4; ibid., 25 October 1978, 4.

[14] Sanjabi, *Omidha va Naomidiha,* 300-302.

[15] This writer's interview with Abdolkarim Anvari, tape 1, London, 13 November 2007; San'ati, "Shapour Bakhtiar," 213-214.

[16] Ibid.

[17] Jamshid Amuzgar, "Majara-ye Vapasin Ruzha-ye Farmanrava'i-ye Shah," (Khatereh'i az Jamshid Amuzgar), *Rahavard,* no. 39 (Summer 1995): 146-148.

[18] Gholam Reza Afkhami, *The Life and Times of the Shah* (Berkeley: University of California Press, 2009), 492- 493.

[19] Amuzgar, "Majara-ye Vapasin Ruzha-ye Farmanrava'i-ye Shah," 146-148.

[20] (DNSA) Memorandum of Conversation, Participants: Dr. Shapour Bakhtiar, National Front; John Stempel, Political Officer, U.S. Embassy, Tehran, September 24, 1978.

[21] Ibid.

[22] Ibid.; Memorandum of files, Participants: Dr. Shapour Bakhtiar, Executive Committee, National Front; John D. Stempel, American Embassy, Tehran; Congressman Stephen Solarz; Stephen Shalom, Friend of the Congressman, 17 October 1978.

[23] Ibid.

[24] Ibid.; Memorandum of Conversation, Participants: Shapour Bakhtiar, Iran Party Leader and Member of Executive Board of the National Front; John D. Stempel, Political Officer; W. Gregory Perett, Political Officer, 22 October 1978.

[25] Ibid.

[26] Afkhami, *The Life and Times of the Shah,* 495- 496; Farah Pahlavi, *An Enduring Love: My Life with the Shah, A Memoir,* translated from the French by Patricia Clancy (New York: Miramax Books, 2004), 291- 292.

[27] Bakhtiar, *Yekrangi,* 143-144; Afkhami, *The Life and Times of the Shah,* 495-496.

[28] Bakhtiar, *Yekrangi,* 145-149; Mohammad Reza Pahlavi, *Pasokh beh Tarikh,* 2nd printing (Los Angeles: Ketab-e Pars, n.d.), 169, 268.

[29] Bakhtiar, *Yekrangi,* 149.

[30] (DNSA) Memorandum of Conversation, American Embassy, Tehran, 27 November, 2 December 1953.

[31] Bakhtiar, *Yekrangi,* 144; *Ettela'at,* 6 January 1979, 2.

[32] (United Kingdom, The National Archives) TNA. FCO/Telegram Number 726 of 31 October 1978.

[33] *Si-yo Haft Ruz Pas az Siy-o Haft Sal: Chand Goft-o Gu ba Dr. Shapour Bakhtiar darbareh-ye Dowran-e Zamamdariyash* (Paris: Radio Iran Publishers, 1982), 35-36; unpublished interview of Keyvan Dadjou with Shapour Bakhtiar, Suresnes, France, tape 1, October 1986.

[34] Abbas Milani, *The Shah* (New York: Palgrave Macmillan, 2001), 398- 401; Afkhami, *The Life and Times of the Shah*, 495- 496; Pahlavi, *An Enduring Love,* 489-491; Hushang Nahavandi, *Akherin Ruzha: Payan-e Saltanat va Dargozasht-e Shah*, 2nd printing, translated by Behruz Sur-Esrafil and Maryam Seyhun (Los Angeles: Sherkat-e Ketab, 2005), 195, 300.

[35] *Khaterat-e Mozaffar Baqa'i*, edited by Habib Ladjevardi, Iranian Oral History Project, Harvard University Center for Middle Eastern Studies, Bethesda, MD, tape 2, 25 June 1976.

[36] Cyrus Kadivar's interview with Sirus Amuzgar, 4 March 2003: http://www.iranian.com/CyrusKadivar/2003/March/37days/; TNA. FCO/ PREM 16/1720. Telegram Number 1046 of 31 December 1978.

[37] Bakhtiar, *Yekrangi*, 147; "Man Morgh-e Tufanam," Dr. Shapour Bakhtiar quoted from the website of the National Resistance Movement of Iran: http://www.namir.info/Neuer%20Ordner/05-Spalte%20Links/Bakhtiar/16-10-10-man%20morghe%20toofanam.htm.

[38] This writer's interview with Hamid Zonnur, Paris, 11 December 2007; this writer's interview with Javad Khadem, Paris, 12 December 2007; unpublished interview of Keyvan Dadjou with Shapour Bakhtiar, Suresnes, France, October 1986.

[39] *Surat Jalasat-e Kongereh-ye Jebheh-ye Melli-ye Iran*, compiled by Amir Tayerani (Tehran: Gam-e No Publishers, 2009), 216-226.

[40] TNA. FCO8/3189.Internal Political Situation in Iran, Telegram number 966 of 12 December 1987.

[41] *Ettela'at*, 6 January 1979, 2; ibid., 7 January 1979, 7.

[42] Ibid., 6 January 1979, 6.

[43] *Keyhan*, 6 January 1979, 2.

[44] Ibid.

[45] Ibid., 7 January 1979, 7.

[46] This writer's interview with Mohammad Moshiri-Yazdi, Paris, 21 February 2008; ibid., 13 December 2007; this writer's interview with Sirus Amuzgar, Paris, 13 December 2007.

[47] *Khaterat va Yaddashtha-ye Arteshbod Fereydun Jam*, compiled by Dr. Morteza Moshir (Los Angeles: Sherkat-e Ketab, 2000), 277.

[48] http://www.bbc.co.uk/persian/iran/2011/08/110802_l78_bakhtiar_20th_anniv_sirous_amoozgar.shtml; http://www.iranian.com/CyrusKadivar/2003/March/37days/.

[49] http://www.bbc.co.uk/persian/iran/2011/08/110802_l78_bakhtiar_20th_anniv_sirous_amoozgar.shtml.

[50] This writer's telephone conversation with Mohammad Moshiri-Yazdi, Paris, 17 August 2013.

[51] This writer's interview with Mohammad Moshiri-Yazdi, Paris, 21 February 2008.

[52] This writer's interview with Pari Kalantari, Paris, 24 April 2012.

[53] This writer's interview with Mohammad Moshiri-Yazdi, Paris 21 February 2008.

[54] This writer's interview with Sirus Amuzgar, Paris, 13 December 2007; this writer's interview with Mohammad Moshiri-Yazdi, Paris, 21 February 2008.

[55] This writer's interview with Hamid Zonnur, Paris, 11 December 2007; this writer's interview with Rahim Sharifi, Paris, 11 December 2007; this writer's interview with Manuchehr Razmara, Paris, 22 February 2008.

[56] This writer's interview with Sirus Amuzgar, Paris, 13 December 2007.

[57] Quoted from the BBC Persian language website: http://www.bbc.co.uk/persian/iran/2011/08/110802_l10_bakhtiar_20th_anniv_majlis_speech.shtml.

[58] *Ettela'at*, 7 October 1978, 4, quoted in Mostafa Rahimi, *Qanun-e Asasi va Osul-e Demokrasi* (Tehran: Amir Kabir Publishers, 1978), 225.

[59] This writer's interview with Manuchehr Razmara, Paris, 22 February 2008; ibid, 26 April 2012.

[60] TNA.FCO/ PREM 16/1720, Telegram Number 1629 of 29 December.

[61] This writer's interview with Javad Khadem, Paris, 12 December 2007.

[62] *Keyhan*, 28 January 1979, 2.

[63] This writer's interview with Javad Khadem, Paris, 12 December 2007.

[64] This writer's interview with Mohammad Moshiri-Yazdi, Paris, 21 February 2008; ibid., 26 April 2012.

[65] This writer's interview with Manuchehr Razmara, Paris, 26 April 2012.

[66] This writer's interview with Mohammad Moshiri-Yazdi, Paris, 21 February 2008; ibid., 21 and 26 April 2012; http://www.radiozamaneh.com/35480.

[67] This writer's interview with Manuchehr Razmara, Paris, 22 February 2008; *Siy-o Haft Ruz Pas az Siy-o Haft Sal: Chand Goft-o Gu ba Dr. Shapour Bakhtiar darbareh-ye Dowran-e Zamamdariyash*, 27.

[68] *Keyhan*, 28 January 1979, 8.

[69] TNA. FCO/ PREM 16/1719, Telegram Number 4, November 1978.

[70] Abbas Qarahbaghi, *E'terafat-e Zheneral: Khaterat-e Arteshbod Abbas Qarahbaghii, Akherin Ra'is-e Setad-e Bozorg Arteshdaran va Ozv-e Showra-ye Saltanat (Mordad-Bahman 57)* (Tehran: Ney Publishers, 1987), 145-147.

[71] *Keyhan*, 24 January 1979, 1.

[72] *A'in-e Eslam*, vol. 7, no. 4 (Khordad 1329): 3, 38.

[73] *Ettela'at*, 21 January 1979, 7.

[74] Ibid., 19 October 1978, 4; ibid., 11 January 1979, 3; ibid., 16 January 1979, 5; ibid., 21 January 1979, 5; ibid., 22 January 1979, 4; ibid., 24 January 1979, 3; ibid., 29 January 1979, 5; ibid., 30 January 1979, 5; ibid., 5 February 1979, 5; ibid., 6 February 1979, 2; ibid., 8 February 1979, 4; ibid., 11 February 1979, 7; *Keyhan*, 24 January 1979, 3; ibid., 10 February 1979, 3-4; ibid., 20 January 1979, 5; ibid., 5

February 1979, 3; ibid., 8 February 1979, 3; ibid., 10 March 1979, 6; *Namehha, Zendeginameh, Asnad va Namehha-ye Ayatollah Haj Seyyed Reza Zanjani* edited by Behruz Tayerani, 2ⁿᵈ printing (Tehran: Samadiyeh Publishers, 2009), 85.

[75] Baqer Aqeli, *Ruzshomar-e Tarikh-e Iran*, vol. 1 (Tehran: Goftar Publishers, 1993), 554; Hasan Arsanjani, *Yaddashtha-ye Siyasi-ye Siyom-e Tirmah 1331*, compiled by Pirayeh Bamshad, 2ⁿᵈ printing (Tehran: Atash Printing House, 1956), 56.

[76] *Ettela'at*, 20 January 1979, 7; ibid., 5 February 1979, 7; ibid., 21 January 1979, 2; *Keyhan*, 29 January 1979, 2; ibid., 1 February 1979, 5; ibid., 8 February 1979, 3.

[77] *Ettela'at*, 22 January 1979, 6; ibid., 1 February 1979, 8; ibid., 4 February 1979, 2; ibid., 10 February 1979, 8; *Keyhan*, 29 January 1979, 2; ibid., 4 February 1974, 4.

[78] Boris Groys, "Sprachversagen: zur Arbeit des Künstlers und Theatermachers Christoph Schlingensief," *Lettre International*, 90 (Herbst 2010): 114-116.

[79] Qarahbaghi, *E'terafat-e Zheneral*, 313-314, 318-319; this writer's interview with Sirus Amuzgar, Paris, 22 February 2008.

[80] *Keyhan*, no. 10367, 13 February 1979, 8; Abbas Qarahbaghi, *E'terafat-e Zheneral: Khaterat-e Arteshbod Abbas Qarahbaghii, Akherin Ra'is-e Setad-e Bozorg Arteshdaran va Ozv-e Showra-ye Saltanat (Mordad-Bahman '57)* (Tehran: Ney Publishers, 1987), 326-327.

[81] This writer's interview with Manuchehr Razmara, Paris, 22 February 2008.

[82] *Ettela'at*, no. 15782, 11 February 1979, 8.

[83] This writer's interview with Sirus Amuzgar, Paris, 13 December 2007; ibid., 22 February 2008; Bakhtiar, *Yekrangi*, 205;
http://www.bbc.co.uk/persian/iran/2011/08/110802_l78_bakhtiar_20th_anniv_sirous_amoozgar.shtml;
http://www.iranian.com/CyrusKadivar/2003/March/37days/; *Ettela'at*, 11 February 1979, 8.

[84] This writer's interview with Pari Kalantari, Paris, 24 April 2012; ibid., telephone interview, 22 December 2013.

[85] This writer's interview with Mohammad Moshiri-Yazdi, Paris, 26 April 2012.

[86] This writer's interview with Pari Kalantari, Paris, 24 April 2012; ibid., telephone interview, 22 December 2013.

[87] "Revayat-e Hashemi-Rafsanjani az Ta'sis-e Madreseh-ye Refah," Aftab news website: http://aftabnews.ir/vdcceoqp.2bqem8laa2.html; *Baray-e Tarikh Miguyam: Khaterat-e Mohsen Rafiqdust*, compiled by Sa'id Allamiyan (Tehran: Sureh-ye Mehr Publishers, 2013), 20-21; Hamid Karamipur, *Karnameh-ye Siyasi va Farhangi-ye Dabirestanha-ye Kamal-e Narmak, Refah, Alavi* (Tehran: Markaz-e Asnad-e Enqelab-e Eslami, 2010), 73-76, 81-83, 90-91, 94.

[88] Jamaran news and information outreach website, 3 February 2010: http://www.jamaran.ir/fa/NewsContent-id_13558.aspx.

89 "Revayat-e Hashemi-Rafsanjani az Ta'sis-e Madreseh-ye Refah," Aftab news website: http://aftabnews.ir/vdcceoqp.2bqem8laa2.html; interview with Engineer Ali Danesh-Monfared about "The Imam's Presence at Refah School," Jamaran news and information outreach website, 3 February 2010: http://www.jamaran.ir/fa/NewsContent-id_13558.aspx; http://www.parsine.com/fa/news/137358.

90 Quoted from *Parsine* website. News item code 137358, 3 August 2013: http://www.parsine.com/fa/news/137358.

91 *Baray-e Tarikh Miguyam: Khaterat-e Mohsen Rafiqdust*, 43-45, 47.

92 Omid, Borumand Foundation website: http://www.iranrights.org/farsi/memorial-case--3306.php.

93 This writer's interview with France Bakhtiar, Washington, D.C., 16 April 2008; this writer's interview with Human Bakhtiar, Washington, D.C., 16 April 2008; this writer's interview with Mohammad Moshiri-Yazdi, Paris, 26 April 2012.

94 Bakhtiar, *Yekrangi*, 212.

95 This writer's interview with Human Bakhtiar, Washington, D.C., 16 April 2008; this writer's interview with France Bakhtiar, Washington, D.C., 16 April 2008; Bakhtiar, *Yekrangi*, 213, 215.

96 This writer's interview with France Bakhtiar, Washington, D.C., 16 April 2008.

97 The website of Iranian nationalists: http://www.melliun.org/nehzat/n05/payambakh.htm.

98 Ibid.

99 Ibid.

100 Ibid.

101 Ibid.

102 This writer's interview with Manuchehr Razmara, Paris, 26 April 2012; this writer's telephone interview with Shahintaj Bakhtiar, 15 and 16 December 2013; Bakhtiar, *Yekrangi*, 216-218.

103 *Kudeta-ye Nuzheh*, 5th printing (Tehran: Mo'asseseh-ye Motale'at va Pazhuheshha-ye Siyasi, 2008); Mark J. Gasiorowski, "The Nuzhih Plot and Iranian Politics," *International Journal of Middle East Studies* 34 (4) (November 2002): 645-666.

104 This writer's telephone interview with Shahintaj Bakhtiar, 15 December 2013.

105 This writer's interview with France Bakhtiar, Washington, D.C., 16 April 2008.

106 This writer's interview with Sirus Amuzgar, Paris, 13 December 2007; this writer's interview with Javad Khadem, Paris, 12 December 2007.

107 *Iran Tribune* weekly, n. p., n. d., 13-14, 24.

108 This writer's interview with Shahintaj Bakhtiar, 15 and 16 December 2013.

109 (DNSA) Secret 1800202, Oct 79, Staff Cite Director 534442. To: Paris Info. London, Geneva, Tehran, FR/Washington.

110 This writer's interview with Sirus Amuzgar, Paris, 13 December 2007.

111 Ibid.

[112] This writer's interview with Javad Khadem, Paris, 12 December 2007.

[113] *Keyhan*, 3 March 1979, 6.

[114] Mahshid Amirshahi, *Dar Safar* (Los Angeles: Ketab Corporation, 1995), 87.

[115] *Iran Tribune Weekly*, 2; this writer's interview with Sirus Amuzgar, Paris, 13 December 2007.

[116] This writer's telephone interview with Mohammad Moshiri-Yazdi, 22 December 2013.

[117] This writer's interview with Shahintaj Bakhtiar, 15 and 16 December 2013; ibid., 16 December 2013.

[118] This writer's interview with Abbasqoli Bakhtiar on 14 March 2008 in Vancouver, Canada.

[119] This writer's interview with Pari Kalantari, Paris, 22 April 2010; this writer's interview with Fereydun Amir-Ebrahimi, London, 12 November 2007.

Explanatory Notes

Afsharid Dynasty: or Afshar Dynasty, a tribal Turkic dynasty founded in 1736 by its best-known member, Nader Shah Afshar, who ruled the entire country and made military conquests of the Mughal Empire in South Asia. Although the dynasty survived to the latter decade of the 18ᵗʰ century, Nader Shah's successors were unable to sustain their control over the country and ruled certain provinces only for short periods of time.

Ahmad Shah: The last Qajar king, Ahmad Shah (1898-1930), was about eleven years old when he succeeded his deposed father, Mohammad Ali Shah, who had tried to reverse the course of the Constitutional Revolution and reestablish dictatorial rule.

Amir Kabir: Mirza Taqi Khan Farahani (1807-1852), usually referred to as Amir Kabir, was the grand vizier of Naserddin Shah Qajar. He is credited with initiating many reformist measures and attempts at modernizing the country, including the establishment of Darolfonun, the first modern school in Persia.

Aref: Abolqasem Aref-Qazvini (1882-1934), with the pen name of Aref, was a popular constitutionalist poet and song writer.

Ashura: The 10ᵗʰ day of the Islamic lunar month of Moharram and the anniversary of the martyrdom of the third imam of Shi'ites, Hoseyn. For Shi'ites, Ashura is the most important religious mourning day of the year.

Atabaks: Atabaks were the rulers of Lorestan in the Zagros Mountains in the late middle ages.

Bahar: Mohammad Taqi Bahar (1886-1951) was Iran's poet laureate in the first half of the 20ᵗʰ century; he composed his work mostly in classical style. Having been active during the Constitutional Revolution, Bahar also became a politician, a cabinet member, and later on, a professor at the University of Tehran.

Bahonar: Mohammad Javad Bahonar (1933-1981) was a cleric and politician who served as Iran's prime minister for a few weeks in August 1981 before he was assassinated in a bombing.

Banisadr, Abolhasan: The first president of the Islamic Republic of Iran, Banisadr (1933-) was impeached by the parliament in June 1981, less than a year and a half into his four-year presidential term, and fled the country.

Battle of Karbala: Occurred in the year 680, when the small army of the Prophet Mohammad's grandson, Hoseyn, fought against the much larger forces of the Omayyad caliph, Yazid I, during which Hoseyn and his supporters were killed.

Battle of Kheybar: This early Islamic battle occurred in 628 between Moslems and the Jews living in the oasis of Kheybar, located in the northwestern part of the Arabian Peninsula.

Bazargan, Mehdi: The founder of the Freedom Movement, Bazargan (1907-1995) was educated in France and appointed prime minister of the provisional government in 1979, after the Islamic Revolution. In his books, he usually tried to explain scientific phenomena in terms of Islamic ideas.

Beheshti, Ayatollah: One of the important religious figures to gain prominence after the Islamic Revolution, Ayatollah Mohammad Beheshti (1928-1981) served as the secretary general of the Islamic Republican Party and was assassinated along with a number of other members in a bombing at the headquarters of that party.

Black Friday: The name given to 8 September 1978 when in a confrontation between the protestors and martial law troops, dozens of people were killed and wounded.

Borujerdi, Ayatollah: Grand Ayatollah Hoseyn Borujerdi (1875-1961) was the Shi'ite source of emulation for more than two decades and is considered one of the most prominent Shi'ite scholars in the 20th century.

Committees: In Persian, *Komitehs,* or Islamic Revolution Committees, were initially pro-revolution vigilante-style groups that were formed during and after the Islamic Revolution in many neighborhoods around the country. In the early 1990s, they were merged with the police and gendarmerie forces of the new regime.

Companions of the Sire of the Martyrs: Reference to the supporters of Imam Hoseyn (popularly believed to have been 72 in number) in the Battle of Karbala.

Consortium Agreement: In 1954, soon after the overthrow of Prime Minister Mosaddeq, a consortium of companies, which included British Petroleum, Gulf Oil, Royal Dutch Shell, and Compagnie Française des Pétroles, continued the monopoly of Iranian oil into the 1970s.

Constitutional Revolution: The uprisings known as the Constitutional Revolution began in 1905 and resulted in the establishment of the first parliament in Persia in 1906. Mohammad Ali Shah, who succeeded Mozaffareddin Shah, bombed the parliament in 1908. This revolution ended in 1911, when the second parliament concluded its term.

Construction Jihad: *Jehad-e Sazandegi* in Persian, is an organization that was created after the Islamic Revolution in 1979. This organization later became a part of the Ministry of Agriculture Jihad.

Coup d'état of 1953: The joint plan by the British government and the American administration to overthrow Mosaddeq's government and return the Shah to power.

Darolfonun School: See Amir Kabir.

Dashti, Ali: Literary critic, historian, journalist, and novelist, Ali Dashti (1897-1982), who had been educated in Islamic traditions in Iraq, also served as a senator.

Davar: Ali Akbar Davar (1885-1937) served as minister of justice during the reign of Reza Shah Pahlavi. He is credited with having established the foundations of the modern judicial system in Iran.

Derafsh Kaviyani Organization: Sometimes referred to as the Organization of Kaviyani Banner, is a monarchist group that opposes the government of the Islamic Republic.

Devotees of Islam: See Self-Sacrificing Devotees of Islam.

Ershad Religious Center: In Persian, *Hoseyniyeh-ye Ershad*, or Ershad Institute, is a privately donated building in Tehran that was a gathering place for some anti-Shah religious groups prior to the Islamic Revolution. Its fame is partly due to Ali Shari'ati, who delivered a series of lectures at that center.

Eshqi: Mirzadeh Eshqi (1893-1924) was a poet, playwright, and journalist during the constitutional era who was murdered in 1924.

Feast of Ghadir-e Khom: *Eyd-e Ghadir* in Persian, is the celebration of the anniversary of the day in the year 632 on which Ali, the first imam of the Shi'ites, is believed to have been designated by the Prophet of Islam as his successor.

Feda'iyan-e Eslam: See Self-Sacrificing Devotees of Islam.

Gilani, Ayatollah: Ayatollah Mohammad Mohammadi-Da'avi-Sara'i (1928-2014), known as Ayatollah Mohammadi-Gilani, served in several important positions in the Islamic regime including the head of the Islamic Revolution Courts of the Judicial Branch of the capital.

Grand Seyyeds: or the "two Grand Seyyeds," refers to two clerics, Ayatollah Mohammad Tabataba'i (1842-1920) and Seyyed Abdollah Behbahani (1840-1910), who were among the leaders of the constitutional movement.

Guard Corps of the Islamic Revolution: or *Sepah-e Pasdaran-e Enqelab-e Eslami* in Persian, was established soon after the Islamic Revolution in 1979 as a branch of the regime's armed forces and played a major role in the Iran-Iraq War.

Haddad-Adel, Gholamali: Among other high positions, Haddad-Adel (1945-) has served as a member of the Assembly for the Discernment of the Expediency of the Regime, president of the Persian Language and Literature Academy, and speaker of the Islamic Consultative Assembly.

Hashemi-Rafsanjani: One of the most influential clerics in the Islamic Revolution, Akbar Hashemi-Rafsanjani (1934-2017) served in a variety of positions, including speaker of the parliament and two terms as president of Iran.

Herat War: or the siege of Herat by the army of Mohammad Shah Qajar (1808-1848), was the Qajars' first attempt in 1838 to take back the territories they had a claim to; but they were defeated, since the city had sought protection from the British in India.

Hira Cave: A cave near Mecca where Moslems believe the first revelations of the Koran were made to the Prophet Mohammad in 610, when he was visited by Archangel Gabriel.

Hojjat ol-Eslam: A clerical title for a Shi'ite seminarian who has completed his preliminary and seminar studies.

Illumination philosophers: Followers of the philosophy of Shahaboddin Sohrevardi, a 12th century Persian philosopher who founded the Iranian school of Illuminationism or Illuminism, an important school in Islamic philosophy that was inspired by Zoroastrian and Platonic ideas.

Imam of the Age: The 12th Shi'ite imam, Mahdi, who is believed to be alive and in occultation, and who will emerge at the end of time to bring peace and justice to the world.

Incident of the Gowharshad Mosque: or the event of the Gowharshad Mosque, refers to the clerics' and people's sit-in protest and rebellion in 1935 in opposition to the modern dress code edict issued by

Reza Shah Pahlavi, in which many were killed when the government forces suppressed the rebellion. Gowharshad Mosque is a part of Imam Reza's shrine complex in the city of Mashhad in northeastern Iran.

Iran-Iraq War: Began with the invasion of Iran by the Iraqi military of Saddam Hussein on 22 September 1980 and lasted until 20 August 1988.

Islamic Revolution Guard Corps: See Guard Corps of the Islamic Revolution.

Kashani, Ayatollah: Ayatollah Abolqasem Kashani (1882-1962) was an anti-British cleric and politician who initially joined forces with Prime Minister Mosaddeq. He served as the speaker of the parliament during that period, but later turned against Mosaddeq and supported the Shah.

Kasravi, Ahmad: Historian, linguist, and legal expert, Ahmad Kasravi (1890-1946) was initially trained to become a cleric; he denounced the religious establishment in his lectures and writings, which resulted in his assassination by members of Navvab-Safavi's group, the Devotees of Islam.

Kalileh and Demneh: The translation of an ancient Indian collection of animal fables, *Panchatantra,* which was translated into Middle-Persian in the 6th century and later into other languages.

Khajeh: An archaic male honorific used for persons of distinguished social standing and affluence. It was also used for eunuchs who served in royal harems.

Khalkhali, Sheykh Sadeq: Mohammad Sadeq Khalkhali (1926-2003) was a cleric who headed the Islamic Revolution Courts following the 1979 revolution, whose swift rulings for the execution of the functionaries of the monarchical regime and opposition forces to the Islamic regime earned him the title of the country's "hanging judge."

Khaz'al, Sheikh: Khaz'al (1863-1936) was the ambitious chief of the Bani Kaab Arab tribe. Supported by the British government and the Anglo-Persian Oil Company, he was brought to Tehran, where he remained under house arrest for the remainder of his life.

Komeyl prayer: A prayer of supplication which is often recited in a tone of lamentation.

Lor tribal pants: Bakhtiari tribal trousers, which are long, usually black trousers with very wide legs, each made of several meters of cotton cloth.

Mahmud Afghan: An Afghan rebel who put a siege on Isfahan in the early 18ᵗʰ century and forced the abdication of the weak Safavid king, Shah Soltan Hoseyn. Shortly afterward, he was defeated by Nader Afshar (see Afsharid Dynasty).

Majlis: in Persian, *Majles*, usually refers to the National Consultative Assembly, or parliament.

Maleki, Khalil: One of the leaders of the Tudeh Party of Iran (see Tudeh Party), Maleki (1901-1969) split from the party and formed a party known as the Third Force.

Mansur, Hasan Ali: (1923-1965), prime minister of Iran from 1964 to 1965. Mansur served during the White Revolution of Mohammad Reza Shah Pahlavi and was assassinated by the Devotees of Islam.

Marhab: Marhab ibn al-Harith was a Jewish knight and warrior who defended the Jews against the Islamic forces in the Battle of Kheybar in 628. Shi'ites believe that he was killed by their first imam, Ali ibn Abitaleb.

Ministry of Culture: Up to around the mid-20ᵗʰ century, in Iran, the ministry in charge of education was called the Ministry of Culture.

Modarres: An important clerical figure, Hasan Modarres (1870-1937) served in the Iranian parliament for several terms. Later, he was sent into exile due to his opposition to Reza Shah Pahlavi.

Mosaddeq: An offspring of Qajar kings on his mother's side, Mohammad Mosaddeq (1882-1967) was born into a prominent family of high officials. After receiving a doctoral degree in law from Switzerland and returning to Iran, he was appointed governor of Fars Province. Mosaddeq also served in several other positions, including minister and parliamentary deputy, before he served twice as prime minister between 1951 and 1953. Later, he was exiled to Ahmadabad village in northern Iran.

Mostowfiyolmamalek: Title of Mirza Hasan Ashtiyani (1871-1932), an important figure of the Qajar era who held many high positions, such as prime minister, including his premiership in 1910 and 1911, during the reign of Ahmad Shah Qajar.

Motahhari, Ayatollah: Ayatollah Morteza Motahhari (1919-1979) is considered to have shaped the institutions of the Islamic Republic. He was assassinated by the Forqan, an underground militant Shi'ite anti-clerical Islamic group.

Musavi, Mir Hoseyn: Mirhoseyn Musavi (1942-) was the last prime minister of Iran from 1981 to 1989, before the constitutional change that abolished that position. His presidential candidacy in 2009 in opposition to Mahmud Ahmadinezhad resulted in widespread protests against the Islamic regime and the birth of the "Green Movement."

Nasereddin Shah: The reigning sovereign of Persia for nearly half a century, Nasereddin Shah (1831-1896) ruled from 1848 until his death, when he was assassinated by Mirza Reza Kermani, a commoner, an event that had been unprecedented in Persia's history.

National Consultative Assembly: *Majles-e Showra-ye Melli* in Persian, was the lower house of parliament in Iran, all the members of which, according to the Constitution, were supposed to be elected by the direct vote of the people, unlike the senate (*Majles-e Sena*), half of the members of which were appointed by the king.

Pahlavi Dynasty: The Pahlavi Dynasty was founded by Reza Shah in 1925, when the Persian parliament voted him the Shah of the Imperial State of Persia. This dynasty ruled Iran until 1979, when Reza Shah's son, Mohammad Reza (1919-1980), was overthrown by the Islamic Revolution.

Pahlavi, Reza Shah: Although in practice he was the ruler of Persia from 1921 as the minister of war, he officially became the Shah of Iran as Reza Shah Pahlavi (1878-1944) in 1925. After the occupation of Iran by Allied forces in August of 1941, he was forced into exile.

Qa'ani: Mirza Habibollah Shirazi, known as Qa'ani (1808-1856), was one of the best-known poets of the Qajar era.

Qajar Dynasty: Similar to most Persian dynasties since the Islamic invasion of Persia in the 7th century, the Qajars were a Turkic tribal dynasty and the first dynasty after the Safavids to hold continuous power in Persia for over a century. It was founded by Agha Mohammad Khan Qajar in 1789, when he overthrew the Zand Dynasty.

Qanat: An ancient Persian water source and irrigation system consisting of a gently upward-sloping tunnel dug horizontally into rising ground in a valley such that from deep within the earth, water runs out to the surface for drinking and farming in a village below.

Qashqa'i Tribe: Similar to the Bakhtiari tribe, the Qashqa'is are members of a nomadic tribe that consists of several clans living in central and southern Iran, mostly in the mountainous areas of Fars Province, although their territories sometimes overlap those of the Bakhtiari tribe.

Qavamossaltaneh: The Qajar title of Ahmad Qavam (1873-1955), who came from an important influential family and held many positions, including that of prime minister several times during the Qajar and Pahlavi Dynasties.

Qom Feyziyeh Seminary: *Madreseh-ye Feyziyeh-ye Qom* in Persian, is today the most important Shi'ite seminary in Iran.

Qorban Feast: *Eyd-e Qorban* in Persian and *Eid al-Adha* in Arabic, or the Feast of the Sacrifice, is the day in the Islamic lunar calendar on which Moslems honor the Prophet Abraham's act of obedience to God.

Raja'i: Mohammad Ali Raja'i (1933-1981) was the second president of the Islamic Republic, who served in that office for 28 days in 1981, when he was assassinated in a bombing.

Reza Khan: See Reza Shah Pahlavi.

Rial: The official currency of Iran. In the 1940s and 1950s the rate of exchange was approximately 75 *rials* per U.S. dollar.

Safavid Dynasty: Considered one of the most powerful dynasties since the Islamic conquest of Persia in the 7ᵗʰ century, the Safavids ruled from 1501 through the second decade and part of the third decade of the 18ᵗʰ century. The Safavids, whose origin was a Sufi sect in Ardabil in northern Iran, made Twelver Shi'ite Islam the official religion of Persia.

SAVAK: Persian acronym for the Organization of National Intelligence and Security, was the secret police of Mohammad Reza Shah; it was established in 1957. It was disbanded during the premiership of Bakhtiar and later replaced with a new organization after the 1979 Islamic Revolution in Iran.

Savushun: A novel by the famous Iranian writer, Simin Daneshvar.

Self-Sacrificing Devotees of Islam: *Feda'iyan-e Eslam* in Persian, was a terrorist Shi'ite group founded in 1946 by Navvab-Safavi, whose members carried out a series of meticulous assassinations of well-known Iranians, including prime ministers.

Sepah-e Pasdaran-e Enqelab-e Eslami: See Guard Corps of the Islamic Revolution.

Seyyed: Male honorific that precedes the names of those who trace their ancestry to the Prophet Mohammad through his grandsons, Imam Hasan or Imam Hoseyn.

Shah Tahmasb: The second monarch of the Safavid Dynasty, Tahmasb I (1514-1576), was crowned king at the age of 10 and had the longest reign in that dynasty.

Shari'ati, Ali: A French-educated sociologist by training, Ali Shari'ati (1933-1977) is sometimes referred to as the "ideologue" of the Islamic Revolution. He is known for his anti-Shah lectures at the Ershad Religious Center before the Islamic Revolution.

Shari'atmadari, Ayatollah: Ayatollah Mohammad Kazem Shari'atmadari (1905-1986) was the most notable grand ayatollah in Iran during the Islamic uprising of 1978-1979. Soon after the Islamic Revolution, he was placed under house arrest to the end of his life.

Sharif-Emami, Ja'far: A career politician who served as the head of the Iranian Senate, Ja'far Sharif-Emami (1910-1998) also served as prime minister for nearly a year in 1961 and 1962, and again in 1978 for a little over two months, before the Islamic Revolution.

Sire of the Martyrs: See Battle of Karbala.

Sire of the Oppressed: See Battle of Karbala.

Source of emulation: *marja'-e taqlid* in Persian, refers to fully-qualified Shi'ite grand ayatollahs who have reached the apex in the hierarchy of theological status to interpret Islamic laws and whose religious decrees are followed by a large number of people.

Tabataba'i, Seyyed Ziya'oddin: A journalist, Tabataba'i (1889-1969) became the prime minister of Persia under Ahmad Shah Qajar, after Reza Khan's Persian Cossack Brigade coup d'état of 1921.

Takhti, Gholamreza: An Iranian Olympic gold-medalist wrestler, Takhti (1930-1968) was considered the most popular athlete of Iran in the 20th century.

Taqizadeh: Hasan Taqizadeh (1878-1970) was one of the best-known figures during and after the Constitutional Revolution. Although he had begun his career as a cleric, he soon advocated the "Westernization of Iran, both outwardly and inwardly." Taqizadeh served in a variety of positions, including as a parliamentary representative, minister of finance, ambassador to England, and the head of the Senate.

Tasu'a: The 9th day of the Islamic holy month of Moharram, the day before "Ashura," the 10th day, which is commemorated by Shi'ite Moslems as the anniversary of the martyrdom of Imam Hoseyn and his supporters in the Battle of Karbala in 680.

Teymurtash: Abdolhoseyn Teymurtash (1883-1933) was one of the most visible and influential politicians in Iran, especially in the wake of the Constitutional Revolution and during the earlier part of the Pahlavi Dynasty. Although admired by the elite and the public alike, he fell out of favor with Reza Shah and was sentenced to prison by the government, where he was killed.

Third Force: The movement that was established by Khalil Maleki.

Tudeh Party: Initially a leftist party that later became a pro-Soviet communist political party that played an important role during the movement for the nationalization of the Iranian oil industry. It was banned in Iran following the 1949 assassination attempt against the Shah.

Tuman: Unofficial currency of Iran, equivalent to 10 *rials*.

Voice and Vision of the Islamic Republic: The government controlled national radio and television network of the Islamic Republic of Iran.

Vosuqoddowleh: The title for Hasan Vosuq (1868-1951), who was from a most prominent Iranian family and who served during both the Qajar and Pahlavi Dynasties in a variety of positions, including that of prime minister.

White Revolution: or the "Revolution of the Shah and the People," consisted of a series of reforms by Mohammad Reza Shah Pahlavi in 1963 that included land reform and women's right to vote.

Zahedi: General Fazlollah Zahedi (1892-1963), who had served in the Persian Cossack Brigade under Reza Khan (later Reza Shah), held many important positions during the reigns of Reza Shah and Mohammad Reza Shah. Zahedi staged the 19 August 1953 coup d'état and replaced Mosaddeq as prime minister.

Zand Dynasty: Founded by Karim Khan of the Zand tribe, the Zand Dynasty at various times ruled parts or most of the provinces of Persia during the 18th century, until it was overthrown by the Qajar rulers.

Zand, Karim Khan: The founder of the Zand Dynasty who, with the exception of Khorasan Province in the northeastern part of Iran, ruled the entire country from 1751 to 1779.

Bibliography

Abrahamian, Ervand. *Iran Between Two Revolutions*. Princeton: Princeton University Press, 1982.

Afkhami, Gholam Reza. *The Life and Times of the Shah*. Berkeley: University of California Press, 2009.

Afshar, Iraj. *Parvandeh-ye Saleh (dar bareh-ye Allahyar Saleh)*. Tehran: Abi Publishers, 2005.

Alam, Mostafa. *Naft, Qodrat, va Osul, Peyamadha-ye Kudeta-ye 28 Mordad*, translated by Gholamhoseyn Salehyar. Tehran: Chapakhsh Publishers, 1998.

Amanollahi-Baharvand, Sekandar. *Kuchneshini dar Iran: Pazhuheshi darbareh-ye Ashayer va Ilat*. Tehran: Agah Publishers, 2009.

Amini, Iraj. *Bar Bal-e Bohran: Zendegi-ye Siyasi-ye Ali Amini*. Tehran: Mahi Publications, 2009.

Amir'ala'i, Shamsoddin. *Mojahedan va Shahidan-e Rah-e Azadi*. Tehran: Dehkhoda Publishers, 1979.

Amirshahi, Mahshid. *Dar Safar*. Los Angeles: Ketab Corporation, 1995.

Amuzgar, Jamshid. "Majara-ye Vapasin-e Ruzha-ye Farmanrava'i-ye Shah," (Khatereh'i az Jamshid Amuzgar). *Rahavard*, no. 39 (Summer 1995): 146-148.

Amuzgar, Zhaleh. "Ostureh-ye Zendegi-ye Zartosht." *Kelk, Mahnameh-ye Farhangi va Honari*, no. 20 (October/November 1991).

Aqeli, Baqer. *Ruzshomar-e Tarikh-e Iran az Mashruteh ta Enqelab-e Eslami*, vol. 1. Tehran: Goftar Publishers, 1993.

Aramesh, Ahmad. *Khaterat-e Siyasi*, ed. by Gholamhoseyn Mirza-Saleh. Tehran: Danesh Publishers, 1990.

Arsanjani, Hasan. *Yaddashtha-ye Siyasi-ye Siyom-e Tirmah 1331*, 2nd printing. Compiled by Pirayeh Bamshad. Tehran: Atash Printing House, 1956.

Asnad-e Jonbesh-e Daneshju'i dar Iran (1329-1357), Majmu'eh-ye Asnad-e Tarikhi, vol. 1. Compiled and edited by Deputy President's Office of Management and Information Services. Tehran: Printing and Publication Organization of the Ministry of Islamic Culture and Guidance, 2001.

Asnadi az Ahzab-e Siyasi-ye Iran (Hezb-e Iran-Hezb-e Sa'adat-e Melli-ye Iran). "Moqaddameh." Tehran: Office of the Vice President for Management and Information Dissemination, n.d.

Astarabadi, Mohammad Mehdi Khan. *Tarikh-e Jahangosha-ye Naderi,* ed. by Mitra Mehrabadi. Tehran: Donya-ye Ketab, 2011.

Azarang, Abdolhoseyn. "Ali Amini va Rishehha-ye Shekast-e Eslahat." *Bokhara, Majalleh-ye Farhangi va Honari,* no. 55 (November 2006): 108-114.

Azododdowleh, Ahmad Mirza. *Tarikh-e Azodi: Sharh-e Hal-e Zanan va Dokhtaran va Pesaran va Motozammen-e Si va Hasht Sal Saltanat va Navader Ahval-e Fathali Shah Qajar.* Gowhardasht, Karaj: Sarv Publishing Company, 1983.

Bakhtiar, Chapour. *Ma fidélité.* Paris: Albin Michel, 1982.

Bakhtiar, Shapour. *Yekrangi,* trans. by Mahshid Amirshahi. Paris: Khavaran Publishers, 1982.

————Ph.D. dissertation. "Essai sur Les rapports entre le pouvoir et la religion dans la constitution des sociétés."

Bakhtiari, Aliqoli Khan, Sardar As'ad. *Tarikh-e Bakhtiari.* Tehran: Farhangsara Publishers, 1984.

Bakhtiari, Roshanak. "Zendegi va Marg-e Shahid-e Bozorg-e Azadi, Khan Babakhan As'ad." In Gholamabbas Nowruzi-Bakhtiari,

Tarikh va Tamaddon-e Bakhtiari, Vizheh-ye Farhang va Honar, vol. 1. Tehran: Anzan Publishers, 1995.

Bakhtiari, Sardar Zafar. *Yaddashtha va Khaterat-e Sardar Zafar Bakhtiari*. Tehran: Yasavoli, Farhangsara Publishers, 1983.

Banijamali, Ahmad. *Ashub: Motale'eh'i dar Zendegi va Shakhsiyat-e Dr. Mohammad Mosaddeq*. Tehran: Ney Publishers, 2007.

Baqi, Emadoddin. *Jonbesh-e Daneshjui'i-ye Iran az Aghaz ta Enqelab-e Eslami*, vol. 1. Tehran: Jame'ah-ye Iranian Publishers, 2000.

Bara-ye Tarikh Miguyam: Khaterat-e Mohsen Rafiqdust. Comp. by Sa'id Allamiyan. Tehran: Sureh-ye Mehr Publishers, 2013.

Bargatzky, Walter. *Hotel Majestic: Ein Deutscher im besetzten Frankreich*. Feriburg im Breigau: Herder, 1987.

Bayat, Kaveh. "Daneshgah-e Tehran, Avval-e Bahman 1340." *Goft-o Gu, Faslnameh-ye Farhangi va Ejtema'i*, no. 5 (Autumn 1994): 48-50.

Mehdi Bazargan, Mehdi. *Enqelab-e Iran dar Do Harekat*. Tehran: Bazargan Publishers, 1984.

———. *Eshq va Parastesh ya Termodinamik-e Ensan*, 3rd printing. Houston, Texas: Daftar-e Pakhsh-e Ketab, 1979.

———. *Shast Sal Khedmat va Moqavemat, Khaterat-e Bazargan, Goft-o Gu ba Sarhang Golamreza Nejati*. Tehran: Khadamat-e Farhangi-ye Rasa, 1996.

Berr, Hélène. *Pariser Tagebuch, 1924-1944*. München: Deutscher Taschenbuch Verlag, 2011.

Bertholet, Denis. *Paul Valéry: Die Biographie*. Berlin: Insel Verlag, 2011.

Binder, Leonard. *Iran: Political Development in a Changing Society*. Berkeley: University of California Press, 1962.

Bloch, Marc. *Die seltsame Niederlage: Frankreich 1940: Der Historiker als Zeuge.* Frankfurt am Main: Fischer, 1995.

Bonakdarian, Mansour. *Britain and the Iranian Constitutional Revolution of 1906-1911: Foreign Policy, Imperialism, and Dissent.* Syracuse: Syracuse University Press, 2006.

Buchner, Carl H. und Eckhardt Köhn (Hrsg.) *Herausforderung der Moderne. Annäherung an Paul Valéry.* Frankfurt am Main: Fischer Taschenbuch Verlag, 1991.

Chehabi, Houchang E. *Iranian Politics and Religious Modernism: The Liberation Movement of Iran under the Shah and Khomeini.* Ithaca, New York: Cornell University Press, 1990.

Cronin, Stephanie. *Tribal Politics in Iran: Rural Conflict and the New State, 1921-1941.* New York: Routledge, 2007.

Curzon, George N. "The Karun River and the Commercial Geography of South-west Persia." *Proceedings of the Royal Geographical Society* 12 (9) (September 1890): 514-515, 526-528.

Curzon, George N. *Persia and the Persian Question. Volume I.* London: Longmans, Green, and Co., 1892.

Daryaee, Touraj. *Sasanian Persia: The Rise and Fall of an Empire.* London: I.B. Tauris, 2009.

Davani, Ali. *Nehzat-e Ruhaniyun-e Iran*, vol. 3. Tehran: Bonyad-e Farhangi-ye Imam Reza Publishers, 1981.

Ehmann, Dieter. *Bahtiyaren: Persische Bergnomaden im Wandel der Zeit.* Wiesbaden: Dr. Ludwig Reichert Verlag, 1975.

Elwell-Sutton, L.P. *Persian Oil: A Study in Power Politics.* London: Lawrence and Wishart Ltd, 1955.

Eraqi, Mehdi. *Nagoftehha: Khaterat-e Shahid Haj Mehdi Eraqi.* Ed. by Mahmud Moqaddasi, Mas'ud Dehshur, and Hamid Reza Shirazi. Paris: Mo'sseseh-ye Khadamat-e Farhangi-ye Rasa, 1987; Tehran: 1991.

Fabvre, Lucien. "Ein Historiker prüft sein Gewissen." *Wie Geschichte geschrieben wird*, mit Beiträgen von Fernand Braudel, Natalie Zemon Davis, Lucian Febvre, Carlo Ginzberg, Jacues Le Goff, Reinhard Koeselleck, Arnoldo Momigliano. Berlin: Wagenbach Verlag, 1990.

Firuz, Shahrokh. *Zir-e Sayeh-ye Alborz*. Washington, DC: Mage Publishers, 2011.

Firuzan, T. "Darbareh-ye Tarkib va Sazman-e Ilat va Ashayer-e Iran." *Ilat va Ashayer*. Tehran: Agah Publishers, 1983.

Galt, Charles Alexander, et al. *Il-e Bakhtiari*. Translated by Kaveh Bayat and Mahmud Taherahmadi. Tehran: Shirazeh Research and Publication, 2008.

Garthwaite, Gene R. "The Bakhtiyari Khans, the Government of Iran, and the British, 1846-1915." *International Journal of Middle East Studies* 3 (1) (January 1972).

Gasiorowski, Mark J. "The Nuzhih Plot and Iranian Politics." *International Journal of Middle East Studies* 34 (4) (November 2002): 645-666.

Gnoli, Gherardo. *Iran als erligiöser Begriff im Mazdaismus*. Opladen: Westdeutscher Verlag, 1993.

Gozareshha-ye Mahramaneh-ye Vezarat-e Omur-e Kharejeh-ye Engelis dar Bareh-ye Enqelab-e Mashruteh-ye Iran az Tarikh-e Ordibehesht 1288 ta Azar1288, 20 Rabi'ossani 1327 ta 16 Ziqa'deh 1327, 11 May 1909 ta 30 November 1909, vol. 3. Ed. by Ahmad Bashiri. Tehran: No Publisher, 1984.

Groys, Boris. "Sprachversagen: zur Arbeit des Künstlers und Theatermachers Christoph Schlingensief." *Lettre International*, 90 (Herbst 2010): 114-116.

Hadis-e Moqavemat: Asnad-e Nehzat-e Moqavemat-e Melli-ye Iran, vol. 1. Comp. by Nehzat-e Moqavemat-e Melli-ye Iran. Tehran: Nehzat-e Moqavemat-e Melli-ye Iran, 1984.

Hakim, Mohammad Taqi Khan. *Ganj-e Danesh: Joghrafiya-ye Tarikhi-ye Shahrha-ye Iran*. Ed. by Dr. Mohammad Ali Sowti and Jamshid Kiyanfar. Tehran: Tehran Publishers, 1987.

Hedayat, Mehdiqoli Khan. *Khaterat va Khatarat*. Tehran: Zavvar Publishers, 1996.

Hezb-e Iran, Majmu'eh'i az Asnad va Bayaniyehha 1322-1323. Comp. by Mas'ud Kuhestaninezhad. Tehran: Shirazeh Publishers, 2000.

Ibn Khaldun. *Moqaddameh*, vol. 1. Trans. by Mohammad Parvin-Gonabadi. Tehran: Bongah-e Tarjomeh va Nashr-e Ketab, 1966.

Issawi, Charles (ed.). *The Economic History of Iran, 1800-1914*. Chicago: University of Chicago Press, 1971.

Jäckel, Eberhard. *Frankreich in Hitlers Europa: die deutsche Frankreichpolitik im Zweiten Weltkrieg*. Stuttgart: Deutsche Verlags-Anstalt, 1966.

Jazani, Bizhan. *Tarikh-e Si Saleh: Tarh-e Jame'ahshenasi va Mabani-ye Esteratezhi-ye Jonbesh-e Enqelabi-ye Khalq-e Iran*. Np: np, nd.

Jebheh-ye Melli beh Revayat-e SAVAK. Tehran: Markaz-e Barrasi-ye Asnad-e Tarikhi-ye Vezarat-e Ettela'at, 2000.

Kamran, Ramin. "Bakhtiar, Bist Sal Ba'd." *Sahand*, no. 30 (February 2012): 25-46.

Karamipur, Hamid. *Karnameh-ye Siyasi va Farhangi-ye Dabirestanha-ye Kamal-e Narmak, Refah, Alavi*. Tehran: Markaz-e Asnad-e Enqelab-e Eslami, 2010.

Kasravi, Ahmad. *Darbareh-ye Siyasat*, 2nd printing. Tehran: Daftar-e Parcham Publishers, 1945.

Kasten, Bernd. *"Gute Franzosen": die französische Polizei und die deutsche Besatzungsmacht im besetzten Frankreich 1940-1944.* Sigmaringan: Jan Thorbecke Verlag, 1993.

Katouzian, Mohammad Ali Homayoun. *Mosaddeq va Nabard-e Qodrat.* Trans. by Ahmad Tadayyon, 2nd printing. Tehran: Mo'asseseh-ye Khadamat-e Farhangi-ye Rasa, 1993.

Katuziyan (Haj-Seyyed-Javadi), Kiyan. *Az Sepideh ta Sham.* Tehran: Abi Publishers, 2002.

Kemp, Norman. *Abadan: A First-hand Account of the Persian Oil Crisis.* London: Allen Wingate, 1953.

Ketabcheh-ye Khaterat-e Hoseynqoli Khan Ilkhani Bakhtiari. Ed. by Ahmad Tadayyon, 1st printing. Np: Mo'asseseh-ye Pazhuhesh va Motale'eh-ye Farhangi, 1994.

Khaterat va Yaddashtha-ye Arteshbod Fereydun Jam. Comp. by Dr. Morteza Moshir. Los Angeles: Sherkat-e Ketab, 2000.

Khaterat-e E'temadossaltaneh, Ruznameh-ye Khaterat-e E'temadossaltaneh. Ed. by Iraj Afshar. Tehran: Mo'asseseh-ye Amir Kabir Publishers, 1998.

Khaterat-e Mas'ud Hejazi: Ruydadha va Davari, 1329-1339. Tehran: Nilufar Publishers, 1996.

Khaterat-e Mozaffar Baqa'i. ed. by Habib Ladjevardi. Iranian Oral History Project, Harvard University Center for Middle Eastern Studies, Bethesda, MD, tape 2, 25 June 1976.

Khaterat-e Sardar Maryam Bakhtiari, az Kudaki ta Aghaz-e Enqelab-e Mashruteh. Ed. by Gholamabbas Nowruzi-Bakhtiari. Tehran: Anzan Publishers, 2003.

Khaterat-e Shapour Bakhtiar, Nokhost Vazir-e Iran (1357). Ed. by Habib Ladjevardi. Iranian Oral History Project, Harvard University Center for Middle Eastern Studies, Bethesda, MD, 1996.

Khaterati az Allahyar Saleh. Ed. by Seyyed Morteza Moshir. Tehran: Mehrandish Publishers, 2003.

Khazeni, Arash. *Tribes and Empire on the Margins of Nineteenth-Century Iran.* Seattle: University of Washington Press, 2009.

Kudeta-ye Nuzheh, 5th printing. Tehran: Mo'asseseh-ye Motale'at va Pazhuhcshha-ye Siyasi, 2008.

Ladjevardi, Habib. *Labor Unions and Autocracy in Iran.* Syracuse: Syracuse University Press, 1985.

Lambton, Ann. "Tarikh-e Ilat-e Iran." In *Ilat va Ashayer.* Trans. by Ali Tabrizi. Tehran: Mo'asseseh-ye Entesharat-e Agah, 1983.

Lambton, Ann. *Malek va Zare' dar Iran,* 3rd printing. Trans. by Manuchehr Amiri. Tehran: Markaz-e Entesharat-e Elmi va Farhangi, 1983.

Layard, Sir Austen Henry. *Safarnameh-ye Layard: Nabard-e Mirza Taqi Khan Bakhtiari ba Hokumat-e Qajariyeh.* Trans. by Mehrab Amiri. Tehran: Anzan Publishers, 1997.

Liakos, Antonis. "Griechenland und Europa. Im Knäuel der Krisenreaktionskräfte – Vorurteile und Richtigstellungen." *Lettre International,* 95 (Winter 2011): 20.

Louis, William Roger. *The British Empire in the Middle East, 1945-1951: Arab Nationalism, the United States, and Postwar Imperialism.* Oxford: Clarendon Press, 1984.

Luther, Hans. *Der französische Widerstand gegen die deutsche Besatzungsmacht und seine Bekämfung.* Tübingen: Institut für Besatzungsfragen, 1957.

Maalouf, Amin. *Der Mann aus Mesopotamien.* Frankfurt am Main: Suhrkamp Verlag, 2003.

Makki, Hoseyn. *Khaterat-e Siyasi.* Tehran: Elmi Publishers, 1989.

Maleki, Khalil. *Khaterat-e Siyasi.* Europe: Kushesh baray-e Pishbord-e Nehzat-e Melli-ye Iran, 1981.

Mansuri, Javad. *Tarikh-e Qiyam-e 15 Khordad beh Revayat-e Asnad,* vol. 1. Tehran: Markaz-e Asnad-e Enqelab-e Eslami, 1998.

Mehraban, Rasul. *Barrasi-ye Mokhtasar-e Ahzab-e Borzhuazi-ye Melli-ye Iran dar Moqabeleh ba Jonbesh-e Kargari va Enqelabi-ye Iran.* Tehran: Peyk-e Iran Publishers, 1980.

Michelet, Jules. *Geschichte der Französischen Revolution.* Aus dem Französischen von Richard Kühn. Frankfurt am Main: Zweitausendeins, 2009.

Milani, Abbas *The Shah.* New York: Palgrave Macmillan, 2001

Mirzadeh, Vahid. *Tadavom-e Hayat-e Siyasi dar Ekhtenaq, Tarikh-e Shafahi-ye Nehzat-e Moqavemat-e Melli.* Tehran: Selk Publishers, 2000.

Mosaddeq, Gholamhoseyn. *Dar Kenar-e Pedaram: Khaterat-e Dr. Gholamhoseyn Mosaddeq.* Comp. and ed. by Sarhang Gholamreza Nejati. Tehran: Rasa Cultural Services Institute, 1990.

Movahhed, Mohammad Ali. *Khab-e Ashofteh-ye Naft, Dr. Mosaddeq va Nehzat-e Melli-ye Iran.* Tehran: Karnameh Publishers, 2005.

Nahavandi, Hushang. *Akherin Ruzha: Payan-e Saltanat va Dargozasht-e Shah,* 2nd printing. Trans. by Behruz Sur-Esrafil and Maryam Seyhun. Los Angeles: Sherkat-e Ketab, 2005.

Nameh-ye Tansar. Ed. by Mojtaba Minovi. Tehran: Majles Print House, 1932.

Namehha, Zendeginameh, Asnad va Namehha-ye Ayatollah Haj Seyyed Reza Zanjani, 2nd printing. Ed. by Behruz Tayerani. Tehran: Samadiyeh Publishers, 2009.

Nejati, Gholamreza. *Mosaddeq: Salha-ye Mobarezeh va Moqavemat,* vol. 2. Tehran: Mo'asseseh-ye Khadamat-e Farhangi-ye Rasa, 1997.

————. *Tarikh-e Siyasi-e Bist-o Panj Saleh-ye Iran (az Kudeta ta Enqelab).* Tehran: Mo'asseseh-ye Khadamat-e Farhangi-ye Rasa, 1992.

Pahlavi, Farah. *An Enduring Love: My Life with the Shah, A Memoir.* Trans. from the French by Patricia Clancy. New York: Miramax Books, 2004.

Pahlavi, Mohammad Reza Shah. *Enqelab-e Sefid.* Np. Nd.

Panj Daheh pas az Kudeta Asnad Sokhan Miguyand, vol. 1. Trans. by Dr. Ahmad Ali Raja'i and Mahin Soruri (Raja'i). Tehran: Qalam Publishers, 2004.

Parsa, Asghar. *Farzand-e Khesal-e Khishtan.* Comp. by Ali Parsa. Tehran: Ney Publishers, 2009.

Paul Valéry, Werke, Band 2: Dialoge und Theater. Herausgegeben von Karl Alfred Blühner. Frankfurt am Main: Insel Verlag, 1990.

Payam-e Iran, vol. 11, no. 410 (November 1991).

Pazhuheshi dar Bab-e Monasebat-e Engelis ba Khanha-ye Bakhtiari az Aghaz-e Saltanat-e Mozaffareddin Shah ta Soqut-e Qajariyeh. Tehran: Mo'asseseh-ye Motale'at-e Tarikh-e Iran, 2011.

Pishdad, Amir and Mohammad Ali Homayoun Katouzian, *Namehha-ye Khalil Maleki.* Tehran: Markaz Publishers, 2002.

Porseshha-ye Bipasokh dar Salha-ye Estesna'i: Khaterat-e Mohandes Ahmad Zirakzadeh. Ed. by Dr. Abolhasan Ziya'-Zarifi and Dr. Khosrow Sa'idi. Tehran: Nilufar Publishers, 1997.

Pozzi, Catherine. *Paul Valéry, Glück, Dämonen, Verrückter: Tagebuch 1920-1928.* Frankfurt am Main: Suhrkamp, 1998.

Pur-Bakhtiar, Ghaffar. "Qatl-e Hoseynqoli Khan, Ilkhan-e Bakhtiari va Naqsh-e Mo'tamedoddowleh, Hakem-e Fars dar An." *Faslnameh-ye Tahqiqat-e Tarikhi,* vol. 13 (Autumn and Winter, 2003): 76-78.

Pur-Bakhtiar, Ghaffar. "Sardar As'ad Bakhtiari va Kusheshha-ye Farhangi." *Faslnameh-ye Tahqiqat-e Tarikhi va Motale'at-e Arshivi*, vol. 18 (2008): 19-24.

Qarahbaghi, Abbas. *E'terafat-e Zheneral: Khaterat-e Arteshbod Abbas Qarahbaghii, Akherin Ra'is-e Setad-e Bozorg Arteshdaran va Ozv-e Showra-ye Saltanat (Mordad-Bahman '57)*. Tehran: Ney Publishers, 1987.

Radisch, Iris. Camus: *das Ideal der Einfachheit. Eine Biographie*. Reibek bei Hamburg: Rowohlt, 2013.

Rahbani, Majid. "Hezb ya Jebheh: Nokhostin Kongereh-ye Jebheh-ye Melli-ye Iran (Dey 1341)." *Jahan-e Ketab*, nos. 251-252, vols. 1 and 2 (Farvardin-Ordibehesht 1389): 38-44.

Raphael, Lutz. "Navigieren zwischen Anpassung und Attentismus: die Pariser Universität unter deutscher Besatzung 1940-1944." In Stefan Martens und Maurice Vaïsse (Hrsg.), *Frankreich und Deutschland im Krieg (November 1942-Herbst 1944): Okkupation, Kollaboration, Rèsistance*. Bonn: Bouvier, 2000.

Reed, John. *Ten Days that Shook the World*. New York: Boni & Liveright, 1919.

Rejal-e Asr-e Pahlavi, Shapour Bakhtiar beh Revayat-e Asnad-e SAVAK. Tehran: Center for the Examination of Historical Documents of the Ministry of Information, 2011.

Ruhani (Ziyarati), Seyyed Hamid. *Barrasi va Tahlili az Nehzat-e Imam Khomeyni*. Tehran: Rah-e Emam Publishers, 1986.

Sadiqi, Gholamhoseyn. *Jonbeshha-ye Dini-ye Irani dar Qarnha-ye Dovvom va Sevvom-e Hejri*. Ed. by Yahya Mahdavi. Tehran: Pazhang Publishing Company, 1993.

Safahati az Tarikh-e Mo'aser-e Iran: Asnad-e Nehzat-e Moqavemat-e Melli, vol. 5. Compiled by Nehzat-e Azadi-ye Iran. Tehran: Nehzat-e Azadi-ye Iran, 1984.

Safarnameh-ye Ibn Batuteh, vol. 1. Trans. by Mohammad Ali Movahhed. Tehran: Agah Publishers, 1991.

Safarnameh-ye Rezaqoli Mirza Nayeboleyaleh, Naveh-ye Fathali Shah. Editorial supervision of Iraj Afshar. Tehran: Asatir Publishers, 1982.

Sahabi, Ezzatollah. *Nim Qarn Khatereh va Tajrebeh: Khaterat-e Mohandes Ezzatollah Sahabi az Dowran-e Kudaki ta Enqelab-e 57*, vol. 1. Tehran: Farhang-e Saba Publishers, 2007.

San'ati, Mohammad Hoseyn. "Shapour Bakhtiar." *Faslnameh-ye Motale'at-e Tarikhi*, no. 6 (Spring 2005): 206-208.

Sanjabi, Karim. *Omidha va Naomidiha (Khaterat-e Siyasi)*. London: Jebheh-ye Melliyun-e Iran Publishers, 2007.

Sardar Bahador, Ja'farqoli Khan. *Khaterat-e Sardar As'ad Bakhtiari*, 2nd printing. Ed. by Iraj Afshar. Tehran: Asatir Publishers, 1999.

Sekandari, Pari. *Dar Dadgah-e Mottahaman beh Qatl-e Bakhtiar*, 2nd printing. Paris: Khavaran Publishers, 2006.

Sepehr, Lesanossaltaneh. *Tarikh-e Bakhtiari*. Tehran: Sazman-e Shahanshahi-ye Khadamat-e Ejtema'i, 1947.

Sepehr, Mohammad Taqi Lesanolmolk. *Nasekhottavarikh: Tarikh-e Qajariyeh az Aghaz ta Payan-e Saltanat-e Fathali Shah*, vols. 1 and 2. Tehran: Asatir Publishers, 1998.

Shahmoradi, Bizhan. "Boridan-e Gisvan dar Sugvariha-ye Bakhtiari." *Iran Nameh*, vol. 22, nos. 3 and 4 (Autumn-Winter, 2005): 283-299.

Shayegan, Seyyed Ali. *Zendeginameh-ye Siyasi: Neveshtehha va Sokhanraniha*, vol. 1. Comp. by Ahmad Shayegan. Tehran: Agah Publishers, 2006.

Siy-o Haft Ruz Pas az Siy-o Haft Sal: Chand Goft-o Gu ba Dr. Shapour Bakhtiar darbareh-ye Dowran-e Zamamdariyash. Paris: Radio Iran Publishers, 1982.

Surat Jalasat-e Kongereh-ye Jebheh-ye Melli-ye Iran. Comp. by Amir Tayerani. Tehran: Gam-e No Publishers, 2009.

Tafazzoli, Ahmad. "Chahar Katibeh-ye Kardir, Mubad va Mosmer." *Kelk, Mahname-ye Farhangi va Honari*, no. 40 (July 1993): 148-151.

Tafazzoli, Ahmad. "Kartir va Siyasat-e Ettehad-e Din va Dowlat dar Dowreh-ye Sasani." *Iran Nameh*, vol. 17, no. 2 (Spring 1999): 302-303.

Tajadod, Nahal. *Die Träger des Lichts*: Magier, Ketzer und Christen im alten Persien. Düsseldorf: Walter Verlag, 1995.

Tajrebeh-ye Mosaddeq dar Cheshmandaz-e Ayandeh-ye Iran. Ed. by Houshang Keshavarz-Sadr and Hamid Akbari. Bethesda, MD: Ibex Publishers, 2005.

Theil, Veronika. *Die Bretagne, "a l'heure allemande."* Dresden: Technische Universität Dresden, 2005/2006.

Umbreit, Hans. *Der Militärbefehlshaber in Frankreich, 1940-1944.* Boppard am Rhein: Harald Bolldt Verlag, 1967.

Va'ez (Shahrestani), Nafiseh. *Siyasat-e Ashayeri-ye Dowlat-e Pahlavi-ye Avval.* Tehran: Tarikh Publisher, 2009.

Vahman, Fereydoun. "Pishgoftar." *Iran Nameh*, vol. 17, no. 2 (Spring 1999).

Valéry, Paul. *Cahiers/Hefte 1*, Auf der Grundlage der von Judithe Robinson besorgten französischen Ausgabe Herg von Hartmut Köhler und Jürgen Schmidt-Radefeldt, Übersetz von Markus Jakobs, Hartmut Köhler, Jürgen Schmidt-Radefeldt, Corona Schmiele, Karin Wais. Frankfurt am Main: Fischer Verlag, 1987.

Vargas Llosa, Mario. *Die Wahrheit der Lügen, Essays zur Literatur.* Frankfurt am Main: Suhrkamp Verlag, 1990.

Von Choltitz, Dietrich. *Brennt Adolf Hitler: Tatsachenbericht des letzten deutschen Befehlshabers in Paris.* Mannheim: UNA Weltbücherei, 1950.

Wuthenow, Ralph-Rainer. *Paul Valéry zur Einführung.* Hamburg: Junius Verlag, 1997.

Yadnameh-ye Ostad Dr. Gholamhoseyn Sadiqi. Comp. and ed. by Dr. Parviz Varjavand. Tehran: Chapakhsh Publishers, 1993.

Yadnameh-ye Yadollah Sahabi. Comp. by Mohammad Torkaman. Tehran: Qalam Publishers, 1998.

Yarshater, Ehsan. "Moruri bar Tarikh-e Siyasi va Farhangi-ye Iran-e Pish az Eslam." *Iran Nameh,* vol. 17, no. 2 (Spring 1999): 185-213.

Yazdi, Ebrahim. *Akherin Talashha dar Akherin Ruzha: Matalebi Nagofteh Piramun-e Enqelab-e Eslami-ye Iran.* Tehran: Qalam Publishers, 1984.

Yekrangiyan, Sartip Mirhoseyn. *Seyri dar Tarikh-e Artesh-e Iran, az Aghaz ta Payan-e Shahrivar 1320.* Tehran: Khojasteh Publishers, 2005.

Zelossoltan, Mas'ud Mirza. *Tarikh-e Sargozasht-e Mas'udi: Zendeginameh va Khaterat-e Zelossoltan Hamrah ba Safarnameh-ye Farangestan.* Tehran: Babak Publishers, 1983.

Index